Islam and Global Studies

Series Editors
Deina Abdelkader, University of Massachusetts Lowell
Lowell, MA, USA
Nassef Manabilang Adiong, Co-IRIS (International Relations
and Islamic Studies Research Cohort), Quezon City, Central Luzon
Philippines
Raffaele Mauriello, Allameh Tabataba'i University, Tehran, Iran

Islam and Global Studies series provides a platform for the progression of knowledge through academic exchanges based on multidisciplinary socio-political theory that studies the human condition and human interaction from a global perspective. It publishes monographs and edited volumes that are multidisciplinary and theoretically grounded and that address, in particular, non-state actors, Islamic polity, social and international justice, democracy, geopolitics and global diplomacy. The focus is on the human condition and human interaction at large. Thus cross-national, cross-cultural, minority and identity studies compose the building block of this series; sub-areas of study to which Islamic theory and socio-political praxis can provide an alternative and critical lens of inquiry. It explores Islam in history and in the contemporary world through studies that:

a) provide comprehensive insights of the intellectual developments that have defined Islam and Muslim societies both in history and in the contemporary world;

b) delineate connections of pre-colonial Muslim experiences to their responses, adaptations and transformations toward modernity;

c) evaluate old paradigms and emerging trends that affect Muslims' experiences in terms of political state system, democracy, secularization, gender, radicalism, media portrayals, etc.;

d) show empirical cases of intra-Muslim and Muslim–Non-Muslim relations.

R. Charles Weller

'Pre-Islamic Survivals' in Muslim Central Asia

Tsarist, Soviet and Post-Soviet Ethnography in World Historical Perspective

R. Charles Weller
Department of History
Washington State University
Pullman, WA, USA

ISSN 2524-7328   ISSN 2524-7336 (electronic)
Islam and Global Studies
ISBN 978-981-19-5696-6   ISBN 978-981-19-5697-3 (eBook)
https://doi.org/10.1007/978-981-19-5697-3

© The Editor(s) (if applicable) and The Author(s), under exclusive license to Springer Nature Singapore Pte Ltd. 2023
This work is subject to copyright. All rights are solely and exclusively licensed by the Publisher, whether the whole or part of the material is concerned, specifically the rights of translation, reprinting, reuse of illustrations, recitation, broadcasting, reproduction on microfilms or in any other physical way, and transmission or information storage and retrieval, electronic adaptation, computer software, or by similar or dissimilar methodology now known or hereafter developed.
The use of general descriptive names, registered names, trademarks, service marks, etc. in this publication does not imply, even in the absence of a specific statement, that such names are exempt from the relevant protective laws and regulations and therefore free for general use.
The publisher, the authors, and the editors are safe to assume that the advice and information in this book are believed to be true and accurate at the date of publication. Neither the publisher nor the authors or the editors give a warranty, expressed or implied, with respect to the material contained herein or for any errors or omissions that may have been made. The publisher remains neutral with regard to jurisdictional claims in published maps and institutional affiliations.

This Palgrave Macmillan imprint is published by the registered company Springer Nature Singapore Pte Ltd.
The registered company address is: 152 Beach Road, #21-01/04 Gateway East, Singapore 189721, Singapore

"A critical, deeply researched work on a long and still debated theme within and beyond Kazakh scholarship. Weller's book is an erudite exploration of Tsarist, Soviet, Western (European and American), Turkish and modern Kazakh writing on the spread and role of Islam and other religious systems in Kazakh society. As such, it is essential reading for all who are interested in the history of religion in Central Asia and in particular of Islam in Kazakhstan."
—Peter B. Golden, *Professor Emeritus of History, Turkish and Middle Eastern Studies, Rutgers University*

"This the first book-length study of the concept of 'pre-Islamic survivals' among the Kazakhs and other Muslim societies of Central Asia. Weller's painstaking research draws on medieval and modern primary sources, including twenty-first century developments. ...Focused primarily on the Kazakhs, the book opens doors to a broader discussion of Muslim populations of Central Asia and the former Russian Empire in the context of colonial scholarship and the global reach of knowledge production."
—Marina Tolmacheva, *Professor Emerita, Middle Eastern & Islamic History, Washington State University and President Emerita, American University, Kuwait*

"Weller's study of the concept of 'pre-Islamic survivals' in Central Asia is an erudite and thought-provoking book. On the basis of wide-ranging research and deep engagement with Kazakh-language sources, he argues that the paradigms through which a number of (especially Western) scholars have—implicitly or explicitly—understood religiosity in Central Asia do not adequately explain Central Asian religious beliefs and customs. His arguments merit careful study and engagement by scholars of Central Asian history and the history of religion alike."
—Ian W. Campbell, *Associate Professor of History, University of California-Davis, California*

"A comprehensive volume which offers fresh perspectives and ideas... Scholars of Islamic, religious, cultural and historical studies will find much of interest on the problems of 'syncretism' and 'conversion,' especially in relation to the study of religious identity in Central Asia and its developing trends."
—Ainura D. Kurmanaliyeva, *Professor & Department Chair, and Nurlykhan K. Aljanova, Senior Lecturer & Vice-Chair on Science and International Cooperation, Department of Religious & Cultural Studies, Al-Farabi Kazakh National University (Almaty)*

"This is an insightful work, rich in detail; scholars from many disciplines will benefit from it."
—Razia Sultanova, *Research Fellow, Cambridge Muslim College, UK, and Visiting Professor, Charles University, Prague, Czech Republic*

For my mother, for all her years of love & care, an inspiration for, and positive influence upon my life in immeasurable ways.

PREFACE

This study[1] is closely tied to an article I published in the *Journal of Islamic Studies* in 2013–2014 treating "Religious-Cultural Revivalism as Historiographical Debate: Contending Claims in the Post-Soviet Kazakh Context."[2] That article emerged from a number of years of prior research which were eventually given significant shape during my visiting fellowship at Yale University (2010–2011) when I lectured on the topic at both Yale and Princeton and then again, in revised form, several years later at UCLA. I have drawn from the introduction and conclusion to that article in framing the introduction, conclusion and other select parts of this work. The main body of that article, in revised and expanded form, is also included as a final chapter in Part Three of this present book. Various portions of the material in Chapters four, five and six were also presented at two different annual conferences of the Central Eurasian Studies Society (CESS) in 2016 and 2018, with particularly helpful feedback from the discussant for the 2016 panel, Tomohiko Uyama (Hokkaido University). Appendix One represents a revised, updated paper presented at the annual conference of the World History Association (WHA) in 2015. That chapter treats the late nineteenth-, early twentieth-century historiographical debate between two members of the Orenburg Scientific Archival Commission—the Orthodox church historian and missionary N.M. Chernavsky and the colonial administrator and veterinarian A.I. Dobrosmyslov—addressing the question of the impact of Catherine II's policies of religious toleration on Kazakh Islamic history and identity. All of the material has been reworked across the years and fit together within the context of this present study.

This volume is dedicated to a foundational, prolegomenous topic within the study of Central Asian religious history and identity. As a history of a central ethnographical and theoretical construct (or concept) within the study of Central Asian religious-cultural history, and the related historiographical debates which emerged across the late Tsarist, Soviet and post-Soviet periods, this study provides an essential backdrop to more straightforward religious-cultural histories.

Although the subtitle of this book employs only the term "ethnography," cultural anthropology and historiography are also in view. Attempting to squeeze all such terms into not only the title, but every sentence in which one or the other of those terms appears would not have been reasonable, so the reader should, as a general rule, understand all three terms to be in view on most occasions when any one of those terms is employed. This remains true for 'cultural anthropology' in particular, even though I typically limit my choice of terms to either 'ethnography' or 'historiography' throughout. Although I have training in theology, philosophy, religious-cultural studies and anthropology, history is my primary field. 'Historiography' is, therefore, my main interest. I define that term here for purposes of this study as 'the construction of historical narratives,' with a view to understanding and analyzing their underlying assumptions and implications. Inasmuch, however, as ethnography, cultural anthropology, theology and religious-cultural studies, among much else, all contribute essential source material as well as theoretical orientations and approaches which shape the construction of historical narrative, there remains a close, overlapping and reflexive relationship between them all.

I do not intend this book as the, or even a, final word on this otherwise very complex and much debated topic. I am deeply indebted to the very rich and pioneering scholarship of many others in various relevant fields, even those whose positions I may at times critique. It should also be borne in mind that whatever points of critique I do raise pertain only to the specific, limited points raised and not the vast, rich entirety of any particular scholar's contributions to the field. As the late UNESCO-honored nineteenth-century Kazakh Muslim reformer, Abai Kunanbaiuhli (1845–1904), put it: "study with clear and noble aims, not to acquire learning so as to be able to argue with other people. Now, arguments within reason help to strengthen one's convictions, but, excessive zeal for them can only spoil a person."³ My aim, as always, is to contribute collegially and respectfully to continuing dialogue and, where needed, debates on particular issues which I attempt here to bring into sharper focus. I can only hope the work will be received in that spirit and make some small contribution toward that end.

Pullman, USA   R. Charles Weller

Notes

1. I acknowledge that my system of transliteration throughout the volume is not entirely consistent. This has to do with several factors, some of them historical, which I will not take time or space here to justify. I will only note that I was originally planning to convert all the transliteration of Kazakh and Russian to Cyrillic or the recently adopted Latin script, but have only done so for the bibliography, not all of the endnotes. I accept that this is perhaps an academic 'sin' or 'crime' of some sort on my part, albeit hopefully only a misdemeanor in the eyes of most. I can only regret whatever minor inconvenience it might cause; it should not otherwise impact the study in any significant way. Those who know the languages should readily be able to understand the transliterations within context. The transliterated citations within the endnotes are all keyed to transliterations of the author's last names in parentheses within the bibliography at the head of the citations in order to ensure clear reference/connection between them, and between references and bibliographies within other studies.
2. "Religious-Cultural Revivalism as Historiographical Debate: Contending Claims in the Post-Soviet Kazakh Context." *Journal of Islamic Studies*, Vol. 25, No. 2 (May 2014): 138–177. DOI: 10.1093/jis/ett058 (Published online Nov 12, 2013. http://jis.oxfordjournals.org/content/25/2/138).
3. Abai Kunanbaiuhli (c. 1900), "Word Thirty-Two," in *Book of Words*, Leneshmidt Translations Resource Library (URL: http://www.leneshmidt-translations.com/book_of_words_abai_kunanbaev_english/32.htm). Cf. Garifolla Yesim ([1994] 2020), "Word Thirty-Two: The Requisites of Learning," in *An Insider's Critique of the Kazakh Nation: Reflections on the Writings of Abai Kunanbaiuhli (1845–1904)*, tr. and ed. R. Charles Weller (Boston, MA: Asia Research Associates), pp. 211–212.

Acknowledgements

I am grateful, first and foremost, to Deina Abdelkader, Nassef Manabilang Adiong and Raffaele Mauriello as editors of the *Islam and Global Studies* Series with Palgrave Macmillan for their interest in and support for this volume. This is the second book I have published in this series, the first being a co-edited volume with Anver Emon on *Reason, Revelation and Law in Islamic and Western Theory and History* in 2021. Thanks also to the blind reviewers for their critical feedback on the original proposal and full manuscript. Their suggested revisions have been invaluable in helping to improve the quality of the work. And thanks to Palgrave Macmillan for their support for this project as well, particularly Ananda Kumar Mariappan, Sandeep Kaur, Arun Prasath, Misao Taguchi and the other editorial and production staff who have worked patiently with me on several projects, including now this one, providing expert guidance throughout the entire contract, submission and production process.

I likewise owe a debt of thanks to Peter Golden, Marina Tolmacheva, Stefan Berger, Razia Sultanova, Richard Foltz, Ainur Kurmanaliyeva, Nurlykhan Aljanova and Tomohiko Uyama for reading through (various parts of) the manuscript and offering their endorsement and/or critical feedback. Their suggestions have likewise been invaluable in helping to improve the quality of this study, though I of course remain responsible for the final content and views expressed herein. Blind peer reviewers at the *Journal of Islamic Studies* along with Geoff Humble, Will Tuladhar Douglas, Willard Sunderland, Nathaniel Knight, Michael David-Fox,

Colum Leckey and Jonathan Bone have all made helpful suggestions on various portions of this study across the past five or so years, including some of the primary and secondary source material, for which I am likewise thankful. Beyond this, I am of course indebted to all those whose scholarship I have drawn on, past and present, in order to produce the present study.

I would also like to express my gratitude to Dr. Mohammad Ghaedi and Abdollah Ghaffari for their research assistance with Persian-Iranian Farsi sources, both classical and modern. Dr. Ghaedi's assistance along these lines has been particularly noteworthy. Christopher W. Card also deserves thanks for his research assistance in locating select sources relating to Nauryz (Nowruz) and Islam in particular.

I am grateful always for the ongoing support of al-Farabi Kazakh National University (KNU, Almaty, KZ) and Washington State University (WSU, Pullman, WA, USA), especially the Department of Religious and Cultural Studies within the Faculty of Philosophy and Political Science at KNU and the Department of History within the College of Arts and Sciences at WSU. Special thanks are, likewise, due to both the KNU and WSU libraries and their staff for helping to locate and supply an essential wealth of primary source material, without which this study would not have been possible, particularly during the pandemic.

And finally, the support of a number of family, friends and colleagues for this work has meant a great deal. There are too many to name here, though I will make special mention of Viveka Raol, Shiv Rajurs, David Kalivas and, organizationally, the World History Association, among a good many others.

Contents

1 Introduction: Framing the Study 1
    Background and Context 1
    The Question of Kazakh Religious-Cultural History and
    Identity: An Illustrative Case Study 2
    Concluding Reflections and Overview of Chapters and Sections 9

Part I   Historical Sources of Tsarist 'Survivals' Ethnography

2 Religious-Cultural 'Survivals' in Euro-American
    and Euro-Slavic Christian and Secular Sources 15
    E.B. Tylor and Protestant Anti-Catholic Polemicists
    as Sources for Soviet 'Survivals' Ethnography? 15
    Tylor and 'Survivals' Historiography in the Nineteenth-
    Century: Monotheistic Degenerational versus Evolutionary
    Developmental Theories of Early Human History 16
    'Survivals' Historiography in Seventeenth-Century German
    Enlightenment Sources 20
    Hebrew-Jewish and Christian Sources of 'Survivals'
    Historiography 22
    Nineteenth-Century Romantic Nationalism and the Russian
    Orthodox Tradition of 'Dual Faith' 26
    Concluding Reflections 31

3 Middle Eastern and Central Asian Islamic Sources of 'Survivals' Ethnography   33
Qur'anic and Middle Eastern Islamic Sources   33
Eleventh-Century Karakhanid and Other Turkic Sources   35
Sixteenth-Century Central Asian Sources   42
Western (Christian) Orientalist Scholarship   45
Concluding Reflections   46

4 'Pre-Islamic Survivals' Among the Kazakhs in Tsarist Russian and Kazakh Colonial Ethnography, 1770–1917   49
Early Tsarist Colonial Ethnographers of Kazakh Religious Identity, 1770–1860   50
The First Kazakh Colonial Ethnographer, Shokan Ualihanuhli (1863–1865)   55
"Remnants" Historiography and 'the Kazakh of Kazakhs,' Abai, in the Later Nineteenth and Early Twentieth Centuries   59
The Terminological Shift to "Perezhitki" in Early Twentieth-Century Writings of Tsarist Russian Missionaries   61
Part One Conclusion: Summary of Tsarist Historical Sources   63

Part II Historical Sources of Soviet 'Survivals' Ethnography

5 Sources and Aims of Soviet 'Survivals' Ethnography in Its Initial (Pre-World War Two) Phases   67
The Persistence of 'Survivals' Ethnography in Russian Orthodoxy   68
'Survivals' Ethnography in Marx, Engels, Lenin and Stalin   68
Tylor, Frazer and Other Euro-American Sources of Influence   72
Early Soviet 'Survivals' Ethnography of Kazakh and Central Asian Islamic History, 1920s–40s   74
Concluding Reflections   80

6 Transformations in Soviet 'Survivals' Ethnography in the Post-World War Two Period   83
Soviet "Theoretical and Practical Narrowness in Evaluating the Beliefs and Rituals of the Peoples of Central Asia"?: G.P. Snesarev's Late-Coming Challenge   83
Revisiting the Marxian-Engelsian Framework   86

The Curious Absence of Concern for 'Pre-Islamic Survivals' in Soviet Anti-Islamic Propaganda Literature in the Pre-World War Two Period 88
Snesarev and the Soviet Deployment of 'Pre-Islamic Survivals' for Renewed Anti-Religious Propaganda Efforts in the Post-World War Two Period 94
Clarifying the Chronological Frame of Soviet 'Survivals' Ethnography 98
The Importance of Kazakh Nomadic Steppe Culture in Snesarev's Understanding and Deployment of 'Pre-Islamic Survivals' Among Other Central Asian Muslim Peoples 101
Part Two Conclusion: Summary of Soviet Historical Sources 102

Part III Historiographical Constructions of and Debates Over Kazakh Religious History and Identity in Soviet and Post-Soviet Kazakh Scholarship

7 The Framing of Kazakh Religious History and Identity in Post-World War Two Soviet Kazakh Publications 107
Kakimzhanov, About the Reactionary Essence of the Religion of Islam *(1953)* 108
Bisenov, The Origin of Islam and Its Class Significance *(1955)* 113
Duisenbin, About the Religion of Islam and Its Current State *(1961)* 121
K. Mashrapov Devotion to Islam—A Detrimental Survival *(1962)* 124
Concluding Reflections 125

8 Religious-Cultural Revivalism as Historiographical Debate: Post-Soviet Kazakh Perspectives on Their Past 129
Framing the Essential Issues 131
Tengrist Historiography 132
Islamic Approaches and Christian Interludes 140
Concluding Reflections 157

Part IV International Post-Soviet 'Survivals' Scholarship in Global Historical Perspective

9 Divergent Views on the Historical and Present Relation of Shamanism and Islam in International Post-Colonialist Scholarship   163
Sultanova, Zarcone and Hobart on Female Musical and Healing Traditions in Post-Soviet Studies of Shamanism and Sufism   164
Deweese's Critique of Turkish, French and Soviet Scholarship   166
Revisiting the Evidence from Privratsky, Muslim Turkistan   168
Historically Interactive and Transformational Understandings and Definitions of 'Islam' and 'Shamanism'   173
Concluding Reflections   177

10 Retrospect and Prospect: Situating Post-Soviet "Survivals" Scholarship Within a World Historiographical Frame   181
Post-Colonialist Agendas and the Historian's Task   181
Debates Over Terminology: Beyond 'Syncretism' and 'Pre-Islamic' Constructs?   184
Continuities and Discontinuities in Colonialist vs. Post-Colonialist Historiography   187
In Search of the Historical End Point of Conversion   189
Distinguishing Historical Fact from Fiction: Description vs. Analysis vs. Thesis   190
Historiographical Trends in the Post-World War Two Era   193
'Survivals' as Historical Heritage, 'Remnants' of Crosscultural Contact and Exchange   197
'Religious Survivals', 'Dual Faith' and "Integral" Religious Identities   201

Conclusion: A Summary of the Main Points of the Study	205
Appendices	211
Notes	243
Bibliography: Primary Sources	347
Index	385

CHAPTER 1

Introduction: Framing the Study

BACKGROUND AND CONTEXT

Studies of Central Asian religious history and identity are enmeshed in a complex web of religious, cultural, linguistic, economic and political dynamics taking shape in the international arena, particularly those triggered by the Soviet collapse, the post-911 'War on Terror,' the rise of China and the reassertion of expansionist ambitions in Russia, most recently in Ukraine. Closely related to or emerging from these large-scale developments and trends have been the rise of ISIS as well as the Ukrainian 'Orange,' Georgian 'Rose' and Kyrgyz 'Tulip' revolutions together with related confrontations in a 'New Great Game' or 'neo-Cold War' involving Russia, China, the North Atlantic (cf. 'Western') world and Turkey over Crimea, Ukraine, the Uighurs, Chechnya and other Central Eurasian regions, resources and peoples. Central Asian religious identity and its developing trends remain therefore, as they have throughout their history, intimately tied to broader Central Eurasian and Middle Eastern Islamic ones.[4] And this long-time transregional exchange goes on both reflexively shaping and being shaped by the dynamics of the broader Asian and international worlds.

Against this more complex transregional and international backdrop, the historical formation of Central Asian religious identity in relation to its emerging trends today remains, as it has from at least the early nineteenth century down to the present, deeply debated. Concerning

© The Author(s), under exclusive license to Springer Nature Singapore Pte Ltd. 2023
R. C. Weller, *'Pre-Islamic Survivals' in Muslim Central Asia*, Islam and Global Studies,
https://doi.org/10.1007/978-981-19-5697-3_1

questions of Islamic identity in particular, Devin Deweese, in his detailed study of *Islamization and Native Religion* among the Central Asian peoples, noted "a persistent fear and hostility toward Islam...combined with general unfamiliarity with the Inner Asian world" which resulted in "contradictory dismissals of Islam as either ungenuine or uncivilized."[5] Preoccupation in the West with Islam as a potentially violent religion reinforce this dichotomist approach, leaving little room for normalized conceptions of Muslim faith and practice. A long history of alleged 'clashes' between essentialized constructions of Western and Islamic 'civilizations' traced as far back as the very rise of Islam serve, within Western historiographical interpretations, as grounds for perpetuating such views. The rise of ISIS provides the latest proof for this paradigm. Islam remains primarily a 'security' issue for the Western, Russian and Chinese (cf. also Israeli) powers. Representatives of both the business and religious missionary interests of these world powers share that concern and, therefore, also desire to stem Islamic influence across not only the Middle East and North Africa, but Central Asia and the broader world. It is within this regional and global context[6] that the nearly two-centuries-old debates over religious history and identity in Central Asia take on renewed though transformed meaning and urgency. These debates concern, at their heart, the question of the historic and present relation of Islam to 'pre-Islamic' traditions within Central Asia. Although Islam is clearly the predominant faith tradition of all the Central Asian peoples, questions as to how that predominance has been achieved and maintained, and how it relates to 'survivals' of various 'pre-Islamic' traditions, remain front and center.

The Question of Kazakh Religious-Cultural History and Identity: An Illustrative Case Study

While the question of 'pre-Islamic survivals' has remained relevant among the Uzbeks, Tajiks, Tatars and other Central Asian peoples to varying degrees, debates over the issue in relation to the Kazakhs (and Kyrgyz) have received fairly sustained and notable attention, both in national- and foreign-language scholarship, from at least the early nineteenth-century onward. My own domain of linguistic expertise also resides in Kazakh. I thus focus my main attention within this study on the question in relation to the Kazakhs, though highlight other Central

Asian peoples at key junctures along the way. Much of the deeper history of historiography and ethnography covered in the main chapters of Part One, in particular, also pertain to all of the Central Asian peoples in general, so that my focus upon the question in relation to Kazakh religious history and identity occurs primarily in Parts Three and Four as well as here in the Introduction to the volume. The question of Kazakh religious history and identity serves as both a topic of specialized focus and an illustrative case study within the broader field of Central Asian studies.

Discussions of Kazakh and broader Central Asian religious-cultural identity must be understood against the backdrop of a complex religious-cultural history involving multiple traditions emanating from both within and beyond Central Asia. Some of the most prevalent traditions which preceded Islam by many centuries and remained for long centuries beyond its initial spread into the region include Shamanism, Tengrism (indigenous 'Sky-God'[7] worship), Zoroastrianism, Judaism, Buddhism and Christianity.[8]

From the Tsarist through the Soviet and on into the post-Soviet periods, questions have typically focused on just how genuine Kazakh Muslim identity and practice has been: Were the Kazakhs introduced to Islam early or late in their history and, relatedly, should they be counted 'true, devout' or only 'casual' Muslims 'in name only'? Tursin Hafiz Gabitov, a professor of religious, cultural and philosophical studies at al-Farabi Kazakh National University,[9] in his discussion of "Relational Dynamics of Religious Systems among the Kazakhs," overviews the main, competing perspectives as follows:

1. "The Kazakhs accepted Islam formally only late in their history, and it had a negative impact on the national culture" (missionary point of view);
2. "In traditional Kazakh culture the influence of shamanism, Zoroastrianism, and Tengrism is more predominate than Islam, so these earlier religions need to be revived anew" (archaistic [cf. 'veneer'] point of view);
3. "Though Muslim mentality is predominate in the south of Kazakhstan, in other regions Islam was not spread so widely; some of the people of those regions are even the descendants of Buddhists, Nestorian Christians, and Manicheans" (separatist point of view);

4. "Kazakhs accepted the religion of Islam under the influence of people of Central Asia [i.e. Uzbeks in the south] and those along the Volga River [i.e. Tatars from the north]" (the theory of outside influence); and

5. "The religion of the Kazakhs has never gone beyond the level of ancient mythology and ritual" (myth-ritual [cf. 'veneer'] point of view).

Among recent Muslim scholars located in the West, one of the more prominent writers on Islamic history in Central Asia, Adeeb Khalid, holds that "the Islamization of the Kazakhs was...completed only in the late nineteenth century."[10] While he does not explicitly state that the Kazakhs held to 'pre-Islamic' beliefs and practices up to this point, it is clearly implied. Among Western and presumably non-Muslim scholars continuing to locate primary religious identity for the Kazakhs in various 'pre-Islamic' religious-cultural traditions, Richard Foltz, in his study of *Religions of the Silk Road*, considers Islam a shallow overlay covering deeper historical traditions. He, thus, suggests that "[t]o this day among the Kazakhs one can find shamans who perform traditional shamanistic rituals using the Qur'an, Arabic letters, and such."[11] In similar fashion, James Thrower, in his study of *The Religious History of Central Asia from the Earliest Times to the Present Day*, holds that "[t]he Kazakhs, who were not finally converted to Islam until well into the nineteenth century, are the least Islamicised of all the Turkic peoples of Central Asia, continuing to observe much of their traditional religion even to the present-day. ...It was, in fact, the Russians who encourage[d] the Kazakhs to become Muslims..."[12] Likewise, Ira M. Lapidus, within his original as well as recently revised study of the history of *Islamic Societies to the Nineteenth Century*, advances the view that among the Kazakhs, "Islam...probably made little headway until the eighteenth century, when Tatar merchants, missionaries, secretaries, and teachers helped construct mosques and schools" and even then "[t]heir practice of Islam... merged ancient folk beliefs and traditions with new religious practices."[13]

These serve as just a few examples from several prominent scholars writing on Central Asian religious history.[14] All of these works, it should be noted, are general introductions or broad surveys, not specialized studies of Kazakh religious history and identity. Thrower's work provides the most comprehensive coverage—though broadly of Central Asia, not specifically the Kazakhs. Even more, it is a draft manuscript published posthumously on his behalf by a colleague. It relies heavily on secondary Russian and English sources. And Thrower's main expertise was Soviet atheism and its historiographical and ethnographical treatment of early world religious history, not Central Asian religious history.

Following trends in post-colonialist historiography, other Western scholars have assessed these inherited Tsarist- and Soviet-influenced perspectives more critically. They counter by defending an authentically (cf. "integral") Islamic identity for the Kazakhs, albeit one still often distinguished as a unique but genuine expression of Islam which preserves and integrates numerous Central Asian religious-cultural traditions. Chief among these is Devin Deweese. His primary works treat issues of religious conversion and identity among Central Asian Muslims in the Mongol and post-Mongol periods, preceding but historically related to the later rise of the Kazakhs. In his study of *Islamization and Native Religion*, Deweese denounces "a litany of uncritically accepted pronouncements on Islamization" as "clearly flawed by a remarkable misunderstanding both of the nature of Islam and of the indigenous religious conceptions that preceded Islamization" while "at the same time" being "patently uninformed by any of the conceptual tools developed over the last century for the humanities and social sciences by the field of *Religionswissenschaft*." This is, Deweese insists, largely because scholars "have rarely looked further than nineteenth-century descriptions, and, more important, have never 'listened' to indigenous accounts of intertwining religious and ethnic identities." For Deweese, "[i]t is the critical value of such indigenous accounts of conversion that must be stressed" because they provide "our *only* access to the *meaning* of conversion for those peoples."[15]

Deweese expresses concern that Central Asian "historical identities" have never been "seriously examined in [their] historical context." One should not think because of this, however, that he is concerned with the actual history of conversion as it took place. In his view,

> even a thorough reconstruction of the historical setting and events that occurred, and even a precise description of 'what happened' could not convey the *significance* of the conversion understood and felt, religiously, by the adherents of the new faith and their communal heirs. The 'conversion' happened, and had historical antecedents and consequences, but in and of itself was at the same time beyond the ken of historical constructions.[16]

Correspondingly, his work is not a history of Islamization in Central Asia, but an in-depth analysis of one particular conversion narrative—namely Otemish Hajji's mid-sixteenth-century account of the early fourteenth-century conversion of Ozbek Khan of the Golden Horde, its "meaning of conversion for those peoples," and "its many echoes" among various Central Asian Muslim peoples across the ages.[17] Deweese's study follows the comparative history of religions school epitomized by Mircae Eliade[18] as well as the 'cultural turn' in historiography pioneered by Clifford Geertz and other anthropologists in the 1970s.[19] It is vast and rich, thoroughly informed and persuasive, a monumental and impressive contribution to the field. Certain of his comparative interpretational suggestions, however, driven as they are by foundational assumptions and goals shaped by the post-colonial, particularly post-Soviet debates he is addressing, raise important questions about his thesis.

Following Deweese, and completing his doctoral work under him, Allen J. Frank has done more than any other scholar to-date to address issues of religious history and identity among the Kazakhs (as well as certain other Central Asian Muslim peoples). Particularly noteworthy here would be, first, his chapter on "Islamic Transformation on the Kazakh Steppe, 1742–1917: Toward an Islamic History of Kazakhstan under Russian Rule." He also published a volume titled *Muslim Religious Institutions in Imperial Russia: The Islamic World of Novouzensk District and the Kazakh Inner Horde, 1780–1910*. It is a study "based primarily on a single manuscript...written in 1910" by a Muslim scholar of the time. Beyond this, he worked with Mirkasyim A. Usmanov to produce a co-edited volume titled *An Islamic Biographical Dictionary of the Eastern Kazakh Steppe, 1770–1912* which, with an introduction, provides a translation of a 1912 manuscript originally published by another Muslim scholar of the time. Along with his chapter surveying developments between the late eighteenth and early twentieth centuries, Frank (with assistance from Usmanov) provides an enormous wealth of detail to help clarify major gaps as well as correct Tsarist and Western misrepresentations of the crucial period covered. At the same time, crucial questions are raised by uncritical dependence on certain of his sources as well as his attempts to make broad, sweeping generalizations about issues of broader religious history and identity based on the limited, local historical sources and periods he treats.

Heavily influenced by the work of both Geertz and Deweese, Bruce G. Privratsky produced an in-depth study of *Muslim Turkistan: Kazak*

Religion and Collective Memory (2001). Privratsky, like Deweese and Frank, takes up the cause of answering Tsarist, Soviet and Western approaches which deny the essential "integrity" of Kazakh Muslim identity. He thus makes his main aim to defend "the premise that the Kazak ancestors were Muslim." However, whereas Deweese takes a cultural and comparative history of religions approach centered in the post-Mongol era, and Frank, methodologically and disciplinarily, a more conventional historical approach concentrating on the late Tsarist age, Privratsky utilizes the tools of cultural anthropology to demonstrate the authentic and integral Muslim nature of Kazakh religious identity and practice in the post-Soviet period, interspersing within the first two chapters limited critical discussion of the nineteenth-century historiographical paradigms he seeks to set straight. Privratsky's work, like that of Deweese, follows the 'cultural turn' in anthropological and historical studies (see Chapter 10, Conclusion). In doing so, he walks a very fine, ambivalent line between downplaying the need for "a religious ethnohistory [to] be reconstructed in detail" and "cultural pressures, whether native or foreign, demanding that a people build its identity honorably from genuine historical sources."[20]

Three additional works which have followed Privratsky's anthropological approach and carry the discussion beyond the Kazakhs to other Central Asian peoples, particularly the Uzbeks and Kyrgyz, are, first, Maria E. Louw's 2007 study of *Everyday Islam in Post-Soviet Central Asia*. In a review of the work published in the *Journal of Islamic Studies*, Deweese commended Louw's work for being, in his own estimation, "free of the influence of interpretative models entrenched during Soviet times, and gratifyingly unsullied by the unfruitful approaches to religion, and especially the focus on political Islam, characteristic of the Sovietological literature on Islam in Central Asia."[21] Louw foregrounded the 'Muslim' identity of her subjects over and above their ethnic-national or cultural identities. She drew her primary anthropological data from observations and interviews conducted in and around Bukhara, where a 'Bukharan' identity is still emphasized in large measure among both Uzbeks and Tajiks living there, over against their distinct ethnic or national identities, harkening back to the Bukharan Emirate, as a means of maintaining peace, harmony and friendship. The latter reflects ongoing influence of Soviet concerns reappropriated in a post-Soviet context. A shared history, together with a shared territory and a shared 'Muslim' identity, all serve as focal points of their shared and thus harmonious identity.[22] How these historical-cultural, linguistic, religious and geo-political factors influenced the outcomes of Louw's study are not clear. Neither are they grappled with in Deweese's review, which praises her for prioritizing 'Muslim' over cultural, ethnic and/or national identity.

In contrast, David Montgomery's 2016 study of *Practicing Islam: Knowledge, Experience, and Social Navigation in Kyrgyzstan* aimed to construct an 'anthropology of religious knowledge,' yet insisted that it is misleading to use any one "common denominator," including religious (particularly 'Muslim') identity, to describe how various people understand themselves and navigate everyday life accordingly. When 'Muslimness' played a role in his 'informants' lives, he highlighted various understandings of 'Islam' among even family members and friends, definitions and understandings which almost always involved their own personal as well as local–regional contexts. Though focused on Kyrgyzstan, particularly the regions of Osh and Naryn, Montgomery's work includes ethnic Uzbeks living there. He conducted his fieldwork on various visits between 1999 and 2013, with particular emphasis given to an extensive survey conducted in 2005. It should be noted that elsewhere, in his chapter on "Religion" within his edited volume on *Central Asia: Contexts for Understanding* published in 2022, Montgomery asserted that "[r]emnants of the earlier traditions are largely that: remnants. Islam remains the most prevalent of the confessional traditions…"[23] While he clearly minimizes "remnants" (cf. 'survivals') within post-Soviet Central Asia, he does not dismiss them entirely, and does not offer any indication of what he perceives the balance between "the earlier," i.e., 'pre-Islamic,' "traditions" and Islam to be.

One year after Montgomery, Julie McBrien published a study titled *From Belonging to Belief: Modern Secularisms and the Construction of Religion in Kyrgyzstan*. She was concerned with elucidating both the distinction as well as intersecting relations between secularism, religion and national identity from a uniquely post-Soviet as opposed to Eurocentric point of view. She teased out tensions which have developed as post-Soviet approaches to Islam grounded primarily in 'belief' have confronted former Soviet communal emphases of religious-cultural identity. She drew primarily from fieldwork conducted in 2003–2004 in the Ferghana Valley in southern Kyrgyzstan where the encounter of these approaches was particularly noticeable.

All three of these works lack deeper historical grounding, though they provide varying limited measures of broader historical context. Like

Privratsky, they follow a cultural anthropological approach which concerns itself more with self-understandings of 'Muslim' identity and practice in the present, i.e., the post-Soviet context in this case, rather than conclusions drawn from a more thorough-going historical study based in all the available historical sources, primary and secondary. In this respect, they are concerned more with 'history as (collective) memory,' or 'history and (collective) memory,' than with actual history. They thus yield understandings of and implications for 'Muslim identity' which have more psychological-social than historical groundings. While these types of studies are certainly important and have their own validity, the distinctions remain necessary and significant.

With a view to more conventional historical scholarship, two other works merit mention here in closing out this overview: First, an edited volume on *Kazakhstan: Religions and Society in the History of Central Eurasia* which features various contributions from noteworthy Central Asian as well as Western scholars.[24] It covers the earliest beginnings down to the mid-twentieth century, supplying, among much else, new archival research on Kazakh and Central Asian Muslim identity in the post-Mongol period within a framework emphasizing religious pluralism in the heartland of the 'Silk Roads.' Finally, Robert D. Crews' chapter on "Nomads into Muslims" in *For Prophet and Tsar: Islam and Empire in Russia and Central Asia* is probably the most fair and balanced treatment to-date of the debate over Kazakh religious history and identity in nineteenth-century Tsarist Russia.[25] He offers in-depth analysis of the views of Levshin, Malov, Babadzhanov, Valihanov and other key voices of the age adorned with liberal quotes from their works, wisely and skillfully leaving the 'critical tension' inherent in the debate unresolved, as indeed it was and remains.

CONCLUDING REFLECTIONS AND OVERVIEW OF CHAPTERS AND SECTIONS

All of the works highlighted above grapple with the question of 'pre-Islamic survivals' among the Central Asian peoples—the Kazakhs in particular—and the role that Tsarist and Soviet ethnography played in shaping the interpretations of their religious identity in direct connection to those alleged 'survivals.'

Because of their centrality in the study of Kazakh and broader Central Asian religious history and identity, this work is concerned with understanding, first, the origins and aims of both Tsarist and Soviet historiography and ethnography of Central Asia. Of particular interest is their shared focus on 'pre-Islamic survivals'—or 'remnants,' 'vestiges,' 'traces,' 'relics,' etc. cf. also 'remains,' 'ruins'; Russian: остатки, следы, пережитки, реликты; cf. also сохранили; Kazakh: сарқыны, қалдықтары—and their distinctive appropriations of those interrelated constructs (or concepts) for religious missionary, social-legal, political identity and other imperial purposes. When, why and how did the Tsarist and Soviet ethnographic traditions each begin distinguishing between 'pre-Islamic' and 'Islamic' identity in Central Asia via the conceptual apparatus of 'remnants/survivals' and what is the historical relation between these two historiographical/ethnographic schools, as well as the historical relation of each to other European, Middle Eastern and Central Asian traditions of both religious and secular historiography? As the ensuing study will demonstrate, the answer to these questions involves placing Tsarist and Soviet scholarship within a broader global frame of 'remnants/survivals' historiography and ethnography tracing its roots back to Hebrew-Jewish, Christian and Islamic sacred texts and the cultural-civilizational traditions which they helped shape.

Parts One and Two (Chapters 2–6) of this study thus trace the historical roots of the conceptual lens of 'survivals' from the late nineteenth-century theories of E.B. Tylor, James Frazer and others, in debate with monotheistic 'degenerationists' and Protestant anti-Catholic polemicists, back to their origins in Jewish, Christian and Muslim traditions—inclusive of Russian Orthodoxy—as well as later more secularized forms in the German Enlightenment and Romanticist movements, down to their appropriations by both Tsarist and Soviet ethnographers of Muslim Central Asia for their respective religious missionary, social-legal, political identity and other imperial purposes. A close, careful reading of these chapters reveals that what may appear on the surface (by way of a more cursory reading) as various, disparate historiographies are, in fact, historically interconnected strands all tying into Tsarist and Soviet appropriations of 'pre-Islamic survivals' within their respective historiographies and ethnographies of the Central Asian peoples.

Part Three (Chapters 7 and 8) moves on to analyze historiographical depictions and related debates over Kazakh and broader Central Asian religious identity among Soviet and post-Soviet Kazakh (as opposed to Russian) sources in particular. Once again here, though the primary focus is upon the Kazakhs, the historiographical depictions and related debates contain both reference to and relevance for other Central Asian Muslim peoples. While the phrasing "pre-Islamic survivals" is not always explicitly employed in all the historiography covered in Part Three, the question of "pre-Islamic survivals" in relation to Kazakh (and other Central Asian) Islamic identity is always central.

Parts One and Two are thus concerned with the history of the concept (or construct) of "pre-Islamic survivals" while Part Three is focused upon the resulting historiography, where the concept is not always explicitly employed but is always nonetheless implicitly present. Appendix One ties in closely with Part Three inasmuch as it covers a historiographical debate between two late nineteenth-, early twentieth-century Tsarist figures over the question of Kazakh religious identity in relation to the impact of the late eighteenth-century liberal Enlightenment policies of Catherine II on their Islamization.

Part Four (Chapters 9 and 10) of the volume addresses the central issues raised in the volume by revisiting the problem of "pre-Islamic survivals" in post-Soviet international scholarship. It raises critical points about some of the more influential Western scholarship in particular, in direct relation to Central Asian national sources. Picking up from especially Chapters 7 and 8, Chapter 9 pays special attention to the problem of "Shamanism and Islam." Chapter 10 then expands the discussion by highlighting the complexity of the overall problem of "pre-Islamic survivals" within broader world historiographical trends, both those emerging and taking shape within the Western world in the post-World War Two era as well as Turkish and Iranian traditions grappling with some of the same points of debate over the question of "pre-Islamic survivals."

The study includes comparative analysis of Edvard Westermarck's 1933 study of *Pagan Survivals in Mohammedan Civilisation*, historiographical debates over "pre-Islamic Survivals" among Black African and South Asian Muslim Peoples, and critique of the legacy of Clifford Geertz and Western post-colonialist scholarship in relation to diverging trends of historiography in the post-World War Two era, particularly UNESCO's "History of Humanity" project. The latter intentionally aimed to counter the exclusivist-oriented nationalist and racist historiographical trends which fed into Nazi Germany and the resulting Holocaust, Apartheid South Africa and the segregationist United States, along with other colonialist-imperialist projects.

Drawing from European, Central Asian, Middle Eastern and world history, the fields of ethnography and anthropology, as well as Christian and Islamic studies, this volume contributes to scholarship on 'syncretism' and 'conversion'; definitions of Islam; history as identity and heritage; religion, ethnicity and nationalism; pluralism and multiculturalism; interreligious relations; crosscultural contact and exchange in world history; and more. It adds to discussions taken up by L.R. Rambo and C.E. Farhadian, eds., *The Oxford Handbook of Religious Conversion* (2014), A.M. Leopold and J.S. Jensen, eds., *Syncretism in Religion* (2014), W.H. Harrison, *In Praise of Mixed Religion: The Syncretism Solution in a Multifaith World* (2014), Elana Jefferson-Tatum, "Beyond Syncretism and Colonial Legacies in the Study of Religion" (2020), S. Ahmed, *What Is Islam? The Importance of Being Islamic* (2015), L. Stenberg and P. Wood, eds., *What is Islamic Studies? European and North American Approaches to a Contested Field* (2022), J.H. Bentley, *Old World Encounters: Cross-Cultural Contacts and Exchanges in Pre-Modern Times* (1993), J.T. Davidann and M.J. Gilbert, *Cross-Cultural Encounters in Modern World History, 1453-Present* (2018), S. Berger, *The Past as History: National Identity and Historical Consciousness in Modern Europe* (2015), UNESCO's *History of Humanity* project (1946–2009) and more.

This marks the first extended study of "survivals" to-date as it pertains specifically to Tsarist and Soviet historiographical and ethnographical traditions within Central Asia. It is one of the few studies to focus on 'survivals' as a conscious conceptual lens for the study of human history and culture since Margaret Hodgen, *The Doctrine of Survivals: A Chapter in the History of Scientific Method in the Study of Man* (1936). It builds upon the seminal work of Stella Rock, *Popular Religion in Russia: 'Double Belief' and the Making of an Academic Myth* (2007), along with foundational inquiries into Tsarist and Soviet ethnography of Islamic Central Asia by Francine Hirsch (2005), Vladimir Bobrovnikov (2011), Devin Deweese (2011), John Schoeberlein (2011) and S.S. Alymov (2013). It adds significantly to the historical depth and scope of these investigations while also revising certain suggestions advanced within their seminal scholarship. It is carefully grounded in original research based on primary source material, interacting with relevant secondary scholarship in various fields, including a wealth of Kazakh and other Central Asian national scholarship.

PART I

Historical Sources of Tsarist 'Survivals' Ethnography

While on the surface, the chapters in Part One may appear to treat various, disparate historiographies, they are all historically interconnected strands tying into Tsarist and Soviet appropriations of 'pre-Islamic survivals' among the Central Asian peoples. The various strands treated within this opening (second) chapter in particular require special attention with respect to their historical-chronological relationship: I begin the chapter by critically analyzing Devin Deweese's suggested eighteenth- and nineteenth-century sources for E.B. Tylor's theory of 'survivals,' demonstrating that the picture is far more complicated than Deweese has proposed. It was not, in fact, Protestant anti-Catholic polemicists who inspired Tylor, but monotheistic 'degenerationists' whose agenda reached well beyond the Protestant-Catholic controversies, and concerned the very origins of religious faith among humanity, a paradigm which both Protestants and Catholics (as well as Muslims) in fact shared. (Indeed, many, though not all, within these monotheistic traditions still today explain 'other' religions within the world and its history as 'corrupted survivals' of an allegedly original form of monotheism revealed to Adam in the Garden of Eden.) I then push the search historically deeper into the sixteenth and seventeenth centuries in Dutch and German Enlightenment writings which feed into both Western as well as Eastern European traditions, including Tsarist Russia directly. From this point, in lieu of the centrality of various Christian and Christian-offshoot sources and agendas so prevalent within the storyline, I go all the way back to the historical roots of these Western and Eastern

European traditions, namely the Hebrew-Jewish and Christian scriptural and later church sources which eventually fed into all of the various strands treated in both Chapters 2 and 3. This includes, within Chapter 2, the Reformation and counter-Reformation sources. The latter in particular—drawing from long-established traditions reaching back to the scriptural sources and the various church controversies of 'pagan survivals' which they spawned—tie back into the original discussion regarding Tylor and the eighteenth- and nineteenth-century debates over 'survivals' which shaped the formulation of his theory. Tylor's theory eventually served, alongside the earlier developing Greek and Russian Orthodox and European romanticist/folk nationalist (as well as Middle Eastern and Central Asian Islamic) schools in particular, as major influences on late nineteenth-century Tsarist and early twentieth-century Soviet historiography and ethnography.

In spite of the primary focus on religious-cultural sources and related matters throughout these explorations, readers should keep their eye on broader historical comparisons to and ties with both Western and Eastern European nationalist historiography, especially as religious-cultural identity issues tie into debates over national history and identity. The close tie between religious and nationalist historiography becomes particularly evident later in Chapter 8, but is latent throughout the study.[26]

CHAPTER 2

Religious-Cultural 'Survivals' in Euro-American and Euro-Slavic Christian and Secular Sources

E.B. TYLOR AND PROTESTANT ANTI-CATHOLIC POLEMICISTS AS SOURCES FOR SOVIET 'SURVIVALS' ETHNOGRAPHY?

Devin Deweese, in his study of "Survival Strategies: Reflections on the Notion of Religious 'Survivals' in Soviet Ethnographic Studies of Muslim Religious Life in Central Asia," suggests an epistemic genealogy for Soviet ethnography which traces its roots from early eighteenth-century Protestant polemics against Catholics. Deweese analyzes two Protestant works and draws broad comparisons to Soviet 'survivals' ethnography of Muslim Central Asia. First is the 1729 work of Conyers Middleton, *... the Exact Conformity between Popery and Paganism: or, The Religion of the Present Romans to be derived entirely from that of their Heathen Ancestors* (1729). Middleton complains upon his visit to Rome that all the ceremonies of the Roman Catholic Church "appeared plainly to have been copied from the *Rituals of Primitive Paganism*, as if handed down by an uninterrupted Succession from the *Priests of old* to the *Priests of New Rome...*"[27] The second is the 1774 work of Reverend Joseph Brand, who attacked three types of 'survivals' in Catholicism: "beliefs and rites linked to the yearly cycle of the calendar; life-cycle rites of rural folk, 'from christening to wake'; and beliefs about witches, charms, ghosts, etc." Deweese notes in the latter case—quite accurately—that these are the essential "categories of rites and beliefs typically 'explained'

© The Author(s), under exclusive license to Springer Nature Singapore Pte Ltd. 2023
R. C. Weller, *'Pre-Islamic Survivals' in Muslim Central Asia*, Islam and Global Studies,
https://doi.org/10.1007/978-981-19-5697-3_2

in terms of religious survivals in Central Asian contexts as well." He then argues that these Protestant anti-Catholic polemics helped shape Edward Burnett Tylor's 1871 work on *Primitive Culture: Researches into the Development of Mythology, Philosophy, Religion, Language, Art, and Custom* and other late nineteenth-century 'history of religions' scholars. Tylor thus becomes the conduit by which early eighteenth-century Protestant polemics against Catholics serve as the suggested historical roots for Soviet ethnography of the Central Asian peoples. But Deweese offers only "[t]he widespread currency, in Europe, of such attitudes toward religion and ritual" as broad, circumstantial evidence for the alleged influence of these Protestant approaches on "the evolutionary models of religious and cultural development formulated in the second half of the nineteenth century," particularly those of Tylor, highlighting also Tylor's anti-Catholic Quaker background.[28]

There are two related but distinct questions which Deweese's hypothesis raises: the first concerns the question of the alleged influence of early eighteenth-century Protestant polemics against Catholics—particularly that of Middleton and Brand—on Tylor, and the second concerns the alleged influence of Tylor on Soviet ethnography, especially that concerned with the peoples of Central Asia. Couched between is the question of Tsarist ethnography and its relation to these various schools as well. I will deal primarily though not exclusively with the latter question in this and the following two chapters (Part One), detailing a complex epistemic genealogy lying behind the Tsarist ethnographic tradition(s) which eventually merges with Tylorean and other streams, including that of Marx and Engels, to feed into the Soviet school(s). The Soviet sources will then be taken up in Part Two.

Tylor and 'Survivals' Historiography in the Nineteenth-Century: Monotheistic Degenerational versus Evolutionary Developmental Theories of Early Human History

While the broader Protestant-Catholic polemical context to which Deweese appeals certainly has some merit, circumstantial though it be, Tylor does not in fact leave the question open as to where his influences came from. He explicitly cites Middleton's 1729 work in *Primitive Culture*,[29] demonstrating beyond question his awareness of Middleton's publication. And yet, Middleton was only one of multiple sources which

Tylor cited, with Joseph Brand nowhere referenced. One important additional source which Tylor did reference, however, but left out of the picture by Deweese, was Joseph Priestley (1733–1804), the English scientist and religious historian who, in 1794, moved to the United States (Pennsylvania) and became one of the most influential figures to shape the religious views of Thomas Jefferson, John Adams, Benjamin Franklin and other American 'founding fathers.'[30] Tylor in fact placed Priestley among those he considered, by way of their books, to be some of the most influential figures of the time, each of whom were to be viewed "not for and by himself, but occupying his proper place in history." He thus named Priestley together in a list of six which included Gottfried Leibniz, René Descartes, John Dalton, John Milton and Homer.[31] Although Tylor did not name the specific book(s) by Priestley which he had in view, he doubtless knew of Priestley's famous treatment of *An History of the Corruptions of Christianity* originally published in 1782. In seeking "the recovery of the genuine doctrines of christianity [sic]," Priestley concerned himself with tracing out essential "departure[s] from the original standard of christian faith or practice" by identifying corruptions which had "left considerable vestiges in some christian churches."[32] Priestley references the work of Middleton some fifteen or more times throughout both volumes of his work (though not strictly Middleton's 1729 work on *Popery and Paganism*). It is entirely possible, even probable, therefore, that Tylor discovered Middleton via Priestley. It should also be noted that Priestley himself was not so much a 'Protestant anti-Catholic polemicist' as an anti-Trinitarian polemicist whose lectures and writings on religious, particularly Christian, history made seminal contributions to the founding of Unitarianism, though his approach was clearly an offshoot of the Protestant anti-Catholic tradition.

Minimizing Middleton's importance even further, Tylor originally introduced the concept of 'survivals' before ever referencing Middleton or any other Protestant anti-Catholic (or Unitarian) polemicist in the writing of *Primitive Culture*. He introduced it two years earlier in a "Lecture at University College, London," offered in April 1869 on the subject of "Survival of Savage Thought in Modern Civilization."[33] The sources he cites in his lecture do not include Middleton, Brand or Priestley. Neither does he cite Middleton, Brand or Priestley in his 1865 work, *Researches into the Early History of Mankind and the Development of Civilization*. While it is certainly possible that Tylor was already aware of Middleton and other Protestant anti-Catholic (and Unitarian) polemicists, it would be more in line with the historical evidence to argue that Tylor's later citation of Middleton (as well as Priestley) in *Primitive Culture* simply served to supplement and strengthen, not originally inspire, Tylor's already formulated theory.

Beyond this lineage, Protestant anti-Catholic polemicists were not the only ones using the concept of 'survivals' (or 'remnants'). For example, the preeminent commentator on English law, William Blackstone, argued in 1768 that certain British customs "may be the remnant of that pastoral state of our British and German ancestors which Caesar and Tacitus describe."[34] Here, Blackstone was leaning toward (proto-) romanticist appropriations of the concept of 'remnants,' using them to identify pre-Christian strands of English legal heritage. This early romanticist approach was more in line with the approach later emerging in Tylor and others, though certainly not with the same ultimate ethno-cultural aims in view (see below).

More importantly on the question of Tylor's sources, Margaret Hodgen, *The Doctrine of Survivals: A Chapter in the History of Scientific Method in the Study of Man* (1936), correctly observes that Tylor, in writing both the 1865 and 1871 works, was not guided or inspired by Protestant anti-Catholic polemic, but rather driven by his determination to disprove the 'anti-progressionist,' 'degenerationist' theories which had gained prevalence in his own (later) time through the writings of Richard Whately (1787–1863) and Whately's followers.[35] This was indicated in *Primitive Culture*. In that work, his chief motive and aim in emphasizing 'survivals' was to prove that their "appearance...seems to fit not so well with degradation from a high as with survival from a low civilization."[36] Tylor, in arguing against the notion of an original "high" God, i.e., monotheism, is undermining Protestant anti-Catholic polemics here, not drawing from or supporting them. This same line of thinking was already evident six years prior, in his 1865 *Researches into the Early History of Mankind*, when he cites the 1839 work of a "Bavarian traveler," Dr. Martius, which details life among South American Indians. After quoting Martius—"when I considered that so complex a superstition was but the *remnant* of an originally pure worship of nature, and what a chain of complications must have preceded such a degradation"—Tylor retorts:

> I cannot but think that Dr. Martius's deduction is the absolute reverse of the truth. Looking at the practices of sorcery among the lower races as a whole, they have not the appearance of mutilated and misunderstood

fragments of a higher system of belief and knowledge. ... There is a remarkable peculiarity by which the sorcery of the savage seems to repudiate the notion of its having come down from something higher, and to date itself from the childhood of the human race.[37]

Likewise elsewhere near the end of the original 1865 work, Tylor emphasizes that.

> [t]he chapter on "Images and Names"...is in the strongest opposition to the view strongly advocated by degenerationists, that these superstitious practices are mutilated *remnants* of a high system of belief which prevailed in former times. So far as may be judged from the scanty and defective evidence which has as yet been brought forward, I venture to think the most reasonable opinion to be that the course of development of the lower civilization has been on the whole in a forward direction, though interfered with occasionally and locally by the results of degrading and destroying influences.[38]

By 1871, in *Primitive Culture*, Tylor could articulate his own counter-argument as follows:

> Among evidence aiding us to trace the course which the civilization of the world has actually followed, is that great class of facts to denote which I have found it convenient to introduce the term 'survivals.' These are processes, customs, opinions, and so forth, which have been carried on by force of habit into a new state of society different from that in which they had their original home, and they thus remain as proofs and examples of an older condition of culture out of which a newer has been evolved.[39]

Accordingly—and once again reversing the 'degenerationist' apologetic—Tylor became convinced that "Survival in Culture...sets up in our midst primaeval monuments of barbaric thought and life" by "placing all along the course of advancing civilization way-marks full of meaning to those who can decipher their signs."[40] In other words, he believed 'survivals' (or 'remnants') were key to reconstructing the early history (cf. 'primitive culture') of humankind in precisely the opposite direction of the 'degenerationist' argument which was a presumed position of Judeo-Christian (and Islamic) monotheism. "Moreover," said Tylor, "there have to be included as partial survivals the mass of cases where enough of the old habit is kept up for its origin to be recognizable, though in taking a new form it has been so adapted to new circumstances as still to hold its place on its own merits."[41]

Given the above development of Tylor's thinking, I argue that Tylor did not, in fact—as he claims, and others have simply believed—"introduce" the concept of 'survivals' to the study of human civilizational history. The source of Tylor's doctrine, at least as he formulates it, comes directly from the 'anti-progressionist, degenerationist' proponents who originally sought to employ the concept in their own cause, long before Tylor made use of it. This also means that Deweese's suggestion regarding the influence of Protestant anti-Catholic polemic on Tylor's (and others') later doctrine of 'survivals' falls well short of explaining the historical origins of nineteenth-century Western as well as later (Tsarist and) Soviet 'survivals' ethnography. The concept of 'survivals' (or 'remnants') which Tylor came to employ so centrally in his own work, which then influenced numerous others, traces its roots by way of Martius (1839), followed by the 1840 work of William Cooke Taylor, *The Natural History of Society in the Barbarian and Civilized State*, and the 1854 pamphlet of Richard Whately, *On the Origin of Civilization*.[42] Tylor likewise evidenced certain romanticist notions and strategies of appropriation, though in Tylor's case, he applied them not to the nation, but the entire human race (see below).

'SURVIVALS' HISTORIOGRAPHY IN SEVENTEENTH-CENTURY GERMAN ENLIGHTENMENT SOURCES

Even beyond these lineages however, we can trace various historical strands feeding into Tylorean conceptions and appropriations back even earlier, from out of the same Western European Christian tradition, through the lines of Dutch and German Pietists playing a role in the (Dutch and) German Enlightenment. Han F. Vermeulen, *Before Boas: The Genesis of Ethnography and Ethnology in the German Enlightenment* (2015), highlights the work of Nicolaas Witsen (1641–1717), "a Dutch politician, geographer, and collector" who engaged extensively with Tsarist Russia in the late seventeenth and early eighteenth centuries. Witsen traveled to various parts of the Russian empire, developed networks of exchange with numerous Russians and befriended Peter the Great, aiding him in his Westernization of Russia. Witsen wrote an account of the Tatars and Siberia titled *North and East Tartarye*. It was published originally in 1692, based on his own travels as well as earlier writings he consulted.[43] In Witsen's 1692 work, he proposed "that the northern [Native] Americans descend from the Tartars, …[as] appears from many remnants of manners and customs (overblijfzelen van zeden en gewoonten) of the northern and eastern Tartars that are still found among the northern [Native] Americans in the present day."[44] Witsen, in fact, uses the Dutch term for 'remnants' ('overblijfzelen,' cf. also 'survivals,' 'vestiges') on numerous occasions throughout the work, including later references to "the honorable old remnants of the Christian Faith" and "honored vestiges of Idols."[45] One or both of these latter two references may actually be the physical 'remains' of buildings, statues or visible structures, since the majority of his usages are, in fact, archeological in nature. But given the clear appropriation of the term in relation to "manners and customs," the "remnants of the Christian faith" may include Christian rituals and other practices. Elsewhere he speaks of "remnants of Jews who called themselves Israelites" and "the present remnants of Christians." He thus uses the term of both "customs and manners" and of the people themselves who observe those "customs and manners" (an important point to which I will soon return).[46]

With Witsen's reference to the "many remnants of manners and customs" of Central Asian Tatars preserved, as he saw it, among Native Americans, we have the appropriation of a 'remnants/survivals' historiography which, despite Witsen's Dutch Christian pietism, is not religiously polemical; there is no reference to or even hint of 'pagans' or 'idolatry' of any kind in the phrasing. Nor is it concerned with a 'degenerationist' view, which was also mainly a Christian-based interpretation sharing ideas of 'pagan idolatry' with Christian polemicists. And while it foreshadows in certain ways Tylor and the late nineteenth-century human civilizationist as well as 'history of religion' schools, it is not explicitly concerned with the reconstruction of 'primitive cultures,' though it does allude to 'the early history of mankind and the development of civilization' by shedding light on cultural links between peoples forged through migration in early human history. Witsen's reference thus assumes that the "remnants" of the Tatars of which he is speaking are 'pre-Islamic remnants,' since he clearly acknowledges Tatar Muslim identity in his own day elsewhere. This point will resurface later in the study. For now, it should be noted that Witsen's appropriation of a 'remnants' historiography not only precedes, but feeds historically into the views of later eighteenth-century romantic nationalists (see below), which may have, in turn, in remotely Hegelian fashion, provoked a degenerationist response, followed by the further response of Tylor and company's nineteenth-century human civilizationist school. Certainly Witsen's usage evidences affinities with both the romantic nationalist and human civilizationist appropriations of 'remnants/survivals' historiography, with the historical genealogy only put forward here as a hypothesis awaiting further research.

HEBREW-JEWISH AND CHRISTIAN SOURCES OF 'SURVIVALS' HISTORIOGRAPHY

With a history reaching back to at least the late 1600s, the insufficiency of Hodgen's study of 'survivals' historiography—important though it be—is clearly exposed. Hodgen argued that, "[o]wing to the British source of the doctrine and the singularly repetitious character of the vast literature to which it gave rise throughout the world of scholarship, it has seemed wise for brevity's sake to restrict discussion to English materials."[47] In fact, the paradigm and its history run far deeper and wider, well beyond Deweese's suggestion of the eighteenth-century Protestant 'pagan survivals' polemic against Catholics or the late seventeenth-century Dutch and German pietistic enlightenment tradition glimpsed in the work of Witsen. These are only several of a number of complex intermingling strands of influence converging across the centuries, even millennia.

The wellsprings giving rise to these various historiographies of religious-cultural 'survivals' can be traced back some 1800–3500 years (depending on manuscript and oral tradition dating)[48] to the Hebrew and offshoot Christian (as well as later Islamic) scriptural and legal traditions themselves. The earliest examples of this can be traced back to the Hebrew Bible when it portrays God warning Israel that he "will cut off the remnant (Heb. הָרָאשׁ) of Baal from this place, and the names of the idolatrous priests (mixed in) among the priests."[49] While the passage is, in fact, speaking of the priests of Baal themselves as the 'remnants' to be "cut off," it is through them that 'idolatrous' or 'pagan remnants' (as rituals practiced among the previous Canaanite peoples) survive among the Israelites. Note also the allusion to 'syncretism' in the mixing together of these two traditions. Just as we see later in the Western Christian, Tsarist Orthodox and secular as well as Soviet 'remnants/survivals' traditions, the concept is used of both people and religious-cultural practices, with both often tied together and even used as a means of identification via association of people and practice. Both the peoples and their practices can play both positive and negative roles. That is to say, both 'righteous' and 'unrighteous' (i.e., 'idolatrous, pagan') remnants are identified, depending on the context and purpose of the narrator.

Ideas of 'pagan survivals' are also glimpsed in the call for Israel, in the time of Joshua, to "put away the gods that your ancestors served beyond the River and in Egypt, and serve the LORD."[50] While the Hebrew term for 'remnant/survival/vestige' does not appear explicitly in the passage, there is clear allusion to the concept, accompanied by the typical charge of 'syncretism' (and 'idolatry'). Along with this and other examples, the case of the Samaritans and 'the foreign peoples' with whom they intermingled is perhaps the best known, spanning both the Hebrew and Christian scriptural traditions. Thus the biblical writers complained that, "[t]o this day they do according to the earlier customs…They feared the Lord and served their own gods according to the custom of the nations from among whom they had been carried away into exile. …their children likewise and their grandchildren, as their fathers did…".[51]

To what extent these ancient Hebrew-Jewish and Christian (as well as later Islamic) scriptural traditions were independently shared with, influenced by or perhaps themselves influenced surrounding Middle Eastern or even broader Asian, African and Native American peoples and cultures is a question beyond the scope of this particular study, though one worth pursuing. The question has, likewise, been raised as to what kinds of distinctions might exist between the various monotheistic traditions which emerged in succession from out of the Middle Eastern context and the non-monotheistic traditions arising historically in other parts of the world. In close connection, what distinctions are there, if any, between "world religious" traditions and those which have remained more rooted in local, regional or even particular tribal or ethnic communities.[52]

Moving beyond the Hebrew-Jewish and Christian scriptural canons themselves, St. Augustine, in a sermon preached sometime after 396 CE, noted that "in celebration of a pagan superstition, Christians came to the sea and there they baptized themselves." He does not use the term 'remnant', 'survival' or otherwise, nor does he explicitly frame the practice in terms of a 'continuation' from 'pre-Christian' times, but the practice was most likely ancient and the concern with distinguishing between Christian and un-Christian practices is clear.[53] Indeed, the line between 'un-Christian' and 'pre-Christian' is often blurred and overlapping.

Augustine's reference is just one example. Tracing out all the various branches of this paradigm and its particular expressions within not just Western, but broader world Hebrew-Jewish and Christian history, would require a full-length monograph or even series of monographs. Some work along these lines has, in fact, already been done. For example, along with an earlier co-edited volume on *Paganism and Christianity, 100–425 CE: A Sourcebook* (1992), Ramsay MacMullen, *Christianity and Paganism in the Fourth to Eighth Centuries* (1997), has already studied "the determination of the Christian leadership to extirpate" what they perceived to be pagan survivals in the ancient Latin Christian church.[54] MacMullen's work elucidates how, especially in the early stages, 'pagan survivals' were understood more in terms of distinct competing religious practices which Christianity was attempting to overcome. That is, the question of how a 'pagan' world was converted to Christianity. But it is in that very process that 'pagan idolatrous practices' not only 'survive' distinctly in parallel, but are eventually imported into the church, becoming maintained by and/or intermingled with the practices of those who convert to Christianity from those 'pagan' backgrounds.

Adding to the contributions of MacMullen and others, Bernadette Filotas, *Pagan Survivals, Superstitions, and Popular Cultures in Early Medieval Pastoral Literature* (2005), covers "the aspects of popular religion and culture that the ecclesiastical hierarchy perceived as survivals of paganism and superstitions." Overlapping but extending the period covered by MacMullen, she treats Latin Christianity—particularly the Latin, Germanic and Celtic peoples in the northwestern half of the Roman Empire—between 500 and 1000 CE. Within her work, she cites, for example, from the Council of Tours in 567 CE, which expressed concern over professing Christians "persisting" in "the errors of the pagans," including the offering of food to deceased ancestors after returning home from participating in the church's feast of the Chair of St. Peter. The latter church feast, like Christmas, had been established on a former Roman holiday in order to try to displace it, in this case the Roman feast of *Caristia* which involved 'sacrifices' and dedications of food to household gods as well as their ancestral dead held on February 22. Thus Christian customs were themselves, in some cases, re-dressed 'remnants' of 'pre-Christian' practices. The Council of Tours also noted "those who keep pagan customs" such as visiting "chosen [read: sacred] places," particularly "rocks, trees or springs."[55] In another related study done by Ruth Mazo Karras, "Pagan Survivals and Syncretism in the Conversion of Saxony" (1986), she records that some 500–600 years later, in Saxony, Archbishop Unwan of Hamburg-Bremen "ordered all pagan rites, of which the superstition still flourished in the region, to be utterly banished," in particular "tree worship."[56] Although Unwan and the Council of Tours do not use the same Tylorean terminology of 'survivals,' 'remnants,' etc., the idea of 'pre-Christian' practices still continuing (cf. 'surviving') is clear in both, with the phrasing that I am citing here coming from the original sources themselves, not the later authors (i.e., Filotas or Karras) who are citing them (in English translation).

One unique and related example worth discussing here comes from yet a later period, namely the sixteenth-century Spanish Inquisition. The practice of forced conversions—from both Judaism and Islam to Spanish Catholic Christianity—raised the unavoidable question of whether those conversions were genuine. The Spanish Inquisition was concerned, at its heart, with distinguishing between (and then rooting out) 'pre-Christian' versus authentically 'Christian' beliefs and practices. These questions of Muslim versus Christian identity in the Spanish Inquisition extended well beyond the Iberian peninsula into the Spanish American colonies.[57] Note here carefully the relevance to debates over 'genuineness' as well as 'forced conversions' in treatments of 'pre-Islamic' versus 'Islamic' beliefs and practices in the Central Asian context. Similar questions plagued the Tsarist Russian empire, particularly in the forced conversions of Tatar and other Volga-Ural Muslims to Russian Orthodox Christianity in the eighteenth century (and earlier). Within the Euro-American trajectory, along with the opposition to pagan survivals highlighted above, the broader European Inquisitions reaching globally across the eleventh to the eighteenth centuries—from the onset of the Crusades down to the 'Salem witch trials' in the offshoot American colonies[58]—serve as further historical antecedents feeding into the eighteenth-century Protestant anti-Catholic polemic highlighted by Deweese.[59]

With respect to the historical development of a Protestant anti-Catholic polemic framed (in part) around a 'pagan survivals' historiography, it should be noted that the examples above come from the Catholic era, mostly prior to the Protestant Reformation. The Spanish Inquisition is the sole exception, emerging as it did in the earliest phases of the Reformation, itself a predominantly counter-Reformation movement. As the Spanish Inquisition sought to cleanse pre-Christian practices from their Jewish and Muslim converts, John Calvin penned his *Treatise on Relics* in 1543, shortly after returning to Geneva, Switzerland for his final twenty-plus years of ministry (1541–1564). Amid numerous denunciations of the entire practice of "worshipping" relics (cf. 'remnants,' 'survivals,' 'vestiges') of Christ and the saints, including supposed remnants of the wood from Jesus' cross, Calvin condemned it all as "a diabolical doctrine, expressly reproved by St Ambrose as a Pagan superstition." He thus rejected the entire 'cult of the saints.' In his reference to St. Ambrose, Calvin was implying that these 'pagan superstitions' had somehow survived via the Catholic Church since the fourth century. Ultimately Calvin pleaded: "it would be most important to abolish from amongst us Christians this pagan superstition of canonising relics, either of Christ or of his saints, in order to make idols of them; for this is a defilement and an impurity which should never be suffered in the Church."[60]

Calvin's work links back to the late nineteenth-century period when Tylor was in process of constructing his notions. Calvin's 1543 *Treatise on Relics* had been translated and re-published by Count Valerian Krasinski in 1870, together *With An Introductory Dissertation On the Miraculous Images, as Well as Other Superstitions, of the Roman Catholic and Russo-Greek Churches*. Krasinski was a Polish Calvinist who served as both an aristocratic politician and nationalist historian. His treatise was one of several to appear in the latter nineteenth century in both England and America. Others included an 1868 work by George Duncan on *Iconology: Papal Idolatry: Or, Modern Romanism: A Development of Ancient Paganism* (1868) and Abram Herbert Lewis's *Paganism Surviving in Christianity* (1892). Both Duncan and Krasinski's works were prior to Tylor's 1871 study of *Primitive Culture*, though neither were referenced by Tylor therein. Krasinski explicitly tied this appropriation of 'survivals' historiography as a strategy of Protestant anti-Catholic polemic back to the historical fathers of the Protestant Reformation.

Nineteenth-Century Romantic Nationalism and the Russian Orthodox Tradition of 'Dual Faith'

In spite of the historical depth and force of the respective Catholic and Protestant struggles against 'pagan survivals,' the historically related yet distinct problem of 'dual faith' (Russian: двоеверие, *dvoeverie*) as it emerged within the Eastern, especially Russian, Orthodox tradition was much nearer and more influential in shaping Russian historiography of Islamic Central Asia.

From early on, Nestor, famed author of *The Russian Primary Chronicle* (also known as *The Tale of Bygone Years*), chronicled Russian Orthodox hagiography and history between approximately 1080 and 1120. He thus wrote just one century after the famed conversion of Vladimir the Great in 988 CE, detailing the history both leading up to and following from that conversion, down to his own time. In his coverage of events in the year "6576," i.e., 1068, Nestor highlighted the "barbarian incursion" of a "multitude of nomads known as the Polovcians" who "attacked the land of the Rus'." He explained it as God's judgment against them for living "like pagans." This "pagan" life included the attachment of "superstitious significance" to various encounters, or to sneezing, and "other similar customs." "The churches still stand," he noted, "but when the hour of prayer is come, few worshippers are found in the church."[61] Earlier in his Chronicle, Nestor had detailed numerous "pagan customs" of various Slavic peoples who formed the Rus'.[62] Nestor also noted that, following his own exalted conversion from Russian paganism, Vladimir had "ordained that wooden churches should be built and established where pagan idols had previously stood," thus inseparably intermixing the historic traditions together for generations to come.[63]

Stella Rock has delved into this history in her study of *Popular Religion in Russia: 'Double Belief' and the Making of an Academic Myth* (2007), though curiously she offers little analysis of Nestor's work itself. She nonetheless provides an in-depth study which is highly relevant—both comparatively and historically—to the debates over 'pre-Islamic survivals' in the Central Asian Muslim context. Part of that in-depth study includes tracing out the comparative and historical relation of 'pagan survivals' within the Western and Eastern branches of Christendom. Among much else unveiled by that particular avenue of inquiry, she gives attention to the continuing debates and tensions over 'pagan survivals' between certain of the more puritanical Russian Orthodox clergy and the popular Russian peasantry across the seventeenth and eighteenth centuries.[64]

Rock starts off Chapter Three, "A History of Historians," by noting that the actual history behind "the academic concept of double-belief"—which she defines as "the preservation of pagan elements within the religious faith of the Russian *norod* or 'folk'"—"preceded," she says, "the appearance of the term itself in the scholarship of Russian history."[65]

In short, the history of the phenomenon preceded the later coining of the academic terminology employed to analyze it. The technical usage of the term emerged, in fact, within the romantic nationalist context of the late eighteenth, early nineteenth century coming into Russia via two channels. One was the influence of Euro-American 'Bible Societies,' particularly in this case the British and Foreign Bible Society, which inspired the founding of the Russian Bible Society in 1813. These emphasized the importance of 'national (cf. also folk) languages.'[66] The other was Johann Gottfried Herder and company who, from their own Western Protestant Christian perspective, concerned themselves with the history and nature of "folk culture and religion." As Rock explains in relation to the Russian Orthodox tradition:

> In terms of *dvoeverie*, the myth that the 'folk', unspoiled by modern, enlightened ideas, preserved pure and unchanging cultural and religious traditions rooted in the primitive, pre-Christian past, has had the greatest impact. This perception of the peasantry (generally equated with the 'folk') as bearers of an essentially static national culture led to the belief that pre-Christian religion could be reconstructed by the study of peasant belief and culture, and an obsession with identifying 'pagan survivals' with peasant religiosity.[67]

Among early Russians contributing to the development of these romantic notions were the court poet Vasily Trediakovsky (1703–1769). As early as 1735, he was drawing the attention of his Russian homeland to the "natural, ages-old poetry of the simple people." Mikhail Dmitrievich Chulkov (1743–1792) had likewise "published several large collections of fairy tales and folk songs in the 1760s and 1770s."[68]

Although Rock locates the origins of these ideas among Western European Christian thinkers, she points not to the Protestant anti-Catholic polemicists, but the romantic nationalists, particularly those in Russia. It would seem that both the Protestant polemicists and romantic nationalists are heirs to the same scripturally rooted tradition and its earlier historical outworking within Latin Christianity highlighted above, though the romantic nationalists clearly turned the concept on its head, employing it for purposes of reconstruction and affirmation rather than deconstruction and denial. Some of both of these purposes can be glimpsed in the Tsarist as well as Soviet ethnographical traditions, which distinguished, however arbitrarily, between 'national' and 'religious' history and identity. The Greek (and other Eastern) Orthodox branches of Christianity developed their own concern for 'pagan survivals' which fed into the Russian branch of this tradition, though further exploration of the Byzantine, particularly pre-Russian, strains of that history has yet to be undertaken.

Whatever its precise streams of influence, Rock goes on to highlight Russian figures conducting the "initial research into... 'pagan survivals'." Among these were the works of Mikhail V. Lomonosov, *Old Russian History* (1766), J. M. Snegirev, *Festivals and Superstitious Rituals of the Russian Common People* (1837) and A. V. Tereshchenko, *Life of the Russian People* (1848). With respect to the latter work, one essential figure which Rock passes over is K. D. Kavelin (1818–1885). Kavelin not only wrote a seminal review of Tereshchenko's, *Life of the Russian People*, but two years earlier, in 1846, penned "A Look at the Legal Life of Ancient Russia." Writing over a century later in 1956, the Soviet ethnographer Sergei A. Tokarev (1889–1985), saw in Kavelin's work "that 'method of survivals' that is usually associated with the name of Edward Tylor and which was actually developed later by an English scientist."[69] This in spite of Kavelin never using the term "survivals" ("perezhitki") explicitly. The question of whether he employed other Russian terms such as "sledy" or "ostatki" (i.e., "remnants, traces," etc.), which were more common prior to the later shift to explicit Tylorean "survivals" historiography, can only be answered by more extensive analysis of his works. But the essential concept is there. Indeed, Kavelin held that an entire "historical world" could be revealed in "living facts, daily, normal, natural conditions of life," so that "our customs and rituals represent the...ruins of epochs separated by centuries, monuments of concepts and beliefs" from days gone by. "Folk customs," he insisted, "are the key to the history of a people."[70] The latter idea reflects the influence of German and broader European Romantic nationalist ideas on Kavelin's paradigm and approach. Kavelin was in fact one of the early nineteenth-century liberal "Westernizers." He was also an early member of the same Russian Geographical Society to which A. I. Levshin, Matvei N. Yastrebov and Shokan Ualihanuhli (Russian: Valikhanov) belonged, with all three of the latter playing seminal roles in the formulating of theories and approaches to ethnography among the Kazakhs (see below).

Meanwhile, of particular importance for Soviet ethnology, Rock discusses "[t]he model of the resistant masses struggling for a long period to preserve their own [pre-Christian] beliefs in the face of an alien Christianity rooted in an elite culture." This unique interpretation—reflecting more the romantic nationalist than the polemical anti-syncretistic variety—was introduced by Sergei M. Solov'ev, *History of Russia from the Earliest Times*. It was a 29-volume work published originally in St. Petersburg between 1851 and 1879 and re-published in Moscow between 1959 and 1966. Representing a more polemical Russian Orthodox perspective, an 1861 article most likely emanating from a teacher at the Kazan Theological Academy—the main training grounds for educators who were being sent to teach at Kazakh-Russian schools on the Kazakh steppe—foreshadowed "an influential collection" of essays published the following year in 1862 titled *Sermons and teachings against pagan beliefs and rituals*. Metropolitan Makarii Bulgakov (1816–1882) then commenced work some fifteen years later on a multi-volume work on Russian church history which he published between 1877 and 1889. It became a foundational source for all subsequent Russian church history studies. Makarii displays and perpetuates the same basic concern among Russian Orthodox clergy and missionaries for being "Christian in name only" and "perform[ing] the external rites of the holy Church" while "preserv[ing] at the same time the superstition and rituals of their [pagan] fathers." E. E. Golubinskii, *History of the Russian Church* (1880–1904), following Makarii, displayed this concern as well. M. Azbukin then carried on this tradition by producing a five-part "Essay on the Literary Struggle of Representatives of Christianity with the Remnants (Russian: *Ostatkami*) of Paganism among the Russian People" which appeared in *Russian Philological Bulletin* between 1892 and 1898.[71] It was a "systematic exposition of *dvoeverie* ['double belief'], outlining [its] various stages of development." By the early twentieth century, S. I. Smirnov offered a feminist interpretation of sorts, though not necessarily a positive one: he wrote an "influential" monograph entitled *Impious Women* (1909) "which identified women as the main preservers and protectors of pagan beliefs and rituals after the establishment of Christianity in Rus." Smirnov also wrote a *History of Spirituality in the East* (1906) and *An Investigation into the History of Church Life* (1913), presumably with similar attention to issues of pagan survivals.[72] E. V. Anichkov, *Paganism and Old Rus* (1914), as well as N. Gal'kovskii,

The Struggle of Christianity with Pagan Survivals in Old Rus (1915), both continued in this tradition. Meanwhile, George Vernadsky (1878–1973)—who studied in Moscow and St. Petersburg between 1905 and 1917 as the Tsarist Empire breathed its last—carried this view to the United States when he fled Soviet Russia in 1926–1927 via Prague. In his multi-volume *History of Russia*, he retained the view that "[p]agan influences long persisted in popular beliefs" with "Christian churches... built upon the former places of pagan worship" and "paganism [holding] its ground for a long time under a thin veneer of Christian rites."

All of the sources outlined above, and more, make plain that a 'remnants/survivals' historiography was fairly widespread in Russian Orthodox sources from at least the mid-1700s on, with certain of these works even re-published in the Soviet period.[73]

Concluding Reflections

Although the Russian Orthodox 'dual faith' tradition has undoubtedly exerted the greatest influence on the later emerging Tsarist as well as Soviet ethnographic schools, the various Euro-American and Euro-Slavic Christian and secular sources reveal a long and diverse history of 'survivals' historiography which significantly complicate attempts to ascribe Tsarist and Soviet traditions to any single source among them, particularly that of E.B. Tylor. Tylor's own conception of 'survivals,' along with those of the late nineteenth-century British anthropological and broader 'history of religions' schools which have drawn significantly from his work, as well as the views of Marx and Engels, must likewise be understood against the backdrop of these much longer, deeper historical roots. Even then, the complex history unearthed in Euro-American and Euro-Slavic Christian and secular sources do not provide a comprehensive view. They tie into Islamic sources emanating from the Middle East, Central Asia and beyond, as the next chapter attempts to outline.

CHAPTER 3

Middle Eastern and Central Asian Islamic Sources of 'Survivals' Ethnography

Although the term 'dual faith' did not take on a clearly articulated definition and apologetic sense prior to the nineteenth century, Tsarist ethnography and history was clearly steeped in a worldview which commonly distinguished between 'pre-Christian' and 'Christian' beliefs and practices and recognized 'remnants/survivals' within Russian history well before that time. This in itself is significant. But one additional 'remnants/ survivals' tradition must also be considered in order to round out the broader world historical context of Tsarist and later Soviet 'remnants/ survivals' ethnography in Central Asia. As a third and later branch of the Middle Eastern monotheistic (cf. 'Abrahamic') faiths, Islam shared a concern for distinguishing between 'remnants of pagan idolatry' and authentic Islamic devotion. Hints of it surface within the Qur'an itself. They become explicitly evident in numerous Islamic societies as Islam spread among the many peoples and cultures of the Afro-Eurasian networks, with the Middle Eastern and Central Asian traditions being most relevant for the question of 'pre-Islamic survivals' in Muslim Central Asia.[74]

QUR'ANIC AND MIDDLE EASTERN ISLAMIC SOURCES

R. Michael Feener, in a chapter on "Muslim Cultures and Pre-Islamic Pasts: Changing Perceptions of "Heritage,"" offers, among other things, a survey of various "Muslim interpretations of Qur'anic verses" which

© The Author(s), under exclusive license to Springer Nature Singapore Pte Ltd. 2023
R. C. Weller, *'Pre-Islamic Survivals' in Muslim Central Asia*,
Islam and Global Studies,
https://doi.org/10.1007/978-981-19-5697-3_3

direct the faithful "to reflect on the visible traces of pasts connected with traditions of pre-Islamic Arabia and biblical literature." He also includes diverse responses among various Muslims across the ages to the Egyptian Pyramids, pre-Islamic remains still visible at Javanese Islamic shrines, and more.[75] This focus on "visible traces of pasts" ties into the present study of religious-cultural 'survivals,' but it is a distinct dimension which raises questions pertaining more to archeological 'remains' or 'ruins' than intangible beliefs and practices.

With respect to the latter, the first traces of religious-cultural 'survivals' can be discerned in the Qur'an itself, in verses such as: "It was not God who instituted (superstitions like those of) a slit-ear she camel, or a she camel let loose for free pasture, or idol sacrifices for twin births in animals, or stallion camels freed from work. It is blasphemers who invent a lie against God" (5:106), and "They said: ...Dost thou (now) forbid us the worship of what our fathers worshipped?" (11:62). There is clear reference here to long-standing pre-Islamic Arab religious-cultural practices, though if we accept the traditional dating of the Qur'an, in its original oral form, to Muhammad's lifetime, these practices could not have had much time at this point to 'survive' together in any syncretic fashion. Some—particularly those wishing to uphold a more 'purist' point of view—may even argue that the verses represent two distinct opposing options which were not mixed together but rather competing with one another. The application (and even exegesis in at least one case) could go in either direction, with the paradigm undergirding a "remnants (cf. 'continuations') of pre-Islamic practices" inherent within the passages regardless.

Beyond the Qur'an itself, those in the Hanbali legal tradition—especially the Syrian-born scholar Ibn Taimiyah (also Taymiyyah, 1263–1328)[76] and, much later, the puritanical reformist of Arabia, Muhammad ibn Abd al-Wahhab (1703–1792)[77]—stand out as the more vocal interpreters expressing opposition to certain aspects of 'the cult of saints' and other 'pagan vestiges' among Muslim communities of their day.[78]

In terms of actual evidence for certain 'pre-Islamic' practices, Hazem Hussein Abbas Ali, Hazem Hussein Abbas Ali, in a chapter titled "Casting Discord: An Unpublished Spell from the Egyptian National Library," has noted the following:

> Some of the pre-Islamic papyri...confirm that the practice of *tafrīq* in Egypt preceded Islam. Modern-day practices confirm that many centuries of disapproval by Islamic orthodoxy, especially of the kind of magical ritual or spell that this paper documents (combining Qur'anic verses and calling upon God

besides other spiritual beings and aiming to alter someone's situation by harming others), have not led to the abandonment or oblivion of such practices.[79]

Among other examples of what he himself calls "manifestations of a monotheistic reaction in Islam against pagan survivals," Ignaz Goldziher (1850–1921) relates the story of a youth in the Mu'ayyad mosque in early 1700s Cairo usurping the pulpit and declaring: "All these graves of saints must be destroyed, those who kiss the coffins are infidels,…"[80] The idea of 'pagan survivals' is implicit in the youth's distinguishing between what his society knows to be long-standing practices throughout the Middle East which predate the rise of Islam and the true path of Islam as he (and others like him) interpret it. The 'cult of the saints' also became the object of condemnation by supposedly Wahabi-influenced schools in nineteenth-century India, as reflected in the tract *Al-Bulagh al-Mubin* and others.[81] There is, likewise, the case of Usman dan Fodio (1754–1817), the Fulani founder of the Sokoto Caliphate in Northern Nigeria, who saw "the mixing of the old religious Hausa belief in *bori*, with its many spirits and Islamic monotheism…as the ideal condition for a Jihad, a call to one God, Allah, through preaching, teaching, and where this fails, through acts of war and conquest."[82]

Eleventh-Century Karakhanid and Other Turkic Sources

Within Central Asia, Devin Deweese, in *Islamization and Native Religion*, has already offered a thorough analysis of self-understandings among Central Asian Muslims, particularly as these concerned the relation of 'pre-Islamic' and Islamic traditions within the process(es) of their own conversion. As per Deweese, this involved "asserting the centrality of Islam in their own conceptions of communal origin, identity, and solidarity."[83] It is important historically, however, to situate the mindset reflected in Otemish Hajji's mid-sixteenth-century account of the early fourteenth-century conversion of Ozbek Khan of the Golden Horde within its post-Mongol (as well as its later Safavid-Ottoman Shia-Sunni) context. The thirteenth-century Mongol (and Crusader) "devastation" of the Islamic Middle East and Central Asia had a significant impact on revivalist trends among both Buddhists and Muslims in eastern and western Central Asia respectively. Islam had been slowly but surely taking root among the Central Asian Turkic peoples since especially the ninth and tenth centuries. It had effectively gained ascendancy by the time the Mongol onslaught hit. But that ascendancy had been negotiated through a long, complex historical process. The post-Mongol (and post-Crusade) revivals were set on re-establishing a lost Islamic ascendancy, with a revised view toward "pagan" Mongol (and Christian) traditions.[84] There are reasonable, historical grounds for suggesting that a different mindset existed during the earlier, pre-Mongol spread of Islam throughout the region, when Islam was still viewed as a relatively recent religious-cultural tradition in relation to Central Asian traditions which had roots reaching back long centuries—Shamanism, Tengrism and Zoroastrianism in particular.

Peter Golden, in *Central Asia in World History*, says that Yûsuf Khâss Hâjib of Balasaghun recommended "the shaman's amulets and incantations" alongside the physician's medicines.[85] But Robert Dankoff, who Golden cites as his source, translates the term as "diviner" not "shaman."[86] This touches directly into the question at hand, with evidence here reaching back to 1069, when Balasaghuni wrote his now-famous *Kutadgu Bilig* (*Blessed Wisdom* or *Knowledge*). And it raises the very questions of the historical processes of conversion and thus interreligious interaction which lie at the heart of these continuing debates. Certain forms of Shamanism, of course, continued in these regions down to this time, and well beyond. Meanwhile, the Karakhanid leader, Satuq Bughra Khan (d. 955), is said to have been converted to Islam in 934. Recent Chinese scholarship suggests revising this date to approximately 950.[87] Either way, it is just a decade or two earlier to the conversion of the Seljuk tribes who would soon migrate into the Middle East as mercenary soldiers. This leaves roughly one century, give or take, for the processes of conversion (i.e., Islamization) to take place among the Karakhanids by the time Balasaghuni wrote.

The original terms which Balasaghuni used in the passage in question are "*afsûnçılar*" and "*emçiler*." The latter corresponds to the modern Kazakh "емші" ("*emshi*") or "healer." The former corresponds to the modern Kazakh term "сиқыршылар" ("*syqirshilar*") and Tatar term "сихерчеләр" ("*syqercheler*"), i.e., "magician, sorcerer, diviner."[88] There are of course nearly 1000 years between the original use in the Karakhanid context and modern Kazakh (and Tatar) usage, but a historical connection remains by way of *emçiler* in particular. More importantly here, the Karakhanid Turkic terms employed by Balasaghuni are not derived from an Arabic etymology, nor is the main personal noun in question—"*afsûnçılar*"—drawn from the Turkic term for "diviner" or "magician" as identified by Mahmud Kashgari (1005–1102) in his eleventh-century *Compendium of the Turkic Dialects* (*Dīwān Lughāt al-Turk*). Kashgari was, like Balasaghuni, writing from within the Karakhanid khanate. In providing a fairly extensive dictionary of Karakhanid Turkic terms, he gives *qa'm* for "diviner" and *yelwici* (cf. 'emshi') for "magician."[89]

Balasaghuni's choice of "*afsûnçılar*" in this particular case is traced back to Persian (Farsi: *afsūn*, نوسفا, or *fisūn*, نوسف).[90] The *Comprehensive Persian-English Dictionary* defines the most relevant forms of these Persian terms as "magician, enchanter, conjurer, wizard," with no mention of any connections to Sufism or Islam.[91] These underlying Persian terms were, for example, employed by Firdausi (or Firdowsi, Ferdowsi) in his classic Persian work, the *Shahnameh (Book of Kings)*. Firdousi completed his *magnum opus* between 977 and 1010 CE, over half a century prior to Balasaghuni's *Blessed Wisdom*. Inclusive of all the derivative forms of *afsūn* and *fisūn*, Firdausi uses the term(s) a total of 152 times.[92] Twelve of these are directly relevant to the passage in Balasaghuni, where Firdausi speaks of "sorcerers," "magicians," "wizards," etc., depending on the context and English translation.[93] "Diviners," used by Dankoff for his English translation of Balasaghuni, is of course a closely related English synonym. All of Firdausi's usages are in relation to pre-Islamic magicians or sorcerers (cf. also diviners). This includes, for example, the Turanian (Central Asian Turkic) magician Bazur who cast a spell and unleashed a snow storm on the Persian hero Rostam. Zal, a magician who fought on Rostom's side, used his magical powers to help bring healing to Rostam after a major injury nearly left him and his great horse for dead. The mythological nature of these passages makes no difference in establishing the meanings and range of usages of the Persian term which underlies Balasaghuni's reference to "diviners" who "utter spells" and use "amulets" and "incantations" to help heal sickness.

Elsewhere in Persian classical literature, in a rather unique, vague reference, the Persian scholar and poet Nasir Khusraw (c. 1003–1077) commends the "*fesoongar*" who "heals the wounds of patients with kind words."[94] Given Khusraw's own background as a *faqih* (religious scholar), it is doubtful that he has Sufi masters in view here. He rather, within context, seems to be encouraging any and all believers to take on the role of an "enchanter" who brings healing to those with heavy hearts through the kindness of their words. This touches into a sense of the term comparable to, but much milder than (i.e., stopping well short of) the role of the "diviners" which Balasaghuni recommends to his readers. Still, Khusraw is somehow combining 'pre-Islamic' and Islamic ideas together. It is a reasonable question to ask how much Firdausi's *Shahnameh* may have influenced Khusraw's choice to reference such a historical-cultural figure as a model for believers.

Meanwhile, these same Persian terms are only rarely used in relation to Sufi (or any other Islamic) holy men who perform healings, miracles and related phenomena. This is precisely the boundary that Khusraw drew in limiting his reference to 'kind words of healing.' The well-known Persian Sufi poet, Mahmoud Shabestari (1288–1340), told how "he (the symbol of love and unity) went to the khaneghah drunk at night and turned the *fesoon* (magic) of the Sufists into *afsoon* (myth)." Shabestari implies here, in the later fourteenth century, that such "magic" was not considered part of the authentic Sufi heritage and was thus rejected.[95] His sentiment remains widely shared. When, on occasion, these terms are still applied today within the Iranian-Farsi context, they remain highly controversial, precisely because of their typical meaning encountered in the *Shahnameh* and elsewhere, as reflected in ongoing debates in Iran.[96]

Until further research reveals otherwise, the overall evidence as it stands supports the conclusion that Balasaghuni was most likely referring to traditional Central Asian "diviners," otherwise known as "magicians, wizards, sorcerers, enchanters" and the like. Given that these are all terms quite fitting for the Central Asian shaman, especially from the viewpoint of the neighboring Persians, and the shaman was the main traditional healer (cf. 'medicine man') prior to the influx of Islamic "doctors" and related medicines and hospitals pioneered by al-Razi and others, Peter Golden's use of "shaman" for the reference in Balasaghuni has strong historical backing; indeed the greater weight of historical-linguistic evidence supports it.

This has important implications for not only our own modern understandings of the conversion (i.e., Islamization) process among Central Asian Turkic peoples, the Karakhanids here in particular, but for our understanding of their own views of that process as well. Balasaghuni's *Blessed Wisdom* can be compared in certain ways to Firdausi's *Shahnameh*, as an affirmation of traditional Turkic language, culture and spirituality amid their conversion to Islam, over a century after that conversion had begun.[97] This is not a Marxist-Soviet 'anti-Islamic resistance' thesis. The Karakhanid Turks were rather preserving traditional modes of medicine and healing as they embraced Islam.[98] In spite of what certain scholars may want the evidence to say, Balasaghuni's reference to "diviners" offers no clear indication in either direction as to whether this was alongside their Islamic faith (cf. 'double faith') or integrated into it. If the latter case, then the shamanic *afsûnçılar* might be using Qur'anic references and prayers in their "spells" and "incantations" and written verses and prayers in their "amulets."[99]

In further support of this interpretation, there is one other additional piece of linguistic evidence from Balasaghuni's *Blessed Wisdom*, namely his choice to use the Turkic term *Tangri* throughout his entire volume when making reference to "God." The Arabic *Allah* does not appear. Albeit without the citation of any supporting evidence, Bruce Privratsky has argued as follows: "That Tengri is the least common word for God in Kazak speech suggests that Kazak religion long ago distanced itself from the cult of the sky god in early Turkic religion..."[100] While it may mean that Islamic conceptions of God came to predominate, as they surely did, it does not necessarily mean the Kazakhs had "distanced themselves" from their Tengrist heritage; many continue viewing it as an integrated and still 'surviving' part of their Islamic faith (see Chapter 8).

A number of interpreters place significant emphasis on the prominence of Islamic terminology in the Turkic Central Asian languages, including even greetings, as presumed proof of thoroughgoing Islamization (see esp., Chapter 9). Directly relevant to the discussion here, these arguments focus at times on particular vocabulary items. These kinds of linguistic-terminological arguments are, however, far more semantically and historically complex than 'meets the eye.' The fact that Soviet-era and even post-Soviet atheists regularly use(d) the phrase "slava Bogu" (слава Богу, "praise God"), for decades, even nearly a century now, does not serve as proof of how thoroughly steeped they were/are in Russian Orthodox theological conviction. Russian-speaking Central Asian Muslims have and still do at times employ the phrase as well. This in itself demonstrates that language borrowed from another religious domain can quite easily be given new shades of meaning when situated within a new and different religious context. The same holds true for Arabic terms making their way historically into other languages, or even people of non-Islamic faiths who speak and use Arabic as their 'mother tongue.' Among the latter would be Middle Eastern Arab Christians, including those in Lebanon, Palestine and elsewhere. While there is much theologically that they share in common, there are also essential distinctions, most notably trinitarian conceptions of 'Allah.'[101] Among non-Arabic speakers, the Mari of Siberia, also at times called

Cheremis, are a Volga Finnic people inhabiting the Volga-Kama region in Tatarstan and Bashkiria. They have, through sustained historical contact with the Central Asian Islamic world around them, adopted the Arabic-Islamic term '*keremet*' (керемет, 'amazing,' 'miraculous') for their chief evil diety-spirit as well as a sacred place for offerings. This diety-spirit is pre-Islamic and their understanding of the spirit remains predominantly spiritistic according to ancient Mari worldview, not Muslim, though this does not mean that Islamic conceptions of the 'miraculous' have not found their way into the Mari worldview in some sort of 'synthesized' or 'integrated' fashion.[102] As per Peter Golden, "[t]he term is also found in other Volga Finnic languages (Udmurt *keremet*, Mordvin *kerämet*' [керэметь] and Turkic Chuvash *kiremet/keremet* 'a god, holy place.'"[103] A similar linguistic phenomenon is evident in Hindi, where both Arabic and Persian vocabulary has, over the long centuries of interaction between Turko-Persian Muslim and South Asian Hindu peoples, become mainstream among Hindu speakers of Hindi.[104] In spite of Arabic (and Persian) Islamic terms being deeply integrated into their vocabulary, no persuasive argument can be made that Hindus of the subcontinent, particularly in the more northern regions, have been thoroughly Islamized; to the contrary, they have thoroughly 'Hinduized' the Arabic-Islamic terms, though here again some added Islamic influence may have seeped in over the centuries.[105]

Within Kazakh itself, the Arabic-derived term *aruaq* (аруақ) is one of the most telling examples. It carries the very specific and delimited meaning of 'ancestral spirit' within the Kazakh semantic domain. And its meaning is likewise singular, in clear distinction from its Arabic counterpart; it is made plural by appending the standard Kazakh plural ending 'tar,' i.e., *aruaqtar*. '*Aruaq*' (or *arwah*, أرواح) is an Arabic term already in its plural form, derived from the singular root '*ruh*' (or '*ruq*', روح). And the Arabic term is not delimited like the Kazakh to 'ancestral spirit.' The Arabic term itself in fact has no sense of 'ancestral' inherently in it, it requires the explicit added modifying term 'ancestral' to carry such a meaning. Kazakhs here have clearly taken an Arabic spiritual term and re-appropriated it in ways which clearly differ from the original Arabic. This supports the argument that the Kazakhs have not simply adopted and adapted the Arabic-Islamic meanings of the various terms which have come into their language, but in this case in particular have replaced a pre-existing Turkic (or other) term with a new though modified Arabic-Islamic one, applying that new, modified Arabic-Islamic term to their pre-existing (cf. 'pre-Islamic') 'ancestor cult.' Kazakh attitudes toward devotional practices in relation to the '*aruaq*' have, no doubt, been placed within an Islamic context, but this does not mean that they have lost their 'pre-Islamic' notions entirely. They have rather, more likely, been thoroughly integrated together across the long centuries.

In spite, then, of the complexity of linguistically based historical arguments, it is reasonable to see the Karakhanid usage of *Tangri* as, not "distanc[ing] themselves" from Islam, but rather most likely indicating the continuing predominance of their traditional Tengrist modes of understanding integrated together with the later Islamic views. This integration is, likewise, reflected in Kashgari's *Compendium of the Turkic Dialects* where he affirms "*tangri*" as the term used—and in the spirit of Kashgari, proudly one might add—among Turks for "God."[106] If, following Privratsky, stress is to be laid upon the fact that a people's "religious vocabulary is thoroughly Islamic and is unlikely to have become so recently,"[107] the same line of reasoning should apply when we observe that for both Kashgari and Balasaghuni, their "religious vocabulary is thoroughly" Turkic. As just noted above, there are important cautions to be minded in making such arguments, but overall, Kashgari and Balasaghuni among the Turks, and Firdausi among the Persians, all represent integrative affirmations and even re-assertions of their own national cultures amid (and not in Soviet-style opposition to) the Islamization processes underway in the pre-Mongol period of Central Asia. This historical-contextual fact, more than the mere terminology itself, supports these conclusions.

In addition to the evidence from the Karakhanid Turkic literature, among the Oghuz Turks of Central Asia, "there was a gray-bearded, gray-haired, very clever old man, a reasonable, wise man, a magician" known as "Ulug-Turluk" who served under their legendary ruler Oghuz-Kagan. This too appears, then, to be during the process of Islamization, though further research needs to be done on the precise Oghuz Turkic term lying behind the English translation of "magician" here.[108]

Along similar lines, the terms "Tangri" and "Allah" are intermixed within the 14th–15th-century Book of Korkut Ata (or Dede Korkut), as evidenced in the various surviving manuscripts. This includes the later Gonbad manuscript which represents a transition from old Oghuz Turkic into later Persian Azerbaijani between the sixteenth and eighteenth centuries. If we follow again the lines of argument employed by Privratsky and others, the overall evidence supports the conclusion that Turkic peoples retained a distinctly "Tengrist" understanding of God well beyond their early conversion period.[109] There is no good reason to believe that after long centuries of integration into their worldview that the Tengrist conceptions necessarily disappeared (cf. "Tengrist Historiography" in Chapter 8).

Sixteenth-Century Central Asian Sources

With respect to the Kazakhs in particular, the evidence from the Persian Muslim historian Fazl Allah ibn Ruzbihan Isfahani (1455–1521) is well-known. Isfahani was a protected guest of the Bukharan khan at the time. He was a Sunni scholar taking refuge from the Shia persecutions being carried out under Shah Ismail in Iran (r. 1501–1524). He was known for his participation in debates over Islamic law and theology.[110] As a Sunni Islamic legal scholar and supporter of the Bukharan khanate in its military struggles against the Kazakhs at the time, Isfahani noted in the early 1500s that the Kazakhs were still engaged in what he described as essentially the "apostasy" of sun worship. Isfahani noted that the Kazakh practice here was observed with the coming of spring and the renewed ability to produce the centuries-old (cf. 'pre-Islamic') traditional drink of the steppe nomads, *qumis* (cultured mare's milk). They bowed to the sun before their drinking of the first spring *qumis*.[111] This practice has typically been taken as a reference to what Kazakhs and others have come to call 'Tengrism,' or 'the worship of heaven,' or more literally 'worship of the (blue) skies,' which includes 'nature (as well as ancestral spirit) veneration.' Soviet and even post-Soviet Kazakhs later interpreted it in this manner.[112]

There is a distantly similar case of "Sun-worshipers, called Shammasi" whom the Chagatai ruler of Kashmir, Mirza Muhammad Haidar Dughlat (d. 1551), in his 1547 *History of the Moghuls of Central Asia*, identified as among the false religious groups in Kashmir at roughly the same time. These so-called Sun-worshipers were, it would appear, an offshoot or consequence of Mir (Shaykh) Shams-ud-Din Iraqi (d. 1526) and his Nurbakshi Sufi teachings which Shams-ud-Din had carried to the Kashmir valley region from out of Iran in the 1480s.[113] Dughlat, as a military and political leader, imposed—by "punishment of death" in certain cases—a Sunni orthodox Central Asian Muslim presence in the region from 1540 down to at least the time of his own death in 1551.

He condemned Shams-ud-Din and the various related Sufi groups associated with him, an interpretation which, like Isfahani, involved political as well as religious allegiances. As for Shams and associates, the Arabic term for 'the sun,' 'ash-shams' (الشمس) is the name of the 91st Qur'anic Sura, while another Qur'anic passage says that when Abraham "saw the sun (ٱلشَّمْسَ) rising in splendor, he said: 'This is my Lord; this is the greater (or greatest) [one].'"[114] More importantly for the Kashmiri Sufi groups, the name of the influential Sufi missionary in Kashmir, "Shams-ud-Din," means "The Sun of Faith (or The Sun or Light of the Religion)," a point noted by Dughlat. It is not clear whether such "Sun-worshipers" within Islamic Sufi history have possible roots linking back to the worship of the female sun Goddess "Shams, the lady of Mayfa'a" or "Shams 'Aliyyat" in pre-Islamic Arabia,[115] Dughlat makes no reference to those or any other possible historical ties. Whatever its historical roots however, and whatever its precise link with Shams-ud-Din Iraqi, the apparently Sufi sect was condemned by the explicitly Sunni zeal of Dughlat in a manner even stronger than Isfahani's condemnation of the Kazakhs.[116]

The 'Silk Road' trade connections between the Central Asian Muslim nomads and the Turkic Muslim Mughals of India, who themselves hailed from Turkic Muslim Central Asia, are well-known. These included links into Kashmir, which was closely connected with the Mughals and eventually came under their rule in the late 1500s. There were Hindustani merchants resident in Astrakhan. The trade in horses was especially high, with literally thousands of horses, some possibly from the Kazakh steppes, filling the stables of the Mughal emperors.[117] What religious influences may have passed between them remains yet to be explored in greater depth.

The possibility of any direct historical links here between the "Sun-worshipers" of Dughlat and Isfahani's reference to the Kazakhs remains, until further research, remote (i.e., unlikely) at best. But the mere presence of this group within Dughlat's narrative raises questions about possible Sufi or other Islamic-related influences and/or understandings behind the Kazakh practice of sun worship. Historically, Shams-ud-Din and the Nurbakshi order were linked back to lineages emerging from Yusuf Hamadani (d. 1140) and the Kubrawi Sufi order which spread into Central Asia.[118] There was also a branch of the Kubrawi order in Kashmir. The Yasawi order likewise ties into Hamadani's lineage. The imagery of the sun, including the rising of the sun, played a significant role in not only pre-Islamic Arabia and the Qur'an, but Sufi traditions in particular, including the work of Rumi as well as the Kubrawi and Nurbakshi,[119] and perhaps the Yasawi orders. Although the Kazakh practice of "sun worship" was clearly rejected from Isfahani's own Islamic theological and cultural-political viewpoint, a possible Islamic-related interpretation would reorient the entire discussion about Isfahani's observation of Kazakh sun worship in terms of its implications for Kazakh religious identity. Assuming that it was, in fact, "worship" of the sun has to take into consideration Isfahani's own theological and political biases. And it remains entirely possible that Sufi teachings drawing on the imagery of the sun and sunrise became intermingled with Turkic steppe Tengrism, which further complicates the questions involved. But this is a theory just as grounded in the historical evidence as any exclusivist thesis based in either Tengrism or Sufism.[120]

Whether Tengrism, Sufism or an integrated combination of both however, the concept of 'pre-Islamic pagan survivals' is implicit in Isfahani's view of the practice, with the 'pre-Islamic' in this case being practices leftover from the time prior to Kazakh conversion (as opposed to prior to the rise of Islam).[121] Indeed, his use of the term "apostasy" implies what he considers to be a former (i.e., forfeited) Muslim identity. Whether he used the term "pagan" in relation to this practice awaits a closer look at the full context of his statement and other works, but the idea is implicit, a paradigm shared with Russian Orthodoxy and the broader Christian "dual faith" tradition. The same is essentially true of Dughlat's evaluation of the "Sun-worshipers" of Kashmir.

In contrast to Isfahani's religious indictment of the Kazakhs and Dughlat's own condemnation of the Kashmiri "Sun-worshipers," Dughlat seems to count the Kazakhs unquestionably Muslim, apparently not aware of their sun-worshiping practice. His affirmation of Kazakh Muslim identity can be deduced from the fact that in his introduction, Dughlat declares: "Of those Moghuls who were not Musulmans, I have not mentioned more than the names; for an infidel, though he attain to the spledour of Jamshid or Zohhak, is not worthy of having his life commemorated."[122] He then goes on to include the Kazakhs at fairly generous length within his account, with special emphasis upon Kasim Khan (r. 1511–1521).[123] Whereas Isfahani—hosted by the Uzbeks, political enemies of the Kazakhs at the time—condemns the Kazakhs as 'apostates,' Dughlat and other Moghuls who stood in Sunni religio-political alliance with them, counted them, without question, genuine Muslims.[124] This kind of 'all or nothing' attitude is, in fact, common, not only among various Muslims, but multiple other religious groups in their respective infighting. As in the Protestant anti-Catholic polemic (see above) and multiple other cases, one group is inspired in the face of religious-political struggles to declare that their opponents are 'infidels' by finding some kind of religious grounds for condemning them as 'heretics,' in spite of their opponent's own clear claims to the contrary. Where Isfahani and Dughlat draw clear lines in opposite directions is precisely where, historically, much of the debate over Kazakh Muslim identity occurs. They together (though particularly Isfahani) provide the kind of historical 'evidence' which is later used by Tsarist, Soviet and other historians, ethnographers and anthropologists to argue for 'late' or 'incomplete' and thus often 'disingenuous' conversion to Islam, typically tied to assertions of 'pre-Islamic remnants' from these and other still earlier eras.[125]

Other examples could be cited, but these suffice to show that even if the precise phrasing was not used, ideas of 'pre-Islamic remnants' and 'pagan survivals' have long been implicit in the language of certain Muslims across the centuries—Middle Eastern, Central Asian and others—as far back as Mohammad himself. The aim here is not to suggest that such interpretations are either wrong or right, but rather trace out the historical roots of Tsarist and Soviet 'survivals' ethnography from all possible angles.

Western (Christian) Orientalist Scholarship

The materials above provide several related lines from within the Islamic tradition, what we might call 'emic' or 'internal' lines. The other is the 'etic' or 'external,' that is, the history of Western interpretations of 'pre-Islamic pagan survivals.' Such interpretations go back at least as far as the Christian writer John of Damascus (676–749) who views the Muslim practice of worship at the Ka'aba as reflecting pre-Islamic idolatry.[126] Much later, in the modern period, Joseph White (1745–1814), Laudian Professor of Arabic and later Regius Professor of Hebrew at Oxford University, spoke in 1784 of "those numerous and irksome observances with which the Mahometan ritual is burdened...derived from less pure and venerable sources; ...from the superstitious customs of the barbarous and pagan Arabs."[127] 'Pre-Islamic survivals' are, in White's view, inherent within the religion of Islam itself. White's approach to Islam's historical formation as a religious tradition was common within modern Western (including Russian) critical schools of interpretation from the seventeenth or eighteenth century onward. It, in fact, historically parallels the Protestant polemic against Catholics as well as developing trends in Tsarist Russian historiography (see Chapter Two).

Finally, in the latter part of the nineteenth century, 'founding fathers' of modern Euro-American 'Islamic studies' employed Tylorean 'survivals' historiography in their interpretations of Islamic history. The German Orientalist Theodor Nöldeke (1836–1930) thus makes one sole reference in 1883 to the "survival of Arab heathenism" when discussing the rise of Islam.[128] In this, Nöldeke shares the view of both John of Damascus and Joseph White, among others. Likewise, as alluded to earlier, the Hungarian scholar Ignaz Goldziher appropriated 'survivals' historiography in his two-volume *Muslim Studies* published in 1889–1890. There he speaks of "true survivals of pagan cults at the grave of the saint which were preserved in the immodest customs hallowed by popular superstition, customs the connection of which...recall the lascivious religious customs of paganism, the last vestiges of which are preserved" among various Muslim peoples in various places. These are, in Goldziher's eyes, "remnants of pre-Islamic popular customs," "surviving remnants of conquered religions" or "survivals of the old religions" with "their manifestly pagan character," against which many Muslims themselves reacted.[129]

Concluding Reflections

The Islamic tradition(s) within the Middle East, Central Asia and beyond had a conceptual apparatus for distinguishing between corrupt and pagan 'pre-Islamic' versus authentically 'Islamic' beliefs and practices which was shared with the Hebrew-Jewish and Christian traditions, most likely even originally influenced by and then continuously interacting across the centuries with those earlier Middle Eastern monotheistic paradigms. These perspectives surface within the Qur'an and then take clearer, fuller shape in subsequent centuries all across Islamic lands, including the Middle East and Central Asia. Based on the evidence of Central Asian sources, such as the works of Firdousi, Balasaghuni and Kashgari, it can even be argued that the Iranian and Turkic ethno-national traditions, likewise, distinguished between their own 'pre-Islamic' and 'Islamic' religious-cultural traditions in a 'proto-romanticist' and/or 'proto-folk nationalist' manner. Inasmuch as these historically culturally inclusivist-integrationist, 'preservationist' approaches among the Central Asian peoples sought to synthesize and harmonize the traditions as opposed to separate, condemn and 'cleanse' one from the other, they were distinct from the original theologically and legally exclusivist paradigms of the Middle Eastern monotheistic traditions which were grounded in ideas of necessarily 'pure' divine revelation enshrined in sacred scriptures.

When considering all the Euro-American and Euro-Slavic Christian and secular, the Islamic Middle Eastern and Central Asian and the Central Asian indigenous sources, it is clear that a rather complex variety of 'remnants' (or 'survivals') ethnographies and historiographies long pre-dated and fed into later Tsarist conceptualizations and appropriations of 'survivals' among the Muslim peoples of Central Asia. Those that have been treated above in Chapters 2 and 3 are not disparate histories or historiographies, they are interconnected strands intersecting in various overlapping ways. These then fed into the Soviet ethnographical tradition(s), both indirectly via the Tsarist (as treated in the next chapter) and directly by way of their own participation in and influence upon the Soviet school(s), as the following chapters will now demonstrate.

CHAPTER 4

'Pre-Islamic Survivals' Among the Kazakhs in Tsarist Russian and Kazakh Colonial Ethnography, 1770–1917

A wide variety of interpretive schemes employing a framework of 'pre-Christian' and 'pre-Islamic survivals' in Western Euro-American, Eastern Euro-Slavic and Islamic Middle Eastern and Central Asian sources were—by the late 1700s, and increasingly throughout the 1800s into the early 1900s—widely known among and readily available to key Tsarist officials, historians and ethnographers of Kazakh (and broader Central Asian) religious history and identity, including Rychkov, Levshin, Ualihanuhli, Il'minskii, Haruzin, Zeland, Poyarkov, Radlov,

---

For broader historical context for this chapter, see esp., Robert D. Crews, "Nomads into Muslims," in *For Prophet and Tsar: Islam and Empire in Russia and Central Asia* (Cambridge, MA, and London: Harvard University Press, 2006), pp. 192–240. Cf. also Ian W. Campbell, *Knowledge and the Ends of Empire: Kazak Intermediaries & Russian Rule on the Steppe, 1731–1917* (Ithaca, NY and London: Cornell University Press, 2017), and S.M. Mashimbaev and G.S. Mashimbaeva, *Patshalik Resei zhanye Kenges Imperialarining Kazakstandagi Ruhani Otarlau Sayasatining Zardaptari (XIX gasirding 70–80 zhildari—XXI gasirding basi)* [*Consequences of the Policies of Spiritual Colonization in Kazakhstan under the Russian and Soviet Empires (1870–80s—the Beginning of the 21st Century)*] (Almaty, KZ: Kazakh Universitesi, 2013), along with my English-language review of this work in Central Asian Survey , Vol. 34, No. 4 (2015): 585–588.

© The Author(s), under exclusive license to Springer Nature Singapore Pte Ltd. 2023
R. C. Weller, *'Pre-Islamic Survivals' in Muslim Central Asia*, Islam and Global Studies,
https://doi.org/10.1007/978-981-19-5697-3_4

Bukeihanuhli, Barthold and others. As the present chapter demonstrates, the appropriation of both the explicit construct and (at times implicit) interpretational scheme involving 'pre-Islamic survivals' among Tsarist Russian and Kazakh ethnographers, missionaries and other colonial agents from the late 1700s down to the end of the Tsarist Empire both reflexively draw from and contribute to the continuation of much broader world historiographical traditions and trends. It should, likewise, be borne in mind that the views of Marx and Engels as well as, slightly later, Tylor, were all forged during this same era, albeit within the Western European context, with the earliest works of Lenin drawing, very late in the period, from both the Western Euro-American and Eastern Euro-Slavic streams, interacting as they did with the Central Asian Islamic.

EARLY TSARIST COLONIAL ETHNOGRAPHERS OF KAZAKH RELIGIOUS IDENTITY, 1770–1860

Captain N.P. Rychkov, military officer and adjunct instructor at the Imperial Academy of Sciences, was already, in the late eighteenth century, speaking of ancient religious-cultural 'survivals' among the Kazakhs. Writing in his *Daily Travel Notes...in the Kirghiz-Kaisakh Steppe,* in 1771, he insisted that:

> All the rituals conducted by the Kirghiz [Kazakh] peoples during weddings and during the burial of the deceased are the remnants (*остатки*) of the oldest known peoples, namely the pagan peoples who lived within the limits of the vastness of Asia; and they [the Kazakhs] accepted the faith of Mahomed much later. I will describe them [the remnants of the wedding and burial rituals] here, so as to depict the natural simplicity of the ancient centuries.[130]

This extrapolation of "the natural simplicity of the ancient centuries" from "the remnants" of Kazakh wedding and burial practices reflects Tylorean concerns a century before Tylor and company come along.[131] Rychkov cites no sources, presumably because he is recording "daily notes" and not writing an academic treatise. If we were to look for Western European influence on Rychkov, it most likely would have come in his day via the Prussian scientist P.S. Pallas (1741–1811) who worked in Russia and whom Rychkov accompanied on an expedition among the Tatars, Bashkirs, Kazakhs and others in 1769–1770. Pallas was heir to the same late seventeenth-century Dutch and German pietistic enlightenment tradition as Witsen, who also had forged close ties with Russian colleagues, even the Tsar of Russia himself (at the time), Peter the Great. Witsen, in his historiography of the Tatars, was already employing the concept of "remnants of [ancient] manners and customs" preserved over not only long centuries, but migrations of peoples across continents. His allusion to migrations in ancient history transcending the Bering Straits seems to presume a 'pre-Islamic' context (see Chapter Two). As for the Kazakhs, Witsen actually provides a brief description of them later within his work. There he does not use the Dutch term for 'remnants/survivals,' but does employ a 'dual faith' paradigm when he asserts that "[t]he Kirghiz [Kazakh] peoples hold to the same idolatry as the Kalmyks, though there are also Mohammedans (among them)."[132] Part of Witsen's influence comes from the 1558 account of the English traveler Anthony Jenkinson, though Jenkinson makes no reference to the Kazakhs explicitly, only the "Tatars" and "Turkmen" among Central Asian Turkic peoples, and only as "Mohammedans" when doing so. Then again, Witsen's view may have come from the Russian colleagues he interacted with over the course of many years. From this vantage, Russian influence on Euro-American 'survivals' historiography should not be ruled out. Wherever Witsen gets his view however, it is articulated in 1692, with historical ties to both Pallas and Rychkov, though there is no clear evidence that the latter drew directly from either of them. But however 'scientific' their perspectives may appear, they both employ a well-established Christian paradigm, including specific terminology, of a 'dual faith' marked by "remnants" of "pagan" and "idolatrous" practices. Rychkov served together under Catherine the Great in the late eighteenth century, with his 'pagan remnants' paradigm standing in harmony with the prevailing views of the (if at times 'noble') 'savage' Kazakh nomads reflected in the reports of Aleksei Tevkelev and O.I. Igelstrom.[133] All these together helped to shape Catherine's religious policies toward the Kazakhs, including her choice to send Tatar Muslim merchants and missionaries among them to help further (or 'fully') Islamize them (see Appendix One).

If we were to search for the beginnings of this kind of historiography earlier than Catherine, we are told that the Empress "Anna Ioanovna banned in 1736 the re-building of mosques among the Bashkirs. It can be assumed that the Empress did not want to attach the Bashkirs to Islam, since then they were almost strangers to Mohammedanism, and held a shamanic, pagan error."[134] So claims Evfimii A. Malov (1835–1918), a

Russian Orthodox missionary who served as a Professor in the division of 'Anti-Muslim Studies' at the Kazan Theological Academy. Malov, however, was writing in 1867 and, therefore, possibly anachronistically interpolating prevailing views of his time back into Bashkir history in order to buttress his own case at the time of writing. That case involved an argument against the continuing policy of Catherine the Great, namely that of providing governmental support for the building of mosques among Muslim peoples. Malov was among a growing number of voices across the nineteenth century who opposed this practice, particularly when it might facilitate the (further) conversion of peoples like the Kazakhs whose religious history and identity were, in Malov's time, coming under increasing debate. Rychkov was writing, however, before those debates began taking shape. His views supported, not opposed, the policies of Catherine. It was A.I. Levshin who would apply them within a changing context nearly a half-century later, with Malov significantly influenced by Levshin's work, as well as that of Yastrebov and Valikhanov who also, in the 1850s and 1860s, followed Levshin's earlier lead.

This brings us to A.I. Levshin, who published a volume in 1832 titled *A Description of Kirghiz-Kaisak, or Kirghiz-Kazakhstani Hordes and Steppes*. This work was based on his 1822 ethnographic expedition into the Kazakh steppe for the Ministry of Foreign Affairs. One of his chapters was devoted to the subject of "Faith and Superstitions" among the Kazakhs. There he describes how certain Kazakhs "combine the teaching of Islamism with remnants (остатками) of ancient idolatry."[135] He does not reference any particular sources for this view. He simply sets it forth in the beginning of the chapter as one of three different ways in which, according to his interpretation, Kazakhs understood and practiced their religious traditions. While—of little surprise—he does not cite works of Russian church history when treating Kazakh religion, his phrasing reflects, I suggest, like that of Rychkov, Russian Christian flavoring. Additionally, the sources he does cite at various other points include a number of foreign works: a German work by Johann Eberhard Fisher titled *Siberian history* (1768), which was translated into Russian in 1774; a study written in Latin and Arabic by Edvardo Pocockio (1604–1691), *Specimen historiae Arabum*, which was "commenced by the father Edward Pococke (1604–1691) but attributed to the son (1648–1727)" and eventually published under the editorship of Joseph White at Oxford in 1806 (see Chapter Three); the travel account by William of Rubruck based on his journeys across the Kazakh steppe

4 'PRE-ISLAMIC SURVIVALS' AMONG THE KAZAKHS IN TSARIST RUSSIAN ...   53

en route to the Mongol court in 1253; and a French work by Ignatius Mouradgea d'Ohsson on *The Current State Of The Ottoman Empire* (1787–1820).[136] Since, again, Levshin leaves us without specific reference for his 'pre-Islamic remnants' ethnography, the best we can say is that both the Western Euro-American and Russian traditions (as well as possibly the Muslim perspective, particularly that of Tatar, Uzbek and other Central Asian Muslims toward the Kazakhs and Kirgiz) may have shaped his interpretation, with the Russian Orthodox 'dual faith' paradigm being, most likely, the primary lens through which he viewed Kazakh religious identity and practice.

The Russian colonialist context in which Levshin carried out his ethnographical study of the Kazakhs—namely the 'Speransky Reforms,', viewed within the broader 'Great Game' against the British—is important for understanding Levshin's motives and aims,[137] but Russian Orthodox and Tsarist ethnographical ideas of 'dual faith' with their corresponding historiographies appropriating both 'pre-Christian' and 'pre-Islamic survivals' clearly preceded as well as followed Levshin,[138] so the particular historical context does not explain its origins, only its particular application. This same fundamental distinction between 'historical origins' versus later 'historical appropriation' is important to keep in view within the Soviet period as well.

Levshin's publication became a standard reference for Kazakh studies in not only the Tsarist but Soviet period. Important here to note, however, is that Levshin himself does not portray the entire Kazakh population as mixing 'remnants' of earlier beliefs and practices with Islam; he limits this assessment to only one portion of the population. Levshin later served as a founding member of the Russian Geographical Society in 1845.

Some two decades after Levshin published his ethnographical study of the Kazakhs, Matvei N. Yastrebov (1826–1853)—a teacher of history and geography in the Troitsk and Chelyabinsk schools and an ethnographer for the Russian Geographical Society—wrote an article on "Kirgiz [Kazakh] Shamans" which he published in 1851. While Yastrebov does not use the specific Russian terms for 'dual faith' and its closely related idea of 'remnants,' 'survivals,' etc., he portrays the Kazakhs very much along the same lines as Levshin, as holding to a 'dual faith' marked by their native (cf. pre-Islamic) shamanism coexisting with Islam. The former is, according to his interpretation, their true, heartfelt faith, while Islam was, much later, forced upon them, so that they did not embrace it deeply or sincerely. Yastrebov had already demonstrated his interest in pre-Christian beliefs and practices among Russians in the regions where he taught in a previous article on "Folk beliefs, Superstitions, Witchcraft, Tales, etc., in the Troitsk and Chelyabinsk Districts" published (it would seem) sometime in the late 1840s. Accordingly, Yastrebov explicitly expresses his own Christian faith in his treatment of Kazakh religious identity and practice. It does not appear, however, that Yastrebov embarked, as had Levshin, on any long-term or detailed expedition, but rather simply observed the Kazakhs of the far northwestern region near Troitsk as they came down to their winter pastures after the early frosts began to set in.[139]

One additional Tsarist ethnographer who contributed to studies of 'pre-Islamic' customs among the Kazakhs was the Polish Court Counsellor Iosif (Efim) Yakovlevich Osmolovskii (1820–1862). Osmolovskii graduated from the Oriental Faculty of Kazan University, going on to serve in the Asiatic Department of the Ministry of Foreign Affairs starting from 1844. He was appointed administrator for the local Kazakh population for the Orenburg frontier commission in 1853 and served in that capacity until his death in 1862. Osmolovskii had been serving in Orenburg as a translator since 1848, with knowledge of a number of Central Asian languages, including Kazakh.[140] Osmolovskii's relationship with the Russian Geographical Society awaits further clarification, but one of his more significant projects in his work among the Kazakhs was production of a digest of Kazakh customary law (*adat*) by way of a number of ethnographic research expeditions among them between 1849 and 1853. Within his work, Osmolovskii interpreted Kazakh customary law as having undergone "a complex process of transformation under the influence of internal and external factors that had changed conceptions of Kazakh identity," presumably in a more Islamic direction. He identified what he considered to be "earlier legal traditions" in contradistinction to those which supposedly traced their roots to later "interactions between Kazakhs, Khivans and Bukharans."[141] One of Osmolovskii's imperial aims was, of course, to distance the Kazakhs from those allegedly more radical Islamic societies to the south, so his interpretations must be viewed in that light. Whether he used, in his original Russian, the specific terminology of 'remnants,' 'survivals' or otherwise at this still early stage awaits further clarification, but his conceptual approach reflects it.

The First Kazakh Colonial Ethnographer, Shokan Ualihanuhli (1863–1865)

Another decade on, Shokan Ualihanuhli (Russian: Chokan Valihanov, or Valikhanov) became a fellow member with Levshin and Yastrebov in the Russian Geographical Society. He offered similar interpretations of Kazakh religious history and identity in a number of different essays. Writing between 1863 and 1864 in his treatise "On the Muslim Faith in the Steppe," he, much like Levshin and Yastrebov before him, claimed that "[t]here are many among the Kyrgyz [Kazakhs] who still do not know even the name of Mohammed, and our shamans in many areas of the Steppe have not lost their significance."[142] Indeed, Valikhanov titled a seminal essay, written just one or two years earlier, "Vestiges (следы) of Shamanism among Kyrgyz [Kazakhs]." There he identified what he considered to be "traces (следов) of respect for" the 'sun god' and other ancient beliefs and practices.[143] According to his analysis, he explained this condition of his own Kazakh nation by saying: "We are currently in the dual faith [Rssn: двоеверия] period in the Steppe, as it was in Rus during the times of Saint Nestor."[144]

Consciously following the work of Nestor and Russian Orthodox historiography (see Chapter Two), Valikhanov set forth this "dual faith" paradigm in the fourth line of the opening paragraph of his treatment of "Muslim Faith in the Steppe." It served as one of the primary prisms through which he interpreted Kazakh religious history and identity. It is none other than what Stella Rock, *Popular Religion in Russia*, identifies as "the academic concept of double-belief, meaning the preservation of pagan elements within the religious faith" of the people (see Chapter Two).

Following from this, in his second paragraph, Valikhanov framed this Russian dual faith paradigm within an Enlightenment progressivist approach with the ultimate aim of "gaining access to European civilization." But he dreaded the thought of "going through a Tatar period" to get there, in the same way that "the Russians went through a Byzantine period" of hegemony.[145] "However repellant Byzantine hegemony was," he argued, "it nevertheless introduced Christianity, an indisputably enlightening force." If Valikhanov himself did not convert to Russian Orthodoxy, as many Kazakh scholars maintain, he was nonetheless clearly favorable to the conversion of Kazakhs to Russian Orthodoxy, not necessarily for salvation, but as a vehicle for civilizational enlightenment. By contrast, "the impressionable Kirghiz [Kazakh]" would not gain anything "from [Muslim] Tatar culture, except dead scholasticism, capable only of inhibiting the development of thought and feeling." Valikhanov was thus adamant: "We must at any price avoid a Tatar period, and the [Tsarist] government must help us to do so."[146]

Valikhanov reflected this same progressivist view of European civilizational superiority being achieved by way of passing through various "periods" or "stages" of historical development in his view of the Central Asian Muslim peoples to the south, i.e., "modern Bokhara, Khiva and Kokan." This was evident in a collection of works by "Russian Travellers," including, as per his Russianized name, "Chokan Valihanov," Mikhail Veniukov and others, which was translated into English in 1865 and published in London under the title *The Russians in Central Asia*. There Valikhanov spoke of "Central Asia, in its present stage of social organization," as representing "a truly mournful spectacle" because "her present stage of development" was that of "a wild and barbarous race, demoralized by Islamism."[147] His anti-Islamic sentiment is clear enough; the main point here however is his progressivist Enlightenment view of cultural-civilizational history which passes through various "periods" or "stages" on the way to achieving an 'advanced' status exemplified by modern liberal Europe inclusive of Russia. Christianity, particularly in this case Russian Orthodoxy, was an integral part of that 'advanced civilizational' status in Valikhanov's view and he welcomed it among the Kazakhs, in clear preference over Islam.

In positing such a progressivist advance of civilization in stages, Valikhanov was building on Tsarist Russian discourse which had taken clear shape by the 1760s in distinct relation to the Kazakhs vis-à-vis Russia.[148] The modernizing, Westernizing liberal reforms being carried out under Alexander II (r. 1855–1881) following Russia's defeat in the Crimean War (1853–1856) gave the Russian progressivist narrative new and transforming relevance. Valikhanov was further in sync with not only Levshin and Yastrebov, but the work of Kavelin in the later 1840s (see Chapter Two), with all four of them fellow members in the Russian Geographical Society. Marx and Engels were just beginning to evidence similar trends in their works, particularly Engels (see next chapter), but they were heading in a much more critical, anti-imperial direction which significantly revised the envisioned path for European progress. Still, there were clear parallels in their respective approaches which would eventually converge, especially Valikhanov's approach of distinguishing pre-Islamic 'pagan' practices from Islamic ones as a basis for denying the Kazakhs an integral Muslim identity, which then served as grounds for bypassing such unwanted, allegedly harmful stages by socially controlling and helping to advance development along the presumably progressive historical path toward the Russian Empire's conceived end-goal. Indeed, precursors to later Soviet views and approaches were clearly visible in the combined work of Valikhanov and Solov'ev (see Chapter Two), along with Kavelin and the others who all appropriated and situated a 'remnants' (or 'traces,' 'survivals') ethnography within various combinations of Russian Orthodox 'dual faith,' Enlightenment progressivist and romantic nationalist historiographies.

They all developed these views and approaches prior to and independent of Marx, Engels and Tylor, and even potentially contributed to this developing ethno-historiography by way of reciprocal international exchange. Valikhanov, in fact, provides one of two examples of the general reciprocal influence taking place between Western Euro-American secular scientific approaches to the 'history of religion' and nineteenth-century Tsarist schools. These exchanges occurred within the context of the 'Great Game' being played out between the Tsarist and British empires across the nineteenth and early twentieth centuries.[149] The first example is Valikhanov's contribution to the volume which was translated into English in 1865 and published in London under the title *The Russians in Central Asia* (see above). Of specific relevance here, the concept of "remnants" is employed by Valikhanov in this work when he speaks of "traces of antiquities," though this is in reference to his search for the physical remnants of "a large idol carved out of a block of stone" near Lake Issyk-kul in Kyrgyzia. It occurs in the context of discussing the "Propagation and Suppression of Christianity" in the area, with his noted failure to find any "traces of antiquities" of idol worship. The lack of any such traces was used as proof of the Muslim Kyrgyz suppression of non-Muslim faith traditions.[150] The translation of Valikhanov's work into English in London, at the same time Tylor was busy formulating his ideas in England, may even have, however distantly, impacted Tylor's work, though Tylor does not explicitly reference Valikhanov. They were nonetheless both part of the trans-imperial exchanges in which such constructs took shape, with Tylor engaging Protestant-offshoot traditions in both their anti-Catholic and anti-progressivist (i.e., degenerationist) forms. In the opposite direction, F. Max Müller, *Lectures on the Science of Language* (1861–1866), was translated into Russian in 1866 and published in the first Russian scientific linguistic magazine *Philological Notes* [*Филологические Записки*]. While this specific work does not employ 'survivals' historiography,

Müller was one of the contributing founders of the entire nineteenth-century 'history of religion' school, impacting the work of Tylor and others. And the tracing of linguistic etymologies became central to questions of religious-cultural influence as well as 'survivals.'

Importantly here, however, and contra Bruce G. Privratsky's claims in *Muslim Turkistan: Kazak Religion and Collective Memory*, Müller did not influence the work of Shokan Valikhanov or the earlier Buryat scholar Dorzhi Banzarov (cf. 1822–1855). Privratsky asserts that they both "learned from Max Müller" naturalist theories about religion which led them to their conclusions regarding shamanism as a natural and even necessary corollary to nomadism.[151] Privratsky's source, however—namely Christopher Atwood—names both "Wilhelm Schwartz and Friedrich Max Müller" as simply "contemporaries" of Banzarov, crediting the development of the theory to Banzarov, not Schwartz or Müller. Atwood in fact clarifies in a footnote that "Banzarov's work preceded these influential nineteenth-century German theorists and has to be seen as a case of intellectual parallelism within a similar Zeitgeist, rather than as a case of direct influence."[152]

Privratsky likewise claims that Banzarov influenced Valikhanov, with Müller's influence apparently coming through Banzarov. Valikhanov had, in fact, ranked Banzarov in importance with Levshin in terms of impact on future studies. He considered Banzarov's study of Mongolian shamanism "the sole systematic and best scholarly research on this religion" available at the time. But he by no means embraced all of Banzarov's analysis or conclusions. Rather, he considered Banzarov's study of Mongolian shamanism inadequate as a source for studying the phenomena of Kazakh shamans and related *baqsi* figures, particularly because "the major part of data for his [Banzarov's] essay" had been "borrowed from shamanic prayers, collected by Lamas in special books and in its transformed form adapted to Buddhism."[153] Privratsky is certainly correct in recognizing a "two-tier theory" in Valikhanov's work, but he mislocates its sources in the work of Banzarov by way of Müller and other Western European scholars instead of the Russian Orthodox dual faith tradition which Valikhanov himself explicitly referenced, in combination with romanticist appropriations of the construct situated within an Enlightenment progressivist historical frame. This historical scheme was only beginning to take on emerging evolutionary notions by the time Valikhanov wrote, just several years after the publication of Darwin's *Origin of Species* (1859).[154]

These are essential points in tracing out the epistemic genealogies of later Soviet ethnographers in particular, since Valikhanov was one of the most influential sources on Soviet ethnography of the Kazakh and, by extension, other Central Asian Muslim peoples. Tylor and company were more of an addendum to an already existing and developed paradigm and approach from which Tylor himself had, in its Western Protestant form, originally borrowed and then inverted for his own purposes.

"Remnants" Historiography and 'the Kazakh of Kazakhs,' Abai, in the Later Nineteenth and Early Twentieth Centuries

Returning, then, to Tsarist interpreters of Kazakh religious history and identity, N.L. Zeland, writing in 1885, observed that "Muslim rituals are mixed with remnants [остатками] of paganism" among the Kazakhs. A.N. Haruzin, in his 1889 "anthropological and ethnological essay" on "Kirghiz [Kazakhs] of the Bukei Horde," did not use the terms 'pre-Islamic,' 'remnant,' 'survival' or otherwise, but nonetheless described "the struggle between old paganism with the Mohammedanism [recently] entering" among the Kazakhs. F. Poyarkov, writing in 1891, in an essay titled "From the Realm of Kirgiz Beliefs," included both of these quotes in his treatise. He also spoke of others who "wrote that they preserved the remnants [следы] of fire-worship, etc." He himself employed this paradigm, albeit with a different Russian term, in reference to Kazakhs "who follow the remnants [остатки] of old pagan beliefs." Among these, he considered it "obvious that worshipping spirits of ancestors is the remnant [остатокъ] of the previous Kara-Kirgiz religion."[155]

Writing sometime between the late nineteenth and early twentieth century, not long after Poyarkov, one of the greatest national figures in Kazakh history, Abai Kunanbaiuhli (Russian: Kunanbaev, 1845–1904), briefly, in one passage, outlined Kazakh and broader Central Asian religious history as follows:

> many Islamic religious teachers came to Central Asia with soldiers from Arabia, and while they were turning the attention of the peoples to the new religion..., ...due to their [the Central Asian peoples'] shamanistic beliefs and customs of fire and candle worship (remaining still) from (long) before (бұрыннан),[156] they were not able to quickly understand and transition to Islam. ...We, too, have seen in certain places the remnants

(саркынын) of customs of an observed religion in which phenomena in the world that are inexplicable are made into (a) god:...[157]

Abai immediately goes on to describe the oil and fire ritual carried out by the daughter-in-law upon her entrance into her new family home, where she is made to exclaim "'Mother of fire, mother of oil, bless!,'... we've dedicated this unto the deceased ancestral spirits (өлген аруаққа арнадық)."[158] "Superstitions such as these," Abai then says, "were once plentiful, [but] thanks be to God, these days it seems they are steadily decreasing."[159]

Abai here speaks in two related yet distinct ways of "remnants" (cf. 'survivals') of past beliefs: the first is in the original coming of Islam to Central Asia when the "beliefs and customs ... (remaining still) from (long) before" were not only surviving, but still thriving and predominant to the point that the Central Asians "were not able to quickly understand and transition to Islam." Although Abai says a few lines between this and his statement about "the remnants of religious customs in certain places" which he himself and others of his time have seen, the latter are clearly holdovers from the former. In Abai's perspective then, these "remnants" still around in his time had remained since the original coming of Islam.

Importantly though, these pre-Islamic "survivals" were, from Abai's vantage, "steadily decreasing" in his day. Abai thus holds a progressivist view of the steadily increasing spread of Islam among the Kazakhs, moving from a time when superstitious religious customs "were once plentiful" to their clear, observable steady decline as adherence to Islam gained ascendancy. A key question of interpretation here is whether Abai is signifying that he himself witnessed, at some point earlier in his life, the period when these pre-Islamic "survivals...were once plentiful." If so, it would have to be at some point between about age 10, in 1855, down to perhaps 1870 or 1880. It would seem doubtful on these grounds that Abai intends to claim witness to that period. Regardless, however, of the answer to that particular question, it does not change the fact that he clearly witnessed them "steadily decreasing," so the interpretational point is only a matter of relative, not absolute consequence, i.e., it is only a matter of how long and late they remained "plentiful" and thus how quickly they were "steadily decreasing."

Abai thus clearly uses the concept as well as explicit terminology of 'pre-Islamic remnants' to delineate Kazakh religious history and identity. Indeed, Abai's viewpoint here accords with and supports nineteenth-century Russian colonial historiography, including that of Shokan Valikhanov, which held that the process of full Islamization was still not complete in the latter part of the nineteenth century, even the early twentieth. He nonetheless, contrary to Valikhanov, sees Islam in the ascendancy, not shamanism or other "remnants," and welcomes the continuing process of Kazakh Islamization. It would appear, in fact, that Abai is implicitly countering Valikhanov's view amid ongoing debates within the Russian Empire as to the proper religious identity of the Kazakhs. Certainly Abai was aware of Valikhanov's study, which had become a primary source of reference on Kazakh religious history and identity by Abai's time. It explicitly included reference to the same "pre-Islamic" ritual which Abai cited, that of the daughter-in-law throwing oil on the hearth fire and invoking ancestral blessings. Abai is not, however, dependent on Valikhanov for his knowledge of the ritual, but rather attests to seeing it still in practice himself in his own day. And in spite of his more modernist-reformist views, he did not see it as an integral part of Kazakh Islamic faith and practice.[160] On this latter point, he was in agreement with more conservative Islamic legal and theological scholars. He was also, in limited measure, in agreement with Valikhanov and his ethnographic school, though it is clear that Abai did not simply adopt and perpetuate Valikhanov's views. As this and other evidence both above and below demonstrates, the historiography is far more complex than a simplistic line running unchanged and unchallenged from Valikhanov down to the post-Soviet era.

The Terminological Shift to "Perezhitki" in Early Twentieth-Century Writings of Tsarist Russian Missionaries

A number of Russian Orthodox missionaries and Tsarist ethnographers carried the 'remnants' paradigm into the early twentieth century.[161] A.N. Sedelnikov, writing in 1903 about the "Ethnographic Composition and Culture" of the Kazakhs, noted the "survival [пережитокъ] of a past tradition" which was part of Kazakh marriage customs.[162] Although the other standard Russian terms such as "ostatki" and "sledi," as well as occasionally "relikti," continued to be used, Sedelnikov was among the first to begin using the Russian term "perezhiktki" (and its variations), apparently signaling the rising influence of the Tylorean paradigm which had been taking shape in the latter quarter of the nineteenth century.

Several pages on, in describing religious beliefs and practices, he suggests that "[t]he Kyrgyz [Kazakhs] are still under the influence of nature" involving, among other things, "some rituals." In clarifying these 'survivals' of ancient practices rooted in 'nature,' he asserts that "[f]rom paganism, the Kyrgyz [Kazakhs] preserved [сохранили] only faith in the *baqsy* (shaman)."[163] It seems, however, that the intended distinction is based on the idea of "faith" as opposed to merely "influence," so that the sense would be 'from among past pagan faith traditions.' As Tsarist (and later Soviet) ethnography did not typically classify Islam as a 'pagan' faith, this phrasing accords with the standard interpretation that shamanism and Islam were the two main competing faith traditions among the Kazakhs, with other 'survivals' being recognized, but not classified as 'faiths' (i.e., 'religions') in and of themselves.[164] Sedelnikov's analysis was part of a multi-volume encyclopedia project detailing all the peoples, cultures and territories of the Russian Empire carried out in the latter years of Tsarist rule between 1899 and 1914.

Within Russian ethnography of Central Asian Muslim peoples other than the Kazakhs, Russian Orthodox missionaries and historians working in the Caucasus from as early as 1839, with roots reaching back nearly a century to 1743, constructed a history of the mountain peoples of the Caucasus which depicted their Islamic faith as a historically shallow veneer masking an original Orthodox faith whose deep medieval roots were still visible in their day. This work was eventually carried forward by the Society for the Restoration of Orthodoxy in the Caucasus (1860–1917). It included identification of the intermixing of Christian, Islamic and surviving "pagan" beliefs and practices.[165] Elsewhere, the Soviet scholar G.P. Snesarev, in an eight-year study of *Survivals [Реликты] of Pre-Islamic Beliefs and Rituals among the Khorezm Uzbeks* (see Chapters 5 and 6), noted several Tsarist-era scholars who provided "[m]uch valuable information, although sometimes quite fragmentary and scattered," regarding 'pre-Islamic survivals' in broader Central Asia. These included A.P Khoroshkhin's 1876 treatise on the Turkestan region, V.P. and M.V. Nalivkin's 1886 article on "the native peoples of Ferghana," and N.P. Ostroumov's study of the Sarts between 1890 and 1895.[166] Meanwhile, M.S. Andreev penned an essay on "Remnants [Остатки] of Pagan Customs among Natives (Uzbeks, Tajiks)" published in 1895.[167] Curiously Snesarev does not cite this particular source, but he does note that Andreev was among the earliest Soviet ethnographers to produce studies of 'survivals' among Central Asian peoples in the 1920s (see below). The work of Andreev, among several others (see next chapter), thus demonstrates continuity between Tsarist and Soviet 'survivals' ethnography as well as clear, direct influence of the former on the latter, significantly complicating the otherwise simplistic theory of Tylorean influence typically put forward. Continuing on with late Tsarist sources, an author which S.P. Tolstov simply identified as "K" titled his 1902 essay "Remnants [Остатки] of Shamanism among the Sarts."[168] Snesarev, for his part, goes on to highlight A.A. Divaev's *Ethnographic Materials* on the Syr Daria region between 1891 and 1907, A.A. Semenov's 1903 *Ethnographic Essay* on Tajik mountain peoples, A. Shishov's 1904–1905 study of the Sarts of the Syr Daria region, and N.S. Lyoshkin's 1916 work titled *Half a Lifetime in Turkestan: Essays on the Life of the Native Peoples*.[169] Five years earlier, in 1911, and thus well before the Soviet period, M.S. Andreev had teamed together with A.A. Polobtsov to address "Remnants [Остатки] of the Old Social Order" in a volume containing *Materials on the Ethnography of the Iranian Tribes of Central Asia*.[170] Snesarev had passed over this work as well. All these latter works together sufficiently demonstrate that the concept of 'remnants/survivals' was quite familiar to and abundantly employed by Russian Tsarist ethnographers from at least the last quarter of the nineteenth century.

Part One Conclusion: Summary of Tsarist Historical Sources

The most immediate and influential source informing Tsarist 'pre-Islamic survivals' ethnography was initially the 'dual faith' paradigm of Russian Christian history, inherited as it was from the Byzantine and broader Western Christian tradition, reaching all the way back to the Hebrew-Jewish and Christian scriptural sources themselves. The Islamic branch of this Middle Eastern monotheistic historical thread also played a secondary role, entering Central Asia and eventually being applied to the Kazakh case by way of the Uzbeks and Tatars in particular. In the face of increasing religious, cultural, legal and political crises across the nineteenth century, which involved questions of religious history and identity among various peoples of the empire, including the question of Islam and the Kazakhs, Levshin and Yastrebov, as Russians schooled in the 'Orthodoxy, Autocracy, and Nationality' period of conservatism under Alexander I (1825–1855), and Valikhanov, as a Kazakh 'convert' to Russian progressivist civilization, inclusive of Russian Orthodoxy, all served to lay the foundations for this heritage, which was then passed on for generations to come, down through the Soviet and post-Soviet periods. This historiographical-ethnographical tradition was later supplemented by and even shrouded within the emerging secularized scientific 'history of human and religious origins' schools taking shape from the mid-nineteenth century in Western Europe. Though originally appropriated within Russian ethnography of the Kazakhs, it was eventually applied to other Central Asian Muslim peoples in the latter part of the 1800s.[171] This came by way of Tylor, Frazer and company's influence on late Tsarist and Soviet scholars, with the Russian tradition reciprocally making its own unique contributions to the work of Tylor and others through international networks of dialogue and exchange.

It must be borne in mind, however, that not all those framing the histories and identities of the various nationalities in Tsarist Russia employed a 'survivals' paradigm. This included the Muslim populations of Central Asia. As Elena Campbell has amply demonstrated, Tsarist Russian views of and approaches to Islam, particularly in the latter years of the empire, were marked by "[r]egional diversity, ministerial rivalry, governmental fear of popular response, as well as different opinions within tsarist officialdom."[172] This is significant because it begs the question of what is meant by the term 'Tsarist ethnography.' That is to say, there was no one standardized version of 'Tsarist ethnography' which always interpreted and responded to the Muslim peoples of the Russian Empire in the same way. As we shall see in the following chapter, Soviet ethnographers worked within a more restricted historiographical frame, though the situation was far from static or entirely uniform.

PART II

Historical Sources of Soviet 'Survivals' Ethnography

CHAPTER 5

Sources and Aims of Soviet 'Survivals' Ethnography in Its Initial (Pre-World War Two) Phases

This chapter continues the quest to understand the origins and aims of both Tsarist and Soviet historiography and ethnography of Central Asia, especially their shared focus on 'pre-Islamic remnants' or 'survivals' (cf. also 'vestiges,' 'relics,' etc.) and their respective appropriations of that construct. Given the clear pre-existence of a well-established tradition of 'survivals' historiography and ethnography between the late eighteenth and early twentieth centuries in Tsarist Russia, with a closely related tradition of 'double faith' going back to the eleventh century, (see Chapter 2), the question arises of the relation of Soviet views and approaches to former Tsarist Russian historiography, both in terms of how they compare with one another on theoretical and practical levels and in terms of how the Tsarist tradition may have shaped the Soviet. Central to addressing these issues are the questions of when, why and how Soviet ethnography began distinguishing between 'pre-Islamic' and 'Islamic' identity in Central Asia via the conceptual apparatus of 'survivals' and what sources the various authors of Soviet 'survivals' ethnography specifically cite within their studies. Two main traditions of Tsarist 'survivals' ethnography are the most immediately relevant and obvious in terms of potential influence—namely the Russian Orthodox 'double faith' and the secular scientific versions—though Euro-American sources also played a significant role, as did Islamic ones.

© The Author(s), under exclusive license to Springer Nature Singapore Pte Ltd. 2023
R. C. Weller, *'Pre-Islamic Survivals' in Muslim Central Asia*, Islam and Global Studies,
https://doi.org/10.1007/978-981-19-5697-3_5

The Persistence of 'Survivals' Ethnography in Russian Orthodoxy

Regarding the Russian Orthodox sources in the Soviet era, Stella Rock notes that

> Soviet scholarship enthusiastically embraced the academic concept of double-belief. Soviet historians tended to focus on pagan survivals as evidence of active resistance by the people to the institution of the Church and the ruling classes who helped impose Christianity [cf. also Islam] on the populace...[,] as an unconscious desire to preserve the religious pattern of the ancestors, or as a creative response to needs unfulfilled by the new religion.[173]

N.M. Nikol'skii, *History of the Russian Church* (1930), George P. Fedotov, *The Russian Religious Mind* (1946), D.S. Likhachev (1953), B. Grekov, *Kiev Rus* (1959) and B.A. Rybakov, *Paganism in Ancient Rus* (1981) were among those who embraced and applied this deeply rooted tradition in the Soviet cause.[174] As indicated by the dates of publication, most of these were produced in the post-World War Two period (see Chapter 6). To what degree, they followed the same pathway of development as, and/or possibly interacted with, Soviet approaches to Islam is a question which must be left to another study. It is important, nonetheless, to note the continuation of a 'remnants/survivals' historiography within the Russian Orthodox tradition throughout the entire Soviet period.

'Survivals' Ethnography in Marx, Engels, Lenin and Stalin

Before discussing the Tsarist scientific stream (which itself had also originally drawn from the Russian Christian 'dual faith' paradigm) and its relation to Soviet 'survivals' ethnography, I return to the work of E.B. Tylor from 1865 onward, particularly his 1871 study of *Primitive Culture*, which also played an important role. Tylor's views went on to influence those of James Frazer and a number of other late nineteenth- and early twentieth-century 'history of religion' scholars in the Euro-American domain which then, in dynamic reciprocal fashion, impacted both the late Tsarist and Soviet ethnographic schools. This took place via two routes: One, their influence on especially Freidrich Engels and his subsequent foundational authority for Lenin, Stalin and the entire Soviet ethnographical tradition and, two, by way of direct influence on (late Tsarist and) Soviet ethnographers themselves, particularly in the latter's formational period.

First, with respect to Marx and Engels as foundational figures, we should bear in mind that they are not themselves 'Soviet,' but represent a Western European tradition taking shape in parallel with late Tsarist ethnography. With this in mind, James Thrower argues that Tylor's views clearly and directly shaped those of Engels in particular.[175] Three important things must, nonetheless, be acknowledged when considering Thrower's contention: First, Thrower notes that Engels never explicitly cited Tylor. Second, when Thrower cites the main, relevant passage where (according to Thrower's estimation) Engels summarizes the heart of Tylor's work—namely his 1886 critique of the views of Ludwig Feuerbach in relation to Hegel—Engels offers a sweeping overview of the entire "development of religions," from the earliest "personification of natural forces" down to "the idea of the one exclusive god of the monotheistic religions"; but he nowhere mentions the idea of 'survivals.'[176] And third, Thrower himself supplies no grounds for concluding that Tylor's influence on Engels explicitly included the idea of 'survivals.'

There is in fact, though, at least one passage where Engels utilizes the term 'survival' in a Tylorean sense, and it occurs in the same treatise where (according to Thrower) he summarizes Tylor, though it is some eight paragraphs later. In that later passage, Engels contends that "the Hegelian premundane existence of the 'absolute idea,' the 'pre-existence of the logical categories' before the world existed, is nothing more than the fantastic survival of the belief in the existence of an extramundane creator...."[177] But three more observations are vital here: one, Engels does not have 'pre-Islamic' versus 'Islamic' manifestations specifically in view; two, Engels does not cite Tylor, so specific attribution to any particular writer, Tylor or otherwise, is impossible; and three, this supplies us with only one lone, albeit general, reference.

Beyond this, Engels speaks elsewhere, in 1882, of "Islam itself...preserving its specifically Oriental ritual" in its very origins and practice.[178] The idea of 'pre-Islamic survivals' is at least implicit here. This view of Islam's borrowings from pre-Islamic sources—Arab, Greek, Roman-Byzantine, Persian, Jewish, Christian, Zoroastrian and more—was shared by numerous other (especially non-Islamic) interpreters both in and even before Engel's day. It approximates, though does not explicate, the positions of John of Damascus, Joseph White and Theodor Nöldeke (see Chapter 3). As early as 1853, however—that is, well before the influence of Tylor, Frazer and company[179]—Engels posited that debates involving 'syncretism' were the very grounds for the rise of Islam, saying: "[the Islamic religion] seems to me to bear the character of a Bedouin reaction against the settled but degenerating fellaheen of the towns, who at that time had also become very decadent in their religion, mingling a corrupt nature-cult with corrupt Judaism and Christianity."[180] Syncretism of course implies the 'survival' of two or more traditions mixed together. It, likewise, implies the ability to distinguish the various mixed traditions from one another. Important here, however, is, as Thrower points out, that, "[a]s men of the nineteenth century," Marx and Engels held "opinions—derived for the most part...from the anthropology of their day." Thrower describes these opinions as being mainly "about the origin and early forms of religion,"[181] but Marx and Engels also addressed the relation of earlier to later forms of religion, distinguishing (however inaccurately) between three essential stages of religious history. This progressive interpretation of world religious history has, as we shall see, important ramifications for 'pre-' and 'post-world religious' forms.

V.I. Lenin and Joseph Stalin both spent their formative years in the late Tsarist period, but served as the ultimate sources of authority for what would eventually become the Soviet historiographical school. Like Marks and Engels, they were both 'men of their times,' shaped in various ways, pro and con, by the prevailing views of their day. These included not only thinkers like Tylor, Frazer and other late-nineteenth, early twentieth-century Euro-American 'history of religion' scholars, but the clear, direct influence of Marx and Engels as the main, general authorities for their views on religion (and most everything else). Whether by influence of Marx and Engels, or some other source(s), both Lenin and Stalin speak of 'survivals,' 'remnants' or 'relics' of the past. These references included religion, but religion was viewed as one of numerous 'remnants' or 'survivals' of the feudalist or capitalist world order.

Lenin, in his 1905 article on "Socialism and Religion," spoke of "proletarians who have preserved certain remnants (остатки) of old prejudices" in direct relation with "the religious question."[182] This was part of "the struggle against the Middle Ages, including, among other things, the old, official religion and with all attempts to update it or justify it anew or otherwise, etc."[183] This religion is among "the remnants (остатки) of serfdom," "the dying, departing remnants (остатки) of the old" which he wishes to actively help kill off completely.[184] Lenin uses the Russian term 'perezhitkii' ('пережитки') frequently in like manner, that is, primarily of feudal or medieval 'remnants' or 'survivals.'[185]

As for Stalin, in discussing the Jews in relation to "the Georgians, Daghestanians, Russians and Americans respectively," he suggests that,

> if there is anything common left to them, it is their religion, their common origin and certain remnants (остатки) of the national character. All this is beyond question. But how can it be seriously maintained that petrified religious rites (что окостенелые религиозные обряды) and fading psychological remnants (остатки) affect the 'destiny' of these Jews more powerfully than the living social, economic and cultural environment that surrounds them?[186]

As with Lenin, therefore, Stalin also aims at "the destruction of feudal remnants (остатков)" in order to resolve these and other issues,[187] though neither Lenin nor Stalin speaks of any 'pre-Islamic' or even Islamic remnants specifically. Neither do they typically employ the Russian term for "paganism" ("язычества") in relation such "survivals," suggesting that their own personal influence came more from Marx, Engels and other secular sources such as Tylor as opposed to Russian Orthodox historiography.[188]

Overall then, the views of Marx and Engels, as well as Lenin and Stalin, all took shape within the late nineteenth-, early twentieth-century milieu which gave rise to progressivist 'survivals' historiography in both the Euro-American and Euro-Slavic traditions. Chinese communist propaganda later drew from these same and other more complex sources in what Peter Stearns calls their attack upon "capitalist remnants that were exploiting older beliefs and rituals in order to survive."[189] Though the authority of these four socialist thinkers was unquestionable, it seems doubtful that their influence on broader Soviet 'survivals' historiography and ethnography was decisive or exclusive. Numerous Soviet scholars and propagandists drew from various sources, including Tsarist most immediately, both religious and secular. They nonetheless form one (or perhaps two closely related) additional stream(s) of thought among many in the multiple, criss-crossing historical influences all feeding into Soviet 'survivals' ethnography at the broader level.[190] Given that their discussions of religious history largely drew from and revolved around Christianity in both its Western and Eastern European forms, particularly in relation to European feudalism, I suggest that, along with the secular scientific school of Tylor and company, these respective Christian traditions helped to shape their perspectives on questions of broader religious history and identity, including Islamic.

Tylor, Frazer and Other Euro-American Sources of Influence

Regarding direct influence from Euro-American sources (other than Marx and Engels) on Soviet ethnographers themselves, particularly in the latter's formational period, I will draw primarily from Thrower's overview, supplemented by additional material along the way. As early as 1919, Ivan Skvortsov-Stepanov—a dedicated Bolshevik and participant in the October Revolution—had translated into Russian the work of the German ethnographer and sociologist Heinrich Cunow (1862–1936), *The Origin of Religion and Faith of God*. Since Thrower is not concerned with Tylor's influence in this case, or with Soviet 'survivals' ethnography, he makes no mention of either, but Cunow references the work of Tylor in relation to "animism" near the beginning of his study and then later speaks of "remnants" (German: 'reste') of totemism at least once.[191]

Five years later, Thrower suggests that Anatoly V. Lunacharsky (a playwright and journalist who also served as the first Soviet Minister of Education) was "probably under the influence of...James Frazer" in writing his *Introduction to the History of Religion*. But this is Thrower's own estimation. Thrower references the second edition of Lunacharsky's work published in 1924, but the book was first published in 1923, based on lectures delivered in St. Petersburg in 1918. Lunacharsky later published a third edition, with no date of publication.[192] Whether starting from the lectures in 1918, the original 1923 edition, or one of the other two revisions, Lunacharsky does reference the work of Tylor, though not in connection to 'survivals.'[193]

Building on these contributions, V.K. Nikol'sky, a historian of religion at Moscow University, published an article in 1926 introducing "New Foreign Work on Primitive Worldviews." Then, in the following decade, "[b]etween 1930 and 1939," under the editorship of V.K. Nikol'sky, "many of the writings of Western anthropologists"—including James Frazer, Edward B. Tylor and Lucien Lévy-Bruhl—"were published in Russian translation."[194] Nikol'sky himself translated Tylor, *Primitive Culture* (1871), in 1939.[195] What precise influence these translation efforts exerted on Soviet 'survivals' ethnography is not clear, but among other works appearing in these early foundational decades, A. Zolotarev published a study in 1934 on *Survivals [Пережитки] of Totemism among the Peoples of Siberia* followed two years later by D.K. Zelenin's 1936 inquiry into *The Cult of the Ongons in Siberia: Remnants [Пережитки] of Totemism in the Ideology of the Siberian Peoples*.[196]

In parallel, between 1925 and 1927, L.Y. Sternberg, "one of the founders of the Soviet Ethnographic School," was lecturing on the topic of *Primitive Religion in the Light of Ethnography* at the University of Leningrad. Drawing from these lectures, Sternberg eventually published a book by that title in 1936, demonstrating his "wide acquaintance with Western anthropological writing on religion."[197] In that work, Sternberg spoke of "remnants (пережитки) of the manifestations of God" in several places.[198] Likewise, whether drawing from Nikol'sky's 1926 article or not, 1926 was the year Frazer inspired V.S. Bogoraz in his "superb study of the myth of the dying and rising 'beast' ('zver') found in many parts of Siberia." Bogoraz, working among the Chukchi people, went on in 1939 to produce "one of the earliest [Soviet] studies of Siberian shamanism." Along with his clear dependence on the Tsarist ethnographer V.M. Mikhailovsky's in-depth look at *Shamanism* released in 1892, "[t]he conceptual apparatus which Bogoraz brought to bear on his study of these peoples was heavily indebted to Frazer, Levi-Bruhl, and Friedrich Boas." Given these sources of influence, Bogoraz was most likely familiar with the concept of 'survivals,' but I leave the question as to the precise role it may have played in his work to other researchers.[199] The importance of that question, however, is reflected in the fact that "[a]lmost all of the future leaders of the Soviet ethnographic school—B.L. Bogayevsky, A.M. Pokrovsky, G.P. Frantsov, V.O. Vasilenko, A.I. Novikov, A.F. Anisimov and L.N. Manuylova—were his pupils." Noteworthy among these, G.P. (also known as Y.P.) Frantsov (1903–1969)—hailed by many as "the single most important scholar in the entire field of 'scientific atheism'"—wrote his doctoral dissertation in 1940 on *Fetishism and the Problem of the Origin of Religion*.[200] While it is not clear just how Frantsov employed 'survivals' ethnography within his work, the influence of Tylor, Fraser and others—directly or indirectly—seems clear by virtue of the main topic he treats.

Meanwhile, Sergei A. Tokarev, in a 1956 article treating "The Contribution of Russian Scientists to World Ethnographic Science," argued that Russian 'survivals' historiography could be traced back well before Tylor, to the work of Russian historians writing in the 1840s, particularly K.D. Kavelin (1818–1885; see Chapters 2 and 4).[201]

Early Soviet 'Survivals' Ethnography of Kazakh and Central Asian Islamic History, 1920s–40s

Overviewing some of the major sources of influence on Soviet 'survivals' ethnography at the broadest level—especially Euro-American influence on Soviet study of the origins and general stages of development of world religious history—provides an essential context for understanding Soviet 'survivals' work on Kazakh and broader Central Asian Islamic history and identity. With respect to the latter, the Soviet scholar G.P. Snesarev noted that—along with the late Tsarist sources he named (see Chapter 4)—a number of Soviet scholars going back as far as the early 1920s had contributed to the study of religious 'survivals' in Central Asia. First among these was M.S. Andreev who, says Snesarev, "assembled exceedingly rich material on relics of ancient beliefs among the peoples of Central Asia." Unnoticed by Snesarev, Andreev had, in fact, already published an article on "Remnants [Остатки] of Pagan Customs among Natives (Uzbeks, Tajiks)" in 1895 (see end of Chapter 4). Continuing this work into the Soviet period, Andreev's ethnographic studies of the Tajiks and peoples of the Samarkand region, among others, emerged from expeditions starting in 1921, with publications dating between 1923 and 1927. In a chapter published in 1925 titled "On Ethnography of the Tajiks," Andreev spoke of the Tajiks as themselves being "surviving remnants (остатки)" of "various Iranian peoples" who lived "in hard-to-reach mountain areas." His concern with these "remnants of Tajiks" was connected with his attempt to trace out various dialects which had "survived (уцелевшим) in the form of a relic (реликта) in our day as a remnant (остатком) of the Sogdian language." All this was central for Andreev in distinguishing "who exactly is Tajik and who is not Tajik in different places of Central Asia."[202] Among them, "in a more complete old form, public assemblies of...mountain Tajiks have survived/been preserved (сохранились) in their homeland, within their villages" where also "the ancient custom of public hospitality is still widely preserved (сохранился)."[203] His interest in "public assemblies" and "public hospitality" seems to draw from his earlier 1911 work with A.A. Polobtsov on "Remnants [Остатки] of the Old Social Order" among Iranian tribes of Central Asia (see Chapter 4). It was only natural then that Andreev would frame Tajik religious customs in these same terms. Indeed, the last eight pages of his chapter were dedicated to showing how

[t]he Tajik, as a Muslim, is not distinguished by great fanaticism, in accordance with the general population of Central Asia, especially, for example, compared with the Muslims of India or Persia. ...A full picture of the old beliefs (прежних верований), with very little elaboration of Tajik folklore from scattered and largely lost small fragments (фрагментам), is not yet possible to restore, especially since under the concept of the "pre-Muslim pagan period" ("до-мусульманского языческого периода") there are in essence the remains of the beliefs (остатки верований) of a number of different epochs and cultures which have come down to us in a very confused and mixed (mess of) people's ideas.[204]

Returning to Snesarev's overview, he notes that A.L. Troitskaya also wrote on "vestiges of shamanism and of ancient beliefs in family life" in articles published in both 1925 and 1935. Likewise, E.M. Peshchereva produced "[e]xceptionally valuable material, particularly on craft cults, vestiges of ancestor worship, and women's rituals," with two different works included in volumes on Tajikistan and Turkistan both released in 1927.[205] Additionally, in 1928, L.P. Potapov focused his attention on "Remnants [Пережитки] of the Cult of the Bear among the Altai Turks,"[206] while Iu.V. Knorozov closed out the decade with a 1929 article on Tajik social-cultural features which made reference to 'pre-Islamic remnants', though only briefly in passing.[207]

Bridging the 1920s and 1930s, the Kazakh historian Sanzhar Zhafarovich Asfendiarov (1889–1938) published two works, one a short booklet on the *Reasons for the Emergence of Islam*, released in 1928, and the other an article on "Islam and Nomadic Economy." The latter appeared in the journal *Atheist* in 1930. In "Islam and Nomadic Economy," Asfendiarov referenced "the works of the famous English ethnographer J. Fraser ('Totemism and Exogamy,' 'Golden Bow')" where "you can find a number of illustrations on" magic and religion. He, likewise, made repeated reference in both works to the Hungarian scholar Ignaz Goldziher, who employed 'survivals' historiography in his two-volume *Muslim Studies* published in 1889–1890 (see Chapter 3).[208] As noted by the modern Kazakh historian Zifa-Alua Auezova, "Conceiving a People's History: The 1920–1936 Discourse on the Kazakh Past," this was in keeping with Asfendiarov's overall approach, which made lavish use of "ancient Greek, Roman and Chinese texts, medieval geographic treatises written in Middle Eastern and European traditions, historical treatises composed within the boundaries of the Mongol Empire, as well as Central

Asian and Russian sources."²⁰⁹ Whatever the precise source(s) of his 'survivals' historiography, he certainly employed it, albeit sparingly, within both these (and presumably other) publications. Thus in relation to the "complex rituals and cults" of "agricultural farming," he suggested that "[t]races ([с]леды) of these rites and beliefs we find in all religions, from ancient agricultural religions to Christianity." He was, likewise, confident that "[w]e can find among the Arabs beliefs and traces (следы) of the influence of agricultural religions, from the ancient patriarchal agricultural religions to Judaic and Christian views." Indeed, "Islam as a religion was formed much later, under the influence of Greco-Byzantine and Persian culture." Note the close relation between crosscultural "influence" and the "traces" of that influence in the various 'pre-Islamic survivals' left as 'evidence.'²¹⁰

But not just religious 'survivals,' Asfendiarov, like other Soviet scholars (cf. e.g., Andreev above) and numerous writers in various traditions of historiography, as far back as the Hebrew biblical, speaks also of portions of ethnic or religious groups themselves as 'survivals.'²¹¹ Thus he says, "[i]n Central Asia, in the region of Katta-Kurgan, we have the remains (остатки) of Bedouin tribes who lost their language, but retained their tribal names and semi-nomadic way of life."²¹² In similar fashion, Asfendiarov's only application of 'survivals' historiography throughout the entire span of *Reasons for the Emergence of Islam* is in reference to non-religious matters. Thus regarding Arab clan relations and "the enormous significance of the nomadic cattle-breeding economy at that time" he proposes that the "[k]inship relations" in view "were not a remnant (пережитком) of a previous era." Nonetheless, "[t]here was a complicated kinship structure, in the presence of clan customs and survivals (пережитком)" which included "the dominance of the merchant aristocracy" and other related components. These 'survivals' were apparently why "in the Koran we find...an attempt to organize a religious (national) community, [and] the destruction of a number of tribal customs and survivals (пережитков), like blood feuding, shooting, contempt for renegades from the clan (whom the Koran calls 'muhajirs'), travelers etc." Ultimately though, in his view, "it is impossible to divide the Arab ideology into a patriarchal, feudal and commercial or clan system as a survival (пережитком) of a nomadic life." And "there is absolutely no indication that the cultural heartlands of Central Arabia were the remnants (остатками) of a once-great culture." While Asfendiarov thus himself employs 'survivals' historiography at certain points, a number of his references actually negate the validity of applying it to the particular situations in view.²¹³

Moving into the 1930s, "[S.P.] Tolstov's researches on problems of the history of religion among the peoples of Central Asia are," says Snesarev, "of exceptional importance."[214] After undergraduate work in mathematics, Tolstov (1907–1976) began studying anthropology in 1923 with an original focus on Russian material culture. In 1929, he transferred to the Historical and Ethnological Faculty of Moscow State University, taking his first trip to Khorezm that year. He completed his 'doksent' (master's equivalent) degree in 1930, at the age of 23, going on to earn his 'kandidat' (doctoral equivalent) degree "from the Leningrad State Academy of the History of Material Culture," with a specialization in "the history and archeology of Central Asia." He was appointed "head of the Faculty of History, Moscow State University, Department of Ethnography" in 1937. After successfully defending his 'doktorant' thesis (equivalent to a post-doctoral monograph) in 1942 on the topic of *Ancient Khorezm*, "he was appointed director of the Institute of Ethnography of the USSR Academy of Sciences," eventually becoming chief editor of the journal *Soviet Ethnography* from 1946 to 1966 as well as an honorary member of the Academy of Sciences of the Uzbek SSR.[215]

One of Tolstov's most important early contributions was on "The Religion of the Peoples of Central Asia," which included a sizable list of recommended sources at the very end. This material is contained in volume one of the two-volume set on *Religious Beliefs of the Peoples of the USSR: a collection of ethnographic materials* published in 1931.[216] V.K. Nikol'skii (or Nikol'sky) was one of two chief editors of these volumes. The importance of this for our purposes is that, while James Thrower did not concern himself with 'survivals' historiography and ethnography, he did note that V.K. Nikol'skii was also the one who oversaw the translation of "many of the writings of Western anthropologists"—including Frazer, Tylor and Lévy-Bruhl—into Russian (see above). It is not surprising, then, to find a number of references to 'pre-Islamic remnants' in these volumes, including Tolstov's work, though this does not mean that Tylor and company were the only sources of influence. In fact, in the long bibliographic list of recommended sources which Tolstov provides at the end of his section, Tylor, Frazer and other such Euro-American anthropologists do not appear. The sources in the list are determined, however, by their direct relevance to Central Asia, so this does not exclude their influence, it only suggests that it is indirect rather than direct, at least in Tolstov's work. Tolstov's recommendations included mostly Tsarist, early Soviet and Islamic, as well as a limited number of Western European sources, a point to which I will return shortly. More important for now is that not only did Tolstov's work itself frame Central Asian religious history and identity in terms of 'pre-Islamic remnants' mixed together in syncretic fashion with Islam, it recommended other works which did the same as key sources for Soviet scholars pursuing studies from the 1930s on. Both Knorozov (see below) and Snesarev themselves are evidence that Tolstov's recommendations continued to impact studies along these lines down to the 1960s and beyond.

As for Tolstov's own historiography of "The Religion of the Peoples of Central Asia," very early in his opening section, he explains that "Islam managed to fuse with the entire complex of pre-Islamic popular beliefs and rituals, and, touching on only the official teachings of Islam," left the roots of those earlier faiths "in the earth," from where they continued to grow alongside and even as part of Islam. "It is important," he argues, "for us to understand...this Central Asian religious syncretism in the process of its composite layering [в процессе его сложения], in the historical context (in which it took shape)."[217] After these and other remarks in his opening two pages, he moves into the remainder of his 138-page study where he covers "Central Asia before Islam," "Religion in Central Asia before Islam," "Central Asia after the Arab Conquests," "The Ethnic Composition of the Central Asian Republics and Kazakhstan," "Central Asian Religious Syncretism" and "Religious Organization," followed by sections dedicated specifically to "The Kazakhs and Kirgiz," "Turkmen," "The Uzbeks and Tajiks" and "Islamism." Midway into the first paragraph of the section on "Religion in Central Asia before Islam," he speaks of "remnants [пережитков] of totemism" recorded among the Scythian-Saka peoples in Herodotus.[218] Later, in discussing the term 'aruak' ('ancestral spirit', see Chapter 3) as a component of "Central Asian Religious Syncretism," Tolstov asserts that "the cult of the same ancestors is modified into a cult of the saints and their graves," implying that 'remnants' of 'the cult of the ancestors' known from ancient times in Central Asia continues on, merging into a 'cult of saints' within Islam.[219] In similar fashion, when discussing "Shamanism," he suggests that:

> In Muslim Central Asia, shamanism continues to live a full life, pushed into the background, but still preserving its face and rather peacefully coexisting with Islam. ...Shamanism is characteristic of almost all the peoples

of Central Asia. It is particularly pronounced among the Kirghiz and Kazakhs, but we find quite distinctive remnants [пережитки] of it among the Uzbeks, Turkmens and Tajiks. It is interesting to trace the merging of shamanism with Islam, which is clearly visible everywhere.[220]

Several pages later, Tolstov dedicates a short section to "Remnants [Пережитки] of Totemism," insisting in his opening declaration that "it is necessary to emphasize a significant number of remnants [пережитков] of totemism" to be found among the Central Asian Muslim peoples. After finishing his brief excursus, he concludes: "Of course, these are only fragments [осколки]. Totemism is a long-gone stage and its vestiges [пережитки] remain as inclusions in other social and ideological fabric. But one must reckon with these vestiges [пережитками]." Perhaps of little surprise, Tolstov went on four years later to dedicate a complete article to the study of the "Remnants [Пережитки] of Totemism and Dual Organization among the Turkmen" (1935),[221] which was still recognized 40 years later, upon his death, as "a significant contribution to the development of the problem of totemism."[222] As for his 1931 study of "The Religion of the Peoples of Central Asia," Tolstov brings it to a close saying:

> Wherever the vestiges [пережитки] of the tribal system are alive, subsistence farming, the patriarchal way of life,...[etc.,], continue to live a full life, sometimes slightly veiled by Muslim terminology, sometimes in its former form - beliefs and rituals peculiar to these ways. Animism, shamanism, the cult of ancestors and ancestral gods, the cult of the hearth, the worship of the pious sanctuaries, agrarian and cattle breeding magic, harmful magic (witchcraft), the cult of spirits - patrons of crafts, fetishism - all this is not yet a relic [пережитком] in Central Asia, but still a very real phenomenon. ...The steady evolution from "pagan" gods and spirits to Muslim prayers in everyday life and production clearly underlies this fact.[223]

Along these same lines, Tolstov's "Essays on Primitive Islam" (1932) interpreted Islam itself as having been based on 'pre-Islamic remnants' absorbed from surrounding religions and cultures. Thus in summing up his lifetime of achievements upon his death in 1976, Tolstov was recognized for having "initiated the study of [a number of] cardinal problems" in Central Asian ethnography, including "the genesis of various customs and rites, the history of Islam and its Central Asian specificity, relics of ancient pre-Islamic religions and beliefs [реликты древних доисламских религий и верований], and so on."[224]

As for other Soviet Central Asian 'survivals' ethnography produced in the 1930s, Snesarev highlights a 1934 article "devoted...specially to vestiges of totemism" and a 1936 monograph on *Traces [Следы] of Primitive Communism among Mountain Tajiks*, both written by N.A. Kisliakov. And I have already noted A.L. Troitskaya's articles on the "vestiges of shamanism and of ancient beliefs in family life" in 1925 and 1935 (see above).[225]

Concluding Reflections

Three points can be made at this juncture based in the preceding survey: First, it is clear that from the very rise of Soviet historiography and ethnography on Central Asia that the 'survivals' approach was well-known and appropriated. Second, as is made clear from the sources cited in the Soviet works themselves—namely, Tsarist (both Christian and secular progressivist), Islamic and Western European secular progressivist—Tylor and other Euro-American scholars cannot be credited as the sole or even primary sources of influence. They formed only one among numerous streams converging through trans-imperial networks of contact and exchange in the late nineteenth to early twentieth centuries.[226] I will not attempt to measure the extent to which each of these various 'survivals' schools exerted an impact, though based on the general balance of references within the works I have consulted, it appears that both Tsarist and Euro-American secular sources predominate. It is not possible, however, to depend solely on explicit references in published materials since numerous undocumented discussions among both fellow Russians—missionaries, diplomats, military personnel, colonists, traders and more—as well as native Central Asian peoples surely shaped their perspectives and approaches.

There seems little, if any, basis, however—by way of my third point—for Eren Tasar's suggestion that the Finnish sociologist Edvard Westermarck's 1933 study of *Pagan Survivals in Mohammedan Civilisation: Lectures on the traces of pagan beliefs, customs, folklore, practises and rituals surviving in the popular religion and magic of Islamic peoples* was a primary source of inspiration to the entire Soviet 'survivals' ethnographical tradition in Central Asia. Indeed, Tasar goes so far as to assert that "Tsarist and early Soviet social scientists borrowed...

Westermarck's ideas wholesale."[227] But he provides no evidence, either by way of references to Westermarck in (late Tsarist or) Soviet ethnographical literature or otherwise, and there appears to be no translation of Westermarck's book into Russian, either in the 1930s or later.[228] A better suggestion might have been Westermarck's earlier study of *Ritual and Belief in Morocco* published in 1926 which highlighted "survivals of ancient Berber practices," "survivals of funeral and mourning customs" and "survivals of totemism," among others.[229] Better still would have been Theodor Nöldeke or Ignaz Goldziher, who, as 'founding fathers' of 'Islamic Studies' in the Euro-American domain, were already applying Tylorean ideas of 'survivals' to Muslim societies as early as the 1880s (see Chapter 3). In fact, in his 1948 work titled *Following the Tracks of Ancient Khorezmian Civilization*, Tolstov cites Nöldeke.[230] Beyond this, until clear evidence is presented otherwise, the argument can only be circumstantial, that is to say, that Goldziher (as well as Westermarck nearly half-a-century later) were part of the same broad trans-imperial networks drawing from some of the same sources as late Tsarist and Soviet scholars. Westermarck's suggested distinction in the historical origins of 'survivals' did, nonetheless, represent a shared perspective among Euro-American and Euro-Slavic scholars, namely, that "[g]enerally speaking, the survivals may be traced to two main sources: first, the Arabic paganism prevalent at the time when Mohammed appeared as the founder of a new religion, and secondly, ideas and practices current in the countries to which it spread."[231]

As for the continuation of Soviet 'survivals' ethnography into the 1940s, Snesarev himself participated in an "Expedition to Central Asia in the Spring of 1940 with the Goal to Study Religious Remnants." Beyond this, he references only an unpublished doctoral dissertation by Iu.V. Knorozov on *Survivals [Пережитки] of Animism among the Plain Tadjiks* (1940), S. Ilyasov's *Survivals of Shamanism among the Kirgiz* (1945) and a later article by Knorozov titled "The Shrine of the Prophet Shamun" (1949). The paucity of sources from the 1940s might be explained by the interruption of the Great Patriotic War, which Snesarev himself, and presumably a number of other Central Asian ethnographers, served in. By the 1950s and beyond, Soviet 'survivals' ethnography increases noticeably. The number which Snesarev highlights from the 1950s are too many to name, with an abundance of 'survivals' publications continuing down to the mid- and even late 1980s.[232]

CHAPTER 6

Transformations in Soviet 'Survivals' Ethnography in the Post-World War Two Period

Soviet "Theoretical and Practical Narrowness in Evaluating the Beliefs and Rituals of the Peoples of Central Asia"?: G.P. Snesarev's Late-Coming Challenge

We might have concluded our inquiry into Soviet 'survivals' ethnography with the previous chapter if Snesarev had not, in his 1969 study, claimed that "Central Asia has almost entirely escaped the attention of students of early forms of religion, although Central Asian ethnography has long had at its disposal material that would be quite useful in solving problems of primitive beliefs and cults." He insisted that "[s]cholars concerned with problems of religion, including primitive beliefs" were not properly seeking "to penetrate the ethnographic region in question." This was, he surmised, due to "a traditional view which considered Central Asia an area of undifferentiated prevalence of an advanced religion—Islam—and, moreover, one brought in from outside. This tradition is very much alive, and has been responsible," Snesarev asserts, "for a certain theoretical and practical narrowness in evaluating the beliefs and rituals of the peoples of Central Asia."[233]

After cautioning several pages later that Central Asian Islam's "significance should not be overestimated" because it was, in certain areas in particular, "unable to sink roots for a long time,"[234] Snesarev adds to his point by suggesting that

© The Author(s), under exclusive license to Springer Nature Singapore Pte Ltd. 2023
R. C. Weller, *'Pre-Islamic Survivals' in Muslim Central Asia*, Islam and Global Studies,
https://doi.org/10.1007/978-981-19-5697-3_6

83

no attempts have been made to look more critically at that entire complex of beliefs and rituals, with all their local features, which together constitutes Central Asian religion, and that *no attempt has been made to introduce the needed differentiation into that complex to distinguish orthodox Islam from pre-Islamic relics having little relationship to it and often existing independently. There were no such efforts made in the literature (with the exceptions referred to above) or, what is most important, in the practical work of culture and adult education.*

This was possibly due, he said, to "the same long-established opinion that Central Asia is a zone of classical Islam in its most characteristic forms." This "superficial approach" led to "atheist activity in Central Asia" which "was oriented entirely toward orthodox Islam," leaving "[t]he entire complex of pre-Islamic vestiges" effectively untouched.[235]

Snesarev himself affirms that, from as early as the 1920s, Soviet ethnographers had recorded survivals of primitive religious beliefs and practices among the peoples of Central Asia, yet, he argues, they provided only incidental and occasional passing reference to the subject.[236] Until—so he contends—his own explicit efforts, "no attempt ha[d] been made to introduce the needed differentiation into that complex to distinguish orthodox Islam from pre-Islamic relics," and the prior 'incidental and passing references' had been "unutilized" with respect to their "practical value for educating people in the spirit of atheism."[237] As noted above, Tolstov, active from 1931 on, was recognized as having "initiated the study of," among other things, "relics of ancient pre-Islamic religions and beliefs" in Central Asia. This recognition, however, was made upon his death in 1976, so Tolstov's eulogizers may have been influenced by the attention which Snesarev began explicitly drawing to the issue just seven years prior. Given the clear contributions of Tsarist and early Soviet ethnographers who preceded Tolstov, it is debatable whether Tolstov actually deserved recognition as 'initiator' of such studies, but such attributions aside, Snesarev and Tolstov's eulogizers were in apparent contention over when the tradition started, at least within Soviet ethnography.

Devin Deweese agrees with Tolstov's eulogizers, naming Tolstov as the first among many Soviet ethnographers of Central Asia who distinguished 'pre-Islamic survivals' from 'normative Islam.' Overall Deweese seems to imply that, from Tolstov in the 1930s onward, all Soviet works concerned with religious 'survivals' had in view an explicit agenda of "'revealing' the origins of particular practices and beliefs as holdovers from pre-Islamic times" in order to demonstrate that "Islam in Central Asia, as a mixture of Islam and pre-Islamic practices, is not really Islam at all, but something else. The notion of survivals thus became a simple shorthand for 'explaining' the defective, substandard, tainted, hybrid Islam determined to be characteristic of Central Asia." He does recognize that Islam itself is viewed as a form of religious 'survival' within an atheistic state, but overall his interpretation of the 'survivals' motif within Soviet ethnography is that it was exploitative from early on, if not from the very beginning, with a specific agenda to undermine Central Asian Islam.[238]

But was this really the case? Granted, Snesarev's allegation that "no attempt ha[d] been made to introduce the needed differentiation into that complex to distinguish orthodox Islam from pre-Islamic relics" seems curious at best, if not exaggerated. Not only Tolstov, but Knorozov, in fact, under Tolstov's direction, had taken up that very cause. After comparing other Muslim shrines to that of the Prophet Shamun in one small section near the end of his 1949 article, Knorozov summed up his comparison by essentially echoing Tolstov when he said:

> The Sanctuary of Jumart is not the only example of the persistence of pre-Islamic cults [домусульманских культов] in the Khorezm oasis. …the cults of the divine patrons of irrigation, fertility, and cattle breeding are the most persistent, which is largely due to the role they played in the economic and domestic life attributed to them by the population. They were connected with the pre-Islamic seasonal holidays, which for a long time were preserved [сохранявшимися] in Khorezm."[239]

More importantly, however, Knorozov claimed in the very opening sentences of his study that, "[t]hanks to the success of socialist construction in Central Asia, the cult of saints and related phenomena have largely lost their significance. Nevertheless, such religious survivals [пережитки] require serious attention, especially having been cut off for such a long time from cultural centers having a role in the everyday life of the population."[240] Snesarev was clearly aware of Knorozov's work, having explicitly cited it, and even seems to be taking up the challenge identified by Knorozov of paying "serious attention" to "such religious survivals." Indeed, Snesarev noted that Knorozov's 1949 article "raises…a number of highly significant questions with respect to pre-Islamic beliefs," but these, from Snesarev's view, were "unfortunately only in passing."[241] Also contrary to Knorozov—who, still a half century later, echoed Abai's belief from the late 1800s or early 1900s that 'survivals' were "steadily decreasing" in his day (see Chapter 4)—Snesarev held that "such religious survivals" had not "largely lost their significance," but to the contrary, had tenaciously endured even in the face of "socialist construction in Central Asia."

Additionally, two things should be noted: First, Snesarev is bemoaning the thought that "Central Asia ha[d] almost entirely escaped the attention of," not ethnographers of Central Asia such as Tolstov and Knorozov, but of "[s]cholars concerned with problems of religion, including primitive beliefs." As per Thrower, most of these scholars worked among what they considered to be 'primitive peoples' in Siberia and elsewhere. Second, Snesarev suggests that this lack of attention to "pre-Islamic relics" by scholars of "early forms of religion" is "because of a traditional view which considered Central Asia an area of undifferentiated prevalence of an advanced religion—Islam."

REVISITING THE MARXIAN-ENGELSIAN FRAMEWORK

AS Engels argued in an 1882 essay:

> Great historical turning-points have been accompanied by religious changes only so far as the three world religions which have existed up to the present—Buddhism, Christianity and Islam—are concerned. The old tribal and national religions, which arose spontaneously, did not proselytize and lost all their power of resistance as soon as the independence of the tribe or people was lost. ...Only with these world religions, arisen more or less artificially, particularly Christianity and Islam, do we find that the more general historical movements acquire a religious imprint.[242]

The Marxist view of the major world religions—particularly Buddhism, Christianity and Islam—was that they had absorbed into their very essence earlier 'primitive' religious traditions such as animism, totemism, shamanism and the like. This reflected a progressive evolutionary view significantly influenced by the comparative history of religion(s) school taking shape in Western Europe in the late nineteenth and early twentieth centuries. Beginning from the early 1920s, Soviet historians of religion worked to identify the stages of early human religious history, though, like their Euro-American counterparts, they eventually, by the late 1930s or 1940s, abandoned the effort to explicitly detail each precise stage. But the main aim of this work in the Soviet context—at least originally, in the pre-World War Two context—was not distinguishing 'pre-Islamic survivals' and 'normative Islam' among the Central Asian Muslim peoples. 'Normative Islam' had absorbed 'pre-Islamic survivals' into its very essence and character. Like their Euro-American counterparts, Soviet ethnographers rather worked among contemporary 'shamanists,' 'animists' and others in order to elucidate early religious history based on the assumption that the forms of these 'primitive' traditions preserved original ones. Although Soviet historians of religion were unable, in the end, to articulate the earliest stages of human religious history, they outlined (however simplistically and inaccurately) the main contours of world religious history by positing that 'primitive' religions led to 'national/folk' religions, eventually giving way to the emergence of the world (or 'universal') religions—Buddhism, Christianity and Islam. What this meant, for all practical purposes from the Marxist-Leninist standpoint, was that the main vehicles of 'survival' for humankind's more 'primitive' religious traditions were the major world religions themselves,[243] representing as they did the final stage of world religious development in connection with the feudalist and capitalist world order. Thus, there was no real surprise or question about pre-Islamic versus Islamic identity from the Soviet point of view. The entire history of religion was, through this syncretistic evolutionary process, destined to eventually fade, together with capitalism, into the sunset and be replaced by the atheistic communist dawn. From both the Marxist and Soviet vantage, no 'survival' of religion was expected or predicted—pre-Islamic, Islamic or otherwise. When dealing, therefore, with peoples adhering to the major world religious traditions (such as those of 'Islamic' Central Asia), the main Soviet strategy, at least in its pre-World War Two phase, focused on countering those later world religious traditions which posed a real threat politically, not the 'survivals of primitive belief' which were thought to be *historically* layered beneath and behind them.

As Engels had argued from as early as 1853, the more urgent concern from a Marxist-Leninist viewpoint was that "Mohammed's religious revolution, like every religious movement, was *formally a reaction.*"[244] Michael Kemper elucidates how this core paradigm worked itself out as Soviet scholarship wrestled with the essential origins and nature of Islam within a Marxian world historical frame for nearly a decade, from the early 1920s down to 1933.[245] While room to argue various interpretations was offered during this period of uncertainty, the delineation of an official party line between 1932 and 1933—one which was in line with the Marxian-Engelsian as well as Leninist-Stalinist view—marked the close to further debate, stifling any creativity in Soviet orientalist scholarship on the subject thereafter. The negotiated settlement depicted Islam as a reactionary instrument of feudal lords imposed upon the masses for purposes of exploitation, oppression and inequality.[246] As per Shoshana Keller, there were, in fact, three main themes which were taking shape from the early 1920s onward, namely: Muslim leaders "worked for oppressing the classes to help exploit workers and peasants; second, Islam brutally oppressed and exploited women; third, religion had developed as a way for primitive man to understand and control incomprehensible forces of nature, and therefore, the 'cure' for it was basic scientific knowledge."[247]

THE CURIOUS ABSENCE OF CONCERN FOR 'PRE-ISLAMIC SURVIVALS' IN SOVIET ANTI-ISLAMIC PROPAGANDA LITERATURE IN THE PRE-WORLD WAR TWO PERIOD

One of the first among a number of anti-religious propaganda publications aimed at various Soviet Muslim peoples throughout the first two decades of Soviet rule was a brief pamphlet by the well-known advocate for an Islamic communist synthesis, Mirsaid (cf. Mirza) Sultan-Galiev (1892–1940). His pamphlet was titled *Methods of Anti-religious Propaganda among Muslims*. It was published in Moscow in 1922 at a cost of 5000 rubles per copy.[248] At the start of the work, Sultan-Galiev insisted on "adopting methods absolutely different from those used among other peoples." He urged "a very careful and skillful approach" which was grounded in "the nature of anti-religious propaganda, and not an anti-religious struggle." We should not, he warned, "conduct any struggle against any religion, but only propagandize our own atheistic views which we have an absolute right to do." In doing so, the Soviets must never forget that, with respect to the Muslim peoples of the domains, "their cultural backwardness and their position as a politically and morally downtrodden people are their main evil." This meant, in Sultan-Galiev's eyes, that the new USSR would have to "make these peoples truly free and equal citizens of the Soviet republic" in order to successfully win them over.[249]

Having laid down this foundational framework and orientation, Sultan-Galiev went on to delineate distinct approaches to each of the Soviet Muslim peoples, devoting specific sections to the "Tatars," "Bashkirs," "Kyrgyz," "Turkestan, Khiva and Bukhara" and "Azerbaijan, highlander Caucasians and Crimeans." Significantly here, he does not mention the Kazakhs explicitly. The question is whether he intended to include them under the broad heading of "nomads" in relation to the Bashkirs and Kyrgyz in particular, or whether he did not, as a Tatar, count them genuinely Muslim. If the latter, it is an implicit judgment on their religious condition as being predominantly identified with "pre-Islamic" traditions, with their Islamic identity a mere veneer. Given his descriptions of "nomadism" in relation to Islam, and his sure knowledge of Kazakh nomadic lifeways, it seems more likely that he intended their condition to be understood in relation to "nomadism," and thus generally categorized together with the Bashkirs and Kyrgyz.

Regarding the Bashkirs and other similar nomadic groups, Sultan-Galiev speaks of "their great susceptibility to superstitions, whose character is that of the remnants of former paganism (остатков прежнего язычества)." Nomadism, he argues, inhibits people from full devotion to their Islamic faith, "especially" their ability "to perform certain religious rites." This was confirmed by "all researchers, both European and Eastern," he claimed. A "class-racial antagonism" between Baskhirs, and presumably Kazakhs, also played a role in the "weak development of religious fanaticism" among them in comparative relation to the other Soviet Muslim groups. His argument regarding the Bashkirs being "less fanatical" here foreshadows in some ways that made three years later by M.S. Andreev in relation to the Tajiks in 1925 (see previous chapter), though Sultan-Galiev and Andreev each had different aims and intents in relation to the differing nature of their studies, i.e., anti-religious propaganda versus ethnographic research respectively. In further distinction, Sultan-Galiev's employment of the term "paganism" ("язычества") in relation to "the remnants" ("остатков") suggests more a Russian Orthodox and Islamic 'double faith' perspective than a secular ethnographic scientific one. Andreev never (explicitly) argued, like Sultan-Galiev, that "Islam bore the character of a superficial, artificially grafted religion."[250]

Importantly here though, whether Andreev implied or assumed a "double faith" perspective, neither he nor Sultan-Galiev made any recommendation to explicitly employ 'pre-Islamic survivals' as part of their anti-Islamic strategy. 'Pre-Islamic survivals' rather functioned for them as a proof of tamer, milder, looser Islamic devotion, which serves to provide, not explicit and specific strategic weaponry to employ ethnographically or historiographically against them, but mainly as proof for hope that they could more easily win them over without great concern for the 'revolutionary character' of Islam necessarily resulting in 'Islamic uprisings.' As per Engels and the general Soviet viewpoint in the pre-World War Two period, "[t]he remnants of former paganism" among them were not typically employed for explicit anti-Islamic propaganda among the Muslim populations themselves; they were rather viewed as an "assimilated" (cf. 'integral') part of their Islamic identity and practice only serving to elucidate broader world historical processes of religious development and help Soviet religious and political leaders to distinguish levels of Islamic devotion in relation to questions of "fanaticism" and potential resistance or uprising in light of their view of Islam as a potential source of reactionary revolution which aimed to exploit and oppress the masses.

Thus in spite of Sultan-Galiev's anti-religious propaganda pamphlet and the ethnographic work of Soviet scholars, 'pre-Islamic survivals' are not employed in pre-World War Two propaganda literature. It was rather the Marxian-Engelsian and Leninist-Stalinist line on Islam which was followed. This is manifest in Soviet Kazakh literature of the 1920s and 1930s. This included the first known small booklet of the 1920s, namely, Gali Begaliev's *How the Religion of Islam was Founded*, published in 1927 or 1928. Following this was a Kazakh translation of Sanzhar Asfendiarov's Bedouin nomadic theory of Islam's origins, *Reasons for the Emergence of Islam*. It was originally published in Russian in 1928 and then in Kazakh in 1930. (As noted above, Asfendiarov also published an article in Russian treating "Islam and Nomadic Economy" in 1928.) Then, in 1938, what appears to have been an author of Ukrainian descent named F. Oleshchik wrote a small, 20-page booklet *On the Reactionary Role of the Followers of Islam*. It was translated from an original Russian version written in 1937, with over 10,000 copies of the Kazakh version printed. That same year (1939), 5000 copies of G. Ibragimov's 43-page booklet on *The Religion of Islam: Instrument of Imperialism* came fresh off the press.[251]

Apart from Begaliev's booklet, which was one of the last Kazakh works to be issued in Arabic script, the others were printed using the Latin script in place of Arabic as part of a second wave of Soviet assaults on Islam from 1928 to 1942.[252] Regardless of script, however, Kazakh was still, like that of any Muslim people, regarded as a 'Muslim' language. Russian was the language of colonization and Sovietization. Works carried greater weight when they were published not only by Central Asian native figures (as in three of the four works noted above), but in 'Muslim' languages. While translated works—if they were known to the reader as such—suffered from 'guilt by association,' they still reached a predominantly Muslim audience via a Muslim language. This was in line with the Marxist-Leninist vision: "national in form, socialist in content."[253] There was also need to transcend the sheer lack of fluency in Russian among the broader Muslim populations.[254]

As for the content of the book(let)s, Begaliev's *How the Religion of Islam was Founded* begins with "The Arabs before Islam" as well as, several chapters later, "Islam before Muhammed" and "Conditions in Arabia before the Spread of Islam in the World." Treating, however summarily, nearly all aspects of the Arabs and Islam both before and during Muhammed's lifetime, Begaliev shows special concern for subjects like "The Era of Expansion," "Military Duties," "Conditions of the Formation of a Political Community" and "The Establishment of Islam and an Islamic State." Begaliev, in fact, concludes the work by returning to the latter topic, with expressed concern for 'pan-Islamic' ideas. He controverts, with a sense of warning, the claim that Islam is not political, insisting that it clearly aimed for and successfully established an Islamic political state, with Muhammed subjugating all of Arabia and regions beyond by military conquest. This is proven by not only historical 'evidence,' but multiple citations from the Qur'an. Nearly the first third of the booklet focuses on the conditions in Arabia before Muhammed and Islam, with Begaliev's interpretation showing how these 'pre-Islamic' conditions shaped the rise of Islam. But this is not in a consciously Tylorean sense. It is simply the prevailing, even necessary, view of an evolutionary interpretation of history, with Begaliev's main aim being to demonstrate precisely the hallmark of Marxian-Engelsian as well as early Soviet historiography on Islam: its politically imperialist and exploitational nature.

Both of Sanzhar Asfendiarov's works, "Islam and Nomadic Economy" and *Reasons for the Emergence of Islam* (see above), have been (justifiably) identified as following the Bedouin nomadic theory of Islam's origins, which he argued for over against the more typical Meccan merchant view. Though the latter accords well with the Marxist emphasis on economic history, and Asfendiarov cites Marx (and Engels) generously, he could appeal specifically to Engels in this case, who held that

Islam "seems to...bear the character of a Bedouin reaction against the settled but degenerating fellaheen of the towns" (see above). Indeed, within Asfendiarov's reconstruction "[t]he internal contradictions of the Arab feudal-clan society would be overcome by way of expanding the economic territory, by way of crushing the Meccan trade-and-consumer capital, by way of discarding clan vestiges (пережитков) and creating a religious (national) community instead of the patrimonial one."[255] Thus economics still factored into his Bedouin nomadic theory. So did the idea of "пережитков" ("remnants/survivals/vestiges"). In proposing, however, that "Asfendiarov's understanding of early Islam was intrinsically linked to his interpretation of the history of his own Kazakh people," Kemper offers only two references in connection with this suggestion, with no discussion or translation of precisely what those references have in view. They are, in fact, a "form of musical and poetic improvisation, so widespread among Bedouins, Kurds, Bashkirs, Kazakhs, Kirghiz and so on" and a "compar[ison] with the Kazakhs of Kzyl-Orda district, engaged in cattle breeding and rice culture."[256] There is nothing clearly or explicitly related to Islam here, particularly not the kind of 'pre-Islamic survivals' historiography or ethnography central to the question at hand. Likewise, to whatever degree Asfendiarov may have "shared his distance to Islam as well as his sympathy for 'traditional' Kazakh lifestyle with the well-known Kazakh intellectual in Russian service, Chokan Valikhanov (1835–1865),"[257] Asfendiarov never explicitly references Valikhanov or his works. True, Asfendiarov did explicitly propose that "the religious indifference of the Arabs, especially among the nomads, was very great," suggesting at one point that "some tribes" with whom Muhammed formed an alliance "even retained their old religion."[258] But Kemper's suggestion that, based on this, Asfendiarov "seems to imply that the Kazakh nomads were Muslim 'in name alone'" raises questions as to what extent Kemper's reading of Kazakh history into the narrative may have been colored by his own acute awareness of and concern for the long-standing debate over Kazakh religious history and identity "which had already been popular in the nineteenth century, and which has not lost its popularity since." The question is of particular relevance when, with respect to that debate, Kemper makes sole reference to the 2001 work of Allen Frank, *Muslim Religious Institutions in Imperial Russia*, which I will discuss later in regard to this precise claim.[259] Kemper's suggestions certainly have merit, but the main question before us here is whether 'pre-Islamic survivals' historiography or ethnography was explicitly employed in early Soviet works for anti-Islamic purposes, including here Asfendiarov's, and the answer in the latter case appears to be 'no.' Rather, Asfendiarov's main focus and concern, in line with Marxist-Leninist historiography, was that "Islam has been completely transformed and become a religion of exploitation, and subsequently a weapon of reaction." This includes explicit concern for "Pan-Islamists like Jamal ad-Din al-Afghani, Musa Begiev, the Young Turks and the Kemalists" as well as "Gasprinskii" who all "built and are building the necessary political or political-religious system supposedly derived from the Koran."[260]

Ibragimov's 1939 booklet, *The Religion of Islam: Instrument of Imperialism*, sums up its main thesis in the title. His primary focus was on the feudal and class context in which Islam originally rose, but it also concerned itself with several features of Russian Islamic history. These included the struggle between Qadimists and Jadidists which emerged in the latter part of the nineteenth century and the role of Muslim political parties working within and as part of the government structures in the post-1905 tumult of Tsarist Russian history. Both these were connected with independence struggles among Muslim peoples, particularly the pan-Islamic and pan-Turkic movements, tied to the Turkestan National Liberation Struggle (Basmachi Rebellion) which continued through the 1930s. All this was aimed at convincing the reader of precisely the three themes noted above in reference to Shoshana Keller's study.

In all these works from the 1920s and 1930s, the Islamic identity of the Kazakhs appears to have been taken for granted and the main Soviet approach to Muslim peoples applied thereto. Indeed, the Kazakhs were targeted in the broader assault on Muslim Central Asia in the period of Soviet consolidation, experiencing the destruction of mosques, confiscation of property and persecution of believers going on simultaneously across the Soviet empire in this period. Conspicuously absent from all these works are any references to former Tsarist-era debates or Shokan Ualihanuhli (Chokan Valikhanov) on pre-Islamic versus Islamic history and identity among the Kazakhs (or any other Central Asian Muslim people). 'Pre-Islamic survivals' and their nineteenth-century ethnographic sources played no significant role in pre-World War Two Soviet anti-Islamic propaganda among the Kazakhs in particular and, I would argue, therefore, among other Central Asian peoples.[261]

Snesarev and the Soviet Deployment of 'Pre-Islamic Survivals' for Renewed Anti-Religious Propaganda Efforts in the Post-World War Two Period

Perhaps Snesarev had a point then. The 'survivals' question in Soviet ethnography did not, at least in the pre-World War Two era, result in or constitute an atheistic assault on Central Asian Islam. The question of "what 'survivals' might have continued into the Soviet period," religious or otherwise, Central Asian or otherwise, was simply part of "certain ethnographic basics."[262] True, Andreev, in the early 1920s, employed 'pre-Islamic survivals' ethnography to show that "[t]he Tajik, as a Muslim, is not distinguished by great fanaticism, in accordance with the general population of Central Asia, especially, for example, compared with the Muslims of India or Persia" (see previous chapter). But was his purpose simply denigrating or denying "the general population of Central Asia" an authentically Islamic identity? His main appeal seems rather to be that, by virtue of the many 'pre-Islamic survivals' which are evident there, Central Asia should not be viewed as posing any major 'Islamic threat.' That Andreev's ethnography was published during the Turkistan National Liberation Struggle—what the Soviets called the 'Basmachi Rebellion'—suggests he was appropriating such ethnography, not to engage in anti-Islamic propaganda among the Tajiks, but to 'take the pressure off his subjects,'[263] or perhaps alleviate Soviet leaders' concerns. Both, in fact, are tied intimately together.

Even if Andreev be interpreted as having an anti-Islamic agenda in his 'pre-Islamic survivals' ethnography—which the evidence does not favor in my view—Tolstov and other pre-World War Two Central Asian ethnographers do not display such an agenda, at least not explicitly. They instead come across rather 'matter-of-fact' about 'pre-Islamic survivals' as a natural and even expected part of a multi-layered evolutionary history. Even when Knorozov suggested, briefly in passing, that 'pre-Islamic survivals' should be taken seriously, it was not for the sake of undermining Islamic identity, but rather—as per Lenin and Stalin, and later Snesarev as well (see below)—facilitating their destruction as distinct manifestations of religious belief and practice in and of themselves. That those manifestations happened to 'survive' within an Islamic context was merely circumstantial. They could just as easily have been, and in fact were, observed in Christian and Buddhist contexts. But all of these, again, were ethnographers, not publishers of anti-religious literature. Besides, Knorozov was writing in 1949, that is, the post-World War Two period.

As Snesarev lamented then, prior to the 1960s, "atheist activity in Central Asia was oriented entirely toward orthodox Islam."[264] Snesarev, however, was—if only slightly—chronologically misinformed. He was apparently unaware that Soviet Kazakh anti-religious publications were targeting 'pre-Islamic survivals' from as early as 1953. But not—as far as my own research reveals—before that date, which is chronologically significant. There is, in fact, a gap in Kazakh anti-religious literature between Ibragimov's 1939 publication and A. Kakimzhanov's 1953 work *About the Reactionary Essence of the Religion of Islam* (see next chapter). Whether a corresponding gap exists in anti-religious literature among other Central Asian peoples awaits further research. But one thing is certain: While Kakimzhanov and others did use the 'pre-Islamic survivals' construct to help in undermining Kazakh Islamic devotion, a specifically 'anti-Islamic' agenda was not the primary aim of Soviet 'survivals' ethnography in the pre-World War Two period. Rather, in line with Snesarev's later claims, the highlighting of 'pre-Islamic survivals' in the pre- and even early post-World War Two period was in order to come to grips with the fact that "certain relic beliefs and rituals continue to exist...and it would be fundamentally false to simply hope for their spontaneous disappearance. That process will proceed more rapidly the more attention is paid in atheist propaganda to pre-Islamic Survivals, and most important, the wider and deeper is the scientific basis on which that propaganda rests." The expeditionary research conducted by Snesarev and his colleagues "was intended to promote the process of disappearance." By laying bare "the genesis of each phenomenon," namely "its sources in the depths of primitive thinking," a concerted Soviet atheistic propaganda campaign could "thereby...lead people to the conclusion that the given phenomenon belongs in its entirety to stages in the development of society that are long past." This, in his view, was "the most correct and productive method of discrediting any relic phenomenon."[265]

This was in accordance with one of the two primary aims of Soviet 'survivals' ethnography as delineated by Lenin and Stalin as they interpreted and applied Marx and Engels: namely the identification and subsequent "destruction of [all] feudal remnants." This was inclusive of Islam, but by no means limited to it, and did not inseparably link 'pre-Islamic survivals' ethnography to an assault on Islam. The other main purpose was, again, elucidating the earliest (cf. 'primitive') stages of world religious history. This was the primary aim of broader pre-World War

Two Soviet ethnography as it concerned itself with religious 'survivals' of all kinds, Islamic or otherwise. As Thrower points out, Soviet religious studies were not brought into harmony with an "explicitly Marxist-Leninist framework" until the post-World War Two period,[266] which is when religious 'survivals' of all kinds lost their more typically benign status and became explicit, intentional objects of atheistic propaganda.

I must agree, then, with S.S. Alymov in his study of "G.P. Snesarev and the Field Study of Religious-Domestic Survivals" when he says that "[t]he suggestion made by DeWeese and Schoeberlein to see in the use of such categories [i.e., 'pre-Islamic survivals'] the concealed design of a specifically anti-Islamic 'deconstruction' seems to me unproven and excessively complicates the motivation of Snesarev and other researchers, especially since...they used the notion of 'survivals' for various forms of culture and social organization..."[267] Indeed, a Georgian student in Tbilisi in the mid-1980s wrote his doctoral dissertation on *Remnants of the Past as a General Sociological Category*.[268] This does not mean that Deweese is wrong about *one* of the ultimate causes to which Soviet 'survivals' ethnography was, in a conscious and intentional manner, applied. It rather provides clarification of the broader historical as well as historiographical frame within which Soviet 'survivals' ethnography took shape, and the aims to which it was applied, in relation to Islamic Central Asia and beyond.

Tasar's contention is doubtful as well, that 'pre-Islamic survivals' functioned in the post-World War Two period as a means for the Council for the Affairs of Religious Cults (CARC), instituted by Stalin in 1944, "to sift through the confusing maze of 'registerable' and 'unregisterable' Muslim practices and institutions in Central Asia, selecting a few that would enjoy tacit legitimacy and protection provided that their observance occurred exclusively under [the Central Asian muftiate] SADUM's auspices."[269] If Soviet 'pre-Islamic survivals' ethnography in the post-World War Two period was applied to this end, Tasar offers no examples or evidence, only a claim. And the literature I have examined reveals no clear aims along these lines.

In connection to Tasar's concerns with how Soviet 'survivals' ethnography factored into international relations in the post-World War Two era, David G. Anderson and Dmitry V. Arzyutov note an important counter-trend in their study of "The Construction of Soviet Ethnography and 'The Peoples of Siberia.'" Soviet scholars involved in the production of the multi-volume series *Peoples of the World* highlighted how their project "differs greatly from other foreign ethnographic works which usually report on backward peoples and concentrate their attention on survivals (пережиточные явления)." Tolstov was one of the chief architects of the project when it was first proposed back in the 1940s. The denial of a 'survivals' approach in this ethnographic project, in contrast with their Euro-American counterparts, was not explicitly articulated until 1967 in a presentation to the Lenin and State Prize Committee given by the newly appointed director of the Institute of Ethnography. Comparatively, Rock likewise notes that "*dvoeverie* was also not accepted unquestionably by Soviet academics." This select group of Soviet scholars thus contributed to "challenging the concept of 'double belief'" which was premised upon the concept of 'survivals.'[270]

Critical views of 'survivals' ethnography were, in fact, gaining ground among both Euro-American and Euro-Slavic ethnographers from the 1950s on in response to the rise of Nazi, Soviet and other white European supremacy-driven ideologies across Europe east and west.[271] Exchanges "between Soviet ethnographers and their American counterparts" taking shape from the mid-1950s on only helped to sharpen the critique, as part of escalating Cold War competition, among each respective side.[272] It is, therefore, inaccurate and misrepresentational to suggest that 'survivals' ethnography was "embedded in Marxist doctrine, and in the nascent Soviet academic establishment" so deeply and thoroughly that the critiques gaining ground from the 1930s on were too late to effect any appreciable, conscious change.[273]

Meanwhile, Snesarev's promotion of the construct may well have been an attempt to counter these trends. Or the claims of those involved in the *Peoples of the World* project were perhaps mere rhetoric in the face of mounting international pressure, reflecting an external as opposed to internal strategy. Whatever the case, 'survivals' historiography became an openly debated methodology among Cold War powers by the 1960s amid ethnic and religious minority rights movements closely tied to decolonization across the globe. This was because it implied not only that the peoples preserving those 'survivals' were still living in the past, following in many cases 'primitive' customs (cf. "backward peoples"), but was situated in a syncretic frame which distinguished between 'foreign' and 'genuine' components of peoples' beliefs and practices, thus denying them a holistic, integral identity. It had also clearly come to serve colonial-imperial agendas of dominance, which post-colonial historiography eventually came to critique, inclusive of these particular Soviet scholars from the 1950s on.

Clifford Geertz and other Euro-American scholars were, thus, in fact products of the rising post-World War Two debates over this contested construct, emerging as they did on the scene in the 1960s and 1970s. They were part of "the cultural turn" in ethnography and historiography taking shape in that period (see Chapter 10).[274] Certain Soviet ethnographers helped to push world ethnographic trends in this direction, which means that this particular critical branch of Soviet ethnography contributed to the newly developing ethnographic and historiographic schools out of which Geertz and his "thick description" methodology emanated. The work of later scholars such as Devin Deweese, Bruce G. Privratsky, John Schoeberlein and other Euro-American scholars who have followed "the cultural turn" in historical and cultural anthropology are thus partly indebted to this more critical branch of Soviet ethnography.

Clarifying the Chronological Frame of Soviet 'Survivals' Ethnography

A clearer picture of the chronological frame of Soviet 'survivals' ethnography thus comes into view. It transitioned from (1) a primary focus on elucidating early (and later) world religious history for the sake of Soviet scholarship in its foundational pre-World War Two period, in accord with Euro-American trends,[275] to (2) increasing tension between growing criticisms and abandonment of the methodology, on the one hand, and intensifying calls for its effective appropriation in the renewed atheistic campaigns of the post-World War Two, post-Stalinist period on the other. But not only this. 'The effective appropriation school' then developed, in the post-World War Two period, from simple to more sophisticated, 'scientific' forms. This scheme of historical development stands in general harmony with that outlined by Vladimir Bobrovnikov in his study of "The Contribution of Oriental Scholarship to the Soviet Anti-Islamic Discourse: From the Militant Godless to the Knowledge Society." Bobrovnikov sets forth a chart comparing the main tactical approaches to the "denunciation of Islam" in the work of Orthodox missionaries prior to 1917, followed by what he terms "Militant Atheism" between the 1920s and 1940s and then "Scientific Atheism" from the 1950s to 1980s. Soon thereafter he explains how, in the latter period in particular, "Islam Becomes a Religious Survival."[276]

From the late 1960s on, Snesarev sought to facilitate the process of methodological sophistication. He urged that what was "most important" was establishing this "atheist propaganda [of] pre-Islamic Survivals" on a much "wider and deeper...scientific basis." This was in order to "offer a competent explanation of...these phenomena" and, thus, "promote the process of disappearance." Snesarev's push in this more scholarly, scientific direction was in accordance with "the Central Committee resolution of 14 August 1967, 'On the Measures of Further Development of Social Sciences and in Increasing Their Role in the Building of Communism'" and "the 1974 Leningrad conference dedicated to 'The Topical Problems of the History of Religion and Atheism in the Light of Marxist-Leninist Scholarship.'"[277] It coincided with two important pendulum swings in Soviet religious policy which followed on the heels of Khrushchev's failed atheistic campaign (1954–1964). The first and overall trend was a softening which eschewed the violence of Khrushchev's approach, though the initial softening was, beginning in the 1970s, intensified through increased publication of anti-religious literature.[278] Khrushchev's campaign had itself, of course, followed a period of Soviet compromise in religious policy in order to garner support during World War Two (1942–1953). The atmosphere of the post-Khrushchev era was marked not by a simple tolerance of religious belief and practice in exchange for political and military patronage, but rather a perceived need "to understand the cause of the persistence of religious belief and its ability to attract contemporary Soviet people." Namely, to "explain why masses of people [still] believe" and then find ways to respond to those reasons and causes in a more effective, scientific way. The ultimate aim was to 'overcome' those beliefs and replace them with atheistic convictions.[279]

This was precisely the approach taken by the Soviet Kazakh scholar Shinbergen Bekpanovich Amanturlin in his 1977 study of *The Survivals of Animism, Shamanism, and Islam and Atheistic Work against Them*. He "aimed to reveal the reasons of animistic and other worldviews in their contemporary stage of development, the essence of those beliefs, and the degree of their spread in village areas of Kazakhstan," insisting that "in order to effectively struggle against diverse superstitions it is very important to know what believers think about their content, how they explain them, and what the reasons are in following these prejudices."[280] Elsewhere, he emphasizes the need to "explain the reasons for the preservation of many archaic animistic beliefs and other superstitions in the isolated, remote area of Kazakhstan" in order to eradicate them entirely.[281] Amanturlin based his own sketch of Kazakh religious history and identity upon both Tsarist and Soviet sources. Among several others, the primary sources used for constructing his overall framework of Kazakh religious history were: A. Levshin, *Description of the Kirgiz-Kaisak Hordes and Steppes* (1822/1832), A. Haruzin, *Kirgiz Peoples of the Bukei Horde* (1889), *The Past of Kazakhstan in the Eastern Sources and Materials* (1935) and E.B. Bekmukhanova, *Unification of Kazakhstan to Russia* (1957).[282]

Amanturlin represents a move toward addressing pre-Islamic 'Survivals' among the Kazakhs in a more scientific manner. He thus bemoans the fact that, still in 1977, "[u]nfortunately, we have only a few works dedicated to explanations of this problem, which is of high importance in our day."[283] He argues that:

> weak educational and enlightening works among the population also contribute to the preservation of the Survivals of the past in the consciousness of the people. ...we must consider how to thoroughly demonstrate the religious Survivals in each region, aiming to reveal the reasons for their tenaciousness in each situation. This will provide an academic approach in the search for a solution to the problem of atheistic education among the working people (ibid.).

He is convinced that it is not enough to simply point out, like Kakimzhanov and others, that 'pre-Islamic survivals' persist among the Kazakhs and then use them to try to convince the people that they are, therefore, not true Muslims. This was an approach still being employed in Amanturlin's own day, as evidenced by a certain Kazakh work published the same year (1977), namely *The Religion of Islam and the Truth of Life* by Husaiin Zeinetdinuhlii Aknazarov. In Chapter 2 of that work, entitled "The Coming (lit. Entry) of Islam into Kazakhstan," Aknazarov draws heavily from Marx and Engels, Shokan Ualihanuhli, Ibirai Altinsarin, Abai Kunanbaiuhli and V.V. Barthold to highlight the Kazakh's heterogeneous religious character, particularly the traditions of Shamanism and Islam, condemning them both, along with the rest, as instruments of patriarchal-feudal aristocrats which dragged down the mentality, social welfare and progress of society.[284] Aknazarov had published another similar work some 13 years earlier, in 1964, entitled *The Religion of Islam and Its Reactionary Essence*, with both of those followed by yet another work hitting the shelves in 1986 as *Unique Aspects of the Spread of Islam in Kazakhstan*.[285] In these, Aknazarov simply carries on the tradition commenced by Kakimzhanov in 1953. Amanturlin aimed rather at what Snesarev had called for: a "wider and deeper...scientific basis on which that propaganda rests."

The Importance of Kazakh Nomadic Steppe Culture in Snesarev's Understanding and Deployment of 'Pre-Islamic Survivals' Among Other Central Asian Muslim Peoples

But scientific or not, the subject of 'pre-Islamic survivals' among the Kazakhs ties into the work of Snesarev in another important, even foundational way as well. Snesarev advanced an important line of reasoning in the "Introduction" to his 1969 study when he argued that Khorezm's close proximity to the nomadic Kazakh steppe was "of substantial significance" because it was "an area of great conservatism" in both its "social institutions...and in ancient beliefs." "The retarded rates of dissemination of Islam among the pastoral nomads" thus supplied, in Snesarev's view, "historical evidence" that the Khorezm Oasis "was always characterized by adherence to ancient beliefs, particularly shamanistic ones." The "constant contact" between the two areas "undoubtedly influenced the fact that many archaic phenomena persisted for a long time in Khorezm itself."[286]

Of interest here is Snesarev's (certainly questionable) assumption that the religious-cultural influence runs in seeming mono-directional flow from north to south, out of the nomadic steppe into the Khorezm Oasis. But he also employs an ahistorical comparative argument based on the shared "milieu" of the two respective geo-cultural domains. Both avenues of reasoning rest on his view of the "ancient beliefs, particularly shamanistic ones[,]" and "retarded rates of dissemination of Islam among the pastoral nomads."

The religious history and identity of the steppe nomads, particularly that of the Kazakhs (and Kirgiz), was the first domain in which Tsarist ethnographers began explicitly applying a 'pre-Islamic survivals' and concomitant 'dual faith' paradigm. That ethnographical-historiographical tradition, reaching as far back as Levshin in the early 1800s (see Chapter 4), continued supplying an essential framework and starting point for other Central Asian peoples, from the latter part of the nineteenth century on. It remained relevant to Snesarev and others as they intensified efforts to eradicate 'pre-Islamic survivals' among the peoples of Central Asia in the late 1960s and beyond.

Part Two Conclusion: Summary of Soviet Historical Sources

Following the changing of the guard, Soviet ethnographers, suspicious of Tsarist scholarship, worked within a more restricted historiographical frame, though the situation was far from static and entirely uniform. It is clear that from the very rise of Soviet historiography and ethnography on Central Asia that the 'survivals' approach was well-known and appropriated. Based on the sources cited in the Soviet works themselves—namely, Tsarist (both Christian and secular progressivist), Islamic and Western European secular progressivist—Tylor and other Euro-American scholars cannot be credited as the sole or even primary sources of influence. They formed only one among numerous streams converging through trans-imperial networks of contact and exchange in the late nineteenth to early twentieth centuries.

In the course of the study, a clearer picture of the chronological frame of Soviet 'survivals' ethnography comes into view. It transitioned from (1) a primary focus on elucidating early (and later) world religious history for the sake of Soviet scholarship in its foundational pre-World War Two period, in accord with Euro-American trends, to (2) increasing tension between growing criticisms and abandonment of the methodology, on the one hand, which provoked intensifying calls for its effective appropriation in the renewed atheistic campaigns of the post-World War Two, post-Stalinist period on the other. But not only this. The effective appropriation school then developed, in the post-World War Two period, from simple to more sophisticated, 'scientific' forms.

Thus, an explicit, intentional concern with 'pre-Islamic survivals' in Central Asia *for anti-Islamic purposes* did not take shape in Soviet ethnography until sometime after World War Two.[287] It arose as a new and explicit strategy employed as part of the revival of atheistic propaganda in the post-World War Two—particularly post-Stalinist—era. Certainly this was the case in the Kazakh context, and appears so overall. It reached popular proportions by the mid-1970s,[288] and continued on to the end of the Soviet Empire (see Chapter 7). Meanwhile, a select group of Soviet scholars who were engaged in international Cold War debates began criticizing and rejecting a 'survivals' approach from the 1950s onward, in tandem with other critical post-colonialist scholarship taking shape across the wider globe.[289] These scholars represented one divergent school which set itself at odds with G.P. Snesarev and his colleagues who intensified their focus on 'pre-Islamic survivals' as a tool of anti-religious and related anti-Islamic propaganda. These developments helped to set the stage for the ensuing approaches to and ongoing debates over the question of 'pre-Islamic survivals' among the Central Asian Muslim peoples in the post-Soviet period (see Chapters 8, 9 and 10).

PART III

Historiographical Constructions of and Debates Over Kazakh Religious History and Identity in Soviet and Post-Soviet Kazakh Scholarship

Having analyzed the history of the construct (or 'conceptual apparatus') of "pre-Islamic survivals" in Parts One and Two, Part Three moves on to analyze historiographical depictions of and related debates over Kazakh religious identity among Soviet and post-Soviet Kazakh sources. Though the primary focus is upon the Kazakhs, the historiographical depictions of and related debates over Kazakh religious identity contain both reference to and relevance for the other Central Asian Muslim peoples. While the phrasing "pre-Islamic survivals" is not always explicitly employed in all the historiography covered in Part Three, the question of "pre-Islamic survivals" in relation to Kazakh Islamic identity is always central. Part Three is thus focused upon the resulting historiography and relevant debates, where the terminological construct itself is not always consciously, explicitly employed but is always nonetheless implicitly present.

CHAPTER 7

The Framing of Kazakh Religious History and Identity in Post-World War Two Soviet Kazakh Publications

This chapter examines how Soviet Kazakh publications framed Kazakh religious history and identity, particularly in the 1950s and early 1960s. The earlier 1920s and 1930s has already been covered in Part Two because those publications encompassed a distinctive approach within Soviet ethnography and historiography of Central Asian Islam in the pre-World War Two period. "Pre-Islamic survivals" did not feature as a main, strategic concern or focus for explicitly anti-religious propagandistic purposes in that earlier era. Likewise, the transition to a softer, more scientific approach in the post-World War Two period from the later 1960s on was also substantiated (see Chapters 5 and 6). This chapter, therefore, provides several primary examples of the appropriation of "pre-Islamic survivals" within the more direct and basic propagandistic approach which initially took shape in the more immediate post-World War Two and particularly post-Stalinist era. I situate the deployment of this stratagem in its larger contexts within each respective publication, with extensive sections offered in translation at certain limited junctures in order to allow the sources to speak for themselves and provide primary source material which other scholars can further analyze and employ in various related though distinct studies.

© The Author(s), under exclusive license to Springer Nature Singapore Pte Ltd. 2023
R. C. Weller, *'Pre-Islamic Survivals' in Muslim Central Asia*, Islam and Global Studies,
https://doi.org/10.1007/978-981-19-5697-3_7

KAKIMZHANOV, *ABOUT THE REACTIONARY ESSENCE OF THE RELIGION OF ISLAM* (1953)

First among Soviet Kazakh anti-religious propaganda pieces issued in the post-World War Two period,[290] A. Kakimzhanov published a short work *About the Reactionary Essence of the Religion of Islam* in 1953. It was a total of 60 pages and enjoyed a press-run of 20,000 copies.[291] As with most such literature of the time, his booklet was put out by the Kazakh State Publishing House. The Table of Contents laid out the main topics for study as follows:

Preface	3
"About the Emergence of the Religion of Islam"	6
"The Religion of Islam—The Enemy of Science and Scholarship"	19
"The Reactionary Essence of the Religion of Islam"	34
"The Religion of Islam—A Remnant of Prior Times in Humanity's Mind"	49

Central to his concern in the preface, Kakimzhanov argued that: "Religious customs and traditions are one of the harmful remains of the past world which have not yet been rooted out of peoples' minds. It is clear to society that the religion of Islam is one of the old leftover religions in our nation."[299] He then offered an extended narrative in his opening chapter "About the Emergence of the Religion of Islam." He essentially overviews the entire history of religious development from its earliest stages up to the emergence of the monotheistic religions, all of course from a strictly Marxist point of view (see Chapters 5 and 6).

Kakimzhanov reaches back to peoples from "early times in the territory of Kazakhstan" and charts their worship of "the sun, moon, stars and fire" as well as "supplication to the spirit of their ancestors." They, so he asserts, "called this religion the religion of shamanism." The "god" of this combined animistic (or polytheistic), ancestral shamanic religion, he then claims, was known as "'tangiri' ('god'), 'kok tangiri' ('the sky god')," with these early peoples "counting everything the work of 'tangiri.'" He refers to the peoples from "these early times" as "Kazakh groups," apparently because they inhabited what later became Kazakhstan. Debates over the origins of 'the Kazakhs' aside, his main point is that they "considered fire to have miraculous power, ...as the dominant force." He is apparently bringing Zoroastrian elements into the mix here, though does not clearly label it as such. Regardless, these early Kazakhs "poured oil on fire, praying, circling sick people and animals around it in order to 'rid' them of their illnesses."[293] He, in essence, surveys, in broad, sweeping fashion, the history of most of the pre-Islamic traditions which would later become "survivals" among the Kazakhs.

While this may appear, at first glance, sheerly a product of Soviet 'survivals' propaganda, Kakimzhanov's survey, in fact, coincides in at least its more general contours with that of the great history of religions scholar Mircea Eliade. This is reflected in Eliade's *History of Religious Ideas* which was published in three volumes in the 1970s, specifically his coverage of "The Religions of Ancient Eurasia: Turko-Mongols, ...," where he likewise surveys "the vicissitudes of creation" together with their worship of "Tängri, the 'Celestial God'" and "Shamanic myths and rituals." While this particular work comes from the 1970s, Eliade's views therein can be traced back to the 1940s–50s.[294]

Whatever precisely Kakimzhanov's sources—which he does not here cite—this combination of religious beliefs and practices among early "Kazakhs," so he goes on to explain,

> originally emerged when people were powerless over their material life conditions, and humans grew more and more subservient to nature. In connection with transformations in peoples' material life conditions, religious conceptions also continually changed. As peoples' scientific knowledge increased little-by-little, in accordance with their progress, religious beliefs lost their former significance, were proclaimed worthless as traditions of faith, and new religious doctrines and precepts repeatedly emerged. Likewise, after the secrets of the objects and phenomena of nature were exposed, they lost their status as 'gods' and made room for new understandings of god to emerge. ...[295]

Humankind's increasing awareness of and mastery over its environment led slowly but surely to the next major transformational phase in world religious history. Although it followed the Soviet interpretations worked out in the 1920s and 30s (see Chapter 5), Kakimzhanov's narrative was here again not simply Marxist; it had become, by the time he was writing in the 1950s, the prevailing view among scholars of religious history throughout the Western world. Scholars in Soviet Russia as well as recently founded communist China were both aware of and tied into broader international interpretations and trends. Secularization theory was coming into its own.[296] Kakimzhanov followed the conventions of the day in portraying the emergence of Islam among the Arabs in the early seventh century in entirely materialistic terms, with of course the Marxian twist of it being an opiate of the masses fabricated for purposes of imperialistic political and economic class exploitation. Thus, Kakimzhanov maintains,

> [t]he religions of our day which are founded upon servanthood to one god emerged in connection with the division of society into classes and the appearance of political states. As the tribal groups of early human societies gave way to political states, the former tribal gods and religions which were based upon them were left behind, giving way to gods and religions which had political significance.[297]

Here he offers the examples of Amon from Egypt and Marduk from Babylon, linking their imperial deities to the pre-Islamic Arabian tribal gods. It was then "the god of the Quraysh tribe of the city of Mecca" was, amid all the various polytheistic options, "eventually...proclaimed god of all of Arabia." Kakimzhanov cites from Engels to the effect that "there...would have been no conception of monotheism" without a supreme political state and its ruler to simultaneously and reciprocally give rise to the need for monotheism and justify the political state and ruler.[298] This in itself was not a distinctly Marxist-Soviet interpretation, though it fit within the Marxist-Soviet historiographical frame. He linked this proposed historical development, however, to "the division of society into classes" wherein "understandings of god also changed" from forces having power primarily over nature to now having power over society itself. Such Gods could no longer be likened therefore to natural phenomena, but had to be conceived as incomparable to any such created thing, "omnipotent" and "omnipresent" as well as "fashionably authoritative and wrathful." This is how "the oppressive classes which held power thought up universal gods...such as the Christian's Sabaoth, the Jew's Yahweh and the Muslim's God and replaced national and ethnic gods...."[299] Kakimzhanov then advances a hallmark interpretation which became central within the Marxist-Soviet view, with certain features likewise shared across much of the broader European and Christian world(s):

Arab rule, which was founded upon violence and national theft, was unstable. In the end, the uprisings of the local peoples against the religion of Islam and the Arab soldiers who depended on the authority of its god brought the caliphate to collapse. ...

...By suppressing the objections of the peoples of the Arab working class who were caught in the shackles of oppression, expanding the nation's trade relations, uniting in order to fight against the attacks of their outside enemies, and then, after uniting, conquering foreign nations, the religion of Islam emerged as an ideological instrument of militant warfare. This religion, like others, became an opium making people crazy in the head,[300] serving a genuinely reactionary role. ...[301]

Having explained the historical rise of Islam against the backdrop of deeper world religious history, Kakimzhanov concludes his historical overview by coming full circle back to the territory of Kazakhstan. His entire thrust is aimed at denying a historically deep and authentic Islamic identity for the Kazakhs, with Fazl Allah ibn Ruzbihan Isfahani and Shokan Valikhanov his two primary sources of authority (see Chapters 3 and 4). "Islam," he insists, "was spread very late" within the history of Kazakhstan. "The claim that Kazakhs have been Muslim from olden times is," Kakimzhanov himself now claims, "false preaching spread by Mullahs." He then proceeds to offer what had become a standard historical narrative of Kazakh Islam, namely that up until "the XI century the religion of Islam covered only the southern regions of Kazakhstan, and even then it was mostly spread among the ruling classes. The vast majority of Kazakhstan's population had not embraced Islam. Gradually, it slowly came to pass that the ruling classes forcibly spread Islam among the Kazakhs." Kakimzhanov thus attributes the supposed later spread of Islam among the more northern regions and larger masses most immediately and directly to Kazakh "ruling classes," not Catherine II's (r. 1762– 1796) policies of religious toleration and/or "Tatar" (i.e., Volga-Ural Muslim) merchants, scribes and other intermediary servants supported by the imperial apparatus down to approximately the 1850s (see Appendix One). This aligns with his 'spread by force' theory. But whether it was via "the strategy[302] of spreading the religion of Islam via force," as in Kakimzhanov's view here, or the combined efforts of Catherine II and the Volga-Ural Muslims, the outcome was still the same, namely that these efforts to spread Islam at this allegedly late date were unable to destroy and do away with the shamanistic religion of the masses. Religious traditions and customs remained unchanged with respect to their meaning, only their names were switched out. The god of the Muslims – "God" continued to be extolled alongside of the gods of the shamanic faith known as "tangir" "kok tangir" ("god" "sky or heavenly god"). Syncretism[303] occurred.[304]

Kakimzhanov invokes Fazl Allah ibn Ruzbihan Isfahani at this juncture, misidentifying him as an "Uzbek ruler," instead of as an Iranian Sunni Muslim scholar, guest of an Uzbek ruler.[305] Isfahani provides evidence, according to Kakimzhanov, that "in the beginning of the XVI century…it was common knowledge among the people that there were still some signs of disbelief in the Islamic faith among the Kazakhs. … images of idols were preserved among the Kazakhs, and they worshipped those images."[306] These things were, Kakimzhanov insists, "contrary to the Muslim faith." He notes specifically how the Kazakhs of Isfahani's time "gazed upon the sun and bowed their heads," saying, "'you have given grass to our cattle'."[307] That is, these sixteenth-century Kazakhs engaged in 'sun-worship.'[308]

Along with Isfahani, Kakimzhanov appeals to the authority of "[p]rogressive thinkers of the Kazakh people" who, so he claims, "have openly shown how much extensive damage the spread of the Islamic religion caused in its time." Among these, it was most notably "Shokan Valikhanov, Abai Kunanbaev and Ibirai Altinsarin" who "called for the Kazakh people not to place their hope in the backwards, reactionary east and its religion, but in the Russian people who had great advanced culture and science and were great masters of progressive thinking." These particular Kazakh thinkers "struggled throughout their lives in order to spread Russian culture among the Kazakh nation and to save them from," not just the religion of Islam, but "the ill effects of" another main Soviet enemy, "Turkic nationalism."

Among the three "progressive thinkers" that Kakimzhanov specifically cites, he places the greatest weight of emphasis on Shokan Valikhanov who, "during the 1860s," held that "the Muslim religion ha[d] not been thoroughly absorbed into our [Kazakh] blood and flesh, but this religion poses a serious threat to mislead and break down our people in the future." Most importantly, Valikhanov, says Kakimzhanov, insisted that steps had to be taken to stop the expanding spread of the Islamic religion and weaken, or if possible, completely eradicate the detrimental impact of the Tatar mullahs and Central Asian sufi saints. For that, [Valikhanov] demanded that, first, they had to give up the practice of supporting mullahs and Islamic ideas and then open Russian schools in place of the Islamic schools among the Kazakhs.[309]

Education was, in Valikhanov's view, key to stopping "the spread of Islam" which "brought harm to the friendship of the Kazakh people with the Russian people." The education which Kakimzhanov had in view was of course not, as per Valikhanov, Tsarist, but Soviet, just as "friendship...with the Russian people" was likewise understood now in Soviet terms.[310]

All in all, "the Islamic religion," Kakimzhanov concluded, "is not a faith which is inherently necessary[311] with Muslims. The people lived for a great many centuries not knowing the Islamic faith. This religion came along at a particular time during the development of humankind's social existence and it will come to an end at a particular time."[312] This vision of "Muslims" devoid of "the Islamic religion" highlights the ethnocultural understanding of "Muslim" which prevailed in Soviet parlance.

BISENOV, *THE ORIGIN OF ISLAM AND ITS CLASS SIGNIFICANCE* (1955)

Just two years after Kakimzhanov, Kh. Bisenov published a short (32-page) booklet on *The Origin of Islam and Its Class Significance* with a press-run of 10,000 copies. Like Kakimzhanov's work, Bisenov's propagandist work was put out by the Kazakh State Publishing House.[313] Early in the booklet, he complains that, "[w]hile socialism has been established in our nation, and socialist ideology founded upon Marxist-Leninist (teachings) is dominant, there are still remnants (калдыктары) of bourgeois ideology in the minds of certain ones among our (Kazakh) people." He repeated the phrase "remnants (калдыктары) of bourgeois viewpoints" for added emphasis.[314]

"One of the harmful remnants (калдыктары) of the old (order)" which Bisenov took special concern with were those of "religious servitude and the worship of blind faith traditions." He pointed to "the war years" as the cause for "some revival of blind religious faith traditions as well as customs and traditions, and, in parallel, a considerable measure of official recognition of everything considered religious, even the activities of church and mosque leaders." The Soviet Union experienced in parallel "the abating of scientifically-grounded atheistic propaganda," so that "religious survivals (діни калдыктары) significantly revived." It was, in fact, "the insufficiency or weakening of ideological activity and, within it, scientifically-grounded atheistic indoctrination" which was "[t]he first and foremost reason for the existence of religious survivals and their revival."[315] Unless "survivals" are completely eradicated, so Bisenov implies, there is always a chance that they might be revived.

Over the next few pages, Bisenov begins recounting early religious history, including its origins, in much the same way as Kakimzhanov, with select quotations from Engels: humankind's weakness, fear and ignorance are the main reasons for religion's rise, with phenomena of the natural world providing the points of reference. As humankind is divided up into social classes and political states arise, political leaders and religious clergy emerge, promoting new understandings of religion—particularly the monotheistic traditions of Judaism, Christianity and Islam—which oppress the masses. Against this backdrop, "the religions which placed [n]atural forces and their phenomena, animals, deceased forefathers and others on par with god continued thriving in ancient Arabia – the land where the religion of Islam emerged – until patriarchal-tribal relations were eliminated."[316]

In Bisenov's view, it was apparently not just some, but all of "[t]he peoples that the Arabs conquered" who "opposed the spreading of the Islamic religion." Either Bisenov's idea of "the peoples" here is more strictly of "the proletariat" or the opposition was only short lived, since he immediately tells us that "those who were rich and the ruling classes embraced the new religion, while the main working-class peoples upheld for a long period their former religions more than the religion of Islam."[317] His reference to "more than" reflects a comparative 'dual faith' perspective (see Chapters 2 and 4). As such, it would be a 'survival' of Tsarist-era Russian Orthodox interpretations now re-appropriated within a Soviet historiographical frame for Soviet causes.[318]

Bisenov's narrative of the historical rise of Islam and the resistance against it by especially "the main working-class peoples" provides an essential backdrop for his transition to a specific focus on Islam within the religious history of Kazakhstan. Here again the essential outline of his narrative, especially his initial brush-stroke overview, follows the same general outlines as that of Kakimzhanov's, with certain differing points of emphasis. "Islam," according to Bisenov, "began spreading into the territory of Kazakhstan in the middle of the VIII century, from the time that the Arabs conquered Central Asia and our present republic's southern area." He is clearly referring here to the Battle of Talas (or Atlah) in 751 CE when the Tashkent Turks called upon the Abbasid Muslim armies in Samarkand and Merv to assist them against their rivals in Ferghana who were allied with T'ang Chinese forces.[319] "From there the Muslim religion spread very slowly," mainly among "the feudalists of the southern farming regions who embraced Islam while the core population of nomadic peoples, especially in central and northern Kazakhstan, entered the Islamic religion later."[320] Unlike Kakimzhanov, Bisenov leaves the precise means of the later spread among the nomadic northern populations opaque, mentioning neither Catherine II, the Tatars or any coercive Kazakh rulers. He does speak elsewhere of "[t]he exploitation of the religion of Islam, and the opening of the way for the distribution of the Qur'an and (Muslim) preaching by the close enemy of all peoples – the Tsarist government,"[321] which most likely encompasses reference to these practices all the way back to the time of Catherine II, but he does not again explicitly name Catherine II here, or the Tatars, nor does he make this allusion within this particular context. It comes much later, mainly in connection to his discussion of the Alash Orda and the politics of Islam and nationalism in the early twentieth-century context of Tsarist reform. As to Islam's earlier spread into Central Asia, Bisenov is, at a later juncture, clear as to the destructive and imperializing nature of the conquests, citing loosely from "[t]he great scholar of Khorezm Al-Beruni [also Al-Biruni] (972–1048)" who "wrote in this way":

> When the Arabs conquered Central Asia, 'they utterly destroyed all the Khorezm people's written records and preserved legends, all their scholars, and everything they had, leaving absolutely nothing; thus, there is no certain knowledge left from their history before the coming of the religion of Islam. ...after this the Khorezm people forgot the art of writing and reading and lost a great deal of knowledge and scholarship...'[322]

It is clear here that Bisenov is not simply parroting Kakimzhanov, which means he is not parroting a mere Soviet template. The narratives share obvious general features, but each author draws from their own select sources to drive their shared Soviet propaganda home. These are

Soviet Kazakh authors who each craft narratives of Soviet atheistic propaganda aimed at convincing their own Kazakh people through whatever 'historical (and other) facts' they deem best suited for the task. They build on one another but also depart and venture down their own paths of approach along the way.

One common point of agreement with Kakimzhanov, though expressed again in Bisenov's own unique way, was that "[w]ithin the lands of Kazakhstan, Muhammed's dogmatic 'teaching' formed a very long alliance with the shamanist religion." Bisenov here, like Kakimzhanov, appeals to "[t]he Kazakh scholar and educator Sh. Ualihanov" who said that "the Kazakhs 'go on confusing the customs and traditions of the Muslim religion with the blind beliefs of the shamanist faith'" and these "'customs and traditions, concepts, and legends of shamanism, which are closely tied to nomadic lifeways, have been fully preserved until this day.'" While citing Valikhanov, Bisenov himself insisted, however—in line with broader Soviet and international secular scholarship on 'the history of religions'—that this 'mixing' of Shamanism and Islam within Central Asia was nothing unusual, for "the religion of Islam is nothing special, no different from other religions. There are, in the Islamic religion, idolatrous practices of the ancient Arabs, and legends of the Hebrew religion, and dogmas of the Christian religion, and remnants (қалдықтары) of early Iranian religion." It was the very nature of Islam (as well as Judaism, Christianity and other 'world religions') to mix with the "remnants" of 'pre-existing' religious traditions which were part of the context into which they were born, whether that 'birth' was, in Islam's case, its original inception in seventh-century Arabia or its later spread into new areas, Central Asia in particular in this case.[323]

Having highlighted select points related to Islam's initial spread into Central Asia, including southern sedentary Kazakhstan, and its later eighteenth- and nineteenth-century spread among the northern nomadic populations, Bisenov turns his attention to early twentieth-century political developments involving the Alash Orda. The Alash Orda leaders, Bisenov asserts, "knew well that for the training and upbringing of obedient, mindless slaves there was no more convenient school than the madrasas of the mullahs."[324] This should be of no real surprise, he argues, because they were not alone in this recognition, they shared it with the Tsarist regime, who in turn shared it with the British and American imperialist powers:

7 THE FRAMING OF KAZAKH RELIGIOUS HISTORY AND IDENTITY ...   117

The exploitation of the religion of Islam, and the opening of the way for the distribution of the Qur'an and (Muslim) preaching by the close enemy of all peoples – the Tsarist government – is self-evidently understandable. (This is) because the Tsarist government used the Qur'an to instigate revolutionary and national independence movements among the oppressed peoples in its eastern regions. For example, in the time of the cruel Stolypin's reforms the "Muslim world" newspaper run by Tsarist hitmen and mullahs, on 11 October 1911, called upon the Muslim intelligentsia not to teach Marx's *Capitalism* among the population, but distribute the Qur'an and Sharia law code.

The (previous) continual reading of passages from the Qur'an on the radio by the British imperialists and, in the present, the regular publishing in the USA of books which indoctrinate (people with) the reactionary preaching of the Qur'an are hardly coincidental activities.[325]

The Cold War context of Bisenov's work comes clear here, and his depiction of British and American activities is generally accurate.

Having covered the spread of Islam into Central Asia and, specifically, Kazakhstan, Bisenov now returns to an earlier theme, namely "the entire range of first-rate people [who] have, throughout the entire history of the religion of Islam, come out against this reactionary ideology." He starts with "the Medieval period itself," during which "first-rate scholars sorely criticized the Qur'anic nonsense against science and scholarship." Along with al-Beruni (see above), these also included

[T]he great Central Asian scholar and thinker Abu-ali ibn-Sina – Avicenna – (980-1037) [who] mocked the Qur'anic preaching that God created the earth, 'mountains', fields and roads. Avicenna demonstrated that the mountains came into being through the movement of the earth and the effect of wind and water which caused the rising of the earth's surface. The Muslim religious authorities severely persecuted the great scholar for his bold scholarly views.

With the weight of medieval Islamic scholars such as al-Beruni and Ibn Sina behind him, Bisenov returns in the next paragraph to "the magnificent educator and scholar of the Kazakhs Shokan Valikhanov" who "was completely opposed to the religion of Islam." Valikhanov demanded, according to Bisenov, that the Tsarist government put an end to its support of the spread of Islam among the Kazakhs. Bisenov emphasizes here Valikhanov's promotion of "the opening of many Russian schools in place of the Muslim medreses and mullahs and the spreading of Russian culture on the Kazakh steppe." He then portrays "[t]he Kazakh's exceptionally noteworthy pedagogue – the educator Ibirai Altinsarin" as being in essential agreement with Valikhanov, claiming that he "wrote that Muslim religious studies had no sacred value whatsoever other than 'pouring sand in people's heads' and nothing in common with wisdom and reflection." There was of course a 'half-truth' in this, though Altinsarin had limited this particular critique to Tatar, Uzbek and other supposedly 'fanatical' Muslim peoples of Central Asia. He did not, however, entirely oppose the spread of Islam among the Kazakhs, but argued instead for a more 'enlightened' form essentially in line with burgeoning Jadid ideas of reform.[326] "The great Abai" as well, says Bisenov, "harshly exposed in nonchalant manner the reactionary dogmas of the greedy Muslim leaders and the religion of Islam."[327]

Bisenov's invocation of Abai marks a transition from a focus on the "first-rate people" who have opposed Islam, to "the reactionary" nature of the religion, as he, through his Soviet lens, sees it. "The history of the religion of Islam itself," Bisenov thus argues, "shows how Muslim leaders have continuously betrayed" not only "the national cause of the peoples," but the great friendship between those national peoples and the Russian peoples in the process. If I reframe Bisenov's sometimes seemingly random and scattered order chronologically, then this history goes back to "when the Tatar-Mongol soldiers entered Central Asia, Kazakhstan, the Caucasus and other nations," where it was the Islamic leadership who "called upon the people not to express any opposition to the soldiers." Much later came "[t]he reactionary movement against the people led by Shamil in the Caucasus, which aimed, in the second quarter of the XIX century, to separate the peoples of the Caucasus from Russia and the Russians." It did so wearing "the mask of a jihad." Likewise, "[t]he close enemy of the Kazak people, the gang leader Kenesari Kasimov engaged in banditry under the banner of leading a 'holy war' against 'the unbelievers' on the Kazakh steppe in the 1830s–40s. This also separated the Kazakhs from Russia, and from the unity of friendship with the great Russian people...." Kasimov was effectively another Shamil in Bisenov's interpretation. Then "[i]n 1916, during the national independence uprising of the peoples of Kazakhstan and Central Asia, the Muslim mullahs played a genuinely villainous role" by, he asserts, "betray[ing] the cause of the people, stirring up ethnic animosity, and weakening those participating in the uprising."[328]

Bisenov's various glosses over these select historical examples all serve, in fact, as a prelude to his twin central concerns within this section, pan-Islamism and pan-Turkism. His coverage of these interrelated historical movements spans the entire first half of the twentieth century, down to 1955 when he is writing, with a focus on the two world wars in particular. Bisenov ties both "pan-Islamism" and "pan-Turkism" to the former Ottoman Turkish Empire and the emerging modern state of Turkey. While he identifies pan-Turkism specifically as "a reactionary political movement aimed at the cause of the bourgeoisie and pomeshiks," i.e., wealthy agricultural land owners, he has, according to Soviet parlance, identified Islam in the same general terms later in his treatment (see below) and elsewhere at various junctures.

As Bisenov comes to the heart of his diatribe, he frames his arguments about pan-Islamism and pan-Turkism within the broader context of Soviet-Western international relations, i.e., in the heat of the Cold War. "The [Western] imperialists," he warns, "are involved in using pan-Islamism and pan-Turkism to justify and fulfill their aggressive plans." "German imperialists" in particular "made use of pan-Islamism and pan-Turkism" throughout the First World War "in order to conquer new Eastern colonies."[329] These "Eastern colonies" included numerous "Turkic peoples, who were Muslim" and "part of Russia," including "Kazakhs, Tatars, Uzbeks and others." They had, proudly and willingly by implication, "begun embracing Russian culture, and the revolutionary traditions of the great Russian people, joining their destiny with the destiny of the Russian people in a common struggle against the Tsarist regime. Separating these peoples from Russia and becoming a partial colony of German imperialism, (or) joining as part of the backward, partially feudal Turkey, would have," Bisenov insists, "led them head on into a reactionary calamity." Meanwhile within Russia, these twin trouble-making movements

> attempted to raise complaints against the Russian people and Russian government and stir up hatred among the Muslims inhabiting Central Asia, Kazakhstan, the Caucasus and other regions. Feudalists and the wealthy, Muslim leaders and bourgeois nationalists were the true heads of pan-Islamism and pan-Turkism. They propagated these degenerate ideas of theirs through their own publishing arms, attempting to poison the minds and hearts of the population with bourgeois nationalist venom, opposing Russian learning and culture in order to hold the peoples in the darkness and ignorance of the black night of Islam.

Coming specifically to World War Two, that is "the Patriotic War of the USSR," Bisenov returns to the link with Western imperialism. "Muslim leaders served as foreign agents for British imperialists, praising the reactionary idea of forming a unified Muslim state" consisting of "the Caucasus, Central Asia's current Soviet Republics and Soviet Kazakhstan." "In the USA," these Western imperialist efforts continued as so-called "'expert' preachers of the Muslim religion are," at the time of his writing in 1955, "being prepared while various publications of pan-Islamism are being issued; they preach, among other things, in the publications that Islamic peoples do not have their own national cultures, they only allegedly have a 'common Muslim' culture."[330]

This specific evidence from the pan-Islamic and pan-Turkic movements[331] serves to prove that "[f]rom the very first days of the Great October socialist revolution the religion of Islam opposed the Soviet government. It eagerly participated with *all* the bourgeois-nationalist counter-revolutionary 'governments' and institutions and organized the Basmachi band using the battle of the Entente (powers) and the intervention of foreign nations."[332]

In spite of such egregious behavior, Bisenov made clear that "[t]he Soviet government severely punished these kinds of religious people, of course, not for their religious service, but...for taking up the cause of internal counter-revolution and international imperialism, directing themselves against the causes of the Soviet people, and engaging in anti-government activities."[333]

After this historical overview of Islam's persistent opposition to Soviet authority and political mission, and the dangers it poses, Bisenov shifts his focus to the destruction of religious "survivals" among the Kazakhs in his own day. He himself provides no break in the flow of his narrative, but the transition is clear as he spotlights the fact that danger still remains because "there are still religious survivals in the hearts and minds of a certain portion of our workers." These "survivals" include, not Shamanism or Tengrism or Zoroastrianism, but practices associated with Islam, particularly "[t]he attending of churches and mosques by certain of our citizens and observing of religious customs and traditions (ait, fast, etc.)." Bisenov assures his readers that "they do not do it because they are genuinely religious, but even though it is only done as a habit, tradition, (or) custom, nonetheless it shows they tolerate the 'leather heels' of religious survivals,[334] and these survivals are not compatible with our communist worldview." He further includes "the practices of taking many wives, and staking inheritance," both of which "are survivals of the religion of Islam." He cites here "*Kazakhstanskaya Pravda*, 12/III No 52, 5/X 1954" as one of the few sources which he references throughout his work. His brief list also embraces "the fast (of Ramadan) which robs people of strength by not allowing them to eat, and they celebrate what is known as 'kurban ait' (that is, 'the feast of sacrifice')."[335] He is careful to limit those observing such 'survivals' to "certain portions of the people of our republic."[336]

Having unleashed his atheistic assault on "the black night of the Islamic religion," including its history and all the various religious 'survivals' that have come to be associated with it across the centuries, Bisenov turns in his conclusion to the imagined democratic glory of the Soviet state and its laws of religious freedom. He presumes the Kazakh population will be persuaded by his propaganda to abandon Islam and all other religious "survivals" and follow the superior Marxist-Leninist ways and views. Writing in the post-Stalinist period, Stalin is given no place in his narrative. Instead:

> As a truly consistent democratic nation, genuine religious freedom is granted in our nation. ...
> The 124th statute of the Soviet Constitution grants freedom of conscience and freedom to conduct anti-religious indoctrination.[337] ...
> Soviet laws severely punish the persecution of people for their religious faith. But our Marxist materialist perspective on the world, our communist morals, and our obligations are not in any way compatible with religious ideology and religious morals. Therefore, every mindful citizen of our nation who counts themselves a lover of Lenin, a mindful builder of communism cannot continue looking with disdain upon the religious survivals in certain peoples' hearts and minds, they must oppose religion among people and conduct reasonable scientific-atheistic work.[338]

While his emphasis is Islam itself, Bisenov thus combines Soviet propaganda against 'pre-Islamic' as well as Islamic 'survivals' in one treatise, distinguishing and singling them both out for eradication.

DUISENBIN, *ABOUT THE RELIGION OF ISLAM AND ITS CURRENT STATE* (1961)

Six years after Bisenov's pamphlet, Zh. Duisenbin published a slightly more substantial work *About the Religion of Islam and Its Current State*. It was 122 pages in length, released, as always, by the Kazakh State Publishing House with a print run of only 6500 on this occasion.[339] Duisenbin laid out the framework for his study as follows:

Preface	3
The Origins and Essence of the Religion of Islam	13
Islam in the East in the Present Period	35
The Religion of Islam – A Remnant of the Past in our Nation	67

In Chapter 3 of his work—"The Religion of Islam—A Remnant of the Past in our Nation"—Duisenbin briefly notes that Islam spread on the Kazakh steppe in the ninth–tenth centuries. He then goes on to place Shokan Ualihanuhli (Valikhanov) among the atheists who were persecuted by the Tsarist government and its Orthodox organs, suggesting that his writings were only published, after much resistance and rejection, because he was a military officer and had written about Kazakh religion.[340]

After referencing Catherine II's establishment and promotion of Muslim institutions, personnel and publications, he asserts that: "In comparison with Central Asia, the Caucasus, and Volga regions, the Islamic religion spread late among the Kazakhs. In particular, the northern Kazakh tribes confessed Islam late." He quotes, without reference, a Central Asian khan who—so he, like Kakimzhanov, alleges—forced Islam upon the Kazakhs in the fifteenth century. He concludes: "These historical facts themselves show the falsehood of the claim of religious fanatics who say that 'the Kazakh people have been Muslim from long ago.'" He turns then again to Valikhanov to explain "the reasons for the lack of depth of the spread of Islam among the Kazakhs."[341]

Duisenbin's use of the term "pagan" to describe "numerous" practices "leftover" from pre-Islamic times points to the influence of old Tsarist Orthodox paradigms underlying Soviet Kazakh 'pre-Islamic remnants' historiography here. Among these allegedly 'pagan leftovers', "shamanism's *baksi* have come to parallel and be the same as the mullahs" with "the shamanic religion thoroughly mixing together with Muslim beliefs." It was "for these reasons that Shokan called the Kazakh people a religiously shallow (шала діңді) people" ripe for progressivist education. It is only because the Tsarist government supported Islam as an "instrument" of empire that "Islamic preaching remained strong among the Kazakhs down to the time of the revolution," giving the Tsar the status of a Sufi saint.[342]

Picking up yet another central, recurring theme, Duisenbin launches from here into a brief historical recounting of how Central Asian Muslims formed political parties within the Tsarist government in the early twentieth century and eventually stood against the Communists. This provides further historical 'evidence' for the Soviet accusation that Islam is a reactionary instrument of imperialism.[343] It was the Great Patriotic War started by "the devoted Hitlerites of Germany" and all the sufferings which it brought that reignited the "religious survivals" leftover from pre-Soviet times. The Soviet expectation—shared widely, and increasingly, across the secularizing Western world, from the Enlightenment to the rise of Tylorean-style social science and beyond into the twentieth century—had not failed; it had simply been 'disrupted' by the tragedy of war. The faith of the Soviets, like that of other Western secularization theorists, itself 'resisted' and 'survived' this challenge. But Duisenbin is nonetheless confident that "there is no religious fanaticism among us." He then provides a number of recent examples from newspapers, journals and other sources of those who, over the past two years (1959–1960), have renounced their religion and 'converted' to atheism.[344]

Duisenbin then returns to earlier Kazakh and Islamic history. The custom of building mausoleums in connection with saint veneration took root, he claims, among the Arabs in the tenth to eleventh centuries, taken over from earlier Middle Eastern practices. The custom spread among Central Asian peoples, including the Kazakhs, between the tenth to fifteenth centuries. They thus appear in the "great cities on Kazakh land from early times," including Taraz, Turkistan, Otirar and Sairam. After discussing these shrines and their related figures for several pages, Duisenbin concludes: "If we come to the truth of it, these structures were erected to retain the glorious reputation of these great religious and prosperous (аукатты) people who have been named above."[345]

Part of my argument here is that, through these kinds of historical excursions within their writings, anti-religious propagandists like Duisenbin aided, however unwittingly, in preserving the Islamic history and thus identity of the Kazakhs and other Central Asian Muslim peoples throughout the Soviet period. While oral tradition kept alive by khojas and other religious figures in connection with these shrines may have contributed, they were not the only sources. Both sources, in fact, served to collaborate one another, in spite of being in competition with one another in their overall aims and agendas.

Ultimately though, according to Duisenbin, it was just as Shokan Ualihanuhli had said, namely that the veneration of saints within Islam, particularly its miraculous aspects, became syncretically mixed together with ancient shamanic practices.[346]

Duisenbin finishes his exposition with "A Few Words Regarding the Survivals within the Customs and Traditions of the Islamic Religion."[347] He says nothing of any historical significance, but rather appeals to the Kazakhs to abandon these survivals and embrace atheism fully, with a view to leaving the past behind and progressing toward the imagined higher ground of enlightened Soviet civilization.

K. Mashrapov *Devotion to Islam—A Detrimental Survival* (1962)

Just one year after Duisenbin, K. Mashrapov released a short (48-page) booklet titled *Devotion to Islam—A Detrimental Survival*.[348] 7000 copies were printed and distributed throughout kiosks, bookstores and elsewhere. Although a short work, Mashrapov included a number of topics set forth in the Table of Contents:

The Worship of Objects of Nature as the Early Original Form of Religion	4
Regarding the "Ancestral Spirit" god	10
What Do Science and Religion say about the "Soul"?	20
Regarding the Fast	26
Religious Festivals of Islam	32
What is the Term Qur'an?	34
Who are the Ones Going About Spreading Religious Faith These Days among the Kazakhs?	42

After a brief introduction calling for Kazakhs to overcome their dependence on religion, Mashrapov begins his treatment of "The Worship of Objects of Nature as the Early Original Form of Religion" with the accusation that those claiming to worship Allah alone "go on worshiping fire, mountains and stones, the Moon, living creatures, and various natural phenomena." Like all the others, Mashrapov argues, "the religion of Islam itself is composed of the early forms of early humankind's religions, namely" totemism, fetishism and animism. Most importantly here, however, is Mashrapov's short section addressing the question: "Who are the Ones Going About Spreading Religious Faith These Days among the Kazakhs?" For all the continuing Soviet efforts to invalidate Islam and convert the Kazakhs to atheism, there remained, somewhat contra Duisenbin, those still spreading Islamic faith among them, and those who continued to hold fast to it until the coming of independence, albeit in forms certainly impacted by 70 years of atheistic propaganda.

Concluding Reflections

Alongside Snesarev's more scientific approach which branched off and evolved in its own direction from the later 1960s onward (see Chapter 6), these types of straightforward confrontational works—with their condemnations of and appeals against the "survivals" of both Islam and various pre-Islamic beliefs and practices which had come to be integrated together with it across the centuries—continued down to the 1980s, and beyond into the early independent period. As with the examples provided here, the later works exhibited only slight variations on the same themes, mainly in terms of the precise historical content and balance of coverage they chose to incorporate in order to convince their audiences to abandon their religious "survivals" and join wholeheartedly in the Soviet atheist cause. As reflected in Mashrapov's final chapter, none of these "survivals," including particularly Islam, died out as expected in the face of the increasing Soviet and broader Western push toward secularization. Indeed, religious revival challenged both the Euro-Slavic and Euro-American versions. The latter's attempt, particularly within America, to coopt religion via a secularized form of more generic and 'civil religion' as part of its anti-communist Cold War strategy (cf. 'In God We Trust') ultimately, like the Soviet hardline approach, failed. Within the post-colonial and post-modernist contexts, both more liberal as well as conservative forms of religious devotion among more codified faiths experienced increasing revivalism alongside indigenous and popular traditions. The Soviet collapse significantly accentuated these trends, though was also, in part, brought about by them.

It should be noted, however, that "pre-Islamic survivals" were not the only or even primary focus of the Soviet atheistic apologetic. They drew on every argument in relation to every aspect of 'Islam', past and present, which was at their disposal, in desperate and far-fetched manner at times. And they did so with the assumption that Islam was the primary faith tradition through which, or at least in intimate relation to which, any and all 'survivals', pre-Islamic or otherwise, had survived. Pan-Islamism, pan-Turkism and other political dimensions of, or related to, the Islamic faith were a central concern, more so than the mere fact of 'religious survivals' themselves. In this, they continued perpetuating the same essential arguments against Islam which marked their pre-World War Two propaganda, only updated with new material from the later decades down to their own times. Indeed, the explicit turn to 'pre-Islamic survivals' in the post-World War Two era may well have been a strategy which aided in distracting attention away from their otherwise direct assault on Islam itself. It served their need to balance anti-Islamic with pro-Islamic propaganda as they strove to foster positive relations with the Middle East and other Islamic countries within the context of the Cold War.

Two other particular observations which are noteworthy in these works: First, while most of the sources do, in some shape or form, make reference to Catherine II's policies and their impact on "late" Kazakh conversion to Islam (cf. Appendix One), it does not, in the balances, play an overly weighty role in their historiographical attempts to convince the Kazakhs that they are not true, genuine Muslims, or at least have not been, so they claim, for very long. Among the sources considered here, Duisenbin is the most explicit and forthright in pressing this historiographical argument, but deeper comparative study of this particular question would be worth pursuing.

Second, reference to 'survivals' of 'Nestorian Christianity' among the Central Asian peoples are conspicuously lacking from the Soviet sources. In spite of drawing from every possible historical argument they could find to counter Islamic identity and practice within Central Asia, the Soviet propagandists did not apparently see it as a significant and viable heritage (cf. 'remnant') of Central Asian religious history and identity. This is not to say that there has not been a certain limited measure of Christian presence among the Turkic Central Asian peoples historically,[349] or that this history and identity does not continue to be important; it certainly does, as indicated by some of the controversial efforts to counter and even deny or suppress it.[350] But it did not play any significant role in Soviet anti-Islamic propaganda, indicating that Soviet scholars and activists did not consider it significant historically.

Meanwhile, the range of historical material that they do employ within their propagandistic narratives is fairly broad and diverse, and, albeit appropriated to Soviet agendas, certainly not devoid of factual accuracy. It was, in fact, through their various historical excursions that anti-religious propagandists aided, however unwittingly, in preserving the Islamic history and thus identity of the Kazakhs and other Central Asian Muslim peoples throughout the Soviet period. The sheer presence and weight of the Islamic heritage in Central Asia made it impossible for Soviet scholars to ignore or dismiss. They were forced to grapple with it in their anti-Islamic apologetics and in doing so aided, in part, in perpetuating the very religious identity and related practices they aimed to destroy. Central Asian Muslims were, after all, well capable of recognizing and ignoring the Soviet propaganda, or perhaps paying it public homage when necessary, while continuing to esteem and preserve it in their hearts. That this was in fact the case is demonstrated by the "survival" of Islam throughout seventy years of Soviet assault.

In the aftermath, the post-Soviet Central Asian peoples were left to sift through their entangled past, separate out historical truth from Soviet propaganda, and work to revise and revive their authentic historical identities.[351] As the next chapter demonstrates, this was and remains far easier said than done. As the subsequent chapters then demonstrate as well, the same was and remains true for broader international scholarship both within and beyond the field of Central Asian studies.

CHAPTER 8

Religious-Cultural Revivalism as Historiographical Debate: Post-Soviet Kazakh Perspectives on Their Past

This chapter examines diverging and competing historiographical interpretations of Kazakh religious identity emanating from key post-Soviet Kazakh intellectuals and scholars.[352] This is accomplished, much as in the

---

The present chapter is a revised version of my article: "Religious-Cultural Revivalism as Historiographical Debate: Contending Claims in the Post-Soviet Kazakh Context," *Journal of Islamic Studies*, Vol. 25, No. 2 (May 2014): 138–177. The revisions come mainly 'around the edges,' especially in the beginning and ending sections, with some of the introductory and concluding material moved to the introduction and other parts of this book, with a revised intro and conclusion for this chapter. Additional sources have also been added at the end of the main body. The material in this chapter stems from work at the Central Asian Historical-Cultural Research Center in Almaty, Kazakhstan and my doctoral work at al-Farabi Kazakh National University (2002–2006) as well as subsequent presentations at the 16th Annual World History Association Conference in Milwaukee, WI (2007) and the 9th Annual Conference of the Central Eurasian Studies Society, Georgetown University, Washington, DC (2008), each emphasizing distinct aspects of the material. Special thanks also to Yale and Princeton universities for the opportunity to further research and lecture on this subject during my time as a visiting fellow at Yale in 2010–2011, and to Richard Foltz, Alfred J. Andrea, John Voll, Bruce Privratsky, Joel Tishken, and the two anonymous reviewers at *JIS* for reading through drafts and offering critical feedback vital to improvement. All views and interpretations remain my own.

© The Author(s), under exclusive license to Springer Nature Singapore Pte Ltd. 2023
R. C. Weller, *'Pre-Islamic Survivals' in Muslim Central Asia*, Islam and Global Studies, https://doi.org/10.1007/978-981-19-5697-3_8

previous chapter, via careful English translations of those sources, garnished with secondary though nonetheless essential material along the way. My own critical analysis is kept minimal in order that the Kazakh voices can speak for and interact among themselves as much as possible.

The various views represented highlight the internal struggle between resurgent Muslim and Tengrist (i.e., 'Native Turkic Religious') and Shamanist positions developing in dynamic interface with lingering atheistic communist and rising Western secular as well as limited measures of Christian (and Buddhist) influence among the Turkic Central Asian peoples. Although the term "pre-Islamic" does not occur within any of the narratives, the question remains central to the interpretations, with Tengrism, Shamanism, animism, 'the cults of saints and ancestors' and other (allegedly) "pre-Islamic" traditions regularly referenced. There is clear overlap between certain of the positions taken by these post-Soviet Kazakh interpreters and those encountered in the Chernavsky-Dobrosmyslov debate (Appendix One) as well as Soviet Kazakh propaganda literature (Chapter 7), though very little critical reflection is offered by the Kazakh authors as to what the precise parallels are and to what extent they are influenced, pro or con, by Tsarist and/or Soviet historiography and ethnography.

The outcomes of these diverging and competing narratives carry implications for not only Turkic Central Asian history and identity, but for interreligious, intercultural and international relations and dialogue between the Western and Central Asian as well as broader Western-Asian, Western-Islamic and Christian-Muslim worlds. They affirm the central importance of historical knowledge and historiographical (re)interpretation particularly within post-colonial and other revivalist settings and, likewise, help to normalize our perceptions of Islam as a participant in such exchanges within the Kazakh as well as broader Central Asian and world communities.

One point worth highlighting in this chapter, which is relevant beyond the Kazakh and even broader Central Asian context, is that revivalism, while no doubt having a strong present and future focus, is grounded in and dependent upon historiographical interpretation, making any analysis of revivalism which fails to pay heed to that fact incomplete at best. A second point is that the Islamic voices participating in the debate, when compared with the Tengrist or other religious proponents, reveal by all means an equally passionate, but by no means peculiarly 'radical' or 'extremist' nature.

Framing the Essential Issues

Garifolla Esim, a nationally recognized scholar and deputy senator in the Kazakhstani government,[353] had long back in 1996 in the second of his 10-volume work on *The Essence of Mind: Reflections on Politics and Culture*, noted how there were those "in our nation" who were

> attempting on occasion to elucidate 'Kazakh-ness' not via the Muslim religion, but by way of the mentality which existed in the days when the worship of Tengrism was followed. What I have to say about this issue is that the days when the Turkic peoples followed Tengrism are history. ...In the present time, however, our Kazakh-ness, as well as our broader Turkic-ness is grounded in the Muslim religion. How...this problem will be resolved is dependent upon the reflections of the scholarly community. Of course, it is doubtless that the scholars who remain stuck in the mindset they were trained up in under the Soviets will [in like manner] brush aside the Muslim religion with a single wave of their hand. That is to say, they will turn Islam into an archaic relic of the past as well. And with the issue now framed this way, what shall our fate be? It is surely necessary to continue the discussions and exchange of ideas regarding this matter.[354]

Though writing in the still-fledgling years of post-Soviet revival, his words have generally remained an accurate appraisal of the continuing exchange of ideas down to recent years. Note here that Esim's concern is with 'Kazakh-ness' and 'Turkic-ness,' that is, ethnic and cultural identity, more than religion.[355] The latter serves to elucidate the former. This also comprises a rare acknowledgment of the fragile ground upon which all historically progressivist appeals stand: the fate of one allegedly dead-in-the-past tradition can easily become the fate of another, begging precisely the question of what revival is all about. Concerning such questions, Esim's openness to ongoing dialogue deserves to be highlighted, as does his ideally communal approach to resolving the matter, clearly mindful of the importance of historiographical debate as central in that process. As evidenced in the analysis below of various Kazakh voices expressed in the ensuing years, "the discussions and exchange of ideas regarding this matter" have, in fact, continued, with a fair range of creative diversity.

Tengrist Historiography

The Kazakh journalist Kurmangazi Karamanuhli[356] has been a well-known advocate of the revival and restoration of Tengrism to a central place in Kazakh cultural and national life following the Soviet collapse. It represents for him, and others like him, the allegedly pure, true, original religion of the Turkic Central Asian peoples prior to the coming of Islam. His approach to the historical and continuing relationship between Islam and Tengrism ostensibly emphasizes peaceful co-existence, yet it has clearly differing outcomes from those promoting a predominantly Islamic history and identity in relation to Tengrism and other 'pre-Islamic' faith traditions in Central Asia. After a long treatise extolling the virtues of Tengrism in close relation to ancestor veneration, nomadism and love of nature, Karamanuhli climaxes his passionate appeal for revival of such traditional nomadic lifeways by trying to assure the proponents of Islam that:

> From the things which have been said above it is clear that no idea has surfaced, of course, which would indicate a devaluing of other religions, particularly Islam. We esteem the religion of Islam, respect the Qur'an, which is the holy book of the Muslims, and place a high price tag upon the spiritually powerful service of the prophet Muhammad, counting the way he devoted himself wholeheartedly to God and in the Middle Ages joined together the various Arab tribes which had fallen into the worship of polytheism as great heroism. Along with that, the religion of Islam is the religion which today our aged and respected fathers and mothers observe. Still more, it has left a deep track in history, and in the days when our people had to walk a narrow and slippery path, it was a shield against the attempts to thoroughly convert them all, spare none, to Christianity. Therefore, we shall never give place to its being put down or subjected to mockery.
>
> No one can separate or dissuade the Kazakhs from Islam. Our purpose is, in practice, to search out and know the living sacred mysteries of the indigenous traditions and customs whose visible manifestations [cf. 'remnants, survivals'] have not disappeared even if their secrets perhaps have, to discover their more progressive as well as dated qualities. They are traditions and customs which are still being observed alongside the ritual practices of Islam. We pursue this aim because, alongside the spiritual benefits of Islam, the national worldview grounded in Tengrism also has a vast sea of benefit to offer today's generation.[357]

Yet Karamanuhli, some 35 pages prior, launched into his quest by painting a less-than-positive picture of Islam's historic arrival among and impact upon the Kazakh peoples and their ancestors: "The religion of Islam was spread on the Kazakh steppe through historical events which, in clutching, powerful waves, raised a fierce storm." He has in view here three waves in particular, the first being "the aggressive Arab invasion" when, between the seventh and ninth centuries, "clutching together the Qur'an and sword...the blood-spilling Arabs" came and "by military force, took over Iran and what today is the territory of Uzbekistan and southern Kazakhstan and forcibly converted them to the religion of Islam." In process, "the aggressors...exerted all their energies toward ridding the people of their customs and traditions, destroying them, and making them change their own personal as well as geographical names."[358] Karamanuhli borrows here from two other Kazakh writers, Kadir Mirzaliev and Toktasin Omirzakov, to add weight to his own sword-like historiographical thrust of pen.[359] His second wave breaks under "the Golden Horde, Berke khan (1255–66) and Ozbek khan (1312–42)" when "[t]heir decree that Islam be made the state religion was, for the most part, fulfilled in the strictest of terms."[360] His choice of vocabulary here ("decree," "strictest of terms") effectively extends the 'forced' nature of Islamic conversion in Central Asia into the second main period of its spread. Finally, "[t]he third mighty wave began when the Kazakh nation passed over into Russian control. In the year 1772, from Queen Catherine II's public treasury, 3600 copies of the Qur'an were printed and distributed at no cost among the Kazakhs..." His interpretation here in this latter third period follows the essential contours of Duisenbin's take on the matter in particular, with all of it standing in general accord with Soviet-era historiography (see previous chapter). All in all, in Karamanuhli's view, the "deep track in history" left by Islam is filled with forced conversion, bloodshed, destruction and unwelcome imperialist domination, with Karamanuhli emphasizing midway: "Never has any people or nation willfully turned its back on its own original faith," which of course for him is Tengrism.[361] It is not by mere coincidence that we will later find both Bulutai and Nurtazina, each advocates of Islam in their own distinctive ways, attempting to answer these kinds of claims and offer a markedly different, more congenial view of Islam's historic spread and acceptance among the Kazakhs.

That Karamanuhli's attempted appeasement of his Muslim kin at the climax of his essay was greeted at best with ambivalent reception, if not downright suspicion, is of little surprise. Neither is the fact that, when speaking at a national conference in 2005 on the Kazakh language issue in relation to repatriating returnees from the Kazakh diaspora,[362] I found myself in a conversation with two of Karamanuhli's colleagues who highlighted his article as representative of their views. They then went on to note the break between Tengrists and Muslims over the national language issue, with each of them ultimately forming separate national language centers aimed at Kazakh national language revival. It reveals the intimate connection between issues of national language, culture and religion in post-Soviet Central Asia, all with political overtones. Certain Tengrists have been determined to restore the ancient runic (Orkhonic Turkic) script, rejecting the Cyrillic, Arabic and Latin as all inseparably tied to foreign imperialist powers and their cultures. Meanwhile certain Muslims have advocated for a return to the Arabic script, rejecting the Cyrillic and Latin on similar grounds, but seeking greater harmony with the broader Islamic world while claiming, contra the Tengrists, that Islam is the true, historic 'way of the Kazakh fathers.'[363] Both Tengrists and Muslims lost their bids in January 2021 when the Kazakhstani government elected to return to a Soviet-era strategy followed between 1928-40, namely a modified Latin script which would help to bring them into closer accord with the international world. Tengrist historiography, however, continued on.

Akseleu Seidimbek, the late well-known and respected Kazakh scholar of clearly Tengrist persuasion, would seem to share much of the heart as well as worldview of Karamanuhli. In his 1997 work on *The Kazakh World: An Ethnocultural Exegesis*,[364] in far greater depth than Karamanuhli, he adds his voice to the debate, expressing dismay with the way in which Islam, with the aid of another destructive power—Tsarist Russia—came, historically, to "spot" and ultimately displace what he conceives to be a previously pristine Turkic world. Seidimbek bemoans the course of events, saying:

> Unfortunately, pure Turkic history, which was handed down via the earlier oral history of the Steppe, has come to be spotted with the history of Islam. ...Through the support of the Russian emperor [read: Catherine II] the religion of Islam – which until that time only a limited number of 'kozha' families held – grew stronger and stronger. With every passing year, dozens of Tatar mullahs, acting as missionaries, began to come, flowing like a river onto the Kazakh Steppe. As unconstrained as the wind they made the Kazakhs bow down in submission, casting the hell of colonization into their consciousness.[365]

It is no accident that both Karamanuhli's and Seidimbek's interpretations of Kazakh Islamic history are built upon the commonly held view that the Kazakhs were forcibly converted to Islam and that, especially in the more northerly reaches, it had not deeply penetrated the Kazakh steppe until the later eighteenth and nineteenth centuries. Such approaches, as noted by Gabitov (see Chapter 1), open the door to possible resurgence of a former 'native' tradition, if indeed their historiographical interpretations hold true. But that is precisely the point: to ascertain the true interpretation of Kazakh history in order to restore it in purest fashion, with a view to the present and future. In pursuing that agenda, Seidimbek reaches back as far in time as one can go, asking:

> ...how can it be said that the world religions of Zoroastrianism, Buddhism, Judaism, [Christianity] and Islam came into the world by mere coincidence in areas bordering on the regions inhabited by the Central Eurasian nomads? Will you deny that the main tenets of the religion of Tengrism became the fabric forming the origins of these world religions? For, in wrapping up the matter, what we call the religion of Tengrism was the original worldview of humankind through which they sought to master time and space and come to terms of agreement with one another in their surrounding shared space. (pp. 95–96)

Islam (together with all world faiths) is thus subjugated to a derived, secondary status, a corrupted religious 'survival' representing degeneration from an originally pure monotheistic Tengrism, with Tengrism itself being extolled as "the original worldview of humankind." And so, with one stroke of the pen, Seidimbek has resolved the entire debate over the origins and history of religion[366] and all humankind is invited, together with the Kazakhs, to return to this pristine source of truth and human vitality. As we shall soon see, the same claim to origins is asserted by certain advocates of Islam among the Kazakhs, just as it has been by multiple other apologists of the various world faiths throughout the centuries, including the 'degenerationists' against which Tylor and his cohorts fought (see Chapter 2).[367]

In both Karamanuhli and Seidimbek, along with other Tengrist advocates, a strong 'naturalist' emphasis can be observed which both draws from and contributes to modern ecological and environmental concerns being expressed in the debates over global warming and climate change while at the same time taking on anti-modernist features.[368]

Appearing the same year as Karamanuhli and Seidimbek (1997) was also Abdizhapar Abdakimuhli, who, within his larger framework of Kazakh history, presented the "[t]he Turkic nomads standing in opposition against the religion of Islam for nearly one thousand years."[369] Not surprisingly, he echoes both Karamanuhli and Seidimbek in dating the penetration of Islam among the Kazakhs late in their history, coming via outside influence from the Uzbek south and Tatar north, with again aid from Tsarist Russia (p. 104). In places "where Islam quickly established its glory," it "conformed the entire essence of culture to what it dictated," with "[t]he religious pietists destroying the Turkic literature, saying they were 'the writings of Satan, the Devil'" (p. 95). This harkens back to al-Biruni's eleventh-century critique of the Arab destruction of Khorezm's cultural, linguistic and literary heritage; it served a similar role as 'historical evidence' marshaled by Bisenov and other Soviet Kazakh writers in their anti-Islamic diatribes (see Chapter 7). It is a specific claim which Bulutai counters from his pro-Islamic position (see below). In taking this approach, Abdakimuhli likens the Islamic conquests of Central Asia to Tsarist and Soviet Russian imperialism, insinuating that both of the latter twin powers actually took inspiration and drew lessons from the former:

> Let us speak simply and straightforwardly with respect to the truth: it is known that, in the view of Christians and those adhering to other religions, at one time the Arabs also in the days of their warring raids held to exactly this kind of political policy. Thus, it is right to understand this political policy of Tsarism as one for which they found support by leaning upon the practical experience of those who went before them. For the political policy of Christianization and Russification, which found a niche for itself and was continued for centuries, came to serve the causes of the Dvoryans and Pomeshchiks of the Tsar's empire, and later of the Bolsheviks who were coming to be awakened.[370]

It should nonetheless be noted that no explicit Tengrist declaration is found in Abdakimuhli. Indeed, in a 2008 article on "Religion and Language," he focused on the idea of 'sacred languages' in relation to the world religious traditions, particularly Buddhism, Christianity and Islam, quoting quite liberally from the Qur'an in a fairly positive manner. One might sense that his views over the years have undergone transformation, possibly bringing about deeper appreciation of Islamic faith in relation to Kazakh culture, which would be quite understandable amidst Islam's increasing ascendancy within the continuing dialogue.[371]

Some five years later, in 2002, a more nuanced, moderating voice would appear placing an affirmative study of Tengrism in positive relation to Islam within the larger context of *The Study of Religion*, both in general terms of the world's various religious traditions and specifically those within the social, cultural and political milieu of Kazakhstan. This was the work of **Serik T. Amirgazin**[372] who dedicated chapter five in his book to "The Religion of Tengrism—the Wellspring of Our Spirituality."[373] There, he insists that "the deep meaning of Tengrism was not just Heaven, but the very religious beginnings which gave birth to the original religious beliefs of the Kazakh people" (p. 54). In this, he echoes Karamanuhli.

Tengrism's essential features—which he suggests are shared with Confucianism and Zoroastrianism and still evident today—are: "1. To place no limits upon the Almighty Creator in Heaven; 2. To earnestly fulfill the traditional ways ('osietter') which the forefathers have handed down; 3. To be a model to and instruct the young generation in the [Kazakh's] traditional lifeways, the lifeways handed down by the forefathers" (p. 53). His emphasis upon the Kazakh ancestors and their traditional ways of life as the heart of Tengrism is clear, which, in his view, should lead to "the living of a worthy life in this world" as "the primary purpose of the religion of Tengrism" (p. 54). The intimate and important connection between these matters is seen later when he explains that: "The worldview which birthed a people's unique ways of life also gives shape to the distinct essence of the religion" (p. 56). "Thus, the custom of respecting nature, and the custom of esteeming people or ancestors is formed from out of the foundations of Tengrism which [itself] has been formed from out of the ethnonational ('ulttik') worldview" (p. 60). In all this, he is directly in line with Seidimbek and Karamanuhli, the latter of whom he draws from explicitly as an "essential" bibliographic source for his chapter.[374]

But not only traditionalism grounded in the way of the forefathers, Amirgazin's association of Tengri, the God of Heaven, with monotheism is likewise clear, a point on which he goes beyond Seidimbek and Karamanuhli. This is glimpsed not only in his enumeration of Tengrism's first essential feature, but is made explicit when he later insists that the cases he highlights "provide the basis for concluding ('tizhirim zhasau') that the religion of the ancient Turks was a monotheistic religion of a single God," citing among other evidences a quote from the tenth-century Arab Muslim geographer al-Maqdisi. He clarified earlier, however, that "while Buddhism is founded upon confession of 'the Four Noble Truths', Christianity 'the one God in three forms', and Islam 'There is no God but Allah, and Muhammad is his prophet', the religion of Tengrism is founded upon acknowledgement of heaven as Father and earth as Mother" (p. 53). From its "very beginnings," "rituals of [animal] sacrifice ('kurbandik shalu') were spread widely in connection to this faith" (p. 57). In the time of the ancient Turk khaganate (6–8th cc.), "this Tengrist religion rose to the level of a state religion" closely associated with the khan, which, through the later Mongols, eventually led to its "reaching the status of a world religion" able to "take its place alongside Christianity, Islam, Buddhism or whichever of the world's religions may have existed at that time" (p. 57). He, however, would seem to differ with Seidimbek in suggesting that, in general, "there is no need to search for the traces of Christianity or Islam from out of Tengrism," though he nonetheless considers that "Murat Adji's opinion about the acceptance of Christ as the son of God ('Tangirining uhli') occurring through the close contact of Christians with the steppe peoples comes close to the truth" (pp. 59–60).[375]

More importantly, Amirgazin's conclusion almost echoes Karamanuhli's:

[A]t present this solidified religious faith is reviving and bringing nourishment to our lives. ...new research about Tengrism is being undertaken, becoming the cause for new perspectives and hypotheses to come forth. For in the present time, even though we claim that we belong to the Sunni Muslim community[376] the traces of Tengrism appear dominant within the process of our [seeking a] pure understanding, within our unique mentality. On top of that, if we call to mind that the primary form of Islamic teaching which has been spread across our territory is that of Akhmet Yasawi's Sufism (a religiously mystical path),[377] then the unique shape of our Eurasian features become ever clearer. ...Therefore we can say with confidence that one of the chief sources of our spirituality in the present day is lying within the conceptual origins of the religion of Tengrism. Still more, when speaking about the traditions of our fathers, our customs and mindset, and our cultural lifeways, the primary problem pressing upon us is that of discovering how, in later years, spiritual subordination ('sabaktastik') occurred only directly with various forms of adherence to Islam. ...It seems the only longings which remain are those saying that with the sorting out of the syncretism (or synthesis) of Islam and that of the faith of the steppe nomads the work is finished.

With these sentiments, Amirgazin ends his treatment of Tengrism and moves into his next chapter on "World Religions." There he treats four main topics: Buddhism, Christianity, Islam and "the impact of the world religions in Kazakhstan." While the entire chapter is engaging, what concerns us here is his coverage of Islam and its 'impact in Kazakhstan.' After first discussing Buddhism and Christianity, he commences his section on Islam, in a manner reminiscent of Gabitov, by highlighting "the multiple myths and erroneous representations of Islamic civilization in the literature of the West and Russian Empire" which are "more than sufficient," noting five in particular which, "more than sincere ignorance of Islam, are fabrications emerging from the perspective of explicit agendas" (pp. 70–71). Again akin to Gabitov, but also Bulutai, he then reminds readers of "the [harmful] impact of the undertakings of the famous Crusades, wars of colonialism, Christian missionaries and 'businessmen'" upon both the Muslim world as well as native peoples of Central Asia, claiming at the same time that: "In contrast, in the Middle Ages within the Islamic Empire the policy of forcibly converting Christian peoples to Islam was not carried out in official manner with harshness like it was in the West. This is because, according to the foundational doctrine of the religion of Islam, a person must accept Allah of their own free will" (pp. 71–72). Indeed, this view is reflected when, several pages later, he treats "the process by which Islam spread" in the territory of Central Asia and Kazakhstan. In stark contrast to Karamanuhli, Abdakimuhli, and Seidimbek (cf. also Baieke below), there is not a hint of the sword, forced conversion, or the destruction of culture; rather, he notes "the importance of the undertakings of missionaries" (p. 74). The closest he comes to mentioning 'force' is in addressing "the main reasons for the spread of Islam on the Kazakh steppe," where, in his fourth of five reasons, he says "the religion of Islam was not simply spread through force and war, Muslim missionaries also have a prominent role in propagating it" (p. 75). But this passing nod is minimized as a contrasting scenario. Between his brief summary of Islam's historical spread in Kazakhstan and the reasons for it, he does, however, note that "it is appropriate for each person to present Islam's coming to the Kazakh steppe from the position of their own perspective" (p. 74). His own view is clearly positive and embracing, perhaps leaving room for his fellow Tengrists to take differing perspectives.

As for Islam's relation to Tengrism, Amirgazin names Islam, at the very start of the chapter, as "the youngest world religious teaching" (p. 63). This prepares the way for his envisioned merging of Islam with Tengrism in the historical outworking of Central Asia's destiny, which reflects a refined approach in comparison with Karamanhuli, one which verges on that of Nurtazina and Esim (see below), though with Tengrism, not Islam, apparently maintaining primacy. Indeed, he anticipates Nurtazina by noting that among the five reasons for its spread among the Kazakhs are "Islam's compatibility with the precepts of a kinship-patriarchal system" and "the non-contradictory nature of Shari'ah law with the rules of Kazakh custom in multiple situations" (p. 75). In similar fashion, "we also agree with the opinion that, 'as social research has shown, religious adherents often embrace Islam like a national custom because the majority of its religious and daily-life rituals are connected to ancient practices of their ancestors" (p. 75). And yet, if after concluding his chapter on Tengrism he leaves us with the impression that Tengrism, not Islam, does and even should take primacy, he draws his chapter on Islam among the world religions to a close on an equally high note, claiming that: "The religion of Islam is found to be the continuation of all the world religions which came before it and the limits to which the process of growing in spiritual perspective can soar" (p. 77).

He, thus, in the end, appears to place Tengrism and Islam on near-equal footing, viewing Tengrism as the historical root and foundation and Islam the capstone and crowning glory of Kazakh spirituality in the post-Soviet period, each continuing together to contribute vital nourishment to the overall well-being of the Kazakh people. Such an approach certainly reflects his views on "The Aims of the Religious Education – Securing Unity and Solidarity," which was the title of a conference paper he presented at a joint Kazakh-Turkish international symposium held in Kazakhstan in 2011.[378]

ISLAMIC APPROACHES AND CHRISTIAN INTERLUDES

A clear and calculated Muslim response to Tengrist as well as Shamanist and Christian missionary historiography was to be found in the work of Murtaza Bulutai, *The Religion of the Fathers*.[379] Bulutai is a returnee from the Kazakh diaspora in Turkey, the son of a mosque leader there. He repatriated to Kazakhstan in 1994 with the explicit purpose of reviving Islam among the Kazakhs[380] as well as other Central Asian Turkic peoples (pp. X–XI). He might, in general, share the preference expressed for Islam by Esim, Gabitov and others, but he takes a decidedly firmer and more exclusivist view. Before addressing Islam's relation to other religions however, he, in the "Foreword" (ibid.), contrasts three main respective interpretations of Islam within Kazakh history which he sees actively competing with one another in the post-Soviet period. The first is the atheistic perspective, a leftover product of the Soviet era. In the eyes of atheists Islam is a backward, archaic hindrance to progress and civilization, one which must be done away with and left behind (cf. Esim above). The second is the Kazakh nationalist perspective which sees Islam as belonging primarily to the national cultural heritage, a central representation and even determiner of 'Kazakhness,' as in the views expressed by Esim and Gabitov. The third, in Bulutai's opinion, is the correct, truly Islamic view, one which, "while maintaining a proper love for its own people and land of birth, is the view of those scholars and authors who consider Islam the greatest treasure of all, those who exalt its humanitarian contributions, who are forward-looking, scholarly and progressive."

But Bulutai goes well beyond this in his detailed discussion of Central Asian religious history, combined as it is with related discussions addressing the proper theological and philosophical as well as historical relation between religion, culture and political state. The whole vast undertaking, nearly 500 pages in all, is aimed at demonstrating beyond all doubt that Islam is, in his eyes, "the greatest treasure of all," not only for his Kazakh and other Turkic Central Asian kin, but the entire world, though he remains clearly focused on convincing the former, not the latter. A cursory glance at some of the topics he addresses helps to elucidate his perspective. They include: "Islam, the True Religion," "Islam's Exceptional Characteristics," "The 'Correctness' ('hak bolui') of Islam," "The Brave Heroism of Muslims," "The Belief of Intelligent People," "The Deficiency of Other Beliefs and Faiths," "The Freedom Granted to Other Religions," "The Truth About Accusations [Against Islam]," "Was Islam Spread by the Sword?..." "Did Muslims Destroy Languages?," "What Kind of Politics were Involved in the Spread of Islam?," "Political 'Fatih' and the Spread of Islam" and "Which is the [True] Religion of Our Fathers?"

Concerning the latter question in particular, Bulutai answers historically, insisting:

> One truth is certain: We can observe the way in which the polytheistic religions in the named region [of Central Asia] came, little-by-little, to vanish away, being replaced by monotheistic faiths, ultimately culminating in the end in the establishment of the true religion of Islam. ...Paying no mind

to the contrary propaganda and unrelenting stubborn resistance of these [other former] religions which was carried on by their members and missionary societies as well as their political and military powers and groups sharing a common cause, Islam overcame all challenges, finding its way into the people's hearts, and in all the inhabited places along the Silk Road – which had turned into an arena of competition for many religions – it emerged victor, sealing its place as the one, unified religion of the region. (pp. 1, 6)

He thus takes a competition-oriented triumphalist approach achieved through a diffusionist-progressivist-fulfillment vision of Central Asian and even broader world history. He believes, like Seidimbek, that all religious expressions of humankind began with an alleged original form, but for Bulutai it is a form of Islam, not Tengrism, referred to as 'hanif dini,' or 'religion of the true believers,' with all subsequent manifestations of religious expression in human history being derived from this original source, devolving into corrupt 'survivals' over time, and ultimately destined to return to and be fulfilled through their properly restored form which came through Muhammad.[381]

He calls all the non-monotheistic faiths "crude" (Kzk. 'turpaii'),[382] counting them idolatrous. Meanwhile, as seen above, all faiths except Islam are viewed in terms of their "contrary propaganda and unrelenting stubborn resistance." For Christianity, he offers a special extended chapter (pp. 133–151) to demonstrate not only its "contrary propaganda and unrelenting stubborn resistance," but its gross theological errors. He climaxes his treatment of it by quoting at length from another well-known Kazakh scholar's work on Turkic history,[383] condemning in the strongest possible terms the Russian Orthodox missions among the Turkic peoples, particularly the Tatars and Kazakhs, in which he highlights the destruction of mosques, forced conversions, confiscation of land, etc. (pp. 150–51). Elsewhere in the book, as well as in other works, he displays a strong distaste for other forms of Western Christianity, American in particular, ridiculing their alleged backward (i.e., anti-scientific and anti-progressive) and 'fundamentalist' tendencies.[384] All this reflects his deep concern with and strong opposition to the rise of Western Protestant (and limited Catholic) missionary efforts among the Kazakhs in the post-Soviet period, coupled with his distaste for Western dominance in world affairs. Indeed, the entire chapter on Christianity, in spite of focusing primarily on the ancient Church of the East (mis-named the

'Nestorian' Church) in Central Asia, seems aimed at undermining any potential influence from or appeal to that historic tradition by modern Christian missionaries, with Bulutai explicitly noting his concern over any such attempts at several junctures.

Indeed, Bulutai saw the writing on the wall, for joining the debate just several years down the road from a Kazakh Christian perspective would be Manarbek Baieke, a Kazakh historian who embraced Christianity in its Protestant Evangelical form and took up the task of researching the history of Christianity in Central Asia in order to use it as grounds for promoting the spread of Christianity in the region in the post-Soviet period, presenting it as the revival of a lost, historic faith. In 2004, he produced an article in Kazakh (with translations into Russian and English) entitled "A Brief History of Religions in Central Asia and Its Significance for the Spread of Christianity in this Region," going on to complete a full-length manuscript on *The History of Christianity in Kazakhstan and Central Asia* in 2006.[385]

Baieke's view of the history of Islam in Central Asia follows the same basic contours found in the more critical Tengrist perspectives of Karamanuhli and Seidimbek highlighted above, namely that it came as a religion of force and oppression converting the Turkic peoples against their will, damaging their traditional culture and never really penetrating that deeply among the Kazakhs until late in their history, if even then (pp. 174–191). In the process of describing that history, Baieke quotes from a hotly contested work published in Almaty in 1993 which claims to be a reprint of a manuscript originally published by a certain Kazakh named Kazibek bek Tauasaruhli in 1776.[386] Some of the central points of debate over that work are precisely the passages quoted by Baieke, namely the author's assertions that: "I do not consider it appropriate the way some pseudo-mullahs go about saying that our forefathers are, in praiseworthy fashion, descended from some Arabs, or Noah. We are the descendants of a people who lived when there was no religion of Islam" (cf. Seidimbek above).[387] The same author likewise insists, with respect to those Kazakhs who had embraced Islam, "you have turned away from (our) religion," adding later, after a scathing critique cast in poetic form of the way in which Muslims behaved and treated others, "if this is what being a Muslim is, we have no need of such."[388] Tauasaruhli associated himself—and not by mere coincidence—with the Kerei and Naiman clans, that is, the two distinct clans from among the Kazakh ancestors documented in the historical records to have converted to Christianity in its eastern form.[389]

Following from his references to Tauasaruhli, Baieke goes on to say:

> The Turks could not (find it within themselves to) cast aside their Christian faith in Jesus which had been solidified among them before Islam's coming and embrace Islam, thus running headlong into a spiritual check on their faith. As the Arabs increased in strength, they placed all kinds of restrictions upon the Turks' (Christian) faith, turning their church buildings into mosques and repressing them socially. Now the Turks, left to wander aimlessly like sheep without a shepherd, mixed together all of the faiths found in their history—Shamanism, Judaism, Tengrism, Zoroastrianism, Buddhism, Manichaeism, and Christianity—filling up the ancient nomad's worship of the God of Heaven, Tengrism, with the Christian symbol of the cross and turning it into their own unique syncretistic religion, reviving that faith for a final time within this confusing epoch of history, and then seeming to vanish away. (p. 192)

This is how he factors Tengrism into the mix, accusing in the process scholars like Murat Adji of "apparently confusing who influenced who," since Adji in several notable publications (released in Kazakh, Russian and English) takes the position that European Christians borrowed the symbol of the cross from the Turks of Central Asia.[390]

After thus recounting Central Asian religious history with an emphasis on the presence of Christianity via the ancient Church of the East (ca. 50–1500 CE),[391] Mongol-era Roman Catholicism (1245–1404 CE),[392] and later European Protestant (ca. 1800–1917 CE)[393] and Russian Orthodox missions (ca. 1865–1917 CE) in the Tsarist era, all topped off by the re-introduction of Christianity among the Kazakhs and other Turkic peoples via Western Protestant and Catholic missions in the post-Soviet period, Baieke concludes his formidable 375-page study, replete with documentation, by claiming: "With that Christianity came back to life in the very place in Eurasia where it was said to have gone off into oblivion in the fifteenth century."[394] It should be noted that Baieke does, along the way, highlight times of peace historically between Christians and Muslims (e.g., p. 199), emphasizing in his conclusion peaceful co-existence within the religious-political conditions of post-Soviet independent Kazakhstan (pp. 365–377).

Bulutai's apologetic against Christianity—formidable in its own right and replete itself with documentation—was thus not without prophetic sense or purpose. Though apparently directed at the Western Christian threat to post-Soviet Islamic revival, his inclusion of and even climax on the destructive nature of Russian Orthodox missions among the Central Asian Muslims contained a clear warning against all forms of that once historic faith in the region.[395]

Only "Shamanism," because of its deep, long historic influence among the Central Asian peoples right down to the present day, receives comparable attention (pp. 103–112), albeit only half that afforded Christianity. This is perhaps surprising since Bulutai, though clearly recognizing and expressing his concern over the reviving appeal of 'Tengrism' among Kazakh neo-traditionalists and cultural nationalists in the post-Soviet era, nonetheless offers comparatively minimal treatment of that historic native tradition. He does not even offer it separate attention via its own distinct chapter, but covers it under the heading of 'polytheism.' His concern with and concentrated apologetic against religious traditions associated with 'Tengrism' comes three years later in 2003. This reflects the mounting influence of the Tengrist position in the early 2000s. Bulutai responds in a small booklet entitled *The Truth About Burkhanism*.[396] The booklet is drawn from a series of newspaper articles which formed a public debate between himself and Murat Auezov, former head of the National Public Library of Kazakhstan and grandson of the well-known Kazakh literary figure Mukhtar Auezov. In it, Bulutai makes a point of calling into question the work of George Soros and his foundation among foreign nations such as Kazakhstan and then quotes Auezov in an interview sponsored by Soros as saying:

> In the mountainous region of Altai there is a tribe called the Kerei who have remained since the days of the era of the ancient Turks. They themselves say that 'we have survived to this day, preserving the heart of the Turkic ways'. And as they say, so it is. They have a religion called 'Burkhanism'. And we can say that this 'Burkhanism', which arose in the 19th and beginning of the 20th centuries, is a new form of Tengrism. (pp. 9–10)

Bulutai (p. 10) asks "why Auezov, working as a servant on behalf of and answerable to the Soros Foundation, gives an extended interview and in place of Islam, the religion of the Kazakhs, preaches a faith like 'Burkhanism', which, like a soup made of three stocks, does not mix with our people?" The intimation is that foreigners—particularly in this case, amidst the recently begun 'War on Terror' and 'Iraq War,'

Americans—are behind certain efforts to undermine the Islamic faith among the Kazakhs. He then goes on (pp. 10–11) to offer five reasons why Auezov is mistaken, pointing out quite correctly that Burkhanism is an indigenous cultural resistance movement which arose in opposition to Tsarist Russian imperialism and which emerged from a mixing of Shamanism and Buddhism in the course of the Altai national independence struggle.[397] It is here that he insists 'Tengrism' and 'Burkhanism' are as far apart as "heaven and earth," having virtually nothing to do with one another. The remainder of the booklet goes on to detail his case against Auezov's assertions[398] in highly accusative and condemning fashion.

More than Tengrism (though often associated with it), Bulutai expresses his concern, even outright opposition, to "The Cult of the Forefathers" (aka "Ancestors"), devoting his entire seventh section (out of nine total) to that "problem" (pp. 382–422). In Bulutai's view: "What we call the cult of the ancestors (ancestral servitude) is the complex of beliefs and practices which have arisen as a result of faith in the establishment of relations between the dead and the living, their communicating with one another, and the preserving of relations between family members" (p. 382). For Bulutai, such a "cult" has always been "a component of especially a polytheistic faith complex" which most typically "takes shape...among primitive societies" (pp. 382 and 384). Bulutai thus adopts, like many such Muslim apologists, Western secular -- including Tsarist Russian -- historiography (see Chapter 2 and 4) as well as Tylor and the nineteenth-century 'history of religion' school, and the later Soviets (see Chapter 2, 6 and 7). Indeed, "idol worship took its start from the grave stones of (national) heroes, of those who remained in the collective memory of the nation" (p. 408). Bulutai thus equates "the cult of the ancestors" with idolatry, responding to those who claim "the Kazakhs are a people who pray to and venerate the spirits of the ancestors" by highlighting that "[t]he Kazakh people emerged upon the stage of history in the fifteenth-sixteenth centuries as a Muslim people" (p. 390). In other words, being Muslim is juxtaposed against 'the cult of ancestor veneration' so that the former leaves no room for the latter. His views are equally applicable to saint veneration, which creates further tension over the passionate devotion and central place awarded to Qoja Akhmet Yasawi and his sacred shrine in Turkistan within the Kazakh and broader Central Asian Islamic world.

That Bulutai continued to maintain and even promote this basic position in the ensuing years is reflected in the opposition expressed in a newspaper-internet article published in September 2012 by Aziret Barbol entitled "Bulutai is going about perverting and corrupting the religion of the fathers."[399] Barbol is clearly playing off the title of Bulutai's book *The Religion of the Fathers* and, indeed, names the book and its author in the first line. But the primary issue for which he takes Bulutai to task is reflected in the two quotes he places front and center at the very start of his piece, the first and most important coming from the then honored leader of Kazakhstan, President Nazarbaev himself:

> "The spirits of the fathers—ancestral spirits—nourish and feed me on a daily basis. A religious sense and faith in (the spirits of) my fathers—this is my main affair. I know that the ancestral spirits have upheld my forefathers, and in the same way I believe in their nourishing and feeding of me. You see, in my understanding the Kazakhs must have lived in this way within traditional, classical Kazakh nomadic society. ...So then, the ideal of our forefathers is in accordance with the most sacred held beliefs and practices of our lives today."[400]

Barbol then goes on to defend Kazakh ancestor veneration contra Bulutai. Reflecting public concern for the controversy, Barbol's article stirred a long discussion thread running from September to November 2012 (ibid.).

Eliciting similar opposition from fellow countrymen and women, Bulutai, in *The Religion of the Fathers*, likewise challenges any and all historical and sentimental attachment the Kazakhs may have to their nomadic heritage, claiming:

> ...we should re-examine the widely held idea that our forefathers were nomads. Nomadic culture is not an advanced, developed step [in the historical-cultural process]. Looking at the cultural (sedentary) lifeway which existed 3000-3500 years ago in Kazakhstan, we can say that our ancient ancestors were not nomads, but cultured peoples. 'Cultured' means sedentary, settled dwellers, inhabitants of the city. 'Cultured' is a word meaning 'city'. To be 'cultured' is to be a city-dweller, sedentary, and 'culture' means the way of life in the city, sedentary life. (pp. 23–24)

He thus confronts head on the nomadic steppe culture which the Kazakhs inherited and preserved throughout nearly the entire span of their existence as a distinct people, from 1466 to the present, with that heritage reaching back into the history of the Central Asian steppe peoples in continuous unbroken succession some 3000 years, surviving down to the early mid-twentieth-century collectivization campaigns under Stalin, with leftover remnants still noticeably lingering into the late twentieth-, early twenty-first-century post-Soviet era.[401] His opposition to nomadism is most likely due to its strong association with Tengrism, Shamanism, ancestor veneration and other socio-religious ideas and practices. Bulutai explicitly grounds his approach in a 'civilizationist' worldview in which 'culture' and 'civilization,' and with them 'cultured' and 'civilized' ways of life, are defined primarily in terms of sedentary city-based existence. This is founded upon the prophet Muhammad's example established via his move (i.e., 'hejira') to and settling of the first Muslim community in the city of Medina, with 'Medina' meaning simply 'City,' from which comes the derived Kazakh term for 'culture' (Kzk. 'madeniet'). As indicated by his use of the phrase "advanced, developed step," Bulutai, like many modern Muslim apologists, mixes this argument with Western secular progressivist historiography.

Tengrism aside, these latter two points—on ancestral veneration and nomadic culture—mark rather radical distinctions in Bulutai's approach to the problem of the relation of Islam and Kazakh culture, one which stands in sharp contrast to and even seeks to overturn the views of Kazakh history and identity in relation to steppe nomadic culture prevalent among much of the Kazakh scholarly and broader national community.

Nazira Nurtazina, in her 2003 work on *Kazakh Culture and Islam*, shares a clearly Islamic heart with Bulutai, but she takes a markedly different approach, insisting that, for the Kazakhs, "[t]he nomadic way of life must be valued as a magnificent phenomenon." [402] She argues for a historically, progressively achieved near-perfect synthesis between Islam and Kazakh nomadic culture inclusive of Tengrism. Indeed, the relationship between the two is entirely natural, almost seamless within the progressive and even foreordained flow of events, for:

> The Turkic peoples considered 'the Lord of Heaven', 'the God of the Sky' to be the most high god. ...If we say that nomadism itself was like a natural-psychological preparation for the religion of Islam, we must also add that the religion of Tengrism as well, in comparison with other world religions, displays a tendency toward monotheism. As time progressed, this

monotheistic tendency grew ever-stronger with the influence of the developed religions and, in the end, joined itself in time with the religion of Islam. In other words, we can see clear foundational principles within the worldview of the nomadic and Turkic peoples which led them to an effortless acceptance of monotheism and the Muslim religion. (ibid.)

Nurtazina comes close here to Amirgazin's view in suggesting such a natural relationship between Central Asian nomadic culture and Islam, though Amirgazin appears to retain Tengrism as dominant in the end. Other Tengrists like Seidimbek use the argument to claim that Islam was a corrupt 'survival' of their own more prior and pristine faith as part of their call for the people of Turkic nomadic heritage to return to the original 'way of their fathers' (see above). But Nurtazina is well aware of the surrounding context of debate in which she is participating, and addresses the issue head on:

Here we consider it appropriate to raise a very important theoretical problem, for opinions which have no basis in scholarship, but are filled with patriotism and nationalism are, in spite of becoming less common in recent days, still being heard, such as 'What need was there, then, for Islam? We had our own magnificent tradition of the ancient Turkic nomads,' 'the Arab-Islamic factor corrupted us'. (ibid.)

Her attempted solution to this dilemma rests on a "strict law of history" which, in her view, requires that "Tengrism had to be exchanged" with Islam as the perceived pinnacle of the "new, ethical religions" represented by the monotheistic faiths. They are "new" in the sense that they allegedly all followed and even arose from Tengrism, posited as it is as a non-ethical religion and, thus, at an allegedly earlier stage in the morally progressive development of humankind. The influence here again of late nineteenth-, early twentieth-century linear-progressivist secular views of history is clear, with Nurtazina even referencing Arnold Toynbee and others in her appeals to such envisioned 'laws of history.' However she achieves it though, it is for her a "necessary conclusion, the fruit of the meeting and joining together in kinship fashion of that traditional heritage and culture and the religion of Islam, which developed in close relationship with nomadic ways and came to be not only the inheritance of the ancient Turks, but a significant spiritual force impacting the entire history of humankind."[403] Nurtazina went on to express all these views in a booklet co-authored with another female Kazakh scholar, N.D. Khasanaeva, entitled *Historical Prerequisites for the Islamization of the Ancient Turks*, published in 2010.[404]

More crucial for the Kazakhs, however, than any general 'law of history' is, in Nurtazina's view, their own law of honoring their ancestors. It is no mere coincidence that both the Muslims and Tengrists brilliantly craft their appeal, to use the title of Bulutai's book, around *The Religion of the Fathers*. Indeed, the Tengrists are essentially writing the same book, only the subtitle of theirs would not be, as Bulutai's, *Why Did the Turks Become Muslims?*, but, as we have seen, *Why Did the Turks Abandon Tengrism?* While the options are certainly more complex, those in particular who have been imbued with the anti-traditionalist mindset of the rationalistic post-Enlightenment West have difficulty appreciating let alone recognizing the importance of this matter within the Central Asian worldview, stoked now as its fires are to even more intense degrees by the collapse of the anti-traditionalist Soviet assault. The stakes are high and the strategies crucial. Thus Nurtazina, like Bulutai, leaves no room for historical mishap or reversal.

Garifolla Esim, as already hinted at in passing comments on the subject in 1996 (see above), develops further, some 11 years later, a 'closed door' approach on the past. He takes the same essential view as Bulutai (and Seidimbek), namely that one, true religion has always existed since the beginning of human history and has never itself changed. The only thing which has changed and, thus, produced corrupted forms (cf. 'survivals') of that religion is human understanding. It is for this reason that Muhammad, whose "light" was known before ever he appeared, came to deliver humanity from its strayed paths. "We can, therefore, say that we have been in the way of Muhammad, that we were Muslims from the very beginning of time."[405] This is why Esim considers as crude and lost those who, as he puts it, claim that "Islam is not the religion of our fathers, in the past we believed in the God of Heaven (Kzk. Kok Tengir), our religion is Tengrism, Islam came and destroyed Tengrism, let us therefore turn away from Islam and once again return to Tengrism." Insisting that the essence of time is change, and that history therefore depends on change, he explains that the idea of reviving the past is what 'renaissance' is all about, and this is precisely why the Kazakh fathers adopted Islam, because it brought the religion of Tengrism to new levels of maturity and development. In other words, in Esim's view the acceptance of Islam by the Kazakh fathers is itself a return to Tengrism, a renewal and revival of it, only in a new and improved form.

We see, then, Bulutai, Nurtazina and Esim (as well as Seidimbek from a Tengrist view) all taking a similar approach to the historical relation of Tengrism and Islam, each with their own unique vantage. In further comparison of their respective approaches, the vision of Islam which both Nurtazina and Esim share is identified primarily through its Sufi mystical and later Jadidist cultural reformist expressions, whereas Bulutai tends to emphasize a city-based 'orthodox' Islam located primarily in scriptures, mosques, medreses and more traditional, conservative scholars. This distinction in approach is perhaps attributable, in part, to the fact that Bulutai is a Kazakh raised in the city-based culture of Turkey with its glorious Ottoman legacy, the son himself of a mosque leader, while Nurtazina and Esim are native Kazakhs of Kazakhstan, with Nurtazina writing from the heart of Kazakh Sufi saint devotion, the holy city of Turkistan, home of the mausoleum of Qoja Akhmet Yasawi (d. 1166), patron saint of the Yasawi Sufi order which became one of the primary vehicles (together with the Naqshbandiya) through which the Turkic steppe nomads were converted to Islam.[406] It is a heritage which Esim likewise deeply esteems. For especially Nurtazina and Bulutai, this marks a distinction in their respective approaches not only in relation to the broader Kazakh nomadic heritage, but to its deep-rooted traditions of 'aruak' (i.e., ancestor) and intimately related saint devotion. Bulutai seeks to significantly downplay those traditions, even calling significant portions of them idolatrous, whereas Nurtazina seems much more willing to embrace and defend them as important components of the Kazakh cultural and Islamic synthesis which she champions. And in her view, that synthesis is vital for the post-Soviet revival of both, for "[i]f the study of Islam is not intentionally combined with the study of what it means to be Kazakh, then the spiritual renaissance which we all long for will remain as empty words, a daydream on the face of a sheet of paper."[407]

Tursin Hafiz Gabitov, a long-time professor of religious, cultural and philosophical studies at al-Farabi Kazakh National University,[408] takes a similar approach, predating Nurtazina by a good many years in a number of his works, which touch on various aspects of the subject. Most explicitly and concisely, Gabitov set forth the complexity of these matters in a chapter treating "Relational Dynamics of Religious Systems among the Kazakhs." There he addresses the historically oriented competition to revive past traditions among his people, noting that "[i] n the last years, many works have been published and many dissertations defended on the topic of these religious systems," namely the Tengrist and Shamanic traditions.[409] Gabitov's suggested solution to the dilemma is in realizing that "the Tengrist religion is discovered to be a religious system which is more suited to the needs of a Eurasian nomadic economico-cultural type of people. The period of its dawning in Turkic history coincides with the time of the union, according to the principal of nationhood, of the Turkic and Mongol tribes and their establishing of steppe empires."[410] His assessment gives Tengrism, in particular, a highly political twist, as indeed it carries, making it all the more a formidable challenger to certain aspirations of Islam within the Central Asian context.[411]

According to the same logic, Islam, in Gabitov's view, established itself among the Kazakhs because it proved better suited to the changing environment of the steppe nomads, thus yielding what might be called a 'Tengrist' and an 'Islamic era' within the framework of Kazakh religious history. But further reflection on Gabitov's view—shared by numerous colleagues—reveals his belief that all the previous religious traditions of the Kazakhs remain, to one degree or another, wrapped up in the present: "The various religious systems of the Kazakh people across the centuries cannot be seen as types that were replacing one another. As a rule, in certain historical periods, religious systems co-existed simultaneously, in syncretism or synthesis, depending on which view is held. One of them typically becomes dominant in relation only to a particular form of spiritual culture."[412] Along these lines, Gabitov and several other Kazakh scholars in a co-authored article on "Islam and the Values of Kazakh Culture" argue that, "in order to be accepted by" the Central Asian Turkic peoples,

> Islam had to accept their initial world outlook and spiritual core. This process was two-sided. ...Tengri and holy aruakhs (ancestral spirits) took on Muslim content. Sky Tengri became Allah, the aruakh turned to (Sufi) pirs... Even shamanism within the context of Kazakh culture became an element of Islam. The dance of the shaman adopted elements from Sufi actions; before his rituals, the shaman made ablutions in an Islamic way; the shaman began his words with a prayer to Allah and to the prophet Muhammad and His khalifs. ...The transformation from native religions to an Islamic form within Kazakh culture covers many centuries...

Such a view makes space for the peaceful ongoing co-existence of various religious traditions, past and present. That Gabitov is concerned to promote such a view is clear from his work with UNESCO in producing *On the Path to a Culture of Peace* in 2000, UNESCO's "International Year for the Culture of Peace."[413]

In spite, however, of Gabitov's skillful, peace-oriented employment of the paradigm of mutual co-existence, Islam remains, in the present period, decidedly dominant in his overall scheme over whatever remnants of Tengrism or other religious traditions might still exist or be revived among the Kazakhs. He thus climaxes his essay with assurance of its enduring power in the face of post-Soviet chaos and its globalizing trends[414]: "But let us turn our attention to one particular cultural and historical detail: there has never been an ethnocultural group in history that has renounced the religion of Islam."[415] Against this backdrop, he and his colleagues suggested that:

> If one is to overcome the Marxist-Soviet thesis that Islam has been imposed upon the Turks by the Arabs, then it is possible to identify the following aspects of this issue: a) Islam has played a civilizational function in the culture of Turkic people; b) on the basis of Islam, the culture of Turkic people in IX-XII centuries blossomed, and the Turkic philosophy of this period occupied one of the leading positions in the world philosophical process; c) under conditions of colonial cultures imposed on the Turkic people of Russia and China, Islam resisted the assimilatory policy of those empires and played a role in preserving their ethnic identity; d) through Arabic-language philosophy Turkic people were familiarized with the ancient (Greek) philosophic heritage.

From this vantage, conversion and ongoing adherence to Islam is concerned primarily with civilizational ethics, a broad and diverse world education, the power and means to stand against colonial oppression and the preservation of Kazakh ethnic identity.[416] Still, implicit within Gabitov's overall view is the possibility that the shifting sands of time might re-arrange the current religious-cultural configuration to achieve a new synthesis, with the door of destiny left hanging open, though not entirely to chance; it is firmly yet elusively in the hands of those seeking to shape and guide it via the very dialogue in which they are participating.

Nagima Baitenova and Kairat Zatov, in a 2006 article on "The Faiths and Beliefs of the Ancient Turks,"[417] take a more subtle approach, though one yielding, however implicitly, a similar conclusion concerning the historic relation and priority of Tengrism, Islam and other essential aspects of Kazakh culture and history. They focus their attention throughout on ancestor devotion, Tengrism and Shamanism. Along the way, the impressive tolerance and inclusiveness of Tengrism is highlighted, suggesting that it demonstrated an ability to embrace whatever faiths or beliefs came along and "synthesize" them into a new unified faith system, with explicit reference to Gabitov on that point (see above). The authors then nod briefly near the end to Buddhism, Zoroastrianism, Christianity and a few other historic faiths of Central Asia, placing Buddhism and Christianity in particular at a distance by associating the former with eastern Central Asia and the latter with foreign Silk Road merchants as opposed to indigenous Turks, with a supporting quote from William of Rubruck as to the Tengrist-Shamanist orientation of the Kazakh ancestors. This 'foreign' view of ancient Central Asian Christianity as well as Buddhism is commonly expressed among Kazakh scholars,[418] paralleling their attitude toward all modern forms of Christianity as well as Buddhism in their midst. Baitenova and Zatov draw their conclusion—and not without significance—in accordance with the balance of emphasis they have shown throughout: The only belief systems which the Turkic peoples of Central Asia have historically held are Tengrism, Shamanism and ancestor devotion with Islam alone managing to form an amenable, synthesized relationship with those "traditional faiths." The whole subtle yet brilliant thrust of the article is, thus, a tolerant, inclusive, embracing attitude toward Tengrism, Shamanism, ancestor devotion and Islam which leaves all others excluded, distant (historically and culturally), "non-traditional" (cf. foreign), and, presumably, undesirable, at least as far as any Turkic peoples are concerned.[419]

Tattygul Kartaeva, another Kazakh scholar at al-Farabi Kazakh National University, devotes an entire (20-page) section in her extensive 2014 two-volume study to "Baqshylyq," which she equates with "Shamanism." She views it as a historical tradition which has been transformed across time in its encounters with Islam and other aspects of modernity. It has nonetheless maintained, in her eyes, its integral place within the Kazakh ancestral heritage. Beyond this, she analyzes the full array of Kazakh beliefs and practices ('nanym-senimder') as well as 'folkways' ('yrym-tyimdar', cf. 'superstitions') and concludes that they all together "play a significant role in Kazakh life, embracing all aspects of that life." With her study focused on the Kazakhs of the Syr region, she holds that their folkways in particular "took their start from the religions of ancient Zoroastrianism, animism, totemism, Tengrism, fetishism and Shamanism and have merged these together with Islam in a continuing cooperative partnership." She then clarifies: "In other words, the remnants (or survivals, Kzk: сарқыншақтары) of the age when polytheism passed to monotheism have been preserved (by the Kazakhs) in the Syr region."[420]

Erke Tamabekkyzy Kartabaeva produced a monograph in 2016 on *Islam zhanye Ortagasyrlyk Turkiler* [*Islam and the Turks of the Middle Ages*]. After explicitly rejecting more radical, dogmatic, exclusivist interpretations of "Islam,"[421] Kartabaeva deals explicitly at length with "the historical-spiritual processes taking place in the region of Central Asia between the VIII-XIII centuries." She considers, for example, "the cult of saints" to be a means by which average, everyday people are able to adhere to their faith in a practical way.[422] Going well beyond this one particular case, she notes that "the spiritual world of the ancient Turks is an extremely complex issue" over which there are multiple disputes and disagreements. Whatever position one takes, Kartabaeva insists that "it is incorrect to pit 'nomadic culture' against 'Islamic culture.'"[423] The Turks did not simply embrace Islam as it came to them from the Arabs, i.e., in its Arab form. Islam and Turkic culture, including the latter's spiritual beliefs and practices, reciprocally shaped one another to forge an authentic synthesis between the two which yielded a uniquely Turkic Central Asian form of Islam. Islam "absorbed" ancient Turkic ways into its very stature.[424] The "synthesis" of the Turkic culture and Islam was, from Kartabaeva's vantage, a step toward the "integration" of the Turkic peoples "into broader humanity."[425]

Finally here, **a team of nine Kazakh historians, with N.D. Nurtazina among them**, cover the topic of "Religious beliefs: Islam in the XIV-XV Centuries: Discrete nature of the process of Islamization of Nomads" in their 2021 text *History of Kazakhstan*. They provide evidence from various sources—primary and secondary; Central Asian, Middle Eastern and 'Western'; Islamic and non-Islamic—which detail that historical "process" from the thirteenth to the fifteenth centuries. Although "the spread of Islam in the Golden Horde was not smooth" due to "open and secret opposition from Shamanists, Christians and Buddhists," "[t]he end of Islamization and consolidation of the authority of this religion [of Islam] in the tradition" came under Uzbek Khan, albeit through "his policy of eradicating separatism and anti-Muslim sentiment" by way of "intolerance, rigidity, and under the threat of punishment demanded to become orthodox Muslims." Beyond Uzbek Khan, "[t]he radical turn to Islam is connected with the name of the Chagataid Togluk Timur," i.e., Tamerlane, who took "decisive measures…to strengthen the position of Islam."[426]

All in all, "the process of Islamization…took about 600 years," from the eighth century on (cf. the Battle of Talas, 751 CE), with the thirteenth-fourteenth centuries marking "its final stage."[427] This "end of Islamization" did not, however, resolve questions of political, economic and other motives involved in the conversion process, which included both "internal and external factors" leading them to "seek for a new religion."[428] Nor did it mean the complete erasure of all 'pre-Islamic' spiritual-cultural traditions of the Central Asian Turkic peoples. It rather meant the "dominance" of Islam, especially as the new, official state religion which "finally superseded various religions and currents that had penetrated the territory of the ulus of Juchi due to different historical circumstances."[429] "The spiritual renaissance of the Golden Horde era" led to "the synthesis of Islam and nomadic cultural ideals."[430]

In spite of all this, it remains "too early to talk about the reconstruction of the spiritual and religious history of the Golden Horde" with any finality. And even once we are able,

> religion and spirituality are so subtle matters that it is impossible to believe that once established in society and the state, Islam functions automatically afterwards and thus preserves its original high status and influence. Unfortunately, many researchers have such a 'mechanistic' view of religion. In fact, especially nomadic societies that do not have stationary cultural centers (if they also fall into unfavorable geopolitical conditions, isolation, etc.) have always had a risk of de-Islamization, which is expressed in a gradual, seemingly imperceptible demoralization of the people at first glance, a decrease in literacy rates, revival of superstitions, etc. Therefore, in the following centuries, partial de-Islamization took place in the history of Kazakhstan. However, despite all contradictory phenomena, the main indicator of Islamic loyalty, i.e., self-consciousness and self-identification of the people, has always remained unchanged.[431]

The authors thus posit a distinction between a more stable psychologically grounded religious identity which may or may not align fully with shifting historical realities across time and space, i.e., the distinction between 'history and memory.' This requires historical researchers to approach their subject(s) with an attitude of flexibility and openness to both the sources and relevant facts they yield, regardless of whether they always square with the "self-consciousness and self-identification of the people." Their interpretation here also represents a unique take on the more typically linear-progressivist views, allowing as it does for ebbs and flows in religious devotion across time in relation to transformations in historical circumstances. In this, they come close to Gabitov's view, albeit with subtle distinctions.

Concluding Reflections

Present- and future-oriented revivalist efforts, at their heart, require deeply rooted historical appeals giving necessary rise to historiographical debate. This is observed in the differing interpretational approaches evidenced among Kazakh scholars and other public figures in relation to the revival of their respective faith traditions in the post-Soviet context. These interpretational approaches clearly draw from past Tsarist and Soviet historiography (see Chapters 4, 5, 6, 7 and Appendix One), each for their own distinctive purposes; but they consciously strive, in Gabitov's words, to "overcome the Marxist-Soviet thesis," as well as former Tsarist agendas, and offer instead innovative, revisionist understandings. The outcomes are shaped by efforts to look back upon their past in order to recover their religious and national identities with a view to living them out in new ways within their present and future global contexts.

It is noteworthy that the Islamic voices participating in the debate, when compared with the Tengrist and other religious proponents, reveal by all means an equally passionate, but by no means a peculiarly 'radical' or 'extremist' nature. De-radicalizing (i.e., normalizing) general representations of Islamic revivalist voices among the Kazakhs (and even more broadly, Central Asians,) in their post-Soviet independent contexts thus appear in order, as does downsizing the proportion of focus fixed on those issues and the 'terrorist threats' associated with them, when treating Kazakh (and Central Asian) Islam.[432] Indeed:

> The 'Islamic explosion' postulated by Western scholars up until the collapse of the USSR never occurred; however, Western policy makers have in the post-Soviet era continued to fear a Khomeinist-style Islamic revolution

in this strategic region. ...the concept of an 'Islamic threat' to Central Asia is in itself a largely Western construct, serving Western interests, and misrepresents the interests of Islam within Central Asia today.[433]

Concern for securitization in the post-9/11 era, which includes the rise of ISIS and numerous other developments, has certainly affected the interpretations and related appropriations of their past in the present. There is noticeable concern for these issues in some of the various sources covered here within this chapter, in terms of both defending more scripturalist, orthodox views of Islam (cf. Bulutai) and in warning against radicalized interpretations (cf. Kartabaeva). Analyzing the impact of these factors in a more in-depth manner would, however, require a distinctive focus detailed in a separate, dedicated chapter or article.[434] Along these lines, it can at least be noted that the efforts to use Islam in order to promote moral-ethical attitudes and behaviors in line with and even controlled by state agendas provides comparative resemblance at points with previous Soviet approaches. This particular issue has little bearing on the question of the historical relation between Islam and "pre-Islamic survivals," though for the majority who understand their history to have culminated in a synthetic integration of the various religious traditions, with Islam as the predominant identity through which all the prior traditions are integrated and preserved, the pre-Islamic traditions are also mined for their moral-ethical value in similar fashion. The Kazakhstani Muftiyat dedicated the year 2014 to the topic of "Religion and Tradition," publishing a book and giving mosque-based sermons under that rubric throughout the year (see Chapter 10). Various imams made concerted "efforts to establish and propagate 'good' Islam—Islam that is based on the orthodoxy recognized in the wider Muslim world and is simultaneously rooted in the body of so-called national traditions as well as fitting existing secular sensibilities and widespread notions of modernity and progress."[435]

Most importantly for the purposes of this particular study, these various narrative exchanges elucidate the ways in which Kazakhs understand their own religious identity in historical perspective, considered comparatively against the 'surviving' legacy of the Tsarist and Soviet ethnographic traditions. The post-Soviet Kazakh narratives reveal the way in which they understand the historical relation of the various religious traditions—"pre-Islamic" and Islamic, in all their various forms and

8 RELIGIOUS-CULTURAL REVIVALISM AS HISTORIOGRAPHICAL DEBATE ... 159

expressions—which are all an integral part of Kazakh as well as broader Central Asian history and identity.

Inclusive of though not necessarily limited to the interpretations encountered in the sources within this chapter, the range of various viewpoints, regarding both past and present, can be roughly grouped into seven or eight overlapping and dynamically shifting positions on a continuum running between: (1) an exclusivist 'orthodox' Sunni Muslim view; (2) a Tengri-inclusivist Sufi-Modernist Muslim view; (3) an exclusivist Tengrist view; (4) a Muslim-inclusivist Tengrist view; (5) a cultural Muslim-predominant pluralist view; (6) a neo-Marxian atheistic progressivist view; and (7) a Western-influenced Kazakh (or Kyrgyz) Christian view, and (8) an egalitarian 'Silk Road' pluralist view.[436] Similar and overlapping, though not always identical, positions and trends have manifested themselves within the unique yet shared post-Soviet contexts of the various Central Asian Muslim peoples.[437]

All studies of Central Asian religious history, including this one, contribute in some fashion to one or another of these viewpoints, even several in terms of both potentially strengthening or weakening the respective positions. It is essential that genuine scholarly inquiry not be driven by any agendas—religious, political or otherwise—to contribute in particular predetermined ways to one or another outcome along these lines, but approach the evidence openly with a view to allowing the evidence to determine its own conclusions and outcomes as much as is reasonably, humanly possible. To this end, these rough and flexible groupings serve only to help analyze various sources, not guide and determine their results.

Beyond this, analysis of these historiographical exchanges carry instructive lessons for not only Kazakh and Turkic Central Asian history and identity, but for interreligious, intercultural and international relations and dialogue among various world religious and cultural communities. They affirm the central importance of historical knowledge and historiographical (re)interpretation (however accurate or inaccurate they be), particularly within post-colonial and other revivalist settings.

PART IV

International Post-Soviet 'Survivals' Scholarship in Global Historical Perspective

CHAPTER 9

Divergent Views on the Historical and Present Relation of Shamanism and Islam in International Post-Colonialist Scholarship

In light of the long, complex history of Tsarist and Soviet ethnography among the Central Asian Muslim peoples, the question of 'pre-Islamic survivals' took on new forms and functions within the post-Soviet context. Freedom from long decades of imperial hegemony, particularly the more immediate past marked by seventy years of Soviet atheistic propaganda, gave way to religious-cultural revival. This was and remains accompanied by historiographical debates which necessarily provide validity and direction to the various contending revivalist claims.[438]

The previous chapter has documented the main contours of these developments among seminal Kazakh (as well as some Kyrgyz and Turkish) scholars. Other scholars, however, both foreign and national, have also weighed in on these matters from varying points of view. I have already covered, in the Introduction to this work (as well as the previous chapter), some of the main outlines of these debates and select scholars who represent, at the simplest binary level, pro and con approaches to 'pre-Islamic survivals' among the Kazakhs in particular. I will now return to and expand upon those narratives, with a view to broader Central Asia. All of the works touched on in the Introduction—both pro and con— were, in fact, post-Soviet productions, and all were from Western scholars. They reach down to the two-thousand-teens. This would suggest that differing viewpoints will most likely continue to be aired, with the critical tensions perhaps ever-shifting but never fully resolved. That is the

© The Author(s), under exclusive license to Springer Nature Singapore
Pte Ltd. 2023
R. C. Weller, *'Pre-Islamic Survivals' in Muslim Central Asia*,
Islam and Global Studies,
https://doi.org/10.1007/978-981-19-5697-3_9

very nature of historical debate and process. My focus here will expand in certain ways upon the previous chapter, drawing instead from various scholars writing in English, Kazakh, Turkish and Farsi and situating the perspectives and various exchanges within a broader world historical and historiographical setting. All of this will be accomplished by focusing in on diverging views and approaches to the problem of the historical relation of Shamanism to Islam within Central Asian and broader Islamic history.

SULTANOVA, ZARCONE AND HOBART ON FEMALE MUSICAL AND HEALING TRADITIONS IN POST-SOVIET STUDIES OF SHAMANISM AND SUFISM

With respect to the question of both the historical and continuing relation of "pre-Islamic" and Islamic traditions within Central Asia, Shamanism has served as a focal point of both ongoing interest and controversary.[439] This is evident among the Kazakh sources (see previous chapter), but extends well beyond them. Distinct from yet closely tied to Tengrism, Shamanism more often serves as a component of the debates, alongside 'ancestor and saint veneration' and other ritual and customary practices, though at times it is treated as a distinct religious tradition standing on its own (cf. Arabic-Turkic 'din').

Along uniquely gendered lines,[440] the Uzbek scholar at Cambridge Muslim College, Razia Sultanova, has addressed the historical relation of Shamanism and Central Asian Islam in a 2011 work titled *From Shamanism to Sufism: Women, Islam and Culture in Central Asia*. In a chapter on the "Interaction of Shamanism and Sufism in Central Asian Female Performance," Sultanova covers various manifestations of Shamanism among women in the rituals and music[441] of the Turkmen, Kazakhs, Tajiks and Uzbeks. Ultimately she argues, among other things, that "pre-Islamic religious practices have been integrated deeply with local traditional culture and art. Shamanism appeared in many forms of esoteric practices, and still does." Some have criticized her work for lacking deeper analysis of Shamanism in its historical and definitional dimensions, but this was not her primary aim. More importantly here for our purposes, she does not use the language associated with 'veneer' or 'two-tier' theories of the relation of Islam and Shamanism, but rather describes them as "deeply integrated," i.e., integral in terms of the "synthesis" produced by Islam's ability "to accommodate Shamanism as well as other indigenous cultural practices and beliefs."[442]

Among Western scholars, Thierry Zarcone and Angela Hobart extended Sultanova's study to the broader Islamic world in *Shamanism and Islam: Sufism, Healing Rituals and Spirits in the Muslim World* (2012). Along with Central Asia and Siberia, which are the main focus of the work, the volume includes chapters on Afghanistan, Iran, Turkey, North Africa, Indonesia and Southeastern Europe. They open the volume, however, with a chapter on "Vladimir Nikolaevich Basilov (1937–1998): A Pioneer of the Study of 'Islamised Shamanism'." They thus reveal the Soviet ethnographic roots from which they primarily draw, though this should not be taken to mean that their interpretations are not sufficiently critical, since they engage a wide range of scholarship. Sultanova draws at a few limited junctures from Basilov as well, though does not display a strong dependence on his work. In spite of its Soviet ethnographic underpinnings, however, Zarcone and Hobart's edited volume could perhaps be taken as confirmation of Bruce G. Privratsky's thesis that many of these so-called pre-Islamic survivals were spread so widely across the Islamic world because they were an integrated (cf. integral) part of the Islamic heritage which came together with the main pillars of "Islamic confession and ritual prayers." Thus Privratsky, pointing to the earlier (1997) work of Devin Deweese, insists that "[m]ost religious beliefs and customs in Turkistan are best understood as contextualizations of Islam, not as survivals of pre-Islam."[443] Later in 2014, Deweese added to this thesis in an extended treatment of "Shamanization in Central Asia." There he referenced a study by Zarcone from 2000 emanating from "French academic circles" which were themselves, so Deweese claims, influenced by Turkish historiography.[444] In balance however, the edited collection by Zarcone and Hobart also highlights how local traditions factored into the final synthetic outcome in each region, which remains an important question of historical research.

As Zarcone and Hobart's volume helps illustrate, studies of and debates over 'pre-Islamic survivals' among Muslim peoples extend beyond post-Soviet Central Asia, both historically and presently, into various other Islamic societies.[445] The studies and debates, likewise, go well beyond the religious, into the cultural, social, economic, political, artistic, musical and other realms of life.[446] The Turks of modern Turkey—originating as they did from out of the Central Asian heartland—and the Persian-Iranian peoples represent two of the most prominent examples of the ongoing efforts to negotiate their own unique respective Turkish and Persian-Iranian histories and identities in relation to their Islamic.[447]

DEWEESE'S CRITIQUE OF TURKISH, FRENCH AND SOVIET SCHOLARSHIP

Deweese, in "Shamanization in Central Asia" (2014), writes off an entire long-standing tradition of Turkish scholarship by accusing it of being "intent on distinguishing an essentialized religious profile for the Turks, on an ethnic and national basis, with affinities for 'heterodox' versions of Islam." These "approaches," Deweese asserts, "find 'shamanic' origins for any and every feature of Turkish religion that appears to lie outside a narrowly construed 'Islamic' framework, and often imagine Central Asia as the venue in which a Turkish shamanism barely touched by Islam survived for many centuries (and indeed might still be found alive)." As the lone example for such Turkish "approaches," he cites one article by a Turkish scholar published in French in 1929, early in Kemal Ataturk's reforms, when French was still lingering as a *lingua franca* in the Turkish academic world.[448] He cited the same work in his 1994 study of *Islamization and Native Religion in the Golden Horde*.[449] This is simply insufficient evidence to write off the entire vast production of Turkish scholarship over the past century, especially when Deweese does not appear to have taken any time over the past twenty-five plus years to do more careful and nuanced analysis of Turkish historiography, particularly from more recent times.

With respect to that Turkish scholarship, Cemal Şener released a work on *Shamanism: The Religion of the Turks before Islam* in 1997, with reprintings in 2003 and 2010. Among numerous other topics, Sener's work includes sections on "Traces of the Shaman in Turkish Culture" and "Prayers of the Kyrgyz-Kazakh Shamans." Özgür Velioğlu published a work in 2005 treating *The Reflection of Beliefs on Turkish Cinema: Shamanism, Sky-god, Animism, Naturism, Totemism, in terms of Islamic Beliefs*. Atilla Bağci put out a study on "The Holiness of the Wolf in Terms of Shaman Mythology in Turkish Culture." Among other things, Bağci argues that "the cult of the wolf and the face of the wolf [which are] blessed in the stories of Grandfather Korkut are not Islamic motifs. They are motifs which belong to the belief of Shamanism." Yilmaz Orhan produced a study on "The Effects of Ancient Turkish Religion (Belief in Heaven) and Shamanism in Alevism."[450]

Turkish scholars have also produced studies of Shamanic "residues" among the Uyghurs in particular. Samire Mömin investigates "what kind of remnants shamanism has left today" among the Uyghurs "and how it has undergone changes within the framework of the religion of Islam, which is widely lived in society, by focusing on different thoughts and taboos about shamanism." Alimcan Inayet argues that Shamanism "continues today" among the Uyghurs "and forms an important part of social life by taking on different forms and disguises among people. On the one hand, Uyghur Shamans maintain their shamanic practices and traditions by adapting them to Islamic understanding, on the other hand, they use Islamic practices and traditions for shamanic purposes."[451] Whether in the end we agree or disagree, all of these (and more) merit due attention and analysis before they are so quickly and easily swept aside with a single, all-encompassing pigeon-holing of their supposed "intent."

Deweese's single reference to two journal articles from 1988 and 2000, respectively, the latter by Zarcone, is also insufficient for writing off all the "French academic circles" which he depicts as having been influenced by this branch of Turkish historiography. Although their work was published a year prior, Deweese does not reference or engage the volume by Zarcone and Hobart noted above, nor Sultanova's work published three years earlier. When he does finally engage Zarcone and Hobart's volume, two years later in a 2016 review, he opens by writing off all of the "volume's fourteen papers" in the same essential manner, i.e., by insisting that they all follow "an essentialized vision of 'orthodox Islam'" which ultimately "presumes," so Deweese claims, "a historical trajectory of development that embeds the 'origins' of these practices in pre-Islamic or non-Islamic frameworks."[452]

But by his own acknowledgement, in "Shamanization in Central Asia," Deweese follows "a dramatically different conceptual framework within which to interpret the data, both newly discovered and long available."[453] It is "a historical trajectory of development that embeds the 'origins' of these practices," or at least their post-conversion development, "in strictly Islamic frameworks." Deweese argues that eighteenth- and nineteenth-century Sufi rituals were misinterpreted by Soviet ethnographers from especially the 1950s onward as 'shamanistic' performances. His aim is to overturn "the interpretative assumption that 'popular' or 'everyday' Central Asian religion in the Soviet era was essentially 'shamanism' with a veneer of Muslim, and Sufi, elements laid atop it."[454]

But several points must be made here: First, while he offers convincing evidence that supposedly 'shamanic-like' practices can be traced back to what had become by that time authentically Sufi practices documented as far back as the thirteenth and fourteenth centuries,[455] he does not adequately demonstrate that no shamanic influence occurred earlier in the history at some point(s). To the contrary, he acknowledges—very briefly, in passing, nearly twenty pages into his discussion—that "[o]ne might still argue that the *zikr's ultimate* origin lies in "shamanism," to be sure…". Within Central Asia, I have shown that Turkic Central Asian shamanic healing practices were interacting with and influencing Islamic (very probably Sufi) ones in the Karakhanid period as documented by Yusuf Balasaghuni (see Chapter 3). The debate here, then, is not about whether (Turkic Central Asian) Shamanism has exerted genuine historical influence on Islamic practices; it is rather about how different frameworks of, or perhaps even differing emphases within historical interpretations yield different outcomes related to the differing aims (cf. agendas) of each. Deweese lays emphasis on the idea that various historical traditions, religious or otherwise, represent "'the thorough identification of the practices in question as part of the 'Muslim' way of life'."[456] While this is certainly true, mere "identification of the practices in question" in Muslim terms cannot be grounds for disregarding or, still more, completely erasing the historical origins of those practices (or beliefs). Nor does it mean that the original traditions did or still do not somehow, in varying transformed contexts across the centuries, authentically "survive" within and through the 're-identification'—or "contextualizing," as Privratsky puts it—of the tradition (see more on this below).

REVISITING THE EVIDENCE FROM PRIVRATSKY, *MUSLIM TURKISTAN*

Privratsky tells us that "[t]he Kazak *baqsıs* [shamans] absorbed the Islamic therapeutic vocabulary precisely because their curing methods depended on an overarching social myth or ideology…"[457] Likewise, "the Turko-Persian term, *pir*, [has been] taken over by the shamans from Sufism" in connection with how "[s]hamanic travel has been absorbed into the Muslim dreamvision (*ayan*)."[458] Within a context of post-Soviet revivalism (see Chapter 8), Privratsky noted what appeared to be efforts "to encourage the association of the [shamanic] healing tradition with Islamic sources." All in all, "[e]lements of Inner Asian shamanship that survive are expressed in Islamic vocabulary by self-consciously Muslim practitioners who use therapies well-known in other Muslim societies."[459]

Privratsky himself seeks, like Deweese, to minimize any ideas of 'survival' in relation to Shamanism (or other 'pre-Islamic' traditions) as much as possible because he wishes to "defend" "the premise that the Kazak ancestors were Muslim."[460] "Everywhere we looked for shamans," Privratsky insists, "we kept coming up with [Muslim] *täwips* instead."[461] While not agreeing with all their premises, Privratsky effectively allies himself with those informants who also wish to minimize or deny the non-Islamic (cf. also 'pre-Islamic') elements within their history and culture in order to uphold and strengthen a 'pure' Islamic identity. Thus, for him, "one cannot escape Jolbarıs Qoja's conclusion that 'their [the Shaman's] seed has dried up'."[462] But Qoja's assessment raises questions about the competition for religious as well as broader social-cultural power and influence, particularly among the Qojas, both past and present.[463] Although Privratsky does not address this potential 'conflict of interest' among his informants, he nonetheless provides clear evidence of contemporary and past Muslim opposition to Shamanism on at least theological grounds. For example, a son of one of his female informants "objected respectfully" to his mother's testimony, insisting that the Kazak *baqsis* (shamans) were possessed by evil, demonic spirits. "This contradiction," Privratsky notes, "was made necessary by Omar's duty… to uphold the way of Islam, which opposed the shamans." Another of his female informants likewise "says the spirits of the *baqsıs* are jinn; she "herself calls them demonic spirits" because "their crazy behavior makes them incompatible with the 'gentle spirits'…by which the Muslim *emshi* heals today." Therefore, "as a Muslim *täwip* she lays no claim to the shamanic heritage." Another of his informants "was required by her husband's family to learn the *namaz* and cut her ties to the shamanic tradition."[464]

Closely linked to Islam's theological rejection of Shamanism was and is its adoption of Western-Russian Enlightenment and scientific historiography undergirded by theories of racial and cultural-civilizational superiority. Islam as a religion having a 'sacred scripture' and law code comparable to and even influenced by that of Moses was held—within these eighteenth- to nineteenth-century Western-Russian views—to be 'more advanced' than the 'primitive, savage, barbaric' nomads with their primitive, barbaric religious traditions such as Shamanism (cf. 'higher' and 'lower cultures'). Thought not all, there are still a substantial number of more progressivist as well as conservative Muslims both in and beyond Central Asia who have developed their own versions of these comparative-progressivist views, with their own faith tradition situated above all others, particularly in this case the presumably demonic and primitive tradition of Shamanism.

But not only has the Shamanic heritage been minimized, denied and/or condemned by those considering it their Islamic duty to do so in the post-Soviet revivalist period, "Muslims and communists" had once "joined hands in pronouncing that shamanism was obsolete."[465] Privratsky's Qoja informant (above) has carried this view into the post-Soviet era. Meanwhile, one Kazakh *baqsi* from the Soviet period "burned many of his books for fear of the police during Brezhnev's time."[466] In spite of these problematic complications within his sources, Privratsky, in one easy sweep, simply writes off those Kazakhs who see Shamanism still 'surviving' into the present day as "[s]till under the spell of Marxist theory."[467] Either this, or "Kazaks who intone Valilkhanov's ideas and claim that their old religion was shamanism are confusing it" with other traditions.[468] This in spite of them being 'indigenous voices' with their own understandings of their own religious history and identity (see below). All in all, as per one of his Qoja informants, "[t]he *baqsïs* were an easy target of the Soviet anti-religious activists, because they healed not in the quiet way of the mullahs and *täwips* with their pulse-taking, breath therapies, and herbal remedies, but with ecstatic trances that could be ridiculed as so much 'shouting and noise'."[469] That Privratsky does not deal with the problem of how this dual-sided persecution and oppression from two dominant and highly influential forces in Central Asia, the Islamic and Soviet, is curious at best. Certainly the shamanic tradition was forced to both hide and transform itself throughout the Soviet era.[470] We should not therefore, as Privratsky has done, look strictly for evidence of how contemporary post-Soviet Shamanism displays "continuity" with the pre-Soviet past and then judge whether it is still authentically "Shamanism" based on that comparison, but rather allow for its expression in transformed and more subdued ways. We should likewise raise legitimate critical questions about sources, living or textual, which have a religious and/or broader social, cultural or even political motive for possibly minimizing, denying or denouncing Shamanism in either its historic or more present-day forms.

Privratsky's self-professed (and post-colonialist) apologetic aim is evident throughout much of his study. It is to "defend" Kazakh Muslim identity, both historically and presently, by demonstrating "the triumph of the 'Islamic synthesis'"[471] in all aspects of Kazakh religious life. He nonetheless provides "images of archaic practice" emanating from the Turkic Central Asian shamanic tradition,[472] including evidence of "traces of the early synthesis of shamanic and Islamic healing practices." "The shamanic texts left to us by Divaev (1899) and Castagné (1923, 1925, 1930)," he observes, "find their historical continuity in reports" from the contemporary informants he interviews. While the "continuity" of these "traces," in Privratsky's own anti-Valikhanovian and anti-Soviet estimation, are "faint" and "fall well short of a living shamanism,"[473] he in fact "encountered a few serious references to living Kazak shamans," acknowledging that "this evidence suggests that shamans survive." Indeed, one revivalist event "implies that there [were] 40 shamans in southern Kazakstan" as of the late 1990s when he did his research. In one case, "it was impossible to determine whether he," the professing *baqsi*, "actually knows the traditional shamanic repertoire, or is just another Muslim *täwip*." Here, then, he did not, with absolute certainty, simply find Muslim *täwips* in every instance. Meanwhile, "[s]everal characteristics of the shamanic trance" were "evident" in some of the descriptions he collected. "Shamanic demonology is," likewise, "featured" in a recital of shamanic texts which had been committed to memory by one practitioner he interviewed, linking them again to the late nineteenth-century studies of Divaev and Castagné and others. He furthermore relates elsewhere that while "[t]he *peri* are usually subsumed into the Quranic *jinn*, ...one that has preserved its identity is the *sū-peri* (water-spirit), a well-known female spirit that tempts men," particularly in relation to swimming in the Syr Daria River. Privratsky's use of the term "preserved" should be noted here as an essential synonym of 'survived', i.e., it represents a 'survival.' From this angle, the pre-Soviet Central Asian shamanic heritage 'survived' the joint Muslim-Soviet assault in certain recognizable forms, though this still requires further reevaluation from an angle looking for how it may also have survived in other transformed and subdued ways thus far overlooked by Privratsky and other scholars.[474]

An additional problem with Privratsky's analysis is that he is not simply looking for 'survivals' of Shamanism which have been integrated into Kazakh Muslim ways of life. He is instead looking for the 'survival' of a full-fledged, "living shamanism" practiced again in full accord with pre-Soviet and even deeper historical forms of Central Asian Shamanism. Against this rather high standard he finds very little which measures up to his expectations. This again leaves the question hanging over this debate of just how Turkic Central Asian Shamanism has been transformed and re-expressed across not only the Soviet period, but even the longer, deeper centuries as it has faced new challenges of resistance and outright rejection by both Islam and the two successive Russian imperial powers, Tsarist and Soviet. This latter angle of approach requires seeing the relationship between Central Asian Shamanism and Islam in terms of 'resistance', namely that of the former to the latter. This is problematic for those emphasizing a 'harmonious' "accommodation" of the one within the other, but both processes can, in fact, be happening simultaneously. Part of the 'resistance' can be the conscious, intentional adaption of the Central Asian Shamans and their heirs to the Islamic healing traditions in order preserve their places and influence within increasingly Islamizing societies.

This historical interpretation, likewise, raises questions about whether Islam served as a mere 'conduit' for Central Asian Shamans to 'survive' in 'Islamic clothing', i.e., the veneer theory. But one does not have to go to this extreme. This is precisely where the lines are drawn, in fact, in the ongoing debates over how to historically explain and depict "accommodation" and "integration" between the two traditions. It should also be recognized here that an interpretational framework of 'resistance' is not uniquely Soviet. It has been employed by numerous Protestant Christian as well as Enlightenment and Romanticist interpreters (see Chapters 2 and 4). Likewise, Muslims and Jews both at times interpret their own history in terms of 'resistance' in relation, for example, to the Spanish Inquisition (see Chapter 2) or Western imperialism. Much of the history of Islam in Central Asia is, in fact, viewed through the lens of 'resistance' to Tsarist and Soviet encroachment. Well beyond this, Chiara Formichi includes an entire chapter on "Islam as Resistance" in her historical survey of *Islam and Asia*.[475] The histories of 'Black Islam' in both the United States and South Africa are, likewise, interpreted through a motif lens of 'resistance' to White Christian oppressors. Even Black Christianity is, in certain respects, interpreted through this motif lens, though it also exhibits clear points of harmony with certain strands of White Christianity. Beyond these are multiple other examples within the histories of Buddhism in East Asia, Hinduism in Indonesia, etc. And just as there are Central Asians today who take differing approaches to these issues, it is not unreasonable to propose, on sociological grounds, that similar multivectored processes were occurring historically. It is too convenient to simply label the 'resistance' interpretation, especially if/ when applied to various 'pre-Islamic' traditions, a 'survival' of 'Soviet' ethnography and historiography so as to write it off in one easy sweep; the matter is much more complicated from a broader and deeper world historical perspective, especially given the clear evidence from Privratsky and elsewhere of certain dominant Muslim opposition to Shamanism in both the Soviet and post-Soviet periods.

HISTORICALLY INTERACTIVE AND TRANSFORMATIONAL UNDERSTANDINGS AND DEFINITIONS OF 'ISLAM' AND 'SHAMANISM'

Whether through 'resistance' or 'harmony,' various forms of Central Asian 'Shamanism' must be granted the same liberality of interpretation offered to Islam (or any other religious traditions), in terms of its ability to adapt and transform to varying cultural and historical circumstances across time and space. Along with Kartaeva's view of Shamanism as a historically transformative tradition (see previous chapter), I quote here at length from Mircea Eliade in his vast studies of Shamanism and other world religious traditions:

> The historical changes in the religions of Central and North Asia—that is, in general, the increasingly important role given to the ancestor cult and to the divine or semidivine figures that took the place of the Supreme Being—in their turn altered the meaning of the shaman's ecstatic experience. Descents to the underworld, the struggle against evil spirits, but also the increasingly familiar relations with 'spirits' that result in their 'embodiment' or in the shaman's being 'possessed' by 'spirits,' are innovations, most of them recent, to be ascribed to the general change in the religious complex. In addition, there are influences from the south, which appeared quite early and which altered both cosmology and the mythology and techniques of ecstasy. Among these southern influences we must reckon, in later times, the contribution of Buddhism and Lamaism, added to the Iranian and, in the last analysis, Mesopotamian influences that preceded them.
> In all probability the initiatory schemes of the shaman's ritual death and resurrection is likewise an innovation, but one that goes back to much earlier times; in any case, it cannot be ascribed to influences from the ancient Near East, since the symbolism and ritual of initiatory death and resurrection are already documented in the religions of Australia and South

America. But the innovations introduced by the ancestor cult particularly affected the structure of this initiatory schema. The very concept of mystical death was altered by the many and various religious changes effected by lunar mythologies, the cult of the dead, and the elaboration of magical ideologies.[476]

Further study of Shamanism from this historically transformational angle, especially during the Soviet period, is in order before any final conclusions are drawn.[477] Although seemingly and not surprisingly in ever-decreasing measure, Privratsky provides evidence from his informants which attest to Kazakh shamans still surviving and practicing their rituals and healings into the 1930s and even beyond, down to 1963 and then on into the Brezhnev era (1964–1982). That this tradition, or at least 'remnants' of it, would 'survive' on into the post-Soviet period, and even experience revival among certain Kazakh groups who see it as part of their historical-cultural heritage, should be no great surprise.[478]

With Privratsky's findings placed more properly in this re-interpreted critical light, I return then to an important second point regarding Deweese's argument against the Soviet interpreters. He convincingly shows in several cases that they rely on questionable, if not demonstrably false historical narratives to explain the origins of the supposedly 'shamanic' practices within Central Asian Islam. But a mistaken understanding of a phenomenon's historical origins does not determine the accuracy or inaccuracy of the comparative analytical observations about the phenomenon itself. Nor does it mean that the assertion of historical influence is in and of itself wrong. For example, the historical influence of Greek Orthodoxy on Russian Orthodoxy remains a historical fact, whether or not the interpreter attributes that historical influence to the proper historical period(s) or sources. It does not matter here in this analogy that both traditions are "Orthodox," it is their distinction as "Greek" and "Russian" which provides the point of comparison. The suggestion of historical influence by way of comparative analysis by Soviet scholars remains (not perfectly, but) generally reasonable and possibly even valid, whether or not they have properly identified the precise point(s) at which historical influence may have occurred. They have studied both traditions and know for a fact (cf. 'contextual' or 'circumstantial evidence') that those traditions have interacted within the deeper history of Central Asia. Soviet scholarship on Shamanism in Islamic Central Asia also drew from prior and broader Tsarist era and

Soviet studies of Siberian and other forms of shamanism, providing them with at least some measure of comparative support for their assertions.[479] Privratsky himself uses this comparative approach, drawing from some of those same earlier sources. If it looks like Shamanism, smells like Shamanism and tastes like Shamanism, then there are at least reasonable grounds for asserting points of possible historical connection (see on the Iranian scholars Atooni, Sharifian and Atooni, "A Comparative Study of Islamic Sufism and Shamanic Mysticism" below). Granted they may be wrong in assuming 'dependent influence' as opposed to 'independent development' in assessing the historical relation between Central Asian Shamanism and Islam. Such assumptions are an inherent danger in comparative religious-cultural studies. But the danger of the assumptions works both ways, i.e., for both Deweese and the Soviet 'survivals' scholarship which he seeks to eradicate. Meanwhile, albeit with great hesitation and reluctance, Deweese nonetheless confesses that "[i]t is perhaps overly fair to acknowledge at least the possibility that in the course of the 1930s and '40s," under various historical pressures, "the face of religious life indeed changed dramatically, leading to the submergence of the complex of rites described in the 1920s, clearly linked with Sufism, and the ascendance of rites genuinely traceable to the postulated 'shamanic heritage' of some Central Asian peoples."[480] Deweese's suggested analysis here of potential historical transformations in both Sufism and Shamanism runs counter to the study of Art Leete who notes that "In the Soviet writings of the 1930s, shamans were always depicted as the main enemies of the communist regime among the indigenous peoples of the North,"[481] but at least these studies together provide some points of departure for further exploration of the various historical transformations possibly experienced by the shamanic tradition during the Soviet period.

In his attempts to reinterpret and identify any and all possible appearances of Shamanism as instead forms of authentic Sufi Islam, with a view, like Privratsky, to defending the purity, authenticity and integrity of Central Asian Islamic identity, Deweese must hold notions as to what defines or constitutes "Islam," otherwise the term loses its viability as a phenomenon properly subject to scholarly analysis. Adeeb Khalid, like others, argues for the validity of multiple understandings of "Islam," based in "multiple and simultaneous sources of authority,"[482] but this presumes clear definitions grounded in those "sources of authority," whatever they happen to be. Debates over definitions of 'Islam' and 'who speaks for Islam' continue down to the present-day,[483] but once

"Islam" is defined, it immediately determines what is properly "Islamic" and "non-Islamic," including "pre-Islamic," relative to whatever definition is posited. Deweese, like all others, inescapably has his own notion of "Islam" which determines its proper borders and boundaries in relation to other faith traditions. Deweese argues for the historical 'purity' of the Islamic tradition he conceives, untainted by Shamanistic or Tengrist or other 'foreign' (cf. 'idolatrous') traditions. He interprets all change within Central Asian Islamic (particularly Sufi) history as being driven by strictly 'internal' as opposed to any 'external' (cf. 'outside,' 'foreign') factors, particularly any religious ones.[484] His "dramatically different conceptual framework" requires that he restrict himself to such an approach.

Yet there remains the possibility that, even after the initial influence of Central Asian Shamanism on Sufism via the Karakhanids (and possibly Seljuks or others), interaction and influence continued to occur. Given the complex nature of historical process, insulating and sealing off any potential shamanic (or other outside, 'foreign') influences or manifestations is highly problematic at best, especially across multiple centuries of religious history. As just one example, possible interaction and influence between Turkic Central Asian Islam and Shamanism appears in Islamic sources from as late as the 1600s.[485] As the team of Kazakh scholars noted in their 2021 overview of the *History of Kazakhstan*, processes of conversion, deconversion and revival are continuously taking place across historical landscapes (see end of Chapter 8). Positing only two possible options, either a 'Shamanistic' or an 'Islamic' interpretation, is a misleading dichotomy which unnecessarily inhibits more nuanced and balanced academic inquiry.

Part of the problem here has been the lack of a detailed, reliable 'history of Shamanism in Central Asia', including one which covers the Soviet era, which then might serve as a reliable point of reference for such a comparative inquiry.[486] These fortunes are, however, changing, particularly with the 2022 publication of an article by two Kazakh scholars, B.M. Atash and M.E. Tanjarov, who treat the "Genesis and Evolution of Shamanism in the Ancient Turkic-Turkic-Kazakh Steppes: Historical and Cognitive Orientations." They divide the history into six distinct "stages" of development, including: "1. the emergence of world shamanism; 2. its entry into the Turkic-Kazakh steppe; 3. the era of the Revival of shamanism; 4. the competitive (parallel) coexistence of shamanism and Islam; 5. the destruction or revival of shamanism in the Kazakh steppe; 6. «an attempt of Neo-Shamanism»." The authors summarize their findings as follows:

9 DIVERGENT VIEWS ON THE HISTORICAL AND PRESENT RELATION ...   177

The chronological time of the emergence of shamanism can be determined only approximately. [The article] reports on the wide spread, deployment of shamanism in the Turkic-Kazakh steppe, [and] about conflicts and convergence in the context of dialogue with Islamic culture. The destruction of shamanism in the Kazakh steppe is associated with the ideology under the Soviet government and examples and analogies have been given by archetypal elements of shamanism in the modern art of the twentieth century, especially in music. As a result of the research, the authors drew attention to the appearance of shamanism, which can be called an integral culture, and came to the conclusion about its viability, in which remnants are preserved [today] in the spheres of public life.[487]

While Atash and Tanjaraov make a significant contribution here to the ongoing discussions, another part of the problem remains the high religious, cultural and political and even gender stakes involved in these debates within the post-colonial and especially post-Soviet context. Meanwhile, the main body of their article is written in Kazakh, unfortunately limiting its access to the wider international academic community. The latter problem is more properly resolved by non-Kazakh-speaking scholars who wish to engage these issues learning Kazakh, or at least hiring a competent Kazakh-speaking research assistant, as opposed to translating this and all other Kazakh material into English or other languages. As for their Kazakh scholarship however, we must ask what happened to the certainly noble concern for "'listen[ing]' to indigenous accounts of intertwining religious and ethnic identities" and "the critical value of... indigenous accounts of conversion" which gives priority to "the *meaning* of conversion for those peoples"?[488] Deweese, Frank, Privratsky and others write off entire swaths of Turkish and Central Asian (as well as, by implication, Iranian) indigenous voices by simply accusing them of either being ethnically or nationalistically motivated, and/or mindlessly following Tsarist (particularly 'Valikhanovian') or Soviet historiographical and ethnographical traditions, or themselves being overly 'Russified.' The matters are far more historically and theoretically complex.

Concluding Reflections

This entire discussion, both here and throughout the book, has much to do with the fact that history is identity. Be that as it may, historically speaking, one thing is certain: To whatever extent broom sweeping and other practices may have been, as Privratsky points out, diffused as an already integrated (cf. integral) part of the Islamic (Sufi) heritage, the ancient Persian New Year *Nauryz* (or, *Nowruz*), the Kazakh fire ritual conducted by the newly married daughter-in-law, and various other religious-cultural components which represent continuing traditions among various Turko-Persian Central Asian peoples are not shared across all Islamic societies, and thus represent "surviving" local and regional (cf. indigenous) traditions.[489] The same can be said for the unique religious-cultural configurations of multiple Islamic societies across the world, each with their own unique debates over 'survivals.'

Meanwhile, certain scholars are essentially conducting, however astutely and academically, and ironically, a 'crusade' or 'jihad of the pen' against "pre-Islamic survivals" in Muslim Central Asia. They are out to eradicate the 'remnants' of Soviet survivals ethnography within post-Soviet scholarship and in Central Asian religious history itself. From this angle, such scholars are following a comparatively similar methodological approach and agenda as the Soviets, they are simply inverting it. A good deal of Western and Islamic post-Soviet scholarship has, in fact, focused on identifying "residues" (cf. 'survivals') of the Soviet legacy in Central Asia and targeting those 'survivals' in order to dismantle, deconstruct and replace them with revised post-colonialist, Western democratic, Islamic or other ideals, values, perspectives or agendas.[490] Not that this is inherently wrong. But it must first be asked how lingering 'survivals' of Western democratic Cold War historiography may be unconsciously or subconsciously influencing the attitudes of Western scholars toward especially Soviet historiography. As Bob Dylan sang in the thick of the Cold War in 1964: "I've learned to hate Russians," particularly Soviet Russians, "all through my whole life." This includes a profound distrust of their 'ideological' scholarship. Not that it is my intent to defend and justify all Soviet scholarship here. The question of our own Western biases must simply be raised in all fairness, in attempting to grapple with our own assumptions, potentially some unconscious ones. Soviet scholarship remains an easy target for Western (and Muslim) scholars in the post-Cold War era, even as that Western scholarship grapples to come to terms with its own colonialist heritage. Meanwhile, whether directly or indirectly, consciously or otherwise, a fair amount of post-colonialist (including post-Soviet) Islamic scholarship draws from Marxist-socialist sources in their critique of modern nation-states and nationalism, rejecting it as a Western imperial imposition which is contrary to Islamic norms, values and ideals. In this, they align themselves with former Soviet views.

Post-Soviet interpretations of Central Asian (and other) history cannot be dismissed as lingering 'survivals' of 'Soviet' ethnography or historiography on the mere grounds that they share certain common features with Soviet sources. This is particularly true in terms of mere historical 'description', as opposed to what makes their 'analysis' and 'arguments' in relation to that history uniquely 'Soviet.' Critical questions regarding Islamic historiography also need to be grappled with more seriously in equal measure, not only in regard to nations and nationalism, but more importantly for our purposes here, Central Asian religious history.

Beyond this, it must also be asked how there can be 'survivals' of the Soviet historiographic-ethnographic legacy, as well as the Tsarist (especially Valikhanovian), not to mention 'survivals' of multiple other influences religiously, culturally, socially, linguistically, politically, economically, etc., within broader world history, yet no "pre-Islamic survivals" in Central Asia? Indeed, much of human history contains 'survivals' of prior generations, both materially and culturally, whether for relatively shorter or much longer spans of time, even centuries or millennia. Cultural 'survivals' are often (though not always or necessarily) the result of crosscultural contact and exchange in world history. An "Islamic studies" approach has its own limitations, including the problem of determining precisely what 'Islamic studies' is in terms of boundaries, foci, approaches, etc.[491] It is a world historical approach which is needed, particularly one grappling with issues of 'crosscultural contact and exchange' in comparative global perspective.[492]

Those scholars specifically and intentionally targeting 'Soviet survivals ethnography' have clearly contributed a vast wealth of scholarship to the field and their challenges raise crucial questions which need to be taken seriously. My own work here (and elsewhere) significantly benefits from that scholarship and so confirms this at multiple junctures. But they have not yet resolved all the complex issues spanning numerous cultures and their historiographical traditions across multiple centuries, including those within Central Asian religious-cultural history.

Soumia Aziz at International Islamic University in Islamabad, Pakistan concluded that Zarcone and Hobart's volume provided "an insightful analysis..., exploring the complexities and variety of rituals, involving music, dance, and, in some regions, epic and bardic poetry, demonstrating the close links between shamanism and the various arts of the Muslim world."[493] The Iranian scholars Behzad Atooni, Mahdi Sharifian and Behrooz Atooni co-authored a "Comparative Study of Islamic Sufism and Shamanic Mysticism" in 2019. They reasoned that "Shamanic rituals and customs bear a striking resemblance to Islamic Sufi customs; to the extent that some even believe that Islamic Sufism was influenced by Shamanism." The article covered the origins of Shamanism; its distinctions from magic, trauma, insanity and the category of primitive religions; and major similarities between shamanism and Sufism (and other mystic religious expressions around the world). Common to both Shamanism and Sufi mysticism are "the states of trance and ecstatic unconsciousness, the importance of music and stomp, soul flight and ascension of the seeker, magical flight, mystical austerity, performing supernatural wonders, and the issue of rebirth." Concerning the question of the historical relation between the two traditions, they waffled between the idea that the similarities were "not necessarily because of the impact of Shamanism's beliefs and rituals on Sufism," while insisting that "the possible influence of Shamanism on Sufism in some of its rituals and dimensions...cannot be neglected or ignored." They themselves seemed to favor, however, that the similarities were to be explained by independent origins grounded in "similarities within the world's mystical schools,"[494] including an "Ishraqi essence," i.e., a form of (divine) illumination within the human soul.[495] A number of more conservative Iranian scholars also reject these kinds of more ecstatic forms of Sufi mysticism as being historically influenced by Shamanism and thus illegitimate.[496]

One (among other) of the questions arising here is, if Turks and Iranians follow a historiographical (and ethnographical) approach which shares certain affinities with and yields certain similar results to the Tsarist and Soviet schools which these scholars target, and yet that Turkish and Iranian historiography has not been significantly shaped or driven by those Russian schools,[497] and are certainly not carrying out scholarship under a looming post-Soviet shadow, then it would seem that the problem is not strictly or directly located in Tsarist and Soviet historiography and ethnography. And if this be the case, then the locus of the critiques need to be revised and redirected, embracing a much wider and more complex web of scholarship historically and globally. That is, in fact, one of the main points of this volume, to establish the much broader, more complicated nature of the debates, both historically and presently, from a world historical perspective. This includes the overly simplistic attribution of Soviet 'survivals' scholarship almost exclusively and repeatedly to E.B. Tylor which likewise yields "a narrowly construed 'Soviet' framework."

CHAPTER 10

Retrospect and Prospect: Situating Post-Soviet "Survivals" Scholarship Within a World Historiographical Frame

POST-COLONIALIST AGENDAS AND THE HISTORIAN'S TASK

Inasmuch as (both Tsarist and Soviet) Russian imperialism and colonialism in Central Asia were oppressive and agenda driven—including specifically here the broadly shared agenda to 'de-Islamize' both the Central Asian peoples and their histories, at least from the mid-nineteenth century onward—the trends and aims of post-Soviet scholarship to 'decolonize' Central Asian history and historiography by helping properly 're-Islamize' it are necessary, good and right. This thrust within the post-Soviet aftermath is, in fact, part of a much longer, deeper trend of post-colonialist historiography going all the way back to the 1960s–70s and manifesting uniquely in various parts of the world as part of the interrelated processes of 'decolonization.' "The agenda"—as one scholar tracing out the history of debates over 'syncretism' put it—has been "to fight the cultural imperialism of First World theologians," historians and other scholars, "and to recover indigenous cultures and values in their traditional religions and cultures denigrated by Christianization and westernization."[499] The latter should be taken, in this case, to include Russification and Sovietization. I support and contribute to the efforts to 'decolonize' Western (including again Tsarist and Soviet) colonialist-imperialist history, as my published scholarship demonstrates (see below). I suggest, however, the need for much more nuanced and diversified

© The Author(s), under exclusive license to Springer Nature Singapore Pte Ltd. 2023
R. C. Weller, *'Pre-Islamic Survivals' in Muslim Central Asia*, Islam and Global Studies,
https://doi.org/10.1007/978-981-19-5697-3_10

approaches which go beyond mere binary oppositional choices, particularly those in this case of a Russian-Soviet versus an Islamic studies approach.

The post-colonialist agenda to 'decolonize' and thus, in this case, 're-Islamize' Central Asian history is, again, necessary and good. This, however, is only part of the story. There is also the need and even shared right of Tengrists, Shamanists, and others to reclaim the past. If (not all, but) a significant measure of Tsarist and Soviet scholarship aimed at 'de-Islamizing' the Central Asian peoples and their histories, as it surely did, it also aimed at 'de-Tengrianizing' and 'de-Shamanizing' them as well. The highlighting of 'pre-Islamic survivals' was not for purposes of strengthening, restoring and supporting them; it was to strategically target them all the same. True, they sought to exploit 'pre-Islamic survivals' for 'de-Islamizing' purposes in the process, particularly in the post-World War Two period, but it again did not mean they supported 'pre-Islamic survivals.' Their ultimate aim was, in the Tsarist era, if not to 'Islamize' the Kazakhs in particular via Catherine's liberal policies, then to (later) Christianize them.[500] The Soviets, likewise, did not highlight 'pre-Islamic (religious) survivals' to help restore and revive them; they aimed to destroy them along with Islam and Christianity, labeling them all 'religious survivals' which were effectively written off as 'opiates of the masses', 'superstitious leftovers of the feudal past.' This is seen clearly, for example, in the Soviet Kazakh propagandist work by Zh. Duisenbin, *About the Religion of Islam and Its Current Standing*. In Chapter 3, "The Religion of Islam—A Remnant of the Past in our Nation," Duisenbin finishes his exposition with "A Few Words Regarding the Survivals within the Customs and Traditions of the Islamic Religion" by appealing to the Kazakhs to abandon these survivals and embrace atheism fully, with a view to leaving the past behind and progressing toward the presumed higher ground of enlightened Soviet civilization (see Chapter 7).[501] As per Privratsky's sources, "the Soviets would take the shamans away and shoot them."[502] Indeed, "shamans were always depicted as the main enemies of the communist regime" in the 1930s and beyond.[503] Both "Muslims and communists joined hands in pronouncing that shamanism was obsolete,"[504] because both were eager to eradicate it from Central Asia. Note also here that Duisenbin views these "survivals" as being, not separate from and outside of Kazakh Islam, but "within the Customs and Traditions of the Islamic Religion." The post-colonialist argument, therefore, applies equally to all these 'religious survivals', not strictly the 'Islamic'. Soviet propagandists understood 'pre-Islamic survivals' to be thoroughly "integrated" into and identified with "the 'Muslim' way of life'" (see on Privratsky and Deweese below). 'Pre-Islamic' and Islamic survivals were all targeted together. If any received special support and treatment, it was more the Islamic and Christian (and, to some degree, Buddhist), both during Tsarist times of 'religious toleration' from the reign of Catherine II (1762–1796) down to approximately the 1850s, when Islam was counted among the more advanced, civilized ways of life in comparison to nomadic primitive Shamanism and animism, and in Soviet times during and after The Great Patriotic War (i.e., World War Two).

The scholar's—and particularly here the historian's—task, therefore, remains, not to privilege any particular one over the other of the Soviet 'religious survivals,' but to sift through the historical—including the Tsarist and Soviet ethnographical as well as Muslim historiographical—evidence and painstakingly try to reconstruct the past as accurately and faithfully as humanly possible.[505] And this we do regardless of whose position it happens to support or not support and what corresponding praise or criticism it may invoke from the various religious (and other social, cultural, linguistic, political) interest groups who have a vested stake in the outcomes.[506] With respect to Islam in particular, the question of how far we should go in 'purifying' or 'cleansing' Central Asian history from references to 'pre-Islamic survivals' now hangs over the interpretation of every historical period. While there is no doubt that Islam has for long centuries been deeply and firmly rooted in Central Asia—including among the Kazakhs and their Turkic ancestors—and remains so to this day, it is unrealistic to expect that human history, including Central Asian history, does not consist of long, complicated and ongoing processes of religious-cultural exchange and negotiation between multiple centuries-long traditions.[507] It remains a very delicate balancing act to restore Islam to its rightful place within Central Asian historiography without completely ignoring, discarding and/or erasing certain historical evidence simply because it happens to agree, to whatever extent, with previous Tsarist and/or Soviet (or other 'Western') scholarship. That, indeed, is another major question hanging in the balances on the other side of the scales.

Debates Over Terminology: Beyond 'Syncretism' and 'Pre-Islamic' Constructs?

The debate over 'pre-Islamic survivals' is part of the ongoing debate over 'syncretism' as a construct which has long been employed within historical studies, particularly within the domains of 'religion' and 'culture.'[508] From the time of Plutarch down to the sixteenth century, 'syncretism' was viewed in primarily positive terms in relation to ideas of 'political unity', i.e., of those holding otherwise politically disparate positions joining together against a more threatening common foe. Even the Renaissance Christian humanist Erasmus held this view. 'Syncretism' took on predominantly negative religious connotations in connection to increasing disputes between Protestants and Catholics over the theological as well as historical 'purity' of 'the (divinely revealed) faith' from the sixteenth century onward. This view became enshrined in two works in particular: the Jesuit scholar Veit Erbermann's *Eirenikon Catholicum* published in 1645 followed by the 1648 work of the Lutheran theologian Johannes Konrad Dannhauer who "wrote a comprehensive monograph on the history of syncretism as the mixing of things which do not belong together." This view was not challenged until the late nineteenth-century history of religions school began to apply the concept to the historical evolution of all religions, including Judaism, Christianity and Islam. Inasmuch as that school aimed at undermining the exclusivist claims of the respective monotheistic faith traditions, 'syncretism' retained a negative connotation in their historiography. Rising debates continued into the twentieth century, with post-colonialist historiography representing one of the latest turns in the storyline.[509] Viewed comparatively in relation to Part One of this volume, this rather cursory glance at the history of the construct of 'syncretism' differs from the history of the construct of 'survivals' precisely because the two constructs are distinct, though they began to distantly merge from the sixteenth century, becoming more closely entangled from the late nineteenth century onward when both constructs took on formal theoretical significance in the study of religious-cultural history.

The history of the theoretical constructs aside, at a deeper level, the debate over 'syncretism' is a debate over precise definitions and the terminology and descriptive language used to convey those definitions within the corresponding historical narrative. Understandings and representations of 'conversion' lie at the heart of the controversy as well.

This includes 'processes' of religious conversion (as well as continuing future transformations) and corresponding, resulting religious identity at each new phase. Like the term 'syncretism' itself, 'pre-Islamic survivals' has come to be viewed as an inherently derogatory term immediately and exclusively associated with 'veneer' or 'two-tier'—i.e., 'syncretistic'—interpretations. This view in direct relation to the presumed overlap between these two constructs is clearly held by a number of post-Soviet Western and Islamic scholars engaging questions of Central Asian religious history and identity.[510] The presumably negative connotations of these two interrelated constructs, based strictly in 'religious studies', and particularly here, 'Islamic studies' paradigms, suggests that these scholars are, in fact, privileging Islamic theological perspectives, in harmony with post-colonialist Western reactions to Western Christian colonialist historiography, within their approaches and interpretations. Meanwhile, it is this overly narrow, singular view which results in the simple dichotomized option between a perceived 'pro-Islamic' and 'anti-Islamic' approach, with a concomitant push to then depict the various Central Asian peoples as thoroughly and purely Islamic as possible from the thirteenth or fourteenth century on, if not earlier. This overly narrow and polemical understanding of the historiographical options continues to not only dismiss but obstruct viable and productive scholarship.

Terminology is certainly important, though it is little more than a bandage on a deeper wound.[511] As noted above, Sultanova, for example, uses terms and phrases such as "deeply integrated" (i.e., integral) as well as "synthesis" and "accommodate." This is very similar to the language encountered in the work of certain Kazakh scholars regarding Islam's "integration" of prior religious traditions or the "process of mutual adaptation" as Islam spread into and encountered "old traditions and customs," wherein the latter "remained" an integral part of a uniquely Central Asian Islam.[512] Privratsky speaks of "contextualizations of Islam." He directly relates this to Deweese's "'thorough identification of the practices in question as part of the 'Muslim' way of life'," which is the precise position Privratsky argues for in concluding his own study of *Muslim Turkistan*.[513]

The *Oxford Handbook of Religious Conversion* supplies important scholarship in this field, much of it not directly addressing but nonetheless still applicable to questions of 'pre-Islamic survivals' in Muslim Central Asia. In a chapter titled "History and Religious Conversion," Marc David Baer analyzes four different cases of conversion as examples of what he terms "acculturation, adhesion, syncretism or transformation."[514] Important here is how Baer grounds his definitions of these terms, and their essential distinctions, in a clearly corresponding historiography. Elana Jefferson-Tatum's extended, critical review article, "Beyond Syncretism and Colonial Legacies in the Study of Religion: Critical Reflections on Harrison's *In Praise of Mixed Religion* and Blanes's *A Prophetic Trajectory*" (2020), notes that Harrison, *In Praise of Mixed Religion*, proposes three categories: "(1) symmetrical syncretism, (2) asymmetrical syncretism and (3) reflexive syncretism." Here, like Baer and certain other scholars, he seeks to retain (and redeem) "syncretism" as a term, but clarify a range of historical interpretations which he illustrates through three corresponding examples. Meanwhile, Jefferson-Tatum challenges this attempt to salvage notions of 'syncretism' as an unwitting means of perpetuating colonialist historiography and its outcomes.[515]

The debates are complex and run deep; they defy simplistic solutions; they instead invite ongoing collegial engagement and cooperation thru continuing dialog.[516] If we take all the various terms and combine them with others encountered in various discussions of the interaction between various religious-cultural traditions, the still incomplete list includes: absorption, accretion, assimilation, amalgamation, syncretism, synthesis, symbiosis, fusion, integration, accommodation, adaptation, contextualization, acculturation, inculturation, indigenization, translation and "displacement,"[517] the latter of which Deweese uses at times.[518] These terms are sometimes used as mere synonyms and other times as explicit, intentional contrasting options employed to represent subtly distinct theoretical views. Until a committee within Central Asian studies takes up the task of perhaps producing a glossary which might be adopted for the field,[519] it is not likely that complete, unanimous agreement will ever be reached on how to precisely define and when (if at all) to use each of these terms, so it remains, most importantly, up to each scholar to define what they mean by them within the context of their studies, and each reader to use that definition when critically engaging each respective scholar's work.

One thing which might benefit the field is agreement to avoid using the term 'pre-Islamic', due not only to its colonialist history, but its explicit connotations which set whatever traditions are in view in contrast (instead of harmony) with 'Islam'. If certain Central Asian traditions which preceded Islam historically 'survived'—in whatever precise form—together with Islam after the latter's spread into the various Central Asian regions, then 'pre-Islamic' is not an adequate, and indeed even a misleading, term to describe the long-term historical processes at work. Here questions must also be raised about just where a specific religious tradition arose—i.e., its 'geo-ethnic' or 'geo-cultural' place of origins—and the history of its spread into various parts of Central Asia and even broader Asia, Siberia and, in certain cases, still wider parts of the world. These questions become very complex, since some of the traditions involved extend well beyond Central Asia and well back into human history.[520] How many decades and even centuries does a tradition have to be present in a region or among a people for it to be considered 'indigenous'? Or if the term 'indigenous' is to be reserved strictly for traditions originating among a particular 'geo-ethnic' or 'geo-cultural' group and/or their ancestors, then can a 'foreign' tradition ever become deeply 'rooted' and sufficiently 'integrated' enough to be embraced as an 'authentic' part of a people's religious-cultural identity and heritage? Islam certainly came into Central Asia from out of Arabia. But its spread involved a long, historical process of 'adoption' by other peoples, particularly Iranian, which eventually led to its deep rootedness and integration into the lifeways of the various Central Asian peoples.[521] Of course, the process of becoming 'rooted' and 'integrated' is part of the ongoing process of not only 'conversion', but continuing religious 'transformations' as part of transforming social, cultural, economic, political and other landscapes (i.e., contexts) across time.

CONTINUITIES AND DISCONTINUITIES IN COLONIALIST VS. POST-COLONIALIST HISTORIOGRAPHY

Whether the term 'survival' can be usefully retained remains central to the discussion here. Meanwhile, as important as debates over terminology are, we are still left with several problems. The first is the comparative relation of all these various terminological descriptions with the nineteenth-century Marxian-Engelsian and later British anthropological views of Tylor, Frazer and company as well as the twentieth-century Soviet perspectives. The Marxian-Engelsian, British and Soviet views all held that pre-Islamic traditions and customs had been incorporated into the religion of Islam at its very foundations through a historical process.

Those 'pre-Islamic' elements thus became 'integrated' into the very essence of Islam as it then spread into the world, including Central Asia. They held the same essential views of Judaism, Christianity, Hinduism, Buddhism and other 'world religions.' What then is the difference between these earlier Marxian-Engelsian, British and Soviet views of Islam's synthesis (or contextualization, or whichever other term we wish to employ here) of various pre-existing traditions and customs during its rise in Arabia when compared with the ideas of "deep integration," "mutual adaptation," "contextualization" or the "'thorough identification of the practices in question as part of the 'Muslim' way of life'" espoused by the various interpreters above within the Central Asian context? One obvious difference in the Marxist and Soviet case is an explicitly atheist vantage. But metaphysical dimensions cannot serve here as the basis for distinguishing these earlier colonialist and later post-colonialist views because both are concerned with explaining human historical not divinely metaphysical processes. Whether one attributes the historical process to the providential guidance of God in some way or not does not change the historical processes themselves. Unless an interpreter is imposing an interpretation on the historical record which is intended to uphold notions of a 'divinely revealed' and thus theologically 'pure' form of a religion, then at the historical level itself there is no great difference conceptually between the colonialist and post-colonialist interpretations, at least with respect to the 'integration' of pre-Islamic elements into the very fabric of whatever they deem ultimately to be 'Islam' and 'Islamic.'

This question of the comparative relation of the former imperial-colonial and later post-colonialist interpretations of Central Asian and general Islamic history raises the further question as to precisely which 'survivals' in Muslim Central Asia Soviet ethnography in particular attributed to Islam's formational period in early seventh-century Arabia versus its later spread into Central Asia? Whether all Soviet historians, ethnographers and/or anti-religious pamphleteers were always consistent between the pre- to post-World War Two periods or even within those respective periods, there was agreement that Islam (like other world religions) had "contextualized" pre-existing traditions in its formational period which they then viewed as an "integral" part of Islam as it spread around the world. If one wishes to object to my use of "contextualization" and "integral" in reference to late nineteenth- and early twentieth-century Marxian-Engelsian, British and Soviet historical interpretations of the rise and formation of Islam, then a clear, convincing case must be made. And I suggest that it would be in that very debate—over what precise terminology should be used to describe the former imperial-colonial versus later post-colonial views—that (at least some of) the finer points of debate over 'pre-Islamic survivals' would be elucidated. In such a case, it would not be sufficient to simply assert that terms like "syncretism" should be used to describe the former imperial-colonial views and terms like "contextualization" should be reserved for later post-colonialist views. It would require clear, precise, distinct definitions of the various terms one would employ based in specific points identified within the corresponding historiographies, as in the work of Baer and Harrison (see above). This highlights the question as to how much these debates are located in the actual historical processes themselves versus the linguistic-semantic (cf. symbolic) choices used to describe those processes.

In Search of the Historical End Point of Conversion

Regarding, then, the actual historical processes, there is, even more importantly, the question of just when and where non-Islamic (cf. 'pre-Islamic') traditions can and should be identified within the history of various Central Asian Muslim peoples. Only up until the Islamic conquests under Qutaybah ibn Muslim (d. 715) during the time of the Umayyad Caliphate? Until the Battle of Talas in 751 CE? Until the rise of the large-scale conversion of Oghuz and Seljuk Turks in the tenth century? Until the time of Ahmed Yasawi (d. 1166?) and his disciples in the twelfth and thirteenth centuries? Until the conversion of Uzbek Khan (1313–41)? Until the rise of Baha'uddin Naqshband Bukhari (d. 1393) and the founding of the Naqshbandi *tariqa*? Until the observation of 'sun worship' among the Kazakhs in the early 1500s by the Persian Muslim historian Fazl Allah ibn Ruzbihan Isfahani (see Chapter 3)? Until the time of Catherine II down to the mid-1800s (see Appendix One)? Down to the time of Abai Kunanbaiuhli (d. 1904), i.e., the late nineteenth, early twentieth century?

At what precise point historically does the process of 'Islamization' reach a perfect one-hundred percent, to the point that all 'pre-Islamic' traditions have entirely disappeared and it becomes historically incorrect and illegitimate to mention them as recognizably distinct historical elements in relation to each of the distinct Muslim peoples of Central Asia? One major response to this question has, I suggest, already been poignantly offered by the team of nine Kazakh historians who co-authored the 2021 *History of Kazakhstan* textbook which notes that "religion and spirituality are so subtle matters that it is impossible to believe that once established in society" they remain forever enshrined thereafter. Flexible, open approaches are required which recognize processes of both 'conversion' and 'de-conversion' which are all part of ongoing historical 'transformation' across space and time (see end of Chapter 8). Distinctions between 'history and (collective) memory' are also important to bear in mind.[522]

DISTINGUISHING HISTORICAL FACT FROM FICTION: DESCRIPTION VS. ANALYSIS VS. THESIS

Abai Kunanbaiuhli recognized the continuation of 'pre-Islamic survivals' among the Kazakhs down to his time, i.e., the late nineteenth, early twentieth century. His interpretation, in fact, implied that 'pre-Islamic survivals' had remained alongside Islam since Islam's initial penetration into Central Asia (see Chapter 4). Adeeb Khalid and other modern scholars who still hold that "the Islamization of the Kazakhs was...completed only in the late nineteenth century" thus have one of the strongest Kazakh historical figures to support their claims.[523] And in Abai's case, the particular 'pre-Islamic survival' which he cited as an example (cf. evidence)—the appeal to *Ot Ana* ("the Mother of Fire") as oil is poured onto the fire and a blessing invoked—was one which Shokan Valikhanov had noted earlier in his mid-nineteenth-century work. Abai's analytical vantage, however, differed from Shokan's. Whereas Shokan saw in the survivals evidence that Islam had not been deeply absorbed into Kazakh beliefs and lifeways, which then served as his justification for his anti-Islamic proposals, Abai, nearly half a century later, saw in them evidence of their continuing decline in direct proportional relation to the deepening spread of Islam among the Kazakh people which he welcomed. True, later Soviet ethnographers sought to exploit both Valikhanov's and Abai's observations in the same manner, as if they were in perfect agreement, but this was exploitative and ungrounded '(pseudo-)analysis' of the historical fact of Abai's expressed viewpoint.

Prior to both Abai and Valikhanov, A.I. Levshin had observed (1822–1832) that some of the early nineteenth-century Kazakhs "think that apart from the good deity that cares for the happiness of people, whom they call *Khudai*, there is also an evil spirit [jinni], or

Shaitan [Shaytan], the source of the evil."[524] There is nothing untenable in Levshin's description here of the 'historical facts.' That is to say, Levshin's ethnography was correct in identifying these beliefs among the Kazakhs. However, his 'analysis' was wrong, because he (appears to have) attributed them to the dualism of Manicheanism or perhaps Persian Zoroastrianism instead of the Qur'anic monotheism of Islam. He then used his misguided analysis as part of the 'evidence' for asserting his 'dual faith' thesis. The available historical evidence supports the conclusion that these elements of belief, for the Kazakhs, were more likely understood as part of their Islamic faith, not Manicheanism or Zoroastrianism. But the elements in and of themselves were, again, generally speaking, genuine and accurate historical observations on the part of Levshin. He, like Valikhanov and Abai both before him, did not simply fabricate them from out of his imagination, he simply interpreted them through a colored lens.

These same issues apply to Muslim historians and ethnographers, as seen in the cases of Fazl Allah ibn Ruzbihan Isfahani and Mirza Muhammad Haidar Dughlat (see Chapter 3). As Dughlat himself explicitly declares and then demonstrates at various junctures, a strong orthodox Sunni bias permeates his 1547 *History of the Moghuls of Central Asia*. He not only consciously excludes "infidels" and heretics from any noteworthy place in his history, he is ready to visit "the punishment of death" upon sects which he deems aberrant from his own views, which follow the conservative Sunni 'ulema of the Mughal courts in India under Humayun (r. 1530–1556). Isfahani, likewise, portrays those he deems as "apostates" (cf. "heretics"), particularly in this case the Kazakhs, in an unfavorable light, excluding them from any rightful Muslim identity. In the latter case, I have suggested, based on reference to Dughlat's work, that there are possible ways to accept Isfahani's description of Kazakh "sun worship" without applying the same analysis or drawing the same conclusion. If my suggested revision of Isfahani's analysis were followed, it would yield a more favorable Muslim (Sufi) identity for the Kazakhs, though this in itself would not necessarily eliminate the probable Tengrist dimensions involved. I would rather (tentatively here) argue for an integrated Sufi-Tengrist view along the lines of Nazira Nurtazina's interpretation (see below and Chapter 8). Qurban-Ali Khalidi's *Biographical Dictionary* covering the Semei region in Kazakhstan from 1770 to 1912 also reveals a bias against understandings of "Islam" which do not meet his own more "pious," orthodox standards. Otherwise there is no good explanation for his exclusion of one of the most well-known and influential Kazakh Muslim voices of his day, Abai Kunanbaiuhli (1845–1904), from a proper place in his dictionary. Abai's reputation was well established, across Semei and far beyond, by the time Khalidi penned his work. It is quite reasonable to conclude that Khalidi excluded Abai because of the latter's essentially Jadid-style critique of the Tatar-dominated mosques and what Abai considered to be a more simple-minded *taqlid*-based (i.e., *madhhad*-based) faith dependent on "the words of the Mullah,"[525] i.e., the very kind of Islamic holy men which Khalidi extolled in his work. It should also be acknowledged that Khalidi's "biographies" (like other Islamic biographical dictionaries) carry hagiographical undertones which situates them all more properly in the realm of religious as opposed to academic historiography.[526] All in all, the claim that Muslim scholarship in Central Asia has been (noticeably) more accurate and reliable (cf. less biased) than Russian scholarship remains yet to be demonstrated with a clear, convincing and in-depth comparative study. The results of this study raise important counterpoints to such a thesis.[527]

Along similar though distinct lines, Peter B. Golden concludes his 1997 study of "Wolves, Dogs and Qipčaq Religion" by noting that

> the indigenous religious cults of the Qipčaqs do not appear to have been very much different from those of the other Turkic peoples of the Middle Ages. As these beliefs were largely unwritten (there was no scriptural orthodoxy), and our sources, invariably stemming from usually hostile sedentary states, mention them only in passing and often didactically to stress the "barbarism" of the uncouth nomads, we can catch only fleeting and sometimes distorted glimpses of the Qipčaq spiritual world. As a consequence, comparative data are extremely important. Qipčaq religion, then, must be viewed not only within the context of steppe traditions, especially including those of the earlier Iranian peoples who inhabited the Eurasian grasslands for over a millennium until the Hunnic era, but also within a global context.[528]

What all these examples point up is an important, fundamental distinction within historical studies between 'description,' 'analysis' and 'thesis', with the latter corresponding to 'appropriation' or 'praxis' as well as 'aim' and 'agenda'. Granted the lines between these various terms are not as clear-cut as they may appear semantically, since for example all description contains some measure of analysis inherently within it and could even be said to imply a certain thesis or argument; but this risks reading too much into 'description' or even 'analysis' simply because of what may in fact be inevitable, unavoidable or, likewise, simply possible implications which are not necessarily the 'agenda' of the historian. The distinction of categories, therefore, remains viable and even necessary. The only alternative here is to argue that everything the Russian and/ or Muslim sources observed and recorded was completely fabricated for strictly propagandistic purposes.[529] This, however, is an extreme, untenable position. What we have left is the very complicated task of having to carefully sift through Tsarist, Soviet, Western and Muslim ethnography and historiography to weed out the 'historical facts' from the faulty 'analysis' and their related policy and other agendas, making use of the former without perpetuating the latter in new forms and ways. Whether, as in some cases just noted (cf. esp., Levshin and Isfahani), certain analytical observations or arguments regarding 'pre-Islamic survivals' should be more properly interpreted as authentically 'Islamic' is certainly necessary, but neither the evidence nor the interpretations can be forced to fit a pre-conceived or pre-desired mold.[530] Setting out to "defend" particular religious identities—whether Muslim, Tengrist, Shamanist or otherwise—is no better than setting out like the Tsarists or Soviets to deny and denigrate them. It only inverts and thus perpetuates the very dimensions of certain Tsarist and Soviet historiography which post-colonialist critiques have helped identify.

Historiographical Trends in the Post-World War Two Era

As demonstrated in the main body of this study, historical 'survivals' have been appropriated in various, even directly opposite ways by various interpreters across the centuries—from both conservative and liberal anti-religious (cf. anti-pagan, anti-Catholic, anti-Islamic, etc.), to monotheistic degenerationist, (social Darwinian) evolutionary progressivist, (romantic) folk-national reconstructionist, world religious and human civilizational reconstructionist,[531] religious revivalist, interdependent humanitarianist, multi-culturalist/pluralist and more. This brings us back to a key point which further complicates the issue. There are more than simply two contrasting, diametrically opposed historiographical options—'pro-Islamic' vs. 'anti-Islamic'—in relation to the question of the academic viability and application of historical 'survivals' in Muslim Central Asia (and beyond). Two of the most important of these are the historical reconstructionist and interdependent humanitarianist. Both of these are closely connected to studies of crosscultural contact and exchange within not only Central Asian, but broader world history.[532]

As I (and others) have documented elsewhere, historiographical trends in the post-World War Two era went in at least—for our purposes here—four distinct, sometimes competing, sometimes complimentary directions. First, post-colonialist historiography would eventually emerge in direct relation to and even as an instrument of the new wave of decolonization movements. Post-colonialist historiography aimed at decolonizing history of its imperialist-colonialist (cf. hegemonic) interpretations and corresponding agendas. Inasmuch as most of the Islamic world had been subject to various forms of Western imperialism and colonialism, the push has been toward correcting (cf. revising) histories of Islam and Islamic societies. This post-colonialist revision of Islam and other non-Western religious traditions was part of a broader effort to correct (cf. revise) indigenous racial, ethnic, national, cultural, civilizational, gender and other related histories. The objective here was to restore the presumably 'true' (cf. 'positive') image and reputation of these various human identity groups who had been subjugated through hegemonic colonialist historiography (cf. discourse) by restoring their respective histories to their 'true' and rightful interpretations. 'History' itself, as a 'scientific discipline,' had been essentially created by Western powers for distinctively Western nationalist and imperialist purposes, but 'history' itself as a discipline did not need to be entirely discarded; it was not deemed inherently corrupt and rotten to the core; it rather needed to be retooled (cf. decolonized, de-Westernized) and thus restored to proper, legitimate ends. Part of the conundrum here was and remains that post-colonialist historiography essentially relies on many of the same historiographical assumptions and approaches as colonialist historiography (cf. archival and other source research, source criticism [understood in the broadest, not more restrictive, disciplinary sense], peer review, etc.). It likewise shared the assumption that their own religious, racial, ethnic, national, cultural and civilizational identities were each distinct, unique 'historical realities' with their own distinct, unique and real, true histories. This means they were more 'exclusivist' as opposed to 'inclusivist' in orientation, with particular contrast to and exclusion of any 'Western' or 'white European' or other 'foreign' sources or identities, in order to counter any interpretations which might reflect 'dependence' on or 'borrowing' from any 'Western civilizational' or other 'foreign' sources, since ideas of 'dependence' and 'borrowing' undergirded arguments of 'superiority' and 'inferiority' as well as 'corrupted, weakened impurity' or 'incapacity' to stand 'independently' and integrally on their own.

Second, post-modernist (cf. post-structuralist) critiques of history and historiography roughly paralleled post-colonialist critiques and shared together the aim to undermine imperialist-colonialist historiography, but post-modernism took a more radical, 'deconstructionist' route. The post-modernist approach called into question the clear, orderly (cf. structured, structuralist) scientific basis of modernist (cf. colonialist) historiography and its interpretations which were based in assumptions of the 'objective' scientific analyses of stable, fixed objective 'reality'. Various racial, ethnic, national, cultural, civilizational and other such 'identities' were, they argued, subjective 'constructs' of their own "imagined" and "invented" (cf. constructivist) fabrication. Likewise, history itself, as a 'scientific discipline,' had been essentially created by Western powers for nationalist and imperialist purposes. This view they shared with the post-colonialist critique. But their conclusion differed, namely that all historiography was, therefore, necessarily subjective and inherently skewed; there was no 'historical reality' which a supposedly objective 'historical narrative' could represent. 'History' as a discipline needed to be re-classified and re-assigned within academic institutions (and the broader public) as types of literary fiction or mythology (cf. 'myth history').[533]

Third, 'subaltern' historiography combined elements of both post-colonialist and post-modernist critiques. So did the 1960s–70s 'cultural turn' in anthropology, ethnography and historiography reflected in the work of Clifford Geertz (and others such as Deweese and Privratsky). Geertzian-influenced approaches have argued—in varying ways and to varying degrees—that straightforward 'historical narrative' is deficient for determining the ultimate meaning and identity of varying religious, cultural, ethnic and other related groups.[534] They instead advocate a 'thick description' approach which gives voice to native and indigenous peoples, allowing them by way of their own (narrative) accounts—both oral and written, past and present—to tell us who they understand themselves to be, as opposed to us determining this for them by way of a supposedly objective historical account. The shift of emphasis and focus is away from 'history' itself to 'collective (historical) memory' and thus away from questions of objective interpretations of the past to the psychological implications of human understandings of the past. While certainly making significant contributions to post-colonialist revisions of colonialist historiography, anthropology and ethnography, this approach nonetheless significantly risks allowing interpretations of history to be driven by (both individual and collective) psychological understandings of the past, so that standard, traditional historical accounts—if they are deemed worth researching and writing at all—are made to at least significantly align with, if not entirely conform to and support conceived and desired psychological identities, rather than vice versa.[535] In this respect, it leaves itself open to some of the same critiques leveled against imperialist-colonialist historiography by both the post-colonialist and post-modernist schools.

Fourth, in the eyes of many, Western nationalist historiographies which had been taking distinct shape since the nineteenth century had helped spark and drive World War Two. Their racist underpinnings had, in the Nazi German case in particular, contributed most acutely and specifically to the Holocaust.[536] They also served to support South African Apartheid, American segregation and more, continuing even down to the present.[537] UNESCO thus launched, in 1945, a History of Humanity project to counter racist and related nationalist historiographies.[538] Their aim was to demonstrate all humanity's interdependence and equality by highlighting the way in which all the various peoples and cultures (including religions) of the world have contributed to the human story, i.e., human civilization as a whole. Although the entire History of Humanity was in view, national and civilizational histories remained a distinct part of their focus. The project thus gave particular attention to those peoples and cultures which had been denigrated by Western colonialist historiography. In this respect, it too had a post-colonialist agenda. Among those peoples and cultures were not only Islam and various Islamic societies, but indigenous peoples and their religious-cultural traditions as well. These of course had been depicted as 'backward, uncivilized, primitive, savage' and the like. They included traditions such as shamanism, totemism, animism and more, including by implication Tengrism. They also included more indigenous, local forms of various world religious traditions. The latter point raises the question of whether it is more appropriate to speak of religious traditions which have spread across ethnic, cultural, linguistic, national, civilizational and other 'borders' in the singular or the plural, i.e., a singular 'Buddhism', 'Christianity' or 'Islam' versus multiple 'Buddhisms', 'Christianities' and 'Islams'. Both, in fact, have their place within historical studies, which emphasize both continuity and discontinuity, i.e., shared, common versus unique distinguishing characteristics.[539]

'Survivals' as Historical Heritage, 'Remnants' of Crosscultural Contact and Exchange

Highlighting the contributions of each religious-cultural tradition requires recognition of those traditions historically. It also begs the question of what influence they may have had in shaping beliefs, values, customs, practices and more in subsequent societies, cultures and civilizations all the way down to the present-day.[540] Ongoing "influence" into subsequent generations is effectively a form of "survival," whether it is "contextualized" or not. Indeed, "contextualization" itself implies a form of authentic "preservation," otherwise it is merely "displacement." There is an intimate relation here between the "survival" and the "preservation" of humankind's cultural-civilizational heritage. This concerns not only properly understanding the human past and present, especially in terms of human interdependence, but of offering due and proper credit, as well as fostering appreciation, respect and admiration, along with, in some cases, the (sometimes far-reaching) implications these dimensions of historical study have for helping foster mutual understanding, peaceful co-existence and continuing dialog and potential cooperation in the present.[541]

Among numerous others, two of the most prominent areas of historical study where these issues are central are the history of medicine, science and technology and the history of law. It is historically accurate and appropriate to recognize that medical, scientific and technological contributions from ancient Africa,[542] the Near-Middle East, Eastern and Central Asia and Native America have contributed to the making of our modern world. This means there is a 'living' historical link between the past and present which remains real and valid, i.e., the past continues to "survive" or be "preserved" down to and live within the present.[543] 'Islamic civilization' has been and remains an integral part of—i.e., it has both benefited from and contributed to—this human historical heritage.

With respect to law,[544] I have addressed these matters in my recent co-edited volume with Anver Emon, *Reason, Revelation and Law in Islamic and Western Theory and History*. In the Introductory chapter on "Reason, Revelation and Law in Global Historical Perspective," I discussed, among other things, the complicated history behind the United Nations Universal Declaration of Human Rights. That history involves charting contributions from multiple world religious, cultural, national and civilizational traditions, including Islamic and various indigenous sources. It involves questions which go well beyond law, into values, ideals, customs and more.[545] In my later chapter treating "The Historical Relation of Islamic and Western Law," I chart the historical sources of Western and Islamic law in relation to one another across fourteen centuries. The emphasis of the article is on the ('surviving') influence of various Islamic sources within and behind various Western legal traditions.[546]

I have likewise lectured on the topic of "Islamic Contributions to Western Civilization" where I have highlighted cultural, legal, medical, scientific, literary, linguistic and numerous other contributions historically. I have drawn from numerous studies published on this topic over the past century or more, with a surge of renewed interest following 9/11. Most notably among these is the volume edited by Nayef R.F. al-Rodhan, *The Role of the Arab-Islamic World in the Rise of the West: Implications for Contemporary Trans-Cultural Relations* (2012).[547] The subtitle of the work very accurately speaks to the issues at stake in these matters of historiographical framing.

In a forthcoming volume on *Mosaic and Sharia Law in American National History and Identity*, I include a section on "European and American Interest in Ibn Tufayl and Islamic Rationalist Views of Divine and Natural Law, 1671–1721." I argue there, among other things, that the historical streams of Islamic rationalist thought, represented by Ibn Tufayl and Ibn Rushd in particular, fed into the founding of the American nation and its ideals based in natural law theory via John Locke and certain other European thinkers as well as Thomas Paine, Thomas Jefferson, James Madison and others. The Islamic rationalist contribution remains (i.e., "survives" as) a recognizable part of the integral heritage of 'Western' and particularly in this case American religious-cultural and sociopolitical ideals and resulting praxis down to the present. It has, however, been largely passed over in silence in most American historiography. This silence is quite possibly intentional in some cases, particularly among American Christian nationalist and 'Western civilizationalist' historians and their audiences who do not wish to grant any recognition or corresponding credit to 'Islamic civilization' for any such contributions, precisely again because of the far-reaching religious, cultural and even political implications for the present-day. A number of American and Western Christian historians want Christianity to retain its predominate (cf. hegemonic) position within Western and American history.

There are both Christian and Muslim (as well as Jewish, Hindu and other religious) scholars engaged in efforts to demonstrate the beneficial "influence" of their respective religious traditions on human history. These assertions imply a lasting "influence" which reaches across centuries, even down to the present. As a number of my various publications demonstrate, I agree that the Islamic tradition, for example, has made beneficial contributions to Western and American civilization which reach (i.e., have been "preserved" or "survived") all the way down to the present. I also agree that they deserve recognition for their contributions, and that this recognition can result in increased appreciation, respect and even a 'debt of gratitude' for what they have contributed. The fostering of such attitudes, in turn, can contribute toward (not perfect or utopian, but nonetheless) increased levels of peaceful co-existence and even cooperation for the further benefit of humanity, locally and globally. The difference, however, between certain of these religious scholars and others, including myself, is the difference between an 'exclusivist' versus an 'inclusivist' approach. A number of these religious scholars wish to privilege their own religious traditions above all others and even seek to make them the sole source of all that is good and right and beneficial for humanity premised on their theological conviction that their own faith tradition is, in their view, 'divinely inspired' and thus represents the only valid source of all that is good, right, true and beneficial for humankind. In taking this approach, they also seek to minimize not only the contributions, but the very presence of what they view as 'competing' and potentially 'corrupting,' especially 'idolatrous' religious traditions.[548] This 'exclusivist' approach reflects a hegemonic historiography which shares much in common with Western imperialist-colonialist historiography. It is perfectly reasonably to ask how such historiographies might be operating in Central Asia amid the ongoing post-Soviet revivalist debates (see Chapter 8).

Academic disciplines, including history, cannot allow the results of their studies to be determined or dictated by theological (or other ideological) beliefs. Humanities scholarship remains inclusivist in its approach, impartially embracing all of human history, including all of its religious and cultural traditions. Whether the analysis of the contributions of those various, respective traditions is 'positive' or 'negative,' or a mix of both in whatever balance, is a separate matter, but it starts from acknowledging their presence if and when the historical evidence merits it. And in cases of debate, it seeks to address those debates openly, fairly and honestly, especially in the classroom and the public domain, as opposed to minimizing or excluding them altogether in an effort to sway public opinion.

Both 'consistency' and 'impartiality' are essential elements in historical scholarship. It is clear that various religious scholars in many parts of the world are eager to highlight the presence and contributions (cf. 'influence') of their own traditions within their historiographies. Certainly this is the case in the way that Muslim scholars accentuate Islamic contributions to Western civilization. And they have much historical evidence to support their arguments. The question is whether the approaches and methodologies which they employ are being consistently and impartially applied when it comes to the influence and contributions of non-Islamic traditions within the histories of 'Islamic societies', including 'Muslim Central Asia'? Are our historiographies religiously or academically driven? The same questions apply to any and all such religious scholars. It would be only naïveté to deny that religiously driven historiographies are a very real and ongoing problem within the historiography of not only Central Asia and other parts of the 'Muslim world,' but across much of 'Western (Jewish and) Christian Civilization', Judaism and especially Christianity in American history, Judaism in Israeli history, Hinduism and Islam in Indian history, ad infinitum. The only solution is consistent and impartial application of proper historical methodology within historical scholarship. Post-colonialist historiography has made substantial contributions toward correcting and rebalancing prior imperialist-colonialist agendas. It cannot allow its own agenda, however, to itself become exclusivist and/or hegemonic in the process of rebalancing those scales.[549]

'Religious Survivals', 'Dual Faith' and "Integral" Religious Identities

Historical interpretations which include reference to 'pre-Islamic survivals' do not, in and of themselves, inherently violate the "integrity" of Central Asian Islam, past or present. Historical interpretations which intentionally downplay, ignore or exclude evidence are the only things which lack "integrity," regardless of which side of the scales they fall on. If a cultural anthropologist or ethnographer asks a Japanese person today whether they consider themselves Shinto or Buddhist, they will encounter a perplexed look followed most likely by a response which explains how they observe both Shinto and Buddhist customs in an "integrated" fashion within the natural course of their lives. A Japanese proverb sums it up well when it says that one is 'born Confucian, married Shinto and buried Buddhist.' Should the cultural anthropologist or ethnographer conclude that they lack "integrity" in their religious identity? Does religious "integrity" demand that we identify only one religious tradition in relation to each individual or people group? Which is more important, the "integrity" of people themselves or the religion? Note here that the question is not about 'religious pluralism', at least not as understood in the Western democratic sense. That is a related but distinct topic. The Japanese have "integrated" Shinto and Buddhism into their singular, "unified" lives, and if we argue for the influence (cf. 'survival') of Confucian ancestor rites within the Buddhist home altar rituals—whether influenced historically in China (and/or Korea) prior to reaching Japan, or in Japan itself—then there are not just two, but three traditions which have been integrated, synthesized, contextualized and unified together within Japanese life, both individual and corporate. True, historically there have been certain periods of intensified competition between Japanese Shinto and Buddhism, particularly from the sixth to eighth centuries during the initial arrival of Buddhism from China and again in the late nineteenth-century Meiji Restoration when Shinto was declared the official 'national religion' in connection with the restoration of the emperor. And there are struggles at times between various Buddhist sects in particular. But overall a harmonious, integral synthesis has been achieved throughout most of Japanese history down to the present (cf. shinbutsu-shūgō, 神仏習合).[550]

My point here is not that the Japanese and Kazakh situations are identitcal, they are not. It is rather to simply say that I find nothing which lacks "integrity" in Tattygul Kartaeva's historical interpretation which holds that "the religions of ancient Zoroastrianism, animism, totemism, Tengrism, fetishism and Shamanism…have merged…together with Islam in a continuing cooperative partnership" (see Chapter 8).[551] Nor is there anything "anti-Islamic" about it. This is from a historian's (as opposed to a theologian's or religious legal scholar's) point of view, particularly a historian focused on questions of (1) crosscultural contact and exchange, (2) historical heritage and (3) the relation of past and present in Central Asian and broader world history. Neither is her interpretation simply mimicking the theories of Shokan Valikhanov and/or Tsarist and Soviet scholarship, though she does draw from Valikhanov's work, among many other sources, primary and secondary, foreign and national. I suggest it should rather be understood from an equally post-colonial, in particular post-Soviet, perspective which seeks to recover and reclaim her own Central Asian, and particularly in this case Kazakh—and either way, indigenous—historical heritage. It is not 'pre-Islamic', since she includes Islam as part of that integral, indigenous heritage and even recognizes its deep historical roots; if anything, it is 'pre-Russian'. That would, in fact, mean she is seeking to 'de-Russify' Kazakh history, which is effectively to 'decolonize' it. In doing so, she distinguishes 'description' of historical fact from 'analysis' and 'agenda' in her sources. This does not address the question of historical accuracy and/or what my own views of the history may or may not be; only methodology, orientation and aim in relation to the general question of whether her interpretation should be considered "unintegral," "anti-Islamic" and/or "Russified."

Though each have their own unique distinctions, the historical interpretations of Tursin Gabitov, Nagima Baitenova, Nazira Nurtazina, Erke Kartabaeva, Kairat Zatov and others allow for the recognition of Kazakh and Central Asian indigenous religious-cultural traditions to be integrated into and/or alongside their Islamic faith in various ways so that their historical roots are somehow still discernable and traceable down to the present (cf. 'survivals'), with all of them together, in integrated fashion, forming part of their Kazakh Muslim identity (see esp., Chapter 8).[552] These interpreters acknowledge many of the same essential traditions and customs observed by Valikhanov and Abai (cf. historical 'description'), though they do not necessarily come to the same conclusions, precisely because there is no one-for-one deterministic relationship between religious-cultural 'survivals' and what they ultimately mean (i.e., what their implications are) to each specific interpreter. The same holds true—in varying ways and to varying degrees—across Muslim Central Asia,[553] indeed throughout much of the wider Islamic world.

One thing is clear for most of these interpreters however: Islam remains the dominant tradition which supplies their main identity and framework for integrating and observing various historic customs and traditions into their present lifeways and worldview. This study is aimed, not at countering or overturning that historic and present though ever-transforming reality, but further elucidating it, especially by furthering the ongoing dialogue on these important and complex historical questions, particularly that of religious-cultural 'survivals' within the historiography of Central Asia.

Conclusion: A Summary of the Main Points of the Study

It has been the aim of this inquiry to advance the study and understanding of Central Asian religious-cultural history and historiography by placing the topic of 'pre-Islamic survivals' within its much broader world historical and historiographical frames. By doing so, this work attempts to open the way to broader, more productive dialog which moves beyond the rather limited range of historiographical options for understanding and dealing with 'pre-Islamic survivals' which have thus far prevailed within certain Western and Islamic scholarly treatments, namely the overly simplified dichotomy between either a 'Soviet' or 'Islamic studies' approach.

This study also holds value for world religious-cultural studies, including ongoing debates over (historical interpretations of) "syncretism" and "conversion" as phenomena recurring in various forms and contexts throughout world history. It has likewise engaged questions about definitions of Islam, history as identity and heritage, pluralism and multiculturalism, interreligious relations and more, both historically and presently.

As noted in the Preface, my engagement with the work of various scholars in this volume is limited to the select, distinct points which have been addressed. Any critical engagement in particular should be read in light of my very deep and genuine respect and appreciation for all of

© The Editor(s) (if applicable) and The Author(s), under exclusive license to Springer Nature Singapore Pte Ltd. 2023
R. Weller, *'Pre-Islamic Survivals' in Muslim Central Asia*, Islam and Global Studies,
https://doi.org/10.1007/978-981-19-5697-3

my fellow colleagues and the otherwise rich and valuable scholarship they have contributed to the various related fields. This volume is not intended as a final word on the subjects it has treated, but an invitation to ongoing peaceful and cooperative academic dialog within Central Asian, Islamic and world historical studies with a view to working together to further enrich the various related and intersecting fields with which it deals. Along with (1) the chapter and section overview at the end of the Introduction (see Chapter 1) and (2) the introductory and concluding reflections to each of the sections and chapters, the following brief outline provides a summary of the central points advanced within this volume:

1. From a world historical vantage, 'survivals' historiography evidences very deep and wide-ranging complexity in terms of the contexts within and purposes to which it is interpreted and appropriated. These include both conservative and liberal anti-religious (cf. anti-pagan, anti-Catholic, anti-Islamic, etc.), to monotheistic degenerationist, (social Darwinian) evolutionary progressivist, (romantic) folk-national reconstructionist, world religious-cultural and human civilizational reconstructionist, religious revivalist, interdependent humanitarianist, multiculturalist/pluralist and more.
2. Tsarist and Soviet 'survivals' historiography and ethnography is informed by much greater diversity than simply E.B. Tylor (and L.H. Morgan). The Russian Orthodox 'dual faith' tradition runs deep and strong; among all the various world historical sources, including that of Tylor and company, the Russian Orthodox has exerted the greatest influence within Russian historiographic and ethnographic traditions, both Tsarist and Soviet. The Russian Orthodox tradition ties into historic streams of both Western and Eastern Christianity as well as later offshoot schools, particularly the folk-national reconstructionist. The Middle Eastern and Central Asian Islamic traditions also played a significant role in helping inform and shape both Tsarist and Soviet ethnographic approaches to the Central Asian Muslim peoples.
3. The appropriation of and debates over 'survivals' historiography in the early twenty-first century extend well beyond the former Tsarist-Soviet domains, into modern Turkey, Iran, black Muslim and Christian Africa, Berber Muslim North Africa, South and Southeast Asia, and more. We cannot view or approach the problem, therefore, as a uniquely 'post-Soviet' issue, especially not one which is framed in simple, dichotomist terms, i.e., as an option

between 'Russified anti-Islamic' scholarship dependent on and perpetuating nothing but old Soviet sources and their interpretations versus 'pro-Islamic' scholarship situated within 'Islamic studies' and dependent upon allegedly more reliable Islamic sources.
4. Post-Soviet Central Asian national (cf. indigenous) scholars draw from a diverse array of sources. Their acquaintance with and expertise in the Russian sources, both Tsarist and Soviet, exceeds that of most Western scholars. Beyond this, they demonstrate sufficient acquaintance with Western (English, German, French, etc.), Central Asian, Middle Eastern Turkish, Arab and Persian Islamic, and other sources. Their interpretations of the historical relation of "pre-Islamic" Central Asian and Islamic traditions are complex, not simple regurgitations of Tsarist and Soviet views. Within the post-Soviet context, influence from Turkish scholarship may in fact be just as great, possibly even greater, than the former Tsarist and/or Soviet sources. Beyond this, the Kazakhs and other Central Asian Muslim peoples, like their Turkish (and Iranian) counterparts, are, likewise, drawing directly from their own indigenous Central Asian traditions, i.e., the historically-culturally inclusivist-integrationist, preservationist approaches, reflected in the work of Firdousi, Balasaghuni, Kashgari and others, which are distinct from the more 'purist, exclusivist' Islamic paradigms emerging from out of the Middle Eastern religious-cultural complex. In doing so they preserve their Islamic identity in uniquely Central Asian fashion.
5. 'Conversion' and 'transformation' cannot be neatly dichotomized and juxtaposed over against one another. 'Conversion' is itself a form of 'transformation'. Both are part of the same historical process of 'religious change over time'. 'Deconversion' is, likewise, a part of the same continuum within the ebb and flow of religious-cultural history.
6. Given the complex nature of historical processes, it is problematic to posit a centuries-long history in which Central Asian Islam remained, after a certain proposed point of conversion, insulated and isolated from "pre-Islamic" Central Asian religious beliefs and customs, including Tengrism, Shamanism, ancestor veneration, etc. 'Purist' and 'isolationist' views—which depend upon paradigms of complete (cf. 'triumphant') 'displacement' of prior by later traditions and/or emphasize only 'internal' developments thereafter, to the downplay or even exclusion of subsequent

'external' influences—share strong affinities with both earlier and later twentieth-century 'civilizational isolationist' views. Likewise, in spite of being focused upon a particular religious tradition, in this case Islam, such 'exclusivist' historiography displays close parallels with the exclusivist nature of European nationalist historiography as it took shape from the later nineteenth century down to World War Two and beyond. Natural historical processes typically evidence significant diversity and complexity; they are influenced by both 'internal' and 'external' factors to varying degrees in each unique historical context. Interpretational 'frameworks' which prejudice in one direction or the other can, in the short run, serve helpful corrective, revisionist purposes, but can also swing too far in reactionary measure to the other extreme, perpetuate unnecessary debate and run the risk of becoming counterproductive to genuine advances in historiography. The influence of not only political ideologies, but also religious theologies which, by their nature, insist on being dominant and thus hegemonic must also be grappled with openly, fairly and honestly.

7. A careful, thorough and up-to-date 'Religious History of Central Asia' remains to be written—one which is not theologically-religiously, ethnically-culturally or politically motivated and guided, is based on (i.e., synthesizes) all currently available sources/scholarship, includes balanced attention to interreligious encounters and exchanges, and makes a special effort to provide a more genuine history of Shamanism within Central Asia, particularly though not exclusively in relation to Islam. 'Histories' of particular sources which elucidate how various peoples have viewed themselves are helpful, they have their own important place within the historiography. They are, however, more properly understood as 'historical anthropologies' or 'historical ethnographies'; they take their place alongside the various cultural anthropological and ethnographic studies focused on the post-Soviet period, as opposed to being more complete and proper histories. Likewise, histories based on particular sources and/or histories of 'Islam in Central Asia' are necessary and make essential contributions, but are also incomplete and insufficient with respect to a more comprehensive 'Religious History of Central Asia.' Until such a history is written, all discussions about the relation between 'pre-Islamic survivals' and Islam within Central Asia, past and present, help advance the dialog, but

remain limited and tentative, including this study. Arguments for and against 'objectivity' apply to all disciplines, so ultimately provide no compelling basis for dismissing such efforts.
8. With respect to Central Asian and particularly Kazakh religious historiography, the historical sources, both primary and secondary, have thus far not provided us with enough conclusive evidence in either direction to resolve the debates over the historical relation of 'pre-Islamic' and Islamic traditions. And those sources may, in the end, prove incapable of doing so. Measured humility which acknowledges uncertainty, remains genuinely and critically open to all the various options—including any necessary revisions along the way—and speaks fairly in terms of possibility and probability will mark the best, most honest scholarship for the foreseeable future.

APPENDICES

Appendix One: The Early Twentieth-Century Chernavsky-Dobrosmyslov Debate—Did Catherine the Great (r. 1762–1796) Help Convert the Kazakhs to Islam?[554]

The Venue of Debate: The Orenburg Scientific Archival Commission and Its Annual Proceedings, 1896–1917
In 1902—amid ongoing debate among Russian scholars, bureaucrats and missionaries concerning the Islamic versus alleged 'pre-Islamic' identity of the Kazakhs and its implications for Tsarist Russian policies as well as Russian Orthodox missionary strategies—A.I. Dobrosmyslov published a defense of Catherine the Great's (1762–1796) 'civilizing mission' and related policy of religious toleration among the Kazakhs. He gave particular attention to the question of whether that 'civilizing mission' and that policy had resulted in the conversion and/or deepening commitment of the Kazakhs to Islam and concomitant resistance to Russification.

Dobrosmyslov's defense was, in fact, a response to a work published two years earlier by N.M. Chernavsky, a colleague within the Orenburg Scientific Archival Commission. The commission was formed with the aim of preserving, researching and publishing findings from "the inventories of the archive of the Orenburg governor-general, abolished in 1881."[555] By 1889, they began publishing some of their findings, eventually issuing annually what they called their *Proceedings* from 1896 down to the end of the empire in 1917.[556] Although in Lubichankovsii's evaluation, "not all of their published works conformed to a sufficiently high academic level," this is a judgment in retrospect, and one colored by the intervening years of Soviet and post-Soviet critical approaches; in their own day, as Lubichankovskii notes, "the Orenburg Scientific Archival Commission became a major and significant feature of the social life of the region."[557] Indeed, they "made an invaluable contribution to the development of literature in the Orenburg region," tapping into a wealth of archival resources which, to this day, still awaits full disclosure.[558]

The importance of the commission's work both within and beyond Orenburg is reflected in the city's historic role as: a major Russian military and trading outpost serving as a hub in east–west and north–south lines of trade, including the later Orenburg-Tashkent line within the imperial railway system; a seat of Russian regional government and a Russian Orthodox archbishopric as well as, later, their regional mission; an administrative seat closely tied with the Orenburg Muslim Spiritual Assembly located to the north in Ufa; a primary source for "the formulation and implementation of the policy of Russia towards the East," including its religious and educational policies[559]; and one of several major centers within the empire for the publishing and distribution of literature, particularly in this case literature related to the Muslim peoples who predominated the region. Situated at this publishing center, "the Commission sent out editions of its work to the Archaeological Institute, the Imperial Archaeological Commission, the Archives of the Ministry of Justice in Moscow, and the Scientific Archival Commissions of Tambovsk, Orlavsk, Simbirsk, Ryazan and other provinces."[560]

One of the stated aims of the *Proceedings* was articulated in its 1897 edition in the following terms:

> Preserving the memory of the past, the love of our history without reason is considered to be the first sign of culture. Studying ourselves, our past, we learn to love our motherland dearly, being those who selflessly love their homeland, and are unwittingly imbued with the desire to improve themselves, their lives, their knowledge, their spiritual development, aiming to contribute to society with their knowledge and feasible labor.

A certain Russian nationalistic spirit thus pervaded the publication, nurtured within the nationalistic atmosphere in which it emerged, namely the conservative turn under Russia's final two tsars, Alexander III (r. 1881–1894) and Nicholas II (r. 1894–1917), who both worked to reverse many of Alexander II's (r. 1855–1881) liberal reforms. This development itself was part of the larger movement toward establishing history as a recognized 'scientific' discipline within the context of rising European nationalism and imperialism, with the discipline of history inseparably harnessed to and effectively controlled by the national state. But as evidenced by the very debate between Dobrosmyslov and his chief opponent and fellow member of the Commission, N.M. Chernavsky, *Proceedings* gave voice to differing, even at times mutually antagonistic positions, evidencing "a wide range of interests and researches from the moment of its inception."[561]

When Dobrosmyslov penned his treatise on Catherine II and the Kazakhs, he was thus debating points originally raised within the earlier, more extensive work of Chernavsky, with Chernavsky also publishing a subsequent rebuttal. This exchange took place within a sequence of volumes (VII, IX, and X) of the *Proceedings of the Orenburg Scientific Archival Commission*. Yet, it is Dobrosmyslov's work alone which is cited by modern scholars as an authority on the subject of Kazakh Islamic versus alleged 'pre-Islamic' history and identity (as well as other subjects).[562] It is thus Dobrosmyslov who is our main concern and with whom we start, elucidating his work within the more immediate as well as broader Tsarist imperial debate of which it was part.[563]

As reflected clearly in the title he chose for his piece—"Concerns of the Empress Catherine II for the Enlightenment of the Kirgiz [Kazakhs]"[564]—Dobrosmyslov's primary aim and focus within his work was a defense of Catherine II and her civilizing mission among the Kazakhs[565] in relation to then current (late-nineteenth, early twentieth-century) debates over Tsarist government policies of religious tolerance toward Muslims. It was not intended to be an in-depth, scholarly examination of Kazakh religious history and its implications for Kazakh Islamic versus alleged 'pre-Islamic' identity. His treatise provided only restricted reference to and personal interpretation of a very select, limited set of events which are part of Kazakh religious history and identity—namely those connected with Catherine II—in necessary relation to his main argument. That argument is summed up in his conclusion as follows:

> Therefore, it seems to us that there is no ground to accuse the Empress Catherine II of inculcating Islam among the Kirgiz; on the contrary, with the help of the Tatars and Bashkirs, we [the Russian state] were able to tame the Kirgiz and make them citizens of the Russian Empire, and upon achieving that, we finally had an opportunity to introduce the Russian culture among them.

This essential thesis is reiterated throughout Dobrosmyslov's treatise, including the opening paragraph where he quotes from a decree of Catherine II issued immediately upon her accession to show that this was, in fact, her own goal, with Dobrosmyslov himself adding emphasis in italics to highlight both Catherine II's and his own central focus:

> Therefore, it has been considered whether it would be possible...to avert them [the Kirgiz] from their barbarian customs and *to instill humaneness and better manners in them*, to lead them to cooperate with the Russians more often; thus persuading them in such a skillful fashion that they have the need for the Russian language and literacy in order to be able to talk with all Russian people without interpreters and write letters to whomever necessary and to read letters from them as well.

The Historical Context: Before and After Catherine's Policies, 1750–1900
As part of the broader question of Russian policies toward the Eastern peoples, proper completion of the goal of 'Russifying' and thus 'civilizing' the Kazakhs in Dobrosmyslov's own time, that is, the early twentieth century, was in fact his main purpose for addressing the debate.[566] The question of the Islamic versus alleged 'pre-Islamic' identity of the Kazakhs and the history undergirding that identity was strictly secondary. The debate involved at its heart the question of the best strategy and approach for achieving this Russo-centric version of the 'civilizing mission', including the eventual Christianization, in its Russian Orthodox form of course, of the Kazakhs (and other non-Russian peoples; see on Valikhanov, Chapter 4).[567] Inasmuch, however, as Kazakh Muslim identity and the history behind it affected, in Dobrosmyslov's time, contemporary Tsarist governmental policies and related strategies which determined success or failure in the cause of Russification, the question of how previous Tsarist policies toward the Kazakhs had affected their religious identity mattered. This is reflected in the final, climactic concern with which Dobrosmyslov leaves his readers:

> I am deeply convinced that the mosques and Kirgiz schools established by the Empress Catherine II are only now a convenient opportunity for those wishing to find an easy explanation for the strengthening of the Kirgiz in Islam in the orders of our government, but who have no desire to consider carefully the meaning of such decrees and the circumstances that caused them.

Those Russian scholars, bureaucrats and missionaries who viewed Muslim faith and identity as a hindrance or, more seriously, an outright threat to the cause of russification opposed any governmental policies which might help foster and/or support Islam. Those who viewed (the tolerable, non-threatening expressions of) Muslim faith and identity as, at least for the time being in some limited capacity, a 'necessary evil' compatible with and, in some views, even a stepping stone along the path toward[568] a Russo-centric civilizing process generally, however readily or reservedly, supported such policies. The policies and their debates revolved around five distinct yet interrelated issues confronting them in the late Tsarist era:

1. Whether to embrace and thus aim for a vision of 'civilization' in relation to 'Russianness' defined according to the more conservative 'Slavophile' or more liberal 'Westernizing' intelligentsia, with variations on both of these classic constructs taking shape across the nineteenth century[569];
2. Whether—in the face of resurgent Russian nationalism spurred on by Alexander III's (r. 1881–1894) reactions against the liberalizing policies of his father Alexander II (r. 1855–1881) and the continuation of those trends under Nicholas II (1894–1917)—to uphold and promote a more liberal enlightenment policy of 'religious toleration' or a more restrictive policy which favored a single state-sanctioned form of Russian Orthodoxy; if 'religious toleration' was to be granted, then should this be put into practice by means of simply 'ignoring' Islam (i.e. non-interference) or subjecting Islam to state control and, with it, possible state subsidies for its institutions[570];
3. Whether, in relation to questions regarding historic Kazakh Islamic versus alleged 'pre-Islamic' identity, to support Islamic shari'a law or Kazakh customary (cf. 'adat') law in relation to legal disputes involving family and other related social matters within local courts[571];
4. Whether to continue to follow the Il'minskii educational method which concentrated on 'secular', non-religious curriculum and employed the national lay-staff from among as well as languages of non-Russian peoples using Cyrillic instead of Arabic script as a bridge or return to a more direct Russian-language approach combined with greater emphasis on incorporating Russian Orthodoxy more explicitly into the imperial educational system[572];

5. Whether to work, if at all, toward conversion of the Kazakhs to Russian Orthodoxy via the more indirect, longer-term approach of the Il'minskii method or a more direct, urgent effort of explicit evangelization whose only concern was whether to use an anti-Islamic polemical versus an animistic/shamanistic-oriented missionary strategy.[573]

These issues and the debates associated with them had been taking shape since the early 1800s, following the first mass defections of Volga-Ural (i.e., Tatar, Bashkir, and other related) Muslims from Russian Orthodoxy back to Islam after having been forcibly converted in the early to mid-1700s in the reigns of those who preceded Catherine II.[574] They were accentuated and given increasing urgency with each mounting confrontation between the Muslim and Western modernist worlds across the nineteenth and early twentieth centuries—not only in the Russian, but the British, French and other European empires which had expanded across Asia and Africa.[575]

Most immediately impacting the Chernavsky-Dobrosmyslov debate would have been the 1898 Andijan Uprising against Tsarist rule led by Muslims in the Turkestan province.[576] In 1899, S.M. Dukhovskoi, the governor-general appointed to Turkestan following the Uprising, used the incident in a report submitted to Tsar Nicholas II (1894–1917) to highlight "anti-European revolts among the Muslims of Asia and Africa." Dukhovskoi singled out the state policy of religious tolerance as a primary cause for discontent in the borderlands.[577] Across the border in China, the Boxer Uprising, beginning in August 1899, only added fuel to the fires of Tsarist concern. On the horizon in 1902 was also an empire-wide celebration to mark the fortieth-year anniversary of the emancipation of the serfs, reflecting as that act did the liberal reformist policies of Alexander II.[578]

Thus while Chernavsky published his original study to commemorate the 100th anniversary of the founding of the Orenburg Eparchy, which had taken place in 1799,[579] other historical factors shaped not only his undertaking during his research and writing of the work between 1898 and 1900, but Dobrosmyslov's response to him as well. Both of their works ultimately stood in a long line of scholarship which, in some form or other, attempted to respond to questions of imperial policy concerning religious tolerance, education, enlightenment and civilization (cf. modernization), and Russification as these pertained to the Kazakhs and the question of their Islamic versus alleged 'pre-Islamic' identity. Such scholarship would include the studies of A. I. Levshin (1822, 1832), Sh. Ualihanuhli (Russian: Ch. Valihanov, 1863–1865), E. Malov (1867–1868), Sh. Ibragimov (1874), N.I. Il'minskii (1891) and more.[580]

The Course of the Debate: Elucidating Essential Points of Agreement-Disagreement
Dobrosmyslov makes no reference, in fact, to any of the earlier seminal works on Kazakh religious identity from the nineteenth century, nor does he direct his defense against them, at least not explicitly. He makes the main object(s) of his treatise clear when stating:

> In conclusion...I must say a few words regarding the fact that among the local intellectuals and the in press, there was an established opinion, which I believe to be incorrect, that 'the policy of religious tolerance' and allegedly even 'patronage of Islam in expectation of political benefits, that were adopted in the reign of Catherine II, had a considerable maleficent effect on the Kirgiz' [Kazakhs].[581]

The source which Dobrosmyslov quotes from here, referenced in a footnote, is: "*N. M. Chernavsky*. Orenburgskaya eparxiya v' proshlom' eya ii nastoyashshem' iizd. 1900 goda, vipusk' tserviii, str. 123 [Orenburg Eparchy in the Past and Present. 1900, No. 1, p. 123]."[582] In fact, Dobrosmyslov provides only six references throughout his twelve-page article: two of them archival sources eminating from Catherine II, one (not in rebuttal to but) as a point of evidence from "A. Meyer (1865)" referring back to an event early in Catherine II's reign, two in direct rebuttal to material quoted from Chernavsky (one of which is the passage quoted above), and the sixth from a source drawn from the particular section (i.e., pages 122–127) of Chernavsky's formidable 354-page well-documented study to which Dobrosmyslov is immediately and directly responding.

It is therefore essential to consider Chernavsky's work within its own broader context in order to properly grasp the aim and intent as well as evaluate the accuracy of Dobrosmyslov's retort. With respect to the section which Dobrosmyslov clearly has in view, namely that entitled "The policy of religious tolerance of Catherine II and its influence on the rise of Islam," Chernavsky sets forth his main point(s) of concern in the opening declaration, where he notes that:

The end of the eighteenth century, then, is characterized not only by a weakening state of missionary work in the Kazan region, but also by the politics of liberal tolerance, almost an indulgence – not deliberate, of course, but with known goals in mind nevertheless – and a strengthening of Islamic influence. By many of its actions, the Government itself aided in the increase of the Islamic influence.[583]

Elsewhere Chernavsky drives home his point, alleging that in pursuing these policies "the Government played into the hand of Islam" (123), that "its impractical actions effectively gave an unprecedented level of church organization to Russian Islam" (122), "even distribut[ing] state subsidies to this end, seemingly sanctioning the Muslim faith" (122).

Chernavsky buttresses his position by citing two cases noted by the State Councilor of the Turgai Regional Board I. I. Kraft in his *Collection of Laws about the Kirgiz People*. One is the recommendation in 1750 of a Military Council to the first Governor-General of Orenburg I. Neplyuev who served under the Empress Elizabeth I (1741–1762) that it was "obscene to build a mosque at public expense, 'especially by Christian hands'."[584] He adds to this in a footnote that.

> during Neplyuev's times, efforts were made to protect the Kirgiz people from Tatar influence; so, for example, in its May 11, 1747 decree, the Council of Foreign Affairs had forbidden marriages between Kirgiz people and Muslims – Baskirs and Tatars from Orenburg, as well as Kazan.[585]

Chernavsky's ultimate point is that in "[c]omparing these directions [of Catherine II] with the former, relating to the middle of the same eighteenth century, we notice a huge difference in attitudes and tactics of the Government in relation to the Kirgiz-Kaisak people" (124).

Dobrosmyslov answers these claims, saying:

> G. Chernavsky found that before Catherine II ascended her throne, the policy in relation to the Kirgiz was different and he adduced a single fact to support that statement, namely when the Council of Foreign Affairs did not agree to satisfy the petition of Nuraly Khan requesting [them] to build a mosque next to the grave of his father, Abul Khair Khan. We should recall that the construction of mosques for the Kirgiz was approved already by the Empress Anna Ioannovna, therefore Russia to a great degree owes it to the Tatar [Kutlu Muhammet] Tevkelev for adoption of Russian citizenship by the Kirgiz of the Little and Middle jüzes, who cooperated with the Kirgiz leaders in the next thirty years in all important cases, and later on, in the XVIII century…[586]

But Dobrosmyslov misrepresents Chernavsky's position here by asserting that he only "adduced a single fact to support that statement," thus attempting to make Chernavsky's position appear weaker than it actually was, even though Chernavsky had in fact provided at least two pieces of supporting evidence. Chernavsky himself, in his later rebuttal to Dobrosmyslov highlighted this same point, saying: "This is an unjustified accusation: we provide other general evidence in support of our findings, not just one fact."[587] Even more, Dobrosmyslov provides no citation for his own claim that "the construction of mosques for the Kirgiz was approved already by the Empress Anna Ioannovna," who reigned 1730–1741. If we search for possible points of historical reference, first, Hamamoto Mami, in her study of "Tatarskaia Kargala in Russia's Eastern policies," notes that:

> According to a record made in 1834, there were 155 mosques in the Orenburg and Buzulugskii districts at that time, and two of these mosques had been built in the 1730s and five had been built between 1750 and 1756, although no mosques had been built in the 1740s. One mosque was built in 1709...[588]

No evidence suggests, however, that the two mosques "built in the 1730s" in the Orenburg or surrounding areas were commissioned by the Empress Anna, particularly not on behalf of the Kazakhs. To the contrary, in the face of the explicit, legally-endorsed atmosphere of anti-Muslim persecution prevailing throughout the general regions of Tatarstan and Bashkortostan between the 1730s and 1750s, which included both destruction of and bans against rebuilding mosques,[589] they may have been constructed illegally. E. Malov, in his extensive 1867–68 study "On Tatar Mosques in Russia," noted that:

> In areas nearby Kazan, there are a host of mosques, which were built illegally, long having been accepted [by local administrators] against the rules. So in 1736 a decree of Anna Ioannovna ordered that mosques and schools in Bashkir lands not be built again without decrees.[590]

Anna's decree was issued on 11 February 1736,[591] in the midst of the 1735–1737 Bashkir uprising against Russian colonial rule.[592] Indeed, Dobrosmyslov himself wrote an entire treatise on the Bashkir uprising which took place in those years, so he was intimately acquainted with both the history and historical sources.[593] This makes his lack of citation concerning his claim all the more questionable, though Chernavsky "published in the *Orenburg. List* for 1901, No. 8, a critical-bibliographical review on his monograph *Bashkir Rebellion in 1735–37*, where we examined the shortcomings and assessed his general writing techniques and erudition with respect to the history of the local region."[594] This makes the Chernavsky-Dobrosmyslov debate being considered here part of a longer series of debates which were, at their heart, historiographical in nature.

Respecting Dobrosmyslov's claim in this most recent debate concerning earlier Tsarist policies toward Islam, Malov makes no mention of any such mosques for the Kazakhs in his detailed study. He also suggests elsewhere that the reason that Anna banned the rebuilding of mosques among the Bashkir is that she "did not want to bind the Bashkir to Islam, since at that time they were almost strangers to Mohammedanism, and held a shamanic, pagan error."[595] This may well be an interpolation of Malov's own mid-nineteenth-century Russian Orthodox missionary perspective back into history in an attempt to lend official credence to his own views, but it must be given the same fair consideration offered Dobrosmyslov or any other Tsarist Russian sources. If Malov's assumption about Anna's perspective is correct, it would stand contrary to Dobrosmyslov's claim, since the Kazakhs were viewed in a similar fashion by the Russian authorities. The debate here is not whether such an interpretation of Bashkir or Kazakh Islam was accurate, but whether Anna commissioned and supported the construction of mosques for the Kazakhs while denying them for the Bashkir, since she probably viewed both, whether accurately or inaccurately, in the same way religiously. The discussion of this point, however, is merely hypothetical, since no evidence is available from the time of Anna's reign (1730–1740) to support Dobrosmyslov's assertion.

With respect to the decades just before and after Anna's reign, Aelita Miniyanova notes that a limited number of madrasas were established in Tatarstan, Bashkortostan, and the surrounding areas: "in 1709 in Suyunduk village; in 1720 in Sterlibash village; and in 1745 in Seitov Posad near Orenburg, to name a few."[596] Based on the correlating data here as well as from other historical records, the founding of the madrasas most likely occurred in conjunction with the construction of mosques. But Suyunduk is roughly 300 miles (480 km) and Sterlibash some 280 miles (450 km) north of the Kazakh borderlands, and both were established prior to the reign of the Empress Anna, so these would not support Dobrosmyslov's reference either. The closest possible case is Miniyanova's latter reference to Seitov Posad (known in Tatar-Turki as Kargali) in the vicinity of Orenburg in 1745. Concerning the construction of this mosque, a Senate Decree was issued on 8 March 1744, "On settlement of the Kazan Tatars in the city of Orenburg, and permission for them to build a mosque in the city,"[597] with actual erection of the mosque occurring one year later in 1745.[598] Note carefully, however, that the permission was for "them," that is, the Kazan Tatars, not the Kazakhs. The latter were not mentioned in relation to the mosque. It was strictly to accommodate the needs of the Tatars, who had been recognized as practicing Muslims under Tsarist rule since the conquest of Kazan by Ivan IV in 1552. No view to support, promote or spread Islamic institutions was involved, not even for the Tatars, particularly not in the face of clear, consistent policies during this period (ca. 1730s–1760s) which otherwise explicitly restricted not only the building of more mosques among the empire's Muslim peoples, but to the contrary facilitated and supported their confiscation and destruction. The decree on Tatar settlement in Orenburg and permission for them to build a mosque there was a rare concession within an otherwise hostile anti-Islamic socio-political milieu. It was concerned primarily with Tsarist economic strategy which sought to harness increasing Tatar commercial success in order for Russia to expand its trade networks throughout the Kazakh steppelands, and from there into the trade networks running through Central Asia and multiple other Asian realms to the south.

The vision for expanding these trade networks was originally espoused by Peter the Great who saw in the Kazakh steppelands east of the Caspian Sea "the key and gate to all the Asian countries and lands" to the south for purposes of Russian trade and strategic imperial expansion (not to mention 'the key and gate' for protecting Russia from potential Jungar attacks from the south).[599] Through reconnaissance missions commissioned by Peter between 1715 and 1719, seven Russian military and trading outposts—Omsk, Zhelezinsk, Dolonsk, Ubinsk, Yamyshevsk (Pavlodar), Semipalatinsk and Ust-Kamenogorsk—were established along the northeastern Kazakh border.[600] The original Orenburg, now renamed Orsk, soon followed in 1734 on the northwestern side, with the Orenburg of Tatar and Kazakh historical fame coming a decade later in 1743 a bit further to the northwest. The histories of Orsk and Orenburg, and similar outposts which followed, are closely tied up with Russian imperial plans involving the Tatars, Bashkir, Kalmyks and Kazakhs. Plans for the latter included official treaties with each of the three Kazakh *zhuz* between 1731 and 1742[601] to make them protectorates in the face of mutual threat from the Jungars (lasting down to 1758), though also with a view to developing Peter's vision for pan-Asian trade. Conspicuously lacking, however, are any plans for strengthening Islamic institutions among the Kazakhs as a means to achieving those ends.

The only other case which might serve as a reference for Dobrosmyslov is the request in 1750 which the Kazakh khan Nurali submitted to Neplyuev asking that the Russian state build a mosque at his father Abulkhair's burial site. But this is doubtful the case Dobrosmyslov had in mind, since it was one of the cases which his opponent Chernavsky had cited as proof of the position Dobrosmyslov was arguing against, namely "a huge difference in attitudes and tactics of the Government in relation to the Kirgiz-Kaisak people" before and after the policies of Catherine II (see above). According to both Chernavsky's and Dobrosmyslov's source—Kraft, *Collection of Laws about the Kirgiz People*—the incident is recorded as follows:

> It was discovered that to build a tomb in the same place where Abulkhair khan was buried was impossible, due to an over-abundance of water [in the area]. Hence khan Nurali suggested to dig up his father's bones and flesh and to bury them near the river Emba, where other nobility had been buried in past. It was decided to build a tomb with the khan's portrait and to build a mosque. However his suggestion was rejected, because it would be built by government expenses and it was not acceptable to build a mosque by Christian aid.[602]

Even if Dobrosmyslov intended this as his point of reference, it would not have been accurate, since the request had no intention of achieving what Dobrosmyslov claimed Russian governmental policies before Catherine II had done, namely strengthening Islamic institutions among the Kazakhs *as a means to civilize them*. It would only have been a concession to a long-standing Central Asian Muslim practice, namely the erection of a shrine or mosque in honor and memory of a noteworthy national or religious figure. This in itself serves as important evidence for establishing Kazakh Muslim identity and practice, at least among the 'white-bone' aristocracy, well before the time of Catherine II.

More decisively against Dobrosmyslov's claim though, as Chernavsky had argued, Khan Nurali's "suggestion was rejected, because it would be built by government expenses and it was not acceptable to build a mosque by Christian aid."

Thus from Peter the Great down to Catherine II, there is no evidence for government plans to strengthen Islamic institutions among the Kazakhs as a means to civilize and thereby incorporate them into the empire. This covers not only the reign of Anna, but Elizabeth I, including her 1744 decree commissioning the construction of the mosque for the Kazan Tatars in Seitov Posad (Kargali), near Orenburg, which was carried out immediately thereafter in 1745, as well as the 1750 request of Nurali. Indeed, Dobrosmyslov, in unwitting contradiction of himself, bears witness to this by emphasizing that Catherine II's strategy to spread Islamic institutions among the Kazakhs via the Tatars in order to 'civilize' and thus 'tame' them was conceived *only after* she attempted to accomplish that 'civilizing mission' directly via the Russians (and other allegedly 'civilized' Slavic and European peoples). In her initial efforts to use the Russians themselves to accomplish these aims, Catherine II was quite naturally continuing the conventional approach inherited from her predecessors. As Dobrosmyslov highlights, it was only after this conventional wisdom failed that she, in her enlightened state, opted to turn to the Tatars and Islam:

> Due to all such circumstances, the Empress Catherine II decided to introduce 'humaneness and better manners' to the non-Russian people *in a different way*: she ordered the Governor in the Ufa and Simbirsk Governorate, the Lieutenant General Ivan Varfolomeyevich Yakobiy (Jacobi) (Decree of 8 July 1782) to build mosques from a design approved by Her on the borders of the Ufa and Tobolsk Governorate...[603]

Dobrosmyslov makes this plain in more succinct fashion when climaxing his study: "Catherine II proceeded to build the mosques and open a Tatar school *only after she saw that there was no Russification of the Kirgiz yet.*"[604]

Chernavsky, in his later rebuttal to Dobrosmyslov, provides further evidence for this interpretation when he cites two previous decrees issued under Catherine II, saying:

Recall, e.g., that although the Imperial Decree of July 21, 1765 allowed 14 illegal Tatar families to remain...it also "resolutely declared that from now on no Kazan or Astrakhan Tatars should ever be allowed to settle in the Orenburg province."[605] Then, a Senate decree of February 8, 1770 ordered to "resettle the Kandaur Tatars and Saltanaul Tatars from Kazan province, under the guise of their own good, to such locations in the Orenburg province from which they could have no relations with Kirgiz-Kaisak people,"[606] as they were seen as a negative influence on the latter...[607]

Along with failed Russian efforts to make headway among the Kazakhs, it was apparently the Pugachev Uprising (1773–1775), Russia's annexation of the Crimea (1774–1783) and Catherine II's personal correspondence with Voltaire (1762–1778), particularly in relation to his views on religious toleration, which eventually caused her to reverse her position. This would accord with the findings of Gulmira Sultangalieva in her study of "The Russian Empire and the intermediary role of Tatars in Kazakhstan," where she notes: "The policy of drawing 'Tatars' into an intermediary role between the state and the Kazakh Steppe acquired an organized character from the start of Catherine II's reign. This allows us to identify a second phase of Tatar penetration into the steppe, extending from the 1770s to the 1850s."[608] Although the first phase (1730–1770) included permission for Tatars to conduct trade in the Kazakh Steppe, it did not, as noted above, envision their role as intermediaries in a 'civilizing mission' aimed ultimately at Russification and integration of the Kazakhs into the empire.

Dobrosmyslov's attempt, therefore, fails when he answers Chernavsky by claiming (falsely) that "the policy in relation to the Kirgiz in the times before Catherine II, as well as during her reign, and for a long time after it, had always been the same" so that "the Empress Catherine II was as much to blame for Islamizing the Kirgiz as any of her predecessors."[609] Both his own contradictory argument within the essay and his inability to cite any historical sources for his claim seal this fate. Whether intentionally or otherwise, Dobrosmyslov once again misrepresented both the historical facts and his opponent's position. And with this, Dobrosmyslov's attempt to discredit "the local intellectuals and... press" he was debating, particularly Chernavsky, also fails and returns back on his own head when he says: "I should note that the comments on the patronage of Islam were based on insufficient knowledge of the history of the Kirgiz nation in general, and the history of this nation after their acceptance of Russian citizenship in particular."[610] Indeed, Chernavsky, in his later rebuttal, points out several historical inaccuracies in Dobrosmyslov's work, even correcting him on one occasion and suggesting that "[s]uch an absurd statement is quite inexcusable for Mr. Dobrosmyslov, who touts himself as the Orenburg-Turgai region's historian."[611]

But Dobrosmyslov's misrepresentations of Chernavsky do not end here. After his assertion that Chernavsky's "comments on the patronage of Islam were based on insufficient knowledge of the history of the Kirgiz nation in general, and the history of this nation after their acceptance of Russian citizenship in particular" (see above), Dobrosmyslov goes on to say:

> It is known that the Kirgiz had been Mohammedan a long time before accepting Russian citizenship, and they would bring their spiritual clergy from Bukhara, Khiva and possibly from other smaller Central Asian Khanates of that time.[612]

Dobrosmyslov thus accuses Chernavsky of not knowing, as an essential part of the history being debated, that the Kazakhs were Muslims before "accepting Russian citizenship." As per his thesis, what Dobrosmyslov juxtaposes against this claim is that Russian governmental policies, whether Catherine II"s or otherwise, were not responsible for Islamizing the Kazakhs. But whether intentionally and deceptively or as a result of poor scholarship, Dobrosmyslov's argument against Chernavsky is a 'straw man', because Chernavsky in fact holds the same position as Dobrosmyslov on this particular point. Chernavsky had already made it plain within his own work that the Kazakhs were "considered Muslim at the time of the adoption of Russian citizenship" (123). Indeed, Chernavsky and Dobrosmyslov agree not only on this quintessential point, but a related one as well, which is summed up by Chernavsky when he says:

> It is a long-established fact (see, for example, Reclus) that in the middle of the eighteenth century, although considered Muslim at the time of the adoption of Russian citizenship, Kirgiz people were Muslim only by name, as they were maintaining their pagan customs in full force (partly, to date), adhering to shamanism and not observing many ceremonial precepts of Mohammedanism. (123)

In his later rebuttal to Dobrosmyslov, Chernavsky summarized his position more fully as follows:

> ...the Kirgiz of the time – and to some extent now – were only so-called Mohammedans. In reality, they did not have their own mosques, but we took care of that for them. There were none literate or spiritual [in the ways of] Islam among them, and so the Tatars and Bukharans filled the void. Their purely pagan beliefs and practices prevailed over Muslim traditions, and they were far from being strict followers of the religion of the Prophet. Had they stayed the same, they would have been better suited for rapprochement with the Russians and more receptive to the truth of Christianity. The Government of Catherine II was naturally concerned with the immediate and urgent matter of keeping the Kirgiz subjects and establishing and maintaining law and order among them. The Government contrived to achieve this goal by, among other things, humanitarian measures, as it saw religion and literacy as the primary means of curbing the willfulness of nomads. Kirgiz people self-identified, if only externally, with Islam and were in this regard like the Tatars. So the Government, acting in accordance with dominant Russian liberal thought, decided to lend support to Islamic notions which were hostile to Christianity in order revive religious consciousness and instill literacy among the Kirgiz, through the Tatars. Thus, the directives were issued for the construction of mosques, mosque schools, the designation of Tatar Mullahs to staff them, publicly-funded dissemination of printed copies of the Qur'an, and so on. The general nature of these directives, which had the ultimate goal to "lessen the barbaric mores of the Kirgiz and instill in them humanity and better manners" (Counc. of Foreign Affairs' Decree, Apr. 8, 1763), clearly shows that the Government relied on [the policy of] strengthening Islam and literacy among the Kirgiz.[613]

Chernavsky was consistent with this position throughout his rebuttal in his usage of "strengthen" (as opposed to "convert") in reference to Tsarist policy and its impact.[614]

As for Dobrosmyslov, far from refuting Chernavsky, he held a very similar view. This is revealed, for example, when, immediately after declaring that "the Kirgiz had been Mohammedan a long time before accepting Russian citizenship," he continues on by clarifying that:

> If the Kirgiz were not so apparently religious in the past and in the present (XIX) centuries, as for instance, the Tatars, who we can constantly observe before our eyes, then it by no means signifies that they were not

Mohammedans. It is known that for most nations, their devoutness is a certain way of self-awareness that covers the sense of their national spirit. It is such self-awareness that most often impedes the change of religion, as it is assumed that the loss of old religion leads to the loss of the national spirit. ...As to the mosques, the Kirgiz do not like to attend them even now, and in that time they probably did not even glance therein entirely.

Chernavsky had likewise acknowledged, with reference to prior scholarship, that the Muslim identity of the Kazakhs was grounded primarily in a psychological-emotional view of themselves as Muslims and not in any steadfast religious observance. He pointed out, together with his earlier reference to their "not observing many ceremonial precepts of Mohammedanism" (see above), that:

> In Rychov's "Orenburg History", it is also noted that although the Kirgiz people recognize themselves as confessors of Mohammedan law, their concept of this law is pathetic, as there are no literate people among them and they have to call upon mullahs and priests from Tashkent and other cities. P. 72[615]

Chernavsky further noted in connection to this that "[e]ven the royally approved chapter of the Siberian Kirgiz People of July 22, 1822 evidences that at this time the faith of Kirgiz people is essentially more pagan than Mohammedan (and therefore expresses hope for their successful conversion into Christianity)."[616]

Concerning this latter point, Dobrosmyslov even shared Chernavsky's hope for the eventual conversion of the Kazakhs to Russian Orthodox Christianity. While not explicitly stating this in the treatise defending Catherine II and her policies, he made it plain elsewhere, particularly in his work on *The Turgai Region: A Historical Study*, where he notes that:

> The Kirgiz people, as experience has shown, can relate to our culture and the truth of Christ the Savior's teaching. Alas, for a long time after their adoption of Russian citizenship, we were unable to commence our task to enlighten the Kirgiz people, as it was necessary, at first, to tame these nomadic people, then to separate them from the neighboring Bashkirs who practiced the same Mohammedan religion, and, finally, to weaken the influence of their coreligionists who lived in Khiva, Bukhara and other small Central Asian emirates.[617]

In spite of Dobrosmyslov's misrepresentations, he and Chernavsky, therefore, both hold the same essential position with respect to not only the psychological-emotional grounding of Muslim identity for the Kazakhs before they were made Russian subjects (i.e., 'citizens'), but their lack of observance of Muslim practices. True, Dobrosmyslov treats Kazakh Muslim identity with greater respect, accepting at face value the Kazakh's own designation of themselves as Muslims whereas Chernavsky does not. Neither, therefore, does Dobrosmyslov explicitly identify the Kazakhs as "pagans" or "shamanists" as Chernavsky does. This is all to Dobrosmyslov's credit and represents an important point of distinction in his versus Chernavsky's views. But the silence of Dobrosmyslov concerning 'pagan', 'shamanistic', 'animistic' or other related practices cannot be taken as a denial on his part of the possible continued observance of those traditions among the Kazakhs.

Dobrosmyslov cannot and should not, therefore, be represented as having definitively answered or overturned the work of Levshin, Ualihanuhli, and other like-minded scholars of the nineteenth and early twentieth century, missionary or otherwise, with respect to the question of Kazakh Islamic versus 'pre-Islamic' identity and practice. He rather displays a significant measure of agreement with them, differing mainly in his willingness to acknowledge the Kazakh's self-designation as 'Muslims'. For example, Dobrosmyslov, like Chernavsky, is in general agreement with Levshin when the latter asserts that:

> The Kirgiz do not observe fasts or ablution, which are rather sensible ordinances of Mohammed, they find it difficult to pray five times a day; they do not have mosques and mullahs chosen among them. Occasionally, the prayers are read by the elderly men in the presence of many others kneeling around them, but mostly everyone prays wherever and whenever he desires. Some do not practice any religious rites. Diligent Muslims are so rare among these people...[618]

Indeed, Dobrosmyslov's interpretation of the Kazakhs as "not so apparently religious" is key to his entire argument, namely that the policies of Russian governmental support for the spread of Islamic institutions among the Kazakhs via the Tatars did nothing appreciable to alter Kazakh Muslim identity or practice. This is clear in Dobrosmyslov's attempt to counter Chernavsky's claims by minimizing the spiritual significance of these policies:

Moreover, the same author [Chernavsky] provided the Decree of the Empress Catherine II ordering to send mullahs as clerks [scribes] to the steppe into the newly opened establishments (the Khan Council, courts), and also saw that as a method of instilling Islam to the Kirgiz, and causing 'considerable difficulties for Russification' of the Kirgiz. Here we need to note that the word mullah does not necessarily imply a spiritual person, but only a person who is literate in Tatar and certainly has knowledge of spoken Russian.

In similar fashion, it is to downplay any religious impact of Catherine II's policies that Dobrosmyslov asserts that "the Kirgiz school [established by Catherine II] had close to no students."[619] He, likewise, describes Kazakh Islamic devotion as remaining consistent both before and after Catherine, both then and even now (in his own time), insisting that "the Kirgiz were not so apparently religious in the past and in the present (XIX) centuries" and, likewise, "[a]s to the mosques, the Kirgiz do not like to attend them even now, and in that time they probably did not even glance therein entirely" (see quote above). Dobrosmyslov, in fact, views Kazakh Muslim identity and practice in essentialist terms—unalterable and unchanging—even in the face of nearly a century of Tatar influence. This is made clear again in his book *The Turgai Region: A Historical Study*, where he asserts that "[o]ne positive characteristic *inherent* in Kirgiz Muslims is that they lack the religious fanaticism that exists in other nations who practice this religion, including our Tatars."[620] In arguing in this fashion, Dobrosmyslov once again contradicts himself since he elsewhere argues for the need to "weaken the influence of their [the Kazakhs'] coreligionists who lived in Khiva, Bukhara and other small Central Asian emirates." Why is it that the Central Asian Muslim peoples to the south were able to influence Kazakh Muslim identity and practice while those to the north (i.e., the Tatar, Bashkir, and others) were not? Indeed, Dobrosmyslov, in the same study, had also asserted that it was necessary "to separate them [the Kazakhs] from the neighboring Bashkirs who practiced the same Mohammedan religion" for fear of the latter's religious influence upon them, whereas in his defense of Catherine II he argues that "with the help of the Tatars and Bashkirs, we were able to tame the Kirgiz and make them citizens of the Russian Empire" (see quote above). In one treatise, he thus brands the Tatars and Bashkirs "fanatics" who must be kept at a distance from the Kazakhs, while in the other he says they were used to influence the

Kazakhs with respect to Russian civilization, but not in any way religiously. Regardless, Dobrosmyslov's argument is precisely that, namely that there had been no appreciable impact resulting from the spread of Islamic institutions, teachings and literature via the Tatars, Bashkirs and others who the Russian state sponsored. Chernavsky was thus justified in his rebuttal when he notes that:

> Dobrosmyslov, however, asserts that Catherine II wanted 'by means of religious sentiment and Tatar literacy' only to tame the Kirgiz, and was far from thinking about strengthening their Islamic faith. It seems as though in this case she fell into a self-contradiction, revealing ignorance: one cannot simply revive religious consciousness on the basis of Islam and yet not strengthen the Islamic faith.[621]

In stark contrast to Dobrosmyslov, Chernavsky makes plain the underlying basis of his thorough-going opposition to any liberal policies of governmental support for Islam in an extended comment in his rebuttal on the nature of Islam and its impact upon the Kazakhs:

> We know that this monotheistic and soullessly abstract religion – with its fatalistic doctrine of predestination and obligatory war with infidels (jihad), with its formalistic and legalistic righteousness that imposes restraints on all things of life, and so on – instills a spirit of religious exclusivity, seclusion and fanaticism into its devoted followers. Placing its followers in a vicious circle of Koranic precepts and Sharia laws, outside of which lies the area of the forbidden, Islam with its doctrine of unbridled devotion to God (Islam) – the basic principle of life and all actions – demands slavish obedience and blind submission from its cohorts. This religion – with a profound spiritual theory but extremely perverted to the point of the loss in human identity and self-awareness – is capable of killing any free thought and intellectual development in a person, causing a person to lose his own properties and abilities and to become a typical despondent Muslim with a fatalistic and deterministic worldview. In addition, there is the Sharia doctrine of the Imamate, according to which there must be one divinely appointed supreme leader of the Muslim world. As the shadow of God on earth, the Imam is an absolute ruler of the entire Muslim community, and thus all of his orders must be complied with as infallible. The Turkish sultan was recognized by our Sunni Muslims as such an Imam – the head of the Muslim world and the custodian of the purity of faith. This doctrine promotes the theocratic nature of Islam, by virtue of which every Muslim must consider himself a loyal subject of the Muslim state under the banner of a single faith. He may happen to live in a different foreign

state, but deep down he must consider himself a member and citizen of one Muslim society, cherishing his irredentist dreams of being under one Muslim religious-political authority, and giving in to such illusions despite having to endure unfavorable conditions... In light of the foregoing, how could one claim that the Tatars, foreign to the Russian culture and civilization, with their Islamic propaganda hostile toward Christianity and, therefore, in the eyes of the common people, toward Russian citizenship, made the Kyrgyz into the "citizens" of our motherland? How can one speak about the Tatars cultural and civic mission among the Kyrgyz, when we know that Islam – with its sense of self-affirmation, which sanctifies with divine authority Koranic precepts and principles that govern the whole life of a Muslim to the smallest detail in the spiritual, social and civic sense – inevitably causes Islamic integration and national self-isolation in the spirit of the Koranic principles, thereby uniting Muslims into one family in a league of its own in a Christian state? How can one, standing on the Russian Orthodox soil, defend this Tatarization, when it was hardly in the interests of the Russian state and its dominant religion?[622]

Chernavsky's views here reflected, in some form or other, those of many Russian statesmen and missionaries not to mention common, everyday citizens. Most immediately and explicitly this is reflected in Dukhovskoi's 1899 report to Nicholas II following the 1898 Andijan Uprising (see above). Beyond the Russian empire, his views accord in general with those of Western Christian Europe throughout most of its encounter with Islam down to the age of Chernavsky. They even echo some of the critical ideas being formulated in his own day by Renan and other Western imperial critiques of Islam interpreted variously through religious, racial, philosophical and political lens.[623]

In the end however, that Chernavsky's critique of Dobrosmyslov's position was not simply retaliation is highlighted by his willingness to affirm sound scholarship even when he does not agree with the conclusions drawn. He, in fact, commended a scholar who had earlier argued along similar lines to Dobrosmyslov, though with much greater balance and consistency when he suggested that:

> The famous ethnographer and publicist N.M. Yadrintsev (1894) is at least more direct and consistent on this subject. Accepting the fact that the government of Catherine II strongly patronized the spread of Islam among the Kirgiz and Buddhism among the Buryats and Kalmyks, Yadrintsev saw in these measures ordinary religious tolerance, political tact, prudence and even wise politics suitable to the circumstances of that time.[624]

If anyone was guilty of retaliation within the debate, Chernavsky considered it not himself, but Dobrosmyslov:

> In the end, we cannot help but point out that Mr. Dobrosmyslov offered such a biased and rigorous criticism of our work after we published in the *Orenburg. List* for 1901, No. 8, a critical-bibliographical review on his monograph "Bashkir Rebellion in 1735-37", where we examined the shortcomings and assessed his general writing techniques and erudition with respect to the history of the local region.[625]

But a biographer of Chernavsky uncovered a deeper dynamic occurring when he noted that:

> In the third issue of *Orenburg Diocesan News* for 1901 he [Dobrosmyslov] had published a review in which he pointed to a number of discrepancies found in the first issue of N.M. Chernavsky's work. The general tone was quite calm, with the author expressing in the conclusion that he wished 'every success in his [Chernavsky's] future work on the study of the history of the Orenburg Diocese and the development of local rich archival material." However, after the publication by Chernavsky in *Orenburg List* of sharp comments on the book *The Bashkir rebellion in 1735-1737 gg.*, ...A.I. Dobrosmyslov decided to make his assessment more severe...and published an extended critique on *The Orenburg Diocese in the Past and Present* in the *Proceedings of the Society of History, Archaeology and Ethnography at the Imperial University of Kazan*.[626] In it he was quite offensive...[627]

The debate between Chernavsky and Dobrosmyslov clearly escalated in the process of exchange. Chernavsky, in fact, appears to be the one to have retaliated first against Dobrosmyslov, with Dobrosmyslov's defense of Catherine II, *as a reprint of the above named critique*, representing a more severe rejoinder, followed by a final overall rebuttal from Chernavsky. However much their tempers may have flared however, the same biographer made the evaluation, with respect to that final rebuttal, that through "a [d]etailed refutation of the critical attacks of Dobrosmyslov, Chernavsky proved most of them unfounded."[628] But he also went on to note that:

> The debate over the merits of N.M. Chernavsky's work continued after the release of the second edition of the book. In the process, it was shown to be true that A.I. Dobrosmyslov had created, in the heat of resentment, a

seemingly subjective idea of inconsistency between the book and its title. This agrees with the professors of the Kazan Theological Academy, where the work was presented for award to the author of the title of Master of Theology. So, associate professor of the Academy [I.] Pokrovsky noted that 'the main and major drawback of Chernavsky's labor is its unsystematic [approach] and lack of literary treatment of rich material on the history of the Orenburg Diocese." Professor F. Blagovidov, analyzing the second edition of the book, simply called it 'an essay lacking many features that characterize scientific historical research.' Looseness of structure, particularly in the detailed study of the dedication of some of the synoptic material, and repeated facts - all this, according to the reviewers, gave reason to call the work more a collection of materials, rather than a monograph or historical research. At the same time, I. Pokrovsky wrote: 'Justice must be said that Chernavsky's work on the history of the Orenburg diocese is very honorable and very valuable for the abundance and diversity of the collected archival materials it contains.'"[629]

Indeed, it is. Thus Chernavsky's work received three other positive reviews from colleagues: I.A. Tihomirov in the *Journal of the Ministry of National Education* (Vol. XII, 1901); B.N. Rudakov in the *Historical Herald* (Vol. II, 1901); and S.G. Rybakov in *Church Bulletin* (1901). While it was, in fact, his master's thesis for his degree, the significance of that degree was greater in Chernavsky's time, and thus required greater effort, as indicated by the 354-page well-documented study he produced. Also, though it was considered a degree in 'theology', Chernavsky's expertise was history, church and missionary history to be precise. While perhaps skewed by his religious perspective, he was nonetheless a trained historian, something Dobrosmyslov could not claim, being instead a veterinarian by training and profession.

Overall it would appear that Chernavsky emerged from the debate with the upper hand. Whether a result of the heated exchange or not is not known, but Dobrosmyslov's critique of Chernavsky would be the last of his works to appear in the *Proceedings of the Orenburg Scientific Archival Commission*. He did go on, however, to produce other publications, including his 1912 study of Tashkent, even though he had retired from imperial service in 1907. His date of death is unknown.[630] Chernavsky's work only appeared in the two subsequent editions of *Proceedings*—namely volumes 11 and 12, both published in 1903—following his rebuttal the previous year in volume 10. After continuing his career as a historian and teacher for the Orthodox Church in the

Orenburg region down to the revolution, he served as a teacher and historian under the Soviets from 1918 to 1931, when he was, according to the minutes of committee, dismissed for "unnecessary and harmful public works of a religious nature and for [interpreting] Pugachev in a religious and monarchical character, completely alien to the Marxist understanding of historical events..."[631] He lived out his days "working as an accountant and bookkeeper in different organizations" until his death in 1940.[632]

Negotiating Tsarist State Agendas for Kazakh Islam: Westernizing Liberal Enlightenment (Dobrosmyslov) Versus Russian Religious Nationalism (Chernavsky)

As Elena Campbell makes plain in her study of *The Muslim Question and Russian Imperial Governance*, the interrelated debates taking place among Russian scholars, bureaucrats and missionaries in the late nineteenth and early twentieth century revealed "a set of conflicting views... about the very modernization of the Russian imperial state."[633] The Chernavsky-Dobrosmyslov debate vividly reflects and contributes to those "conflicting views." In responding to Chernavsky's study, which revealed at its heart a more conservative 'Slavophile' passion wishing to restrict "the politics of liberal tolerance" and, in their place, revive Russian Orthodox missionary work among the predominantly non-Russian peoples of the Orenburg region, particularly in this case the Kazakhs, Dobrosmyslov makes clear that the central burden of his treatise is to defend Catherine II's "politics of liberal tolerance" and their presumed value for ultimately achieving the true 'enlightenment' (i.e., Russification and Christianization) of the Kazakh people.

Chernavsky appears to align with the more conservative views of those such as E. Malov, N.P. Ostroumov, S.M. Dukhovskoi and K.P. Pobedonostsev, the latter being a professor of law, government advisor and the Head (Ober-Procurator) of the Russian Orthodox Church (1880–1907). All of these Russian servants of state, in some form or other, shared Chernavsky's rather negative view of Islam as a whole. Meanwhile, Dobrosmyslov seems to fall somewhere between Russian officials like K.P. von Kaufman and S. Iu. Witte on the one hand, and the followers of Il'minskii on the other. Indeed, Dobrosmyslov may have disagreed with Il'minskii on a number of points, but he shared a measure of common ground with him, since Il'minskii supported, in reserved fashion, a policy of religious toleration and was at times, on that point as well as his educational policies, labeled an 'Enlightenment liberal'.[634]

Wherever precisely he is placed on the scale however, Dobrosmyslov should ultimately be interpreted as standing somewhere among the liberal 'Westernizers' who typically countered the cries for "Autocracy, Orthodoxy, and (Russian) Nationalism" emanating from more conservative 'Slavophile' camps like those represented by Chernavsky.[635] It was a debate which had been developing since the days of Peter the Great, but particularly since the 1830s as a conscious attempt to resist and reverse the conservative swing effected by Nicholas I (r. 1825–1855).[636] After more than a century of predominantly pro-Westernizing Tsars lasting from Peter the Great (r. 1682–1725) down to Alexander I (r. 1802–1825),[637] pro-Westernizing voices suffered a significant setback under Nicholas I. After a reprieve under the liberal reformist policies of Alexander II (r. 1855–1881), a firm conservative reaction such as that reflected in the work of Chernavsky held sway under Russia's final two Tsars, Alexander III (r. 1881–1894) and Nicholas II (r. 1894–1917). This was the overall trend of the era in spite of the brief liberal period from 1906 to 1910 forced upon Nicholas II by popular outcry following Russian defeat in the Russo-Japanese War (1904–5) and, in close connection, 'Bloody Sunday' (January 22, 1905). Dobrosmyslov, writing from the peripheries of empire just before the latter fleeting period of liberal oasis, was therefore among those trying to stem the prevailing conservative tide which, from his vantage, threatened to swallow up and reverse the great strides of progress which Russia had made toward its still distant but hoped for return to world power. It was a return which, for him and those who shared his views, could only come by continuing to pursue the 'modern, enlightened' ways of those who had demonstrated their merit by rising to the pinnacle of world power, namely the Western nations and their allegedly 'enlightened, liberal' empires. Dobrosmyslov later affirmed this position when he spoke of Tashkent as a city as revealing "'two civilizations living side by side – one ancient…the other European'" which "showed the 'natives' the way from an ancient or medieval to a modern and European way of life; and from a static and fatalistic conception of time to one marked by belief in the advance of scientific progress and universal civilization."[638] In Dobrosmyslov's view, this approach and its underlying assumptions had been epitomized by Catherine II and had, therefore, to be defended at all cost.

What Dobrosmyslov set out to demonstrate, therefore, was the enduring legitimacy of Catherine II's liberal enlightenment policies for ultimately attaining the aims of Russian empire, both in her as well as his own day. His main aim was not to prove that the Kazakhs had already been genuine and devout Muslims long before embracing Russian suzerainty and that any scholarship which had asserted otherwise was therefore false. He did not successfully accomplish the former aim and the latter was strictly secondary to it. In the latter endeavor, he only affirmed Kazakh Muslim identity in terms of a psychological-emotional attachment to Islam, judging observance of typical Islamic practices to be negligible among the Kazakhs at best. Dobrosmyslov, therefore, offered, if anything, only a slight corrective to the deeply established traditions of interpretation grounded in the widely recognized work of the Russian scholar A. Levshin (1822, 1832) and the Kazakh scholar Sh. Ualihanuhli (1864–1865, Russian: Chokan Valihanov) and those like Chernavsky who followed their lead. But there is no evidence to suggest he had those earlier seminal works in view. He made the objects of his defense clear: Chernavsky was his main and only explicit target, with others of their own day included only by association with Chernavsky's views. All of this is vital in terms of properly identifying Dobrosmyslov's own stated aims and objectives as well as target audience.

Reassessing Presumptions of Dobrosmyslov's Authority in Modern Scholarship and the Alleged 'Conversion-Transformation' Divide

With respect to evaluating Dobrosmyslov's underlying methodology and reliability, i.e., his quality of scholarship, in terms of its internal consistency and the sources upon which he bases or fails to base his claims, Alton S. Donnelly, in his 1968 study of *The Russian Conquest of Bashkiria, 1552–1740*, considered Dobrosmyslov an "authority on the history of the region."[639] One wonders whether Donnelly was aware that Dobrosmyslov was not, in fact, a trained historian, but a veterinarian serving in the Russian administration. To the contrary, the findings here reveal that Dobrosmyslov's portrayals of his opponents' views and, on at least one occasion, his claims regarding the historical evidence are inaccurate, possibly even dishonest and deceptive. And if the latter, it would not be the only occasion on which his scholarship has been called into question in more recent times. One respected scholar of Russian Central Asian studies, David MacKenzie, described one of Dobrosmyslov's other works as a "dishonest article" which failed to report vital facts pertinent to the topic it addressed.[640]

Certain of Dobrosmyslov's arguments against his opponents—particularly his assertion that Catherine II's policies represented no real break from past Tsarist tradition and his attempts to minimize the religious impact of Catherine II's policies on the Kazakhs—are undermined by internal contradictions within his own treatise. His attempts to minimize the religious impact of Catherine II's policies on the Kazakhs likewise rely, in part, on the untenable assumption that Kazakh Muslim identity and practice remained static across nearly two centuries of ongoing dynamic interaction with the multiple different religious, cultural and political groups surrounding them, including the Persians, Turks, Indians, Uighurs, Uzbeks, Turkmen, Caucasian Muslims, Bashkirs, Tatars, Kalmyks, Jungars, Russians and more. To the contrary, as Allen J. Frank acknowledges in his treatise on "Islamic Transformation on the Kazakh Steppe, 1742–1917: Toward an Islamic History of Kazakhstan under Russian Rule": "we must credit Catherine [II] with establishing the institutional foundation for the Islamic revival that fundamentally transformed Kazakh society over the course of the nineteenth century."[641] There is no doubt that the increasing 'Tatar' (i.e., Volga-Ural) Muslim presence and the related spread of Islamic institutions, teachings and literature among the Kazakhs as supported by Catherine II and those following in her trail between the late eighteenth and mid- to late nineteenth centuries had an appreciable impact on Kazakh Muslim identity and practice. That Dobrosmyslov even attempted to argue against that influence calls his better judgment into question. Dobrosmyslov had, indeed, made a "stilted attempt to prove that the government of Catherine II was in no way responsible for the strengthening of Islam among the Kirgiz."[642] Instead of acknowledging these historical realities himself, Dobrosmyslov misrepresented Chernavsky as portraying Catherine II for being "responsible for the 'Islamization' and 'fanaticization' of the Kazakhs when she embarked on a policy of converting the 'animist' Kazakhs to Islam through the use of Tatar '*mullas*'."[643] Chernavsky is here again shown to be not perfectly, but at least more reasonably sound in his assessment of the impact of Catherine II's policies by way of his recognition that they did not "convert," but contributed to the *ongoing process* of Kazakh Islamization, whereas Dobrosmyslov attempts to severely minimize any possible influences or resulting transformations.

One of the problems involved in the ongoing debates over the history of Kazakh religious identity, particularly in relation to the question of the impact of Catherine II's policies, is an attempted restriction of the meaning of "Islamization" to 'conversion' while dissociating it from the ongoing processes of "transformation." Both 'conversion' and 'transformation' are, in fact, part of one and the same long term, ongoing and in many respects never-ending *process*, which involves ebbs and flows stemming from initial introductions to ever-deepening knowledge and understanding accompanied by ongoing processes of 'acceptance' and 'embrace' of various beliefs and practices. Throughout the entire course of this 'journey of faith' both declines and revivals of observance as well as complex encounters of crosscultural contact and exchange occur resulting in new configurations of relationship between pre-existing and newly entering religious, cultural, linguistic, economic, social and political forces, including sometimes 'deconversion' or 'reconversion'. And these are all taking place at multiple individual as well as larger group levels involving an array of multivectored social networks.[644] While the debate over Kazakh Islamic versus 'pre-Islamic' identity has been greatly aided by Geertz and other scholars of the 'cultural turn' who have provided broader, more flexible definitions of 'Islam', 'Islamic' and 'Muslim',[645] this in and of itself has not resolved the critical tension and resulting confusion over sharply distinguished understandings of 'conversion', which remain largely point-and-time punctuated, and closely related processes of ongoing 'transformation'. This holds true even when the conversion of larger people groups such as the Kazakhs are narrated over extended periods of time since 'conversion' is still so emphatically distinguished from post-conversion 'transformations' in relation to the individuals and smaller groups taking part in the process.

Beyond this, having raised important questions about Dobrosmyslov's scholarship in general, a reassessment of any other modern scholarship uncritically relying on Dobrosmyslov's assumed authority is likewise in order. This would include in particular studies involving not only the Kazakhs, but the Bashkirs and Uzbeks. As for Chernavsky, one does not have to agree with his missionary views or aims to recognize that he, not Dobrosmyslov, was the trained historian and represented much sounder, more honest scholarship within the course of the debate.

At its broadest level, this analysis of the debate affirms the importance of critically examining the methodological and scholarly soundness as well as the historical and political motives and context lying behind the production of primary and secondary source documents. With respect to this latter point, in the case of the treatise by Dobrosmyslov as well as those of Chernavsky examined here, it should be carefully noted that they were penned over a century after Catherine II's time. While they thus constitute 'primary sources' with respect to the late nineteenth-, early twentieth-century debate in which the authors were participating, they should be properly classified 'secondary sources' relative to the main time period with which they deal, that is, the late eighteenth and early nineteenth century.

Appendix Two: Outlines of Central Asian Political and Religious History

Overview of Central Asian Political History[646]
Samanids, 819–1005 (Khurasan & Transoxania, w/Bukhara as capital)[647]
  Qarakhanids, 960–1211[648] (Zhetisu, Kashgaria, Ferghana, Transoxania, w/capitals for eastern branch at Balasaghun, Kashgar and western branch at Uzgend and Samarkand)
  Ghaznavids, 977–1186 (Khurasan, Afghanistan, Hindustan)
  Buyids, 932–1062 (Iran & Iraq, 130 yrs)
  Seljuks, 1038–1194 (Iran & Iraq) (--> 1118 as per Canfield)
  Khorezmshahs, 898/1077–1231 (initially only in Khorezm; later most of Central Asia)
  Qarakhitai, 1141–1211 (Zhetisu, Sinkiang, Transoxania)
  Chingis Khan & Mongols, 1206–1294 (w/capitals at Karakorum and, later, Khanbaliq [Beijing])
  Yuan Ulus, 1260–1368 (capital at Khanbaliq)
  Chaghatay Ulus, 1227–1370/1680 (in Transoxania/Sinkiang; split into two, incl. **Mogulistan**)
  Golden Horde, 1227–1380/1502 (w/capital at Sarai)
  White Horde, 1227–1502 (east Kazakh steppe)
  Ilkhanids, 1256–1335 (Iran & Iraq)[649]
  Timur and Timurid Dynasty, 1370–1507 (w/capital at Samarkand; cf. also Herat)
  (Abulkhayrid) Shaybanids, 1500–1599 (Bukhara, Samarkand, Tashkent, Balkh)
    Ottoman Turks, 1453–1914
    Safavids (of Persia), 1501–1736
    Mughals (of India), 1526–1707 (or 1736 or 1858)

Ashtarkhanids, 1599–1785 (Bukhara)
Zhungarians, 1635–1758
Manghits of Bukhara, 1785–1920 (Bukharan Emirate)
Ming of Khokand, 1710–1876 (Khokand)
Khans of Khiva (Kongirats), 1515–1919
Tsarist Russian conquest & Annexation, 1552–1917 (of the Kazakh steppe, 1731–1917; of 'Central Asia' as an administrative unit, 1864-1917)
Bolshevik Revolution & Soviet Empire, 1917–1991

Overview of Central Asian Religious History
Note that I supply only approximate dates for the origins or entrance of these traditions in(to) Central Asia. I leave aside questions of their decline or cessation in part because they are directly related to the question of 'survivals'.

1. Animism, Totemism, Shamanism and Tengrism, 3rd–2nd mill. BCE --->
2. Judaism, 7th c. BCE --->
3. Zoroastrianism, 7th c. BCE (according to some scholars, 10th c. BCE) --->
4. Buddhism, 2nd c. BCE --->
5. Christianity (Ch. of East, Cath., RO), 1st-16th cc. CE, 13–15th cc., & 19th c. CE --->
6. Manichaeism, mid to late 2nd–15th cc. CE
7. Islam, mid-7–8th c., 10–11th c., 14–15th cc., 18–19th cc. --->
8. Renewed pluralism/Religious revivalism, 1991 --->

Overview of Central Asian Islamic History
650–751 CE: The initial Arab Conquests

- Establishing a foothold: the Arabs conquer Merv, Turkmenistan, AD 649–652
- The push into 'Marawannahr' (Transoxonia), 700s (w/uprisings 'till 11th century')

751–1000 CE: The Seljuk-Oghuz Turkic Conversions in the Arab-Persian Advance (cf. Talas, 751)

1000–1300 CE: The Sufi Penetration into the Turkic Kipchak and Karakhanid Heartlands

1300–1770 CE: Post-Mongol re-consolidation via conversion of (the Il-Khanate of Persia), the Chagatai khanate, the Golden Horde and the Uzbeks

1770–1860 CE: Tatar Missionizing among Kazakhs through Russian Tsarist Ambitions

1860-1920 CE: The Russian Muslim Jadid Reform Movements in Tandem with the Pan-Turkish, Pan-Arab, Pan-Islamic and Pan-Asian Visions of the Ottomans and Japanese

1920-1991 CE: Negotiation of Muslim Identity under Soviet anti-religious Propaganda and Oppression

- Before, During and After 'The Great Patriotic War' (WWII)
- From Gorbachev to Independence

1991–2001 CE: The Push for Revival within the Newly Independent Central Asian Republics

2001–Present: Re-negotiating Revival amid Post-911 Scrutiny

NOTES

1. I acknowledge that my system of transliteration throughout the volume is not entirely consistent. This has to do with several factors, some of them historical, which I will not take time or space here to try to explain. I will only note that I was originally planning to convert all the transliteration of Kazakh and Russian to Cyrillic script, but have only done so for the bibliography, not all of the endnotes. I accept that this is perhaps an academic 'sin' or 'crime' of some sort on my part, albeit hopefully only a misdemeanor in the eyes of most. I can only regret whatever minor inconvenience it might cause; it should not otherwise impact the study in any significant way. Those who know the languages should readily be able to understand the transliterations within context. The transliterated citations within the endnotes are all keyed to transliterations of the author's last names in parentheses within the bibliography at the head of the citations in order to ensure clear reference/connection between them, and between references and bibliographies within other studies.
2. "Religious-Cultural Revivalism as Historiographical Debate: Contending Claims in the Post-Soviet Kazakh Context." *Journal of Islamic Studies*, Vol. 25, No. 2 (May 2014): 138–177. DOI: 10.1093/jis/ett058 (Published online Nov 12, 2013. http://jis.oxfordjournals.org/content/25/2/138).

3. Abai Kunanbaiuhli (c. 1900), "Word Thirty-Two," in *Book of Words*, Leneshmidt Translations Resource Library (URL: http://www.leneshmidt-translations.com/book_of_words_abai_kunanbaev_english/32.htm). Cf. Garifolla Yesim ([1994] 2020), "Word Thirty-Two: The Requisites of Learning," in *An Insider's Critique of the Kazakh Nation: Reflections on the Writings of Abai Kunanbaiuhli (1845–1904)*, tr. and ed. R. Charles Weller (Boston, MA: Asia Research Associates), pp. 211–212.

4. See esp. John Voll, "Central Asia as a Part of the Modern Islamic World," in *Central Asia in Historical Perspective*, ed. Beatrice F. Manz (Boulder, CO: Westview Press, 1994), pp. 62–81 and Robert D. McChesney, "Central Asia's Place in the Middle East: Some Historical Considerations," in *Central Asia Meets the Middle East*, ed. David Menashri (New York and London: Routledge, 1998), pp. 25–51. Cf. the question of influence from and nature of Kazakh Islam in relation to surrounding Central Asian (and Middle Eastern) Islamic traditions?

5. Devin Deweese, *Islamization and Native Religion in the Golden Horde: Baba Tukles and Conversion to Islam in Historical and Epic Tradition* (Pennsylvania State University Press, 1994), pp. 4–5.

6. Beyond this very brief survey, I refer the reader to the edited volume by David W. Montgomery, *Central Asia: Contexts for Understanding* (Pittsburgh, PA: University of Pittsburgh Press, 2022) for precisely what the subtitle indicates.

7. Note that I capitalize the term here in order to give it the same respect and recognition as the monotheistic faith traditions because the use of the lower-case spelling, i.e., 'god,' is directly related to its assigned status as 'pagan idolatry' within those exclusivist monotheistic traditions.

8. Along with Appendix Two, which includes a very brief 'Overview of Central Asian Religious History,' I discuss some of the most important surveys of this religious history below, and reference others throughout the study, so I will leave readers to those sources for more detailed discussions. The very nature of this present study is to assess the historiographical debates raised by all such sources, including any 'survey' I myself might otherwise try to provide here by way of introduction, so it would be contrary to the very aim of this study to try to supply a more

detailed history. Meanwhile, David W. Montgomery's chapter on "Religion" in *Central Asia: Contexts for Understanding*, ed. D. W. Montgomery (Pittsburgh, PA: University of Pittsburgh Press, 2022), pp. 361–377, also supplies a helpful context.
9. Gabitov has served for multiple years, since the mid-1990s, as professor of Philosophy and Culture in the Department of Culture and History of Philosophy et al-Farabi Kazakh þ. He was invited for a three-year visiting professorship at Shahid Beheshti University (formerly National University of Iran) in Tehran in the late 1990s. He has authored or co-authored numerous journal articles, chapters, books and textbooks, as well as local and national newspaper articles (cf. some of the refs in main text above as well as endnotes below).
10. Khalid, *Islam after Communism*, p. 32.
11. Richard Foltz, *Religions of the Silk Road: Premodern Patterns of Globalization*, 2nd ed. (New York: St. Martin's Press, 2010), pp. 133–135 and *Religions of the Silk Road: Overland Trade and Cultural Exchange from Antiquity to the Fifteenth Century*, 1st ed. (New York: St. Martin's Press, 1999), pp. 141–142. Foltz in fact confuses the use of the term 'Kyrgyz' in relation to the 'Kazakh' by locating such usage in pre-Tsarist sources; Dughlat, *Tarikh-i Rashidi*, for example, which Foltz cites, distinguishes clearly between the 'Kyrgyz' and the 'Kazakhs,' calling the former "infidels" and the latter true Muslims (see Chapter 3).
12. James Thrower, *The Religious History of Central Asia from the Earliest Times to the Present Day* (Lewiston, NY, Queenston, Ontario, Canada, and Lampeter, Ceredigion, Wales: Edwin Mellon Press, 1999), p. 27.
13. Ira M. Lapidus, *Islamic Societies to the Nineteenth Century* (Cambridge University Press, 2012), p. 420.
14. Awelkhan Hali, Zengxiang Li, and Karl W. Luckert, "Faith and Fasting," in *Kazakh Traditions of China* (Lanham, MD: University Press of America, 1999), pp. 153ff, likewise insist on the predominance of the animist and shamanist traditions among contemporary Kazakhs. Cf. also Sergei Poliakov, *Everyday Islam: Religion and Tradition in Rural Central Asia* (Armonk, NY: M.E. Sharpe, 1992).
15. Deweese, *Islamization and Native Religion*, p. 9.
16. Ibid., p. 9.

17. Ibid., p. 5; cf. D. Deweese, "Islamization in the Mongol Empire," in *The Cambridge History of Inner Asia: The Chinggisid Age*, ed. N. Di Cosmo, A. J. Frank, and P. B. Golden (Cambridge: Cambridge University Press, 2009), pp. 120–134.
18. Cf. Robert D. Baird, "Interpretative Categories and the History of Religions," *History and Theory*, Vol. 8, No. 8: *On Method in the History of Religions* (1968): 17–30, who notes "the method and scope of history of religions (*Religionswissenschaft*)" that "it is generally agreed that this field of study is divided into two main areas of scholarly concern. One area is systematic, is sometimes called phenomenology of religion, and is represented by such scholars as Van der Leeuw, W. Brede Kristensen, Mircea Eliade, and C. J. Bleeker. The second area is more distinctively historical in orientation and is exemplified by the work of G. F. Moore, Raffaele Pettazzoni, or Joseph Kitagawa (Religion in Japanese History)" (p. 17).
19. See esp. Richard J. Evans, *In Defence of History*, American Edition (New York and London: W. W. Norton & Co., 1998); Ernst Breisach, *On the Future of History: The Postmodernist Challenge and Its Aftermath* (Chicago: University of Chicago Press, 2003) and Georg G. Iggers, *Historiography in the Twentieth Century: From Scientific Objectivity to the Postmodern Challenge* (Middletown, CT: Wesleyan University Press, [1997] 2005).
20. Bruce G. Privratsky, *Muslim Turkistan: Kazak Religion and Collective Identity* (London and New York: Routledge, 2001), pp. 256–257.
21. D. Deweese, "(Review of) *Everyday Islam in Post-Soviet Central Asia*, by Maria E. Louw (London & New York: Routledge, 2007)," *Journal of Islamic Studies*, Vol. 21, No. 1 (January 2010): 157–162, citing from p. 157.
22. Some, though not all of these observations, are based on the fact that I randomly and informally interviewed several 'Bukharan' everyday people during my visit there in 2005 about these very issues. My own sampling revealed in every case, perhaps 6–7 in total, that they considered their language to be shared, in spite of differentiations made by others. See esp., Peter Finke and Meltem Sancak, "To Be an Uzbek or Not to Be a Tajik? Ethnicity and Locality in the Bukhara Oasis," *Zeitschrift für*

Ethnologie (ZfE)/Journal of Social and Cultural Anthropology (*JSCA*) Vol. 137, No. 1 (2012): 47–70.
23. Montgomery, "Religion," in *Central Asia*, p. 368. Note that this is the only use of "remnants," while the term "survivals" does not occur anywhere in the volume.
24. Gian Luca Bonora, Niccolò Pianciola, and Paolo Sartori, eds., *Kazakhstan: Religions and Society in the History of Central Eurasia* (Turin: Umberto Allemandi & Co., 2010).
25. Robert D. Crews, *For Prophet and Tsar: Islam and Empire in Russia and Central Asia* (Boston: Harvard University Press, 2006), pp. 192–240.
26. Comparatively in relation to especially various forms of Christianity in Europe, see Stefan Berger and Christoph Conrad, *The Past as History: National Identity and Historical Consciousness in Modern Europe* (Basingstoke, UK: Palgrave Macmillan, 2015), pp. 123–5; see also Stefan Berger and Chris Lorenz, eds., *The Contested Nation: Ethnicity, Class, Religion and Gender in National Histories* (Basingstoke, UK: Palgrave Macmillan, 2008); Adrian Hastings, *The Construction of Nationhood: Ethnicity, Religion and Nationalism* (Cambridge, UK: Cambridge University Press, 1997); Gokhan Cetinsaya, "Rethinking Nationalism and Islam: some preliminary notes on the roots of 'Turkish-Islamic synthesis' in modern Turkish political thought," *Muslim World*. Vol 89, No 3–4 (July/Oct. 1999), pp 350–76.
27. Conyers Middleton, *A Letter from Rome Showing the Exact Conformity between Popery and Paganism: or, The Religion of the Present Romans to be derived entirely from that of their Heathen Ancestors*, 3rd ed. (London, [1729] 1733), p. 13. I am quoting directly from the third edition. The italics are in the original; they do not represent book titles, as might appear according to present custom, but were the means of emphasis in Middleton's day. Deweese quotes from and draws his analysis of Middleton from the select, limited material provided in Jonathan Z. Smith, *To Take Place: Toward Theory in Ritual* (Chicago and London: University of Chicago Press, 1987).
28. Devin Deweese, "Survival Strategies: Reflections on the Notion of Religious 'Survivals' in Soviet Ethnographic Studies of Muslim Religious Life in Central Asia," in *Exploring the Edge*

of *Empire: Soviet Era Anthropology in the Caucasus and Central Asia*, eds. F. Muhlfried and S. Sokolovskiy (Berlin: LIT Verlag, 2011), pp. 38–39, incl. fn4.

29. Edward Burnett Tylor, *Primitive Culture: Researches into the Development of Mythology, Philosophy, Religion, Language, Art, and Custom*, Sixth Edition (London: John Murray, [1871] 1920), p. 157.
30. See esp. Robert E. Schofield, *The Enlightened Joseph Priestley: A Study of His Life and Work from 1773 to 1804*, Illustrated Edition (State College, PA: Penn State University Press, [1997] 2004). Jefferson and certain other American founding fathers were also familiar with the work of Middleton, most likely via that of Priestley.
31. Tylor, *Primitive Culture* ([1871] 1920), Vol. 1, p. 18.
32. Joseph Priestley, *An History of the Corruptions of Christianity*, Vol. 1, 3rd ed. (Boston: William Spotswood, [1782] 1797), p. viii.
33. Tylor, *Primitive Culture* ([1871] 1920), Vol. 1, in the "Preface to First Edition," p. v, see esp. n1. For the full transcript, see: E. B. Tylor, "On the Survival of Savage Thought in Modern Civilization," in *Notices of the Proceedings at the Meetings of the Members of the Royal Institution, with Abstracts of the Discourses, Vol. V (1866–1869)* (London: William Clowes & Sons, 1869), pp. 522–535. Note that Hodgen's attribution of the 'formal' introduction of the concept of 'survivals' to Tylor, *Primitive Culture* (1871), is thus misleading at best (Margaret Hodgen, "The Doctrine of Survivals: The History of an Idea," *American Anthropologist*, N.S. Vol. 33, No. 3 [1931]: 301).
34. William Blackstone, *Commentaries on the Laws of England*, Book the Second [Vol. 2], 3rd ed. (Oxford: The Clarendon Press, MDCCLXVIII [1768]), p. 84.
35. Margaret Hodgen, *The Doctrine of Survivals: A Chapter in the History of Scientific Method in the Study of Man* (London: Allenson and Co., Ltd., 1936), pp. 26–33 and 54–55. For the broader context of the debate between the 'degenerationist' and 'progressivist' schools of Tylor and Whately, see Daniel Pick, *Faces of Degeneration: A European Disorder, c.1848–c.1918* (Cambridge: Cambridge University Press, 1989), pp. 216–217; cf. also Arthur Herman, *The Idea of Decline in Western History*

(New York: Free Press, 1997), chs. 2 and 4, and J. B. Bury, "The Doctrine of Degeneration: The Ancients and Moderns," in *The Idea of Progress: An Inquiry into Its Origin and Growth* (London: Macmillan and Co., 1920), pp. 78–97. Robert Nisbet, *History of the Idea of Progress* (Piscataway, NJ: Transaction Publishers [Routledge], 1980) also deals, like Bury, with the subject, both specifically in relation to Tylor and the degenerationists of his day, as well as other ideas more ancient and modern.

36. Tylor, *Primitive Culture* ([1871] 1920), p. 45.
37. Edward Burnett Tylor, *Researches into the Early History of Mankind and the Development of Civilization* (Boston: Estes & Lauriat, [1865] 1878), pp. 135–138 (italicized emphasis on "*remnants*" mine).
38. Ibid., pp. 375–376.
39. Tylor, *Primitive Culture* ([1871] 1920), p. 16.
40. Ibid., p. 21.
41. Ibid., p. 72.
42. Tylor, *Researches into the Early History of Mankind* (1865), references Richard Whately, *On the Origin of Civilization* (London: Nisbet, 1854), p. 160; cf. 160fn2). Whately speaks in that essay of "those few rude arts which even savages possess" being "remnants which they have retained from a more civilised state" (Richard Whately, "On the Origin of Civilization" [1854], in *Miscellaneous Lectures and Reviews*, London: Parker, Son, and Bourn, West Strand, 1861, p. 39). The close tie of this theory with mid-nineteenth-century debates over race is evident in Whately stating elsewhere that "savages" themselves "are the degenerated remnants of more civilised races" (p. 43). It further seems tied to the biblical doctrine of 'the remnant of Israel' and related 'remnant of true believers' (cf. pp. 48 and 193ff). As for Taylor, Tylor cites him in 1865, *Researches*, pp. 187 and 281.
43. Han F. Vermeulen, *Before Boas: The Genesis of Ethnography and Ethnology in the German Enlightenment* (Lincoln, NE: University of Nebraska Press, 2015), p. 96, names specifically "Sigmund von Herberstein, Adam Olearius, Eberhard Isbrand Ides, Adam Brand, Lorenz Lange, Georg Johann Uverzagt, …Isaac Massa, Samuel Purchas, and Jean Chardin" as having left accounts about Siberia and related regions prior to Witsen.

44. Nicolaas Witsen, *Noord en Oost Tartarye* [*North and East Tartarye*], 2nd ed. (Amsterdam: François Halma [1692] 1705), p. 157, and Vermeulen, *Before Boas* (2015), p. 98. Though the English rendering of the quote is contained in Vermeulen, I have checked it against the Dutch version and thus provided the precise Dutch phrasing.
45. Witsen, *Noord en Oost Tartarye* ([1692] 1705), pp. 348 and 306–307 respectively.
46. Witsen, *Noord en Oost Tartarye* ([1692] 1705), pp. 325 and 351.
47. Hodgen, *The Doctrine of Survivals*, p. 6.
48. The debates over dating the various sections of the Hebrew-Jewish Bible (Christian 'Old Testament') as well as, to a lesser though still significant extent, the various writings of Christian New Testament are heated and complex. Not only are they historically, archeologically, numismatically and linguistically complex, they are further complicated by questions of bias which pertain to those who are motivated by both religious as well as anti-religious agendas, not to mention various political agendas, particularly those pertaining to questions of Jewish Zionism and the Israeli-Palestinian debates, inasmuch as those latter political debates involve the question of the historicity of the Hebrew Bible. For an excellent, balanced overview, see: Eric H. Cline, *Biblical Archaeology: A Very Short Introduction* (Oxford and New York: Oxford University Press, 2009). For a more liberal, modernist perspective, see esp., Ingrid Hjelm and Thomas L. Thompson, eds., *History, Archaeology and The Bible Forty Years After 'Historicity': Changing Perspectives 6* (London and New York: Routledge, 2016); Hjelm is Associate Professor at the University of Copenhagen and Director of the Palestine History and Heritage Project while Thompson is an American-born Danish biblical scholar, Professor Emeritus at the University of Copenhagen. For a more conservative, traditionalist perspective, see esp., K. A. Kitchen, *On the Reliability of the Old Testament* (Grand Rapids, MI: Eerdman's Publishing Co., 2003); Kitchen is a British biblical scholar, Personal and Brunner Professor Emeritus of Egyptology and Honorary Research Fellow at the School of Archaeology, Classics, and Oriental Studies, University of Liverpool, England.

49. Zephaniah 1:4.
50. Joshua 24:14.
51. Kings 17:24–41; cf. also Ezra 4:2 and John 4:22.
52. Though not treated in this chapter, the broader history of 'pagan survivals' (cf. also 'foreign,' 'impure' or 'barbarian survivals') most likely includes other world religious and cultural traditions. For example, consider the early anti-Buddhist work of a Confucian writer from T'ang China: 韓愈/Han Yu, "論佛骨表/Memorial on the Bones of the Buddha" (819 CE), tr. Geoff Humble (unpublished paper). Han Yu does not use the concept of 'pre-Buddhist survivals', but forewarns that if the spread of Buddhism "is not urgently prohibited, all our temples will be altered, ...Customs will be harmed and conventions degraded," which is to say they will not become completely extinct, but will rather become mere corrupted, intermixed and potentially subsumed within a dominating Buddhist framework (p. 3). The idea of 'remnants' or 'survivals' is not far off here. Han Yu also reflects, however, a concern for 'displacement', which, quite interestingly by way of comparison with debates in the Central Asian context, involves shamans: "The ancient lords, if bringing a corpse back to their country, would first have a shaman use a peachwood broom to expel inauspicious [presences], only then bringing in the body. Now, for no good reason, [Your Majesty is] taking this filthy thing, looking at it in person, without the preparation of a shaman..." (pp. 3–4). Apparently the shamans continued on, in his view, in a 'dual faith' system. For a late twentieth-century perspective on 'pre-Buddhist survivals' in the Tibetan context, see John Myrdhin Reynolds, *Yungdrung Bon - the Eternal Tradition: the Ancient Pre-Buddhist Religion of Central Asia and Tibet: Its History, Teachings, and Literature* (Freehold, NJ: Bompo Translation Project, 1991). My thanks to Geoff Humble and Will Tuladhar Douglas, respectively, for these two references in response to my inquiry on the H-Asia list serve. One pre-publication reviewer of this work has suggested that the idea of 'remnants' or 'survivals' is more characteristic of monotheistic faith traditions. In particular, they have suggested that Han Yu's understanding of the relationship between Buddhism and Confucianism is not comparable to the relationship between 'pre-monotheistic' and monotheistic beliefs

(especially in the 'pre-Islamic' sense covered in later chapters). The argument the reviewer makes is that the Chinese case does not involve the relation between "world religions" and others, but what is internally, authentically Chinese (Confucianism) versus foreign and thus "barbarian" (Buddhism). I suggest that in fact the distinction between what is internally authentic and 'pure' versus foreign and 'barbarian' (cf. also 'primitive' or 'idolatrous') is in fact a shared paradigm between the Middle Eastern monotheistic and East Asian traditions. The epistemological basis of their conceptions certainly differ, in that the monotheistic traditions technically (i.e., theologically) claim to look beyond 'Hebrew' or 'Arab' identity as the source and basis of their distinguishing internally, authentic from foreign, barbaric, idolatrous sources; but even here, essential paradigm remains comparable at heart. Additionally, the way in which ideas of divine revelational purity become closely wed to ideas of 'Hebrew' (cf. also 'Jewish') and 'Arab' ethnic purity are historically manifest and thus also comparable on those grounds to the Chinese.

53. Saint Augustine, "Feast of the Nativity: Sermon 196" and "New Year's Day: Sermon 198," in *The Fathers of the Church: A New Translation: Saint Augustine: Sermons on the Liturgical Seasons*, tr. Sister M. S. Muldowney (New York: Fathers of the Church, Inc., 1959), p. 47; Original Latin: J. P. Migne, ed., *Patrologiae Cursus Completus: Tomus XXXVIII: S. Augustini* (Parisiis: Venit Apud Editorum, 1845), p. 1021; cf. Edvard Westermarck, *Pagan Survivals in Mohammedan Civilisation* (London: Macmillan, 1933), p. 174, who says Augustine "denounces this as a relic of paganism." Westermarck cites this text to demonstrate that certain Berber customs involving fire and water being practiced near the same region were also 'relics of paganism'. Augustine does not necessarily have the idea of 'relic,' 'remnant' or 'survival' in view, but it seems in this case this is what he is referring to, even though he is more immediately concerned in the context with Christians mixing with pagans in their day and "aping their customs and deeds" (Muldowney transl., p. 56).

54. Ramsay MacMullen, *Christianity and Paganism in the Fourth to Eighth Centuries* (New Haven, CT: Yale University Press, 1997), p. iii; see also Ramsay MacMullen and Eugene Lane,

eds., *Paganism and Christianity, 100–425 CE: A Sourcebook* (Minneapolis, MN: Fortress Press, 1992). Cf. Averil Cameron, *Procopius and the Sixth Century* (Berkeley and Los Angeles: University of California Press, 1985): "the anecdotal or miraculous material in [Procopius's] *Gothic Wars*...tends to focus on pagan survivals and mythology (the temple of Janus, the Sibylline books, Aeneas' ship)" (p. 203).

55. Bernadette Filotas, *Pagan Survivals, Superstitions, and Popular Cultures in Early Medieval Pastoral Literature* (Toronto: Pontifical Institute of Mediaeval Studies, 2005), p. 332. The original Latin treatise from which Filotas cites—namely "Concilium Turonense a. 567"—is available in: Charles de Clercq, *Concilia Galliae 511–695* (Turnhout: Brepols, 1991). Cf. also Jean Seznec, *La Survivance des Dieux Antiques* (London: 1940); English transl. *The Survival of the Pagan Gods: The Mythological Tradition and Its Place in Renaissance Humanism Art*, tr. Barbara Sessions (Princeton, NJ: Princeton University Press, 1953). Seznec offers an entire section covering ecclesiastical opposition to pagan survivals in the Renaissance period, though it reflects more a concern with the revival (cf. 'renaissance') rather than the 'survival' of pagan gods through Renaissance art. On a different point, it is noteworthy here that these same kinds of 'pre-Christian remnants' which were condemned by the early church later became the focus of Muslim spiritual leaders who condemned practices tied to a similar and historically-related 'cult of the saints'. The medieval Christian condemnation of visiting 'sacred rocks, trees and springs' likewise closely parallels later condemnation of similar practices among the Kazakh Muslims by various Central Asian Muslim leaders. Though a human anthropological (i.e., 'independent development' based in human nature) rather historically contingent explanation is possible in both cases, there is sufficient evidence for historical contingency in the case of 'the cult of saints'.

56. Ruth Mazo Karras, "Pagan Survivals and Syncretism in the Conversion of Saxony," *The Catholic Historical Review*, Vol. 72, No. 4 (October 1986): 553–572, quoting from pp. 563–564. Karras herself cites from "Adam of Bremen, *Gesta Hammaburgensis ecclesiae pontificum*, II, 48, ed. Bernhard Schmeidler, MGH, SS Rer. Germ., 3rd ed., p. 108".

57. See esp., Karoline P. Cook, *Forbidden Passages: Muslims and Moriscos in Colonial Spanish America* (University of Pennsylvania Press, 2016), pp. 13ff. Cf. Francisco Bethencourt, *The Inquisition: A Global History 1478–1834*, tr. Jean Birrell (Cambridge University Press, 2009).
58. See esp. Jennifer K. Deane, *A History of Medieval Heresy and Inquisition* (Lanham, MD: Rowman & Littlefield Publishers, 2011), though she limits her study to the period between c. 1100 and 1500 CE.
59. Soviet ethnographic agendas in particular are comparable to the Inquisitions, though we could also point to the Tsarist traditions reflected, for example, in Fyodor Dostoevsky's 1880 poem, "The Grand Inquisitor." Cf. Patrick Bergemann, *Judge Thy Neighbor: Denunciations in the Spanish Inquisition, Romanov Russia, and Nazi Germany* (New York: Columbia University Press, 2019).
60. Count Valerian Krasinski, *A Treatise on Relics by John Calvin, Translated from the French Original, With An Introductory Dissertation On the Miraculous Images, as Well as Other Superstitions, of the Roman Catholic and Russo-Greek Churches*, Second Edition (Edinburgh: Johnstone, Hunter & Co., 1870), pp. 173 and 206.
61. Saint Nestor, *The Russian Primary Chronicle*, tr. and ed. Samuel Hazzard Cross and Olgerd P. Sherbowitz-Wetzor (Cambridge, MA: Harvard University Press, [c. 1118, 1930] 1953), pp. 146–148.
62. Nestor, *The Russian Primary Chronicle*, 56–58.
63. Nestor, *The Russian Primary Chronicle*, 117.
64. See chapter four in Stella Rock, *Popular Religion in Russia: 'Double Belief' and the Making of an Academic Myth* (London and New York: Routledge, 2007).
65. Rock, *Popular Religion in Russia*, p. 87.
66. See Judith Cohen Zacek, "The Russian Bible Society and the Russian Orthodox Church," *Church History*, Vol. 35, No. 4 (Dec 1966): 411–437; Stephen K. Batalden, "Printing the Bible in the Reign of Alexander I: Toward a Reinterpretation of the Imperial Russian Bible Society," in *Church, Nation and State in Russia and Ukraine*, ed. Geoffrey A. Hosking (Palgrave Macmillan, 1991), pp. 65–78; and Robert P. Geraci, "Orthodox Missionaries in the Kazakh Steppe, 1881–1917," in *Of Religion*

and Empire: Missions, Conversion, and Tolerance in Tsarist Russia, ed. R. P. Geraci and M. Khodarkovsky (Ithaca and London: Cornell University Press, 2001), pp. 276–277.
67. Rock, *Popular Religion in Russia*, pp. 87–88.
68. Both quotations from Tim Blanning, *The Romantic Revolution: A History* (New York, NY: Random House, 2010), p. 121.
69. С. А. Токарев, "Вклад русских ученых в мировую этнографическую науку [The Contribution of Russian Scientists to World Ethnographic Science]," *Очерки истории русской этнографии, фольклористики и антропологии* [*Essays on the History of Russian Ethnography, Folklore and Anthropology*], (Москва [Moscow]: Наука [Nauka], вып. [Issue] 1, 1956), pp. 5–25, citing from p. 15. My thanks to Nathaniel Knight for drawing my attention to the work of Kavelin as highlighted by Tokarev with respect to the concept and methodology of "survivals."
70. Ibid., 14–15.
71. М. Азбукин, "Очерк Литературной Борьбы Представителей Христианства с Остатками Язычества в Русском Народе (XI-XIV века)" [M. Azbukin, "An Essay on the Literary Struggle of Representatives of Christianity with the Remnants of Paganism among the Russian People (XI–XIV cc.]," *Русский Филологический Вестник* [*Russian Philological Bulletin*], Vol. 28, No. 3 (1892): 133–153; Vol. 35, No. 2 (1896): 222–272; Vol. 37, Nos. 1–2 (1897): 229–273; Vol. 38, Nos. 3–4 (1897): 322–337; Vol. 39, Nos. 1–2 (1898): 246–278.
72. С. И. Смирнов [S. I. Smirnov], "Бабы Богомерзкиия [Women of God]," *Сборник статей, посвященных Василию Осиповичу Ключевскому...*, ed. Я. Л. Барсков [Collection of articles dedicated to Vasily Osipovich Klyuchevsky ..., Ia. L. Barskov] (Moscow, 1909); *Древне-русский духовник: Изследование по истории церковнаго быта* [Ancient Russian confessor. An investigation into the history of church life], (Moscow, 1913); *Духовный Отец в Древней Восточной Церкви. История Духовничества на Востоке* [Spiritual Father in the Ancient Eastern Church. History of Spirituality in the East] (Sergiev Posad, 1906).
73. George Vernadsky, *A History of Russia*, New Revised Edition (New Haven: Yale University Press, 1929–1944), pp. 34 and 42 (cf. pp. 26–27, 33) and Rock, *Popular Religion in Russia*, p. 94.

74. Central Asian interactions with South Asia are also touched upon in this chapter and should be further explored.
75. R. Michael Feener, "Muslim Cultures and Pre-Islamic Pasts: Changing Perceptions of 'Heritage'," in *The Making of Islamic Heritage: Muslim Pasts and Heritage Presents*, ed. T. Rico (Singapore: Palgrave Macmillan, 2017), pp. 24–27.
76. See Ibn Taimiyah, *The Right Way: A Summarised Translation* (Riyadh: Dar-us-Salam, 1996), pp. 64, 70–86. Cf. Cameron Zargar, "Origins of Wahhabism from Hanbali Fiqh," *Journal of Islamic and Near Eastern Law*, Vol. 16, No. 1 (2017): 65–114, esp. pp. 86ff; Diego R. Sarrio, "Spiritual anti-elitism: Ibn Taymiyya's doctrine of sainthood (*walāya*)," *Islam and Christian–Muslim Relations*, Vol. 22, No. 3 (2011): 275–291; Niels H. Olesen, *Culte des saints et pèlerinages chez Ibn Taymiyya (661/1263–728/1328)* [*The Worship of Saints and Pilgrimages in Ibn Taymiyya*] (Paris: P. Geuthner, 1991), and Deweese, "Survival Strategies," p. 41.
77. See Abd Allah Salih al-'Uthaymin, *Muhammad Ibn 'Abd al-Wahhab: The Man and his Works* (I. B. Tauris, 2009), esp. pp. 40, 162n26.
78. See Josef W. Meri, "The Etiquette of Devotion in the Islamic Cult of the Saints," in *The Cult of Saints in Late Antiquity and the Middle Ages: Essays on the Contribution of Peter Brown*, ed. James Howard-Johnston and Paul Antony Hayward (Oxford: Oxford University Press, 2002), pp. 263–286.
79. Hazem Hussein Abbas Ali, "Casting Discord: An Unpublished Spell from the Egyptian National Library," in *Amulets and Talismans of the Middle East and North Africa in Contex: Transmission, Efficacy and Collections*, ed. Marcela A. Garcia Probert and Petra M. Sijpesteijn (Leiden and Boston: Brill Academic, 2022), p. 118.
80. Ignác Goldziher, "Veneration of Saints in Islam," *Muslim Studies*, Vol. 2, ed. S. M. Stern, tr. from German by C. R. Barber and S. M. Stern (London: Allen and Unwin, [1889–1890] 1971), pp. 333–336.
81. See esp. Marc Gaborieau, "A Nineteenth-century Indian 'Wahhabi' Tract against the Cult of the Saints: 'Al-Balagh al-Mubin'," *Islam in India*, Vol. 4, No. 1 (Jan 1989): 198–239.

82. Malami Buba, "The Legacies of the Sokoto Caliphate in Contemporary Nigeria," *History Compass*, Vol. 16, No. 8 (Aug 2018): 1–2; cf. Umar Habila Dadem Danfulani, "Factors Contributing to the Survival of the *Bori* Cult in Northern Nigeria," *Numen*, Vol. 46, No. 4 (1999): 412–447.
83. Devin Deweese, *Islamization and Native Religion in the Golden Horde: Baba Tukles and Conversion to Islam in Historical and Epic Tradition* (Pennsylvania State University Press, 1994), p. 6.
84. The transformation, and what many have considered hardening, of Islamic views is evidenced in the Middle East, for example, in the reiteration of the terms of 'the Covenant of Umar' by the Mamluk clerk al-Qalqashandi (1355–1418) in his *Ṣubḥ al-A ʿshā* (manual for chancery clerks). See Shihāb al-Dīn Aḥmad ibn ʿAlī al-Qalqashandī, *Ṣubḥ al-A ʿshá fī Ṣināʿat al-Inshā'*, 14 Vols (Cairo: al-Maṭbaʿah al-Amīrīyah, 1913–1919), V13:381–386. Though not containing this particular section of al-Qalqashandi's work, see, for context, the recent work by Tarek Galal Abdelhamid, Heba El-Toudy, eds., *Selections from Subh al-A'sha by al-Qalqashandi, Clerk of the Mamluk Court: "Seats of Government" and "Regulations of the Kingdom", From Early Islam to the Mamluks* (New York and London: Routledge, 2017).
85. Peter Golden, *Central Asia in World History* (Oxford and New York: Oxford University Press, 2010), pp. 72–73.
86. Yûsuf Khâss Hâjib, *Wisdom of Royal Glory (Kutadgu Bilig): A Turko-Islamic Mirror for Princes*, tr. Robert Dankoff (Chicago: University of Chicago Press, [1069] 1983), p. 181.
87. Tao Hua, "Satuq Bughra Khan and the Beginning of Islamization in the Tian Shan Region," in *Islam*, ed. Yijiu Jin (Religious Studies in Contemporary China Collection, Volume 6, Leiden: Brill, 2017), pp. 116–134.
88. See Yûsuf Khâss Hâjib, *Kutadgu Bilig Metni* [*The Text of the Kutadgu Bilig*], ed. Turkanitlari (URL: https://kutadgubilig.appspot.com/liii.html), which contains the original 11th c. text in parallel with a modern Turkish translation. Kurtuluş Öztopçu, Zhoumagaly Abouv, Nasir Kambarov and Youssef Azemoun, eds., *Dictionary of the Turkic Languages* (London and New York: Routledge, 1996), provides rather limited coverage of terms, in this case only "cure" is relevant, for which they list differing

Kazakh and Tatar terms (p. 38). Cf. also Privratsky, *Muslim Turkistan*, pp. 193–235, esp. his section on "Today's *Emshi*— Yesterday's Shaman," pp. 231–235, though Privratsky does not trace the terms back to Balasaghuni nor even mention him or the Karakhanids in his study.

89. Mahmud al-Kashgari, *Compendium of the Turkic Dialects (Dīwān Luγāt at-Turk)*, ed. and tr. Robert Dankoff, in collaboration with James Kelly, 3 Vols (Cambridge, MA: Harvard University Press, 1982); see V2:229, V3:125 and V3:221; cf. also V1:236; V2:141; V2:164; V2:307; V2:377; V3:13; V3:260; V3:264.

90. Cf. Nişanyan Sözlük (URL: https://www.nisanyansozluk.com/kelime/efsun), which is based upon Sevan Nişanyan, *Sözlerin Soyağacı: çağdaş Türkçenin etimolojik sözlüğü: etymological dictionary of contemporary Turkish* (2001).

91. Francis Joseph Steingass, *A Comprehensive Persian-English dictionary, including the Arabic words and phrases to be met with in Persian literature* (London: Routledge & K. Paul, 1892), pp. 83 and 929. Hosted online by *Digital Dictionaries of South Asia*, University of Chicago (URL: https://dsal.uchicago.edu/cgi-bin/app/steingass_query.py?qs=%D8%A7%D9%81%D8%B3%D9%88%D9%86&matchtype=default) Steingass (1825–1903), was a British orientalist and linguist of German-Jewish descent. He originally published the work based, in part, on a thorough study of Persian classical literature, including Firdousi's *Shahnameh (Book of Kings)*. It remains a standard reference to this day. For a comparative study on "magic" in world religious and cultural traditions, see: David Frankfurter, ed., *Guide to the Study of Ancient Magic* (Leiden and Boston: Brill Academic, 2019).

92. *Fesoongar* (2x), *afsoongar* (10x), *fesoon* (82x) and *afsoon* (58x).

93. For Farsi, see: شاهنامهٔ فردوسی (ویراست سنجشگرانه)، زیرِ نگرِ یوگنی ا. برتلس، عبدالحسین نوشین و .... مسکو: اکادمی علوم اتحاد شوروی، ۷۱ ،۱۹۶۰. Ferdowsi, *Shahnameh (Critical Edition)*, ed. Eugene A. Bertels, Abdolhossein Noushin, et al. (Moscow: Academy of Sciences of the Soviet Union, 1960–1971). Special thanks to Mohammad Ghaedi for his assistance in conducting this research in the Persian version of Firdousi's *Shahnameh*. The only complete English translation is Firdausi, *The Shahnama of Firdausi*, tr. and ed. Arthur George

Warner and Edmond Warner, 11 Vols (London: Kegan Paul Trench, Trubner & Co., 1905–1910). More recent editions of the Warners' translation have been put out, including in ebook format. Multiple other English translations have been done in abridgment, most notably those by James Atkinson (early nineteenth century), Dick Davis, Helen Zimmern, Ahmad Sadri and B.W. Robinson.

94. The edition of Khusraw's work used for this reference does not seem to be given on the Iranian *Ganjoor* website, but it is widely recognized site using standard editions of Persian-Farsi works. The usage of the specific term within the context of the passage quoted from Khusraw here can be viewed at: https://ganjoor.net/naserkhosro/divann/ghaside-naser/sh149.

95. The material from Firdausi, Khusraw, Rumi and Shabestari, including the quotes translated into English, are based mainly, with thanks, on the research of Mohammad Ghaedi. Abdollah Ghaffari also contributed.

96. See e.g.: Nasser Nikobakht and Seyyed Ali Qassemzadeh, "Specific Methods of Shamanism in Some Sufi Sects," *Mystical Studies*, No. 9, (Spring and Summer 1988): 185–216//
ناصر نیکوبخت و سید علی قاسم زاده، «روش های خاص شمنی گری در برخی از فرقه های صوفیه»، عرفان شناسی، شماره 9، (بهار و تابستان 1367):185-216 .Also: علی ناصری راد, افسون حلقه: نقد و بررسی عرفان حلقه [Ali Naseri Rad, *The Charm of the Ring: A Review of Ring Mysticism*] (1970 / 1390, سایان) (URL: https://ketabnak.com/book/57503/افسون-حلقه-نقد-و-بررسی-عرفان-حلقه). A certain Mohammad Ali Taheri, for example, became the object of major controversy in Iran. Although not himself claiming to be a Sufi, he was labeled a "fesoongar" by certain Iranian clerics and arrested and put in prison two times. He later obtained asylum from Canada. See: "Mohammad Ali Taheri," *Wikipedia* (URL: https://en.wikipedia.org/wiki/Mohammad_Ali_Taheri). My thanks to Abdollah Ghaffari for his assistance with this research.

97. Among numerous treatments of Firdausi and Persian national history and heritage, see: Kolsoum Ghazanfari, *Perceptions of Zoroastrian Realities in the Shahnameh: Zoroaster, Beliefs, Rituals* (Berlin: Logos Verlag, 2011); Mahmoud Omidsalar, *Poetics and Politics of Iran's National Epic, the Shāhnāmeh* (New York: Palgrave Macmillan, 2011); G. M. Wickens, "Persian Literature as an Affirmation of National Identity," *Review of National*

Literatures, selected essays (1970–2001): Emergent and Neglected National Literatures, ed. Ann Paolucci (Middle Village, NY: Published for Council on National Literatures by Griffon House Publications, 2007), pp. 209–237.

98. See the Turkish scholar, Mehmet Turgut Berbercan, "Language and Culture Studies: Old Turkic Christian Texts," *Journal of Turkology*, Vol. 2, No. 27 (Dec 2017): 85–100. He argues that "the Turks, who first came under the influence of Shamanism, then diversified into philosophies such as Buddhism, Brahmanism and Manichaeism, beliefs such as Judaism and Christianity, and finally the first Muslim Turkish state, the Karakhanids.".

99. The use of scriptural verses in amulets within the Abrahamic faith traditions goes back to at least the sixth century BCE. See esp., Gideon Bohak, "Jewish Amulets, Magic Bowls, and Manuals in Aramaic and Hebrew," in *Guide to the Study of Ancient Magic*, ed. David Frankfurter (Leiden and Boston: Brill Academic, 2019), pp. 388–415; cf. also Cline, *Biblical Archeology*, pp. 89ff. Cf. the Book of Isaiah 3:19–21 in the Hebrew-Jewish Bible (i.e., Christian 'Old Testament'). In the Islamic context, see esp., Marcela A. Garcia Probert and Petra M. Sijpesteijn, eds., *Amulets and Talismans of the Middle East and North Africa in Contex: Transmission, Efficacy and Collections* (Leiden and Boston: Brill Academic, 2022).

100. Privratsky, *Muslim Turkistan*, p. 77.

101. See e.g., Khalil Samir and Jørgen S. Nielsen, eds., *Christian Arabic Apologetics during the Abbasid Period, 750–1258* (Leiden: Brill Academic, 1993).

102. See Paul W. Werth, "Big Candles and 'Internal Conversion': The Mari Animist Reformation and Its Russian Appropriations," in *Of Religion and Empire: Missions, Conversion, and Tolerance in Tsarist Russia*, ed. R. P. Geraci and M. Khodarkovsky (Ithaca and London: Cornell University Press, 2001), p. 164ff.

103. Peter B. Golden, "Notes to Weller" (Personal Email Correspondence), 27 July 2022, citing "А. К. Салмин, *Система религии чувашей*, СПб.: Наука, 2007): 404–418." My thanks for this and other clarifications included in my treatment of the Mari.

104. Special thanks to Viveka Raol for her assistance in researching and verifying a fairly extensive list of both Arabic and Persian terms which are still in use among Hindu speakers of Hindi today, particularly in North India (esp., Uttar Pradesh, Madhya Pradesh, Punjab and Haryana). Special thanks also to HH Maharani Samyukta Kumari Gohil of Bhavnagar and Pramilla Mehta for confirming and clarifying the list.
105. See: Tahera Qutbuddin, "Arabic in India: A Survey and Classification of Its Uses, Compared with Persian," *Journal of the American Oriental Society*, Vol. 127, No. 3 (Jul–Sep 2007): 327–328. With respect to how religion, culture and politics within the history of India—especially in the British and post-British era, and particularly in relation to the partition of Pakistan—are impacting Hindi and Urdu, see: Vasudha Dalmia, "Review: The Locations of Hindi (Reviewed Work: *Hindi Nationalism* by Alok Rai)," Economic and Political Weekly Vol. 38, No. 14 (Apr 5–11, 2003): 1377–1384; Rizwan Ahmad, "Urdu in Devanagari: Shifting orthographic practices and Muslim identity in Delhi," *Language in Society*, Vol. 40, No. 3 (June 2011): 259–284; Krisha Hirani, "Hindi and Urdu: A language divided, or a shared history destroyed?," *Cherwell*, 21 Jan 2022. (URL: https://cherwell.org/2022/01/21/hindi-and-urdu-a-language-divided-or-a-shared-history-destroyed/). These historical dynamics have impacted the place of Arabic within Hindi in more recent times in particular, but the points made above still stand.
106. al-Kashgari, *Compendium of the Turkic Dialects*, V3:264; cf. V1:235, where the example "*ol tangrika kertgunsadi*" is given for "He intended to acknowledge the unity of God.".
107. Privratsky, *Muslim Turkistan*, p. 24.
108. Edyge Tursunov, "Jyrau – poets, warriors and strategic minds of the Steppes," Abai Center, Central Asia Program, Institute for European, Russian and Eurasian Studies, The George Washington University, Aug 7, 2020 (URL: https://abaicenter.com/jyrau-poets-warriors-strategic-minds-of-steppes#), citing: Х. Короглы, *Огузский Героический Эпос* [*An Oghuz Heroic Epic*] (Москва: Наука, [1962] 1976). Tursunov also notes the continuing role of "soothsayers" among Crimean Tatars in connection to "jyrau" poets who predict the future.

109. Mahsun Atsız, "Dede Korkut Kitabı'nın Günbet Yazması Üzerine Sentaktik Bir İnceleme," *Korkut Ata Türkiyat Araştırmaları Dergisi*, Vol. 2 (Haziran-June 2020): 188–197, referencing 193–195.
110. See Ümit Gedik, "Fazlullâh b. Rûzbihân-i Huncî ve Mihmân-Nâme-İ Buhârâ'si Üzerine Bir Değerlendirme [Fazlullâh b. An An Evaluation on Rûzbihân-i Huncî and his Mihmân-Nâme-i Bukhara]," *İ.Ü. Şarkiyat Mecmuasi Sayi* 32 (Jan 2018) 95–128. Cf. also Anooshahr, Ali, "Uzbeks and Kazakhs in Fazl Allah Khunji's *Mihmannamah-i Bukhara*," in *Turkestan and the Rise of Eurasian Empires: A Study of Politics and Invented Traditions* (New York and Oxford: Oxford University Press, 2018), pp. 84–113.
111. Meruert Abuseitova, "The Spread of Islam in Kazakhstan from the Fifteenth to the Eighteenth Century," tr. from Russian by M. D. Olynyk, in *Kazakhstan: Religions and Society in the History of Central Eurasia*, ed. Gian Luca Bonora, Niccolo Piancola and Paolo Sartori (Turin, London, Venice and New York: Umberto Allemandi & Co., 2010), p. 133, citing Fazl Allah ibn Ruzbihan Isfahani, *Mihman-name-yi Bukhara*, Institute of Oriental Studies of the Academy of Sciences of the Uzbek Soviet Socialist Republic (IV AN UzSSR), MS 1414, fols. 83r-94v. See: Fazlullah B. Ruzbihan Isfahani, *Mihman-nama-yi Bukhara* (1508–1509). Ed. M. Sotudeh (Tehran, 1962), pp. 43, 169, 170–183; Russian tr. (*Записки Бухарского Гостя*) with Foreword and notes by Р. П. Джалилова (Москва, 1976), pp. 105–106.
112. See Кәкімжанов Ә., *Ислам дінінің реакциялық мәні туралы* [*About the Reactionary Essence of the Religion of Islam*] (Алматы: Қазақ Мемлекет Баспасы, 1953), p. 18: "Religious traditions and customs remained unchanged with respect to their meaning, only their names were switched out. The god of the Muslims— 'God' continued to be extolled alongside of the gods of the shamanic faith known as 'tangir' 'kok tangir' ('god' 'sky or heavenly god'). Syncretism occurred. An Uzbek ruler named Ruzbehan (or Ruzbihan) who in his own time knew well the Kazakhs traditions and customs wrote in the beginning of the XVI century that it was common knowledge among the people that there were still some signs of disbelief in the Islamic faith among the Kazakhs." The "Uzbek ruler" was apparently a Persian historian visiting the Uzbeks, misidentified by Kakimzhanov.

113. See esp.: Shahzad Bashir, *Messianic Hopes and Mystical Visions: The Nūrbakhshīya between Medieval and Modern Islam* (Columbia, SC: University of South Carolina Press, 2003), p. 199. Cf. also Abdul Majid Mattoo, *Kashmir under the Mughals, 1586–1752* (Kashmir: Golden Horde Enterprises, 1988), pp. 149ff and 160–163.
114. Surah 6.78, based on a combination of several English translations hosted by the *Quranic Arabic Corpus*, Language Research Group (University of Leeds, 2009–2017) (URL: https://corpus.quran.com/translation.jsp?chapter=6&verse=78).
115. See esp., Robert G. Hoyland, *Arabia and the Arabs: From the Bronze Age to the Coming of Islam* (New York and London: Routledge, 2001), pp. 94, 164 and 211.
116. Dughlat, Mirza Muhammad Haidar, *Tarikh-i-Rashidi: A History of the Moghuls of Central Asia*, tr. E. Denison Ross, ed. N. Elias (London: Sampson Low, Marston and Company, Ltd., 1895), pp. 434–437. Perhaps the Qur'anic passage—"I found her and her people prostrating to the sun instead of Allah, and Satan has made their deeds pleasing to them and averted them from [His] way, so they are not guided..."— served as the basis for both Dughlat and Isfahani to condemn the respective practices of the Kashmiri Shammasi and the Kazakhs? Surah 27:24, Sahih International translation, *Quranic Arabic Corpus*, Language Research Group (University of Leeds, 2009–2017) (URL: https://corpus.quran.com/translation.jsp?chapter=27&verse=24).
117. A. Burton, "Trade," in *History of Civilizations of Central Asia*, Vol. 5, *Development in Contrast: From the Sixteenth to the Mid-Nineteenth Centuries*, ed. Chahryar Adle, Irfan Habib, and Karl M. Baipakov (Paris: UNESCO, 2004), pp. 412–429, esp. p. 416. Cf. also Janet Martin, "Muscovite Travelling Merchants: The Trade with the Muslim East (15th and 16th Centuries)," *Central Asian Survey*, Vol. 4, No. 3 (1985): 21–38. See also the work of Scot Levi: *Caravans: Indian Merchants on the Silk Road* (New York: Penguin, 2015); *The Indian Diaspora in Central Asia and its Trade, 1550–1900* (Leiden: E. J. Brill, 2002), and ed., *India and Central Asia: Commerce and Culture, 1500–1800* (Oxford and New York: Oxford University Press, 2007).

118. Daniel Beben, "After the Eclipse: *Shaykh Khalīlullāh Badakhshānī and the Legacy of the Kubravīyah in Central Asia*," in *From the Khan's Oven: Studies on the History of Central Asian Religions in Honor of Devin Deweese*, ed. Eren Tasar, Allen J Frank and Jeff Eden (Leiden and New York: Brill Academic, 2022), pp. 181–211, referencing pp. 182–183.
119. Cf. Muhammad Isa Waley, "A Kubrawi Manual of Sufism: The Fusus al-adab of Yahya Bakharzi," in *The Heritage of Sufism: Volume II, The Legacy of Medieval Persian Sufism (1150–1500)*, ed. Leonard Lewisohn (Oxford, UK: Oneworld Publications, 1999), pp. 289–310, esp. 306.
120. Cf. Devin Deweese, "Shamanization in Central Asia," *Journal of the Economic and Social History of the Orient*, Vol. 57 (2014): 327n1, on "some of the conceptual adjustments" which might need to be made in the ongoing post-colonialist, particularly here post-Soviet quest to revise interpretations of Central Asian religious history in new, fresh ways.
121. Distantly related to this point, Peter Golden, *Central Asia in World History* (Oxford and New York: Oxford University Press, 2010), says that Yûsuf Khâss Hâjib of Balasaghuni recommended "the shaman's amulets and incantations" alongside the physician's medicines (72–73). See further discussion of this particular point in the Conclusion.
122. Dughlat, *Tarikh-i-Rashidi*, p. 149.
123. Ibid., pp. 230–231 and 272–273.
134. Of related interest, two paragraphs prior to his emphatic assertion of Muslim identity as central to his criteria of selection (p. 149), Dughlat declares that: "Although the Kirghiz belong to the [confederation] of Moghul they have, on account of their repeated rebellions, become separated from them. All the Moghuls have become Musulmans, but the Kirghiz are still infidels, and hence their hostility to the Moghuls" (p. 148; note that I have replaced the translator's word "tribe" with "confederation" because he explains in a footnote that the original Persian term is 'kaum' and acknowledges that "my impression is that the author means the connection between the two people to be regarded as a political…one"; I am admittedly assuming that the modern Kazakh-Turkic sense of the term applies to this early period, but both the context and the translator's comments support it). Dughlat

is clearly motivated here by a political-military agenda. It could, in fact, be that he is rejecting the Muslim identity of the Kirgiz based on what he and other Moghul Muslims consider 'pagan' practices mixed together with their Islamic devotion. This is of course a debatable interpretation since, one, Dughlat does not explicitly state such a position and, two, because the manuscript *Diya' al-qulub* (*Shining of the Hearts*) penned in 1603 by a 'Black Mountain' Naqshbandi figure, Muhammad 'Iwad, supports the contention of Dughlat, with both regarding the Kirgiz as entirely 'idolators', i.e., 'infidels'. The 1603 work dates the conversion of the Kirgiz to sometime, it would seem, in the latter part of the sixteenth century, after Dughlat had written his work, though the conversion process was possibly already commencing while Dughlat was writing. An analysis of this work and the Kirgiz conversion stories it records is provided by: Joseph Fletcher, "Confrontations Between Muslim Missionaries and Nomad Unbelievers in the Late Sixteenth Century: Notes on Four Passages from the Diya al-Qulub [by Ishaq Effendi]," in *Tractata Altaica*, ed. Walther Heissig (Wiesbaden: Otto Harrassowitz, 1976), pp. 167–174. But two things should be noted: Fletcher notes that the author, by virtue of the language he uses, appears to be "uneducated" (p. 170) and, two, Fletcher never raises the question of shifting political relations and conquests taking place at the time which affected Black Mountain Naqshbandi and Kirgiz relations and, thus, attitudes toward one another. It remains entirely possible that the view reflected in 'Iwad's narrative is along the lines of Dughlat and/or Isfahani.

125. E.g., for anti-religious propaganda purposes, interpreting Isfahani's reference in terms of Tengrism as opposed to Dughlat's Sun-worshipers.
126. See Peter Schadler, *John of Damascus and Islam: Christian Heresiology and the Intellectual Background to Earliest Christian-Muslim Relations* (Leiden and Boston: Brill, 2018), p. 131, and Daniel J. Janosik, *John of Damascus, First Apologist to the Muslims: The Trinity and Christian Apologetics in the Early Islamic Period* (Pickwick Publications, 2016), p. 205.
127. Joseph White, *Sermons Preached before the University of Oxford, in the Year 1784, at the Lecture Founded by the Rev. John Bampton*, First American ed. (Boston: William Greenough [1785] 1793), p. 177.

128. Theodor Nöldeke, *Sketches From Eastern History*, tr. John Sutherland Black (London and Edinburgh: Adam and Charles Black, 1892), p. 66; cf. also "survivals of heathenism" listed in index, p. 286.
129. Goldziher, "Veneration of Saints in Islam," pp. 298, 300 and 309; cf. pp. 306 and 334.
130. Николай Петрович Рычков (1746–1784), *Дневные записки путешествия капитана Николая Рычкова в киргиз-кайсацкой степи в 1771 году* [*Daily Travel Notes of Captain Nikolai Ruchkov in the Kirghiz-Kaisakh steppe, in 1771*] (St. Petersburg: Imp. Akademia Nauk, 1772), pp. 26–27.
131. Cf. Deweese, "Survival Strategies," p. 41, who, apparently following B.G. Privratsky's lead, points back only as far as Valikhanov. Bruce G. Privratsky, *Muslim Turkistan: Kazak Religion and Collective Memory* (Surrey: Curzon Press, 2001), held that "[t]he evaluation of the Kazaks as marginal and syncretizing Muslims derives from Chokan Valikhanov" (p. 11). Privratsky provides important historiographical critique, but does not go back far enough in his search for the origins of these theories and their application within varying contexts across the centuries.
132. Witsen, *Noord en Oost Tartarye* ([1692] 1705), p. 627.
133. Cf. Eren Tasar, *Soviet and Muslim: The Institutionalization of Islam in Central Asia* (Oxford and New York: Oxford University Press, 2017), p. 118, who suggests that the 'survivals' framework was later adopted by the Soviets from Tylor and company because it "confirmed longstanding biases Russian administrators had harbored since the days of Catherine the Great concerning the 'superficial' or 'pagan' form of Islam practiced by Central Asian nomads." Cf. also Ricarda Vulpius, "The Russian Empire's Civilizing Mission in the Eighteenth Century: A Comparative Perspective," in *Asiatic Russia: Imperial Power in Regional and International Contexts*, ed. Tomohiko Uyama (London and New York: Routledge, 2011), pp. 13–31, esp. p. 22, and Dov B. Yaroshevski, "Attitudes Towards the Nomads of the Russian Empire under Catherine the Great," in *Literature, Lives, and Legality in Catherine's Russia*, ed. A.G. Cross and G.S. Smith (Nottingham: Astra Press, 1994), pp. 15–24.

134. Малов, Евфимий А. "О Татарских Мечетях в России" ["About Tatar Mosques in Russia"], Part One, *Православный собеседник* [*The Orthodox Conversationalist*] (Dec 1867): 285–320, quoted material from pp. 311–312.
135. А.И. Левшин [A.I. Levshin], "Вера и Суеверие [Faith and Superstition]," in *Описание Киргиз-Кайсакских, или Киргиз-Казахстанской'их орд и степей* [*Description of Kirghiz-Kaisak, or Kirghiz-Kazakhstani Hordes and Steppes*] (Алматы: Санат [Almaty, KZ: Sanat], [1832] 1996), pp. 313–320; quote from p. 313.
136. Johann Eberhard Fisher, *Sibirische Geschichte...* [*Siberian history from the very discovery of Siberia to the conquest of this land by Russian weapons*], tr. to Russian by V.I. Lebedev (St. Petersburg: Imperial Academy of Sciences, [1768] 1774): "[t]he Russian translation does not include the preface, geographical and historical pointers. ...2400 copies" (see: https://www.prlib.ru/en/node/365150); Edvardo Pocockio, *Specimen historiae Arabum* (Oxford: Clarendon Press, 1806), quoting from: https://archive.org/details/specimenhistoria00pocouoft; William of Rubruck, *The mission of Friar William of Rubruck: his journey to the court of the Great Khan Möngke, 1253–1255*, tr. by Peter Jackson; introduction, notes and appendices by Peter Jackson with David Morgan (London: Hakluyt Society, 1990); Ignatius Mouradgea d'Ohsson, *Tableau Général De L'empire Othoman: L'état Actuel De L'empire Othoman* [*General Table of the Ottoman Empire: The Current State Of The Ottoman Empire*] (Paris, Imp. de monsieur [Firmin Didot], 1787–1820).
137. See Marc Raef, *Siberia and the Reforms of 1822* (Seattle: University of Washington Press, 1956); cf. also David Christian, "The Political Ideals of Michael Speransky," *The Slavonic and East European Review*, Vol. 54, No. 2 (Apr 1976), pp. 192–213; Allen McConnell, *Tsar Alexander I, Paternalistic Reformer* (New York: Thomas Y. Crowell Co., 1970).
138. Around the same time as Levshin, in the 1830s, a Tsarist military officer, V.B. Bronevskii, took part in an expedition to the Kazakh steppes between 1829 and 1830. He published his 'notes' as В.Б. Броневский, *Записки генерал-майора Броневского о киргиз-кайса-ках Средней Орды* [*Notes of Major-General Bronevsky on the Kirghiz-Kaisaks of the Middle Horde*], *Отечественные*

Записки [*Domestic Notes*], Vols. 41, 42, 43 (1830). Bronevskii "paid particular attention to the characteristics of the Kazakh economy, their way of life, customs, spiritual culture" ("Записки генерал-майора Броневского о киргиз-кайсаках Средней орды. Опубликованы в журнале «Отечественные записки» в 1829–30 годах," *MyAktobe*, http://myaktobe.kz/archives/38038), though I have not yet been able to access a copy of the work. Also, Robert Geraci ("Orthodox Missionaries in the Kazakh Steppe, 1881–1917," in *Of Religion and Empire: Missions, Conversion, and Tolerance in Tsarist Russia*, ed. R.P. Geraci and M. Khodarkovsky, Ithaca and London: Cornell University Press, 2001, p. 230) claims Makarii's request to extend Orthodox missions to the Kazakhs in the 1830s was denied "on the grounds that it would be premature, as there were too many 'pagan' vestiges in Kazakh religion for a Christian mission to be effective." He cites T.A. Dogurevich (Т.А. Догуревич, *Свет Азии: Распространение христианства в Сибири* [*The Light of Asia: The Spread of Christianity in Siberia*], Санкт-Петербург, 1897, p. 94) as his source. However, while Dogurevich did describe the Kazakhs as "still real pagans," he never used any Russian terms that would be translated as "vestiges." The full passage reads that Makarii desired to open a mission among the Kazakhs based "on the fact that they are still real pagans and are too savage and undeveloped. During this time, most Kyrgyz [Kazakhs], thanks to the influence of the Tatars, had time to become Muslim, and some of them even claimed to be zealous advocates of Islam. To prevent further spread of Islam among the Kirghiz, the Holy Synod decided to establish a special mission for this purpose. Such a mission was opened in 1882." There is reference here to a condition of 'dual' or mixed faiths, namely pagan and Muslim, though he even here Dogurevich clarifies his intended sense of "pagan" as "too savage and undeveloped." That aside, the use of "still" might be taken in the sense of 'vestiges,' but the fact remains that, even if this were the case, it still leaves us with the problem that the phrasing is Dogurevich's from 1897, not the actual quoted text of an 1830s decree by the Holy Synod. In light of Levshin's estimation of the Kazakhs, it seems reasonable that the Holy Synod could certainly describe Kazakh religious history and identity in these terms at this point, but until the actual decree or letter of the Holy Synod regarding Makarii's mission is checked, I consider the example too complicated by issues of later historiographical interpretation to include in the main narrative.

139. Матвей Никифорович **Ястребов** "Киргизские шаманы. Отрывок из записной книжки" ["Kyrgyz shamans. Excerpt from a Notebook,"], *Москвитянин*, № 8. (1851): 301–312. Additional information re: Yastrebov taken from: "Ястребов Матвей Никифорович," *Troitsk74* (http://troitsk74.ru/history/honorablecitizens/yastrebov/).

140. Alexander Morrison, *The Russian Conquest of Central Asia: A Study in Imperial Expansion, 1814–1914* (Cambridge, UK: Cambridge University Press, 2021), p. 143.

141. The citations and general historical details come, not from Osmolovskii, but the analysis of Pavel Shabley and Paolo Sartori, "Tinkering with Codification in the Kazakh Steppe: ʿĀdat and Sharīʿa in the Work of Efim Osmolovskii," in *Sharīʿa in the Russian Empire: The Reach and Limits of Islamic Law in Central Eurasia, 1550–1917*, ed. Paolo Sartori and Danielle Ross (Edinburgh: Edinburgh University Press, 2020), pp. 220–221. Cf. Paolo Sartori and Pavel Shablei, *Eksperimenty imperii: adat, shariat i proizvodstvo znanij v Kazachskoj stepi* [*Empire Experiments: Adat, Sharia and Knowledge Production in the Kazakh Steppe*] (Moscow: Novoe literaturnoe obozrenie, 2019).

142. Валиханов, "О Мусульманстве в Степи [On Muslim Faith on the Steppe]," 293.

143. Чокан Валиханов, "Следы шаманства у киргизов [Vestiges of Shamanism among the Kirgiz]," in *Чокан Валиханов: Избранные произведения* [*Chokan Valikhanov: Selected Works*] (Москва: Наука, 1986), pp. 298 and 306.

144. Чокан Валиханов, "О Мусульманстве в Степи [On Muslim Faith on the Steppe]," in *Чокан Валиханов: Избранные произведения* (Москва: Наука, 1986), p. 293.

145. It is unclear whether Valikhanov had in view the initial period of Byzantine evangelization under the guidance of Cyril and Methodius in the ninth century or later struggles over Greek versus Russian influence reflected in the reforms of the Patriarch Nikon (r. 1652–1666).

146. Валиханов, "О Мусульманстве в Степи [On Muslim Faith on the Steppe]," 293.
147. Capt. Valikhanof, M. Veniukof, and Other Russian Travellers, *The Russians in Central Asia*, tr. John and Robert Michell (London: Edward Stanford, 1865), pp. 46ff.
148. See Vulpius, "The Russian Empire's Civilizing Mission in the Eighteenth Century," pp. 22–25.
149. With respect to British appropriations of religious-cultural 'survivals' for imperial purposes, see esp., David Chitester, "Savage Survivals," in *Empire of Religion: Imperialism and Comparative Religion* (Chicago and London: University of Chicago Press, 2014), pp. 151–157; cf. also pp. 13, 83–84, 91–113, 121–122, 135–136, 207, 250, 280–307.
150. Capt. Valikhanof, M. Veniukof, and Other Russian Travellers, *The Russians in Central Asia*, tr. John and Robert Michell (London: Edward Stanford, 1865), p. 63.
151. Privratsky, *Muslim Turkistan*, pp. 17–18.
152. Christopher P. Atwood, "Buddhism and Popular Ritual in Mongolian Religion: A Reexamination of the Fire Cult," *History of Religions*, Vol. 36, No. 2 (Nov 1996): 112–139, citing from p. 113.
153. Валиханов, "Следы шаманства у киргизов [Vestiges of Shamanism among the Kirgiz]," p. 298.
154. Cf. Robert D. Crews, *For Prophet and Tsar: Islam and Empire in Russia and Central Asia* (Cambridge, MA and London: Harvard University Press, 2006), p. 211. Crews properly recognizes and explicitly cites Valikhanov's reference to Nestor and the "period of dual faith" which he likened to the "Russians in ancient times.".
155. Ф. Поярков [F. Poyarkov], "Из области киргизских верований [From the Realm of Kirgiz Beliefs]," *Этнографическое обозрение* [*Ethnographic Review*] (Oct–Dec 1891), pp. 22–23, 28.
156. The combined Kazakh word and its post-participle (бұрыннан) most literally and simply means "from before." My translation of it as "(remaining still) from (long) before" is clearly justified by the context.
157. Абай Құнанбайұлы, *Абай: Шығармаларының екі томдық толық жинағы: Екінші том: Өлеңдер мен аудармалар, поэмалар, қарасөздер* [*Abai: A Complete Two-Volume Collection*

of His Writings: Vol 2: Songs and Translations, Poems, and Reflections/Words], ed. Есенбай Дүйсенбайұлы, Ғұсман Жандыбаев (Алматы: Жазушы, 2005), p. 154. Note that in this edition the quote is included as part of 'Word 45.' Numerous other collections place the quoted material in Abai's essay, "A Few Words about the Origins of the Kazakhs," which immediately follows 'Word 45' in most editions, including the 1957 edition edited by Mukhtar Auezov (see pp. 221–222). On a related but distinct note, it is most likely an intended part of later Soviet anti-Islamic propaganda among the Kazakhs that I.K. Кеңесбаев, ed., *Қазақ тілінің түсіндірме сөздігі* [*Explanatory Dictionary of the Kazakh Language*] (Алматы: Қазақ ССР Ғілім Академиясының баспасы, 1959) used this sentence from Abai— "We, too, have seen in certain places the remnants of customs of an observed religion…"—as one of its two examples for illustrating the meaning of the word "сарқын" (p. 247) (see also Chapter 9).

158. See Agila Nurgaliyeva, Zhanna Tastaeva, Alfiya Baibulsinova and Lazzat Serikova, "The Fire Cult and Islam in the Kazakh System of Beliefs," *TRAMES*, Vol. 21 (71/66), No. 2 (2017): 151–160.
159. Ibid., 154 (1957, 221–222).
160. Cf. Privratsky, *Muslim Turkistan*, pp. 136, 152 and 189.
161. It should be noted here that the Siberian-born Tatar Abdurreshid Ibrahim (1852–1944) passed through Kazakhstan during his 1909–1910 tour of Central, East and West Asia. In his travelogue, he did not explicitly employ the terms 'remnants,' 'survivals' or otherwise, but his description of the historical process of Kazakh conversion to and observance of Islam was essentially along these lines. In his short section on "Kazakh History," he asserted that "Islam ha[d] spread among the common Kazakh population…from the time of Catherine II [when] the Russian Tatars entered Kazakhstan." This suggests late conversion occurring 'from the top down' (from elites to the general population) across the late eighteenth down to the early twentieth century, with Islam existing together with their previous religious traditions as the former gradually became predominant throughout this span of more than a century. Several pages later, in a section describing conditions in the Semei region in particular, he observed that "[t]he people of Semei do not want to change

anything from their old habits (eski âdetleri), in submission to their [Islamic] religion." This, again, does not use 'survivals' language explicitly, but approximates it, although it must be acknowledged that his intended meaning of "old habits" is former "habits" of dress and education, not previously existing 'religious customs,' which is the main reason I have not included it as part of the main narrative. 'Abd ur-Reshīd Ibrāhīm, *Alem-i Islam ve Japonyada Intişar-i Islamiyet* [*The World of Islam and the Spread of Islam in Japan*], Vol. 1 (Istanbul: Ahmed Saki Bey Matbaasi, 1328 [1911]), 27–33, quotes from pp. 28 and 33 (URL: http://babel.hathitrust.org/cgi/pt?id=njp.32101077784351;view=1up;seq=1; accessed July 24, 2014); Modern Turkish translation: Abdürreşid İbrahim, *Yirminci Asrın Başlarında Âlem-i İslam ve Japonya'da İslamiyet'ın Yayılması* [*The Islamic World and the Spread of Islam at the Beginning of the Twentieth Century*], tr. Mehmed Paksu (İstanbul: Nesil Yayinlari, 2012), pp. 82–90, quotes material from pp. 84 and 90.

162. А. Н. Седельников, "Распределение Населения Киргизкаго края по Территории, его этнографический состав, быть и культура [Distribution of the Population of the Kirghiz Region in the Territory, its ethnographic composition, and culture]," in *Россия. Полное Географическое Описание Нашего Отечества: Настольная и дорожная книга для русских людей: Томъ Восемнадцатый: Киргизская Край* [*Russia: Full Geographic Description of Our Fatherland: A Desktop and Road Book for Russian People: Vol 18: The Kirgiz Region*], ed. В. П. Семенова (Санкт Петерсбург, 1903), p. 219. She herself insists that "Kyrgyz marriage is not a mystical or sacred rite" (p. 216) in spite of it typically involving Muslim customs and traditions.

163. Both quotations from ibid., p. 222.

164. On Soviet views, cf. Thrower, *Marxist-Leninist 'Scientific Atheism'*, p. 243.

165. Vladimir Bobrovnikov, "The Contribution of Oriental Scholarship to the Soviet Anti-Islamic Discourse: From the Militant Godless to the Knowledge Society," in *The Heritage of Soviet Oriental Studies*, ed. Michael Kemper and Stephan Conermann (London: Routledge, 2011), pp. 76–77; Austin Jersild, *Orientalism and Empire: North Caucasus Mountain*

Peoples and the Georgian Frontier, 1845–1917 (Montreal and London: McGill-Queen's University Press, 2002), pp. 42–47. Bobrovnikov cites Jersild; I have checked and am drawing here from both sources directly.
166. All material in paragraph to this point, including quote, taken from: Г. П. Снесарев, *Реликты домусульманских верований и обрядов у узбеков Хорезма* (Moskva, 1969), translated as G. P. Snesarev, *Survivals of Pre-Islamic Beliefs and Rituals among the Khorezm Uzbeks*, tr. Reinhold Schletzer (Berlin: Schletzer, 2003), p. 11fn15. Note that, true to the Russian spelling, Snesarev's last name is typically transliterated into English with an 's,' though the publishers of the book translation transliterated it as 'z.'.
167. М. С. Андреев (M. S. Andreev), "Остатки языческих обычаев среди туземцев (Узбеки, Таджики)" ["Remains of Pagan Customs among Natives (Uzbeks, Tajiks)"] ("Окраина," 1895), No. 27, pp. 305ff.
168. Сергей Павлович Толстов, "Религия Народов Средней Азии" ["The Religion of the Peoples of Central Asia"], in *Религиозные верования народов СССР: сборник этнографических материалов* [*Religious Beliefs of the Peoples of the USSR: A Collection of Ethnographic Materials*], T. [Vol] 1, ed. V. K. Никольский and М. Г. Левин (Москва: Государственный музей народов СССР, Московский рабочий [Moscow: Moscow Worker], 1931), p. 379.
169. Snezarev, *Survivals of Pre-Islamic Beliefs*, p. 11fn15.
170. Андреев М. С., Половцов А. А. "Остатки прежнего общественного строя" ["Remnants of the Old Social Order"], in *Материалы по этнографии иранских племен Средней Азии: Ишкашим и Вахан* [*Materials on the Ethnography of the Iranian Tribes of Central Asia: Ishkashim and Vakhan*] (Санкт-Петербург, 1911), pp. 8–10.
171. Cf. Mariyam Kerimova, "Russian Ethnology at the End of the 19th—The First Third of the 20th Century: Schools and Methods," *Гласник Етнографског института* САНУ LXIII (1): 167–174; see esp. p. 171 on "the comparative-historical and the remnants methods" taking shape from the 1870s.
172. E. I. Campbell, *The Muslim Question and Russian Imperial Governance* (Bloomington: Indiana University Press, 2015), p. 124.

173. Stella Rock, *Popular Religion in Russia: 'Double Belief' and the Making of an Academic Myth* (London and New York: Routledge, 2007), p. 95.
174. Rock, *Popular Religion in Russia*, p. 116.
175. Cf. also Francine Hirsch, *Empire of Nations: Ethnographic Knowledge and the Making of the Soviet Union* (Ithaca, NY: Cornell University Press, 2005), p. 44; Yuri Slezkine, "The Fall of Soviet Ethnography, 1928–1938," *Current Anthropology*, Vol. 32, No. 4 (1991): 476–484 notes Engels' interest in survivals of social lifeways among Siberians (p. 477n3).
176. James Thrower, *Marxist-Leninist 'Scientific Atheism' and the Study of Religion and Atheism in the USSR* (Berlin and New York: Mouton, 1983), pp. 47–48.
177. Frederick Engels, "Ludwig Feuerbach and the End of Classical German Philosophy" (1886), in *On Religion*, by Karl Marx and Frederick Engels (Mineola, NY: Dover Publications, 2008), p. 230. The Dover English translation "is an unabridged republication of the second impression of the work, originally published by the Foreign Languages Publishing House, Moscow, in 1957" (p. 7). Original German: Friedrich Engels, "Ludwig Feuerbach und der Ausgang der klassischen deutschen Philosophie," in *Karl Marx/Friedrich Engels—Werke* (Berlin: Dietz Verlag, 1975), pp. 283–291.
178. Frederick Engels, "Bruno Bauer and Early Christianity" (1882), *On Religion*, by Marx and Engels, p. 203.
179. Cf. С.А. Токарев, "Вклад русских ученых в мировую этнографическую науку [The Contribution of Russian Scientists to World Ethnographic Science]," *Очерки истории русской этнографии, фольклористики и антропологии* [*Essays on the History of Russian Ethnography, Folklore and Anthropology*], (Москва [Moscow]: Наука [Nauka], вып. [Issue] 1, 1956), pp. 5–25, citing from p. 15.
180. Frederick Engels, "Engels to Marx, Manchester, June 6, 1853," in *On Religion*, by Marx and Engels, pp. 125–126.
181. Thrower, *Marxist-Leninist 'Scientific Atheism'* (1983), p. 237.
182. Владимир Ильич Ленин, "Социализм и религия [Socialism and Religion]" (1905), in *Полное Собрание Сочинений* [*Complete Collection of Writings*], Т. 12 [Vol. 12] (Москва: Издательство Политической Литературы, 1968), p. 146.

183. Владимир Ильич Ленин, "Об Отношении Рабочей Партии К Религии" (1909), in *Полное Собрание Сочинений* [*Complete Collection of Writings*], T. 17 [Vol. 17] (Москва: Издательство Политической Литературы, 1968), p. 425.
184. Ibid., pp. 19, 68 and 130 respectively.
185. He uses the term seven times in volume seventeen of *Полное Собрание Сочинений* alone, though this does not meant that he uses it with the same sense on every occasion.
186. И.В. Сталин, "Марксизм и национальный вопрос" (1913), in *Сочинения* [*Treatises*], T. [Vol.] 2 (Москва: ОГИЗ; Государственное издательство политической литературы, 1946), p. 300; see English transl.: Joseph Stalin, *Marxism and the National Question* (Scottsdale, AZ: Prism Key Press, [1913] 2013), p. 12.
187. Сталин, "Марксизм и национальный вопрос" (1913), p. 319; Stalin, *Marxism and the National Question*, p. 26. Cf. Slezkine, "The Fall of Soviet Ethnography, 1928–1938," pp. 481–482.
188. This is based on initial, limited searches through the writings I have consulted for this study (see citations and bibliography). More research along these more nuanced lines of inquiry might yield greater clarity regarding specific epistemic genealogies of various sources. This does not diminish Rock's assertion that "Soviet scholars" and "Soviet historians" employed the concept of "double faith," as her focus is on Russian Orthodox history and identity in particular. The question remains, nonetheless, as to the dynamic, reciprocal influence of these various strands of historiography and ethnography which together become included under the rubric of "Soviet." The task remains developing a more nuanced understanding how precisely "Soviet" historiography and ethnography initially took shape and then continued to develop over time.
189. Peter Stearns, with Olivia O'Neill and Jack Censer, *Cultural Change in Modern World History: Cases, Causes and Consequences* (London and New York: Bloomsbury Academic, 2018), p. 84; cf. pp. 84ff., for other references to 'survivals' of various Chinese traditions both within and beyond the Chinese communist world. Not all of the references concerns 'survival' in the same sense, but there are nonetheless relevant points within the history covered there.

190. It is worth noting here that in 1873, just one year after Tylor published *Primitive Culture*, William R.S. Ralston introduced the "survivals" theme of Russian paganism to the English-speaking world through his book *Russian Folk-Tales* (London: Smith, Elder, & Co., 1873), see esp. Ch. VI, "Legends," pp. 325ff.; cf. Rock, *Popular Religion in Russia*, p. 91.

191. Heinrich Cunow, *Ursprung der Religion und des Gottesglaubens* [*Origin of Religion and the Faith of God*] (Buchhandlung Vorwärts, 1919), pp. 18 and 137; cf. Thrower, *Marxist-Leninist 'Scientific Atheism'*, p. 240.

192. See "Религия и просвещение: *Луначарский Анатолий Васильевич*, Введение в Историю Религии [Religion and enlightenment: Anatoly Lunacharsky, Introduction to the History of Religion]," *ВикиЧтение* [*WikiQuote*] (https://fil.wikireading.ru/87407).

193. Анатолий В. Луначарский, *Введение в историю религии* [*Introduction to the History of Religion*] (Москва: Директ Медиа [Moscow: Direct Media], 2014), p. 7.

194. Thrower, *Marxist-Leninist 'Scientific Atheism'* (1983), pp. 242–243.

195. Ekaterina Elbakyan, "The Outline of Religious Studies in Russia: Does Soviet Religious Studies Really Exist?," in *Studying Religions with the Iron Curtain Closed and Opened: The Academic Study of Religion in Eastern Europe*, ed. Tomá Bubík and Henryk Hoffmann (Brill Academic Publishing, 2015), p. 276.

196. А. Золотарев, *Пережитки тотемизма у народов Сибири* [*Survivals of Totemism Among the Peoples of Siberia*] (Ленинград, 1934); Д.К. Зеленин, *Культ онгонов в Сибири. Пережитки тотемизма в идеологии сибирских народов* [*The Cult of the Ongons in Siberia: Remnants of Totemism in the Ideology of the Siberian Peoples*] (Ленинград, 1936).

197. Thrower, *Marxist-Leninist 'Scientific Atheism'* (1983), p. 243.

198. Л.И. Стернберг, *Первобытная религия в свете этнографии* [L.Y. Sternberg, *Primitive Religion in the Light of Ethnography*] (Изд-во Ин-та народов Севера ЦИК СССР им. П.Г. Смидовича, 1936), pp. 469–470; cf. pp. 162, 207.

199. Cf. the early twentieth-century study by R.O. Winstedt, *Shaman, Saiva and Sufi: A Study of the Evolution of Malay Magic*

(London: Constable and Co., Ltd., 1925). Winstedt sought to separate out the various interwoven strands of Malay Islamic life along the lines of Tylor and company, discerning, so he argued, threads of animism, Hinduism and Islam all sown together. He made at least three references to "survivals" within his study (pp. 13, 18 and 127). In the earliest of these, he suggested that "many such survivals are gracious and beautiful and maintain the continuity of a civilization. It is to be hoped that modern materialist ideas will not obliterate them entirely and leave Malay culture jejune." If Tylor and others considered 'survivals' leftover residues (cf. superstitions) of earlier stages of human society whose belief and practice needed to be ended for the sake of modern progress, Winstedt took an apparently romantic folk nationalist view and hoped precisely the opposite.

200. All quotes in paragraph from Thrower, *Marxist-Leninist 'Scientific Atheism'* (1983), pp. 244–245.
201. С.А. Токарев, "Вклад русских ученых в мировую этнографическую науку [The Contribution of Russian Scientists to World Ethnographic Science]," *Очерки истории русской этнографии, фольклористики и антропологии* [*Essays on the History of Russian Ethnography, Folklore and Anthropology*] (Москва [Moscow]: Наука [Nauka], вып. [Issue] 1, 1956), pp. 5–25, citing from p. 15.
202. М.С. Андреев, "По этнографии таджиков (некоторые сведения)" ["On Ethnography of the Tajiks (Some Information)"], in *Таджикистан* [*Tajikstan*] (Ташкент, 1925), pp. 151–177, quoted phrases from pp. 153–156, 159.
203. Андреев, "По этнографии таджиков," pp. 164–165.
204. Андреев, "По этнографии таджиков," p. 171. His next sentence continues: "In general, however, the following traits can be noted in more closely conserved traces," wherein he launches into a lengthy description of all the various 'pre-Islamic survivals' found among the Tajiks (pp. 171–177).
205. All references and quoted material in paragraph taken from: Г.П. Снесарев, *Реликты домусульманских верований и обрядов у узбеков Хорезма* (Moskva, 1969), translated as G.P. Snezarev, *Survivals of Pre-Islamic Beliefs and Rituals Among the Khorezm Uzbeks* (Berlin: Schletzer, 2003), pp. 11–13, incl. 11fn15 and 13fn16.

206. Л.П. Потапов, "Пережитки культа медведя у алтайских турок" ["Remnants of the Cult of the Bear Among the Altai Turks"], *Этнограф-исследователь* (1928, Nos. 2–3).
207. Snezarev, *Survivals of Pre-Islamic Beliefs*, p. 10.
208. Санжар Джафарович Асфендияров, "Ислам и кочевое хозяйство" ["Islam and Nomadic Economy"], *Атеист*, No. 58 (1930), with ref to Fraser on p. 5 and Goldziher on pp. 10–11.
209. Zifa-Alua Auezova, "Conceiving a People's History the 1920–1936 Discourse on the Kazakh Past," in *The Heritage of Soviet Oriental Studies*, ed. Michael Kemper and Stephan Conermann (Routledge, 2010), p. 253.
210. All references and quotes to this point from Асфендияров, "Ислам и кочевое хозяйство," pp. 7–8, 15–16.
211. Arnold Toynbee, in his mid-twentieth-century *Study of History*, used the term in the same way, i.e., of peoples themselves as constituting "survivals" (or "remnants") of former ways of life. For example, he asserts in typical condescending British fashion for the time, that "the Appalachian 'mountain people' to-day are no better than barbarians. They have relapsed into illiteracy and witchcraft. They suffer from poverty, squalor and ill health. They are the American counterparts of the latter-day White barbarians of the Old World—Rifis, Albanians, Kurds, Pathans and Hairy Ainus; but, whereas these latter are belated survivals of an ancient barbarism, the Appalachians present the melancholy spectacle of a people who have acquired civilization and then lost it." Arnold J. Toynbee, *A Study of History*, abridgment by D.C. Somervell (London, New York and Toronto: Oxford University Press, 1960), p. 149. It is, however, in this case, the lifeways of these peoples—expressed here for example as "ancient barbarism"—which is the ultimate locus of the "survivals." This underscores, in fact, the close interconnection between the peoples and their lifeways and related appropriation of "survivals" (or "remnants") terminology.
212. Асфендияров, "Ислам и кочевое хозяйство," pp. 15–17. On the preservation of Bedouin tribes in "Turkestan," cf. Санжар Джафарович Асфендияров, *Материалы к изучению истории Востока. Ч.1: Причины возникновения ислама* [*Materials for the Study of the History of the East. Part 1: Reasons for the Emergence of Islam*] (Самарканд, Ташкент: 1928), pp. 41–42. I am using

the Russian version of the latter work. The Kazakh version was published two years later as: Санжар Джафарович Асфендияров, *Исламның пайда болу себептері* (Самарканд: Ташкент, 1930).
213. Асфендияров, ...*Причины возникновения ислама*, with quotations taken from pp. 12, 26, 28, 52 and 53 respectively.
214. Snezarev, *Survivals of Pre-Islamic Beliefs*, p. 13.
215. Т.А. Жданко, М.А. Итина, "Сергей Павлович Толстов (1907–1976)," *Этнографическое обозрение* (1977, No. 2): 3–14.
216. С.П. Толстов, "Религия Народов Средней Азии" ["The Religion of the Peoples of Central Asia"], *Религиозные верования народов СССР: сборник этнографических материалов* [*Religious Beliefs of the Peoples of the USSR: A Collection of Ethnographic Materials*], 2 Т. [2 Vols.], ed. В.К. Никольский and М.Г. Левин. Москва: Государственный музей народов СССР, Московский рабочий [Москва: Московский рабочий], 1931. Both volumes are available on the Russian National Library website at: https://dlib.rsl.ru/viewer/01008780310 and https://dlib.rsl.ru/viewer/01008780314.
217. Толстов, "Религия Народов Средней Азии," р. 242.
218. Note that Tolstov's use of 'remnants' applies not only to religions, but to peoples themselves, as for example his statement that "Remnants [Остатки] of Zoroastrian communities in Central Asia are preserved until the X-XI century, when we find mention of Mazdeism..." (Толстов, "Религия Народов Средней Азии," pp. 246–247). This reflects similar usage by Western Christian scholars, such as White, who uses the original Hebrew and Christian biblical sense of 'remnants' of Israelite-Jews and Christians (see above).
219. Толстов, "Религия Народов Средней Азии," р. 251.
220. Толстов, "Религия Народов Средней Азии," р. 258.
221. С.П. Толстов, "Пережитки тотемизма и дуальной организации у туркмен" ["Remnants of Totemism and Dual Organization Among the Turkmen"], *Проблемы истории докапиталистических обществ* [*Problems of the History of Pre-capitalist Societies*], Nos. 9–10 (1935): 3–41.
222. Жданко, Итина, "Сергей Павлович Толстов (1907–1976)," р. 8.
223. Толстов, "Религия Народов Средней Азии," р. 266.

224. Жданко, Итина, "Сергей Павлович Толстов (1907–1976)," p. 8.
225. Snezarev, *Survivals of Pre-Islamic Beliefs*, pp. 13–14fn16.
226. Hirsch, *Empire of Nations*, offers extensive treatment of Soviet "survivals" ethnography, particularly in the second half of Chapter 5 (pp. 190–227), and then continuing with decreasing frequency of reference in Chapter 6 (pp. 231ff.). Her treatment is excellent overall, though she, like most others, over simplifies the origins of Soviet "survivals" ethnography as being exclusively "derived...from the work of...Tylor" (p. 218). She likewise sees no transformations across time in Soviet "survivals" ethnography, at least not along the lines outlined here as well as in Rock, *Popular Religion in Russia*, and Vladimir Bobrovnikov, "The Contribution of Oriental Scholarship to the Soviet Anti-Islamic Discourse: From the Militant Godless to the Knowledge Society," in *The Heritage of Soviet Oriental Studies*, ed. Michael Kemper and Stephan Conermann (London: Routledge, 2011).
227. Tasar, *Soviet and Muslim*, p. 118.
228. Cf. Timothy Stroup, ed., *Edward Westermarck: Essays on His Life and Works* (Helsinki, 1982) and Knut Pipping, "The First Finnish Sociologist: A Reappraisal of Edward Westermarck's Work," *Acta Sociologica*, Vol. 25, No. 4 (1982): 347–357.
229. Edvard Westermarck, *Ritual and Belief in Morocco*, Vol. II (London: Macmillan and Co., 1926), pp. 39, 158, 363, 504–506, and 513.
230. С.П. Толстов, *По следам древнехорезмийской цивилизации* [*Following the Tracks of Ancient Khorezmian Civilization*], (Москва и Ленинград: АН СССР, 1948), pp. 324ff. Tolstov's work was later translated into English as S.P. Tolstov, *Following the Tracks of Ancient Khorezmian Civilization* (Tashkent: UNESCO Tashkent Office, 2005).
231. Edvard Westermarck, *Pagan Survivals in Mohammedan Civilisation: Lectures on the Traces of Pagan Beliefs, Customs, Folklore, Practises and Rituals Surviving in the Popular Religion and Magic of Islamic Peoples* (London: Macmillan, 1933), p. 1.
232. See Chapter 7 for a study of select Soviet Kazakh sources. More broadly, see: С. Ильясов *Пережитки шаманизма у киргизов* [Vestiges of Shamanism Among the Kirgiz], Труды ИЯЛИ Киргизский филиал АН СССР. Вып.1. [Proceedings IYALI

Kyrgyz Branch of the USSR Academy of Sciences] (Фрунзе, 1945); С.М. Абрамзон, *К характеристике шаманства в старом быту киргизов* [*On the Characterization of Shamanism in the Ancient Kirghiz Homeland*]. // (Москва: КСИЭ, 1958): Вып. 30. С. 143–150; Б.Н. Басилов, "О пережитках тотемизма у туркмен" [About the Survivals of Totemism Among the Turkmen] // Тр. Ин-та истории, археологии и этнографии АН Туркменской ССР. Т. VII. Сер. этнографическая. (Ашхабад, 1963), С. 135–150; Б. Аманалиев, *Доисламские верования киргизов* [Pre-Islamic Beliefs of Kyrgyz]// Религия, свободомыслие, атеизм. Фрунзе. 1967); Ш. Базарбаев, *Современные проявления пережитков ислама и конкретные пути их преодоления (На материалах городов Южной Киргизии)* [*Modern Manifestations of the Survivals of Islam and Specific Ways of Overcoming Them (On materials of Cities in South Kyrgyzstan)*]: Дис. на соиск. учен. степ. канд. филос. наук / Ин-т философии и права (Фрунзе: [Б. и.], 1969); Ш. Д. Абдулкадыров, *О некоторых особенностях борьбы с пережитками ислама в условиях современной чечено-ингушетии* [*Some Features of the Struggle Against Vestiges of Islam Among the Modern Chechen-Ingushetia*], Дис. на соиск. учен. степ. канд. филос. наук / КазГУ им. С. М. Кирова (Алма-Ата: [Б. и.], 1970); Т. Сейтжанов, *Формы и методы с пережитками ислама в условиях современной Каракалпакии* [*Forms and Methods of the Vestiges of Islam in Modern Karakalpakstan*], Дис. на соиск. учен. степ. канд. филос. наук / Науч. рук.: Ж. Т. Туленов, КазГУ им.С.М.Кирова (Алма-Ата: [Б. и.], 1970); Токтобюбю Джунушакунова Баялива, *Доисламские верования и их пережитки у киргизов* [*Pre-Islamic Beliefs and Their Vestiges Among the Kyrgyz*] (Фрунзе: Илим, 1972); А.С. Сурапбергенов, *Объективные и субъективные предпосылки возникновения ислама и его пережитки в современном Казахстане* [*Objective and Subjective Preconditions for the Emergence of Islam and Its Survivals in Modern Kazakhstan*], Дис. на соиск. учен. степ. канд. филос. наук: 09.00.06 / КазГУ им. С. М. Кирова (Алма-Ата: [Б. и.], 1973); Г.П. Снесарев и В.Н. Басилов, eds., *Домусульманские верования и обряды в Средней Азии: Сборник статей* [*Domusul'manskie verovaniia i obriady v Srednei Azii: Sbornik statei, Pre-Muslim*

Beliefs and Rites in Central Asia: A Collection of Articles] (Moscow, 1975). Ш.Б. Амантурлин, *Пережитки анимизма, шаманства, ислама и атеистическая работа [The Survivals of Animism, Shamanism, Islam and Atheistic Work Against Them]* // (Алма-Ата: [б. и.], 1977); Т.Д. Баялиева, *Религиозные пережитки и киргизов и их преодоление [Religioznie perezhitkii ii kirgizov ii ih preodolenie, Religious Vestiges of the Kirghiz and How to Overcome Them]*/ Токтобюбо Джунушакуновна Баялиева [Toktobubo Junushakunovna Bayalieva], (Фрунзе [Frunze]: Илим [Ilim], 1981); Ш.Б. Амантурлин, *Предрассудки и суеверия, их преодоление [Prejudices and Superstitions to How to Overcome Them]: (на материалах изучения сельского населения Казахстана) [(Materials for Study of the Rural Population in Kazakhstan)]* / (Алма-Ата: Казахстан, 1985). Similar studies continued into the early independence era, and beyond: А.Т. Толеубаев, *Реликты доисламских верований в семейной обрядности казахов: (XIX - нач. XX в.)* [*Relics of Pre-Islamic Beliefs in Kazakh Family Rituals (19–20th cc.)*] (Алма-Ата: Гылым, 1991); Раушан Мустафина, *Представления, культы, обряды у казахов (в контексте бытового ислама в южном Казахстане в конце XIX–XX вв.)* [*Representations, Cults, Rituals Among the Kazakhs: In the Context of Everyday Islam in Southern Kazakhstan at the End of the 19th–Twentieth Centuries*] (Алма-Ата, 1992). Cf. В.Н. Басилов, *Культ святых в исламе* [*The Cult of Saints in Islam*] (Mockва, 1970) and С.М. Абрамзон, *Киргизы и их этногенетические и историко-культурные связи* [*The Kirghiz and Their Ethnogenetic and Historical-Cultural Ties*] (Наука, Ленингр. отд-ние, 1971).

233. G.P. Snesarev, *Relikty domusulmanskich verovanii I obriadov u uzbekov Khorezma* (Moskva, 1969), translated as *Survivals of Pre-Islamic Beliefs and Rituals among the Khorezm Uzbeks* (Berlin: Schletzer, 2003), p. 13.

234. Snesarev, *Survivals of Pre-Islamic Beliefs and Rituals*, pp. 15 and 257; cf. also, "The beliefs and rituals of the peoples of Central Asia were on the whole literally saturated with phenomena having little in common with orthodox Islam" (p. 256) and, "Our experience in systematizing and classifying pre-Islamic

Survivals...persuades us that the Survivals of early forms of religion play no less a role in Central Asia than orthodox Islam" (p. 257).
235. Snesarev, *Survivals of Pre-Islamic Beliefs and Rituals*, p. 18; emphasis added.
236. See above in main text where I have cited these sentiments in relation to particular sources (Snesarev, *Survivals of Pre-Islamic Beliefs and Rituals*, pp. 11–12, especially in connection to fn15).
237. Snesarev, *Survivals of Pre-Islamic Beliefs and Rituals*, pp. 13–14.
238. Deweese, "Survival Strategies," pp. 47, 36 and 47fn14 respectively. Tasar, *Soviet and Muslim*, seems to follow suit, claiming that "[a]n obsession with 'vestiges' (Russian, *perezhitki*) of the pre-Islamic past in the everyday practice of Central Asian Muslims became a fixture of Soviet ethnography throughout the USSR's existence" (p. 118).
239. Ю.В. Кнорозов, "Мазар Шамун-Наби" ["The Shrine of the Prophet Shamun"], *Советская Этнография*, No. 2 (1949): 86–97, quote from p. 95.
240. Кнорозов, "Мазар Шамун-Наби," p. 86. Cf. Cf. И. Макатов, *Кул'т святых – пережиток прошлого* [*The Cult of Saints—Relic of the Past*] (Махачкала: Дагкнигоиздат, 1962), who appears, along with Snesarev, to have followed up on Knorozov's suggestion.
241. Snezarev, *Survivals of Pre-Islamic Beliefs*, p. 10.
242. Frederick Engels, "Ludwig Feuerbach and the End of Classical German Philosophy" (1886), in *On Religion*, by Marx and Engels, pp. 239–240; original German: Friedrich Engels: "Ludwig Feuerbach und der Ausgang der klassischen deutschen Philosophie," in *Karl Marx/Friedrich Engels—Werke* (Berlin: Dietz Verlag, 1975), pp. 283–291, quote taken from pp. 285–286.
243. Cf. Thrower, *Marxist-Leninist 'Scientific Atheism'*, p. 228. "Some, however, have become entwined in later and more complex cults, where remnants of the ancient gods survive under other names, and ancient forms have been given new meaning, and a very few have survived into the present, although in a considerably modified form. Such, for example, are Shintoism, Taoism, Confucianism, Hinduism and, of course, Judaism."

244. Frederick Engels, "ENGELS TO MARX [Manchester, approx. May 24, 1853]," in *On Religion*, by Marx and Engels, p. 120. Italics in original.
245. Michael Kemper, "The Soviet Discourse on the Origin and Class Character of Islam, 1923–1933," *Die Welt des Islams*, Vol. 49, No. 1 (2009): 1–48, citing from pp. 3–4.
246. Kemper, "The Soviet Discourse," p. 41.
247. S. Keller, "Conversion to the New Faith: Marxism-Leninism and Muslims in the Soviet Empire," in *Of Religion and Empire: Missions, Conversion, and Tolerance in Tsarist Russia*, ed. R.P. Geraci and M. Khodarkovsky (Ithaca and London: Cornell University Press, 2001), p. 321.
248. The work had originally been published in the journal Жизнь национальностей [*The Life of Nationalities*], No. 29, Issue 127 (14 Dec 1921) and No. 30, Issue 128 (23 Dec 1921).
249. М. Султан-Галиев, Методы антирелигиозной пропаганды среди Мусульман [*Methods of Anti-Religious Propaganda Among Muslims*] (Издание Редакционна-Издательского Отдела Наркомнаца [Edition of the Editorial and Publishing Department of the People's Commissariat of Nationalities], 1922), pp. 3–7. Cf. the anonymous Kazakh work: Дінге қарсы оқуды қалай ұйымдастыру керек [*How Anti-Religious Studies Should Be Organized*] (Алматы: Түрксиб, 1939).
250. Султан-Галиев, Методы антирелигиозной пропаганды среди Мусульман, pp. 9–10.
251. Ғали Бегалиев (Бегалиұлы), Ислам Діні Қалай Құрылды [*How the Religion of Islam Was Founded*] (Қызыл-Орда: Государственное Издательство КССР [State Publishing House of the KSSR], 1928); the catalogue listing for Begaliev's book lists 1927 as the date of publication, though the title page shows 1928; this may indicate that there was an original Russian version published in 1927, but it did not show up in a search for all works by the same author; Санжар Джафарович Асфендияров, *Материалы к изучению истории Востока. Ч.1: Причины возникновения ислама* [*Materials for the Study of the History of the East. Part 1: Reasons for the Emergence of Islam*] (Самарканд: Ташкент, 1928) and Исламның пайда болу себептері (Самарканд: Ташкент, 1930); cf. also Ф. Олещук, *О реакционной роли мусульманского духовенства* (Алма-Ата,

1937) and *Мұсылман руханишыларының реакциясы ролі туралы* (Алматы, 1938); Ғ. Ибрагимов, *Ислам діні империализм құралы* (Алматы, 1939); Ibragimov's work may also have been published in an earlier original Russian version, but if so, it did not show up in a search for all works by the same author. Three other works of a more broadly anti-religious nature were also published in Kazakh in the 1920s–30s: Ғ. Ибрагимов, *Дінге қарсы I-басқыш үйірмелер үшін программа-конспект* [*Programmatic Summary for 1st-Stage Anti-Religious Groups*] (Қызыл Орда, 1928); 4000 copies of this 63-page booklet were printed, authored by the same Ibragimov who published the 1939 work; Chiengaliuhli Kirotip and Galimzhan Alibek Sergali, *Dinge Qarsi Oqu Kitabi: auildi belsendiler men dinsizder uirmeleri ushin* [*A Book of Anti-Religious Studies: For Rural Activists and Atheist Groups*] (Алматы, 1934); the author for this work is listed as "Кротов" in the National Library of Kazakhstan digital catalogue, but the title page shows all the names I've listed in Latin script; it shows them with commas between every name so that there could be five different authors; the work is listed twice, both for 1934, once as a 184-page book with a print run of 3000 copies, the other as a 188-page book with 10,000 copies printed; finally, an anonymous work is listed as: *Дінге қарсы оқуды қалай ұйымдастыру керек* [*How Anti-Religious Studies Should Be Organized*] (Алматы: Түрксиб, 1939).
252. Cf. Z.T. Sadvokasova and A.M. Sadykova, "Comparative Approach to the Study of Policy of Tsarist and Soviet Government in Relation to Islam," *Procedia: Social and Behavioral Sciences*, Vol. 122 (2014): 51 and Serik M. Mashimbaev and Gulshat S. Mashimbaeva, *Patshalik Resei zhanye Keŋges Imperialarining Kazakstandagi Ruhani Otarlau Sayasatining Zardaptari (XIX gasirding 70–80 zhildari – XXI gasirding basi)* [*Consequences of the Policies of Spiritual Colonization in Kazakhstan Under the Russian and Soviet Empires (1870–80s—The Beginning of the 21st Century)*] (Almaty, Kazakhstan, Kazakh Universities, 2013), pp. 212–213.
253. See esp. Walker Connor, "National in Form…," in *The National Question in Marxist-Leninist Theory and Strategy*, Memorial Edition (Pullman, WA: Asia Research Associates, [1984] 2018), pp. 201–253, esp. pp. 240–241n7.

254. Kazakh writers could well have been, and probably at this early stage of the Soviet system, were fluent in both Kazakh and Russian, so 'translation' is not necessarily the most appropriate term, since they could write freely in both languages. The question of variation of meaning between Kazakh and Russian versions is an important one. There are clear examples, such as Ilyas Esenberlin, *The Nomads*, where certain portions covering the history of Islam differ in not only the sense conveyed by the Kazakh versus Russian phrasing, but even the precise content included, with entire sentences sometimes left out of one version. I am preparing an article on one particular case of this in Esenberlin. A more thorough comparative study needs to be undertaken, however, of what seems, at times, to be an intentional manipulation of meaning by Central Asian national authors with a view to their respective audiences. When, where, why and how often do such variances occur and by which writers?
255. Асфендияров, "Ислам и кочевое хозяйство," pp. 12–13.
256. Kemper, "The Soviet Discourse," p. 20 and 20n58 and (Асфендияров, ...*Причины возникновения ислама*, pp. 57 and 66). Note that Kemper does not actually provide the quotations I have included, nor any descriptions of their content, only the page numbers.
257. Kemper, "The Soviet Discourse," p. 21n59.
258. Асфендияров, ...*Причины возникновения ислама*, pp. 28 and 37 respectively.
259. Kemper, "The Soviet Discourse," pp. 20–21, incl. 21n59.
260. Асфендияров, "Ислам и кочевое хозяйство," pp. 16 and 3 respectively, and Асфендияров, ...*Причины возникновения ислама*, p. 59.
261. According to Yemelianova, there were references by the ultra-conservative *Vaisites* in the Volga-Urals to "the corrupted Islam of the majority of the Islamic population" (G.M. Yemelianova, *Russia and Islam: A Historical Survey* [Hampshire and New York: Palgrave, 2002], p. 99). To what extent this may have included pre-Islamic religious practices awaits further investigation.
262. David G. Anderson and Dmitry V. Arzyutov, "The Construction of Soviet Ethnography and 'The Peoples of Siberia,'" *History*

and *Anthropology*, Vol. 27, No. 2 (2016): 183–209, quoted material from p. 188.
263. Cf. Deweese, "Survival Strategies," p. 45.
264. Snesarev's chronological claims perhaps seem questionable, or even contradictory, in light of the fact that he had participated in "the Expedition to Central Asia in the Spring of 1940 with the Goal to Study Religious Remnants" and "the Field Reconnaissance Works of 1954 on the Topic 'Religious Remnants and the Impact of the Socialist Reorganization of the Village on the Departure of the Masses from Religion,' producing reports for both. He likewise stated, in a 1957 work, that "in recent years attention to the overcoming of religious survivals has weakened…in our days religious survivals have lost their former significance" (G.P. Snesarev, О Некоторых Причинах Сохранения Религиознобитовых Пережитков у Узбеков Хорезма (по полевым материалам 1954–1956 гг.): Узбекского отряда Хорезмской археологоэтнографической экспедиции [On some reasons for the preservation of religious relics from the Uzbeks of Khorezm (on the field materials of 1954–1956): The Uzbek detachment of the Khorezm archeological ethnographic expedition], *Sovetskaia etnografiia*, No. 2 (1957): 60, cited in John Schoeberlein, "Heroes of Theory: Central Asian Islam in Post-War Soviet Ethnography," in *Exploring the Edge of Empire: Soviet Era Anthropology in the Caucasus and Central Asia*, ed. F. Muhlfried and S. Sokolovskiy [Berlin: LIT Verlag, 2011], pp. 70–71). Such a statement might be taken to indicate a revivalist view, namely that attention to survivals was previously strong, but died off, and Snesarev was working, with others, to revive it. But it is not clear whether these expeditions and statements are concerned with the 'survival' of religion in general, or with Islam itself, or with pre-Islamic 'survivals.' Either he is contradicting himself for whatever conscious or unconscious reasons, or these earlier statements have Central Asian Islam itself in view as a survival with his field work eventually bringing him to question Central Asian Islamic identity through the discovery of 'pre-Islamic remnants.'
265. Snesarev, *Survivals of Pre-Islamic Beliefs and Rituals*, p. 258.
266. Thrower, *Marxist-Leninist 'Scientific Atheism'* (1983), pp. 245, 251–252.

267. С.С. Алимов, "Г.П. Снесарев и полевое изучение 'религиозно-бытовых пережитков'" ["G.P. Snesarev and the Plural Study of Religious and Domestic Surivals"], *Этнографическое обозрение* [*Ethnographic Review*], Vol. 6 (2013): 69–88, quoted material from p. 85.
268. Лери Георгиевич Хитири, *Пережитки прошлого как общесоциологическая категория* [*Remnants of the Past as a General Sociological Category*]: дис. канд. филос. Наук, Грузинский гос. ун-т; науч.рук. Лутидзе Б.И. (Тбилиси, 1986).
269. Tasar, *Soviet and Muslim* (2017), pp. 117–118.
270. Rock, *Popular Religion in Russia*, p. 108.
271. See esp. Hirsch, *Empire of Nations*, Chapter 6, "State-Sponsored Evolutionism and the Struggle Against German Biological Determinism" (pp. 231ff.). At the very end of Chapter 5, she notes that: "The ethnographers who researched 'survivals' in the 1930s conducted research expeditions that produced a nonbiological, sociohistorical explanation for the persistence of traditional culture and by...[which] helped shape the Soviet response to the external ideological threat of Nazi race science" (p. 227). Soviet "survivals" ethnography was thus closely tied to wider imperialist power struggles across the globe tied to a 'civilizing mission' which came under fire in the post-World War Two period.
272. David G. Anderson and Dmitry V. Arzyutov, "The Construction of Soviet Ethnography and 'The Peoples of Siberia,'" *History and Anthropology*, Vol. 27, No. 2 (2016): 183–209; quoted and other referenced material from pp. 190–192 and 205n20.
273. Deweese, "Survival Strategies," p. 42.
274. Cf. among other sources Daniel Woolf, *A Concise History of History: Global Historiography from Antiquity to the Present* (Cambridge and New York: Cambridge University Press, 2019), pp. 262–280, 290–305.
275. Cf. С. Абашин, *Советский кишлак: Между колониализмом и модернизацией* [*The Soviet Village: Between Colonialism and Modernization*] (Москва: Новое литературное обозрение, 2015), pp. 17–18; cf. also pp. 21–22, 759, and 763.
276. Bobrovnikov, "The Contribution of Oriental Scholarship to the Soviet Anti-Islamic Discourse, pp. 76–81.

277. D.V. Pospielovsky, *A History of Marxist-Leninist Atheism and Soviet Antireligious Policies: Volume 1 of a History of Soviet Atheism in Theory and Practice, and the Believer* (Hampshire and London: Macmillan Press, 1987), pp. 110–111.
278. Pospielovsky, *A History of Marxist-Leninist Atheism and Soviet Antireligious Policies* (1987), p. 109.
279. D.V. Pospielovsky, *Soviet Antireligious Campaigns and Persecutions: Volume 2 of a History of Soviet Atheism in Theory and Practice, and the Believer* (Hampshire and London: Macmillan Press, 1988), p. 109. While this shift in attitude and approach was primarily concerned with Russian Orthodox Christianity, it applied to the phenomenon of religious belief and practice overall. Cf. Alexandre Bennigsen, "The Brezhnev Era Prior to the Soviet Invasion of Afghanistan, 1964–80," in *Soviet Strategy and Islam*, ed. A. Bennigsen (Palgrave Macmillan, 1989), pp. 35–56.
280. Ш.Б. Амантурлин, *Пережитки анимизма, шаманства, ислама и атеистическая работа* [*The Survivals of Animism, Shamanism, Islam and Atheistic Work Against Them*] // (Алма-Ата, 1977), pp. 35 and 43.
281. Amanturlin, *The Remants of Animism, Shamanism, Islam*, p. 52.
282. Sections 1 and 2 of Chapter 2, with the sections titled respectively: "Brief information about the history of the penetration of Islam into the region of Kazakhstan" and "Survivals of animistic and other worldviews and their interrelation with Islam" (Amanturlin, *The Remants of Animism, Shamanism, Islam*, pp. 20–33).
283. Amanturlin, *The Remants of Animism, Shamanism, Islam*, p. 52.
284. Х.З. Акназаров, *Ислам діні және өмір шындығы* [*The Religion of Islam and the Truth of Life*] (Алматы: Қазақстан, 1977), pp. 39–89, esp. 54–55 and 83–89.
285. Х.З. Акназаров, *Ислам діні және оның реакциялық мәні* [*The Religion of Islam and Its Reactionary Essence*] (Алматы: Қазақстан, 1964) and *Қазақстандағы Ислам дінінің таралу ерекшеліктері* [*Unique Aspects of the Spread of Islam in Kazakhstan*] (Алматы: Білім қоғамы, 1986).
286. Snesarev, *Survivals of Pre-Islamic Beliefs and Rituals*, p. 17.
287. Cf. Schoeberlein, "Heroes of Theory": "By the late 1950s and 1960s, scholars operated in a system that had relatively

well-established procedures and norms. In writings from before this time, there are different possible ways to interpret the way ethnographers wrote" (p. 60; cf. pp. 61–62).
288. Cf. Tasar, *Soviet and Muslim* (2017), pp. 117–119, 321–322.
289. Further research on this particular group of scholars would make an important contribution to our understanding of Soviet 'survivals' ethnography in all its complexities.
290. This is of course according to my research; there may be earlier publications in other databases or archives.
291. Кәкімжанов Ә., *Ислам дінінің реакциялық мәні туралы* [*About the Reactionary Essence of the Religion of Islam*] (Алматы: Қазақ Мемлекет Баспасы, 1953).
292. Ibid., p. 5.
293. Ibid., pp. 5–10.
294. Mircea Eliade, "The Religions of Ancient Eurasia: Turko-Mongols, Finno-Ugrians, Balto-Slavs," in *History of Religious Ideas, Volume 3: From Muhammad to the Age of Reforms* (Chicago and London: University of Chicago Press, [1978] 1985), pp. 1–21. While Eliade was a Romanian scholar, he completed his education by the early 1930s, long before the alliance with the USSR in 1944 and later Soviet Communist takeover in 1948. He not only studied with the Sanskrit scholar Surendranath Dasgupta in Calcutta, India in the late 1920s, but took up his professorship at the University of Chicago (USA) in 1956. His work on Shamanism, completed by 1951, was already replete with the language of "survivals," which he imbibed from James Frazer, E.B. Tylor and other British and European scholars much more than Soviet, though he did consult Soviet scholarship as well. In that respect, Eliade serves as one of the best examples of international scholarly exchange during the mid-twentieth century. Becoming one of the most influential scholars of religious studies also helped, for better or worse, spread such views throughout those broader international channels.
295. Кәкімжанов, *Ислам дінінің реакциялық мәні туралы*, p. 11. Kakimzhanov adds a quote from Lenin to the same effect soon after this paragraph in order to substantiate his viewpoint.

296. Cf. William H. Swatos, Jr., and Kevin J. Christiano, "Secularization Theory: The Course of a Concept," *Sociology of Religion*, Vol. 60, No. 3 (Autumn 1999): 209–228.
297. Кәкімжанов, *Ислам дінінің реакциялық мәні туралы*, p. 11.
298. His next paragraph says much the same, but adds angels and demons in relation to assistant leadership positions.
299. Кәкімжанов, *Ислам дінінің реакциялық мәні туралы*, pp. 12–13.
300. Lit. "халықтардың басын айналдыратын" = 'spinning the heads of the people around'.
301. Кәкімжанов, *Ислам дінінің реакциялық мәні туралы*, pp. 17–18.
302. Lit. "саясаты" = politics.
303. Lit. "Қос дінділік" = combined religion; cf. the Russian "двоеверие" = Dual faith (see end of Chapters 2 and 4).
304. The quote here and references in the above paragraph all come from Кәкімжанов, *Ислам дінінің реакциялық мәні туралы*, pp. 17–18.
305. There is no citation by Kakimzhanov, but he is no doubt referencing Fazl Allah ibn Ruzbihan Isfahani, *Mihman-name-yi Bukhara*, Institute of Oriental Studies of the Academy of Sciences of the Uzbek Soviet Socialist Republic (IV AN UzSSR), MS 1414, fols. 83r–94v; cf. Meruert Abuseitova, "The Spread of Islam in Kazakhstan from the Fifteenth to the Eighteenth Century," tr. from Russian by M.D. Olynyk, in *Kazakhstan: Religions and Society in the History of Central Eurasia*, ed. Gian Luca Bonora, Niccolo Piancola, and Paolo Sartori (Turin, London, Venice and New York: Umberto Allemandi & Co., 2010), p. 133.
306. Possibly 'statues.'
307. No quote marks are in the original, I have added them for clarification, since the structure of the Kazakh sentence makes this clear.
308. The references to Isfahani are all taken from Кәкімжанов, *Ислам дінінің реакциялық мәні туралы*, pp. 17–18. See Chapter 3, where I suggest that such 'sun-worship' may have been a form of Sufi Islamic devotion integrated into 'pre-Islamic' Tengrist understandings and practices.
309. Ibid., pp. 18–19.
310. Cf. esp., Saule K. Ualiyeya and Adrienne L. Edgar, "In the Laboratory of Peoples' Friendship: Mixed People in Kazakhstan

from the Soviet Era to the Present," in *Global Mixed Race*, ed. Rebecca C. King-O'Riain, Stephen Small, Minelle Mahtani, Miri Song, and Paul Spickard (New York University Press, 2014), pp. 68–90.
311. Kzk. туа біткен сенім емес.
312. All of the material from endnote 8 down to the end is taken from: Кәкімжанов, *Ислам дінінің реакциялық мәні туралы*, pp. 18ff.
313. Х. Бисенов, *Ислам дінінің шығуы және оның таптық мәні* [*The Origin of Islam and Its Class Significance*] (Алматы: Қазақ Мемлекет Баспасы, 1955).
314. Quoting from "БК(б)П тарихы, кыскаша курс, 325-бет."
315. Бисенов, *Ислам дінінің шығуы және оның таптық мәні* [*The Origin of Islam and Its Class Significance*], pp. 4–5.
316. Ibid. pp. 6–7.
317. Lit. "ислам дінінен," which can be translated as either "more than" or "rather than" (i.e., "as opposed to"). Given the context, especially the "example" offered which follows, I have opted for the former.
318. Бисенов, *Ислам дінінің шығуы және оның таптық мәні* [*The Origin of Islam and Its Class Significance*], pp. 8–9.
319. See e.g., Abdilkhakim Burkhanadin, "The Battle of Atlah and Its Importance in the History of Middle Sirdarya Basin," *Habarshi: Journal of Philosophy, Culture and Political Science*, Vol. 65, No. 3 (2018): 118–128; as noted by Burkhanadin (p. 119b) and others, al-Tabari does not so much as mention the 'Battle of Talas', which is curious given his attention to "the battles which took place in the Eighth century in Central Asia," including his mention of "the king of Taškent as opponent of the Muslims against whom he appealed to China." See Emel Esin, "Ṭabarī's Report on the Warfare with the Türgiš and the Testimony of Eighth Century Central Asian Art," *Central Asiatic Journal*, Vol. 17, No. 2/4 (1973): 135. Cf. Barry Hoberman, "The Battle of Talas," *Aramco World*, Vol. 33, No. 5 (Sept–Oct 1982): 26–31 (https://archive.aramcoworld.com/issue/198205/the.battle. of.talas.htm), and D.G. Tor, "The Islamization of Central Asia in the Sāmānid Era and the Reshaping of the Muslim World," *Bulletin of the School of Oriental and African Studies*, Vol. 72, No. 2 (2009): 279–299.

320. Бисенов, *Ислам дінінің шығуы және оның таптық мәні* [*The Origin of Islam and Its Class Significance*], pp. 9–10.
321. Бисенов, *Ислам дінінің шығуы және оның таптық мәні* [*The Origin of Islam and Its Class Significance*], p. 14.
322. Бисенов, *Ислам дінінің шығуы және оның таптық мәні* [*The Origin of Islam and Its Class Significance*], p. 14. As per Sachau's English translation, Biruni in fact said: "Kutaiba ben Muslim had extinguished and ruined in every possible way all those who knew how to write and to read the Khwarizmi writing, who knew the history of the country and who studied their sciences. In consequence these things are involved in so much obscurity, that it is impossible to obtain an accurate knowledge of the history of the country since the time of Islam (not to speak of pre-Muhammadan times)." (Albiruni, *The Chronology of Ancient Nations: An English Version of the Arabic Text of Athār-Ul-Bākiya of Albiruni, or "Vestiges of the Past," collected and reduced to writing by the author in A.H. 390–1, A.D. 1000*, tr. C. Edward Sachau [London: W.H. Allen & Co.] for The Oriental Translation Fund of Great Britain & Ireland, 1879, p. 42; cf. H.A.R. Gibb, *The Arab Conquests in Central Asia* [London: The Royal Asiatic Society, 1923], pp. 43 and 57n17.) A Russian translation of Biruni's text here must have been available by the time of Bisenov's publication in 1955. S.P. Tolstov (see Chapters 1 and 2) produced *A Collection of Articles* on Biruni in 1950 (С.П. Толстов, *Бируни: сборник статей* [*Biruni: A Collection of Articles*] Москва, Ленинград: Издательство АН СССР, 1950). Two years after Bisenov's work, a full translation of Biruni's *Chronology* was published: Бируни Абу Райхан. *Избранные произведения. т.I, Памятники минувших поколений* (*Хронология*), Ташкент: Изд-во АН УзССР, 1957, pp. 48, 63 (Portions of the Russian transl. available at: http://hbar.phys.msu.ru/gorm/chrons/biruni.htm). I was unable to confirm whether one existed prior to 1955. But Bisenov references no sources, other than "Beruni" in the main text, so it is difficult, if not impossible, to identify his precise source.
323. All refs within the paragraph taken from: Бисенов, *Ислам дінінің шығуы және оның таптық мәні* [*The Origin of Islam and Its Class Significance*], pp. 9–10.

324. Ibid., p. 14.
325. Бисенов, *Ислам дінінің шығуы және оның таптық мәні* [*The Origin of Islam and Its Class Significance*], p. 15.
326. Ibid., pp. 15–16.
327. Ibid., pp. 15–16.
328. Ibid., pp. 16–17.
329. With respect to these dynamics in World War Two, see esp., David Motadel, *Islam and Nazi Germany's War* (Cambridge, MA: Belknap Press, 2014). More broadly, see also Motadel, ed., *Islam and the European Empires* (Oxford and New York: Oxford University Press, 2014).
330. All material on pan-Islamism and pan-Turkism in the paragraphs above, up to the previous endnote, are taken from ibid., pp. 17–19.
331. Bisenov details his 'list' of offenses down to p. 22.
332. I have re-organized the order of the phrases here within the context of my own work, without altering the author's original intended meaning.
333. Ibid., p. 22.
334. Lit. "калдыктардың сірі жанды екендігін." I taking "жанды екендігі" to mean 'have a heart for' in this context. *If* I have translated and understood this phrase correctly then, it refers to the tenacity ('leather heels') of religious survivals. The context clearly supports this interpretation.
335. Lit. "құрман айт," which I take as a misprint for "құрбан айт."
336. All references in paragraph from ibid., pp. 22–24.
337. He quotes here from constitution.
338. Ibid., p. 31.
339. Ж. Дүисенбин, *Ислам діні және оның қазіргі жайы туралы* [*About the Religion of Islam and Its Current State*] (Алматы: Қазақ Мемлекет Баспасы, 1961).
340. Дүисенбин, *Ислам діні және оның қазіргі жайы туралы* [*About the Religion of Islam and Its Current State*], p. 67.
341. Ibid., pp. 67–69.
342. Ibid., pp. 69–71.
343. Both points taken from ibid., pp. 72–73 respectively.
344. Ibid., pp. 77–81.
345. Ibid., pp. 98–99.

346. Ibid., p. 107.
347. Ibid., pp. 114–121.
348. К. Машрапов, *Исламға табыну – зиянды қалдық* [*Devotion to Islam—A Detrimental Survival*].- Алматы, 1962.
349. See esp., Mark Dickens, *Echoes of a Forgotten Presence: Reconstructing the History of the Church of the East in Central Asia* (Münster, Germany: LIT Verlag, 2021).
350. Down to at least 2004, and most likely thereafter, the National Museum in Almaty, for example, harbored a number of Christian burial stones of Turkic Central Asian origin stored in the back vaults, kept back from public display, claiming that they were still 'researching' the rather short inscriptions contained thereon. They placed only one or two of the stones on public display, thus minimizing the visual impact of the historical evidence to the public. The same is true for various other archeological evidence of a distinctly Turkic Christian nature. This can be compared to efforts elsewhere across the globe to suppress certain historical evidence by keeping it locked away and out of public view. I do not know, as of the time of writing here, whether they have ever placed all the stones and other evidence out on full public display and, if so, at what point after 2004 they may have done so. These of course are matters for the field of 'public history' in particular to take up. Regardless, these facts do not revise my assessment of the significance of the Christian historical material in the Soviet Kazakh sources.
351. For additional perspective on this point, see R. Charles Weller, "Introduction: Reason, Revelation and Law in Global Historical Perspective," in *Reason, Revelation and Law in Islamic and Western Theory and History*, ed. R.C. Weller and A. Emon (Singapore: Palgrave Macmillan, 2021), pp. 14–16.
352. For material on broader Central Asia which is related to though distinct from the present chapter, see the recent volume edited by Sophie Roche, *Central Asian Intellectuals on Islam: Between Scholarship, Politics and Identity* (Berlin: Klaus Schwarz Verlag, 2021).
353. Born in 1947, Esim is a professor of Western, Muslim, and Kazakh philosophies and their histories. Along with other professorships, chairs, and deanships in his career, he served for most of the 2000's as Dean of the Faculty of Philosophy and Political

Science et al.-Farabi Kazakh National University in Almaty, Kazakhstan. Among other awards, he has been recognized as an 'Akademik,' the highest rank of scholarship within the country, and granted membership within the National Academy of Sciences of the Republic of Kazakhstan (cf. his profile, in Russian, at: http://bnews.kz/ru/persons/show/14485/). Since the mid-2000's, he has been serving as a member of the Kazakhstani senate. He has, however, been a socially and politically active voice throughout the entire period of Kazakhstan's emergence and development as an independent nation, contributing regularly to national television and radio programs as well as newspaper, magazine and journal publications, including multiple interviews. He has, likewise, published numerous books and articles in both Kazakh and Russian, including *The Elite Scholar Abai* (1994), *The Essence of Mind: Reflections on Politics and Culture* (1995–2007, 10 vols), *A History of Islamic Philosophy* (2000/2004), *Kazakh Philosophy* (2005) and *Kazakh Renaissance* (2006). He has since been honored with a publication in his name entitled *Akademik Garifolla Esim: Bibliografialik korsetkish* (2007). His *Human-ity* (2001) was translated into Turkish, earning him increasing pan-Turkic and international recognition (see Minhac Celik, "Dialogue Eurasia Introduces Kazakh author's 'Adem Zat'," in *Today's Zaman [Today's Times]*, 18 Feb 2010 www.todayszaman.com/newsDetail_getNewsById.action?load=detay&link=201807).

354. G. Esim, *Sana bolmisi: sayasat pen madeniet turali oilar* [*The Essence of Mind: Reflections on Politics and Culture*], vol. 2 (Almaty: Gilim, 1996), p. 65.
355. Cf. Aysegul Aydingun. "Islam as a Symbolic Element of National Identity Used by the Nationalist Ideology in the Nation and State Building Process in Post-soviet Kazakhstan," *JSRI*, No. 17 (Summer 2007): 69–83.
356. After graduating from the Faculty of Journalism at Kazakh State University, Karamanuhli has worked as a journalist, including chief editor, since 1976 for numerous newspapers, magazines, and other publications. In 2008, he was awarded the International 'Alash' Journalist prize.

357. K. Karamanuhli, "Tangirge tagzim" ["The Worship of Tengri"], in *Kazakh tarihinan* [*From Out of Kazakh History*], ed. Yelden Akkoshkarov (Almaty: Zhalin, 1999), pp. 280–281.
358. For a classic study on this 'wave', see H.A.R. Gibb, *The Arab Conquests in Central Asia* (London: The Royal Asiatic Society, 1923). See also M.S. Asimov and C.E. Bosworth, eds., *A History of Civilizations in Central Asia: Vol IV: The Age of Achievement: AD 750 to the End of the Fifteenth Century* (Paris: UNESCO Publishing, 1998).
359. The ref. to Toktasin Omirzakov is from the newspaper *Kazak adebieti* [*Kazakh Literature*], 22 March, 1990.
360. See esp. Devin Deweese, *Islamization and Native Religion in the Golden Horde: Baba Tukles and Conversion to Islam in Historical and Epic Tradition* (State College, PA: Pennsylvania State University Press, 1994).
361. Karamanuhli, "Tangirge tagzim" ["The Worship of Tengri"], pp. 247–248. Within the broader context of his paragraphs treating these three waves of Islamic history, Karamanuhli cites along the way not only Mirzaliev and Toktasin, but S. Ibrashev, "Alpamis batir – Sir boiining perzenti" (in *Zhas Alash*, 6 Jun 1992), an article on "A Brief History of the Kazakhs" in *Zhas Alash* (4 Mar 1993), S. Zimanov, *Russia and Bukhei khandigi* (Almaty, 1982), p. 137; Shokan Ualihanov, *Shigarmalari zhinagi* [*Collectiion of Writings*] (5 vols., vol. 4, pp. 74 and 99), and a general reference to A.I. Levshin, V.V. Barthold, V.V. Radlov, and A.A. Yanushkevich.
362. See R.C. Weller, "Kazak tili oris tiline taueldi bolip kala ma?" ["Will the Kazakh Language Wind Up Remaining Dependent Upon Russian?"], in *Kazak tili zhanye oralman* [*The Kazakh Language and Returnees (from the Kazakh diaspora)*], ed. Sagira Kanahina (Almaty, KZ: Olke: The National Library of the Republic of Kazakhstan and the Language Committee of the Ministry of Culture, Media and Sports of the Republic of Kazakhstan, 2006), pp. 41–45.
363. In the course of his apologetic, Bulutai seeks intentionally to re-infuse Islamic Arabic terminology into Kazakh in order to move the Kazakhs closer to a shared pan-Turkic Islamic language, in some ways similar to the aims of Gasprili and other late nineteenth-, early twentieth-century Jadid reformers. Bulutai's

language in his book on his *The Religion of the Fathers* was, in fact, so much at variance with standard Kazakh that the publishers noted in the beginning that he had insisted on preserving his own style in order to accomplish that goal.

364. A. Seidimbek, *Kazakh alemi: etnomadeni paiimdau* [*The Kazakh World: An Ethnocultural Exegesis*] (Almaty, Kazakhstan, 1997). 3000 copies of this work were printed. Apparently Seidimbek actively expressed opposition to Muslim theses at times, as e.g., at one doctoral defense (http://www.masimkhanuly.kz/2012/12/aqseleu-sejdimbek). After graduating from university, Seidimbek worked as a journalist, including chief editor, from 1976 to 1988, at which time he moved into academics as a scholar, including departmental chair and director, at two different institutes and finally, from 1999 to 2009, at Eurasian National University. See the interview of Seidimbek by T. Batirhan and B. Omaruhli in the newspaper *Aikin* (No. 141 [593]), Thursday, Aug 3, 2006, pp. 10–11. The article (entitled "Oktemdik ustemdik kurgan zamanda adamning beri standartti boladi" ["During the times when the Soviets ruled, all peoples were considered standard-bearers"] was not about the religious debate, but referenced his works, including *Kazak alemi* [*The Kazakh World*], acknowledging their contribution to Kazakh scholarship. Seidimbek passed away in 2009 at age 67. He was honored on national television for his work on what would have been his 70th birthday. He was, likewise, honored at various regional centers, such as the N.V. Gogol World Scholarship Library in Karaganda Oblast.

365. Seidimbek, *Kazakh alemi*, p. 105. It should be noted that the primary concern of Seidimbek's work is not Tengrism, but restoring Kazakh history via Kazakh genealogy and its intimate relation with various customs, including 'zheti atalik,' i.e., the tradition of knowing one's forefathers back to the seventh generation, as a means of determining social relations within and among clans, marriageability, etc. He considers Tengrism integral, however, to historic Turkic steppe culture and identity.

366. On that debate, see esp. E.E. Evans-Pritchard, *Theories of Primitive Religion* (Oxford: Oxford University Press, 1967); Tomoko Masuzawa, *In Search of Dreamtime: The Quest for the*

Origin of Religion (Chicago and London: University of Chicago Press, 1993); Robert N. Bellah, *Religion in Human Evolution: From the Paleolithic to the Axial Age* (Cambridge, MA: The Belknap Press of Harvard University Press, 2011); Eric J. Sharpe, *Comparative Religion: A History*, 3rd ed. (Chicago and La Salle, IL: Open Court, [1975, 1986] 2006); Joseph M. Kitagawa, "The History of Religions (*Religionswissenschaft*) Then and Now," in *The History of Religions: Retrospect and Prospect*, ed. J.M. Kitagawa (New York: Macmillan Publishing Company and London: Collier Macmillan Publishers, 1985), pp. 121–144.

367. Cf. Jamal J. Elias, *This Is Islam: From Muhammad and the Community of Believers to Islam in the Global Community* (Great Barrington, MA: Berkshire Publishing Group, 2011), p. 1, says: "Many devout Muslims would argue that, in actual fact, Islam has always existed...and that the historical Islam that started on the Arabian Peninsula is only the final, definitive form of Islam laid out for human understanding." This belief is typically tied to the belief in the eternality of the Qur'an, including therefore its Arabic language, a view which raises serious problems in relation to the foreign vocabulary of the Qur'an. See esp. Arthur Jeffrey, *The Foreign Vocabulary of the Qur'an* (Leiden: Brill, [1938] 2007). For attempts to substantiate the claim that Christianity represents the original religion of humankind, see: Robert Brow, *Religion: Origin & Ideas* (Downers Grove, IL: Inter-Varsity Press, 1966), and Julian Ries, *The Origins of Religions*, tr. Kate Singleton (Grand Rapids, MI: Wm. B. Eerdmans, 1993).

368. Among other Kazakh scholars showing a favorable attitude toward Tengrism is Zh. Moldabekov, *Kazaktanu* [*Kazakh-ology*, or *The Study of Kazakness*] (Almaty, KZ: Kazak Universiteti, 2003), pp. 76–90. A Kyrgyz scholar taking a Tengrist view similar to that of Karamanuhli and Seidimbek is Dastan Sarigulov, who published a work in 2002 entitled *Tengrism—The Spriitual Knowledge and Worldview of the Kyrgyz People* (D. Sarigulov, *Tengirchilik – kirgizdarding duinu taanimi, tubuluk bilimi*, Bishkek: Tengir Ordo, 2002). Sarigulov is founder of Tengir Ordo, the publisher of his book, headquartered in Bishkek, Kyrgyzstan. The founder and his organization are dedicated to reviving Tengrism among the Central Asian steppe peoples.

To that end, they hosted their "1st International Conference" in November 2003 with the main theme of "Tengrism as the worldview of the Altaic people." It was jointly hosted by The Foundation of Turkic World Research located in Istanbul, Turkey, revealing the extent to which the Tengrist cause permeates the Central Asian Turkic world (for a recent Turkish work treating Tengrism among Turkic Central Asian peoples, with special focus on the Altai peoples, see Günnur Yücekal Arpacı, *Gök Tanrı Inancının Bilinmeyenleri [Unknown Belief in the God of Heaven]* (İstanbul: Cati Yayinlari, 2012); cf. also Mehmet Eröz, *Eski Türk dini (gök tanrı inancı) ve Alevîlik-Bektaşilik [Old Turkish Religion (belief in sky god) and Alevism-Bektashism]* (İstanbul: Türk Dünyası Arastırmaları Vakfi, 1992), and Yıldız Kocasavaş, "Gök Tanrı İnancı," in *Türkler Tarihi*, Vol. 3 (Ankara, 2002), pp. 326–329 and 578–584; special thanks to Prof Ozlem Berk Albachten at Bogazici University for aiding me in obtaining a more complete bibliographic reference on the latter work). Along with Kazakhstan, Kyrgyzstan and Turkey, Tengrist engagement in revivalist efforts across Central Asia can also be seen in Tatarstan, Bashkortistan, Altai and Siberian Buryatia (cf. M. Laurelle, "Religious Revivalism"). Mongolia, if not Turkmenistan and elsewhere, should also be included. As for Sarigulov, I personally met with him in May 2003 in Almaty, Kazakhstan about possible participation in the planned conference. During our talk, he expressed, in the spirit of his Tengrist colleagues, his disdain for the destructive, foreign and imperialist nature of Islam (as well as Christianity and atheism) within the history of the Turkic peoples, insisting that Tengrism represented the original 'natural' religion to which the Turkic peoples needed to return in order to purify themselves of all the damage that has been caused them by these fierce foreign intrusions into their otherwise ecologically balanced, pure, and natural way of living in harmony with their Central Asian steppe environment.

369. A. Abdakimuhli, *Kazakhstan tarihi: erteden buginge deiin [The History of Kazakhstan: From Early Times to the Present]* (Almaty: Respublikalik baspa kabineti, 1997), p. 95. 5000 copies of this work were printed. A revised 2nd ed. of this work was published in 2005 (Almaty: 'Kazakhstan' Publishers). Until I am able to

obtain a copy, I am unable to note any revisions that may have occurred to these passages. The original 1997 edition nonetheless remains an important part of the historiography among post-Soviet Kazakh scholars.
370. Ibid., p. 104.
371. A. Abdakimuhli, "Din zhanye til," *Akikat*, No. 8 (2008): 75–78. See also his article on "Kazirgi tangdagi diniy akhuaoding damuining negizgi bagittari" ["The Main Trends of Developments in the Current Religious Situation"] *Akikat*, No. 12 (2008): 162–164.
372. S.T. Amirgazin, *Dintanu: oku kurali* [*Religious Studies: A Study Aid*] (Astana, 2002). 1000 copies were printed. See also B.K. Kudaibergenov and S.T. Amirgazin, *Diniy Merekeler men Rasimderding Aleumettik Mani* [*The Social Meaning of Religious Celebrations and Rituals*] (Almaty, KZ: Kazak Universiteti, 2004).
373. Kzk. "Tangirlik dini – rukhaniyatimizding bastau bulagi" (pp. 53–62).
374. Along with K. Karamanuhli, "Tangirge tagzim" (*Ana Tili*, 1996), Amirgazin lists: S.G. Klyashtornii, *Mifologicheskii suzheti vdrevneturkskikh pamyatnikakh: Turkologicheskii sb.* (Moskva, 1981); Ch. Omiraliev, *Tangirchilik* (Bishkek, 1994); A.Yu. Nikonov, *Altun bitig: Tengrianstvo* [*The Golden Bough: Tengrism: Myths of the Ancient Turks, Preserved by the Oral and Written Tradition of the Turkic Peoples of the World*] (Almaty, 2000, in Russian) as "Essential-Necessary Literature" at the end of his chapter on Tengrism. Nikonov's intended play on James Frazer's famous work, *The Golden Bough* (1890), should be self-evident. Amirgazin also lists there a work by L.N. Gumilev (Almaty, 1992) and two others without authors. Within the chapter he likewise references "the well-known ('tanimal') French Turkologist Jean-Paul Roux." He cites no particular work, but for those relevant see note 462 below.
375. Along with Adji's Kazakh and Russian works, see in English: M. Adji, *Asia's Europa*, tr. A. Kiselev (Moscow: Izdateltsva, 1996), pp. 307–310.
376. Lit. 'musilmandik ilimning sunnittik mazhabindagi musilmandik umbetke zhatamiz desek te...'.

377. Amirgazin goes on here, in the sentence represented by the break, to associate Russian Orthodoxy with the same roots of spiritual mysticism, that is, the broader geographical-environmental context in which it took shape and for which it is therefore suitable. On the Yasawi tradition, see esp. Ashirbek Muminov, "Yasawiyya bastaulari [Beginnings of the Yasawi Sufi Brotherhood]," in *Yasawi tagilimi* [Studies on the Yasawi Tradtion], ed. M. Mirzahmetov (Turkistan, KZ: Mura, 1996), pp. 22–30.

378. S.T. Amirgazin, "Din egitiminin Gayesi – Birlik ve Beraberligin Saglanmasi" ["The Aim of the Religious Education—Securing Unity and Solidarity"], a paper presented at an *International Symposium on the Teaching of Qoja Akhmet Yasawi and the Problems of Religious Education in Kazakhstan* hosted by the Ministry of Science and Education of the Republic of Kazakhstan, Qoja Akhmet Yasawi International Kazak-Turk University, Ministry of Culture of the Republic of Kazakhstan's Committee for Religious Affairs, and the Local Government of the Oblast of Southern Kazakhstan, Apr 6–9, 2011, Turkistan.

379. M. Zh. Bulutai, *Ata-baba dini: nege turkiler musilman boldi?* (Almaty: Bilim, 2000). 5000 copies of this work were printed. Although Bulutai's scholarship should be classified as 'missionary,' it nonetheless runs deep, drawing on Kazakh, Russian, Turkish, English, (classical and modern) Arabic and other sources, though he depends heavily at times on material such as *Encyclopedia Britannica*. He, nonetheless, has carefully documented his research, well beyond most others treated in this article. See also Bulutai, *Musilman Kazak elimiz [Our Muslim Kazakh Nation]* (Almaty, KZ: Aris, 2001), and Bulutai, *Din zhanye ult [Religion and Ethnos, or Religion and Ethnic Group]* (Almaty: Aris, 2006). A 3-part, 45-min interview with Bulutai which aired on Kazakstan-Shimkent Television is available (in Kazakh) on YouTube at: http://www.youtube.com/watch?v=ZKjHGGtHrDk. It was uploaded in February 2012, apparently the time of the interview, with less than 2000 views in the past 10 years. See background information on Bulutai later in main text above.

380. See Wendell Schwab, "Establishing an Islamic niche in Kazakhstan: Musylman Publishing House and its publications," *Central Asian Survey*, Vol. 30, No. 2 (2011): 227–242.
381. See simplified scheme on p. 297.
382. Cf. esp. pp. 88ff.
383. Rakmankul Berdibai, *Baikaldan Balkanga deiin [From Baikal to the Balkans]* (Almaty, KZ: Kazakhstan, 1996).
384. Although this comes out much more clearly in Bulutai's his later work on *Musilman Kazak Elimiz [Our Muslim Kazakh Nation]* (Almaty, KZ: Aris, 2001), particularly in his chapter on "Diniy (i.e., Religious) Extremism and Terrorism" (pp. 152–164), traces of it appear in *Ata-baba dini [The Religion of the Fathers]*.
385. Manarbek Baieke, *Orta Azia men Kazakstanning masikshilik tarihi* (Almaty, KZ: Litera-M, 2006). 3000 copies were printed. The Kazakh edition was followed a year or so later by a Russian translation. Cf. Mark Dickens, *Echoes of a Forgotten Presence: Reconstructing the History of the Church of the East in Central Asia* (Münster, Germany: LIT Verlag, 2021).
386. Shapirashti Kazibek bek Tauasaruhli, *Tup-tukiannan ozime sheiin [From the Earliest Roots Down to Myself]* (Alamty, KZ: Zhalin, [1776] 1993). Cf. Beksultan Nurzhekeuhli, "Kazibek bek and Kazakh History," in Yelden Akkoshkarov, comp., *Kazakh tarihinan [From Out of Kazakh History]* (Almaty: Zhalin, 1997), pp. 427–454. At least one conference held among Kazakh scholars was dedicated solely to debating Tauasaruhli's book, though the time and place of the conference are currently packed away somewhere in storage within my notes.
387. Baieke, p. 188, quoting Tauasaruhli, *Tup-tukiannan ozime sheiin*, p. 28.
388. Baieke, pp. 188–89, quoting Tauasaruhli, p. 243 and pp. 391–392 respectively.
389. See esp. Alphonse Mingana, "The Early Spread of Christianity in Central Asia and the Far East: A New Document," *The John Rylands Library*, Vol. 9, No. 2 (July 1925): 287–288 and 297–371.
390. Baieke, p. 193. On Adji's position, see esp. "The Mystery of the Cross," in M. Adji, tr. by A. Kiselev, *Asia's Europa* (Moscow: Izdatelstvo, 2005), pp. 307–310; cf. also Amirgazin's affirmation of Adji above in the main text.

391. See esp. Ch 9, "Christians in Central Asia," in *Christians in Asia Before 1500*, ed. Ian Gillman and Hans-Joachim Klimkeit (Ann Arbor, MI: University of Michigan Press, 1999), pp. 205–264; also Wilhelm Baum and Dietmar W. Winker, *The Church of the East: A Concise History* (London and New York: Routledge, 2003).

392. See Christopher Dawson, *Mission to Asia* (New York: Harper & Row, 1966); Peter Jackson, *The Mongols and the West* (Harlow, England: Longman, 2005); Igor de Rachewiltz, *Papal Envoys to the Great Khans* (London: Faber & Faber, 1971).

393. See Herman Jantzen, *Journey of Faith in a Hostile World: Memoirs of Herman Jantzen, Missionary to Turkestan, Caucasus and Bulgaria, Refugee from Bolshevik Russia* (New York: iUniverse, 2008) and Mildred Cable and Francesca French, *George Hunter: Apostle of Turkestan* (London: China Inland Mission, 1948).

394. Baieke is not alone in taking such a historically-oriented approach to the revival of Christianity in Central Asia. After very briefly glossing over the earlier Church of the East and Catholic presence in the region, an anonymous author writing in English on "The History of the Catholic Church in Kazakhstan" offers a divinely-undergirded historiographical leap across the ages, claiming that after a gap of some 500 years, "the history of the Catholic Church in Kazakhstan resumed in the twentieth century when Stalin ordered the deportation to Central Asia of whole peoples of the Catholic tradition. Providence turned a diabolical plan into a missionary event beyond the boldest dreams of even Propaganda Fide or any missionary strategist. From 1930 onwards, many priests were deported and sent to concentration camps in Kazakhstan. Having been released, they settled among the people and began clandestine ministry." No author or publisher is listed for this work is listed, but the copyright is attributed to L'Osservatore Romano, Editorial and Management Offices, Via del Pellegrino, 00120, Vatican City, Europe (URL: www.catholicculture.org/culture/library/view.cfm?recnum=4186).

395. Archbishop Vladimir of the Orthodox Diocese of Bishkek and All Central Asia, addressing the topic of "Christianity and Islam

in Central Asia," in *Islam and Central Asia: An Enduring Legacy or an Evolving Threat?*, ed. Roald Sagdeev and Susan Eisenhower (Washington, DC: Center for Political and Strategic Studies, 2000), pp 95–115, says: "In the minds of the Turkic and Persian peoples, Islam is an inextricable part of their national heritage. ... conversion to another faith would be seen as a betrayal of [their] people. The attempts of certain sectarian evangelizers to shatter this stronghold...are at best naïve; at worst, courting disaster. ... The grand-sounding statements about 'the need for Christian missionary work among the Muslims' express little more than a pipedream. The Russian Orthodox Church has enough to worry about with its own flock..." Although disavowing any authority to speak on behalf of the situation in Kazakhstan, Archbishop Vladimir's remarks represent the position of Russian Orthodoxy across the region, even in Russia itself. Post-Soviet sensitivities to historic tensions—as indicated by Bulutai, Rakmankul whom he quotes, and others—are very real. Issues not only of religion, but of history (esp. Soviet historiography), language, culture and political power all weigh on the scales. Cooperative efforts between the heads of state and the respective Muslim and Orthodox communities are calculated to keep those tensions to an absolute minimum, emphasizing instead peace and harmony.

396 M. Bulutai, *Burkhanism turali shindik* (Almaty, KZ: Aris, 2003). An interview with Muhtar Auezov was first published under the title "Ozimdi Muhtar Auezovting zhazilip bitpegen shigarmasining keiipkerindei sezinemin...," in *Altin Orda*, May 9–15, 2003, with a three-part response from Bulutai then published as "Burkhanism turali shindik," in *Zhas Alash*, July 10, 12 and 15, 2003. These latter three articles were then published as the booklet.

397. Along with Bulutai, see esp. Liudmila I. Sherstova, "Burkhanism in Gorny Altai," in *Religion and Politics in Russia: A Reader*, ed. M.M. Balzer (Armonk, NY and London, England: M.E. Sharpe, 2010), 225–244. See also Agnieska Halemba, "Contemporary Religious Life in the Republic of Altai: The interaction of Buddhism and Shamanism," *Sibirica*, Vol. 3, No. 2 (Oct 2003): 165–182.

398. When asked in an interview by Shadiar Ustemiruhli for *Zhas Kazakh* newspaper on Oct 30, 2010, "you are always talking about Tengrism, Burhanism. What religion do you consider yourself an adherent (lit. representative) of?", Auezov responded, "My forefathers came preaching Islam, I, likewise, consider myself a Muslim." Yet, in a more recent article posted on the *Namys* (Kzk. "Dignity, Honor") newspaper site on Mar 31, 2011, entitled "The Gods Given Birth by Independence" ("Tauelsizdik Tudirgan Tangirler"), Beken Kairatuhli explicitly named Auezov, together with Auezkhan Kodar, as two known examples of "those being led about by this false idea" of Tengrism, going on to argue on behalf of Islam as the true and proper religion. Comments continued to be posted on Kairatuhli's article for more than one year (Mar 31, 2011–Apr 12, 2012). The article has since been taken offline.

399. Әзірет Барбол, "Бұлутай ата дінін бұзып, бұзып жатыр [Bulutai is going about perverting and corrupting the religion of the fathers]," *Abai*, September, 2012.

400. Quoted from: N.A. Nazarbaev, *Tarih tolkininda* [*On the Waves of History*] (Almaty, KZ: Atamura, 2003), p. 41.

401. See esp. Carel van Leeuwen, Tatiana Emeljanenko, and Larisa Popova, *Nomads in Central Asia: Animal Husbandry and Culture in Transition (Nineteenth-Twentieth Century)* (Amsterdam: Royal Tropical Institute, 1995).

402. Nazira Nurtazina, *Kazak Madenieti zhanye Islam: Tarihi-Madeniettanulik Zertteu* [*Kazakh Culture and Islam: Historical-Culturological Research*] (Almaty, KZ: Kazakting Madeniet zhanye Onertanu Gilimi-Zertteu Instituti, 2003), pp. 10–11.

403. Nurtazina, *Kazak Madenieti zhanye Islam*, p. 3. Like Bulutai, Nurtazina actually applies this perspective beyond the Kazakh and Central Asian worlds, claiming that "All of this brings us to the realization that it is a historical necessity for all peoples to move from natural, ancient religions to world religions, especially to the great religion of Islam, which defends and protects the principle of 'tauhid', i.e. God's essential unity. It opens to us the great importance of this historical-cultural turn which, at one time, our forefathers made" (p. 10).

404. Н.Д.Нұртазина және Л.М.Хасанаева, *Ежелгі түріктердің исламдануының тарихи алғышарттары* [*Historical Prerequisites*

for the Islamization of the Ancient Turks] (Алматы: «Қазақ университеті» баспасы, 2010).
405. Garifolla Esim, "Din orkenieti [The Civilization of Religion]," *Egemen Kazakhstan*, Oct 21, 2006, p. 6.
406. Cf. K.A. Nizami, "Popular Movements, Religious Trends and Sufi Influence on the Masses in the Post-Abbasid Period," in *History of Civilizations of Central Asia, Volume 4: The Age of Achievement: A.D. 750 to the End of the Fifteenth Century: Part One: The Historical, Social and Economic Setting*, ed. M.S. Asimov and C.E. Bosworth (Paris: UNESCO, 1998), 365–381, who says: "The Karakhanids encouraged the diffusion of Islam from Transoxania into the Tarim basin and towards the northern steppes. Sufi preachers such as Shaykh Ahmad Ata Yasawı (d. 1166) played an important role in spreading Islam among the nomadic peoples" (p. 371). Deweese, *Islamization and Native Religion in the Golden Horde*, distances Yasawi from the Yasawi Sufi order and emphasizes other factors in the Islamization of the nomadic Turkic steppe peoples. See also: Akira Haneda, "Introduction: Problems of Turkicization, Problems of Islamization," in *Acta Asiatica*, Vol. 34 (1978): 1–21; Richard Frye, "Comparative Observations on Conversion to Islam in Iran and Central Asia," in *Jerusalem Studies in Arabic and Islam*, No. 4 (1984): 81–88; Joseph Fletcher, "Confrontations Between Muslim Missionaries and Nomad Unbelievers in the Late Sixteenth Century: Notes on Four Passages from the Diya al-Qulub [by Ishaq Effendi]," in *Tractata Altaica*, ed. Walther Heissig (Wiesbaden: Otto Harrassowitz, 1976), pp. 167–174; and Ch. 3, "The Turks and Islam to the Thirteenth Century," and Ch. 10, "The Khanate of Kipchak," in *The Empire of the Steppes: A History of Central Asia*, ed. Rene Grousset, tr. Naomi Walford (New Brunswick, NJ: Rutgers University Press, [1939] 1970), pp. 141–170 and 392–408 respectively.
407. Nurtazina (2003), *Kazak Madenieti zhanye Islam*, p 5.
408. Gabitov has served for multiple years, since the mid-1990s, as full professor of Philosophy and Culture in the Department of Culture and History of Philosophy et al.-Farabi Kazakh National University. He was invited for a three-year visiting professorship at Shahid Beheshti University (formerly National University of Iran) in Tehran in the late 1990s. He has authored or

co-authored numerous journal articles, chapters, books and textbooks, as well as local and national newspaper articles (cf. some of the refs in main text above as well as endnotes below).
409. In T.H. Gabitov, Aktolkin Kulsarieva and Zhusipbek Mutalipov, *Madeniettanu* [*Culturology*] (Almaty: Rarity, 2001). 3000 copies of this particular edition were published. 3000 thousand more of the Russian edition were also released, followed in 2005 by 2nd editions. This is an undergraduate textbook influencing thousands of young Kazakh (as well as Russian) students in the universities. Gabitov is also regularly cited as an authority by other authors (as an internet search for his name in both Russian and Kazakh confirms), including Baitenova and Zatov treated near the end of the main text above.
410. Gabitov's view here follows the emphasis in Soviet scholarship on geographical and ecological environment as central in determining religious and cultural beliefs and practices.
411. See Marlene Laurelle, "Religious Revivalism, Nationalism and the 'Invention of Tradition': Political Tengrism in Central Asia and Tatarstan," *Central Asian Survey*, Vol. 26, No. 2 (June 2007): 203–216; see also Aurelie Biard and Marlene Laruelle, "'Tengrism' in Kyrgyzstan: In Search of New Religious and Political Legitimacy," in *Representing Power in Modern Inner Asia: Conventions, Alternatives and Oppositions*, ed. I. Charleux, G. Delaplace, R. Hamayon, and S. Pearce (Bellingham, WA: Center for East Asian Studies, Western Washington University, 2010).
412. T.H. Gabitov, Aktolkin Kulsarieva, and Zhusipbek Mutalipov, *Madeniettanu* [*Culturology*] (Almaty: Rarity, 2001); cf. Kairat Zatov, Tursun Gabitov, Maral Botaeva, Moldagaliyev Bauyrzhan, and Saira Shamahay, "Islam and Values of Kazakh Culture," *International Journal of Social, Behavioral, Educational, Economic, Business and Industrial Engineering*, Vol. 7, No. 6 (2013): 1699.
413. B.G. Nurzhanov, Tursin H. Gabitov, S.Zh. Aidarbaev, K.I. Baizakova, A.S. Ibraeva, and Aktolkyn T. Kulsariyeva, *Beibit Madenieti zholinda* (Almaty: Kazakstan Respublikasining UNESCO zhonindegi Ulttik Kommisiyasi, UNESCO zhanindagi Kazakstan Respublikasining Turakti Okildigi and Al-Farabi Kazakh National University, 2000).

414. Cf. Laura Yerekesheva, "Religious identity in Kazakhstan and Uzbekistan: Global–Local Interplay," *Strategic Analysis*, Vol. 28, No. 4 (2004): 577–588.
415. Cf. Dosmuhammad Kishibekov, *Kazak mentaliteti: keshe, bugin, erteng* (Almaty: Gilim, 1999), p. 109.
416. On the latter point, see esp., Anthony D. Smith, *Chosen Peoples: Sacred Sources of National Identity* (Oxford: Oxford University Press, 2003).
417. N. Baitenova and K. Zatov, "Ezhelgi Turkilerding nanim-senimderi," in *Egemen Kazakhstan*, Aug (?) 5, 2006 (Published online at: http://abai.kz/node/5917, Nov 28, 2010, with a comment posted from June 11, 2017).
418. I encountered the same essential view when speaking with curators at the Kazakh National Museum in Almaty in May 2004 about the two Church of the East grave stones which they had on display.
419. In 2004, with much the same passion and perspective, the editors of the journal *Zhalin* (*Flame*), under the heading "Kazakhs Who Have Forsaken the Religion of the Fathers" ("Ata dininen bezip ketken kazaktar," *Zhalin* [*Flame*], No. 2 (Feb 2004), pp. 56–79), offered about 15 Kazakhs from various walks of life—old and young, women and men, scholars and otherwise—space to express their views on the subject at hand. While the article was aimed against the spread of foreign religions, the question of Tengrism was by all means in the mix. Only one of those who participated championed the Tengrist cause, with all others affirming Islam as the 'the religion of the fathers,' positing various perspectives on the relation of those two historic traditions. Though the editors of the journal may themselves have favored Islam, the ratio seems fairly representative of the larger Kazakh population and illustrates the willingness of these main two claims to nationalist attention to recognize and remain in dialogue with one another.
420. Tattigul Kartaeva, *Syr Öngiri Qazaqtary: Tarıhï-Etnografialyq Zertteu (XIX ğasyrdyng ekinshi jartisy – XX ğasyrdyng basy)* [*Kazakhs of the Syr Region: Historical-Ethnographical Research (from the Second Half of the Nineteenth Century to the Beginning of the Twentieth Century*], Vol 2 (Almaty: Kazakh Universiteti, 2014), pp. 162–212, citing from p. 211. Her treatment of

"Baqshylyq" is on pp. 162-181, with the remaining pages devoted to other beliefs, practices and folkways. Note that I am using the term 'folkways' in order to avoid the historically pejorative presumptions of the term 'superstitions.' For other Kazakh treatments of shamanism, see: M. Taj-Murat, "Shamandik [Shamanism]," in *Turkistan: Halikaralik [International] Encyclopedia*, ed. A. Nisanbaev (Almaty: Kazak Encyclopediasi, 2000), pp. 635-636; Taj-Murat speaks of the continuation of Shamanism down to the nineteenth century and its preservation by way of "Islamization" in Sufism; А.Ш. Әлімжанова, "Шамандық мәтіндердің мәдени ерекшеліктері [The Cultural Uniqueness of Shamanistic Texts]," in *Қазақстанның мәдени мұрасы: жаңалықтары, мәселелері, болашағы* (конф. Материалдары) [*The Cultural Heritage of Kazakhstan: New Findings, Problems and the Future* (Conf. Materials)] (Алматы, 2005), pp. 204-212. Beyond this I have compiled a bibliography of over 80 works in both Kazakh and Russian from the database of the National Library of the Republic of Kazakhstan which I cannot take time or space here to list out in full. Finally here then, see also: Danuta Penkala-Gawecka, "Mentally Ill or Chosen by Spirits? 'Shamanic Illness' and the Revival of Kazakh Traditional Medicine in Post-Soviet Kazakhstan," *Central Asian Survey*, Vol. 32, No. 1 (2013): 37-51.

421. Erke Tamabekkyzy Kartabaeva, *Islam zhanye Ortagasyrlyk Turkiler* [*Islam and the Turks of the Middle Ages*] (Almaty: Kazak Universiteti, 2016), pp. 5-6.
422. Kartabaeva, *Islam zhanye Ortagasyrlyk Turkiler*, p. 250.
423. Kartabaeva, *Islam zhanye Ortagasyrlyk Turkiler*, pp. 142, 146-147.
424. Kartabaeva, *Islam zhanye Ortagasyrlyk Turkiler*, pp. 273-274.
425. Kartabaeva, *Islam zhanye Ortagasyrlyk Turkiler*, pp. 146-147.
426. T. Omarbekov et al., "Religious Beliefs: Islam in the XIV-XV Centuries: Discrete Nature of the Process of Islamization of Nomads," in *History of Kazakhstan (Kazakh Eli): A 4-Volume Textbook. Book 2: Kazakhstan in the XIII Century—The First Quarter of the XVIII Century* (Almaty: Qazaq Universiteti, 2021, in English), pp. 108, 111, 109 and 107 respectively.
427. T. Omarbekov et al., "The Role of Islam in the Process of Kipchakization of Mongols," in *History of Kazakhstan (Kazakh Eli)*, p. 128.

428. T. Omarbekov et al., "Religious Beliefs: Islam in the XIV-XV Centuries," p. 107; cf. also 108, etc.
429. T. Omarbekov et al., "The Role of Islam in the Process of Kipchakization of Mongols," in *History of Kazakhstan (Kazakh Eli)*, p. 128.
430. T. Omarbekov et al., "Religious Beliefs: Islam in the XIV-XV Centuries," p. 112.
431. Ibid., p. 112.
432. Cf. works such as: Roald Sagdeev and Susan Eisenhower, eds., *Islam and Central Asia: An Enduring Legacy or An Evolving Threat?* (Washington, DC: Center for Political and Strategic Studies); Ahmed Rashid, *Jihad: The Rise of Militant Islam in Central Asia* (New Haven & London: Yale University Press, 2002); V.V. Naumkin, *Radical Islam in Central Asia: Between Pen and Rifle* (Rowman & Littlefield, 2005); Eric McGlinchey, *Chaos, Violence, Dynasty: Politics and Islam in Central Asia* (Pittsburgh, PA: University of Pittsburgh Press, 2011). For alternative approaches, see esp. Adeeb Khalid, *Islam After Communism: Religion and Politics in Central Asia: With a New Afterword* (Berkeley, CA: University of California Press, [2006] 2014). See also Hakan Yavuz, "The Trifurcated Islam of Central Asia: A Turkish Perspective" (in J.L. Esposito, J. Voll, and O. Bakar, eds., *Asian Islam in the 21st Century*), who, in the words of the editors, asserts that "the perceptions of Western and Russian Islam inflate the threat that Islamic political activism poses" (p. 6); likewise, Mariya Omelicheva, "Islam in Kazakhstan: A Survey of Contemporary Trends and Sources of Securitization" (*Central Asian Survey*, Vol. 30, No. 2 (2011), pp. 243–256), which, among other things, seeks to "shed light on the worrisome process of the securitization of Islam. The latter phenomenon refers to a discursive practice of presenting Islam as a threat to Kazakhstan despite the prevalence of 'moderate' and apolitical manifestations of Islam in the republic" (abstract).
433. Will Meyer, *Islam and Colonialism: Western Perspectives on Soviet Asia* (London and New York: Routledge, 2002), pp. 2–3. Cf. also Adeeb Khalid, *Islam After Communism: Religion and Politics in Central Asia: With a New Afterword* (Berkeley, CA: University of California Press, [2006] 2014), pp. 1–2.

434. For these issues placed within a broader historical and global context, see especially the updated (2014) edition of Khalid, *Islam after Communism*.
435. Alima Bissenova, "Building a Muslim Nation: The Role of the Central Mosque of Astana," in *Kazakhstan in the Making: Legitimacy, Symbols, and Social Changes*, ed. Marlène Laruelle (*Contemporary Central Asia: Societies, Politics, and Cultures*) (Lanham, MD: Lexington Books, 2016), p. 220.
436. R. Charles Weller, "Religious-Cultural Revivalism as Historiographical Debate: Contending Claims in the Post-Soviet Kazakh Context," *Journal of Islamic Studies*, Vol. 25, No. 2 (May 2014): 138–177, citing from p. 142.
437. E.g., before her untimely passing, the young German scholar, Irene Hilgers, documented (in her 2003–2005 field work) a number of similar perspectives taking shape among Uzbeks in her posthumous monograph *Why Do Uzbeks Have to Be Muslims? Exploring Religiosity in the Ferghana Valley* (Münster, Germany: LIT Verlag, 2009). The Irene Hilgers Memorial Prize continues to be awarded in the journal *Central Asian Survey* (see: https://think.taylorandfrancis.com/journal-prize-pgas-ccas-irene-hilgers-memorial-prize/).
438. Cf. Bruce G. Privratsky, *Muslim Turkistan: Kazak Religion and Collective Identity* (London and New York: Routledge, 2001), p. 14.
439. For select foreign scholarship on Central Asian Shamanism, see: Manabu Waida, "Problems of Central Asian and Siberian Shamanism," *Numen*, Vol. 30, No. 2 (Dec 1983): 215–239; Andrei Znamenski, *Shamanism in Siberia: Russian Records of Indigenous Spirituality* (Boston, MA: Kluwer Academic Publishers, 2003); Marjorie Mandelstam Balzer, ed., *Shamanic Worlds: Rituals and Lore of Siberia and Central Asia* (New York: M.E. Sharpe, 1997); Gary Seaman and Jane S. Day, eds., *Ancient Traditions: Shamanism in Central Asia and the Americas* (University Press of Colorado, Denver Museum of Nature and Science and Ethnographics Press, 1994); V.M. Golovnin and T. Pang, "N.N. Krotkov's Questionnaire to Balishan Concerning Sibe-Solon Shamanism," in *History and Historiography of Post-Mongol Central Asia and the Middle East: Studies in Honor of*

John E. Woods, ed. Ernest Tucker (Wiesbaden, Germany: Otto Harrassowitz Verlag, 2006), pp. 201–209.
440. Another important study of female Shamanism which ties into Sultanova's study is: Lia Zola, "Invisibility or Marginality? Assessing Religious Diversification Among Women Shamans in Eastern Siberia," in *Invention of Tradition and Syncretism in Contemporary Religions: Sacred Creativity*, ed. Stefania Palmisano and Nicola Pannofino (Palgrave Studies in New Religions and Alternative Spiritualities, Cham, Switzerland: Palgrave Macmillan, 2017), pp. 51–68. Comparatively see also: Kyong-geun Oh, "Korean Shamanism—The Religion of Women," *International Journal of Korean Humanities and Social Sciences*, Vol. 2, No. 2 (November), 71–86. https://doi.org/10.14746/kr.2016.02.05.
441. For music as an explicit cultural form through which Tengrism, in connection to Shamanism, has experienced revival within post-Soviet Kazakhstan, see Megan Rancier, "'The Spirit of Tengri': Contemporary Ethnic Music Festivals and Cultural Politics in Kazakhstan," in *Kazakhstan in the Making: Legitimacy, Symbols, and Social Changes*, ed. Marlène Laruelle (*Contemporary Central Asia: Societies, Politics, and Cultures*) (Lanham, MD: Lexington Books, 2016), pp. 229–246.
442. Razia Sultanova, *From Shamanism to Sufism: Women, Islam and Culture in Central Asia* (London: I.B. Tauris, 2011), pp. 24–27.
443. Privratsky, *Muslim Turkistan*, pp. 14–15. Then again, Privratsky questions Zarcone's data from his earlier study in 2000, saying, "Zarcone (2000) mentions two shamans he met in southern Kazakhstan, but only Islamic traits are mentioned in his brief descriptions, leaving the impression that he mistook *täwips* for shamans" (pp. 223–224). Meanwhile, placing Zarcone and Hobart's and other studies in broader global context, see Mariko Namba Walter and Eva Jane Neumann Fridman, eds., *Shamanism: An Encyclopedia of World Beliefs, Practices, and Culture*, 2 Volumes (Santa Barbara, CA: ABC-Clio, 2004).
444. Devin Deweese, "Shamanization in Central Asia," *Journal of the Economic and Social History of the Orient*, Vol. 57 (2014): 326–363, citing from p. 346.

445. Cf. the early nineteenth-century work of R. O. Winstedt, *Shaman, Saiva and Sufi: A Study of the Evolution of Malay Magic* (London: Constable and Co., Ltd., 1925), which interpreted shamanism in a romantic folk nationalist manner.
446. Cf. e.g.: Firas Alkhateeb, *Lost Islamic History: Reclaiming Muslim Civilization from the Past* (London: Hurst & Co., 2017), pp. 30, 115, 149, 170, 172, 176 and 206; Felicitas Becker, "Islamic Reform and Historical Change in the Care of the Dead: Conflicts over Funerary Practice among Tanzanian Muslims," *Africa: Journal of the International African Institute*, Vol. 79, No. 3 (2009): 416–434; Umar Habila Dadem Danfulani, "Factors Contributing to the Survival of the Bori Cult in Northern Nigeria," *Numen*, Vol. 46, No. 4 (1999): 412–447; as noted in Chapter 3 (see n9 and relevant section of main text), the Bori cult in Nigeria relates to the jihads conducted by Usman dan Fodio in the late eighteenth, early nineteenth century; Louis Brenner, "Muslim Divination and the History of Religion in sub-Saharan Africa," *Insight and Artistry: A Cross-Cultural Study of Divination in Central and West Africa*, ed. John Pemberton (Washington, DC: Smithsonian, 2000), pp. 45–59; Sulayman S. Nyang, *Islam, Christianity and African Identity* (Chicago: Kazi Publications, Inc., 2007); Víctor M. Fernández, "Schematic Rock Art, Rain-Making and Islam in the Ethio-Sudanese Borderlands," *The African Archaeological Review*, Vol. 28, No. 4 (Dec 2011): 279–300; and Masahiko Togawa, "Syncretism Revisited: Hindus and Muslims over a Saintly Cult in Bengal," *Numen*, Vol. 55, No. 1 (2008): 27–43.
447. See e.g., on Turkish religious-cultural history and identity: Erol I. Yorulmazoglu, "The Influence of Religion," in *The Turks: The Central Asian Civilization That Bridged the East and the West for Over Two Millennia*, Vol. 1, 2nd ed. (Seattle, WA: Kindle Direct Publishing, 2021), pp. 76–108; Zerrin Günal Öden, *Islam öncesi Türk tarihi ve kültürü* [*Pre-Islamic Turkish History and Culture*] (Ankara: Nobel Paradigma Kitabevi, 2004); Gülçin Çandarlıoğlu, *Islam öncesi Türk tarihi ve kültürü* [*Pre-Islamic Turkish History and Culture*] (Istanbul: Türk Dünyası Araştırmaları Vakfı, 2006); Yaşar Bedirhan, *Islam öncesi Türk tarihi ve kültürü* [*Pre-Islamic Turkish History and Culture*] (Kızılay, Ankara: Nobel Akademik Yayıncılık, 2011); Muhammed Bilal

Çelik, *Islam öncesi Türk tarihi ve kültürü* (Nobel Akademik Yayincilik, 2019); yes, all the same title by differing authors and publishers, obviously a popular topic in Turkish historiography. For Turkish works treating Tengrism among Turkic Central Asian peoples, with special focus on the Altai peoples, see: Günnur Yücekal Arpacı, *Gök Tanrı Inancının Bilinmeyenleri [Unknown Belief in the God of Heaven]* (Istanbul: Cati Yayinlari, 2012); cf. also Mehmet Eröz, *Eski Türk dini (gök tanrı inancı) ve Alevîlik-Bektaşilik* [Old Turkish Religion (belief in sky god) and Alevism-Bektashism] (Istanbul: Türk Dünyası Arastırmaları Vakfı, 1992), and Yıldız Kocasavaş, "Gök Tanrı İnancı [Faith in the God of Heaven]," *Türkler Tarihi*, Vol. 3 (2002): 326–329 and 578–584. On Persian-Iranian religious-cultural history and identity, see e.g.: Richard N. Frye, "Problems in the Study of Iranian Religions," in *Erwin Goodenough Memorial Volume*, ed. Jacob Neusner (Leiden: Brill Academic, 1968), pp. 337–343; Fereshteh Davaran, *Continuity in Iranian Identity: Resilience of a Cultural Heritage* (London and New York: Routledge, 2010); Nasrin Rahimieh, *Iranian Culture: Representation and Identity* (London and New York: Routledge, 2015); Scott Savran, *Arabs and Iranians in the Islamic Conquest Narrative: Memory and Identity Construction in Islamic Historiography, 750–1050* (London and New York: Routledge, 2017).
448. Deweese, "Shamanization in Central Asia," 346. French served as a language of trade, etc., from nineteenth-century Ottoman times.
449. Devin Deweese, *Islamization and Native Religion in the Golden Horde: Baba Tukles and Conversion to Islam in Historical and Epic Tradition* (Pennsylvania State University Press, 1994), p. 596.
450. See e.g.: Cemal Şener, *Şamanizm: Türkler'in Islamiyet'ten önceki dini* [Shamanism: The Religion of the Turks before Islam] (Istanbul: Etik Yayınları [1997] 2010); Ozgür Velioğlu, *Inançların Türk Sinemasına Yansıması: şamanizm, gök-tanrı, animizm, naturizm, totemizm, Islamiyet inançları açısından* [*Reflection of Beliefs on Turkish Cinema: Shamanism, Sky-God, Animism, Naturism, Totemism, in Terms of Islamic Beliefs*] (Kadıköy/Istanbul Es Yayınları 2005); Atilla Bağci, "Türk Kültüründe Kurdun Kutsiyetinin Şaman Mitlerindeki Yeri (The Holiness of the Wolf in Terms of Shaman Mythology

in Turkish Culture)," *Türk Dünyası Dil ve Edebiyat Dergisi* [*Journal of Turkish World Language and Literature*], No. 42 (Dec 13, 2016): 7–15; Yilmaz Orhan, "Alevîlïkte Eskï Türk Dïnï (Göktanri Inanci) ve Şamanïzmïn Etkïlerï [The Effects of Ancient Turkish Religion (Belief in Heaven) and Shamanism in Alevism]," *Akademik Tarih ve Düşünce Dergisi* [*Journal of Academic History and Thought*], Vol. 4, No. 1 (Dec 1, 2014): 1–13.
451. Samire Mömïn, "Şamanïzm ve Günümüzdekï Kalintilari (Uygur Toplumundakï Tabular Üzerïne) [Shamanism and Its Consequential Residues (On Taboos in Uygur Society)," *Ulakbilge: Sosyal Bilimler Dergisi* [*Ulakbilge: Journal of Social Sciences*], Vol. 1, No. 1 (Feb 2015): 79–89; Alimcan Înayet, "Bugünkü Uygurlarda Şamanlık Ve Bir Şaman Duası: Azâîm Koşıkı [Shamanism among Today's Uighurs and a Shaman's Prayer: Azâim Koshıkı]," *Motif Akademi Halkbilimi Dergisi* [*Motif Academy Journal of Folklore*], Vols. 3–4, No. 2 (Dec 1, 2009): 38–52.
452. Devin Deweese, "(Review of) Thierry Zarcone and Angela Hobart ed. *Shamanism and Islam: Sufism, Healing Rituals and Spirits in the Muslim World* (London/New York: I.B. Tauris, 2012)," *International Journal of Turkish Studies*, Vol. 22, No. 1/2 (Fall 2016): 200–201.
453. Deweese, "Shamanization in Central Asia," 327–328.
454. Deweese, "Shamanization in Central Asia," 344.
455. Deweese, "Shamanization in Central Asia," 335n15 and 339n19; cf. also reference to 15th-century evidence on 343.
456. Privratsky, *Muslim Turkistan*, pp. 14–15, citing a 1997 conference paper by Devin Deweese on "The Yasavī Sufi tradition and the problem of shamanic 'survivals.'" Deweese addresses survivals in relation to Yasawi as well in the latter part of his chapter on "Ahmad Yasavi and the Divan-i hikmat in Soviet scholarship," in *The Heritage of Soviet Oriental Studies*, ed. Michael Kemper and Stephan Conermann (London and New York: Routledge, 2011), pp. 262–290.
457. Privratsky, *Muslim Turkistan*, p. 217.
458. Privratsky, *Muslim Turkistan*, pp. 220 and 225 respectively.
459. Both quotes from Privratsky, *Muslim Turkistan*, p. 227.
460. Privratsky, *Muslim Turkistan*, p. 256.

461. Privratsky, *Muslim Turkistan*, p. 225.
462. Privratsky, *Muslim Turkistan*, p. 217.
463. Cf. historically the competition between the Shamanic and Tengrist traditions which, according to Jean-Paul Roux, sometimes emerged. See: Jean-Paul Roux, "Tengri" and "Turkic Religions," tr. Sherri L. Granka, in *The Encyclopedia of Religion*, Vols. 14–15, ed. Mircea Eliade (New York: MacMillan Publishing Co., 1987), V14:401–3 and V15:87–94.
464. Various quotes in second half of paragraph taken from Privratsky, *Muslim Turkistan*, pp. 219, 221, 223, 221 and 220 respectively.
465. Privratsky, *Muslim Turkistan*, p. 217.
466. Privratsky, *Muslim Turkistan*, p. 224.
467. Privratsky, *Muslim Turkistan*, p. 218.
468. Privratsky, *Muslim Turkistan*, p. 17.
469. Privratsky, *Muslim Turkistan*, p. 217.
470. Cf. Olle Sundström, "Is the Shaman Indeed Risen in Post-Soviet Siberia?," *Scripta Instituti Donneriani Aboensis*, Vol. 24 (2012): 350–387, who notes (p. 350n1) that: "To what extent alleged 'shamans' were arrested, incarcerated and executed during this campaign is still not entirely clear. The present article is written within the research project on the 'Repression of "shamans" in the Soviet North from the late 1920s through the 1950s: an archival study', which aims to establish what happened to those accused of being 'shamans'. The project is financed by the Swedish Research Council (Vetenskapsrådet)."
471. Privratsky, *Muslim Turkistan*, p. 121.
472. Privratsky, *Muslim Turkistan*, p. 227.
473. All three previous quotes taken from Privratsky, *Muslim Turkistan*, p. 218.
474. All quotes following previous note down to this point taken from Privratsky, *Muslim Turkistan*, pp. 223–226.
475. Chiara Formichi, "Islam and Resistance," in *Islam and Asia (New Approaches to Asian History)* (Cambridge: Cambridge University Press, 2020), pp. 206–235; cf. also p. 131, where she speaks of "the peak of Islamist anti-Soviet resistance."
476. Mircea Eliade, *Shamanism: Archaic Techniques of Ecstasy*, tr. Willard R. Trask, rev. ed. (Princeton, NJ: Bollingen Foundation and New York: Random House, [1951] 1964), p. 506; cf. Eliade, *Birth and Rebirth: The Religious Meanings of Initiation*

in Human Culture (New York: Harper & Bros., 1958), pp. 61ff., 87ff. See also: Thomas Michael, "Does Shamanism Have a History? With Attention to Early Chinese Shamanism," *Numen*, Vol. 64, Nos. 5–6 (2017): 459–496.

477. Cf. Thomas A. DuBois, "Trends in Contemporary Research on Shamanism," *Numen*, Vol. 58, No. 1 (Jan 2011): 100 –128; Lars Kirkhusmo Pharo, "A Methodology for a Deconstruction and Reconstruction of the Concepts 'Shaman' and 'Shamanism'," *Numen*, Vol. 58, No. 1 (2011): 6–70.

478. For comparison with the Siberian context, see esp., Sundström, "Is the Shaman Indeed Risen in Post-Soviet Siberia?"

479. These include, e.g., V. Verbitskii's observations of Shamanic rituals among the Altaic Turks in 1840, V.M. Mikhailovsky's in-depth look at *Shamanism* published in 1892 as well as V.S. Bogoraz's 1939 study of Shamanism among the Chukchi (see Chapter 5), none of which are discussed by Deweese.

480. Deweese, "Shamanization in Central Asia," 339.

481. Art Leete, "Reconsidering the Role of Shamans in Siberia during the Early Soviet Era," *Shaman*, Vol. 23, Nos. 1–2 (Spring/Autumn 2015): 61.

482. See esp., Adeeb Khalid, *Islam After Communism: Religion and Politics in Central Asia: With a New Afterword* (Berkeley, CA: University of California Press, [2006] 2014), pp. 8–9.

483. Among numerous other works, see esp., the extensive (600-page) study of Shahab Ahmed, *What Is Islam? The Importance of Being Islamic* (Princeton, NJ: Princeton University Press, 2015). Drawing from a host of sources—textual, poetic, artistic, numismatic, mystical-devotional and otherwise—Ahmed challenges simplistic definitions of Islam based almost exclusively in interpretations of the Qur'an and Hadith and/or Islamic law schools. Cf. also John L. Esposito and Dalia Mogahed, *Who Speaks for Islam? What a Billion Muslims Really Think* (New York: Gallup Press, 2007).

484. While I realize that this suggestion may be controversial, I do not intend it as 'polemical' in any way, I simply wish to make what I consider here to be a fair observation: Deweese's view of history in relation to Sufi practices as an expression of 'Islamic civilization' shares significant affinities with the view of 'closed civilizations' espoused by Oswald Spengler in his *Decline of the*

West (1918–1922) and later by Samuel Huntington in his *Clash of Civilizations* (1993 and 1996). To be very clear here: The point of comparison, especially in the latter case, is not the idea of "clash," but again 'closed civilizations' which are sealed off from any outside influences across long centuries of interaction with the larger world around them. I suggest this point needs to be taken seriously and reflected upon constructively. This kind of exclusivist, isolationist view of history likewise parallels religious 'purists' who emphasize only 'internal' and 'independent' developments in order to safeguard doctrines of divine revelation and inspiration from being undermined by 'dependence' upon 'foreign, outside' and thus non-divine influences. However wittingly or unwittingly, Deweese's (as well as Frank's, Privratksy's and other similar) historiography supports such theologically and culturally-civilizationally 'purist' interpretations.

485. Julian Baldick, *Animal and Shaman: Ancient Religions of Central Asia* (Washington Square, NY: New York University Press, 2000), p. 65.
486. The Russian scholar B.N. Basilov published a study of *Shamanism among the Peoples of Central Asia and Kazakhstan*; cf. В.Н. Басилов, *Шаманство у народов Средней Азии и Казахстана* [*Shamanism among the Peoples of Central Asian and Kazakhstan*] (Москва: Наука, 1992). The first chapter covers a brief "History of the Study of Shamanism among the Peoples of Central Asia and Kazakhstan" (pp. 30–47). This provides important background material and sources, but falls short of a history of Central Asian Shamanism. However helpful and important Basilov's work may be, it begs the very questions being raised here in this chapter and other critical post-Soviet scholarship. My call here is for a critical study which engages these issues. Though lacking deeper critical concerns, Baldick, *Animal and Shaman*, provides some limited coverage of the topic; see esp. his chapter on "The Turks" (pp. 38–91). Cf. also Marjorie Mandelstam Balzer, Jan N. Bremmer and Carlo Ginzburg, *Horizons of Shamanism: A Triangular Approach to the History and Anthropology of Ecstatic Techniques*, ed. Peter Jackson (Stockholm, Sweden: Stockholm University Press, 2016); see esp. the "Afterword" by Ulf Drobin (pp. 79–88).

487. Б.М. Аташ and М.И.Танжаров, "Көне Түркі-Түркі-Қазақ Даласындағы Шаманизмнің Генезисі мен Эволюциясы: Тарихи-Танымдық Бағдарлар [Genesis and Evolution of Shamanism in the Ancient Turkic-Turkic-Kazakh Steppes: Historical and Cognitive Orientations]," *Адам Әлемі* [*The Human World*], Vol. 92, No. 2 (2022): 173–187, citation taken from p. 174. Note that I have included minor edits to some of the English grammar.
488. DeWeese, *Islamization and Native Religion*, p. 9.
489. Abai notes that Nauryz was effectively replaced by "*Korban ait*," i.e., Aid al-Adha, the Feast of Sacrifice, with the appellation "Great day of the people" being transferred from one to the other. *Абай: Шығармаларының екі томдық толық жинағы: Екінші том: Өлеңдер мен аудармалар, поэмалар, қарасөздер* [*Abai: A Complete Two-Volume Collection of His Writings: Vol 2: Songs and Translations, Poems, and Reflections/Words*], ed. Есенбай Дүйсенбайұлы, Ғұсман Жандыбаев - Алматы: Жазушы, 2005), p. 156. On Nauryz (Nowruz) and Islam historically, see: Quasem Ahmadi, Fatemeh Lajevardi, and Mohommadreza Adli, "The Influence of Ancient Iranian Culture on Islamic Culture in the Abbasid Period," *Journal of Religious Studies*, Vol. 15, No. 1 (Summer 2021): 1–24; Hamid Ashrafi Kheirabady and Seyed Abolfazi Razavi, "The Revival of Nowruz and Mehregan Celebrations in the Abbasi Court (132–220 AH)," *Journal of Iranian Islamic Period History*, Vol. 12, No. 27 (July 2021): 1–19; Mary Boyce, "NOWRUZ i. In the Pre-Islamic Period," *Encyclopædia Iranica*, online edition, 2016 (URL: http://www.iranicaonline.org/articles/nowruz-i); A. Shapur Shahbazi, "NOWRUZ ii. In the Islamic Period," *Encyclopædia Iranica*, online edition, 2016 (URL: http://www.iranicaonline.org/articles/nowruz-ii); and the Tajik scholar, Hassan Bigonah, "Nowruz in Tradition Transition," *IIOAB Journal*, Vol. 7, No. 3 (September 2016): 491–495; A. M. Malikov, "Celebration of Nowruz in Bukhara and Samarkand in Ritual Practice and Social Discourses (The Second Half of the 19th to Early 20th Centuries)," *Archeology, Ethnology, Anthropology of Eurasia*, Vol. 48, No. 2 (June 2020): 122–129. Special thanks to Christopher W. Card, for his bibliographic research which included these works. Boyce actually traces Persian Zoroastrian roots of Nowruz back to earlier Mesopotamian-Babylonian traditions (Mary

Boyce, *A History of Zoroastrianism: Volume Two: Under the Achaemenids*, Leiden: Brill, 1982, p. 34).

490. Cf. e.g., Khalid, *Islam after Communism*, who highlights how there "remains a substantial residue of the Soviet suspicion of religion and its potential to be put to unhealthy political uses" (p. 121), what he later refers to as "a great residue of the Soviet critique of religion" (p. 132).

491. See esp., Leif Stenberg and Philip Wood, eds., *What Is Islamic Studies? European and North American Approaches to a Contested Field* (Edinburgh University Press, 2022). Among other things, the book, as per its own description, "situates Islamic Studies within broader discussions of the construction of identity and its political implications" and addresses "tensions between normative and non-normative approaches to the study of Islam and Muslims."

492. One possible domain for fruitful inquiry might be, for example, comparative studies of the interactions of Buddhism and Shamanism in Korea with the interactions between Islam and Shamanism in Central Asia. See e.g., Eunsu Cho, "Syncretism of Buddhism and Shamanism in Korea," *The Journal of Asian Studies*, Vol. 62, No. 4, (Nov 2003): 1254–1256; Sung-Eun Thomas Kim, "Korean Buddhist Adoption of Shamanic Religious Ethos: Healing, Fortune Seeking, and the Afterlife," *International Journal of Buddhist Thought and Culture* (*IJBTC*), Vol. 28, No. 1 (2018): 59–85; Antonetta L. Bruno, "The Posal Between the Mudang and Buddhist: In-Between and Bypassing," *Journal of Korean Religions* (Special Issue: *North Korea and Religion*), Vol. 4, No. 2 (Oct 2013): 175–196.

493. Soumia Aziz, "(Review of) *Shamanism and Islam: Sufism, Healing Rituals and Spirits in the Muslim World*, by Thierry Zarcone and Angela Hobart," *Islamic Studies*, Vol. 55, No. 3/4 (Autumn–Winter 2016): 345–346.

494. Cf. Michael York, *Pagan Mysticism: Paganism as a World Religion* (Newcastle-upon-Tyne: Cambridge Scholars Publishing, 2019), pp. 127 and 226ff; cf. also pp. 15, 26, 34, 51, 95, 102, 127, 154, 159, 163, 167n19, 175n34, 185, 206, 241–243, 250–252, 264, 269, 289. See also: Denise Lardner Carmody and John Carmody, *Mysticism: Holiness East and West* (New York: Oxford University Press, 1996); Philip C. Almond,

Mystical Experience and Religious Doctrine: An Investigation of the Study of Mysticism in World Religions (Berlin and Boston: De Gruyter, 2015); Edward Geoffrey Parrinder, *Mysticism in the World's Religions* (Oxford: Oneworld, 1996).

495. Behzad Atooni, Mahdi Sharifian, and Behrooz Atooni, "Comparative Study of Islamic Sufism and Shamanic Mysticism," *Biannual Journal of Mystical Literature*, Vol. 10, No. 19 (2018–2019): 7–26, with the discussion of historical influence on p. 9. The article is in Farsi with an English abstract and title. My thanks to Abdollah Ghaffari for assisting with helping identity key points from the article for my research here.

496. See Chapter 3, n22.

497. This is not to say that they do not cite from them, but they have not been ideologically forced to such conclusions nor steeped almost solely in these traditions.

498. Along with Sultanova's and Kartaeva's works cited above, see: Meruert Abuseitova, "The Spread of Islam in Kazakhstan from the Fifteenth to the Eighteenth Century," in *Kazakhstan: Religions and Society in the History of Central Eurasia*, ed. Gian Luca Bonora, Niccolò Pianciola, and Paolo Sartori (Turin: Umberto Allemandi & Co., 2010), pp. 125–136, esp. pp. 133–134; Tursin Hafizuhli Gabitov, *Qazaq Mädenietining Ruhanï Kengstigi* [*The Spiritual Context of Kazakh Culture*] (Almaty: Raritet, 2013).

499. Anita M. Leopold and Jeppe S. Jensen, "The Historical Background of the Term Syncretism: The Problem of Definition," in *Syncretism in Religion: A Reader* (*Critical Categories in the Study of Religion*), ed. A.M. Leopold and J.S. Jensen (London and New York: Routledge, [2004] 2014), p. 18.

500. Their accommodations of traditional law codes (cf. 'adat') and other cultural customs was, like Soviet nationalities policy, only an ambivalent acquiescence with their longer-term goal in view.

501. Ж. Дүисенбин [Zh. Duisenbin], *Ислам діні және оның қазіргі жайы туралы* [*About the Religion of Islam and Its Current Standing*] (Алматы: Қазақ Мемлекет Баспасы, 1961), pp. 114–121.

502. Privratksy, *Muslim Turkistan*, pp. 216–217.

503. Leete, "Reconsidering the Role of Shamans in Siberia during the Early Soviet Era," 61.

504. Privratksy, *Muslim Turkistan*, p. 217.

505. See esp. Richard J. Evans, *In Defence of History*, American Edition (New York and London: W.W. Norton & Co., 1998); Evans and a team he led served as the primary historical research assistants for the trial of Deborah Lipstadt against the Holocaust denier, David Irving. He helped successfully defend not only Lipstadt, but the historicity of the Holocaust. On post-modernist critiques of history and historiography below in the main text.
506. The task is complicated by the fact that all historical narratives function not only as reconstructions of the past, but to supply humans with varying forms of identity. This is inescapable, whether consciously intended or not. It gives historical narratives a psychological dimension at personal, social, political, gender and other levels. And it is the boundary line between a reasonably objective reconstruction of the past based on the available evidence and its psychological implications which marks the dividing line between history and propaganda, depending on whether the donkey draws the cart or vice versa, i.e., whether the honest and faithful (re)construction of the historical narrative determines the psychological outcomes for human identity or the psychological implications determine, a priori, the (propagandistic) narrative (cf. 'confirmation bias' theory in psychology). Financial, career and other forms of support for historical (and other) scholars by religious, government, institutional and other interest groups deeply complicates this problem and marks the dividing line between genuine academic freedom and constrained or even pre-determined outcomes for research-publication agendas. These dimensions of the problem will never be entirely resolved, but they merit ongoing attention. On 'history as identity', see esp.: James E. Côté and Charles G. Levine, eds., *Identity Formation, Agency, and Culture: A Social Psychological Synthesis* (New York and London: Taylor & Francis—Psychology Press, 2002); Stefan Berger, *History and Identity: How Historical Theory Shapes Historical Practice* (Cambridge and New York: Cambridge University Press, 2022); Stefan Berger and Christoph Conrad, *The Past as History: National Identity and Historical Consciousness in Modern Europe* (Basingstoke, UK: Palgrave Macmillan, 2015); Stefan Berger, ed., *Writing the Nation: A Global Perspective* (Basingstoke, UK: Palgrave Macmillan, 2007); Katharine Hodgkin and Susannah Radstone, eds., *Memory, History, Nation: Contested Pasts* (New York and London: Routledge,

2005); Sahana Mukherjee and Phia S. Salter, eds., *History and Collective Memory from the Margins: A Global Perspective* (Hauppauge, NY: Nova Science Publishers, 2019); Henrik Åström Elmersjö, Anna Clark and Monika Vinterek, eds., *International Perspectives on Teaching Rival Histories: Pedagogical Responses to Contested Narratives and the History Wars* (Cham, Switzerland: Palgrave Macmillan, 2017).

507. Cf. R.C. Weller, "Interview: Islam in the Life of Kazakhs: From Conversion to Current Times," *Central Asian Analytical Network*, March 10, 2017 (URL: http://caa-network.org/archives/8551; in both Russian and English). In the interview, I say: "religious 'conversion' of whole ethnic (or other social) groups is typically a gradual, long-term process, one which in fact never truly ends. Initial 'religious conversion' is too strongly dichotomized with ongoing 'religious transformation'. New forms as well as new understandings of religious faith, all taking shape within new historical circumstances, are continuously evolving and even competing among segments of the population as they slowly spread. Relatedly, conversion to Islam among the Kazakhs, just like conversion to any religion among any population, usually never happens in one single moment of time among the entire population. It is, again, a gradual process of spreading at varying speeds and levels among differing segments of the population. ... religious faith and practice are typically spread through multiple clan and family networks, trade networks, friendship networks, etc. The emphasis here is on various 'social networks', i.e. natural 'channels' of communication and relationship. This is a major part of the problem in the whole debate: arguments are typically simplistic: i.e. 'either' the Kazakhs were Muslim at this or that time, 'or' they were not. The question of exactly how far Islam spread among the Kazakh population at each successive stage of history is difficult to answer. It is a question which will most likely continue to be debated for decades and even centuries to come." For some of the most important dimensions and factors involved in the complex historical process, see esp., Daniel Beben, "Shaykh Khalīlullāh Badakhshānī and the Legacy of the Kubravīyah in Central Asia," in *From the Khan's Oven: Studies on the History of Central Asian Religions in Honor of Devin*

Deweese, ed. Eren Tasar, Allen J. Frank, and Jeff Eden (Leiden and New York: Brill, 2021), pp. 181–211; Ashirbek Muminov, "Islam in the Syr Darya Region from the Twelfth to the Fourteenth Century," in *Kazakhstan: Religions and Society in the History of Central Eurasia*, ed. Gian Luca Bonora, Niccolò Pianciola, and Paolo Sartori (Turin: Umberto Allemandi & Co., 2010), pp. 113–124; Abuseitova, "The Spread of Islam in Kazakhstan from the Fifteenth to the Eighteenth Century" (cited above), and Gulmira Sultangalieva, "The Russian Empire and the Intermediary Role of Tatars in Kazakhstan: The Politics of Cooperation and Rejection," in *Asiatic Russia: Imperial Power in Regional and International Contexts*, ed. Tomohiko Uyama (London and New York: Routledge, 2012), pp. 52–79. Cf. also Devin Deweese, "Re-envisioning the History of Sufi Communities in Central Asia: Continuity and Adaptation in Sources and Social Frameworks, 16th-20th Centuries," in *Sufism in Central Asia: New Perspectives on Sufi Traditions, 15th-21st Centuries*, ed. Devin Deweese and Jo-Ann Gross (Leiden and Boston: Brill, 2018), pp. 21–74, and Ashirbek Muminov and Saipulla Mollakanagatuly, "A First Glimpse at Saduaqas Ghïlmani's (1890–1972) 'Biographies of the Islamic Scholars of Our times'—A Possible Rewriting of the Tsarist and Soviet History of Kazakhstan's Islamic Community," *Asiatische Studien*, Vol. 73, No. 4 (April 2020): 751–759. In terms of a single source, the entire volume edited by Bonora, Pianciola and Sartori covers some of the latest and best research on this topic. For a recent Kazakh monograph treating "the historical-spiritual processes taking place in the region of Central Asia between the VIII-XIII centuries," see: Erke Tamabekkyzy Kartabaeva, *Islam zhanye Ortagasyrlyk Turkiler* [Islam and the Turks of the Middle Ages] (Almaty: Kazak Universiteti, 2016).

508. A.M. Leopold and J.S. Jensen, eds., *Syncretism in Religion: A Reader (Critical Categories in the Study of Religion)* (London and New York: Routledge, [2004] 2014); Geo Widengren, "Culture Contact, Cultural Influence, Cultural Continuity, and Syncretism. Some views based on my previous work," in *Religious Syncretism in Antiquity*, ed. Birger A. Pearson (Missoula, MT: Scholars Press, 1975), pp. 1–20; Eric Maroney, *Religious Syncretism* (London: SCM Press, 2006);

Stefania Palmisano and Nicola Pannofino, eds., *Invention of Tradition and Syncretism in Contemporary Religions: Sacred Creativity* (Cham, Switzerland: Palgrave Macmillan, 2017); David Lindenfeld, *Beyond Conversion & Syncretism: Indigenous Encounters With Missionary Christianity, 1800–2000* (New York, NY: Berghahn Books, 2011); Richard E. Payne, *A State of Mixture: Christians, Zoroastrians, and Iranian Political Culture in Late Antiquity* (Berkeley: University of California Press, 2015).

509. I am drawing here from the helpful overview of the historical development of understandings and appropriations of 'syncretism' as an explicit construct in Kurt Rudolph, "Syncretism: From Theological Invective to a Concept in the Study of Religion," in *Syncretism in Religion: A Reader*, ed. Anita Maria Leopold and Jeppe S. Jensen (*Critical Categories in the Study of Religion* Series) (London and New York: Routledge, [2004] 2014), pp. 68–79, with specific reference to 69–70. For added historical overview, see also: Anita M. Leopold and Jeppe S. Jensen, "The Historical Background of the Term Syncretism: The Problem of Definition," in ibid., pp. 14–22.

510. See e.g., Pavel Shabley and Paolo Sartori, "Tinkering with Codification in the Kazakh Steppe: ʿĀdat and Sharīʿa in the Work of Efim Osmolovskii," in *Sharīʿa in the Russian Empire: The Reach and Limits of Islamic Law in Central Eurasia, 1550–1917*, ed. Paolo Sartori and Danielle Ross (Edinburgh: Edinburgh University Press, 2020), pp. 213–214. They insist that "the term 'syncretism' is derived from the vocabulary of religious studies and conjures up the image of blending and reconciling of religions supposedly at odds." Cf. again esp., Rudolph, "Syncretism: From Theological Invective to a Concept in the Study of Religion," cited above; see also the informed discussion in Chiara Formichi, *Islam and Asia* (*New Approaches to Asian History*) (Cambridge: Cambridge University Press, 2020), pp. 44–45, which draws from Deweese.

511. Cf. esp., Rosalind Shaw and Charles Stewart, "Idiosyncratic Etymology and Syncretistic Controversy," in *Syncretism/Anti-Syncretism: The Politics of Religious Synthesis*, ed. C. Stewart and R. Shaw (London and New York: Routledge, 1994): "Problems with syncretism do not seem to lie with any substantive objection

to the semantics of the term – since hardly anyone would deny that different religious traditions have amalgamated in the past, and continue to interact and borrow from one another today – but with the very word itself and its history of application" (Introduction).
512. See e.g., Kairat Zatov, Tursun Gabitov, Maral Botaeva, Moldagaliyev Bauyrzhan and Saira Shamahay, "Islam and Values of Kazakh Culture," *International Journal of Social, Behavioral, Educational, Economic, Business and Industrial Engineering*, Vol. 7, No. 6 (2013): 1697–1702, citing from p. 1702. See also near the end of the main text and note 51 below.
513. Privratsky, *Muslim Turkistan*, pp. 14–15, citing a 1997 conference paper by Devin Deweese on "The Yasavī Sufi tradition and the problem of shamanic 'survivals.'"
514. Marc David Baer, "History and Religious Conversion," in *The Oxford Handbook of Religious Conversion*, ed. Lewis R. Rambo and Charles E. Farhadian (Oxford and New York: Oxford University Press, 2014), pp. 25–47; cf. Robert D. Baird, "Interpretative Categories and the History of Religions," *History and Theory*, 1968, Vol. 8, No. 8: *On Method in the History of Religions* (1968): 17–30.
515. Elana Jefferson-Tatum, "Beyond Syncretism and Colonial Legacies in the Study of Religion: Critical Reflections on Harrison's *In Praise of Mixed Religion* and Blanes's *A Prophetic Trajectory*," *The Journal of Religion*, Vol. 100, No. 4 (2020): 499–514, citing from p. 501. Cf. William H. Harrison, *In Praise of Mixed Religion: The Syncretism Solution in a Multifaith World* (Montreal: McGill-Queen's University Press, 2014).
516. I propose here that a special conference, or perhaps group of collaborative panels within a conference, with an ensuing special issue journal or edited volume, should be convened to address these matters specifically within the field of Central Asian studies, though interacting with broader scholarship in other regions and fields.
517. Cf. the list in Kurt Rudolph, "Syncretism: From Theological Invective to a Concept in the Study of Religion," in *Syncretism in Religion: A Reader*, ed. Anita Maria Leopold and Jeppe S. Jensen (*Critical Categories in the Study of Religion* Series) (London and New York: Routledge, [2004] 2014), p. 79.

518. Deweese, *Islamization and Native Religion in the Golden Horde*, pp. 179–230 and 290–320.
519. As suggested by various contributors in the volume by Anita M. Leopold and Jeppe S. Jensen, eds., *Syncretism in Religion: A Reader*, definitions need to be tied to particular historical contexts, which means that it would be best for each region to formulate their own definitions, or at least provide their own historical examples for each definition, since all local and regional histories are part of broader world history.
520. Cf. again, e.g., how Mary Boyce actually traces Persian Zoroastrian roots of Nowruz back to earlier Mesopotamian-Babylonian traditions (Boyce, *A History of Zoroastrianism*, p. 34).
521. As I have highlighted in "Religious-Cultural Revivalism as Historiographical Debate," and is reflected in the 7–8 options outlined in the main text above near the beginning of this chapter, there remain a minority of Kazakhs and other Central Asian peoples who continue to view Islam as a 'foreign' invading imperializing presence. This is seen in their historiographies analyzed within the article. The majority reject this view as 'archaistic', wishing to return to a supposedly pristine past which no longer exists. They thus consider it historical digressive as opposed to progressive, with 'progressivist' views remaining influential in their ongoing interpretations, dialogs and responses.
522. T. Omarbekov et al., "Religious beliefs: Islam in the XIV-XV Centuries: Discrete nature of the process of Islamization of Nomads," in *History of Kazakhstan (Kazakh Eli): A 4-Volume Textbook. Book 2: Kazakhstan in the XIII Century—The First Quarter of the XVIII Century* (Almaty: Qazaq Universiteti, 2021, in English), p. 112.
523. Khalid, *Islam after Communism*, p. 32.
524. А.И. Левшин [A.I. Levshin], "Вера и Суеверие [Faith and Superstition]," in *Описание Киргиз-Кайсакских, или Киргиз-Казахстанской'их орд и степей* [*Description of Kirghiz-Kaisak, or Kirghiz-Kazakhstani Hordes and Steppes*] (Алматы: Санат [Almaty, KZ: Sanat], [1832] 1996), pp. 313–320; quote from p. 313.
525. Abai Kunanbaev (ca. 1900), "Word Thirteen," in *The Book of Words* (English transl.) (Leneshmidt Translations Resource

Library, n.d.) (URL: http://www.leneshmidt-translations.com/book_of_words_abai_kunanbaev_english/t13.htm). Cf. Garifolla Yesim, *An Insider's Critique of the Kazakh Nation: Reflections on the Writings of Abai Kunanbai-uhli (1845–1904)* (Boston, MA: Asia Research Associates, [1994] 2020), 190–191, 228.
526. Allen J. Frank and Mirkasyim A. Usmanov, eds., *An Islamic Biographical Dictionary of the Eastern Kazakh Steppe, 1770–1912* (Leiden: Brill, 2004).
527. Among other critiques, cf. also e.g., Tor on the "empirical evidence that the omitting of inconvenient historical facts was indeed practised in Samanid historiography..." D.G. Tor, "The Islamization of Central Asia in the Sāmānid Era and the Reshaping of the Muslim World," *Bulletin of the School of Oriental and African Studies*, Vol. 72, No. 2 (2009): 291-2n53.
528. Peter B. Golden, "Wolves, Dogs and Qipčaq Religion," *Acta Orientalia Academiae Scientiarum Hungaricae*, Vol. 50, Nos. 1/3 (1997): 97; cf. also Golden, "The Shaping of the Cuman-Qipcaqs and Their World," in *Studies on the Peoples and Cultures of the Eurasian Steppes* (An Anthology of essays by) P.B. Golden, ed. C. Hriban (Bucharest: Braila, 2011), pp. 303–332.
529. Privratsky, *Muslim Turkistan*, p. 13, references Marina Tolmacheva as support for the idea that "Soviet ethnographies of the religion of the Central Asian peoples were always the work of short-term expeditions of imposing (usually male) ethnographic teams with an ideological axe to grind against the religious traditions of their (often female) informants." My own reading of Tolmacheva somewhat differs. When she noted that "[t]here are a number of problems with the data," she was directing her critique specifically to data supplied for sociological and anthropological studies of Muslim women in Central Asia, not "the religion of the Central Asian peoples" in general. Along these lines, she says, "most data...seem to have been supplied by men and to men researchers, thus they often are second-hand and to that extent reflective of the outward, observable part of women's religious life; they also may be subject to cultural bias..." (Marina Tolmacheva, "The Muslim Woman in Soviet Central Asia," *Central Asian Survey*, Vol. 12, No. 4 (1993): 531–548, citing from p. 533.

530. This closely relates to but should be distinguished from efforts to provide a theological-doctrinal and/or legal justification for certain Kazakh cultural beliefs or practices, whether that interpretation is imposed upon the past or present. This type of approach is evident, for example, in the declaration of 2014 as the year of "Religion and Tradition" by the Kazakh Muftiyat. Certain Kazakh imams then published a book by that title and gave a series of sermons which provided theological-doctrinal and legal interpretations and justifications for the observance of certain Kazakh religio-cultural practices, including the preparing of *shelpek* (fried bread) "for charity" to "hand out to the poor." While this is true, the imam passed over in silence the fact that many Kazakhs dedicate the *shelpek* to the '*aruak*', i.e., their deceased ancestral spirits. He apparently did not wish to tackle this deeply entrenched and controversial issue which relates directly to the question of "pre-Islamic" beliefs and practices. See Alima Bissenova, "Building a Muslim Nation: The Role of the Central Mosque of Astana," in *Kazakhstan in the Making: Legitimacy, Symbols, and Social Changes*, ed. Marlène Laruelle (*Contemporary Central Asia: Societies, Politics, and Cultures*) (Lanham, MD: Lexington Books, 2016), pp. 219–221.

531. By "historical reconstructionist," I mean simply the 'reconstruction of the historical record' from all available evidence. It should not be confused with the specific period of 'Reconstruction' in American (or any other) history.

532. See e.g., Jerry H. Bentley, *Old World Encounters: Cross-Cultural Contacts and Exchanges in Pre-Modern Times* (Oxford and New York: Oxford University Press, 1993); A.T. Embree and C. Gluck, eds., *Asia in Western and World History: A Guide for Teaching* (Armonk, NY: M.E. Sharpe, 1997); Jon T. Davidann and Marc J. Gilbert, *Cross-Cultural Encounters in Modern World History, 1453-Present*, 2nd ed. (London and New York: Routledge, [2012] 2018); Dirk H. Steinforth and Charles C. Rozier, *Britain and its Neighbours: Cultural Contacts and Exchanges in Medieval and Early Modern Europe* (New York and London: Routledge, 2021).

533. Among numerous responses by professional historians to the challenges of post-modernism, see esp., R.J. Evans, *In Defence of History* (New York and London: W.W. Norton & Co., 1998).

For a salient response to post-modernist critiques of not only history and historiography, but religious-cultural anthropology, see Privratsky, "Challenges to Post-Modernist Epistemology," in *Muslim Turkistan*, pp. 254ff.
534. Cf. the view of Deweese covered near the end of the Introduction to this volume.
535. Cf. Privratsky's handling of the tension between collective historical memory and the evidence of the actual historical record near the end of the Introduction to this volume.
536. When confronted with the question of how their post-modernist denials of historical objectivity related and even lent validity to 'Holocaust denial', Hayden White and others backed off and revised their post-modernist dismissals of the historical enterprise. See Evans, *In Defence of History*, pp. 107–108.
537. See esp., John M. Hobson, "The Clash of Civilizations 2.0: Race and Eurocentrism, Imperialism, and Anti-Imperialism," in *Re-Imagining the Other: Culture, Media, and Western-Muslim Intersections*, ed. Mahmoud Eid and Karim H. Karim (Basingstoke, UK: Palgrave Macmillan, 2014), pp. 75–98.
538. The ethnic cleansings of Stalin, South African Apartheid and U.S. segregation also came to be part of the main 'evidences' of racist inhumane policies and their social-political consequences, but it was most immediately and directly Nazi Germany and the Holocaust. I have already elsewhere addressed how these historiographical trends impacted ideas of the relationship between ethnicity and state (see R.C. Weller, "Foundations of the Western Modernist View of Nations," in *Rethinking Kazakh and Central Asian Nationhood: A Challenge to Prevailing Views* [Los Angeles: Asia Research Associates, 2006], pp. 54–60).
539. I follow those who define 'world religions' not as religions which make a theological claim to be universally valid and true, but which have historically spread across the globe, crossing ethnic, cultural, linguistic and related boundaries. From this vantage, Buddhism, Christianity and Islam qualify most clearly. In the cases of Judaism and Hinduism, for example, their global spread is tied most closely to the Jewish and Hindu diaspora communities who have migrated to various parts of the world, not the missionary spread of the faiths into other ethnic, cultural and/or language groups.

540. As just one example here, see: Peter Stearns, with Olivia O'Neill and Jack Censer, *Cultural Change in Modern World History: Cases, Causes and Consequences* (London and New York: Bloomsbury Academic, 2018), pp. 125–131, concerning the 'survival' of traditional beliefs related to death and dying as medical scientific discoveries altered the mental landscape of Western societies in particular, from the late nineteenth century onward.

541. These latter ideas begin to cross over from historical methodology to philosophy of history, as reflected in the work of Nayef R.F. Al-Rodhan, *Sustainable History and the Dignity of Man: A Philosophy of History and Civilizational Triumph* (Zürich, Switzerland and Berlin, Germany: LIT Verlag, 2009). There remains, nonetheless, a close connection between 'philosophy of history' and 'historical theory (or theories)'.

542. I am including Egypt within Africa, although debate still surrounds whether it should properly be viewed as 'Near Eastern'. Both views, in fact, have historical merit.

543. See esp. Scott L. Montgomery and Alok Kumar, *A History of Science in World Cultures: Voices of Knowledge* (London and New York: Routledge, 2016).

544. Along with what follows, cf. also the recent works by Mahmood Kooria, *Islamic Law in Circulation: Shāfi'ī Texts across the Indian Ocean and the Mediterranean* (Cambridge, UK and New York, NY: Cambridge University Press, 2022) and Mahmood Kooria and Sanne Ravensbergen, eds., *Islamic Law in the Indian Ocean World: Texts, Ideas and Practices* (Abingdon and New York, NY: Routledge, 2022). Kooria's work argues for "the spread and survival of Islamic legal ideas" via not only legal texts, but language. In order to demonstrate the "survival" of the Shafi 'i legal tradition, he argues, in part, that along with texts, particular terms, phrases and concepts reflect and thus must necessarily draw from and preserve that legal tradition. Note here the need to make comparative links (i.e., relation) between the vocabulary of legal texts and other sources. It is the same comparative historical methodology which is involved in questions of the supposed links or relation between past and present forms of shamanism, Tengrism, etc., within the Central Asian context.

545. R.C. Weller, "Introduction: Reason, Revelation and Law in Global Historical Perspective," in *Reason, Revelation and Law*

in Islamic and Western Theory and History, ed. R.C. Weller and A. Emon (Cham, Switzerland: Palgrave Macmillan, 2021), pp. 1–24, esp. pp. 5–10.

546. R.C. Weller, "The Historical Relation of Islamic and Western Law," in *Reason, Revelation and Law in Islamic and Western Theory and History*, ed. R.C. Weller and A. Emon (Singapore: Palgrave Macmillan, 2021), pp. 25–43.

547. R. Charles Weller, "Islamic Contributions to Western Civilization," *Malcolm Renfrew Interdisciplinary Colloquium* Lecture, University of Idaho, Mar 2, 2021. (URL: https://youtu.be/RePQ0FimaXU). And Nayef R. F. al-Rodhan, ed., *The Role of the Arab-Islamic World in the Rise of the West: Implications for Contemporary Trans-Cultural Relations* (Basingstoke, UK and New York: Palgrave Macmillan, 2012).

548. Along with Weller, "Introduction: Reason, Revelation and Law in Global Historical Perspective," pp. 7–10, see: R.C. Weller, "'Western' and 'White Civilization': White Nationalism and Eurocentrism at the Crossroads," in *21st-Century Narratives of World History: Global and Multidisciplinary Perspectives*, ed. R.C. Weller (Cham, Switzerland: Palgrave Macmillan, 2017), pp. 61–62.

549. As referenced earlier, Elana Jefferson-Tatum, "Beyond Syncretism and Colonial Legacies in the Study of Religion," has raised important critical questions which relate to this entire topic. Her critique of William H. Harrison, *In Praise of Mixed Religion: The Syncretism Solution in a Multifaith World*, is particularly relevant. She is especially concerned about reproducing "colonial discourses of contact and empirical othering" by showing "how discourses of syncretism often either directly or inadvertently construct local and indigenous religious traditions as problematically other" (abstract). Or, as she puts it elsewhere, she takes issue with how scholars "participate in and even perpetuate the bordermaking and othering that presently precludes the existence of a mutual multireligious world" (p. 500). This is a different, almost opposite, concern than I am raising here in this sub-section, however.

550. Cf. Tokihisa Sumimoto, "Religious Freedom Problems in Japan: Background and Current Prospects," *International Journal of Peace Studies*, Vol. 5, No. 2 (Autumn/Winter 2000): 77–86.

334   NOTES

551. Note that I am not simplistically assuming that these two examples are equivalent in all aspects or dimensions. All comparisons/analogies contain both similarity and difference. Both the degree to and the manner in which the respective historical faith traditions in the Japanese and Kazakh cases relate together and are appropriated differ in various respects. There are nonetheless points of comparison to be made, and the main point which I am making here concerns the question of religious 'integrity.' Beyond this, I have already treated the question of the comparative and even historical relation of the Middle Eastern monotheistic versus East Asian traditions in Chapter 2 (see esp. note 51 and the related discussion in the main text).

552. Tursin H. Gabitov, "'Relational Dynamics of Religious Systems Among the Kazakhs," in *Madeniettanu* [*Culturology*], by T.H. Gabitov, Aktolkin Kulsarieva and Zhusipbek Mutalipov (Almaty: Rarity, 2001); T.H. Gabitov, "Kazakting diniy madenieti," in *Kazak Madenietining Tarihi* (Almaty: Kazak Universiteti, 2016), pp. 221–231; T.H. Gabitov and Galyia Kasymova, "The Role of the Shamanistic Musician in Kazakh Folk Culture" and Tursun Gabitov, Khairat Zatov, and Bakytzhan Satershinov "Islam and Values of Kazak Culture," in *Kazak Culture: Theory and History*, ed. T.H. Gabitov (Almaty: Kazak Universiteti, 2022, in English), pp. 48–60 and 201–208; Nazira Nurtazina, *Kazak Madenieti zhanye Islam: Tarihi-Madeniettanulik Zertteu* [*Kazakh Culture and Islam: Historical-Culturological Research*] (Almaty: Kazakting Madeniet zhanye Onertanu Gilimi-Zertteu Instituti, 2003); Н.Д.Нұртазина және Л.М.Хасанаева, *Ежелгі түріктердің исламдануының тарихи алғышарттары* [*Historical Prerequisites for the Islamization of the Ancient Turks*] (Алматы: «Қазақ университеті» баспасы, 2010); Khairat Zatov, "Islam Orkenieti Ayasindagi Qazaq Madenieti [Kazak Culture within the Embrace (or Bounds) of Islamic Civilizaton]," in <u>Qazaq Mädenietining Ruhani Kengstigi</u> [*The Spiritual Context of Kazakh Culture*], by Tursin Gabitov (Almaty: Raritet, 2013); Gabitov is the main author, but Zatov is credited as sole, independent author of Ch 4; T. Omarbekov et al., "Religious Beliefs: Islam in the XIV-XV Centuries: Discrete Nature of the Process of Islamization of Nomads" and "The Role of Islam in the Process of Kipchakization of Mongols," in *History of Kazakhstan (Kazakh*

Eli): A 4-Volume Textbook. Book 2: Kazakhstan in the XIII Century – the First Quarter of the XVIII Century (Almaty: Qazaq Universiteti, 2021, in English), pp. 107–113 and 127–133.

553. See somewhat recently Galina Yemelianova, "How 'Muslim' Are Central Asian Muslims? A Historical and Comparative Enquiry," *Central Asian Affairs*, Vol. 4, No. 3 (Jul 2017): 243–269. As summed up in the abstract, she covers how: "Over many centuries, Central Asians developed a particular form of Islam based on a productive and fluid synergy among Islam per se, their tribal legal and customary norms, and Tengrian and Zoroastrian beliefs and practices. It is characterized by a high level of doctrinal and functional adaptability to shifting political and cultural environments, the prevalence of mystical Islam (Sufism) and oral, rather than book-based, Islamic tradition. These qualities have defined distinctive Islamic trajectories in post-Soviet Central Asia, which differ significantly from those in other Muslim-majority countries and in Muslim communities in the West. At the same time, the common Eurasian space and lengthy shared political history of Central Asians and other peoples of Muslim Eurasia are also reflected in the considerable similarities in their Islamic trajectories." See also the earlier work of M. Tolmacheva, "The Muslim Woman in Soviet Central Asia," p. 533.

554. This is a revised version of a paper presented at the 24th Annual World History Association Conference (June 30–July 2, 2015, Savannah, GA). Thanks are due to Willard Sunderland and two blind reviewers for offering important critical input on the original draft edition. Steven Kale also read through and offered general comments from a Europeanist perspective. The author takes full responsibility for its final form and content. Concerning the length of quoted material, I am aware of current academic trends to minimize quotes (particularly indented ones), and I do agree in general. I make two exceptions however: (1) I consider it beneficial to provide translations of as much original primary source material as is reasonable, and (2) I consider it important to provide as much of an original quote as possible, including sufficient context in as fair and balanced a manner as possible, for readers to evaluate my analysis. I have also left some of the longer quotes in raw, extended form due to the fact that this is an appendix, not a main chapter in the volume.

555. С.В. Любичанковский (Lubichankovskii), "Научно-публикаторская деятельность Оренбургской ученой архивной комиссии (конец XIX — начало XX века)" ["Scientific and Publishing Activity of the Orenburg Scientific Archival Commission (End of XIX - Early XX Century)"], *Вестник Оренбургского Государственного Педагогического Университета*, Vol. 12, No. 4 (2014): 120 (URL: http://vestospu.ru/archive/2014/articles/14_12_2014.pdf).

556. Along with Lubichankovskii, "Оренбургской ученой архивной комиссии," see also E.R. Khasanov, *Orenburgskaya uchenaya archivnaya komissiya: vozniknovenie i rabota nauchnogo obshchestva na Yuzhnom Urale (konets XIX - nachalo XX. vv.)* [*The Orenburg Scientific Archival Commission: The Appearance and Operation of the Scientific Community in the South Urals*] (Ufa: Sterlitamak, 1998) for a general survey of the Commission's work. Among their many other contributions, U.T. Akhmetova notes that the "Orenburg Scientific archival commission, [which was] created and worked during the period 1887–1918 in Orenburg, played a great role in development of archeological science in Kazakhstan" ("Kazakh Archeology: History of Investigation and Today's Development," *Qazaqstan Tarihy*, 09 September 2013; URL: http://e-history.kz/en/contents/view/1378).

557. Lubichankovskii, "Orenburgskoi uchenoi archivnoi komissii," 121.

558. Ibid., 122.

559. Ibid., 124; cf. Elena I. Campbell, *The Muslim Question and Russian Imperial Governance* (Indiana University Press, 2014).

560. Lubichankovskii, "Orenburgskoi uchenoi archivnoi komissii," 122.

561. Ibid., 120.

562. Of particular note here would be A.J. Frank, *Muslim Religious Institutions in Imperial Russia: The Islamic World of Novouzensk District and the Kazakh Inner Horde, 1780–1910* (Leiden: E.J. Brill, 2001), p. 275.

563. With respect to the more immediate context, namely the debate with Chernavsky within the *Proceedings of the Orenburg Scientific Archival Commission*, this study introduces, for the first time in Western English-based scholarship, the work of both the Orenburg Scientific Archival Commission and, within it, Chernavsky.

564. A.I. Dobrosmyslov, "Zaboty imperatritsy Ekateriny II o prosveshchenii kirgizov," *Trudy Orenburgskoi Uchenoi Arkivnoi Komissii IX* (1902): 51–63. Note that the Kazakhs were called 'Kirgiz' (or sometimes 'Kirgiz-Kaisaks') by Tsarist Russian ethnographers and officials. I have left the term 'Kirgiz' when it occurs in quotations from Tsarist Russian sources, which should be understood in reference to the Kazakhs.
565. See Willard Sunderland, "Enlightened Colonization," in *Taming the Wild Field: Colonization and Empire on the Russian Steppe* (Ithaca and London: Cornell University Press, 2004), pp. 55–96; see also Ricarda Vulpius, "The Russian Empire's Civilizing Mission in the Eighteenth Century: A Comparative Perspective," in *Asiatic Russia: Imperial Power in Regional and International Contexts*, ed. Uyama Tomohiko (Routledge, 2012), pp. 13–31.
566. On Russification, see: Theodore R. Weeks, "Russification: Word and Practice, 1863–1914," *Proceedings of the American Philosophical Society*, Vol. 148, No. 4 (Dec 2004): 471–489; idem., *Nation and State in Late Imperial Russia: Nationalism and Russification on the Western Frontier, 1863–1914* (DeKalb, IL: Northern Illinois University Press, 1996); Anatolii Remnev, "Colonization and 'Russification' in the Imperial Geography of Asiatic Russia: from the Nineteenth to the Early Twentieth Centuries," in *Asiatic Russia*, pp. 102–128; and J.F. Hutchinson, "Russification," in *Late Imperial Russia, 1890–1917*, pp. 30–33.
567. See esp. Steven Sabol, *"The Touch of Civilization": Comparing American and Russian Internal Colonization* (Denver, CO: University of Colorado Press, 2017).
568. On this point, Chernavsky, in his later Rebuttal to Dobrosmyslov, cited two sources. In direct relation to Catherine II's policies in relation to the Kazakhs, he cited "M.A. Miropiev, *On the State of the Non-Christian Subjects [Inorodtsy] in Russia* (1901): 'Not far removed from being pagan shamanists,' we read on p. 375, 'the Kirgiz increasingly became Muslims under the initiative of our empress, Catherine II, who thought enthusiastically about Islam's spread among them and saw it as *a transitional stage from paganism to Christianity.*'" The other, a more general reference, was "A. Krymsky's essay, *Islam and its Future*, 1899: 'Some [experts] consider it quite possible and historically

natural that at some point Muslims will accept European civilization and join in the general family of enlightened nations. Thus, Cardinal Kherdenreter in his *History of the Church* allows himself to assert the following: 'in order to rid the wild tribes of fetishism and bring them to our high religion, we must first ease them in by using transition steps corresponding to the lower level of their culture and simplistic morality. The transition stage that leads to conversion from paganism to Christianity is Islam" (p. 110).—Interestingly, the idea of Islam being a transitional stage from paganism to Christianity, in the philosophical-evolutionary sense, was also expressed in the final conclusion by our philosopher V. Soloviev in his essay: "Mohammed, his Life and his Religious Teaching" (78)," citing A.E. Krymsky, *Musul'manstvo i ego budushchnost [Islam and Its Future]*, (Moscow: Knizhnoe delo Publishing House, 1899), p. 110. Applying Darwinian ideas to the history of religion, the idea was prominent across the European Christian world of the nineteenth and early twentieth centuries (see e.g. W.G. Mombasa, "Islam not a Stepping Stone to Christianity," *The Muslim World*, Vol. 1, No. 4 [1911]: 365–372).

569. See esp. James M. Edie, James P. Scanlan, and Mary-Barbara Zeldin, eds. *Russian Philosophy: Volume 1: The Beginnings of Russian Philosophy, the Slavophiles, the Westernizers* (Chicago: Quadrangle Books, 1969); Howard F. Stein, "Russian Nationalism and the Divided Soul of the Westernizers and Slavophiles," in *Ethos*, Vol. 4, No. 4 (1976): 403–438; Alexander Chubarov, "The 'Great Debate'," in *Fragile Empire: A History of Imperial Russia* (New York: Continuum, 1999), pp. 60–64; David Saunders, "The Emergence of the Russian Intelligentsia," in *Russia in the Age of Reaction and Reform, 1801–1881* (London and New York: Longman, 1992), pp. 148–172; David MacKenzie and Michael W. Curran, *A History of Russia, the Soviet Union, and Beyond*, 5th ed. (Belmont, CA: West/Wadsworth, 1999); and Mark Steinberg, "Lecture 11: The Birth of the Intelligentsia" and "Lecture 12: Westernizers: Vissarion Belenskii," in *A History of Russia: From Peter the Great to Gorbachev* (New York: Random House Audible, The Great Courses, 2003).

570. For the broader context of this issue, see esp. Campbell, "Dilemmas of Regulation and Rapprochement: The Problem of Muslim Religious Institutions," in *The Muslim Question*, pp. 106–125; cf. also Paul Werth, *The Tsar's Foreign Faiths: Toleration and the Fate of Religious Freedom in Imperial Russia* (Oxford University Press, 2014).
571. In relation to the Kazakhs, see esp. Virginia Martin, *Law and Custom in the Kazakh Steppe: The Kazakhs of the Middle Horde and Russian Colonialism in the Nineteenth Century* (Routledge, 2001); cf. also Robert D. Crews, "Nomads into Muslims," in *For Prophet and Tsar: Religion and Empire in Russia and Central Asia* (Harvard University Press, 2006), pp. 192–240.
572. See Robert P. Geraci, "The Il'minskii System under Siege," in *Window on the East: National and Imperial Identities in Late Tsarist Russia* (Ithaca and London: Cornell University Press, 2001), pp. 223–263; Wayne Dowler, *Classroom and Empire: The Politics of Schooling Russia's Eastern Nationalities, 1860–1917* (Montreal: McGill-Queen's University Press, 2001), and Agnes N. Kefeli, *Becoming Muslim in Russia: Conversion, Apostacy, and Literacy* (Ithaca and London: Cornell University Press, 2014).
573. See Robert Geraci, "'Going Abroad or Going to Russia?' Orthodox Missionaries in the Kazakh Steppe, 1881–1917," in *Of Religion and Empire: Missions, Conversion, and Tolerance in Tsarist Russia*, ed R. Geraci and M. Khodarkovsky (Ithaca, NY: Cornell University Press, 2001), pp. 274–310; Paul W. Werth, *At the Margins of Orthodoxy: Mission, Governance, and Confessional Politics in Russia's Volga-Kama Region, 1827–1905* (Ithaca, NY: Cornell University Press, 2002).
574. See esp. Werth, *At the Margins of Orthodoxy*.
575. See David Motadel, ed.
576. See esp. Aftandil S. Erkinov, *The Andijan Uprising of 1898 and Its Leader Dukchi-Ishan Described by Contemporary Poets* (Tokyo: University of Tokyo, 2009) and Campbell, *The Muslim Question*, pp. 91–99.
577. Campbell, *The Muslim Question*, p. 95.
578. J. F. Hutchinson, *Late Imperial Russia, 1890–1917* (London and New York: Longman, 1999), p. 30.
579. Chernavsky, p. 18.

580. A.I. Levshin, "Vera i Sueverie" ["Faith and Superstitious Beliefs"], in *Opisanie kirgiz-kazakhskikh ili kirgiz-kaisatskih ord i stepei* [*Description of the Kirghiz-Kazakh or Kirgiz-Kaisak Hordes and Steppes*] (St. Petersburg, 1832), pp. 52–67 (reprint edition with notes and commentary ed. M.K. Kozibaev, Almaty, KZ: Sanat, 1996, pp. 313–320); Ch. Valihanov, "Tenkri (Bog)" ["God"], "Musul'manstve v Stepii" ["On Islam in the Steppe"], and "Sledi Shamanstva u Kirgizov" ["Traces of Shamanism among the Kirghiz"], in *Chokan Valihanov: Izbrannie Proiizvedeniya*, ed. A.H. Margulana (Moscow: Nauka, 1986), pp. 226–233, 293–298, and 298–318 (original writings 1858–1865); E. Malov, "O tatarskikh mechetiakh v Rossii" ["On Tatar Mosques in Russia"], *Pravoslavnii sobesdnik* (Dec 1867): 285–320 and (Mar? 1868): 3–45; Sh. Ibragimov, "0 mullakh v kirgizskoi stepi ["On Mullahs in the Kirgiz Steppes"]," in *Materialy dlia statistiki Turkestanskogo kraia*, ed. N. A. Maev (St. Petersburg: Tipografiia K. V. Trubnikova, 1874), pp. 353–361; and N.I. Il'minskii, *Vospominaniia ob I.A. Altynsarine* [*Memories of I.A. Altinsarin*] (Kazan: V.M. Kliuchnikova, 1891).
581. Dobrosmyslov, "Concerns of the Empress Catherine II," p. 60.
582. Ibid., p. 60, n6.
583. Chernavsky, p. 122.
584. Chernavsky, p. 125, citing Kraft, suppl. 30th page, refer. No. 102.
585. Chernavsky, p. 125, n2, citing Kraft, suppl., refer. No. 78.
586. Dobrosmyslov, "Concerns of the Empress Catherine II," p. 62.
587. Chernavsky, Rebuttal, 8–6, n1.
588. H. Mami, "Tatarskaia Kargala in Russia's Eastern policies," in *Asiatic Russia*, p. 49, n87.
589. See E. Malov, "O tatarskikh mechetiakh v Rossii," *Pravoslavnii Sobesdnik* (Dec 1867), p. 295.
590. E. Malov, "O tatarskikh mechetiakh v Rossii," p. 295. Malov was preceded in his study by Antonii Amfiteatrov, archbishop of Kazan; his work was also paralleled by the Orenburg governor-general at the time, N.A. Kryzhanovskii (cf. Campbell, *The Muslim Question*, pp. 120–121).
591. PSZ (*Polnoe sobranie zakonov Rossiiskoi imperii, C' 1649 Goda: Tom IX: 1733–1736* [*Complete Collection of Laws of the Russian Empire: From the Year 1649: Vol IX (1733–1736)*, (Ego Imperatorskago Velichestva Kantselyarii, 1830), No. 6890, pp. 741–745.

592. See esp. Alton S. Donnelly, *The Russian Conquest of Bashkiria, 1552–1740* (New Haven and London: Yale University Press, 1968).
593. A.I. Dobrosmyslov, "Bashkirskii Bunt v 1735, 1736 i 1737 godi," *Trudy Orenburgskoi Uchenoi Arkhivnooi Kommissii*, No. 8 (Orenburg: 1900).
594. Chernavsky, Rebuttal, 8–19.
595. Malov, "O tatarskikh mechetiakh v Rossii," pp. 311–312.
596. Aelita Miniyanova, "Pedagogical Innovations and the Reinvention of 'Old' Pedagogy in Muslim Schools in Russia," in *Muslim Education in the 21st Century: Asian perspectives*, ed. Sa'eda Buang and Phyllis Ghim-Lian Chew (Routledge, 2014), p. 181, citing M.N. Farhshatov, *Public Education in Bashkirya (1860–1890)* (Moscow: Science, 1994).
597. PSZ, Vol. XII (1744–1748), No. 8893, pp. 39–41.
598. Cf. Gulmira Sultangalieva, "The Russian Empire and the Intermediary Role of Tatars in Kazakhstan: The Politics of Cooperation and Rejection," in *Asiatic Russia*, p. 54; cf. p. 72, n11, citing Petr Rychkov, *Istroriya Orenburgskaya* (Orenburg, 1896), p. 12, and A.I. Dobrosmyslov, *Turgaiskaia oblast': Istoricheskii ocherk* (Orenburg, 1898), 220.
599. Donnelly, *The Russian Conquest of Bashkiria, 1552–1740*, p. 44, citing *Vremennik Imperatorskago moskovskago obshchestva istorii I drevnostei rossiishikh*, kn. XIII, "Smes'" (bumagi tevkeleva), p. 15.
600. Donnelly, *The Russian Conquest of Bashkiria*, p. 41.
601. Dobrosmyslov had elsewhere, in another source treating different aspects of Chernavsky's work, criticized him for an alleged discrepancy in dating the Russian-Kazakh treaties 1738 instead of 1731, to which Chernavsky in his rebuttal responded, demonstrating an impressive grasp on the details of that history beyond not only Dobrosmyslov, but many other historians, past and present, who reference these events. Chernavsky thus answers Dobrosmyslov's criticism, saying: "on page 45 we literally attribute the beginning of the Kirgiz allegiance to 1731. That is, when on February 19, a response charter from the empress, Anna Ioannovna, in which she consented to accept the Kirgiz into sovereign allegiance, was sent with the Kirgiz ambassadors to the famous Khan Abul-Khair; and also when, at the same time, a mission headed by Murza Mehmet Tevkelev, an interpreter

from the Council of Foreign Affairs, was sent to the Horde. He succeeded, in the same 1731, to swear-in Khan Abul-Khair, and then, with the Khan's assistance, to swear-in both Khan Shemayk of the Middle Horde and the Karakalpak Khan. However, it was merely a provisional oath – although it established the act of allegiance to Russia, it was not considered official by the Russian government; which is why the government requested a new oath of allegiance for a final and official acceptance of the Kirgiz people into the "true allegiance confirmed by an oath" in a solemn ceremony commensurate with the importance of such an act. This was consequently followed through by the Kirgiz of the Small Horde—through Khan Abul-Khair in August of 1738, by the Kirgiz of the Middle Horde—through Khan Abulmamet in August of 1742, and by the Karakalpaks in 1742, respectively. As such, we briefly presented a history of acceptance of Russian citizenship by the Kirgiz in accordance with the true state of things and in line with the contemporary historian I.I. Rychkov, not in the least persuaded by the opposing views of Mr. Dobrosmyslov" (Chernavsky, *Rebuttal*, 6–7).

602. I.I. Kraft, *Shornik Uzakonenij o Kirgizah Stepnyh oblastei* [*Collection of Laws about the Kirgiz Steppe Regions*] (Orenburg: P.N. Zhariova, 1898), appendix, p. 31.
603. Dobrosmyslov, "Concerns of the Empress Catherine II," p. 53 (italics added).
604. Ibid., p. 63 (italics added).
605. Chernavsky cites here: "P.C.Z., 1765, No. 12437: comp. issue 1, p. 55, fn."
606. Chernavsky cites here: "Issue 1, p. 61, fn. 1," referring it would seem to the volume 1 of the *Proceedings of the Orenburg Scientific Archival Commission*, which was dedicated to the topic of the "Decrees of the Orenburg Military Governors of Empress Catherine II (1764) and the Emperor Paul I (1797–1800)."
607. Chernavsky, Rebuttal, 8–9 & 8–10; cf. also in the main text above that in a "1747 decree, the Council of Foreign Affairs had forbidden marriages between Kirgiz people and Muslims – Baskirs and Tatars from Orenburg, as well as Kazan."
608. Sultangalieva, "The Russian Empire and the Intermediary Role of Tatars in Kazakhstan," p. 54. Chernavsky points to what he considers to be the decisive turning point in Tsarist policy on

this matter, noting that: "In 1859, Orenburg general-governor A.A. Katenin visited the Kirgiz steppe of the Orenburg agency. He made inquiries among the Kirgiz and found out that despite their nomadic lifestyle, they did not shun education – receiving it through the neighborhood Mullahs, or Mohammedan schools in Bukhara or the Orenburg madrasas. Katenin then submitted a project proposal for the establishment of Russian schools for the Kirgiz in the four fortifications of the steppe. This project was approved by a High Decree in the Committee of Ministers on February 9, 1860 (P.S.Z. No. 35158). Katenin expressly asserted in his presentation that 'the education provided in the Mohammedan schools is focused on teaching the intricacies of Mohammedan laws; and the more a Mohammedan knows about the spirit of his religion, the more likely he is to develop an ignorant fanaticism and to despise and hate all non-Muslims, all of which interferes with the successful development of good citizenship and is otherwise dangerous in countries with Christian values.' According to Katenin, in order to counteract the harmful effects on the Kirgiz not yet infected by the Mohammedan fanaticism by means of education received by the children in the Mohammedan schools and through Mullahs, and at the same time spread the Russian influence in the Kirgiz Steppe, it was necessary to establish our governmental schools – to teach young Kirgiz the Russian literacy without the undesirable moral foundations. To read more about these schools, please *see* A.V. Vasiliev's 'Histor. Essay about Russian Education in the Turgai Region and its Current Status', 1896." (8–17, n2) This decisive moment would shape the views of Sh. Ualihanuhli and I. Altinsarin in the coming decades.

609. Dobrosmyslov, "Concerns of the Empress Catherine II," p. 62.
610. Ibid., p. 60.
611. According to Chernavsky, Dobrosmyslov "alleges that Bakhmetev had held both governorship positions – military and civilian – during 1797–1802. Such an absurd statement is quite inexcusable for Mr. Dobrosmyslov, who touts himself as the Orenburg-Turgai region's historian: as many as three civilian governors served consecutively within that time – Duke I.M. Barataev, former vice-governor, I.O. Kurisa and Glazenan." Rebuttal, 8–1.

612. Dobrosmyslov, "Concerns of the Empress Catherine II," p. 61.
613. Chernavsky, Rebuttal, 8–7 & 8–8.
614. Ibid., 8–3, 8–5, 8–7, 8–9, 8–10, 8–12.
615. Chernavsky, Orenburg Eparchy, p. 124, n1.
616. Ibid., p. 124.
617. A.I. Dobrosmyslov, *Turgaiskaya Oblast: Istoricheskii Ocherk*, pp. 220–221, fn144.
618. Levshin, *Opisanie kirgiz-kazakhskikh ili kirgiz-kaisatskih ord i stepei*, pp. 54–55.
619. Dobrosmyslov, "Concerns of the Empress Catherine II," p. 61. (? Check ref) M. Khodarkovsky cites Dobrosmyslov as his sole authority on this point in his study of *Russia's Steppe Frontier: The Making of a Colonial Empire, 1500–1800* (Bloomington and Indianapolis: Indiana University Press, 2002), p. 242, n102.
620. A.I. Dobrosmyslov, *Turgaiskaya Oblast: Istoricheskii Ocherk*, pp. 220–221, fn144. Emphasis added.
621. Chernavsky, Rebuttal, 8–10.
622. 8–13, 8–14; cf. Dukhovskoi; cf. Islam as 'alien'.
623. See A. Hourani, "Islam and the Philosophers of History," *Middle Eastern Studies*, Vol. 3, No. 3 (Apr 1967): 206–225 and 250ff; cf. also S.R. Arjana, *Muslims in the Western Imagination* (Oxford University Press, 2015) and R. Armour, "Islam in the Eyes of the Medieval West" and "Modern Views of Islam," in *Islam, Christianity, and the West: A Troubled History* (Maryknoll, NY: Orbis Books, 2004), pp. 50–60 and 133–146.
624. Ibid., 8–10, n3, citing N.M. Yadrintsev, *Sibirskie inorodtsi* [*Siberian peoples*], (St. Petersburg, 1891), pp. 211–218.
625. Chernavsky, Rebuttal, 8–19.
626. A.I. Dobrosmyslov, *Известия Общества археологии, истории и этнографии при Императорском Казанском университете* [*News of the Society of Archeology, History and Ethnography at the Imperial University of Kazan*], Vol. XVII, No. 2–3 (1901). (This critique was "re-published (without reference to the original publication) in the *Orenburg List* (Sep 1901)."
627. V.C. Bozhe, ed., *Letopistsi zemli Uralskoi: Materiali k istorii Chelyanbinskogo kraevedeniya* (Chelyabinsk: Tsenter istorikokul'turnogo naslediya, 1997) (excerpt taken from: http://chel-history.ru/pages-view-67.html).
628. Ibid.

629. Ibid.
630. "Добросмыслов Александр Иванович (1854 — дата смерти неизв.), краевед [Dobrosmyslov Alexander Ivanovich (1854 - date of death unknown), local historian]." (URL: http://myaktobe.kz/archives/38809).
631. "Чернавский Николай Михайлович [Chernavskaya Nikolai Mikhailovich]," Древо: Открытая Православная Энциклопедия (URL: http://drevo-info.ru/articles/23906.html).
632. Ibid.
633. Campbell, *The Muslim Question*, p. 223.
634. Robert P. Geraci, *Window on the East: National and Imperial Identities in Late Tsarist Russia* (Ithaca and London: Cornell University Press, 2001), p. 248.
635. Cf. Howard F. Stein, "Russian Nationalism and the Divided Soul of the Westernizers and Slavophiles," *Ethos*, Vol. 4, No. 4 (Winter, 1976): 403–438, citing from 421.
636. See Nicholas Riasanovsky, *Nicholas I and Official Nationality in Russia, 1825–1855* (Berkeley: University of California Press, 1967).
637. Cf. esp. Robert D. Crews, *For Prophet and Tsar*, p. 200: "Alexander I continued Catherine's policy of treating Islam as a means to transform Kazakhs into imperial subjects." More generally, Alexander I's reign was marked by seemingly contradictory positions, policies, and trends along the scale from 'liberal' to 'conservative' (see esp. A.M. Martin, *Romantics, Reformers, Reactionaries: Russian Conservative Thought and Politics in the Reign of Alexander I*, DeKalb, IL: Northern Illinois University Press, 1997).
638. Robert D. Crews, "Civilization in the City: Architecture, Urbanism, and the Colonization of Tashkent," in *Architectures of Russian Identity, 1500 to the Present*, ed. James Cracraft and Daniel Rowland (Cornell University Press, 2003), p. 120.
639. Alton S. Donnelly, *The Russian Conquest of Bashkiria, 1552–1740* (New Haven and London: Yale University Press, 1968), p. 180.
640. David MacKenzie, *The Lion of Tashkent: The Career of General M.G. Cherniaev* (University of Georgia Press, 1974), p. 218, n37, referencing A.I. Dobrosmyslov, "Turkestanskaia publichnaia biblioteka i muzei," *Sredniaia Aziia* (Feb. 1910). Mackenzie states that: "This dishonest article failed to mention that Cherniaev had abolished the old Public Library."

641. A.J. Frank, "Islamic Transformation on The Kazakh Steppe, 1742–1917: Toward an Islamic History of Kazakhstan under Russian Rule," in *The Construction and Deconstruction of National Histories in Slavic Eurasia*, ed. Tadayuki Hayashi (Sapporo: Slavic Research Centre, Hokkaido University, 2003), 261–289 p. 270.
642. Chernavsky, Rebuttal, 8–7.
643. Frank, *Muslim Religious Institutions in Imperial Russia*, p. 75.
644. See esp. Lewis R. Rambo and Charles E. Farhadian, "Introduction," Marc D. Baer, "History and Religious Conversion," Robert L. Montgomery, "Conversion and the Historic Spread of Religions," Henri Gooren, "Anthropology of Religious Conversion," Heinz Streib, "Deconversion," and Marcia Hermansen, "Conversion to Islam in Theological and Historical Perspectives," in *Oxford Handbook of Religious Conversion*, ed. L.R. Rambo and C.E. Farhadian (Oxford University Press, 2014), pp. 632-666.
645. Clifford Geertz, *Islam Observed: Religious Development in Morocco and Indonesia* (University of Chicago Press, 1971). See the Conclusion to this volume for clarification of 'the cultural turn' within twentieth-century historiography.
646. Based on Svat Soucek, *A History of Inner Asia*, Appendix 1.
647. Fom 874 as per McEvedy, *The Penguin Atlas of Medieval History* (New York: Penguin, 1992), p. 48, who includes the Tahirids, 822–873.
648. 999–1140, as per R.L. Canfield, ed., *Turko-Persia in Historical Perspective* (Cambridge University Press, [1991] 2002).
649. Based on *Yuri Bregel*, "The Role of Central Asia in the History of the Muslim East."

Bibliography: Primary Sources

Arabic, Persian-Farsi, Turkic
al-Qalqashandī, Shihāb al-Dīn Aḥmad ibn ʿAlī [شهاب الدين أحمد بن علي بن أحمد القلقشندي].
   Ṣubḥ al-Aʿshá fī Ṣināʿat al-Inshāʾ [*Daybreak for the Night-Blind*]. 14 Volumes.
   Cairo: al-Maṭbaʿah al-Amīrīyah, 1913–1919.
Ibrāhīm, ʿAbd ur-Reshīd. *Alem-i Islam ve Japonyada Intişar-i Islamiyet* [*The World of Islam and the Spread of Islam in Japan*]. Volume 1. Istanbul: Ahmed Saki Bey Matbaasi, 1328 [1911].
İbrahim, Abdürreşid. *Yirminci Asrın Başlarında Âlem-i İslam ve Japonya'da İslamiyet'in Yayılması* [*The Islamic World and the Spread of Islam at the Beginning of the Twentieth Century*]. Translated by Mehmed Paksu. İstanbul: Nesil Yayinlari, [1909–10] 2012.
Isfahani, Fazlullah B. Ruzbihan. *Mihman'nama-yi Bukhara* [*Memoir of a Bukharan Guest*] (1508–9). Translated and edited by M. Sotudeh Tehran, 1962. Russian translation: *Zapiski Buharskogo Gostya*. Foreword and notes by R. P. Dzhalilova. Moscow, 1976.
Ferdosi, Abolghasem. *Shahname* [شاهنامه]. Edited by Abdol Hossein Noushin and Evgenii Eduardovich Bertels. Moscow, Soviet Union: Academy of Sciences of the Soviet Union, 1960–71.
شاهنامهٔ فردوسی (ویراست سنجشگرانه)، نه پوشینه. زیرِ نگر یوگنی ا. برتلس، عبدالحسين نوشين و ... . مسکو: اکادمی علوم اتحاد شوروی، ۷۱–.۱۹۶
Quranic Arabic Corpus. Leeds: Language Research Group, University of Leeds, 2009–2017. (URL: https://corpus.quran.com/).

English & Other European Sources (incl. Translations)

al-Kashgari, Mahmud. *Compendium of the Turkic Dialects (Dīwān Luyāt at-Turk)*. Edited and translated by Robert Dankoff, in collaboration with James Kelly. 3 Volumes. Cambridge, MA: Harvard University Press, 1982.

Augustine, Saint. "Feast of the Nativity: Sermon 196" and "New Year's Day: Sermon 198." In *The Fathers of the Church: A New Translation: Saint Augustine: Sermons on the Liturgical Seasons*. Translated by Sister M.S. Muldowney, 45–59. New York: Fathers of the Church, Inc., 1959.

Blackstone, William. *Commentaries on the Laws of England*. Book the Second [Volume 2]. Third Edition. Oxford: The Clarendon Press, MDCCLXVIII [1768].

Cunow, Heinrich. *Ursprung der Religion und des Gottesglaubens* [*Origin of Religion and the Faith of God*]. Buchhandlung Vorwärts, 1919.

d'Ohsson, Ignatius Mouradgea. *Tableau Général De L'empire Othoman: L'état Actuel De L'empire Othoman* [*General Table of the Ottoman Empire: The Current State of the Ottoman Empire*]. Paris, Imp. de monsieur [Firmin Didot], 1787–1820.

Dughlat, Mirza Muhammad Haidar. *Tarikh-i-Rashidi: A History of the Moghuls of Central Asia*. Translated by E. Denison Ross. Edited by N. Elias. London: Sampson Low, Marston and Company, Ltd., 1895.

Engels, Friedrich. "Ludwig Feuerbach und der Ausgang der klassischen deutschen Philosophie." In *Karl Marx/Friedrich Engels – Werke*, 283–291. Berlin: Dietz Verlag, 1975.

Ferdowsi, Abul-Qâsem. *Shahnameh* [*Book of Shahs*] (*Critical Edition*). Edited by Eugene A. Bertels, Abdolhossein Noushin, et al. Moscow: Academy of Sciences of the Soviet Union, 1960–71.

Goldziher, Ignác. "Veneration of Saints in Islam." In *Muslim Studies*. Volume 2. Edited by S. M. Stern. Translated from German by C. R. Barber and S. M. Stern, 255–341. London: Allen and Unwin, [1889–1890] 1971.

Hâjib, Yûsuf Khâss. *Wisdom of Royal Glory (Kutadgu Bilig): A Turko-Islamic Mirror for Princes*. Translated and edited by Robert Dankoff. Chicago: University of Chicago Press, [1069] 1983.

———. *Kutadgu Bilig Metni* [*The Text of the Kutadgu Bilig*]. Edited by Turkanitlari. (URL: https://kutadgubilig.appspot.com/liii.html).

Krasinski, Count Valerian. *A Treatise on Relics by John Calvin, Translated from the French Original, With An Introductory Dissertation On the Miraculous Images, as Well as Other Superstitions, of the Roman Catholic and Russo-Greek Churches*. Second Edition. Edinburgh: Johnstone, Hunter & Co., 1870.

Kunanbaiuhli, Abai. *Book of Words*. Leneshmidt Translations Resource Library, (URL: http://www.leneshmidt-translations.com/book_of_words_abai_kunanbaev_english/32.htm). Original Kazakh work from late 19th, early 20th century.

BIBLIOGRAPHY: PRIMARY SOURCES   349

Marx, Karl and Frederick Engels. *On Religion*. Mineola and New York: Dover Publications, 2008 (Translated from the Russian version published by Moscow: Foreign Languages Publishing House, 1957).

Middleton, Conyers. *A Letter from Rome Showing the Exact Conformity between Popery and Paganism: Or, the Religion of the Present Romans to Be Derived Entirely from That of Their Heathen Ancestors*. Third Edition. London, [1729] 1733.

Migne, J.P., editor. *Patrologiae Cursus Completus: Tomus XXXVIII: S. Augustini*. Parisiis: Venit Apud Editorum, 1845.

Nestor, Saint. *The Russian Primary Chronicle*. Translated and edited by Samuel Hazzard Cross and Olgerd P. Sherbowitz-Wetzor. Cambridge, MA: Harvard University Press, [c. 1118; 1930] 1953.

Nöldeke, Theodor. *Sketches from Eastern History*. Translated by John Sutherland Black. London and Edinburgh: Adam and Charles Black, 1892.

Pocockio, Edvardo. *Specimen historiae Arabum*. Oxford: Clarendon Press, 1806.

Priestley, Joseph. *An History of the Corruptions of Christianity*. Volume 1. Third Edition. Boston: William Spotswood, [1782] 1797.

Ralston, William R.S. *Russian Folk-Tales*. London: Smith, Elder, & Co., 1873.

Reynolds, John Myrdhin. *Yungdrung Bon—The Eternal Tradition: The Ancient Pre-Buddhist Religion of Central Asia and Tibet: Its History, Teachings, and Literature*. Freehold, NJ: Bompo Translation Project, 1991.

Rubruck, William of. *The Mission of Friar William of Rubruck: His Journey to the Court of the Great Khan Möngke, 1253–1255*. Translated by Peter Jackson. Introduction, notes and appendices by Peter Jackson with David Morgan. London: Hakluyt Society, 1990.

Snesarev, G.P. *Survivals of Pre-Islamic Beliefs and Rituals among the Khorezm Uzbeks*. Translated by Reinhold Schletzer. Berlin: Schletzer, [1969] 2003.

Stalin, Joseph. *Marxism and the National Question*. Scottsdale, AZ: Prism Key Press, [1913] 2013.

Tolstov, Sergei P. *Following the Tracks of Ancient Khorezmian Civilization*. Tashkent: UNESCO Tashkent Office, [1948] 2005.

Toynbee, Arnold J. *A Study of History*. Abridgement by D.C. Somervell. London, New York and Toronto: Oxford University Press, 1960.

Tylor, Edward Burnett. *Researches into the Early History of Mankind and the Development of Civilization*. Boston: Estes & Lauriat, [1865] 1878.

———. "On the Survival of Savage Thought in Modern Civilization." In *Notices of the Proceedings at the Meetings of the Members of the Royal Institution, with Abstracts of the Discourses. Volume V (1866–1869)*, 522–535. London: William Clowes & Sons, 1869.

———. *Primitive Culture: Researches into the Development of Mythology, Philosophy, Religion, Language, Art, and Custom*. Sixth Edition. London: John Murray, [1871] 1920.

Valikhanof, Capt., M. Veniukof and Other Russian Travellers. *The Russians in Central Asia.* Translated by John and Robert Michell. London: Edward Stanford, 1865.

Vernadsky, George. *A History of Russia.* New Revised Edition. New Haven: Yale University Press, 1929–1944.

Firdausi. *The Shahnama of Firdausi.* Translated and edited by Arthur George Warner and Edmond Warner. 11 Volumes. London: Kegan Paul Trench, Trubner & Co., 1905–10.

Westermarck, Edvard. *Ritual and Belief in Morocco.* Volume II. London: Macmillan and Co., 1926.

———. *Pagan Survivals in Mohammedan Civilisation: Lectures on the Traces of Pagan Beliefs, Customs, Folklore, Practises and Rituals Surviving in the Popular Religion and Magic of Islamic Peoples.* London: Macmillan and Co., 1933.

Whately, Richard. *On the Origin of Civilization.* London: Nisbet, 1854.

White, Joseph. *Sermons Preached before the University of Oxford, in the Year 1784, at the Lecture Founded by the Rev. John Bampton.* First American Edition. Boston: William Greenough, [1785] 1793.

Winstedt, R.O. *Shaman, Saiva and Sufi: A Study of the Evolution of Malay Magic.* London: Constable and Co., Ltd., 1925.

Witsen, Nicolaas. *Noord en Oost Tartarye* [*North and East Tartarye*]. Second Edition. Amsterdam: François Halma [1692] 1705.

Yu, Han (韓愈), "論佛骨表 /Memorial on the Bones of the Buddha." Translated by Geoff Humble. Unpublished paper, originally dated to 819 CE.

Kazakh

(Aknazarov) Ақназаров, Х.З. *Ислам діні және оның реакциялық мәні* [*The Religion of Islam and Its Reactionary Essence*]. Алматы: Қазақстан, 1964.

———. *Ислам діні және өмір шындығы* [*The Religion of Islam and the Truth of Life*]. Алматы: Қазақстан, 1977.

———. *Қазақстандағы Ислам дінінің таралу ерекшеліктері* [*Unique Aspects of the Spread of Islam in Kazakhstan*]. Алматы: Білім қоғамы, 1986.

(Begaliev) Бегалиев (Бегалиұлы), Ғали. *Ислам Діні Қалай Құрылды* [*How the Religion of Islam was Founded*]. Қызыл-Орда: Государственное Издательство КССР [State Publishing House of the KSSR], 1928.

(Duisenbin) Дүисенбин, Ж. *Ислам діні және оның қазіргі жайы туралы* [*About the Religion of Islam and Its Current Standing*]. Алматы: Қазақ Мемлекет Баспасы, 1961.

(Ibragimov) Ибрагимов, Ғ. Ғ. Ибрагимов, *Дінге қарсы I-басқыш үйірмелер үшін программа-конспект* [*Programmatic Summary for 1st-Stage Anti-Religious Groups*]. Қызыл Орда, 1928.

———. *Ислам діні – империализм құралы.* Алматы, 1939.

(Kengesbaev) Кеңесбаев, І.К., бас редактор. *Қазақ тілінің түсіндірме сөздігі* [*Explanatory Dictionary of the Kazakh Language*]. Алматы: Қазақ ССР Ғілім Академиясының баспасы, 1959.

Kirotip, Chiengaliuhli and Galimzhan Alibek Sergali. *Dinge Qarsi Oqu Kitabi: auildi belsendiler men dinsizder uirmeleri ushin* [*A Book of Anti-Religious Studies: For Rural Activists and Atheist Groups*]. Алматы, 1934 (Published in Soviet Latin script).

(Kunanbaiuhli) Құнанбайұлы, Абай. *Абай: Шығармаларының екі томдық толық жинағы: Екінші том: Өлеңдер мен аудармалар, поэмалар, қарасөздер* [*Abai: A Complete Two-Volume Collection of His Writings: Vol 2: Songs and Translations, Poems, and Reflections/Words*]. Edited by Есенбай Дүйсенбайұлы, Ғұсман Жандыбаев. Алматы: Жазушы, [1855–1904] 2005.

(N.A.) *Дінге қарсы оқуды қалай ұйымдастыру керек* [*How Anti-Religious Studies Should be Organized*]. Алматы: Түрксиб, 1939.

Russian

(Abdulkadirov) Абдулкадыров, Ш. Д. *О некоторых особенностях борьбы с пережитками ислама в условиях современной чечено-ингушетии* [*Some Features of the Struggle against Vestiges of Islam among the Modern Chechen-Ingushetia*]. Дис. на соиск. учен. степ. канд. филос. Наук, КазГУ им. С. М. Кирова. Алма-Ата: [Б. и.], 1970.

(Abramzon) Абрамзон, С.М. *К характеристике шаманства в старом быту киргизов* [*On the Characterization of Shamanism in the Ancient Kirghiz Homeland*]. Москва: КСИЭ, 1958: Вып. 30. С. 143–150.

———. *Киргизы и их этногенетические и историко-культурные связи* [*The Kirghiz and Their Ethnogenetic and Historical-Cultural Ties*]. Наука, Ленингр. отд-ние, 1971.

(Azbukin) Азбукин, М. "Очерк Литературной Борьбы Представителей Христианства с Остатками Язычества в Русском Народе (XI-XIV века)" ["An Essay on the Literary Struggle of Representatives of Christianity with the Remnants of Paganism among the Russian People (XI–XIV cc.]." *Русский Филологический Вестник* [*Russian Philological Bulletin*], Volume 28, Number 3 (1892): 133–153; Volume 35, Number 2 (1896): 222–272; Volume 37, Numbers 1–2 (1897): 229–273; Volume 38, Numbers 3–4 (1897): 322–337; Volume 39, Numbers 1–2 (1898): 246–278.

(Alimov) Алимов, С.С. "Г.П. Снесарев и полевое изучение 'религиозно-бытовых пережитков' [G.P. Snesarev and the Plural Study of Religious and Domestic Surivals]." *Этнографическое обозрение* [*Ethnographic Review*], Volume 6 (2013): 69–88.

(Amanaliev) Аманалиев, Б. *Доисламские верования киргизов* [*Pre-Islamic Beliefs of Kyrgyz*]: *Религия, свободомыслие, атеизм*. Фрунзе, 1967.

(Amanturlin) Амантурлин, Ш.Б. *Пережитки анимизма, шаманства, ислама и атеистическая работа* [*The Survivals of Animism, Shamanism, Islam and Atheistic Work against Them*]. Алма-Ата: [б. и.], 1977.

———. *Предрассудки и суеверия, их преодоление (на материалах изучения сельского населения Казахстана)* [*Prejudices and Superstitions and How to Overcome Them (Materials for study of the Rural Population in Kazakhstan)*]. Алма-Ата: Казахстан, 1985.

(Andreev) Андреев, М.С. (M.S. Andreev). "Остатки языческих обычаев среди туземцев (Узбеки, Таджики) [Remains of Pagan Customs among Natives (Uzbeks, Tajiks)]." *Окраина*, No. 27 (1895): 305ff.

———. "По этнографии таджиков (некоторые сведения) [On Ethnography of the Tajiks (Some Information)]." in *Таджикистан* [*Tajikstan*], 151–177. Ташкент, 1925.

(Andreev) Андреев, М.С. и Половцов А.А. "Остатки прежнего общественного строя [Remnants of the Old Social Order]." In *Материалы по этнографии иранских племен Средней Азии: Ишкашим и Вахан* [*Materials on the Ethnography of the Iranian Tribes of Central Asia: Ishkashim and Vakhan*], 8–10. Санкт-Петербург, 1911.

(Asfendiarov) Асфендияров, Санжар Джафарович. *Материалы к изучению истории Востока. Ч.1: Причины возникновения ислама* [*Materials for the study of the history of the East. Part 1: Reasons for the Emergence of Islam*]. Самарканд, Ташкент: 1928.

———. *Исламның пайда болу себептері*. Самарқанд; Ташкент, 1930.

———. "Ислам и кочевое хозяйство" ["Islam and Nomadic Economy"]. *Атеист*, No. 58 (1930): 1–17.

(Bazarbaev) Базарбаев, Ш. *Современные проявления пережитков ислама и конкретные пути их преодоления (На материалах городов Южной Киргизии)* [*Modern Manifestations of the Survivals of Islam and Specific Ways of Overcoming Them (On materials of cities in South Kyrgyzstan)*]. Дис. на соиск. учен. степ. канд. филос. Наук, Ин-т философии и права. Фрунзе: [Б. и.], 1969.

(Basilov) Басилов, В.Н. "О пережитках тотемизма у туркмен [About the Survivals of Totemism among the Turkmen]." *Тр. Ин-та истории, археологии и этнографии АН Туркменской ССР*, 135–150. Т. VII. Сер. этнографическая. Ашхабад, 1963.

———. *Культ святых в исламе* [*The Cult of Saints in Islam*]. Mockva, 1970.

(Bayaliva) Баялива, Токтобюбю Джунушакунова. *Доисламские верования и их пережитки у киргизов* [*Pre-Islamic Beliefs and Their Vestiges among the Kyrgyz*] Фрунзе: Илим, 1972.

———. *Религиозные пережитки и киргизов и их преодоление* [*Vestiges of the Kirghiz and How to Overcome Them*]. Фрунзе [Frunze]: Илим [Ilim], 1981.

(Bronevskii) Броневский, В.Б. *Записки генерал-майора Броневского о киргиз-кайса-ках Средней Орды* [*Notes of Major-General Bronevsky on the Kirghiz-Kaisaks of the Middle Horde*]. *Отечественные Записки* [*Domestic Notes*], Volumes 41, 42, 43 (1830).

(Valikhanov) Валиханов, Чокан. "О Мусульманстве в Степи [On Muslim Faith on the Steppe]." In *Чокан Валиханов: Избранные произведения* [*Chokan Valikhanov: Selected Works*], 293–298. Москва: Наука, 1986.

―――. "Следы шаманства у киргизов [Vestiges of Shamanism among the Kirgiz]." In *Чокан Валиханов: Избранные произведения* [*Chokan Valikhanov: Selected Works*], 298–318. Москва: Наука, 1986.

(Dobrosmyslov) Добросмыслов А.И. *Тургайская область. Исторический очерк.* Оренбург, 1898.

―――. "Башкирский бунт в 1735, 1736 и 1737 гг. [Bashkir revolt in 1735, 1736 and 1737]." *Труды Оренбургской Ученой Архивноой Комиссии*, No. 8. Оренбург: 1900.

―――. *Известия Общества археологии, истории и этнографии при Императорском Казанском университете* [*News of the Society of Archeology, History and Ethnography at the Imperial University of Kazan*], Т. XVII, No. 2–3 (1901).

―――. "Заботы императрицы Екатерины II о просвещении киргизов [Concerns of Empress Catherine II about the Enlightenment of the Kirghiz]." *Труды Оренбургской Ученой Архивноой Комиссии, No. IX* (1902): 51–63.

―――. «Туркестанская публичная библиотека и музей», *Средняя Азия* [*Central Asia*], (Февраль [February], 1910).

(Dogurevich) Догуревич, Т.А. *Свет Азии: Распространение кристианства в Сибири* [*The Light of Asia: The Spread of Christianity in Siberia*]. Санкт-Петербург [St. Petersburg], 1897.

(Zhdanko) Жданко, Т.А. и М.А. Итина. "Сергей Павлович Толстов (1907–1976)." *Этнографическое обозрение*, No. 2 (1977): 3–14.

(Zelenin) Зеленин, Д.К. *Культ онгонов в Сибири. Пережитки тотемизма в идеологии сибирских народов* [*The Cult of the Ongons in Siberia: Remnants of Totemism in the Ideology of the Siberian Peoples*]. Ленинград, 1936.

(Zolotarev) Золотарев, А. *Пережитки тотемизма у народов Сибири* [*Survivals of Totemism among the Peoples of Siberia*]. Ленинград, 1934.

(Ibragimov) Ибрагимов, Ш. «О муллах в киргизской степи [On Mullahs in the Kirgiz Steppes]» // *Материалы для статистики Туркестанского края*. Ред. Н. А. Маев, 353–361. Санкт-Петербург: Типография К. В. Трубникова, 1874.

(Il'minskii) Ильминский, Н.И. *Воспоминания об И.А. Алтынсарине* [*Memories of I.A. Altinsarin*]. Казань: В.М. Клиучникова, 1891.

(Iliyasov) Ильясов, С. *Пережитки шаманизма у киргизов* [Vestiges of Shamanism among the Kirgiz]. Труды ИЯЛИ Киргизский филиал АН СССР. Вып.1. [Proceedings IYALI Kyrgyz Branch of the USSR Academy of Sciences]. Фрунзе, 1945.
(Knorozov) Кнорозов, Ю.В. "Мазар Шамун-Наби [The Shrine of the Prophet Shamun]." *Советская Этнография*, No. 2 (1949): 86–97.
(Korogli) Короглы, Х. *Огузский Героический Эпос* [*An Oghuz Heroic Epic*]. Москва: Наука, [1962] 1976.
(Kraft) Крафт, И.И. *Сборник Узаконений о Киргизах Степных областей* [*Collection of Laws about the Kirgiz Steppe Regions*]. Оренбург: П.Н. Жариова, 1898.
(Levshin) Левшин, А.И. "Вера и Суеверие [Faith and Superstition]." In *Описание Киргиз-Кайсакских, или Киргиз-Казахстанской'их орд и степей* [*Description of Kirghiz-Kaisak, or Kirghiz-Kazakhstani Hordes and Steppes*], 313–320. Алматы: Санат [Almaty, KZ: Sanat], [1832] 1996.
(Lenin) Ленин, Владимир Ильич. "Социализм и религия [Socialism and Religion]" (1905). In *Полное Собрание Сочинений* [*Complete Collection of Writings*]. Т. [Volume] 12. Москва: Издательство Политической Литературы, 1968.
———. "Об Отношении Рабочей Партии к Религии [On the Attitude of the Labor Party towards Religion]" (1909). In *Полное Собрание Сочинений* [*Complete Collection of Writings*], Т. [Volume] 17. Москва: Издательство Политической Литературы, 1968.
(Lunacharskii) Луначарский, Анатолий В. *Введение в историю религии* [*Introduction to the History of Religion*]. Москва: Директ Медиа [Moscow: Direct Media], [1923] 2014.
(Makatov) Макатов, И. *Кулʼт святых – пережиток прошлого* [*The Cult of Saints – Relic of the Past*]. Махачкала: Дагкнигоиздат, 1962.
(Malov) Малов, Евфимий А. "О Татарских Мечетях в России [About Tatar Mosques in Russia], Part One." *Православный собеседник* [*The Orthodox Conversationalist*], (Dec 1867): 285–320.
(Oleshchik) Олещук, Ф. *О реакционной роли мусульманского духовенства* (Алма-Ата, 1937) and *Мұсылман руханишыларыныӊ реакциясы ролі туралы*. Алматы, 1938.
(Potapov) Потапов, Л.П. "Пережитки культа медведя у алтайских турок" ["Remnants of the cult of the bear among the Altai Turks"]. *Этнограф-исследователь*, Nos. 2–3 (1928).
(Poyarkov) Поярков, Ф. "Из области киргизских верований [From the Realm of Kirgiz Beliefs]." *Этнографическое обозрение* [*Ethnographic Review*] (Oct–Dec 1891): 21–43.
(PSZ) ПСЗ (*Полное собрание законов Российской империи, С' 1649 Goda: Tom IX: 1733–1736*) [*Complete Collection of Laws of the Russian Empire: From the*

Year 1649: Vol. X (1733–1736)]. No. 6890, 741–745. Эго императорского величества канцелярии, 1830.

———. Том XII: 1744–48, No. 6890, 39–41. Эго императорского величества канцелярии, 1830.

(Richkov) Рычков, Николай Петрович. *Дневные записки путешествия капитана Николая Рычкова в киргиз-кайсацкой степи в 1771 году* [*Daily Travel Notes of Captain Nikolai Ruchkov in the Kirghiz-Kaisakh steppe, in 1771*]. St. Petersburg: Imp. Akademia Nauk, 1772.

(Richkov) Рычков, Петр. *Истрория Оренбургская* [*History of Orenburg*]. Оренбург, 1896.

(Sedelnikov) Седельников, А. Н. "Распределение Населения Киргизкаго края по Территории, его этннографический состав, быть и культура [Distribution of the Population of the Kirghiz Region in the Territory, its ethnographic composition, and culture]." In *Россия. Полное Географическое Описание Нашего Отечества: Настольная и дорожная книга для русских людей: Томъ Восемнадцатый: Киргизская Край* [*Russia: Full Geographic Description of Our Fatherland: A Desktop and Road Book for Russian People: Volume 18: The Kirgiz Region*]. Отредактировано В. П. Семенова, 173–222. Санкт Петербург, 1903.

(Seitzhanov) Сейтжанов, Т. *Формы и методы с пережитками ислама в условиях современной Каракалпакии* [*Forms and Methods of the Vestiges of Islam in Modern Karakalpakstan*], Дис. на соиск. учен. степ. канд. филос. Наук, Науч. рук.: Ж. Т. Туленов, КазГУ им.С.М.Кирова. Алма-Ата: [Б. и.], 1970.

(Smirnov) Смирнов, С.И. *Древне-русский духовник: Изследование по истории церковнаго быта* [*Ancient Russian Confessor. An Investigation into the History of Church Life*]. Москва, 1913.

———. "Бабы Богомерзкиия [Women of God]." *Сборник статей, посвященных Василию Осиповичу Ключевскому* [*Collection of articles dedicated to Vasily Osipovich Klyuchevsky*]. Отредактировано Я.Л. Барсков (Moscow, 1909)

———. *Духовный Отец в Древней Восточной Церкви. История Духовничества на Востоке* [*Spiritual Father in the Ancient Eastern Church. History of Spirituality in the East*]. Sergiev Posad, 1906.

(Snesarev) Снесарев, Г.П. "О Некоторых Причинах Сохранения Религиознобитовых Пережитков у Узбеков Хорезма (по полевым материалам 1954–1956 гг.): Узбекского отряда Хорезмской археологоэтнографической экспедиции [On some reasons for the preservation of religious relics from the Uzbeks of Khorezm (on the field materials of 1954–1956): The Uzbek detachment of the Khorezm archaeological ethnographic expedition]." *Sovetskaia etnografiia*, No. 2 (1957).

———. *Реликты домусульманских верований и обрядов у узбеков Хорезма* [*Survivals of Pre-Islamic Beliefs and Rituals among the Khorezm Uzbeks*]. Moskva, 1969.

(Snesarev) Снесарев, Г.П. и В.Н. Басилов, редакторы. *Домусульманские верования и обряды в Средней Азии: Сборник статей* [*Pre-Muslim Beliefs and Rites in Central Asia: A Collection of Articles*]. Moscow, 1975.

(Stalin) Сталин, И.В. "Марксизм и национальный вопрос [Marxism and the National Question]" (1913). In *Сочинения* [*Treatises*], Т. [Volume] 2. Москва: ОГИЗ; Государственное издательство политической литературы, 1946.

(Sternberg) Стернберг, Л.И. *Первобытная религия в свете этнографии* [*Primitive Religion in the Light of Ethnography*]. Изд-во Ин-та народов Севера ЦИК СССР им. П.Г. Смидовича, 1936.

(Sultan-Galiev) Султан-Галиев, М. *Методы антирелигиозной пропаганды среди Мусульман* [*Methods of Anti-religious Propaganda among Muslims*]. Издание Редакционна-Издательского Отдела Наркомнаца [Edition of the Editorial and Publishing Department of the People's Commissariat of Nationalities], 1922. (Originally published in the journal *Жизнь национальностей* [*The Life of Nationalities*], No. 29, Issue 127 (14 Dec 1921) and No. 30, Issue 128 (23 Dec 1921).)

(Surapbergenov) Сурапбергенов, А.С. *Объективные и субъективные предпосылки возникновения ислама и его пережитки в современном Казахстане* [*Objective and Subjective Preconditions for the Emergence of Islam and Its Survivals in Modern Kazakhstan*]. Дис. на соиск. учен. степ. канд. филос. наук: 09.00.06, КазГУ им. С. М. Кирова. Алма-Ата: [Б. и.], 1973.

(Tokarev) Токарев, С.А. "Вклад русских ученых в мировую этнографическую науку [The Contribution of Russian Scientists to World Ethnographic Science]." *Очерки истории русской этнографии, фольклористики и антропологии* [*Essays on the History of Russian Ethnography, Folklore and Anthropology*], (Москва [Moscow]: Наука [Nauka], вып. [Issue] 1, 1956.

(Toleybaev) Толеубаев, Абдеш Ташкенович. *Реликты доисламских верований в семейной обрядности казахов: (XIX - нач. XX в.)* [*Relics of Pre-Islamic Beliefs in Kazakh Family Rituals*]. Алма-Ата : Гылым, 1991.

(Tolstov) Толстов, Сергей Павлович. "Религия Народов Средней Азии (The Religion of the Peoples of Central Asia)." In *Религиозные верования народов СССР: сборник этнографических материалов* [*Religious Beliefs of the Peoples of the USSR: A Collection of Ethnographic Materials*]. Т. [Vol] 1. Отредактировано V.К. Никольский и М.Г. Левин. Москва: Государственный музей народов СССР, Московский рабочий [Москва: Московский рабочий], 1931.

———. "Пережитки тотемизма и дуальной организации у туркмен" ["Remnants of Totemism and Dual Organization among the Turkmen"], *Проблемы истории докапиталистических обществ* [*Problems of the History of Pre-capitalist Societies*], Nos. 9–10 (1935): 3–41.

---. *По следам древнехорезмийской цивилизации* [*Following the Tracks of Ancient Khorezmian Civilization*]. Москва и Ленинград: АН СССР, 1948.
(Fisher) Фишеръ, Іоганнъ Эбергардъ [Fisher, Johann Eberhard]. *Сибирская исторія съ самаго открытія Сибири до завоеванія сей земли россійскимъ оружіемъ* [*Sibirische Geschichte...* // *Siberian history from the very discovery of Siberia to the conquest of this land by Russian weapons*]. Translated to Russian by В.И. Лебедев. При Императорской Академіи наукъ, [1768] 1774.
(Khitiri) Хитири, Лери Георгиевич. *Пережитки прошлого как общесоциологическая категория* [*Remnants of the Past as a General Sociological Category*]. Дис. канд. филос. Наук, Грузинский гос. ун-т; науч.рук. Лутидзе Б.И. Тбилиси, 1986.
(Yadrintsev) Ядринцев, Н.М. *Сибирские инородцы* [*Siberian peoples*]. Санкт-Петербург, 1891.
(Yastrebov) Ястребов, Матвей Никифорович. "Киргизские шаманы. Отрывок из записной книжки [Kyrgyz shamans. Excerpt from a Notebook]." *Москвитянин*, No. 8. (1851): 301–312.

Chinese
韓愈 / Han Yu."論佛骨表 /Memorial on the Bones of the Buddha"(819 CE). Translated by Geoff Humble (unpublished paper).

Bibliography: Secondary Sources

Abuseitova, Meruert. "The Spread of Islam in Kazakhstan from the Fifteenth to the Eighteenth Century." Translated from Russian by M.D. Olynyk. In *Kazakhstan: Religions and Society in the History of Central Eurasia*. Edited by Gian Luca Bonora, Niccolo Piancola and Paolo Sartori. Turin, London, Venice and New York: Umberto Allemandi & Co., 2010.
Adji, Murad. *Asia's Europa*. Translated by A. Kiselev. Moscow: Izdateltsva, 1996.
Ahmad, Rizwan. "Urdu in Devanagari: Shifting orthographic practices and Muslim identity in Delhi." *Language in Society*, Volume 40, Number 3 (June 2011): 259–284.
Ahmadi, Quasem, Fatemeh Lajevardi and Mohommad Reza Adli. "The Influence of Ancient Iranian Culture on Islamic Culture in the Abbasid Period." *Journal of Religious Studies*, Volume 15, Number 1 (Summer 2021): 1–24.
Ahmed, Shahab. *What Is Islam? The Importance of Being Islamic*. Princeton, NJ: Princeton University Press, 2015.
Akhmetova, U.T. "Kazakh Archeology: History of Investigation and Today's Development." *Qazaqstan Tarihy*, 09 September 2013 (URL: http://e-history.kz/en/contents/view/1378).

Ali, Hazem Hussein Abbas. "Casting Discord: An Unpublished Spell from the Egyptian National Library." In *Amulets and Talismans of the Middle East and North Africa in Contex: Transmission, Efficacy and Collections*. Edited by Marcela A. Garcia Probert and Petra M. Sijpesteijn, 107–125. Leiden and Boston: Brill Academic, 2022.

Alkhateeb, Firas. *Lost Islamic History: Reclaiming Muslim Civilization from the Past*. London: Hurst & Co., 2017.

Almond, Philip C. *Mystical Experience and Religious Doctrine: An Investigation of the Study of Mysticism in World Religions*. Berlin and Boston: De Gruyter, 2015.

Al-Rodhan, Nayef R.F. *Sustainable History and the Dignity of Man: A Philosophy of History and Civilizational Triumph*. Zürich, Switzerland and Berlin, Germany: LIT Verlag, 2009.

———, editor. *The Role of the Arab-Islamic World in the Rise of the West: Implications for Contemporary Trans-Cultural Relations*. Basingstoke, UK and New York: Palgrave Macmillan), 2012.

Anderson, David G. and Dmitry V. Arzyutov. "The Construction of Soviet Ethnography and 'The Peoples of Siberia.'" *History and Anthropology*, Volume 27, Number 2 (2016): 183–209.

Anooshahr, Ali. "Uzbeks and Kazakhs in Fazl Allah Khunji's *Mihmannamah-i Bukhara*." In *Turkestan and the Rise of Eurasian Empires: A Study of Politics and Invented Traditions*, 84–113. New York and Oxford: Oxford University Press, 2018.

Archbishop Vladimir of the Orthodox Diocese of Bishkek and All Central Asia. "Christianity and Islam in Central Asia." In *Islam and Central Asia: An Enduring Legacy or an Evolving Threat?* Edited by Roald Sagdeev and Susan Eisenhower, 95–115. Washington, DC: Center for Political and Strategic Studies, 2000.

Arjana, Sophia Rose. *Muslims in the Western Imagination*. Oxford University Press, 2015.

Armour, R. *Islam, Christianity, and the West: A Troubled History*. Maryknoll, NY: Orbis Books, 2004.

Asimov, M.S., and C.E. Bosworth, editors. *A History of Civilizations in Central Asia: Vol IV: The Age of Achievement: AD 750 to the End of the Fifteenth Century*. Paris: UNESCO Publishing, 1998.

Atwood, Christopher P. "Buddhism and Popular Ritual in Mongolian Religion: A Reexamination of the Fire Cult." *History of Religions*, Volume 36, Number 2 (November 1996): 112–139.

Auezova, Zifa-Alua. "Conceiving a People's History The 1920–1936 Discourse on the Kazakh Past." In *The Heritage of Soviet Oriental Studies*. Edited by Michael Kemper and Stephan Conermann, 241–261. London and New York: Routledge, 2010.

Aziz, Soumia. "(Review of) *Shamanism and Islam: Sufism, Healing Rituals and Spirits in the Muslim World*, by Thierry Zarcone and Angela Hobart." *Islamic Studies*, Volume 55, Number 3/4 (Autumn-Winter 2016): 345–346.

Baer, Marc David. "History and Religious Conversion." In *The Oxford Handbook of Religious Conversion*. Edited by Lewis R. Rambo and Charles E. Farhadian, 25–47. Oxford and New York: Oxford University Press, 2014.

Baird, Robert D. "Interpretative Categories and the History of Religions." *History and Theory*, Volume 8, Number 8: *On Method in the History of Religions* (1968): 17–30.

Baldick, Julian. *Animal and Shaman: Ancient Religions of Central Asia*. Washington Square, NY: New York University Press, 2000.

Balzer, Marjorie Mandelstam, editor. *Shamanic Worlds: Rituals and Lore of Siberia and Central Asia*. New York: M.E. Sharpe, 1997

Bashir, Shahzad. *Messianic Hopes and Mystical Visions: The Nūrbakhshīya between Medieval and Modern Islam*. Columbia, SC: University of South Carolina Press, 2003.

Batalden, Stephen K. "Printing the Bible in the Reign of Alexander I: Toward a Reinterpretation of the Imperial Russian Bible Society." In *Church, Nation and State in Russia and Ukraine*. Edited by Geoffrey A. Hosking. Basingstoke: Palgrave Macmillan, 1991.

Baum, Wilhelm, and Dietmar W. Winker. *The Church of the East: A Concise History*. London and New York: Routledge, 2003.

Beben, Daniel. "After the Eclipse: *Shaykh Khalīlullāh Badakhshānī and the Legacy of the Kubravīyah in Central Asia*." In *From the Khan's Oven: Studies on the History of Central Asian Religions in Honor of Devin Deweese*. Edited by Eren Tasar, Allen J. Frank and Jeff Eden, 181–211. Leiden and New York: Brill Academic, 2022.

Becker, Felicitas. "Islamic Reform and Historical Change in the Care of the Dead: Conflicts over Funerary Practice among Tanzanian Muslims." *Africa: Journal of the International African Institute*, Volume 79, Number 3 (2009): 416–434.

Bellah, Robert N. *Religion in Human Evolution: From the Paleolithic to the Axial Age*. Cambridge, MA: The Belknap Press of Harvard University Press, 2011.

Bennigsen, Alexandre. "The Brezhnev Era Prior to the Soviet Invasion of Afghanistan, 1964–80." In *Soviet Strategy and Islam*. Edited by A. Bennigsen, 35–56. Palgrave Macmillan, 1989.

Bentley, Jerry H. *Old World Encounters: Cross-Cultural Contacts and Exchanges in Pre-Modern Times*. Oxford and New York: Oxford University Press, 1993.

Berbercan, Mehmet Turgut. "Language and Culture Studies: Old Turkic Christian Texts." *Journal of Turkology*, Volume 2, Number 27 (December 2017): 85–100.

Bergemann, Patrick. *Judge Thy Neighbor: Denunciations in the Spanish Inquisition, Romanov Russia, and Nazi Germany*. New York: Columbia University Press, 2019.

Bethencourt, Francisco. *The Inquisition: A Global History 1478–1834*. Translated by Jean Birrell. Cambridge: Cambridge University Press, 2009.

Biard, Aurelie, and Marlene Laruelle. "'Tengrism' in Kyrgyzstan: In Search of New Religious and Political Legitimacy." In *Representing Power in Modern Inner Asia: Conventions, Alternatives and Oppositions*. Edited by I. Charleux, G. Delaplace, R. Hamayon and S. Pearce, 55–96. Bellingham, WA: Center for East Asian Studies, Western Washington University, 2010.

Bigonah, Hassan. "Nowruz in Tradition Transition." *IIOAB Journal*, Vol. 7, No. 3 (September 2016): 491–495.

Bissenova, Alima. "Building a Muslim Nation: The Role of the Central Mosque of Astana." In *Kazakhstan in the Making: Legitimacy, Symbols, and Social Changes*. Edited by Marlène Laruelle, 211–228. Contemporary Central Asia: Societies, Politics, and Cultures Series. Lanham, MD: Lexington Books, 2016.

Blanning, Tim. *The Romantic Revolution: A History*. New York, NY: Random House, 2010.

Bobrovnikov, Vladimir. "The Contribution of Oriental Scholarship to the Soviet Anti-Islamic Discourse: From the Militant Godless to the Knowledge Society." In *The Heritage of Soviet Oriental Studies*. Edited by Michael Kemper and Stephan Conermann, 66–85. London and New York: Routledge, 2011.

Bohak, Gideon. "Jewish Amulets, Magic Bowls, and Manuals in Aramaic and Hebrew." In *Guide to the Study of Ancient Magic*. Edited by David Frankfurter, 388–415. Leiden and Boston: Brill Academic, 2019.

Bonora, Gian Luca, Niccolò Pianciola and Paolo Sartori, editors. *Kazakhstan: Religions and Society in the History of Central Eurasia*. Turin: Umberto Allemandi & C., 2010.

Boyce, Mary. *A History of Zoroastrianism: Volume Two: Under the Achaemenids*. Leiden: Brill, 1982.

———. "NOWRUZ i. In the Pre-Islamic Period." *Encyclopædia Iranica*, online edition, 2016 (URL: http://www.iranicaonline.org/articles/nowruz-i).

Breisach, Ernst. *On the Future of History: The Postmodernist Challenge and Its Aftermath*. Chicago: University of Chicago Press, 2003.

Brenner, Louis. "Muslim Divination and the History of Religion in sub-Saharan Africa." *Insight and Artistry: A Cross-Cultural Study of Divination in Central and West Africa*. Edited by John Pemberton, 45–59. Washington, DC: Smithsonian, 2000.

Brow, Robert. *Religion: Origin & Ideas*. Downers Grove, IL: Inter-Varsity Press, 1966.

Bruno, Antonetta L. "The Posal between the Mudang and Buddhist: In-between and Bypassing." *Journal of Korean Religions* (Special Issue: *North Korea and Religion*), Volume 4, Number 2 (October 2013): 175–196.

Buba, Malami. "The Legacies of the Sokoto Caliphate in Contemporary Nigeria." *History Compass*, Volume 16, Number 8 (August 2018): 1–9.

Burkhanadin, Abdilkhakim. "The Battle of Atlah [Talas] and Its Importance in the History of Middle Sirdarya Basin." *Habarshi: Journal of Philosophy, Culture and Political Science*, Volume 65, Number 3 (2018): 118–128.

Burton, A. "Trade." In *History of Civilizations of Central Asia*, Vol. 5, *Development in Contrast: From the Sixteenth to the Mid-Nineteenth Centuries*. Edited by Chahryar Adle, Irfan Habib and Karl M. Baipakov (Paris: UNESCO, 2004.

Bury, J.B. "The Doctrine of Degeneration: The Ancients and Moderns." In *The Idea of Progress: An Inquiry into Its Origin and Growth*, 78–97. London: Macmillan and Co., 1920.

Campbell, Elena I. *The Muslim Question and Russian Imperial Governance*. Bloomington: Indiana University Press, 2015.

Campbell, Ian W. *Knowledge and the Ends of Empire: Kazak Intermediaries & Russian Rule on the Steppe, 1731–1917*. Ithaca, NY and London: Cornell University Press, 2017.

Cameron, Averil. *Procopius and the Sixth Century*. Berkeley and Los Angeles: University of California Press, 1985.

Canfield, Robert L., editor. *Turko-Persia in Historical Perspective*. Cambridge: Cambridge University Press, [1991] 2002.

Carmody, Denise Lardner, and John Carmody. *Mysticism: Holiness East and West*. New York: Oxford University Press, 1996.

Cetinsaya, Gokhan. "Rethinking Nationalism and Islam: Some Preliminary Notes on the Roots of 'Turkish-Islamic Synthesis' in Modern Turkish Political Thought." *Muslim World*, Volume 89, Numbers 3–4 (July/October 1999): 350–376.

Chitester, David. *Empire of Religion: Imperialism and Comparative Religion*. Chicago and London: University of Chicago Press, 2014.

Cho, Eunsu. "Syncretism of Buddhism and Shamanism in Korea." *The Journal of Asian Studies*, Volume 62, Number 4 (November 2003): 1254–1256.

Christian, David. "The Political Ideals of Michael Speransky." *The Slavonic and East European Review*, Volume 54, Number 2 (April 1976): 192–213.

Cline, Eric H. *Biblical Archaeology: A Very Short Introduction*. Oxford and New York: Oxford University Press, 2009.

Connor, Walker. *The National Question in Marxist-Leninist Theory and Strategy*. Memorial Edition. Pullman, WA: Asia Research Associates, [1984] 2018.

Cook, Karoline P. *Forbidden Passages: Muslims and Moriscos in Colonial Spanish America*. University of Pennsylvania Press, 2016.

Côté, James E., and Charles G. Levine, editors. *Identity Formation, Agency, and Culture: A Social Psychological Synthesis.* New York and London: Taylor & Francis - Psychology Press, 2002.
Berger, Stefan. *History and Identity: How Historical Theory Shapes Historical Practice.* Cambridge and New York: Cambridge University Press, 2022.
Berger, Stefan, editor. *Writing the Nation: A Global Perspective.* Basingstoke, UK: Palgrave Macmillan, 2007.
Berger, Stefan, and Chris Lorenz, editors. *The Contested Nation: Ethnicity, Class, Religion and Gender in National Histories.* Basingstoke, UK: Palgrave Macmillan, 2008.
Berger, Stefan, and Christoph Conrad. *The Past as History: National Identity and Historical Consciousness in Modern Europe.* Basingstoke, UK: Palgrave Macmillan, 2015.
Cable, Mildred, and Francesca French. *George Hunter: Apostle of Turkestan.* London: China Inland Mission, 1948.
Crews, Robert D. "Civilization in the City: Architecture, Urbanism, and the Colonization of Tashkent." In *Architectures of Russian Identity, 1500 to the Present.* Edited by James Cracraft and Daniel Rowland, 117–133. Ithaca and London: Cornell University Press, 2003.
———. *For Prophet and Tsar: Islam and Empire in Russia and Central Asia.* Boston: Harvard University Press, 2006.
Dalmia, Vasudha. "Review: The Locations of Hindi (Reviewed Work: *Hindi Nationalism* by Alok Rai)." *Economic and Political Weekly*, Volume 38, Number 14 (April 5–11, 2003): 1377–1384.
Danfulani, Umar Habila Dadem. "Factors Contributing to the Survival of the Bori Cult in Northern Nigeria." *Numen*, Volume 46, Number 4 (1999): 412–447.
Davaran, Fereshteh. *Continuity in Iranian Identity: Resilience of a Cultural Heritage.* London and New York: Routledge, 2010.
Davidann, Jon T., and Marc J. Gilbert. *Cross-Cultural Encounters in Modern World History, 1453–Present.* Second edition. London and New York: Routledge, [2012] 2018.
Dawson, Christopher. *Mission to Asia.* New York: Harper & Row, 1966.
Deane, Jennifer K. *A History of Medieval Heresy and Inquisition.* Lanham, MD: Rowman & Littlefield Publishers, 2011.
de Clercq, Charles. *Concilia Galliae 511–695.* Turnhout: Brepols, 1991.
de Rachewiltz, Igor. *Papal Envoys to the Great Khans.* London: Faber & Faber, 1971.
DeWeese, Devin. *Islamization and Native Religion in the Golden Horde: Baba Tukles and Conversion to Islam in Historical and Epic Tradition.* State College, PA: Pennsylvania State University Press, 1994.
———. "Islamization in the Mongol Empire." In *The Cambridge History of Inner Asia: The Chinggisid Age.* Edited by N. Di Cosmo, A.J. Frank and P.B. Golden, 120–134. Cambridge: Cambridge University Press, 2009.

———. "(Review of) *Everyday Islam in Post-Soviet Central Asia*, by Maria E. Louw (London & New York: Routledge, 2007)," *Journal of Islamic Studies*, Volume 21, Number 1 (January 2010): 157–162.

———. "Survival Strategies: Reflections on the Notion of Religious 'Survivals' in Soviet Ethnographic Studies of Muslim Religious Life in Central Asia." In *Exploring the Edge of Empire: Soviet Era Anthropology in the Caucasus and Central Asia*. Edited by F. Muhlfried and S. Sokolovskiy, 35–58. Berlin: LIT Verlag, 2011.

———. "Ahmad Yasavi and the Divan-i hikmat in Soviet Scholarship." In *The Heritage of Soviet Oriental Studies*. Edited by Michael Kemper and Stephan Conermann, 262–290. London and New York: Routledge, 2011.

———. "Shamanization in Central Asia," *Journal of the Economic and Social History of the Orient*, Volume 57 (2014): 326–363.

———. "(Review of) Thierry Zarcone and Angela Hobart ed. *Shamanism and Islam: Sufism, Healing Rituals and Spirits in the Muslim World* (London/New York: I.B. Tauris, 2012)." *International Journal of Turkish Studies*, Volume 22, Numbers 1/2 (Fall 2016): 200–206.

———. "Re-envisioning the History of Sufi Communities in Central Asia: Continuity and Adaptation in Sources and Social Frameworks, 16th-20th Centuries." In *Sufism in Central Asia: New Perspectives on Sufi Traditions, 15th-21st Centuries*. Edited by Devin DeWeese and Jo-Ann Gross, 21–74. Leiden and Boston: Brill, 2018.

Dickens, Mark. *Echoes of a Forgotten Presence: Reconstructing the History of the Church of the East in Central Asia*. Münster, Germany: LIT Verlag, 2021.

Donnelly, Alton S. *The Russian Conquest of Bashkiria, 1552–1740*. New Haven and London: Yale University Press, 1968.

DuBois, Thomas A. "Trends in Contemporary Research on Shamanism." *Numen*, Volume 58, Issue 1 (January 2011): 100–128.

Elbakyan, Ekaterina. "The Outline of Religious Studies in Russia: Does Soviet Religious Studies Really Exist?" In *Studying Religions with the Iron Curtain Closed and Opened: The Academic Study of Religion in Eastern Europe*. Edited by Tomá Bubík and Henryk Hoffmann, 276–314. Brill Academic Publishing, 2015.

Eliade, Mircea. *Shamanism: Archaic Techniques of Ecstasy*. Translated by Willard R. Trask. Revised edition. Princeton, NJ: Bollingen Foundation and New York: Random House, [1951] 1964.

———. *Birth and Rebirth: The Religious Meanings of Initiation in Human Culture*. New York: Harper & Bros., 1958.

———. "The Religions of Ancient Eurasia: Turko-Mongols, Finno-Ugrians, Balto-Slavs." In *History of Religious Ideas, Volume 3: From Muhammad to the Age of Reforms*, 1–21. Chicago and London: University of Chicago Press, [1978] 1985.

Elias, Jamal J. *This is Islam: From Muhammad and the Community of Believers to Islam in the Global Community.* Great Barrington, MA: Berkshire Publishing Group, 2011.

Elmersjö, Henrik Åström, Anna Clark and Monika Vinterek, editors. *International Perspectives on Teaching Rival Histories: Pedagogical Responses to Contested Narratives and the History Wars.* Cham, Switzerland: Palgrave Macmillan, 2017.

Embree, A.T., and C. Gluck, editors. *Asia in Western and World History: A Guide for Teaching.* Armonk, NY: M.E. Sharpe, 1997.

Esin, Emel. "Ṭabarī's Report on the Warfare with the Türgiš and the Testimony of Eighth Century Central Asian Art." *Central Asiatic Journal*, Volume 17, Numbers 2/4 (1973): 130–149.

Esposito, John L., and Dalia Mogahed. *Who Speaks for Islam?: What a Billion Muslims Really Think.* New York: Gallup Press, 2007.

Evans, Richard J. *In Defence of History.* American Edition. New York and London: W.W. Norton & Co., 1998.

Evans-Pritchard, E.E. *Theories of Primitive Religion.* Oxford: Oxford University Press, 1967.

Farhshatov, M.N. *Public Education in Bashkirya (1860–1890).* Moscow: Science, 1994.

Feener, R. Michael. "Muslim Cultures and Pre-Islamic Pasts: Changing Perceptions of "Heritage."" In *The Making of Islamic Heritage: Muslim Pasts and Heritage Presents.* Edited by Trinidad Rico, 23–46. Singapore: Palgrave Macmillan, 2017.

Fernández, Víctor M. "Schematic Rock Art, Rain-Making and Islam in the Ethio-Sudanese Borderlands." *The African Archaeological Review*, Volume 28, Number 4 (December 2011): 279–300.

Filotas, Bernadette. *Pagan Survivals, Superstitions, and Popular Cultures in Early Medieval Pastoral Literature.* Toronto: Pontifical Institute of Mediaeval Studies, 2005.

Finke, Peter, and Meltem Sancak. "To Be an Uzbek or Not to Be a Tajik? Ethnicity and Locality in the Bukhara Oasis." *Zeitschrift für Ethnologie (ZfE) / Journal of Social and Cultural Anthropology (JSCA)*, Volume 137, Number 1 (2012): 47–70.

Fletcher, Joseph. "Confrontations Between Muslim Missionaries and Nomad Unbelievers in the Late Sixteenth Century: Notes on Four Passages from the Diya al-Qulub [by Ishaq Effendi]." In *Tractata Altaica.* Edited by Walther Heissig, 167–174. Wiesbaden: Otto Harrassowitz, 1976.

Foltz, Richard. *Religions of the Silk Road: Premodern Patterns of Globalization.* Second Edition. New York: St. Martin's Press, 2010. Originally published as: *Religions of the Silk Road: Overland Trade and Cultural Exchange from Antiquity to the Fifteenth Century.* First Edition. New York: St. Martin's Press, 1999.

Formichi, Chiara. *Islam and Asia (New Approaches to Asian History)*. Cambridge: Cambridge University Press, 2020.

Frank, A.J. *Muslim Religious Institutions in Imperial Russia: The Islamic World of Novouzensk District and the Kazakh Inner Horde, 1780–1910*. Leiden: E.J. Brill, 2001.

———. "Islamic Transformation on The Kazakh Steppe, 1742–1917: Toward an Islamic History of Kazakhstan under Russian Rule." In *The Construction and Deconstruction of National Histories in Slavic Eurasia*. Edited by Tadayuki Hayashi, 261–289. Sapporo: Slavic Research Centre, Hokkaido University, 2003.

Frankfurter, David, editor. *Guide to the Study of Ancient Magic*. Leiden and Boston: Brill Academic, 2019.

Frye, Richard N. "Problems in the Study of Iranian Religions." In *Erwin Goodenough Memorial Volume*. Edited by Jacob Neusner, 337–343. Leiden: Brill Academic, 1968.

———. "Comparative Observations on Conversion to Islam in Iran and Central Asia." *Jerusalem Studies in Arabic and Islam*, Number 4 (1984): 81–88.

Gabitov, Tursin H. "Relational Dynamics of Religious Systems among the Kazakhs." In *Madeniettanu [Culturology]*. By T.H. Gabitov, Aktolkin Kulsarieva and Zhusipbek Mutalipov. Almaty: Rarity, 2001.

———. "Kazakting diniy madenieti." In *Kazak Madenietining Tarihi*, 221–231. Almaty: Kazak Universiteti, 2016.

Gabitov, T.H., and Galyia Kasymova. "The Role of the Shamanistic Musician in Kazakh Folk Culture." In *Kazak Culture: Theory and History*. Edited by T.H. Gabitov, 48–60. Almaty: Kazak Universiteti, 2022.

Gabitov, Tursun, Khairat Zatov and Bakytzhan Satershinov. "Islam and Values of Kazak Culture." In *Kazak Culture: Theory and History*. Edited by T.H. Gabitov, 201–208. Almaty: Kazak Universiteti, 2022.

Gaborieau, Marc. "A Nineteenth-century Indian 'Wahhabi' Tract against the Cult of the Saints: 'Al-Balagh al-Mubin'." *Islam in India*, Volume 4, Number 1 (January 1989): 198–239.

Geertz, Clifford. *Islam Observed: Religious Development in Morocco and Indonesia*. University of Chicago Press, 1971.

Ghazanfari, Kolsoum. *Perceptions of Zoroastrian Realities in the Shahnameh: Zoroaster, Beliefs, Rituals*. Berlin: Logos Verlag, 2011.

Geraci, Robert P. *Window on the East: National and Imperial Identities in Late Tsarist Russia*. Ithaca and London: Cornell University Press, 2001.

———. "Orthodox Missionaries in the Kazakh Steppe, 1881–1917." In *Of Religion and Empire: Missions, Conversion, and Tolerance in Tsarist Russia*. Edited by R.P. Geraci and M. Khodarkovsky, 274–310. Ithaca and London: Cornell University Press, 2001.

Gibb, H.A.R. *The Arab Conquests in Central Asia.* London: The Royal Asiatic Society, 1923.
Gillman, Ian, and Hans-Joachim Klimkeit. "Christians in Central Asia." In *Christians in Asia Before 1500*, 205–264. Ann Arbor, MI: University of Michigan Press, 1999.
Golden, Peter B. "Wolves, Dogs and Qipčaq Religion." *Acta Orientalia Academiae Scientiarum Hungaricae*, Volume 50, Number 1/3 (1997): 87–97.
———. *Central Asia in World History.* Oxford and New York: Oxford University Press, 2010.
——— "The Shaping of the Cuman-Qipcaqs and Their World." In *Studies on the Peoples and Cultures of the Eurasian Steppes.* (An Anthology of essays by) P.B. Golden. Edited by Catalin Hriban, 303–332. Bucharest: Braila, 2011.
———. "Notes to Weller" (Personal Email Correspondence). 27 July 2022.
Golovnin, V.M., and T. Pang. "N.N. Krotkov's Questionnaire to Balishan Concerning Sibe-Solon Shamanism. "In *History and Historiography of Post-Mongol Central Asia and the Middle East: Studies in Honor of John E. Woods.* Edited by Ernest Tucker, 201–209. Wiesbaden, Germany: Otto Harrassowitz Verlag, 2006.
Grousset, Rene. *The Empire of the Steppes: A History of Central Asia.* Translated by Naomi Walford. New Brunswick, NJ: Rutgers University Press, [1939] 1970.
Hali, Awelkhan, Zengxiang Li and Karl W. Luckert. *Kazakh Traditions of China.* Lanham, MD: University Press of America, 1999.
Ḥalidī, Qurbān-ʿAlī. *An Islamic Biographical Dictionary of the Eastern Kazakh Steppe, 1770–1912.* Edited by Allen J. Frank and Mirkasyim A. Usmanov. Leiden: Brill, 2004.
Haneda, Akira. "Introduction: Problems of Turkicization, Problems of Islamization." *Acta Asiatica*, 34 (1978): 1–21.
Harrison, William H. *In Praise of Mixed Religion: The Syncretism Solution in a Multifaith World.* Montreal: McGill-Queen's University Press, 2014.
Herman, Arthur. *The Idea of Decline in Western History.* New York: Free Press, 1997.
Hilgers, Irene. *Why Do Uzbeks have to be Muslims?: Exploring religiosity in the Ferghana Valley.* Münster, Germany: LIT Verlag, 2009
Hirani, Krisha. "Hindi and Urdu: A language divided, or a shared history destroyed?" *Cherwell*, 21 January 2022. (URL: https://cherwell.org/2022/01/21/hindi-and-urdu-a-language-divided-or-a-shared-history-destroyed/).
Hirsch, Francine, *Empire of Nations: Ethnographic Knowledge and the Making of the Soviet Union.* Ithaca, NY: Cornell University Press, 2005.

"History of the Catholic Church in Kazakhstan, The." L'Osservatore Romano, Editorial and Management Offices, Via del Pellegrino, 00120, Vatican City, Europe (URL: www.catholicculture.org/culture/library/view.cfm?recnum=4186).

Hjelm, Ingrid and Thomas L. Thompson, editors. *History, Archaeology and The Bible Forty Years After 'Historicity': Changing Perspectives 6.* London and New York: Routledge, 2016.

Hoberman, Barry. "The Battle of Talas." *Aramco World,* Volume 33, Number 5 (September–October 1982): 26–31. (URL: https://archive.aramcoworld.com/issue/198205/the.battle.of.talas.htm).

Hobson, John M. "The Clash of Civilizations 2.0: Race and Eurocentrism, Imperialism, and Anti-Imperialism." In *Re-Imagining the Other: Culture, Media, and Western-Muslim Intersections.* Edited by Mahmoud Eid and Karim H. Karim, 75–98. Basingstoke, UK: Palgrave Macmillan, 2014.

Hodgen, Margaret. "The Doctrine of Survivals: The History of an Idea." *American Anthropologist, N.S.* Volume 33, Number 3 (1931): 307–324.

———. *The Doctrine of Survivals: A Chapter in the History of Scientific Method in the Study of Man.* London: Allenson and Co., Ltd., 1936.

Hodgkin, Katharine, and Susannah Radstone, editors. *Memory, History, Nation: Contested Pasts.* New York and London: Routledge, 2005.

Hourani, Albert. "Islam and the Philosophers of History." *Middle Eastern Studies,* Volume 3, Number 3 (April 1967): 206–268.

Hoyland, Robert G. *Arabia and the Arabs: From the Bronze Age to the Coming of Islam.* New York and London: Routledge, 2001.

Hua, Tao. "Satuq Bughra Khan and the Beginning of Islamization in the Tian Shan Region." In *Islam.* Edited by Yijiu Jin. *Religious Studies in Contemporary China Collection.* Volume 6. Leiden: Brill, 2017.

Hutchinson, J. F. *Late Imperial Russia, 1890–1917.* London and New York: Longman, 1999.

Ibn Taimiyah. *The Right Way: A Summarised Translation* [اقتضاء الصراط المستقيم]. Riyadh: Dar-us-Salam, 1996.

Iggers, Georg G. *Historiography in the Twentieth Century: From Scientific Objectivity to the Postmodern Challenge.* Middletown, CT: Wesleyan University Press, [1997] 2005.

Jackson, Peter. *The Mongols and the West.* Harlow, England: Longman, 2005.

Janosik, Daniel J. *John of Damascus, First Apologist to the Muslims: The Trinity and Christian Apologetics in the Early Islamic Period.* Pickwick Publications, 2016.

Jantzen, Herman. *Journey of Faith in a Hostile World: Memoirs of Herman Jantzen, Missionary to Turkestan, Caucasus and Bulgaria, refugee from Bolshevik Russia.* New York: iUniverse, 2008.

Jefferson-Tatum, Elana. "Beyond Syncretism and Colonial Legacies in the Study of Religion: Critical Reflections on Harrison's *In Praise of Mixed Religion* and Blanes's *A Prophetic Trajectory*." *The Journal of Religion*, Volume 100, Number 4 (2020): 499–514.
Jeffrey, Arthur. *The Foreign Vocabulary of the Qur'an*. Leiden: Brill, [1938] 2007.
Jersild, Austin. *Orientalism and Empire: North Caucasus Mountain Peoples and the Georgian Frontier, 1845–1917*. Montreal and London: McGill-Queen's University Press, 2002.
Karras, Ruth Mazo. "Pagan Survivals and Syncretism in the Conversion of Saxony." *The Catholic Historical Review*, Volume 72, Number 4 (October 1986): 553–572.
Keller, Shoshana. "Conversion to the New Faith: Marxism-Leninism and Muslims in the Soviet Empire." In *Of Religion and Empire: Missions, Conversion, and Tolerance in Tsarist Russia*. Edited by R.P. Geraci and M. Khodarkovsky, 311–334. Ithaca and London: Cornell University Press, 2001.
Kemper, Michael. "The Soviet Discourse on the Origin and Class Character of Islam, 1923–1933." *Die Welt des Islams*, Volume 49, Number 1 (2009): 1–48.
Kerimova, Mariyam. "Russian Ethnology at the End of the 19th—the First Third of the 20th Century: Schools and Methods." Гласник Етнографског института САНУ, No. LXIII (1): 167–174.
Khalid, Adeeb. *Islam after Communism: Religion and Politics in Central Asia: With a New Afterword*. Berkeley, CA: University of California Press, [2006] 2014.
Kheirabady, Hamid Ashrafi, and Seyed Abolfazi Razavi. "The Revival of Nowruz and Mehregan Celebrations in the Abbasi Court (132–220 AH)." *Journal of Iranian Islamic Period History*, Volume 12, Number 27 (July 2021): 1–19.
Kim, Sung-Eun Thomas. "Korean Buddhist Adoption of Shamanic Religious Ethos: Healing, Fortune Seeking, and the Afterlife." *International Journal of Buddhist Thought and Culture (IJBTC)*, Volume 28, Number 1 (2018): 59–85.
Kitagawa, Joseph M. "The History of Religions (*Religionswissenschaft*) Then and Now." In *The History of Religions: Retrospect and Prospect*. Edited by J.M. Kitagawa, 121–144. New York: Macmillan Publishing Company and London: Collier Macmillan Publishers, 1985.
Kitchen, K.A. *On the Reliability of the Old Testament*. Grand Rapids, MI: Eerdman's Publishing Co., 2003.
Kooria, Mahmood. *Islamic Law in Circulation: Shāfi'ī Texts across the Indian Ocean and the Mediterranean*. Cambridge, UK and New York, NY: Cambridge University Press, 2022.
Kooria, Mahmood, and Sanne Ravensbergen, editors. *Islamic Law in the Indian Ocean World: Texts, Ideas and Practices*. Abingdon and New York, NY: Routledge, 2022.

Laurelle, Marlene. "Religious Revivalism, Nationalism and the 'Invention of Tradition': Political Tengrism in Central Asia and Tatarstan." In *Central Asian Survey*, Volume 26, Number 2 (June 2007): 203–216.

Lapidus, Ira M. *Islamic Societies to the Nineteenth Century*. Cambridge, UK and New York: Cambridge University Press, 2012.

Leete, Art. "Reconsidering the Role of Shamans in Siberia during the Early Soviet Era." *Shaman*, Volume 23, Numbers 1–2 (Spring/Autumn 2015): 61–80.

Leopold, Anita M., and Jeppe S. Jensen, editors. *Syncretism in Religion: A Reader (Critical Categories in the Study of Religion)*. London and New York: Routledge, [2004] 2014.

Levi, Scot. *The Indian Diaspora in Central Asia and its Trade, 1550–1900*. Leiden: E. J. Brill, 2002.

———, editor. *India and Central Asia: Commerce and Culture, 1500–1800*. Oxford and New York: Oxford University Press, 2007.

———. *Caravans: Indian Merchants on the Silk Road*. New York: Penguin, 2015.

Lindenfeld, David. *Beyond Conversion & Syncretism: Indigenous Encounters with Missionary Christianity, 1800–2000*. New York, NY: Berghahn Books, 2011.

Louw, Maria E. *Everyday Islam in Post-Soviet Central Asia*. London & New York: Routledge, 2007.

MacKenzie, David. *The Lion of Tashkent: The Career of General M.G. Cherniaev*. University of Georgia Press, 1974.

MacMullen, Ramsay. *Christianity and Paganism in the Fourth to Eighth Centuries*. New Haven, CT: Yale University Press, 1997.

MacMullen, Ramsay and Eugene Lane, editors. *Paganism and Christianity, 100–425 CE: A Sourcebook*. Minneapolis, MN: Fortress Press, 1992.

Malikov, A. M. "Celebration of Nowruz in Bukhara and Samarkand in Ritual Practice and Social Discourses (The Second Half of the 19th to Early 20th Centuries)." *Archeology, Ethnology, Anthropology of Eurasia* Volume 48, Number 2 (June 2020): 122–129.

Mami, H. "Tatarskaia Kargala in Russia's Eastern Policies." In *Asiatic Russia: Imperial Power in Regional and International Contexts*. Edited by Tomohiko Uyama, 32–51. London and New York: Routledge, 2011.

Maroney, Eric. *Religious Syncretism*. London: SCM Press, 2006.

Martin, A.M. *Romantics, Reformers, Reactionaries: Russian Conservative Thought and Politics in the Reign of Alexander I*. DeKalb, IL: Northern Illinois University Press, 1997.

Martin, Janet. "Muscovite Travelling Merchants: The Trade with the Muslim East (15th and 16th Centuries)." *Central Asian Survey*, Volume 4, Number 3 (1985): 21–38.

Mattoo, Abdul Majid. *Kashmir under the Mughals, 1586–1752*. Kashmir: Golden Horde Enterprises, 1988.

Masuzawa, Tomoko. *In Search of Dreamtime: The Quest for the Origin of Religion*. Chicago and London: University of Chicago Press, 1993.

McBrien, Julie. *From Belonging to Belief: Modern Secularisms and the Construction of Religion in Kyrgyzstan*. Pittsburgh, PA: University of Pittsburgh Press, 2017.

McChesney, Robert D. "Central Asia's Place in the Middle East: Some Historical Considerations." In *Central Asia meets the Middle East*. Edited by David Menashri, 25–51. New York and London: Routledge, 1998.

McConnell, Allen. *Tsar Alexander I, Paternalistic Reformer*. New York: Thomas Y. Crowell Co., 1970.

McEvedy, Colin. *The Penguin Atlas of Medieval History*. New York: Penguin, 1992.

McGlinchey, Eric. *Chaos, Violence, Dynasty: Politics and Islam in Central Asia*. Pittsburgh, PA: University of Pittsburgh Press, 2011.

Meri, Josef W. "The Etiquette of Devotion in the Islamic Cult of the Saints." In *The Cult of Saints in Late Antiquity and the Middle Ages: Essays on the Contribution of Peter Brown*. Edited by James Howard-Johnston and Paul Antony Hayward, 263–286. Oxford: Oxford University Press, 2002.

Meyer, Will. *Islam and Colonialism: Western Perspectives on Soviet Asia*. London and New York: Routledge, 2002.

Michael, Thomas. "Does Shamanism Have a History? With Attention to Early Chinese Shamanism." *Numen*, Volume 64, Numbers 5–6 (2017): 459–496.

Mingana, Alphonse. "The Early Spread of Christianity in Central Asia and the Far East: A New Document." *The John Rylands Library*, Volume 9, Number 2 (July 1925): 287–288 and 297–371.

Miniyanova, Aelita. "Pedagogical Innovations and the Reinvention of 'Old' Pedagogy in Muslim Schools in Russia." In *Muslim Education in the 21st Century: Asian Perspectives*. Edited by Sa'eda Buang and Phyllis Ghim-Lian Chew, 180–194. Routledge, 2014.

"Mohammad Ali Taheri." *Wikipedia* (URL: https://en.wikipedia.org/wiki/Mohammad_Ali_Taheri).

Montgomery, David W. *Practicing Islam: Knowledge, Experience, and Social Navigation in Kyrgyzstan*. Pittsburgh, PA: University of Pittsburgh Press, 2016.

———. Editor. *Central Asia: Contexts for Understanding*. Pittsburgh, PA: University of Pittsburgh Press, 2022.

Montgomery, Scott L., and Alok Kumar. *A History of Science in World Cultures: Voices of Knowledge*. London and New York: Routledge, 2016.

Morrison, Alexander. *The Russian Conquest of Central Asia: A Study in Imperial Expansion, 1814–1914*. Cambridge, UK: Cambridge University Press, 2021.

Motadel, David. *Islam and Nazi Germany's War*. Cambridge, MA: Belknap Press, 2014.
———. Editor. *Islam and the European Empires*. Oxford and New York: Oxford University Press, 2014.
Mukherjee, Sahana, and Phia S. Salter, editors. *History and Collective Memory from the Margins: A Global Perspective*. Hauppauge, NY: Nova Science Publishers, 2019.
Muminov, Ashirbek. "Islam in the Syr Darya Region from the Twelfth to the Fourteenth Century." In *Kazakhstan: Religions and Society in the History of Central Eurasia*. Edited by Gian Luca Bonora, Niccolò Pianciola, and Paolo Sartori, 113–124. Turin: Umberto Allemandi & Co., 2010.
Muminov, Ashirbek and Saipulla Mollakanagatuly. "A First Glimpse at Saduaqas Ghïlmani's (1890-1972) "Biographies of the Islamic Scholars of Our times"—A Possible Rewriting of the Tsarist and Soviet History of Kazakhstan's Islamic Community." *Asiatische Studien*, Volume 73, Number 4 (April 2020): 751–759.
Naumkin, V.V. *Radical Islam in Central Asia: Between Pen and Rifle*. Rowman & Littlefield, 2005.
Nisbet, Robert. *History of the Idea of Progress*. Piscataway, NJ: Transaction Publishers (Routledge), 1980.
Nizami, K.A. "Popular Movements, Religious Trends and Sufi Influence on the Masses in the Post-Abbasid Period." In *History of Civilizations of Central Asia, Volume 4: The Age of Achievement: A.D. 750 to the End of the Fifteenth Century: Part One: The Historical, Social and Economic Setting*. Edited by M.S. Asimov and C.E. Bosworth, 365–381. Paris: UNESCO, 1998.
Nurgaliyeva, Agila, Zhanna Tastaeva, Alfiya Baibulsinova and Lazzat Serikova, "The Fire Cult and Islam in the Kazakh System of Beliefs." *TRAMES*, Vol. 21 (71/66), No. 2 (2017):151–160
Nyang, Sulayman S. *Islam, Christianity and African Identity*. Chicago: Kazi Publications, Inc. 2007.
Oh, Kyong-geun. "Korean Shamanism – The Religion of Women." *International Journal of Korean Humanities and Social Sciences*, Volume ??, Number 2 (November): 71–86.
Olesen, Niels H. *Culte des saints et pèlerinages chez Ibn Taymiyya (661/1263–728/1328)* [*The Worship of Saints and Pilgrimages in Ibn Taymiyya*]. Paris: P. Geuthner, 1991.
Omarbekov, T., and B.B. Karibaev. "Religious Beliefs: Islam in the XIV–XV Centuries: Discrete Nature of the Process of Islamization of Nomads" and "The Role of Islam in the Process of Kipchakization of Mongols." In *History of Kazakhstan (Kazakh Eli): A 4-Volume Textbook. Book 2: Kazakhstan in the XIII Century—The First Quarter of the XVIII Century*, 107–113 and 127–133. Almaty: Kazak Universiteti, 2021.

Omelicheva, Mariya. "Islam in Kazakhstan: A Survey of Contemporary Trends and Sources of Securitization." *Central Asian Survey*, Volume 30, Number 2 (2011): 243–256.

Omidsalar, Mahmoud. *Poetics and Politics of Iran's National Epic, the Shāhnāmeh*. New York: Palgrave Macmillan, 2011.

Öztopçu, Kurtuluş, Zhoumagaly Abouv, Nasir Kambarov and Youssef Azemoun, editors. *Dictionary of the Turkic Languages*. London and New York: Routledge, 1996.

Palmisano, Stefania, and Nicola Pannofino, editors. *Invention of Tradition and Syncretism in Contemporary Religions: Sacred Creativity*. Cham, Switzerland: Palgrave Macmillan, 2017.

Parrinder, Edward Geoffrey. *Mysticism in the World's Religions*. Oxford: Oneworld, 1996.

Payne, Richard E. *A State of Mixture: Christians, Zoroastrians, and Iranian Political Culture in Late Antiquity*. Berkeley: University of California Press, 2015.

Penkala-Gawecka, Danuta. "Mentally Ill or Chosen by Spirits? 'Shamanic Illness' and the Revival of Kazakh Traditional Medicine in Post-Soviet Kazakhstan." *Central Asian Survey*, Volume 32, Number 1 (2013): 37–51.

Pharo, Lars Kirkhusmo. "A Methodology for a Deconstruction and Reconstruction of the Concepts 'Shaman' and 'Shamanism'." *Numen*, Volume 58, Issue 1 (2011): 6–70.

Pick, Daniel. *Faces of Degeneration: A European Disorder, c.1848–c.1918*. Cambridge: Cambridge University Press, 1989.

Pipping, Knut. "The First Finnish Sociologist: A Reappraisal of Edward Westermarck's Work." *Acta Sociologica*, Volume 25, Number 4 (1982): 347–357.

Poliakov, Sergei. *Everyday Islam: Religion and Tradition in Rural Central Asia*. Armonk, NY: M.E. Sharpe, 1992.

Pospielovsky, D.V. *A History of Marxist-Leninist Atheism and Soviet Antireligious Policies: Volume 1 of a History of Soviet Atheism in Theory and Practice, and the Believer*. Hampshire and London: Macmillan Press, 1987.

———. *Soviet Antireligious Campaigns and Persecutions: Volume 2 of a History of Soviet Atheism in Theory and Practice, and the Believer*. Hampshire and London: Macmillan Press, 1988.

Privratsky, Bruce G. *Muslim Turkistan: Kazak Religion and Collective Identity*. Surrey: Curzon Press and London and New York: Routledge, 2001.

Probert, Marcela A. Garcia, and Petra M. Sijpesteijn. Editors. *Amulets and Talismans of the Middle East and North Africa in Contex: Transmission, Efficacy and Collections*. Leiden and Boston: Brill Academic, 2022.

Qutbuddin, Tahera. "Arabic in India: A Survey and Classification of Its Uses, Compared with Persian." *Journal of the American Oriental Society*, Volume 127, Number 3 (July–September 2007): 315–338.

Raef, Marc. *Siberia and the Reforms of 1822.* Seattle: University of Washington Press, 1956.
Rahimieh, Nasrin. *Iranian Culture: Representation and Identity.* London and New York: Routledge, 2015.
Rambo, L.R., and C.E. Farhadian, editors. *Oxford Handbook of Religious Conversion.* Oxford University Press, 2014.
Rashid, Ahmed. *Jihad: The Rise of Militant Islam in Central Asia.* New Haven and London: Yale University Press, 2002.
Remnev, Anatolii. "Colonization and 'Russification' in the Imperial Geography of Asiatic Russia: From the Nineteenth to the Early Twentieth Centuries." In *Asiatic Russia: Imperial Power in Regional and International Contexts.* Edited by Tomohiko Uyama, 102–128. London and New York: Routledge, 2011.
Reynolds, John Myrdhin. *Yungdrung Bon—The Eternal Tradition: The Ancient Pre-Buddhist Religion of Central Asia and Tibet: Its History, Teachings, and Literature.* Freehold, NJ: Bompo Translation Project, 1991.
Riasanovsky, Nicholas. *Nicholas I and Official Nationality in Russia, 1825–1855.* Berkeley: University of California Press, 1967.
Ries, Julian. *The Origins of Religions.* Translated by Kate Singleton. Grand Rapids, MI: Wm. B. Eerdmans, 1993.
Roche, Sophie, editor. *Central Asian Intellectuals on Islam: Between Scholarship, Politics and Identity.* Berlin: Klaus Schwarz Verlag, 2021.
Rock, Stella. *Popular Religion in Russia: 'Double Belief' and the Making of an Academic Myth.* London and New York: Routledge, 2007.
Roux, Jean-Paul. "Tengri" and "Turkic Religions." Translated by Sherri L. Granka. In *The Encyclopedia of Religion.* Volumes 14–15. Edited by Mircea Eliade, V14:401-3 and V15:87-94. New York: MacMillan Publishing Co., 1987.
Rudolph, Kurt. "Syncretism: From Theological Invective to a Concept in the Study of Religion." In *Syncretism in Religion: A Reader.* Edited by Anita Maria Leopold and Jeppe S. Jensen, 68–85. *Critical Categories in the Study of Religion* Series. London and New York: Routledge, [2004] 2014.
Sadvokasova, Z.T. and A.M. Sadykova. "Comparative Approach to the Study of Policy of Tsarist and Soviet Government in Relation to Islam." *Procedia: Social and Behavioral Sciences,* Vol. 122 (2014): 51
Sagdeev, Roald, and Susan Eisenhower, editors. *Islam and Central Asia: An Enduring Legacy or an Evolving Threat?* Washington, D.C.: Center for Political and Strategic Studies, 2000.
Samir, Khalil and Jørgen S. Nielsen, editors. *Christian Arabic Apologetics during the Abbasid Period, 750–1258.* Leiden: Brill Academic, 1993.
Sarrio, Diego R. "Spiritual anti-elitism: Ibn Taymiyya's Doctrine of Sainthood (*walāya*)." *Islam and Christian–Muslim Relations,* Volume 22, Number 3 (2011): 275–291.

Savran, Scott. *Arabs and Iranians in the Islamic Conquest Narrative: Memory and Identity Construction in Islamic Historiography, 750–1050*. London and New York: Routledge, 2017.

Schadler, Peter. *John of Damascus and Islam: Christian Heresiology and the Intellectual Background to Earliest Christian-Muslim Relations*. Leiden and Boston: Brill, 2018.

Schoeberlein, John. "Heroes of Theory: Central Asian Islam in Post-War Soviet Ethnography." In *Exploring the Edge of Empire: Soviet Era Anthropology in the Caucasus and Central Asia*. Edited by F. Muhlfried and S. Sokolovskiy, 59–79. Berlin: LIT Verlag, 2011.

Schofield, Robert E. *The Enlightened Joseph Priestley: A Study of His Life and Work from 1773 to 1804*. Illustrated Edition. State College, PA: Penn State University Press, [1997] 2004.

Schwab, Wendell. "Establishing an Islamic niche in Kazakhstan: Musylman Publishing House and its publications." In *Central Asian Survey*, Volume 30, Number 2 (2011): 227–242.

Seaman, Gary, and Jane S. Day, editors. *Ancient Traditions: Shamanism in Central Asia and the Americas*. Denver: University Press of Colorado, Denver Museum of Nature and Science and Los Angeles, CA: Ethnographics Press, 1994.

Seznec, Jean. *La Survivance des Dieux Antiques*. London, 1940.

———. *The Survival of the Pagan Gods: The Mythological Tradition and Its Place in Renaissance Humanism Art*. Translated by Barbara Sessions. Princeton, NJ: Princeton University Press, 1953. (English transl. of *La Survivance des Dieux Antiques*).

Shabley, Pavel, and Paolo Sartori. "Tinkering with Codification in the Kazakh Steppe: 'Ādat and Sharī'a in the Work of Efim Osmolovskii." In *Sharī'a in the Russian Empire: The Reach and Limits of Islamic Law in Central Eurasia, 1550–1917*. Edited by Paolo Sartori and Danielle Ross, 208–238. Edinburgh: Edinburgh University Press, 2020.

Shahbazi, A. Shapur. "NOWRUZ ii. In the Islamic Period." *Encyclopædia Iranica*, online edition, 2016 (URL: http://www.iranicaonline.org/articles/nowruz-ii).

Shams-ud-Din, editor. *Nationalism in Russia and Central Asian Republics: Unfinished Democratic Revolution*. New Delhi: Lancers Books, 1999.

Sharpe, Eric J. *Comparative Religion: A History*. Third edition. Chicago and La Salle, IL: Open Court, [1975, 1986] 2006.

Shaw, Rosalind, and Charles Stewart, editors. *Syncretism/Anti-Syncretism: The Politics of Religious Synthesis*. London and New York: Routledge, 1994.

Slezkine, Yuri, "The Fall of Soviet Ethnography, 1928–1938." *Current Anthropology*, Volume 32, Number 4 (1991): 476–484.

Smith, Anthony D. *Chosen Peoples: Sacred Sources of National Identity*. Oxford: Oxford University Press, 2003.

Smith, Jonathan Z. *To Take Place: Toward Theory in Ritual.* Chicago and London: University of Chicago Press, 1987.

Stearns, Peter, with Olivia O'Neill and Jack Censer. *Cultural Change in Modern World History: Cases, Causes and Consequences.* London and New York: Bloomsbury Academic, 2018.

Stein, Howard F. "Russian Nationalism and the Divided Soul of the Westernizers and Slavophiles." *Ethos*, Volume 4, Number 4 (Winter, 1976): 403–438.

Steinforth, Dirk H., and Charles C. Rozier. *Britain and its Neighbours: Cultural Contacts and Exchanges in Medieval and Early Modern Europe.* New York and London: Routledge, 2021.

Steingass, Francis Joseph. *A Comprehensive Persian-English dictionary, including the Arabic words and phrases to be met with in Persian literature.* London: Routledge & K. Paul, 1892. Hosted online by *Digital Dictionaries of South Asia*. University of Chicago (URL: https://dsal.uchicago.edu/dictionaries/steingass/).

Stenberg, Leif, and Philip Wood, editors. *What is Islamic Studies? European and North American Approaches to a Contested Field.* Edinburgh, Scotland: Edinburgh University Press, 2022.

Stroup, Timothy, editor. *Edward Westermarck: Essays on His Life and Works.* Helsinki, 1982.

Sultangalieva, Gulmira. "The Russian Empire and the Intermediary Role of Tatars in Kazakhstan: The Politics of Cooperation and Rejection." In *Asiatic Russia: Imperial Power in Regional and International Contexts.* Edited by Tomohiko Uyama, 52–78. London and New York: Routledge, 2011.

Sultanova, Razia. *From Shamanism to Sufism: Women, Islam and Culture in Central Asia.* London: I.B. Tauris, 2011.

Sumimoto, Tokihisa. "Religious Freedom Problems in Japan: Background and Current Prospects." *International Journal of Peace Studies*, Volume 5, Number 2 (Autumn/Winter 2000): 77–86.

Sunderland, Willard. *Taming the Wild Field: Colonization and Empire on the Russian Steppe.* Ithaca and London: Cornell University Press, 2004.

Sundström, Olle. "Is the Shaman indeed risen in post-Soviet Siberia?" *Scripta Instituti Donneriani Aboensis*, Volume 24 (2012): 350–387.

Swatos, William H., Jr., and Kevin J. Christiano. "Secularization Theory: The Course of a Concept." *Sociology of Religion*, Volume 60, Number 3 (Autumn 1999): 209–228.

Tasar, Eren. *Soviet and Muslim: The Institutionalization of Islam in Central Asia.* Oxford and New York: Oxford University Press, 2017.

Tatari, Eren, and Renat Shayhutdinov. "State Response to Religious Revivalism in Central Asia." In *European Journal of Economic and Political Studies*, Volume 3, Number 2 (2010): 85–110.

Thrower, James. *The Religious History of Central Asia from the Earliest Times to the Present Day.* Lewiston, NY, Queenston, Ontario, Canada, and Lampeter, Ceredigion, Wales: Edwin Mellon Press, 1999.

Togawa, Masahiko. "Syncretism Revisited: Hindus and Muslims over a Saintly Cult in Bengal." *Numen*, Volume 55, Number 1 (2008): 27–43.

Tolmacheva, Marina. "The Muslim Woman in Soviet Central Asia." *Central Asian Survey*, Volume 12, Number 4 (1993): 531–548.

Tor, D.G. "The Islamization of Central Asia in the Sāmānid Era and the Reshaping of the Muslim World." *Bulletin of the School of Oriental and African Studies*, Volume 72, Number 2 (2009): 279–299.

Tursunov, Edyge. "Jyrau—Poets, Warriors and Strategic Minds of the Steppes." Abai Center, Central Asia Program, Institute for European, Russian and Eurasian Studies, The George Washington University, Aug 7, 2020 (URL: https://abaicenter.com/jyrau-poets-warriors-strategic-minds-of-steppes).

Ualiyeya, Saule K., and Adrienne L. Edgar. "In the Laboratory of Peoples' Friendship: Mixed People in Kazakhstan from the Soviet Era to the Present." In *Global Mixed Race*. Edited by Rebecca C. King-O'Riain, Stephen Small, Minelle Mahtani, Miri Song and Paul Spickard, 68–90. New York University Press, 2014.

van Leeuwen, Carel, Tatiana Emeljanenko, and Larisa Popova. *Nomads in Central Asia: Animal Husbandry and Culture in Transition (19th–20th century).* Amsterdam: Royal Tropical Institute, 1995.

Vermeulen, Han F. *Before Boas: The Genesis of Ethnography and Ethnology in the German Enlightenment.* Lincoln, NE: University of Nebraska Press, 2015.

Voll, John. "Central Asia as a Part of the Modern Islamic World." In *Central Asia in Historical Perspective.* Edited by Beatrice F. Manz, 62–81. Boulder, CO: Westview Press, 1994.

Vulpius, Ricarda. "The Russian Empire's Civilizing Mission in the Eighteenth Century: A Comparative Perspective." In *Asiatic Russia: Imperial Power in Regional and International Contexts.* Edited by Tomohiko Uyama, 13–31. London and New York: Routledge, 2011.

Waida, Manabu. "Problems of Central Asian and Siberian Shamanism." *Numen*, Volume 30, Issue 2 (December 1983): 215–239.

Waley, Muhammad Isa. "A Kubrawi Manual of Sufism: the Fusus al-adab of Yahya Bakharzi." In *The Heritage of Sufism: Volume II, The Legacy of Medieval Persian Sufism (1150–1500).* Edited by Leonard Lewisohn, 289–310. Oxford, UK: Oneworld Publications, 1999.

Walter, Mariko Namba, and Eva Jane Neumann Fridman, editors. *Shamanism: An Encyclopedia of World Beliefs, Practices, and Culture*, 2 Volumes. Santa Barbara, CA: ABC-Clio, 2004.

Weeks, Theodore R. *Nation and State in Late Imperial Russia: Nationalism and Russification on the Western Frontier, 1863–1914.* DeKalb, IL: Northern Illinois University Press, 1996.

———. "Russification: Word and Practice, 1863–1914." *Proceedings of the American Philosophical Society*, Volume 148, Number 4 (December 2004): 471–489.

Weller, R. Charles. "Kazak tili oris tiline taueldi bolip kala ma?" ["Will the Kazakh Language Wind Up Remaining Dependent Upon Russian?"]. In *Kazak tili zhanye oralman* [*The Kazakh Language and Returnees (from the Kazakh diaspora)*]. Edited by Sagira Kanahina, 41–45. Almaty, KZ: Olke: The National Library of the Republic of Kazakhstan and the Language Committee of the Ministry of Culture, Media and Sports of the Republic of Kazakhstan, 2006.

———. "Foundations of the Western Modernist View of Nations." In *Rethinking Kazakh and Central Asian Nationhood: A Challenge to Prevailing Views*, 54–60. Los Angeles: Asia Research Associates, 2006.

———. "Religious-Cultural Revivalism as Historiographical Debate: Contending Claims in the Post-Soviet Kazakh Context." *Journal of Islamic Studies*, Volume 25, Number 2 (May 2014): 138–177. DOI: https://doi.org/10.1093/jis/ett058 (Published online Nov 12, 2013—http://jis.oxfordjournals.org/content/25/2/138).

———. Review of *Patshilik Resei zhanye Kenges Imperialarining Kazakstandagi Ruhani Otarlau Sayasatining Zardaptari (XIX gasirding 70–80 zhildari – XXI gasirding basi)* [*Consequences of the Policies of Spiritual Colonization in Kazakhstan under the Russian and Soviet Empires (1870–80s—the Beginning of the 21st Century)*, by S.M. Mashimbaev and G.S. Mashimbaeva (Almaty, KZ: Kazakh Universitesi, 2013). *Central Asian Survey*, Volume 34, Number 4 (2015): 585–588. (Published online 15 Jul 2015; DOI: https://doi.org/10.1080/02634937.2015.1062614).

———. "Interview: Islam in the life of Kazakhs: From Conversion to Current Times." *Central Asian Analytical Network*, March 10, 2017. (URL: http://caa-network.org/archives/8551; in both Russian and English.)

———. "'Western' and 'White Civilization': White Nationalism and Eurocentrism at the Crossroads." In *21st-Century Narratives of World History: Global and Multidisciplinary Perspectives*. Edited by R.C. Weller. Cham, Switzerland: Palgrave Macmillan, 2017.

———. "Introduction: Reason, Revelation and Law in Global Historical Perspective." In *Reason, Revelation and Law in Islamic and Western Theory and History*. Edited by R.C. Weller and A. Emon, 1–24. Singapore: Palgrave Macmillan, 2021.

——— "The Historical Relation of Islamic and Western Law." In *Reason, Revelation and Law in Islamic and Western Theory and History*, ed. R.C. Weller and A. Emon, 25–43. Singapore: Palgrave Macmillan, 2021.

———. "Islamic Contributions to Western Civilization." *Malcolm Renfrew Interdisciplinary Colloquium*. University of Idaho, Mar 2, 2021. (URL: https://youtu.be/RePQ0FimaXU).

Wickens, G.M. "Persian Literature as an Affirmation of National Identity." *Review of National Literatures, selected essays (1970–2001): Emergent and Neglected National Literatures.* Edited by Ann Paolucci, 209–237. Middle Village, NY: Published for Council on National Literatures by Griffon House Publications, 2007.

Widengren, Geo. "Culture Contact, Cultural Influence, Cultural Continuity, and Syncretism. Some views based on my previous work." In *Religious Syncretism in Antiquity.* Edited by Birger A. Pearson, 1–20. Missoula, MT: Scholars Press, 1975.

Woolf, Daniel. *A Concise History of History: Global Historiography from Antiquity to the Present.* Cambridge and New York: Cambridge University Press, 2019.

Yaroshevski, Dov B. "Attitudes Towards the Nomads of the Russian Empire under Catherine the Great." In *Literature, Lives, and Legality in Catherine's Russia.* Edited by A.G. Cross and G.S. Smith, 15–24. Nottingham: Astra Press, 1994.

Yavuz, Hakan. "The Trifurcated Islam of Central Asia: A Turkish Perspective." In *Asian Islam in the 21st Century.* Edited by J.L. Esposito, J. Voll, and O. Bakar, 109–143. Oxford and New York: Oxford University Press, 2008.

Yemelianova, G.M. *Russia and Islam: A Historical Survey.* Hampshire and New York: Palgrave, 2002.

———. "How 'Muslim' are Central Asian Muslims? A Historical and Comparative Enquiry." *Central Asian Affairs,* Volume 4, Number 3 (July 2017): 243–269.

Yerekesheva, Laura. "Religious Identity in Kazakhstan and Uzbekistan: Global-local interplay." In *Strategic Analysis,* Volume 28, Number 4 (2004): 577–588.

Yesim, Garifolla. *An Insider's Critique of the Kazakh Nation: Reflections on the Writings of Abai Kunanbaiuhli (1845–1904).* Translated and edited by R. Charles Weller. Boston, MA: Asia Research Associates, [1994] 2020.

York, Michael. *Pagan Mysticism: Paganism as a World Religion.* Newcastle-upon-Tyne: Cambridge Scholars Publishing, 2019.

Yorulmazoglu, Erol I. "The Influence of Religion." In *The Turks: The Central Asian Civilization That Bridged the East and the West for Over Two Millennia.* Volume 1. 2nd edition, 76–108. Seattle, WA: Kindle Direct Publishing, 2021.

Zacek, Judith Cohen. "The Russian Bible Society and the Russian Orthodox Church." *Church History,* Volume 35, Number 4 (December 1966): 411–437.

Zarcone, Thierry, and Angela Hobart, editors. *Shamanism and Islam: Sufism, Healing Rituals and Spirits in the Muslim World.* London and New York: I.B. Tauris, 2012.

Zargar, Cameron. "Origins of Wahhabism from Hanbali Fiqh." *Journal of Islamic and Near Eastern Law,* Volume 16, Number 1 (2017): 65–114.

Zatov, Kairat, Tursun Gabitov, Maral Botaeva, Moldagaliyev Bauyrzhan and Saira Shamahay. "Islam and Values of Kazakh Culture." *International Journal of Social, Behavioral, Educational, Economic, Business and Industrial Engineering*, Volume 7, Number 6 (2013): 1697–1702.

Znamenski, Andrei. *Shamanism in Siberia: Russian Records of Indigenous Spirituality*. Boston, MA: Kluwer Academic Publishers, 2003.

Zola, Lia. "Invisibility or Marginality? Assessing Religious Diversification Among Women Shamans in Eastern Siberia." In *Invention of Tradition and Syncretism in Contemporary Religions: Sacred Creativity*. Edited by Stefania Palmisano and Nicola Pannofino, 51–68. *Palgrave Studies in New Religions and Alternative Spiritualities*. Cham, Switzerland: Palgrave Macmillan, 2017.

Kazakh

(Abdakimuhli) Абдакимұлы, Абдижапар. *Қазақстан тарихы: ертеден бүгінге дейін* [*The History of Kazakhstan: From Early Times to the Present*]. Алматы: Республикалық баспа кабинеті, 1997.

———. «Дін және тіл» [Religion and Language]. *Ақиқат*, No. 8, 2008, 75–78 бб.

———. «Қазіргі таңдағы діни ахуалдың дамуының негізгі бағыттары [The Main Trends of the Developments in the Current Religious Situation].» *Ақиқат*, No. 12, 2008, 162–164 бб.

(Alimzhanova) Әлімжанова, А.Ш. "Шамандык мәтіндердің мәдени ерекшеліктері [The Cultural Uniqueness of Shamanistic Texts]." In *Қазақстанның мәдени мұрасы: жаңалықтары, мәселелері, болашағы* (конф. Материалдары) [*The Cultural Heritage of Kazakhstan: New Findings, Problems and the Future* (Conf. Materials)], 204–212. Алматы, 2005.

(Amirgazin) Амиргазин, С.Т. "Дін егітімінің Гаеси - Бірлік ве Бераберлигин Сагланмаси / Din egitiminin Gayesi – Birlik ve Beraberligin Saglanmasi [The Aim of the Religious Education—Securing Unity and Solidarity]." Қожа Ахмет Яссауи мен Қазақстандағы діни білім мәселелері атты халықаралық симпозиум. ҚР БҒМ. Қожа Ахмет Яссауи атындағы Халықаралық қазақ-түрік университеті. ҚР Мәдениет министрлігінің Діни істер бөлімі және Оңтүстік Қазақстан облысының әкімшілігі [A paper presented at an *International Symposium on the Teaching of Qoja Akhmet Yasawi and the Problems of Religious Education in Kazakhstan*, Ministry of Science and Education of the Republic of Kazakhstan, Qoja Akhmet Yasawi International Kazak-Turk University, Ministry of Culture of the Republic of Kazakhstan's Committee for Religious Affairs, and the Local Government of the Oblast of Southern Kazakhstan]. April 6–9, 2011, Turkistan.

———. *Дінтану: оқу құралы* [*Religious Studies: A Textbook*]. Астана, 2002.

(Atash) Аташ, Б.М., and М.И. Танжаров. "Көне Түркі-Түркі-Қазақ Даласындағы Шаманизмнің Генезисі мен Эволюциясы: Тарихи-Танымдық Бағдарлар [Genesis and Evolution of Shamanism in the Ancient

Turkic-Turkic-Kazakh Steppes: Historical and Cognitive Orientations]," *Адам Әлемі* [*The Human World*], Vol. 92, No. 2 (2022): 173–187.

(Auezov) Әуезов, Мұхтар (сұхбар). «Өзімді Мұхтар Әуезовтің жазылып бітпеген шығармасының кейіпкеріндей сезінемін... [I Feel Like the Character in Mukhtar Auezov's Unfinished Work]», *Алтын Орда*, 9–15 мамыр, 2003.

(Baieke) Байеке, Манарбек. *Орта Азия мен Қазақстанның масихшылық тарихы* [*The History of Christianity in Central Asia and Kazakhstan*]. Алматы, КЗ: Литера-М, 2006.

(Baitenova) Байтенова, Нагима, Кайрат Затов. "Ежелгі Түркілердің наним-сенімдері [The Faiths and Beliefs of the Ancient Turks]." *Егемен Қазақстан*, 5 тамыз, 2006. (URL: http://abai.kz/node/5917, 28 қараша, 2010)

(Barbol) Барбол, Әзірет. "Бұлутай ата дінін бұзып, бұзып жатыр [Bulutai is going about perverting and corrupting the religion of the fathers]." *Abai*, September 2012.

(Batirhan) Батырхан, Т., Б. Омарұлы. "Ақселеу Сейдімбекпен сұхбат [An Interview with Akselu Seidimbek]." *Айқын*, No. 141(593), Бейсенбі, 3 тамыз [Thursday, August 3], 2006, 10–11 бб.

(Berdibai) Бердібай, Рахманқұл. *Байкалдан Балканға дейін* [*From Baikal to the Balkans*]. Алматы, КЗ: «Казахстан», 1996.

(Bulutai) Бұлұтай, Мұртаза Ж. *Ата-баба діні: Неге Түркілер мұсылман болды?* [*The Religion of the Forefathers: Why Did the Turks Become Muslims?*]. Алматы: Білім, 2000.

———. Мұсылман қазақ еліміз [*Our Muslim Kazakh Nation*]. Алматы, КЗ: Арыс, 2001.

———. Бұрханизм туралы шындық [*The Truth about Burkanism (Tengrism)*]. Алматы, КЗ: Арыс, 2003. (Originally published in three parts in Жас Алаш, 10, 12 және 15 шілде, 2003).

———. Дін және ұлт [*Religion and Ethnos, or Religion and Ethnicity*]. Алматы: Арыс, 2006.

(Yesim) Есім, Ғарифолла. "Дін өркениеті [Religious Civilization]." *Егемен Қазақстан*, 21 казан [October], 2006, 6-б.

(Gabitov) Ғабитов, Тұрсын Хафизұы. *Қазақ Мәдениетінің рухани кеңістігі* [*The Spiritual Context of Kazakh Culture*]. Алматы: Раритет, 2013.

(Kairatuhli) Қайратұлы, Бекен. "Тәуелсіздік тудырған тәңірлер [The Gods Given Birth by Independence]." *Намыс*, 31 наурыз [March], 2011.

(Karamanuhli) Қараманұлы, К. "Тәңірге тағзым [The Worship of Tengri]." *Қазақ тарихынан* [*From Out of Kazakh History*]. Ред. Елден Аққошқаров, 242–282. Алматы: Жалын, 1999.

(Kartabaeva) Қартабаева, Ерке Тамабекқызы. Ислам және ортағасырлық түркілер [*Islam and the Turks of the Middle Ages*]. Алматы: Қазақ университеті, 2016.

(Kartaeva) Картаева, Таттигул. *Сыр өңірі қазақтары: тарихи-этнографиялық зерттеу (XIX ғасырдың екінші жартысынан XX ғасырдың басы)* [*Kazakhs of the Syr Region: Historical-Ethnographical Research (from the second half of the 19th century to the beginning of the 20th century*]. 2-Том [Volume 2]. Алматы: Қазақ университеті, 2014.

"Ата дінінен безіп кеткен қазақтар [Kazakhs Who Have Forsaken the Religion of the Fathers]." *Жалын* [*Flame*], No. 2 (ақпан, 2004): 56–79.

(Kishibekov) Кішібеков, Досмұхаммад. *Қазақ менталитеті: кеше, бүгін, ертең* [*Kazakh Mentality: Yesterday, Today and Tomorrow*]. Алматы: Ғылым, 1999.

(Kudaibergenov) Құдайбергенов, Б.К., С.Т. Амиргазин. *Діни мерекелер мен рәсімдердің әлеуметтік мәні* [*The Social Meaning of Religious Celebrations and Rituals*]. Алматы, КЗ: Қазақ университеті, 2004.

(Mashimbaev) Машимбаев, Серік М., Гүлшат С. Машимбаева. *Патшалық Ресей және Кеңес империяларының Қазақстандағы рухани отарлау саясатының зардаптары (XIX ғасырдың 70–80 жылдары-XXI ғасырдың басы)* [*Consequences of the Policies of Spiritual Colonization in Kazakhstan under the Russian and Soviet Empires (1870–80s—The Beginning of the 21st Century)*]. Алматы, Қазақстан, Қазақ университеті, 2013. (See my review of this work in English listed above.)

(Moldabekov) Молдабеков, Ж. *Қазақтану* [*Kazakh-ology*, or *The Study of Kazakness*]. Алматы, КЗ: Қазақ университеті, 2003.

(Muminov) Муминов, Аширбек. «Яссауи бастаулары [Beginnings of the Yasawi Sufi Brotherhood]». // *Яссауи тағылымы* [Studies on the Yasawi Tradtion]. Ред. М. Мирзахметов, 22–30. Түркістан, КЗ: Мұра, 1996.

(Nurzhanov) Нуржанов, Б.Г., Турсын Х. Габитов, С.Ж. Айдарбаев, К.И. Байзакова, А.С. Ибраева және Актолкын Т. Кулсариева. *Бейбіт мәдениет жолында* [*On the Path to Peace*]. Алматы: Қазақстан Республикасының ЮНЕСКО жөніндегі ұлттық коммисиясы, ЮНЕСКО жанындағы Қазақстан Республикасының тұрақты өкілдігі және Әл-Фараби Қазақ ұлттық университеті, 2000.

(Nurtazina) Нуртазина, Назира. *Қазақ мәдениеті және ислам: тарихи-мәдениеттанулық зерттеу* [*Kazakh Culture and Islam: Historical-Cultural Research*]. Алматы: Қазақтың мәдениет және өнертану ғылыми-зерттеу институти, 2003.

(Nurtazina) Нұртазина, Н.Д., Л.М. Хасанаева. *Ежелгі түріктердің исламдануының тарихи алғышарттары* [*Historical Prerequisites for the Islamization of the Ancient Turks*]. Алматы: «Қазақ университеті» баспасы, 2010.

(Nurzhekuhli) Нұржекеұлы, Бексұлтан. «Қазыбек бек және қазақ тарихы [Kazibek bek and Kazakh History]. // *Қазақ тарихынан* [*From Out of Kazakh History*]. Құрастырған Елден Аққошқаров, 427–454. Алматы: Жалын, 1997.

(Omiraliev) Омиралиев, Ч. *Тәңгірчилик* [*Tengrism*]. Бишкек, 1994. (Кыргыз)

(Omirzakov) Өмірзаков, Тоқтасын. Қазақ әдебиеті [*Kazakh Literature*]. 22 наурыз, 1990.

(Sarigulov) Саригулов, Дастан. *Тенгирчилик - киргиздардин дуину тааними, тубулук билими* [*Tengrism—The Spriitual Knowledge and Worldview of the Kyrgyz People*]. Бишкек: Тенгир Ордо, 2002. (Kyrgyz writer/activist)

(Seidimbek) Сейдімбек, Ақселеу. Қазақ элемі: етномәдени пайымдау [*The Kazakh World: An Ethnocultural Exegesis*]. Алматы,Қазақстан, 1997.

(Tai-Murat) Тай-Мурат, М. «Шамандык [Shamanism]». *Туркістан: Халықаралық Энциклопедиа* [*Turkistan: Halikaralik [International] Encyclopedia*]. Ред. А. Нысанбаев, 635–636. Алматы: Қазақ Энциклопедиясы, 2000.

(Tauasaruhli) Тауасарұлы, Шапырашты Қазыбек бек. *Түп-тұқияннан өзіме шейін* [*From the Earliest Roots down to Myself*]. Алматы, КЗ: Жалын, [1776] 1993.

(Zatov) Затов, Кайрат. «Ислам өркениеті аясындағы қазақ мәдениеті [Kazak Culture within the Embrace (or Bounds) of Islamic Civilizaton]». Қазақ мәдениетінің рухани кеңістігі [*The Spiritual Context of Kazakh Culture*]. Турсын Габитов (және Кайрат Затов), 190–308. Алматы: Раритет, 2013.

Russian

(Abashin) Абашин, Сергей. *Советский кишлак: Между колониализмом и модернизацией* [*The Soviet Village: Between Colonialism and Modernization*]. Москва: Новое литературное обозрение, 2015.

(Basilov) Басилов, Владимир Николаевич. *Шаманство у народов Средней Азии и Казахстана* [*Shamanism among the Peoples of Central Asian and Kazakhstan*]. Москва: Наука, 1992.

(Bozhe) Боже, В.С., редактор. *Летописцы земли Уральской: Материалы к истории челябинского краеведения* [*Chroniclers of the Ural Land: Materials for Local Chelyabinsk history*]. Челябинск: Центр историко-культурного наследия, 1997.

(Dobrosmyslov) "Добросмыслов Александр Иванович (1854 — дата смерти неизв.), краевед [Dobrosmyslov Alexander Ivanovich (1854–date of death unknown), local historian]." (URL: http://myaktobe.kz/archives/38809).

(Khasanov) Хасанов, Е.Р. Оренбургская ученая архивная комиссия: возникновение и работа научного общества на Южном Урале (конец XIX-начало XX. вв.) *[The Orenburg Scientific Archival Commission: The Appearance and Operation of the Scientific Community in the South Urals]*. Уфа: Стерлитамак, 1998.

(Klyashtornii) Кляшторный, Сергей Г. *Мифологические сюжеты вдревнетюркских памятниках: Тюркологический сб.* [*Mythological plots in ancient Turkic monuments: Turkological collection*]. Москва, 1981.

(Lubichankovskii) Любичанковский, С.В. "Научно-публикаторская деятельность Оренбургской ученой архивной комиссии (конец XIX — начало XX века)" ["Scientific and Publishing Activity of the Orenburg Scientific Archival Commission (End of XIX - Early XX Century)"]. *Вестник Оренбургского Государственного Педагогического Университета*, Vol. 12, No. 4 (2014).

(Mustafina) Мустафина, Раушан. *Представления, культы, обряды у казахов (в контексте бытового ислама в южном Казахстане в конце XIX–XX вв.)* [*Representations, Cults, Rituals among the Kazakhs: in the context of everyday Islam in southern Kazakhstan at the end of the 19th–20th centuries*]. Алма-Ата, 1992.

(Nikonov) Никонов, А.Ю. *Алтун битиг: Тенгрианство: мифы древних тюрков, сохраненные устным и письменным преданием тюркских народов мира* [*The Golden Bough: Tengrism: Myths of the Ancient Turks, preserved by the oral and written tradition of the Turkic peoples of the world*]. Алматы, 2000.

"Религия и просвещение: *Луначарский Анатолий Васильевич*, Введение в Историю Религии [Religion and enlightenment: Anatoly Lunacharsky, Introduction to the History of Religion]," *ВикиЧтение* [*WikiQuote*] (https://fil.wikireading.ru/87407).

(Sartori) Сартори, Паоло и Павел Шаблеи. *Эксперименты империи: адат, шариат и производство знаний в Казахской степи* [*Empire Experiments: Adat, Sharia and Knowledge Production in the Kazakh Steppe*]. М.: Новое литературное обозрение, 2019.

"Чернавский Николай Михайлович [Chernavskaya Nikolai Mikhailovich]," Древо: Открытая Православная Энциклопедия (URL: http://drevo-info.ru/articles/23906.html).

Iranian-Persian-Farsi

Atooni, Behzad, Mahdi Sharifian and Behrooz Atooni. "Comparative Study of Islamic Sufism and Shamanic Mysticism [بررسی تطبیقی تصوف اسلامی و عرفان شامانی]." *Biannual Journal of Mystical Literature* [دوسالانه ادبیات عرفانی], Volume 10, Number 19 (2018–2019): 7–26.

ناصر نیکوبخت و سید علی قاسم زاده، «روش های خاص شمنی گری در برخی از فرقه های صوفیه»، عرفان شناسی، شماره ۹، (بهار و تابستان ۱۳۶۷): ۱۸۵–۲۱۶. // Nikobakht, Nasser and Seyyed Ali Qassemzadeh. "Ecstatic Methods of Shamanism in Some Sufi Sects." *Mystical Studies*, Number 9 (Spring and Summer 1988): 185–216.

علی ناصری راد، افسون حلقه: نقد و بررسی عرفان حلقه [Ali Naseri Rad, *The Charm of the Ring: A Review of Ring Mysticism*] (۱۳۹۰ / ۱۹۷۰, سایان) [Tehran, Iran: Sayan, 2011]. (URL: https://ketabnak.com/book/57503/افسون-حلقه-نقد-و-بررسی-عرفان-حلقه)

Turkish

Arpacı, Günnur Yücekal. *Gök Tanrı İnancının Bilinmeyenleri* [*Unknown Belief in the God of Heaven*]. Istanbul: Cati Yayinlari, 2012.

Atsız, Mahsun. "Dede Korkut Kitabı'nın Günbet Yazması Üzerine Sentaktik Bir İnceleme." *Korkut Ata Türkiyat Araştırmaları Dergisi*, Volume 2 (Haziran-June 2020): 188–197.

Bedirhan, Yaşar. *İslam öncesi Türk tarihi ve kültürü* [*Pre-Islamic Turkish History and Culture*]. Kızılay, Ankara: Nobel Akademik Yayıncılık, 2011.

Bagci, Atilla. "Türk Kültüründe Kurdun Kutsiyetinin Şaman Mitlerindeki Yeri (The Holiness of the Wolf in Terms of Shaman Mythology in Turkish Culture)." *Türk Dünyası Dil ve Edebiyat Dergisi* [*Journal of Turkish World Language and Literature*], Number 42 (December 13, 2016): 7–15.

Çandarlıoğlu, Gülçin. *İslam öncesi Türk Tarihi ve Kültürü* [*Pre-Islamic Turkish History and Culture*]. Istanbul: Türk Dünyası Araştırmaları Vakfı, 2006.
Çelik, Muhammed Bilal. *İslam öncesi Türk tarihi ve kültürü* [*Pre-Islamic Turkish History and Culture*]. Ankara: Nobel Akademik Yayincilik, 2019.
Eröz, Mehmet. *Eski Türk Dini (gök tanrı inancı) ve Alevîlik-Bektaşilik* [*Old Turkish Religion (belief in sky god) and Alevism-Bektashism*]. Istanbul: Türk Dünyası Arastırmaları Vakfı, 1992.
Gedik, Ümit. "Fazlullâh b. Rûzbihân-i Huncî ve Mihmân-Nâme-İ Buhârâ'si Üzerine Bir Değerlendirme [Fazlullâh b. An An Evaluation on Rûzbihân-i Huncî and his Mihmân-Nâme-i Bukhara]." *İ.Ü. Şarkiyat Mecmuasi Sayi*, Volume 32 (January 2018): 95–128.
İnayet, Alimcan. "Bugünkü Uygurlarda Şamanlık ve Bir Şaman Duası: Azaîm Koşıkı [Shamanism among Today's Uighurs and a Shaman's Prayer: Azâim Koshıkı]." *Motif Akademi Halkbilimi Dergisi* [*Motif Academy Journal of Folklore*], Volumes 3–4, Number 2 (December 01, 2009): 38–52.
Kocasavaş, Yıldız. "Gök Tanrı İnancı [Faith in the God of Heaven]." In *Türkler Tarihi* [*History of the Turks*], Volume 3 (2002): 326–329 and 578–84.
Mömin, Samire. "Şamanîzm ve Günümüzdeki Kalintilari (Uygur Toplumundakî Tabular Üzerîne) [Shamanism and Its Consequential Residues (On Taboos in Uygur Society)." *Ulakbilge: Sosyal Bilimler Dergisi* [*Ulakbilge: Journal of Social Sciences*], Volume 1, Number 1 (Feb 2015): 79–89.
Öden, Zerrin Günal. *İslam öncesi Türk tarihi ve kültürü* [*Pre-Islamic Turkish History and Culture*]. Ankara: Nobel Paradigma Kitabevi, 2004.
Orhan, Yilmaz. "Alevilikte Eski Türk Dini (Göktanri Inanci) ve Şamanîzmîn Etkîlerî [The Effects of Ancient Turkish Religion (Belief in Heaven) and Shamanism in Alevism]." *Akademik Tarih ve Düşünce Dergisi* [*Journal of Academic History and Thought*], Volume 4, Number 1 (December 01, 2014): 1–13.
Şener, Cemal. *Şamanizm: Türkler'in İslamiyet'ten önceki dini* [*Shamanism: The Religion of the Turks before Islam*]. Istanbul: Etik Yayınları [1997] 2010.
Velioglu, Özgür. *İnançların Türk Sinemasına Yansıması: şamanizm, gök-tanrı, animizm, naturizm, totemizm, İslamiyet inançları açısından* [*Reflection of Beliefs on Turkish Cinema: Shamanism, Sky-god, animism, naturism, totemism, in terms of Islamic beliefs*]. Kadıköy/İstanbul Es Yayınları 2005.

INDEX

A
Abbasid Muslims, 115
Abdakimuhli, Abdizhapar, 136, 139
ablution, 228
About the Reactionary Essence of the Religion of Islam (Kakimzhanov), 95, 108–113
About the Religion of Islam and Its Current Standing (Duisenbin), 182
About the Religion of Islam and Its Current State (Duisenbin), 121–124
Abu-ali ibn-Sina (Avicenna), 117
Adams, John, 17
Adji, Murat, 138, 144
al-Afghani, Jamal ad-Din, 93
agrarian magic, 79
agricultural religions, 76
Ahmed, S., 12
Aknazarov, Husaiin Zeinetdinuhlii, 100
Alash Orda, 115, 116
Al-Bulagh al-Mubin, 35

Alexander I, 63, 235
Alexander II, 56, 215, 216, 235
Alexander III, 212, 215, 235
Ali, Hazem Hussein Abbas, 34
Almaty, 143
Altai national independence struggle, 146
altar rituals, 201
Altinsarin, Ibirai, 112, 118
Alymov, S.S., 12, 96
Amanturlin, Shinbergen Bekpanovich, 99
Amirgazin, Serik T., 137–140, 149
Amon, 110
ancestors, cult of, 146
ancestral shamanic religion, 108
ancestral spirits/gods, 40, 42, 60, 78, 79, 124, 147, 151, 152
ancestral veneration, 148
Ancient Khorezm, 77
Anderson, David G., 96
Andijan Uprising, 216, 231
Andreev, M.S., 62, 63, 74, 89, 94
Anichkov, E.V., 30

animism, 79, 124
animistic (or polytheistic) religion, 108
Anisimov, A.F., 73
anti-Islamic agenda in his 'pre-Islamic survivals' ethnography, 94
anti-Islamic polemical versus an animistic/shamanistic-oriented missionary, 216
anti-Islamic resistance thesis, 38
anti-Muslim persecution, 219
anti-religious activists, 170
anti-religious propagandists, 123
apostasy, 42, 44
Arab Christians, Middle Eastern, 39
Arabic (and Persian) Islamic terms, 40
Arabic script, 90, 215
Arabs, 114
   and Bedouin tribes, 76
   conquering Central Asia, 115
   emergence of Islam among, 110
   feudal-clan society, 92
   heathenism, 46
   pagan, 45
   tribal gods, pre-Islamic, 110
   tribes, polytheism worship by, 132
Art Leete, 175
aruakhs. *See* ancestral spirits/gods
Aruaq, 40
Arzyutov, Dmitry V., 96
Asfendiarov, Sanzhar Zhafarovich, 75, 90, 91
Astrakhan Tatars, 224
Atash, B.M., 176
Ataturk, Kemal, 166
atheism, 98, 123
Atheist (journal), 75
atheistic education, 100
atheistic propaganda, 124
Atooni, Behrooz, 179
Atooni, Behzad, 179
Atwood, Christopher, 58

Auezov, Mukhtar, 145
Auezov, Murat, 145
Auezova, Zifa-Alua, 75
Avicenna, 117
Azbukin, M., 30
Azerbaijani, 41
Aziz, Soumia, 179

B
Baal, 22
Babadzhanov, Mukhaminad-Salikh, 9
Baer, Marc David, 185
Bagči, Atilla, 166
Baieke, Manarbek, 143–146
Baitenova, Nagima, 153–154, 202
Balasaghuni, Yusuf, 36, 38, 41, 168, 207
Banzarov, Dorzhi, 58
baqsi figures, 58, 170
baqsy (shaman), 62
Barbol, Aziret, 147
Barthold, V.V., 50
Bashkir Rebellion, 232
The Bashkir rebellion in 1735–1737 gg, 232
Bashkir Rebellion in 1735–37 (Chernavsky), 220
Bashkirs, 50, 51, 89, 218, 227, 229, 237
Basilov, Vladimir Nikolaevich, 165
Basmachi band, 120
Basmachi Rebellion, 94
Battle of Talas (or Atlah), 115, 189
Bazur (magician), 37
Bedouin nomadic tribes, 76, 90–92
Before Boas: The Genesis of Ethnography and Ethnology in the German Enlightenment (Vermeulen), 20
Begaliev, Gali, 90
Begiev, Musa, 93

INDEX 387

Bekmukhanova, E.B., 100
beliefs, 137
   Kirgiz, 59
   pagan, 30, 59, 62, 80, 226
   shamanistic, 59
Bentley, J.H., 12
Berber practices, 81
Berger, S., 12
Bering Straits, 51
Berke khan, 133
al-Beruni, 117
Beyond Syncretism and Colonial Legacies in the Study of Religion, 12
bias
   against understandings of "Islam", 191
   Sunni, 191
Bible Societies, 28
Biographical Dictionary (Khalidi), 191
Bisenov, Kh., 113–121
Black Christianity, 172
Black Islam, 172
Blackstone, William, 18
Blagovidov, F., 233
Blanes, Ruy, 186
Blessed Wisdom (Balasaghuni), 37–39
"Bloody Sunday", 235
Boas, Friedrich, 73
Bobrovnikov, Vladimir, 12, 98
Bogayevsky, B.L., 73
Bogoraz, V.S., 73
Bolsheviks, 136
Book of Korkut Ata (or Dede Korkut), 41
Boxer Uprising, 216
Brand, Joseph, Reverend, 15, 17
Brezhnev, Leonid, 170, 174
Buddhism/Buddhists, 3, 58, 201
   Central Asian, 154
   influence on Shamanism, 173
Bukeihanuhli, Bukenbay, 49

Bukei Horde, 59
Bukharan identity, 7, 42, 54, 225, 227, 229
Bukhari, Baha'uddin Naqshband, 189
Bulgakov, Makarii, 30
Bulutai, Murtaza, 133, 136, 139
   on Western Christian threat to post-Soviet Islamic revival, 140–143, 144–148
   scholars and historiographical interpretations, 140–143
burial practices, Kazakh, 50
Burkhanism, 145
Buryats, 231

C
Calvin, John, 25
Campbell, Elena, 64, 234
Canaanite peoples, 22
Capitalism (Marx), 117
Caristia, 24
Castagné, J., 171
Catherine II, Queen, 111, 115, 133, 183, 189
   establishment and promotion of Muslim institutions, 122
   religious policies towards Kazakhs, 51
Catherine the Great, debate over policies of, 211–239
   before and after Catherine's policies, historical context, 214–217
   Dobrosmyslov's underlying methodology and reliability, 236–239
   essential points of agreement-disagreement, 217–234
   Orenburg Scientific Archival Commission, 211–214
   Tsarist state agendas for Kazakh Islam, 234–236
Catholics, 15, 16, 184

cattle breeding magic, 79
Caucasian Muslims, 62, 237
Central Asia: Contexts for Understanding (Montgomery), 8
Central Asia in World History (Golden), 36
Central Asian emirates, 227, 229
Central Asian Khanates, 225
Central Asian sources, 42–45
Central Asian traditions, 10, 33, 36, 186, 207
Chagatai rulers, 42
Cheremis, 40
Chernavsky, G., 218
Chernavsky, N.M., 228, 239
  Chernavsky-Dobrosmyslov debate, 211–239
  on nature of Islam and its impact upon Kazakhs, 230–234
  on Russian religious nationalism, 234–236
China, 216
Christianity, 3, 27
  and interpretations of Islam within Kazakh history, 141–157
  Central Asian, 154
  dogmas of, 116
Christianity and Paganism in the Fourth to Eighth Centuries (McMullen), 24
chronological frame of Soviet 'survivals' ethnography, 98–101
Chukchi people, 73
Chulkov, Mikhail Dmitrievich, 28
Church Bulletin, 233
Church of the East, 144
co-existence, 132, 144, 153, 197, 199
Collection of Laws about the Kirgiz People (Kraft), 218, 222
collective memory, 146, 190
collectivization campaigns, 148

colonialist vs. post-colonialist historiography, 187–189
Compendium of the Turkic Dialects (Dīwān Lughāt al-Turk) (Kashgari), 36, 41
Comprehensive Persian-English Dictionary, 37
Confucianism, 137, 201
conversions. *See* religious conversions
Cooke Taylor, William, 20
Council for the Affairs of Religious Cults (CARC), 96
Council of Tours, 24
Crews, Robert D., 9
Crimea, Russia's annexation of, 224
Crimean War, 56
crosscultural contact and exchange, 197–200
Cross-Cultural Encounters in Modern World History, 1453–Present, 12
crosscultural "influence" and pre-Islamic survivals, 76
cult, 146, 174
  indigenous religious, 192
  of ancestors, 79, 146
  of hearth, 79
  of spirits, 79
  pre-Islamic, 85
The Cult of the Ongons in Siberia: Remnants [Перееежитки] of Totemism in the Ideology of the Siberian Peoples, 73
cultural anthropology, 7
cultural-civilizational superiority, 169
Cunow, Heinrich, 72
The Current State Of The Ottoman Empire (d'Ohsson), 53
customs, 21, 23, 24, 27, 29, 45, 46, 51, 54, 59–61, 74, 76, 79, 81, 97, 108, 112, 114, 116, 120, 123, 132, 137, 138, 140, 165, 180, 188, 201. *See also* rituals

D

Daily Travel Notes...in the Kirghiz-Kaisakh Steppe, in 1771, 50
Dalton, John, 17
Dankoff, Robert, 36
Dannhauer, Johannes Konrad, 184
Davidann, J.T., 12
death, mystical, 174
debates over terminology, pre-islamic constructs, 184–187
demonology, 171
Descartes, René, 17
Description of the Kirgiz-Kaisak Hordes and Steppes (Levshin), 100
A Description of Kirghiz-Kaisak, or Kirghiz-Kazakhstani Hordes and Steppes (Levshin), 52
Devotion to Islam—A Detrimental Survival (Mashrapov), 124
DeWeese, Devin, 2–7, 12, 15, 22, 25, 35, 84, 96, 98
  argument against Soviet interpreters, 174–176
  critique of Turkish, French & Soviet Scholarship, 166–168
  Shamanization in Central Asia, 165
  terms used for religious-cultural traditions, 186
disbelief in Islamic faith, 112
Divaev, A.A., 63, 171
Dobrosmyslov, A.I.
  authority in modern scholarship, 236–239
  westernizing liberal enlightenment, 234–236
The Doctrine of Survivals: A Chapter in the History of Scientific Method in the Study of Man (Hodgen), 12, 18
Donnelly, Alton S., 236
dual-faith paradigm, 51, 53, 58, 201–203
  and Soviet 'survivals' historiography, 26–31
  post-Soviet "survivals" scholarship, 201–203
  Valikhanov on, 55–59
d'Ohsson, Ignatius Mouradgea, 53
Dughlat, Mirza Muhammad Haidar, 42, 191–192
Duisenbin, Zh., 121–124, 182
Dukhovskoi, S.M., 216, 234
Duncan, George, 26
Dvoryans, 136

E

Egyptian Pyramids, 34
Eirenikon Catholicum (Erbermann), 184
Eliade, Mircea, 6, 109, 173
Elizabeth I, Empress, 218, 223
Emon, Anver, 198
emshi, 169
Engels, Freidrich, 69, 95, 110, 114
  on world religions, 86–88
  Soviet 'Survivals' Ethnography, 68–71
Enlightenment interpreters, 172
Enlightenment progressivist approach, 55
Erasmus, 184
Erbermann, Veit, 184
Esim, Garifolla, 131, 140, 141, 150, 151
Essays on Primitive Islam (Tolstov), 79
The Essence of Mind: Reflections on Politics and Culture (Esim), 131
ethnic animosity, 118
Ethnographic Essay (Semenov), 63
Ethnographic Materials (Divaev), 63
Euro-American ethnographers, 97

Euro-American sources of influence on Soviet ethnographers, 72–73
Euro-American 'survivals' historiography, Russian influence on, 26, 51. *See also* Soviet 'survivals' historiography and Tylor
European Protestants, 144
Euro-Slavic ethnographers, 26, 97. *See also* Soviet 'survivals' historiography and Tylor
evangelization, 216
Everyday Islam in Post-Soviet Central Asia, 7
evil spirit (jinni), 190

F
faqih (religious scholar), 37
Farhadian, C.E., 12
fasts, 121, 228
Fedotov, George P., 68
Feener, R. Michael, 33
female musical & healing traditions, 164–165
Ferghana, 115
Festivals and Superstitious Rituals of the Russian Common People (Snegirev), 29
fetishism, 124
Fetishism and the Problem of the Origin of Religion (Frantsov), 73
Feuerbach, Ludwig, 69
Filotas, Bernadette, 24
Firdousi, 37, 207
fire rituals, 178
fire rituals/worship, 59
Fisher, Johann Eberhard, 52
Fodio, Usman dan, 35
Following the Tracks of Ancient Khorezmian Civilization, 81
Foltz, Richard, 4
Formichi, Chiara, 172

For Prophet and Tsar: Islam and Empire in Russia and Central Asia, 9
Frank, Allen J., 6, 92, 177, 237
Franklin, Benjamin, 17
Frantsov, G.P., 73
Frazer, James, 68, 70, 72, 73, 75, 77
French scholarship, Deweese's critique of, 166–168
From Belonging to Belief: Modern Secularisms and the Construction of Religion in Kyrgyzstan (McBrien), 8
From the Realm of Kirgiz Beliefs (essay), 59
funeral customs, 81

G
Gabitov, Tursin Hafiz, 3, 135, 139, 141, 151–153, 202
Gal'kovskii, N., 30
Geertz, Clifford, 6, 11, 98, 195, 238
German enlightenment sources, 20–22
Gilbert, M.J., 12
Golden Horde, 6, 35, 133, 156
Golden, Peter B., 36, 38, 40, 192
Goldziher, Ignaz, 35, 46, 75, 81
Golubinskii, E.E., 30
Gonbad manuscript, 41
Great Patriotic War, 81, 123
Greco-Byzantine culture, 76
Greek Orthodoxy, 174
Grekov, B., 68

H
hagiography, Russian Orthodox, 27
Hâjib, Yûsuf Khâss, 36
Hajji, Otemish, 6, 35
Hakim(s) ('Elite' scholar), 296

Half a Lifetime in Turkestan: Essays on the Life of the Native Peoples (Lyoshkin), 63
Hamadani, Yusuf, 43
Hanbali legal tradition, 34
Han Yu, 251
Harrison, W.H., 12, 186
Haruzin, A.N., 49, 59, 100
Hausa belief, 35
healing practices, shamanic, 168, 171
Hebrew Bible, 22, 76
Hebrew-Jewish and Christian Sources of 'Survivals' Historiography, 22–26
Hebrew religion, 116
Herder, Johann Gottfried, 28
Hinduism, 40, 43, 200
Hirsch, Francine, 12
Historical Herald, 233
Historical Prerequisites for the Islamization of the Ancient Turks (Nurtazina and Khasanaeva), 150
The History of Christianity in Kazakhstan and Central Asia, 143
History of Humanity project, 11, 12, 196
History of Kazakhstan, 155, 176, 190
History of Religious Ideas (Eliade), 109
History of Russia (Vernadsky), 31
History of Russia from the Earliest Times (Solov'ev), 30
History of Spirituality in the East (Smirnov), 30
An History of the Corruptions of Christianity (Priestley), 17
History of the Moghuls of Central Asia (Dughlat), 42, 191
History of the Russian Church (Golubinskii), 30
History of the Russian Church (Nikol'skii), 68

Hobart, Angela, 165, 167, 179
Hodgen, Margaret, 12, 18, 22
Homer, 17
How the Religion of Islam was Founded (Begaliev), 90, 91
Humayun, 191

I
ibn Abd al-Wahhab, Muhammad, 34
ibn Muslim, Qutaybah, 189
Ibn Rushd, 198
ibn Ruzbihan Isfahani, Fazl Allah, 42, 44, 111, 112, 189, 191–192
Ibn Taimiyah, 34
Ibn Tufayl, 198
Ibragimov, G., 90, 93, 95
Ibragimov, Sh., 217
Iconology: Papal Idolatry: Or, Modern Romanism: A Development of Ancient Paganism (Duncan), 26
idolatry, 45, 51, 52, 146
idol worship, 57, 112, 146
Igelstrom, O.I., 51
Il'minskii, N.I., 49, 215, 217, 234
Ilyasov, S., 81
Imam, 230
Impious Women (Smirnov), 30
In Praise of Mixed Religion: The Syncretism Solution in a Multifaith World (Harrison), 12, 186
Inayet, Alimcan, 167
inclusivist interdependent humanitarianist historiography, 197–200
Indians, 237
indigenous cultural resistance movement, 146
indigenous peoples, 195
Inner Asian shamanship, 168
integral culture, 177
integral religious identities, 201–203
interreligious interaction, 36

Introduction to the History of Religion (Frazer), 72
An Investigation into the History of Church Life (Smirnov), 30
Ioannovna, Anna, Empress, 51, 218, 219
Iranian peoples, 46, 74, 165, 173, 180, 187, 192
Iranian religion, 116
Iraqi, Shams-ud-Din, 42, 43
Islam and Asia, 172
"Islam and Nomadic Economy" (Asfendiarov), 75
Islamic approaches towards religious-cultural revivalism, 140–157
Islamic ascendancy, 35
An Islamic Biographical Dictionary of the Eastern Kazakh Steppe, 1770–1912 (Frank), 6
Islamic confession and ritual prayers, 165
Islamic identity, pure, 169
Islamic loyalty, 156
Islamic preaching among Kazakhs, 122
Islamic Rationalist Views of Divine and Natural Law, 1671–1721, 198
Islamic-related influences, 43
Islamic shrines, Javanese, 34
Islamic societies to the Nineteenth Century, 4
Islamic sources
  Middle Eastern, 33–35
  Qur'anic, 33–35
Islam, Soviet assaults on, 90, 127, 150, 171
Islamization, 41, 61, 155–157, 189, 190, 237–239
Islamization and Native Religion in the Golden Horde (Deweese), 2, 5, 35, 166

Islam zhanye Ortagasyrlyk Turkiler [Islam and the Turks of the Middle Ages] (Kartabaeva), 155
Ivan IV, 221

J
Jadid ideas of reform, 118
Jadidists, 93
Jefferson, Thomas, 17, 198
Jefferson-Tatum, Elana, 12, 186
Jenkinson, Anthony, 51
Jensen, J.S., 12
jinn, 171
John of Damascus, 45, 70
Joshua, 23
Journal of Islamic Studies, 7
Journal of the Ministry of National Education, 233
Judaism, 3, 200
Jungars, 222

K
Ka'aba, 45
Kakimzhanov, A., 95, 101
Kalmyks, 51, 231
Kandaur Tatars, 224
Karakhanid sources, 35–42
Karakhanid Turks, 38, 41, 176
Kara-Kirgiz religion, 59
Karamanuhli, Kurmangazi, 132–134, 139, 140
Karras, Ruth Mazo, 24
Kartabaeva, Erke Tamabekkyzy, 155, 202
Kartaeva, Tattygul, 154, 173, 202
Kashgari, Mahmud, 36, 41, 207
Kashmir
  religious groups in, 42–43
  Sun-worshipers of, 44

Kasimov, Kenesari, 118
Kaufman, K.P. von, 234
Kavelin, K.D., 29, 57, 73
Kazakh colonial ethnographer, first, 55–59
Kazakh Culture and Islam (Nurtazina), 148
Kazakh customary law, 54, 215
Kazakh nomads, 51, 101–102, 148
Kazakh religious identity, 2–9, 44–45
Kazakh religious identity, historiographical interpretations of, 129–157
  essential issues, 131
  Islamic approaches and Christian interludes, 140–157
  Tengrist historiography, 132–140
Kazakh religious practice, 42
Kazakh(s), 295
Kazakh semantic domain, 40
Kazakhstan, 296
Kazakhstan: Religions and Society in the History of Central Eurasia, 9
Kazakhstanskaya Pravda, 121
Kazakh Steppe, 52
  culture and 'pre-Islamic survivals', 101–102
  destruction of Shamanism in, 177
  'holy war' against 'the unbelievers' on, 118
  spreading of Russian culture on, 118
  spread of Islam on, 122, 133, 139
  trade networks in, 43, 221, 224
Kazak religion, 39
The Kazakh World: An Ethnocultural Exegesis (Seidimbek), 134
Kazan Tatars, 221, 223
Kazan Theological Academy, 30, 52, 233
Keller, Shoshana, 88
Kemalists, 93
Kemper, Michael, 87, 92

Kerei clans, 143
Kerei tribe, 145
keremet (керрееемеет, 'amazing,' 'miraculous'), 40
Khalid, Adeeb, 4, 175, 190
Khalidi, Qurban-Ali, 191
Khan, Abul Khair, 218, 222
Khan, Kasim, 44
Khan, Nuraly, 218, 222
Khan, Ozbek, 6, 35
Khan, Satuq Bughra, 36
Khan, Uzbek, 155, 189
Khasanaeva, N.D., 150
Khiva, 225, 227, 229
Khivans, 54
khojas, 123
Khorezm Al-Beruni, 115
Khorezm oasis, 85
Khoroshkhin, A.P., 62
Khrushchev, Nikita, 99
Khudai, 190
Khusraw, Nasir, 37
Kiev Rus (Likhachev and Grekov), 68
Kirgiz-Kaisak people, 218, 224
Kirgiz peoples, 57, 59, 79
Kirgiz Peoples of the Bukei Horde (Haruzin), 100
Kisliakov, N.A., 80
Knorozov, Iu.V., 75, 78, 81, 85
kok tangiri ('the sky god'), 108, 112
Koran. *See* Qur'an
Korkut, 166
kozha families, 134
Kraft, I.I., 218
Krasinski, Valerian, Count, 26
Kubrawi Sufi, 43
Kunanbaev, Abai, 112
Kunanbaiuhli, Abai, 59–61, 86, 118, 189, 190, 192
Kunanbaiuhli, Abai (Ibrahim, 1845–1904), 296

394 INDEX

'kurban ait' (that is, 'the feast of sacrifice'), 121
Kutadgu Bilig (*Blessed Wisdom or Knowledge*), 36
Kyrgyz, 1, 7, 55, 62, 89, 231

L
Lake Issyk-kul, 57
Lamaism, 173
Lamas, 58
land confiscation, 142
languages
   Central Asian, 54
   Kazakh, 54, 134
   Russian, 39
   Turkic, 39
   Volga Finnic, 40
Lapidus, Ira M., 4
Latin Christianity, 24
Latin script, 90
Lectures on the Science of Language (Müller), 57
Leibniz, Gottfried Wilhelm, 17
Lenin, V.I., 68–71, 95
Leningrad conference, 98
Leopold, A.M., 12
Levshin, A.I., 9, 29, 49, 52, 100, 190, 217, 228, 236
   Russian colonialist context, 53–54
   Russian Orthodox 'dual faith' paradigm, 53
Lévy-Bruhl, Lucien, 72, 73, 77
Lewis, Abram Herbert, 26
Life of the Russian People (Tereshchenko), 29
Likhachev, D.S., 68
linguistic etymologies, 58
Locke, John, 198
Lomonosov, Mikhail V., 29
Louw, Maria E., 7
Lubichankovsii, 212

Lunacharsky, Anatoly V., 72
Lyoshkin, N.S., 63

M
MacKenzie, David, 236
MacMullen, Ramsay, 24
Madison, James, 198
madrasas, establishment of, 220
magical ideologies, 79, 174
Mahometan rituals, 45
al-Maksidi, 137
Malov, Evfimii A., 9, 51–53, 217, 219, 220, 234
Mami, Hamamoto, 219
Manicheanism, 3, 191
Manuylova, L.N., 73
Marduk, 110
Mari of Siberia, 39, 40
marriage customs, Kazakh, 61
Martius, 18, 20
Marx, Karl, 95
   Soviet 'Survivals' Ethnography, 68–71
   view of the major world religions, 86
Marxian-Engelsian views on pre-Islamic survivals, 187
Mashrapov, K., 124
Materials on the Ethnography of the Iranian Tribes of Central Asia, 63
mausoleums, building, 123
McBrien, Julie, 8
Medina, 148
Meiji Restoration, 201
Mesopotamian influences on Shamanism, 173
Methods of Anti-religious Propaganda among Muslims (pamphlet), 88
Meyer, A., 217
Middleton, Conyers, 15, 16
migrations in ancient history, 51

Mikhailovsky, V.M., 73
Militant Atheism, 98
Milton, John, 17
Miniyanova, Aelita, 220
Mir (Shayk) Shams-ud-Din Iraqi, 42
Mirzaliev, Kadir, 133
missionaries
　Christian, 143
　Muslim, 139
missionaries, Christian. *See* Russian Orthodox missionaries
Moghuls and Kazakhs, political alliance, 44
Mohammad, prophet, 34, 81, 87, 92, 116, 132, 142, 148, 150
Mohammedanism, 51, 225
Mohammedans, 51
Moïmin, Samire, 166
Mongol court, 53
Mongol Empire, 75
Mongolian shamanism, 58
Mongol tribes, 152
monotheism, 18
Monotheistic Degenerational versus Evolutionary Developmental Theories of Early Human History, 16–20
monotheistic degenerationist, 193
monotheistic traditions, 114
Montgomery, David, 8
Mosaic and Sharia Law in American National History and Identity (Weller), 198
Moses, 169
mosques
　building of, 52, 219, 221
　destruction of, 142
　mosque-based sermons, 158
　Mu'ayyad mosque, 35
　Tatar-dominated, 192
mourning customs, 81
Mu'ayyad mosque, 35

Muftiyat, 158
Mughal courts in India, 191
mullahs, Tatar, 113, 134, 237
Müller, Friedrich Max, 57, 58
Muslim missionaries, 139
The Muslim Question and Russian Imperial Governance, 234
Muslim Religious Institutions in Imperial Russia: The Islamic World of Novouzensk District and the Kazakh Inner Horde, 1780–1910 (Frank), 6, 92
Muslim-Soviet assault, 171
Muslim Studies (Goldziher), 46, 75
Muslim Turkistan: Kazak Religion and Collective Memory (Privratsky), 6, 58, 168–173, 185
Muslim versus Christian identity, 25

N
Naiman clans, 143
Nalivkin, M.V., 62
Nalivkin, V.P., 62
Naqshbandi tariqa, 189
Nation(hood), national, 296
nationalist historiography, 14, 208
Native Americans, 21
The Natural History of Society in the Barbarian and Civilized State (Taylor), 20
nature and ancient practices, 62
Nauryz (or, Nowruz), Persian New Year, 178
Nazarbaev, Nursultan, 147
Neplyuev, I., 218, 222
Nestor, Saint, 27, 55
Nestorian Christianity, 3, 126
Nicholas I, 235
Nicholas II, 212, 215, 216, 231, 235
Nikol'skii, N.M., 68

Nikol'sky, V.K., 72, 73, 77
Nöldeke, Theodor, 46, 70, 81
nomads, 89, 115
  Bedouin tribes, 76, 92
  Central Asian Muslim, 43, 116
  culture of, 101–102, 147–149, 156
  Eurasian nomadic economico-cultural type of people, 152
  Kazakh, 51, 89, 92, 101–102, 147
  steppe, 42, 138, 147, 152
  Turkic, 136, 149, 151
  worship of the God of Heaven, 144
non-Muslim faith traditions, suppression of, 57
North and East Tartarye (Witsen), 20
Novikov, A.I., 73
Nurbakshi order, 43
Nurbakshi Sufi teachings, 42
Nurtazina, Nazira, 133, 140, 148–151, 191, 202

O
Oghuz-Kagan (ruler), 41
Oghuz Turks of Central Asia, 41, 189
Old Russian History (Lomonosov), 29
Old World Encounters: Cross-Cultural Contacts and Exchanges in Pre-Modern Times, 12
Oleshchik, F., 90
Omirzakov, Toktasin, 133
On the Origin of Civilization (Whately), 20
On the Path to a Culture of Peace, 153
On the Reactionary Role of the Followers of Islam (Oleshchik), 90
oral tradition, 123
Orenburg Diocese, 233
The Orenburg Diocese in the Past and Present in the Proceedings of the Society of History, Archaeology

and Ethnography at the Imperial University of Kazan, 232
Orenburg Eparchy, 216
Orenburg. List, 220, 232
Orenburg Scientific Archival Commission, 211–214
Orhan, Yilmaz, 166
The Origin of Islam and Its Class Significance (Bisenov), 113–121
The Origin of Religion and Faith of God (Cunow), 72
Origin of Species (Darwin), 58
Osmolovskii, Iosif (Efim) Yakovlevich, 54–55
Ostroumov, N.P., 62, 234
Otirar, 123
Ottoman Turkish Empire, 119
The Oxford Handbook of Religious Conversion, 12, 185
Ozbek khan, 133

P
pagan beliefs, 30, 59, 62, 80, 226
pagan customs, 27
pagan error, 51
pagan faith traditions, 36, 62
pagan idolatry, remnants of, 21, 33
paganism, Russian, 27
Paganism and Christianity, 100–425 CE: A Sourcebook, 24
Paganism and Old Rus (Anichkov), 30
Paganism in Ancient Rus (Rybakov), 68
Paganism Surviving in Christianity (Lewis), 26
pagan practices, remnants of, 22, 35, 51
Pagan Survivals in Mohammedan Civilisation: Lectures on the traces of pagan beliefs, customs, folklore,

INDEX 397

practices and rituals surviving in the popular religion and magic of Islamic peoples (Westermarck), 11, 80
Pagan Survivals, Superstitions, and Popular Cultures in Early Medieval Pastoral Literature (Filotas), 24
Paine, Thomas, 198
Pallas, P.S., 50, 51
The Past as History: National Identity and Historical Consciousness in Modern Europe, 12
The Past of Kazakhstan in the Eastern Sources and Materials (Haruzin), 100
patriarchal-tribal relations, 114
Patriotic War of the USSR, 120
Peoples of the World, 96, 97
perezhiktki survival paradigm, 61–62
persecutions
  and religious fait, 121
  anti-Muslim, 219
  by Tsarist government, 122
  Shia, 42
Persians, 76, 165, 237
Peshchereva, E.M., 75
Peter the Great, 20, 51, 221, 235
Philological Notes (magazine), 57
Philosophy, philosophical, 295
pietistic enlightenment tradition, 51
Plutarch, 184
Pobedonostsev, K.P., 234
Pococke, Edward, 52
Pocockio, Edvardo, 52
Poiarkov, F., 49, 59
Pokrovsky, A.M., 73, 233
Politics, political, 295
Polobtsov, A.A., 63, 74
Polovcians, 27
Pomeshchiks, 136
Popery and Paganism (Middleton), 17

Popular Religion in Russia: 'Double Belief' and the Making of an Academic Myth (Rock), 12, 27, 55
post-colonialist historiography, 187–189, 200
post-colonialist scholarship. *See* Shamanism and Islam, historical relation of
post-Mongol (and post-Crusade) revivals, 35
post-Soviet approaches to Islam, 8
post-Soviet Kazakh intellectuals and scholars, 129, 140. *See also* Kazakh religious identity, historiographical interpretations of
post-Soviet "survivals" scholarship, 174. *See also* Soviet scholarship
  beyond 'syncretism' and 'pre-islamic' constructs, 184–197
  continuities & discontinuities in colonialist vs. post-colonialist historiography, 187–188
  dual faith, 201–204
  historical end point of conversion, 189–193
  historiographical trends in the post-world war two era, 193–197
  inclusivist interdependent humanitarianist' historiography, 197–200
  integral religious identities, 201–205
  post-colonialist agendas & historian's task, 186–189
  religious survivals, 201–205
post-world war two era, historiographical trends in, 193–197
Potapov, L.P., 75
Practicing Islam: Knowledge, Experience, and Social Navigation in Kyrgyzstan (Montgomery), 8
prayers, 228

pre-Islamic Arabian tribal gods, 110
pre-Islamic Arab religious-cultural
    practices, 34
pre-islamic constructs, debates over
    terminology, 184–187
pre-Islamic cults, 85
pre-Islamic 'pagan' practices, 56
pre-Islamic relics, 84
pre-Islamic remains, 34
pre-Islamic survivals, 44
    in Soviet anti-Islamic propaganda
        literature, 88–93
    Soviet deployment and, 94–99
    Western interpretations of, 45–46
Priestley, Joseph, 17
Primitive Culture (Tylor), 16, 17, 19,
    26, 68, 72
*Primitive Religion in the Light of
    Ethnography*, 73
Privratksy, Bruce G., 6, 39, 41, 58, 98,
    165, 168, 182
    providing evidence on Kazakh sha-
        mans' rituals and healings, 174
    views on Historical & Present
        Relation of Shamanism &
        Islam, 168–173
*Proceedings of the Orenburg Scientific
    Archival Commission*, 213, 233
propaganda, Soviet anti-Islamic
    atheistic, 124
    in the Post-World War Two Period,
        94–99
    literature, 88–93
A Prophetic Trajectory (Blanes), 186
Protestants, 172
    Anti-Catholic Polemicists and Tylor,
        15–16
    anti-Catholic polemics, 16
    European, 144
    polemics, 15
    Reformation, 25

publications. *See* Soviet Kazakh
    publications
Pugachev Uprising, 224

Q
Qadimists, 93
Qipčaq religion, 192
Qoja informants, 169, 170
Qur'an, 76, 91, 93, 117, 132, 136,
    230
    distribution among Kazakhs, 133
    religious-cultural 'survivals' in the,
        34
Qur'anic Islamic sources, 33–35
Qur'anic Sura, 43
Quraysh tribe, 110

R
racial-civilizational superiority, 169
Radlov, V.V., 49
Rambo, L.R., 12
al-Razi, 38
*Reason, Revelation and Law in Islamic
    and Western Theory and History*
    (Emon), 198
Reasons for the Emergence of Islam
    (Asfendiarov), 75, 76, 90, 91
*The Reflection of Beliefs on Turkish
    Cinema: Shamanism, Sky-god,
    Animism, Naturism, Totemism, in
    terms of Islamic Beliefs* (Velioğlu),
    166
religio-cultural tradition, 36
*The Religion of Islam and Its
    Reactionary Essence* (Aknazorov),
    100
*The Religion of Islam and the Truth
    of Life by Husaiin Zeinetdinuhlii
    Aknazarov*, 100

The Religion of Islam: Instrument of Imperialism (Ibragimov), 90, 93
The Religion of the Fathers (Bulutai), 140, 147, 150
Religions of the Silk Road (Foltz), 4
Religionswissenschaft, 5
religious allegiances, 43
Religious Beliefs of the Peoples of the USSR: a collection of ethnographic materials, 77
religious connotations, 184
religious conversions, 52, 142
   and Dobrosmyslov's authority in modern scholarship, 236–239
   forced, 25
   historical end point of, 189–190
   Russian Orthodoxy and Kazakhs' conversion, 56
   theoretical constructs of, 184
religious-cultural influence, 58
religious-cultural revivalism. *See* Kazakh religious identity, historiographical interpretations of
religious fanaticism, 123
religious freedom, 121
The Religious History of Central Asia from the Earliest Times to the Present Day (Thrower), 4
religious indictment, 44
religious influences, 43
religiously-driven historiographies, 200
religious-political authority, 231
religious survivals, 74, 201–206. *See also* post-Soviet "survivals" scholarship; Soviet 'survivals' ethnography
   and Tsarist Russian missionaries, 61–62
   in the Qur'an, 34
religious toleration, 111, 183, 215
religious vocabulary, 168
remnants historiography, 33, 59–62. *See also* pagan idolatry, remnants of
Remnants [ОссОтаатки] of Pagan Customs among Natives (essay), 62
Remnants of the Past as a General Sociological Category, 96
Researches into the Early History of Mankind and the Development of Civilization (Tylor), 17, 18
Reynolds, John Myrdhin, 251
Ritual and Belief in Morocco, 81
rituals, 50, 60–61, 83. *See also* Snesarev, G.P., evaluating beliefs and rituals of the Peoples of Central Asia
   altar, 201
   fire, 178
   Mahometan, 45
   shaman's ritual death and resurrection, 173
   Sufi, 167
   Tengrism, 140
Rock, Stella, 12, 27, 28, 30, 55, 68, 97
al-Rodhan, Nayef R.F., 198
The Role of the Arab-Islamic World in the Rise of the West: Implications for Contemporary Trans-Cultural Relations (al-Rodhan), 198
Roman Catholicism, 144
Roman feast of *Caristia*, 24
Romanticist interpreters, 172
Romantic nationalism, 26–31
Rostam (Persian hero), 37
Rudakov, B.N., 233
runic (Orkhonic Turkic) script, 134
Rus, 55
Russian (language, culture, history), 296

Russian Bible Society, 28
Russian Christians, 52
Russian churches and Kazakh religion, 52
Russian citizenship, 225–226, 231
The Russian Conquest of Bashkiria, 1552–1740 (Donnelly), 236
Russian Geographical Society, 53–55
Russian Orthodox Christianity, forced conversion to, 25
Russian Orthodox missionaries, 98, 144
   and Tsarist ethnographers, 61–62
   survival paradigm, 61–62
Russian Orthodox tradition of dual faith, 26–31
Russian Orthodoxy, 174
   and Kazakhs' conversion, 56
   Soviet 'survivals' ethnography in, 68
Russian Philological Bulletin, 30
The Russian Religious Mind (Fedotov), 68
The Russians in Central Asia (Valikhanov), 56, 57
Russo-Japanese War, 235
Rybakov, B.A., 68
Rybakov, S.G., 233
Rychkov, N.P., 49–52

S
Sabaoth, 110
sacred scriptures, 47
SADUM, 96
saint veneration, 123
Sairam, 123
Salem witch trials, 25
Saltanaul Tatars, 224
Samarkand region, people of, 74
Sanctuary of Jumart, 85
Sarts, 62
Schoeberlein, John, 12, 96, 98

scholars and historiographical interpretations, 140–156
   Baieke, Manarbek, 143–145
   Baitenova, Nagima, 153–154
   Bulutai, Murtaza, 140–148
   Gabitov, Tursin Hafiz, 151–155
   Kartabaeva, Erke Tamabekkyzy, 155–159
   Kartaeva, Tattygul, 155
   Nurtazina, Nazira, 148–151
   Zatov, Kairat, 153–154
Schwartz, Wilhelm, 58
Science, scientific, 296
Scientific Atheism, 98
Scythian-Saka peoples, 78
Secularization theory, 109
Sedelnikov, A.N., 61
Seidimbek, Akseleu, 134, 139, 142, 149
self-consciousness, 156
self-identification, 156
Seljuk tribes, 36
Seljuk Turks, 189
Semei region, 191
Semenov, A.A., 63
Şener, Cemal, 166
sermons and teachings, 30, 158
Shabestari, Mahmoud, 38
Shah Ismail, 42
Shahnameh (Firdausi), 38
Shaitan (Shaytan), 191
shaman, 38
Shamanic myths and rituals, 109
Shamanism, 3, 36, 120
   coexistence with Islam, 53
   in Kazakh steppe, destruction of, 177
   Islam's theological rejection of, 169
   Mongolian, 58
   rituals in, 4
   Siberian, 73, 175
   Tolstov on, 78

understandings & definitions of, 173–177
Shamanism and Islam, historical relation of, 164–177
Deweese's Critique of Turkish, French & Soviet Scholarship, 166–168
Hobart, Angela, 156
'Islam' and 'Shamanism', understandings and definitions, 173–177
Privratsky, Muslim Turkistan, evidence from, 168–175
Sultanova, Razia, 164–177
Zarcone, Thierry, 165
Shamanism and Islam: Sufism, Healing Rituals and Spirits in the Muslim World (Sultanova), 165
Shamanism: The Religion of the Turks before Islam (Şener), 165
Shamil, 118
Shammasi, 42
Shamun, Prophet, 85
Sharia laws, 230
Sharifian, Mahdi, 179
Shia persecutions, 42
Shinto, 201
Shishov, A., 63
Siberia, 165
Siberian history (Fisher), 52
Siberian shamanism, 73, 175
Silk Road merchants, 43, 154
Silk Road pluralist view, 159
Skvortsov-Stepanov, Ivan, 72
Sky Tengri, 152
Slavic peoples, 27
Slavophile, 215, 234
Smirnov, S.I., 30
Snegirev, J.M., 29
Snesarev, G.P., 62, 74, 75, 77, 80
  evaluating beliefs and rituals of the Peoples of Central Asia, 83–85
  methodological sophistication of Soviet 'Survivals' ethnography, 98
  on importance of Kazakh nomadic Steppe culture, 101–102
Society for the Restoration of Orthodoxy in the Caucasus, 62
Sokoto Caliphate, 35
Solov'ev, Sergei M., 30, 57
Soros, George, 145
sources. *See* Soviet 'survivals' ethnography
Soviet anti-Islamic propaganda literature, 88–93
Soviet Constitution, 121
Soviet encroachment, 172
Soviet ethnographers, 15
  misinterpretation of Sufi rituals, 167
Soviet Ethnography (journal), 77
Soviet Kazakh publications, 107–124
  About the Reactionary Essence of the Religion of Islam (Kakimzhanov), 108–113
  About the Religion of Islam and Its Current State (Duisenbin), 121–124
  Devotion to Islam–A Detrimental Survival (Mashrapov), 124
  The Origin of Islam and Its Class Significance (Bisenov), 113–121
Soviet scholarship
  Deweese's critique of, 166–168
  on Shamanism, 174–175
Soviet scholarship, Deweese's critique of. *See* post-Soviet "survivals" scholarship
Soviet 'survivals' ethnography, 61, 67–81. *See also* Tsarist Russian and Kazakh Colonial Ethnography, 1770–1917

in Marx, Engels, Lenin and Stalin, 68–71
in Russian Orthodoxy, 68
of Kazakh and Central Asian Islamic history, 1920s–40s, 74–80
Tylor, Frazer and Other Euro-American sources of influence, 72–73
Soviet 'survivals' ethnography, transformations in, 83–102
chronological frame of Soviet 'survivals' ethnography, 98–101
concern for 'pre-Islamic survivals, 88–93
G.P. Snesarev's late-coming challenge, 83–86
importance of Kazakh nomadic Steppe culture, 101–102
Revisiting the Marxian-Engelsian framework, 86–88
Snesarev and the Soviet deployment of 'pre-Islamic survivals', 94–98
Soviet 'survivals' historiography and Tylor
and Protestant Anti-Catholic Polemicists, 15–16
Hebrew-Jewish and Christian Sources of 'Survivals' Historiography, 22–36
Nineteenth-Century Romantic Nationalism and the Russian Orthodox Tradition of 'Dual Faith', 26–31
'Survivals' Historiography in Seventeenth-Century German Enlightenment Sources, 20–22
Spanish Catholic Christianity, forced conversion to, 25
Spanish Inquisition, 25, 172
Specimen historiae Arabum (Pocockio), 52
Speransky Reforms, 53

spirituality, 138, 140, 156, 228
St. Augustine, 23
Stalin, Joseph, 68–71, 70, 95, 96, 121, 148
Sternberg, L.Y., 12, 73
Stolypin reforms, 117
The Struggle of Christianity with Pagan Survivals in Old Rus (Gal'kovskii), 30
The Study of Religion, 137
Sufi customs, 180
Sufi influences, 43
Sufi pirs, 152
Sufi rituals, 167
Sufi saints, 113
Sufism, 138, 164–165, 176
Sultan-Galiev, Mirsaid (cf. Mirza), 88–90
Sultangalieva, Gulmira, 224
Sultanova, Razia, 164–177, 185
Sunni Muslims, 230
Sunni 'ulema, 191
Sun-worshipers, 42, 112, 189, 191
"Survival Strategies: Reflections on the Notion of Religious 'Survivals' in Soviet Ethnographic Studies of Muslim Religious Life in Central Asia", 15
Survivals [Пережитки] of Animism among the Plain Tadjiks, 81
Survivals [Пережитки] of Totemism among the Peoples of Siberia, 72
Survivals [РееРликты] of Pre-Islamic Beliefs and Rituals among the Khorezm Uzbeks (Snesarev), 62
The Survivals of Animism, Shamanism, and Islam and Atheistic Work against Them (Amanturlin), 99
Survivals of Shamanism among the Kirgiz (Ilyasov), 81
syncretism, 22, 70, 78
as a construct, 184–187

debates over terminology, 184–187
of Islam, 138
Syncretism in Religion, 12
Syr region, Kazakhs of, 155

T
T'ang Chinese forces, 115
tafrīq, 34
Tajiks, 63, 74–75, 79
The Tale of Bygone Years (Nestor), 27
Tängri (the "Celestial God"), 39, 41, 108, 109, 112
Tanjarov, M.E., 176
Taraz, 123
Tasar, Eren, 80
Tashkent Turks, 115
Tatar (Kutlu Muhammet) Tevkelev, 218
Tatars, 4, 21, 50, 237
 forced conversions of, 25
 from Orenburg, 218
 merchants and spread of Islam, 111
 mullahs, 113, 134, 226
 Muslim identity, 21
Tauasaruhli, Kazibek bek, 143
täwip, 169, 171
Taylor, Edward, 29
Tengri, 39
Tengrism, 3, 36, 44, 120
Tengrism and Islam, historical relation, 145, 151. *See also* Bulutai, Murtaza; Esim, Garifolla; Nurtazina, Nazira
Tengrist historiography, 42, 132–140
Tengrist modes, 41
Tengrist-Shamanist orientation of the Kazakh ancestors, 154
Tereshchenko, A.V., 29
Tevkelev, Aleksei, 51
Thrower, James, 4, 69, 72, 77, 96
Tihomirov, I.A., 233

Timur, Chagataid Togluk, 156
Tokarev, Sergei A., 73
Tolstov, S.P., 63, 77–80, 84
totemism, 79, 81, 124
Toynbee, 149
Traces [ССледы] of Primitive Communism among Mountain Tajiks (Kisliakov), 80
transformations. *See* religious conversions
Treatise on Relics (Calvin), 25
Trediakovsky, Vasily, 28
Troitskaya, A.L., 75, 80
The Truth About Burkhanism (Bulutai), 145
Tsarist ethnographers, Russian Orthodox missionaries and, 61–62
Tsarist government, 51
 support for Islamic preaching, 122
Tsarist Orthodox, 22
Tsarist Russian and Kazakh Colonial Ethnography, 1770–1917, 49–63, 74. *See also* Soviet 'survivals' ethnography
 Kunanbaiuhli, Abai, 59–61
 of Kazakh religious identity, 1770–1860, 50–54
 survival paradigm, 61–63
 Valihanov, Chokan (1863–65), 55–59
The Turgai Region: A Historical Study (Dobrosmyslov), 229
Turkestan National Liberation Struggle, 93
Turkic Chuvash kiremet/keremet, 40
Turkic movements, 93, 120
Turkic Muslim Mughals of India, 43
Turkic nationalism, 112
Turkic peoples, 35, 38, 51, 79, 140, 144, 152, 156, 237
Turkic sources, 35–42

Turkish scholarship, Deweese's critique of, 166–168
Turkistan, 123
Turkistan National Liberation Struggle, 94
Turk khaganate, 138
Turko-Mongols, 109
Turko-Persian Muslim, 40
Tylor and Soviet 'survivals' historiography, 46
  and Protestant Anti-Catholic Polemicists, 15–16
  Hebrew-Jewish and Christian sources, 22–26
  monotheistic degenerational versus evolutionary developmental theories of early human history, 16–20
  Nineteenth-Century Romantic Nationalism and the Russian Orthodox Tradition of 'Dual Faith', 26–31
  'survivals' historiography, 20–22
Tylor, Edward Burnett, 16, 57, 70, 72, 77, 180
  and Soviet 'survivals' ethnography, 72–73

U
Ualihanuhli, 55. *See also* Valikhanov, Chokan
Uighurs, 237
Ulug-Turluk, 41
Umayyad Caliphate, 189
UNESCO, 11, 12, 196
Unification of Kazakhstan to Russia (Bekmukhanova), 100
Unique Aspects of the Spread of Islam in Kazakhstan, 101
Unitarianism, 17
United Nations Universal Declaration of Human Rights, 198

Usmanov, Mirkasyim A., 6
Uyghurs
  Shamanic "residues" among, 166
Uzbeks, 4, 7, 79, 237

V
Valikhanov, Chokan, 9, 49, 52, 55, 58, 61, 92, 93, 111, 112, 116, 117, 170, 190, 202, 217, 228, 236
  interpretations of Kazakh religious history and identity, 55–59
  on conversion of Kazakhs to Russian Orthodoxy, 55–58
  on dual-faith paradigm, 55–59
  persecution by Tsarist government, 122
Vasilenko, V.O., 73
Velioğlu, Özgür, 166
Veniukov, Mikhail, 56
Vermeulen, Han F., 20
Vernadsky, George, 31
Vladimir the Great, 27
vocabulary
  Arabic and Persian, 40
  Islamic, 41, 133, 168
Volga Finnic languages, 40
Volga Finnic people, 40
Volga-Ural Muslims, 111
  defections of, 216
  forced conversion of, 25
Voltaire, 224

W
Wahabi-influenced schools, 35
wedding rituals, Kazakh, 50
Westermarck, Edvard, 11, 80
Western (Christian) Orientalist Scholarship, 45–46
Western imperialism, 120
Western interpretations of 'pre-Islamic pagan survivals', 45–46

Western Protestant (and limited Catholic) missionary, 142
Western-Russian Enlightenment, 169
Whately, Richard, 18, 20
What Is Islam? The Importance of Being Islamic, 12
What is Islamic Studies? European and North American Approaches to a Contested Field, 12
White Christians, 172
White, Joseph, 45, 52, 70
William of Rubruck, 52
witchcraft, 79
With An Introductory Dissertation On the Miraculous Images, as Well as Other Superstitions, of the Roman Catholic and Russo-Greek Churches (Calvin), 26
Witsen, Nicolaas, 20–22, 51–52
Witte, S. Iu., 234
Wood, P., 12
world religions, 138–139, 188
World War II, 99
worship of the pious sanctuaries, 79

Y

Yadrintsev, N.M., 231
Yahweh, Jew, 110
Yakobiy, Ivan Varfolomeyevich, 223
Yasawi, Qoja Akhmet, 44, 138, 146, 151, 189
Yasawi Sufi order, 151
Yastrebov, Matvei N., 29, 52, 53
Young Turks, 93

Z

Zal (magician), 37
Zarcone, Thierry, 165, 167, 179
Zatov, Kairat, 152–153, 202
Zeitgeist, 58
Zeland, N.L., 49, 59
Zelenin, D.K., 72
Zolotarev, A., 72
Zoroastrianism, 3, 36, 108, 120, 137, 191